If you're a fool
Everything will
happen to you

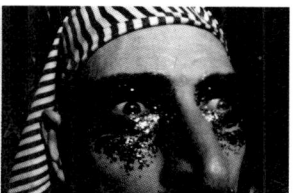

JACK SMITH: Flaming Creature
His Amazing Life and Times

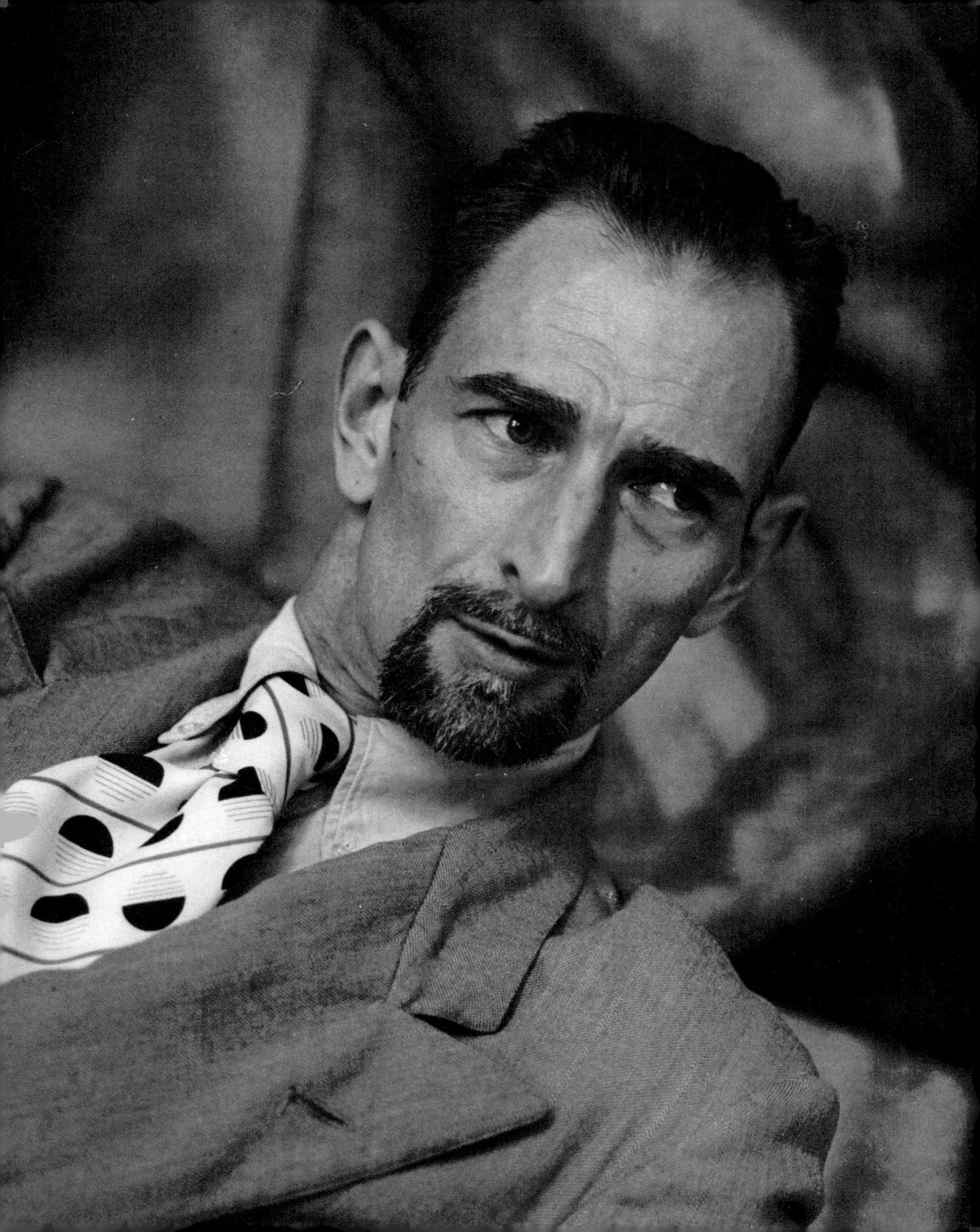

Flaming Creature

Jack Smith

His Amazing Life and Times

– Edited by
Edward Leffingwell, Carole Kismaric, Marvin Heiferman

– Essays
Nayland Blake, J. Hoberman, Edward Leffingwell,
Lawrence Rinder, Ronald Tavel

– Commentaries
Penny Arcade, Stefan Brecht, Richard Foreman, Jonas Mekas,
Susan Sontag, Jerry Tartaglia

a lookout book
The Institute for Contemporary Art, P. S. 1 Museum
Serpent's Tail

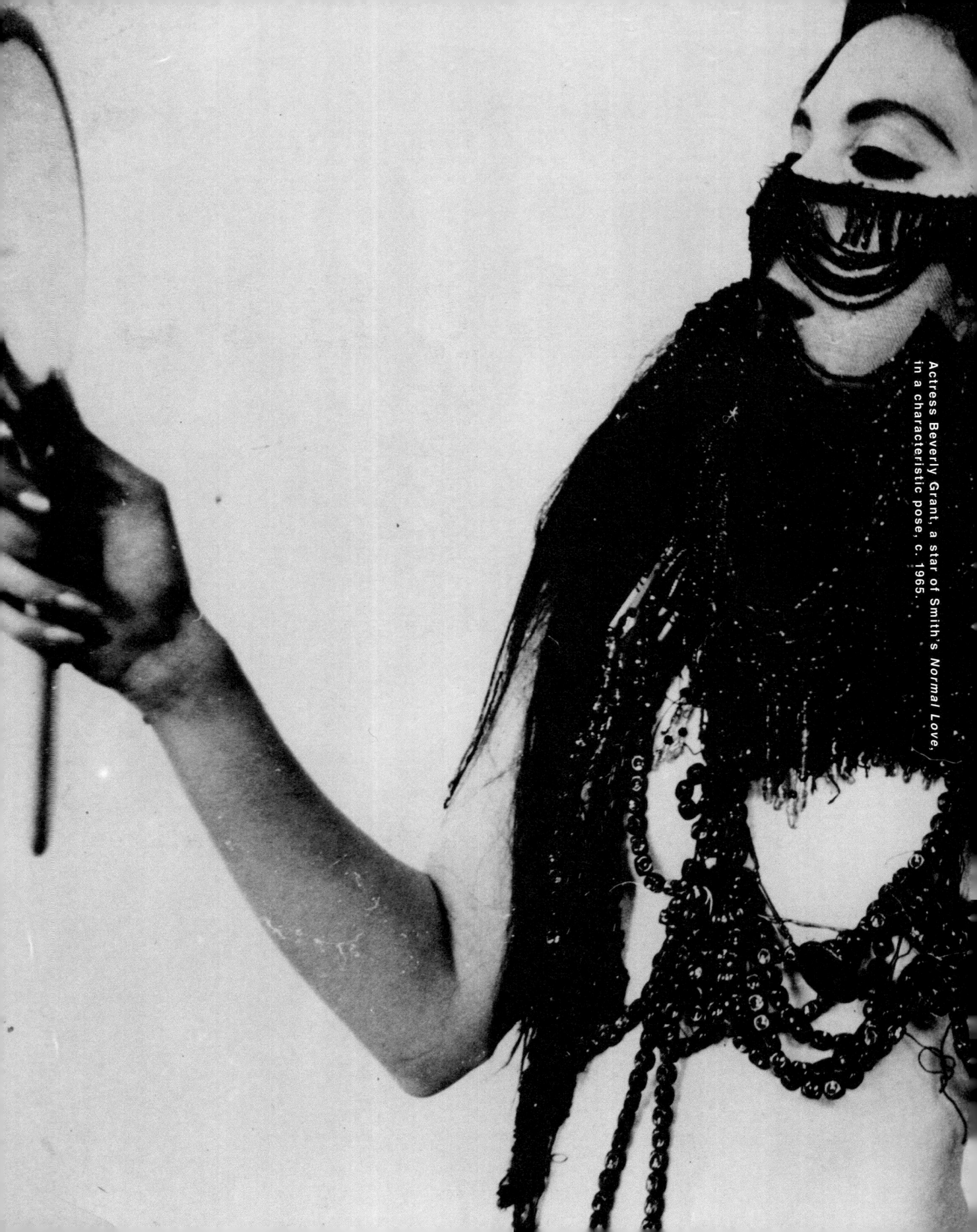

Actress Beverly Grant, a star of Smith's *Normal Love,* in a characteristic pose, c. 1965.

contents

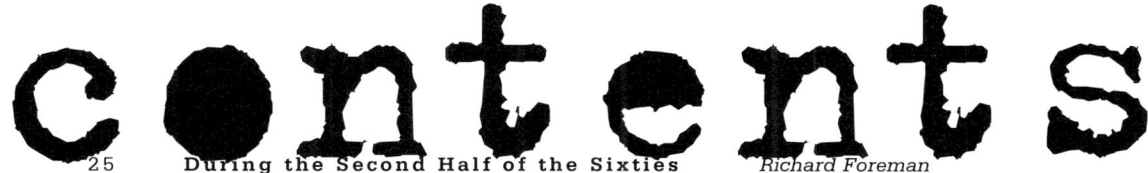

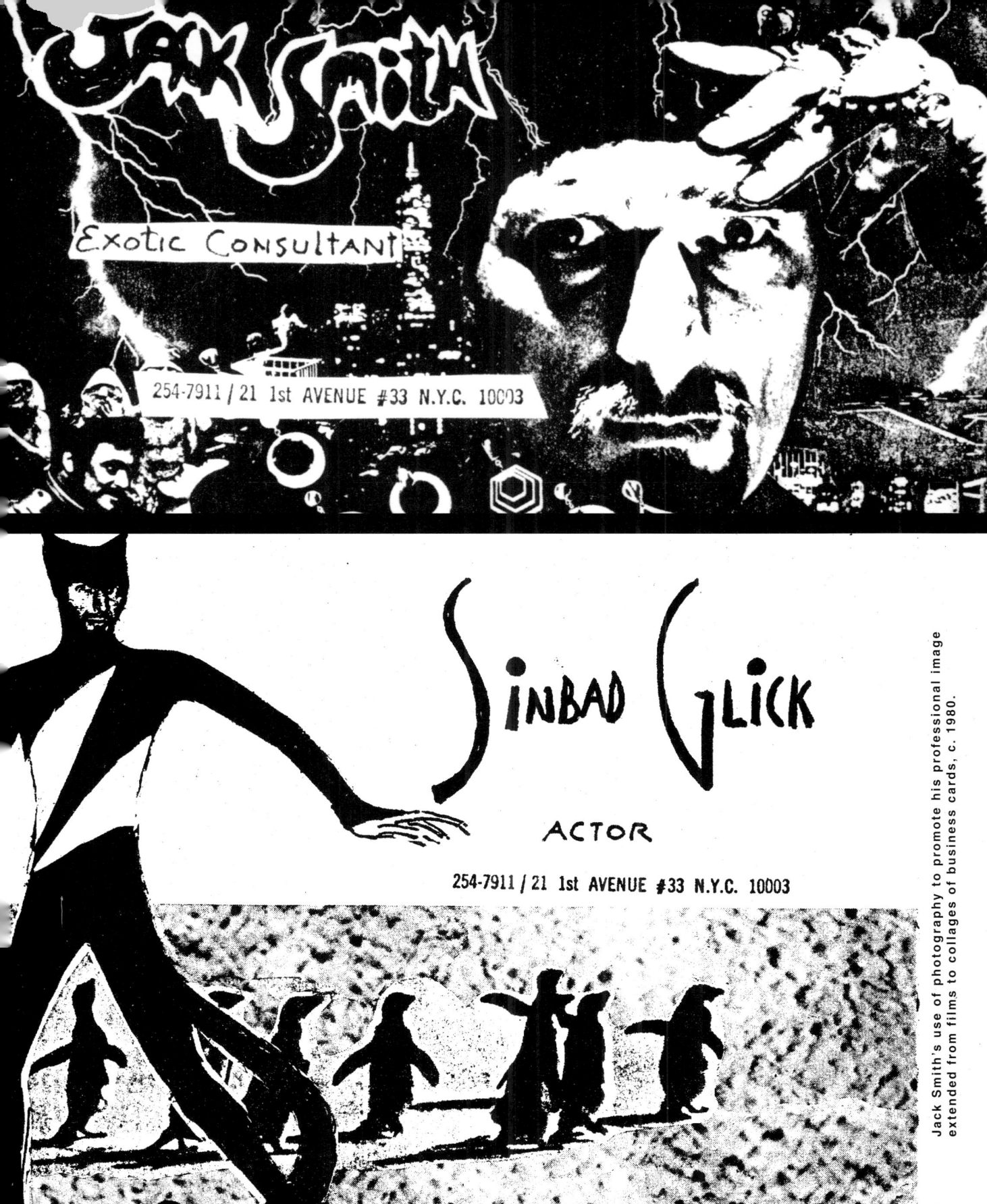

Jack Smith — Exotic Consultant

254-7911 / 21 1st AVENUE #33 N.Y.C. 10003

Sinbad Glick — ACTOR

254-7911 / 21 1st AVENUE #33 N.Y.C. 10003

Jack Smith's use of photography to promote his professional image extended from films to collages of business cards, c. 1980.

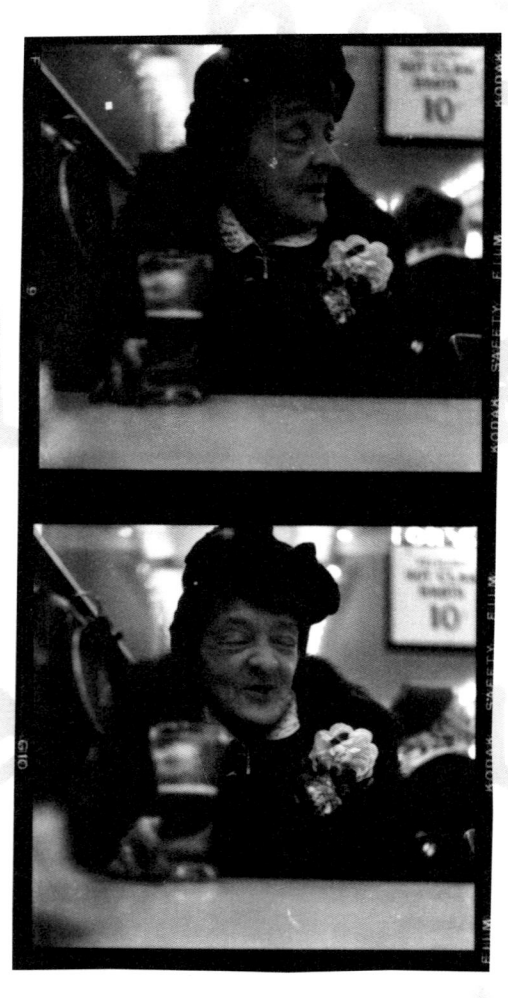

Smith's photographs, and later his films, reflected his fascination with aspects of everyday life that reveal how style or fashion express character, as in this street portrait, c. 1960.

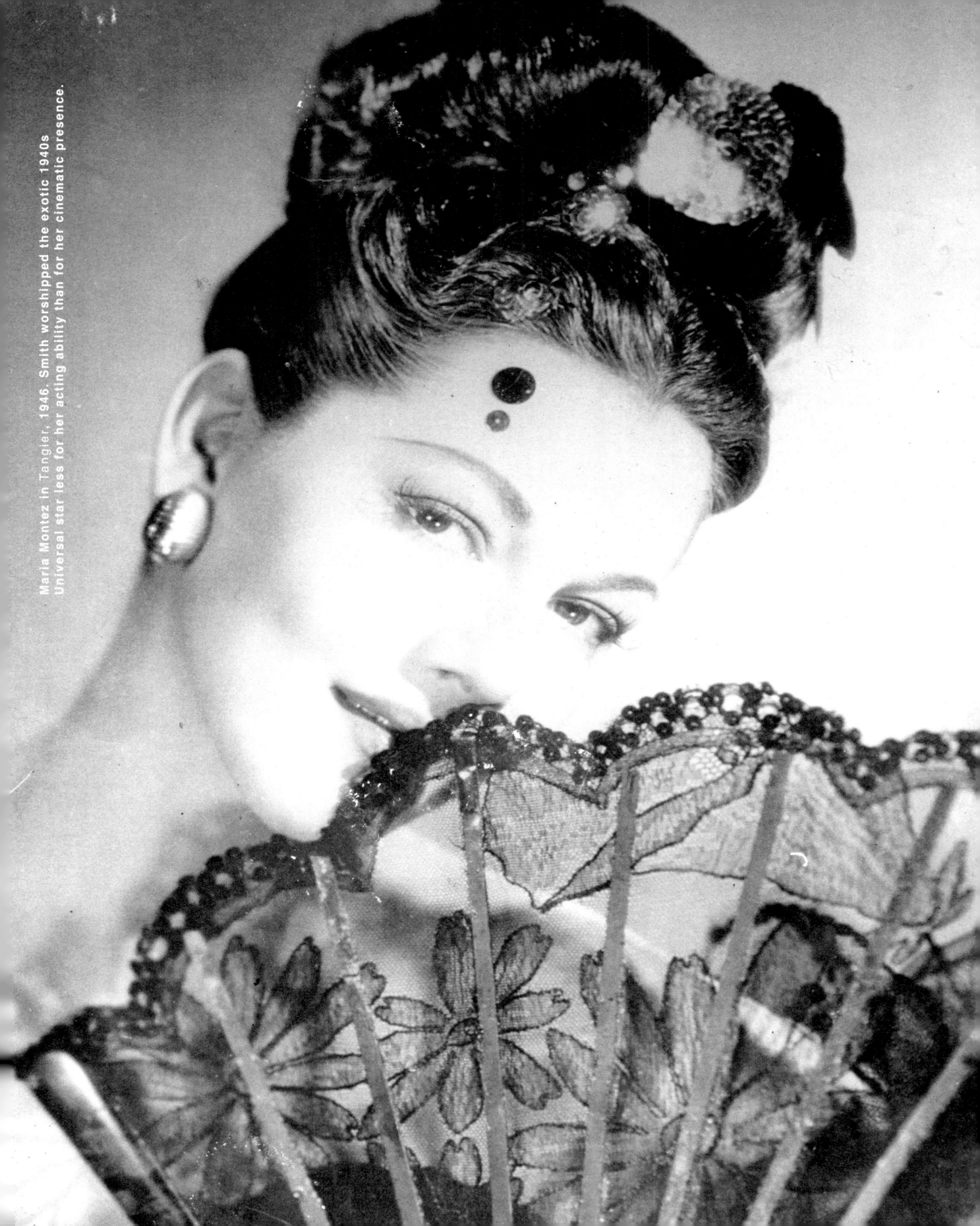

I am really an extremely maternal
person—I'm the only normal man in Baghdad.

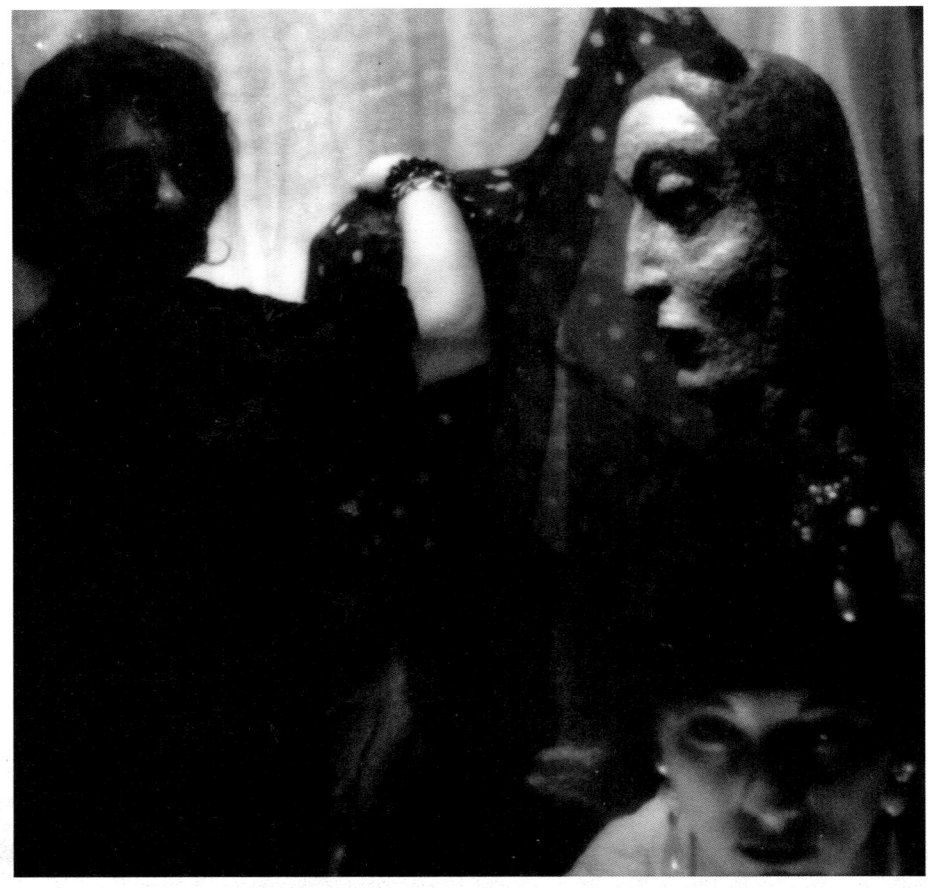

In studio tableaux vivants, Smith explored the narrative and compositional possibilities of the still image, which he later applied to motion pictures, c. 1960.

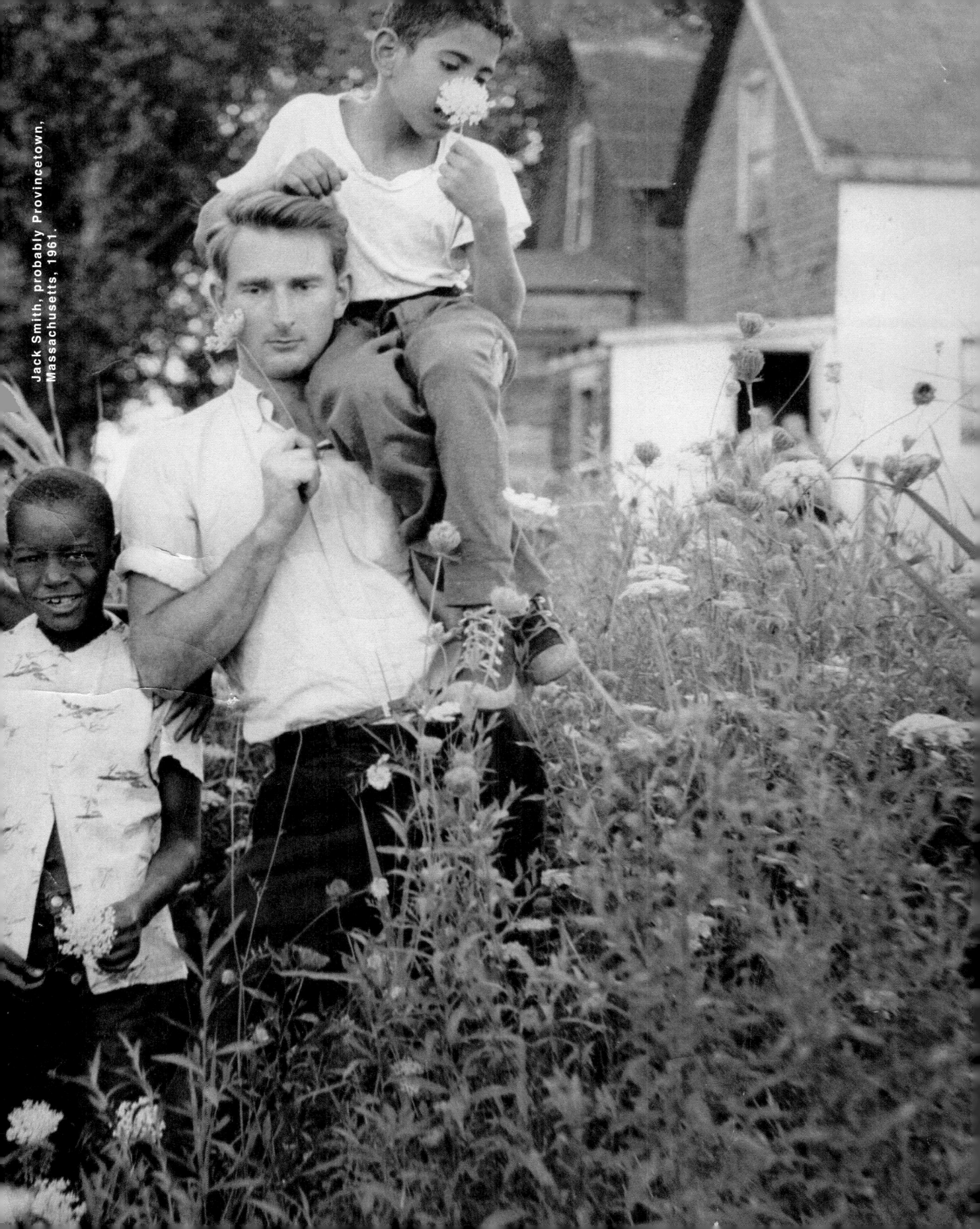

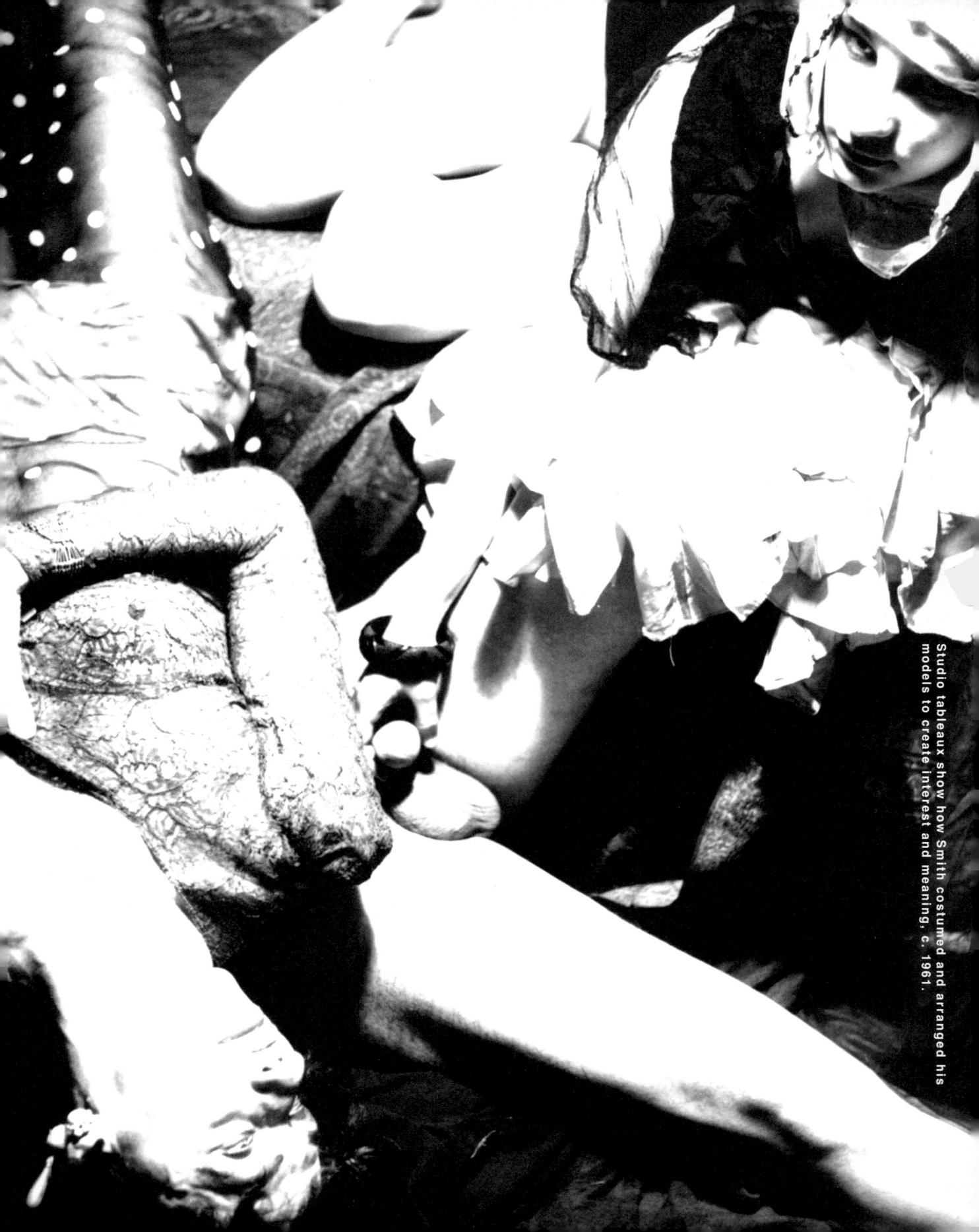

Studio tableaux show how Smith costumed and arranged his models to create interest and meaning, c. 1961.

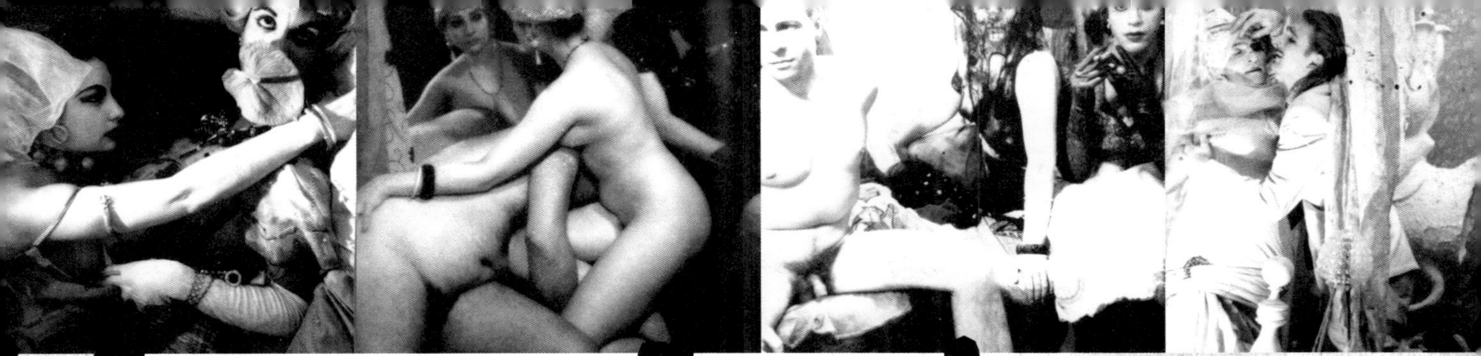

the dying

Moon Pool Vapours

In the Eighteenth Century it was a custom for the Royalty to dress up as shepherds & shepherdess and rush out across the rolling hills at dawn.

gasp of

Moon Pool Vapours

In the 18th century after partying all night the Royals would change into shepherd & shepherdess costumes at dawn and run out across the fields to milk the cows.

Baroness Horsecock

the rec—

tangle

the Embalmed Horsecock

~~the Death bed~~
THE TITLE   God's Body
              ~~or overstimulated~~

Early that morning I could see that
it would be an ordeal day. The Cretins
were ~~so~~ most excitable and openly
masturbated, overstimulating the
pinheads. Today they would put on
their shepherd & shepherdess costumes
and run across the fields with their
sand-pails to milk the cows. I
rode shotgun on them in my floor length
black leather jacket and ~~needle~~ ~~spiked~~-keeled
opera hip boots made of wildebeest
leather with tufted tops. I lingered
over my toilette, admiring my enormous three foot long ~~thick~~ six inch
thick cock; I posed before my glass,
throwing it first over this shoulder,
then the other. Finally, overstimulated
I fucked the tufted tops. However I
was unsatisfied so I lunged ~~at my~~
My noble horsecock rageingly tumes-
cent, ~~I wildly fucked a jagged~~
~~hole in the mirror I smashed~~
a ~~giagantic jagged hole in it which~~
    at my mirror.
I smashed through the mirror and
whirling about I stuffed my cock
in the jagged hole and I fucked
it 'til I was all bloody and ~~so~~.
torn up. Then, to get ~~the~~ maximum
sensation out of my cock I stomped
it in my boots, ~~and stuffed it~~

Smith's notations, essays, and scripts illustrate his adventures in creative writing. A version of this erotic journal entry appeared in *The Floating Bear*, published by poets Diane di Prima and LeRoi Jones, 1963.

8

flinging handsful of meat tenderizing
salts upon it.

Herding the freaks across the fields:
A fly lighted upon my cheek and I
started to think about my body. A pretty
young cretin girl: I prodded her with
my whip and made her sprawl on
the ground. Her hoop skirt flung up
exposing her pink dimpled pasties
to the heavens. ~~She squealed and rolled~~
In a second I was upon her, nudging
her ~~between~~ the buns with my
riding crop. She squealed and rolled
upon her back thrusting her ~~crisp~~
~~knitted~~ pouting quim into my
face. I whipped out my now
flaming organ ~~and going stepping~~
~~to~~ but ~~she~~ her skirt was over her
face and she couldn't see it. I ran
back a few paces, aimed my cock
and charged her but my horse
galloped in before me and impaled
her on his raging rod. Slightly
disappointed I charged my horses
ass hole and jumping up, I transfixed him in midair as ~~he~~ he
was ploughing the cretin girl. My
cock sank deliciously into his
bowels, reaming them out straight
and he ~~galloped and~~ reared and

bolted, causing me to spend even
more deliciously. The little cretin
shepherdess was now ruined for
normal sex and she ran amok among
the other freaks inflaming them. Soon ~~seething~~
the whole hillside ~~was~~ one gigantic
cretin, mongolian and pinhead orgy.

Delighted I rushed to where my
horse lay and snatched my elephant
gun off the pack. I opened up
~~point blank on the melee and~~
on the ~~melee~~ swirling churning carnival of freaky sex and fired ~~point~~
blank into its midst; ~~until I was~~
~~exhausted and could come when~~
~~I had come was twice I lost con-~~
~~sciousness and sank exhausted to~~
~~the ground.~~ Presently I sank delirious
to the ground, gasping and creaming
and blazing away at the freaks.

God sat majestically on the zircon
and rhinestone throne frowning sternly.
We must have been in heaven. He
ordered us all to line up, ~~drop our~~
turn around, drop our pants and
bend over. We meekly obeyed. He walked
up and down paddling us with a
ping pong paddle. He concentrated
chiefly upon the plump pasties, I
noticed. I then noticed that he
had a rather lovely well rounded

bum himself and was probably

rather young ~~he self~~ despite his long golden coloured beard. For the first time homo longings clogged in my throat. ~~He I was~~ Soon God was emitting ~~loud~~ mad giggles and rushing from one plastic to the other ~~or being~~ ~~them with the handle of the~~ ~~paddle teasing them and flicking~~ ~~his tongue up into their cracks~~ ~~and reaming them with his flick-~~ ~~ing tongue~~ paddling shit out of them and ~~then bathing his face~~ ~~in it and greedily stuffing it~~ ~~in his mouth~~ throwing handsful of it all over the place. The freaks ~~suddenly~~ became overstimulated and soon God was in the middle of a gang fuck which spread over all heaven. Angels, ~~saints~~, cupids, dicked each other with their wands - Nuns threw their legs open - ~~Popes screw~~ Archangels laid a pope, A mother superior ~~threw her legs up~~ ~~for quick god~~ - the skies dripped come lightning & thunder crackled and ~~they~~ climaxed, ~~a delicious breeze~~ ~~blew up and~~ and I took adv- antage of the uproar to slip it to god.

173

We left him mouldering behind

the Zircon and Rhinestone throne where he may still be if no- body has ever swept behind there ran slaughing and masturbating ~~back~~ ~~this scene in the eighteenth~~ ~~century about~~ ~~to milk the cows~~ to the moon pool to breath the vapours.
The End

[signature]

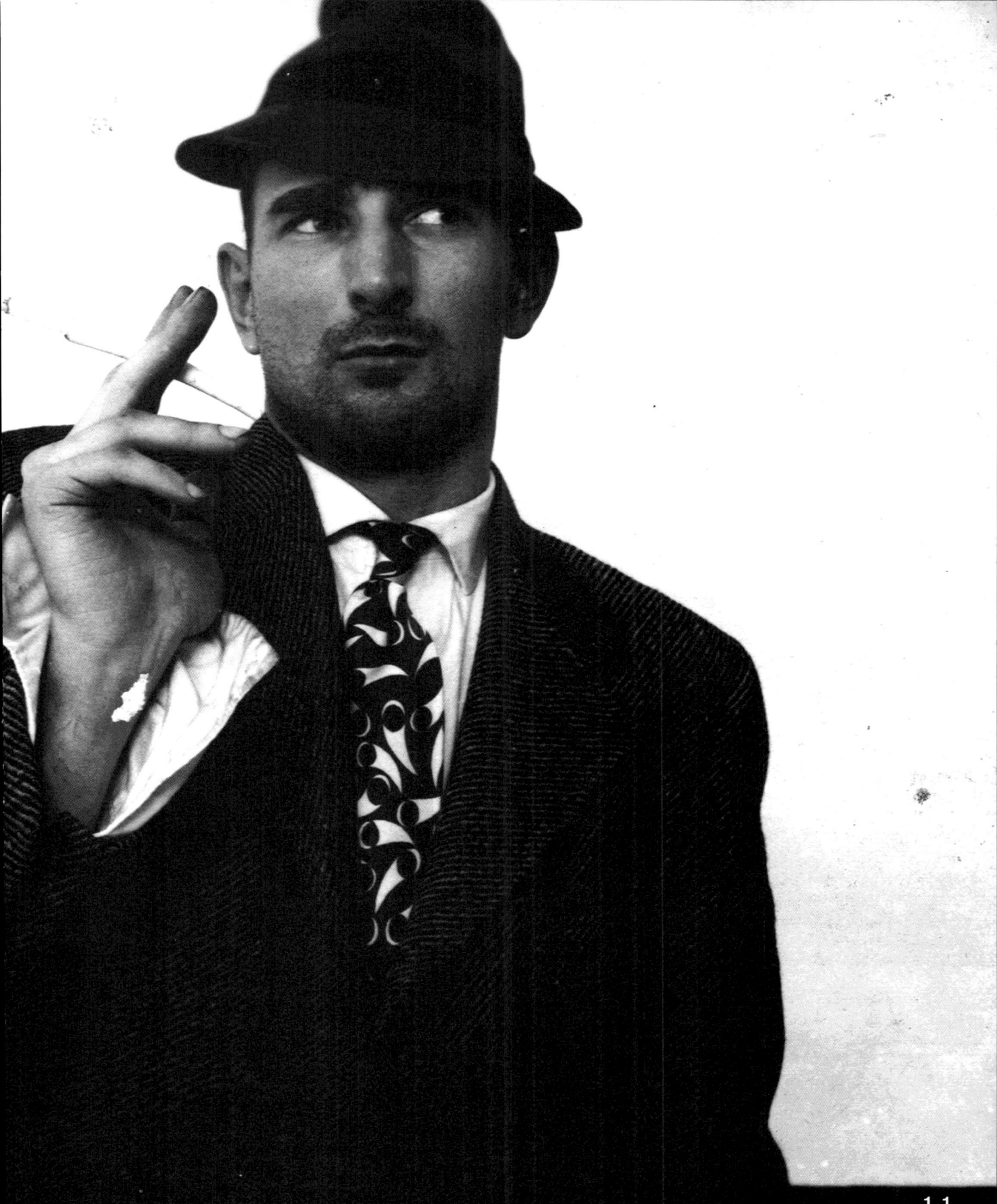

11

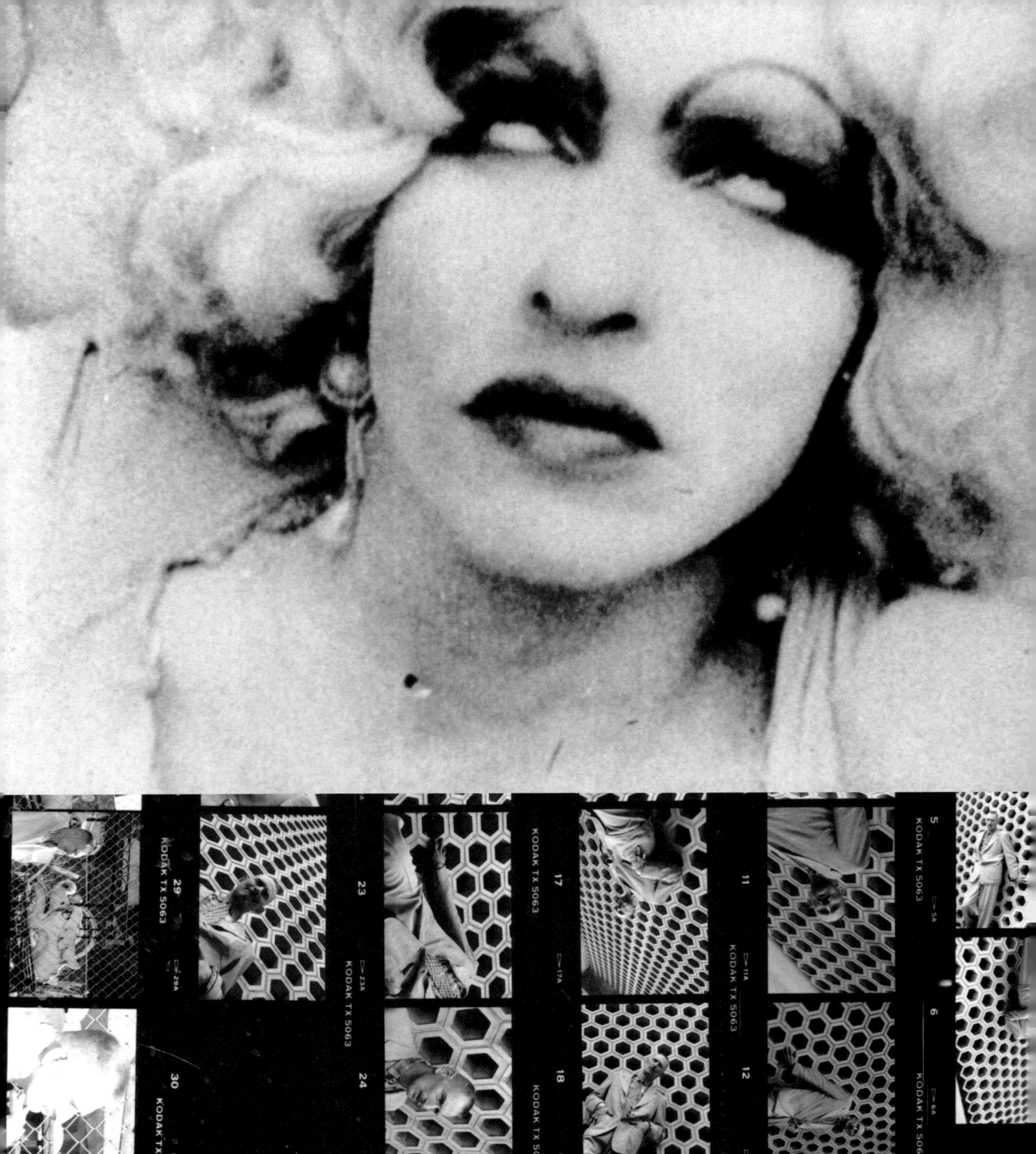

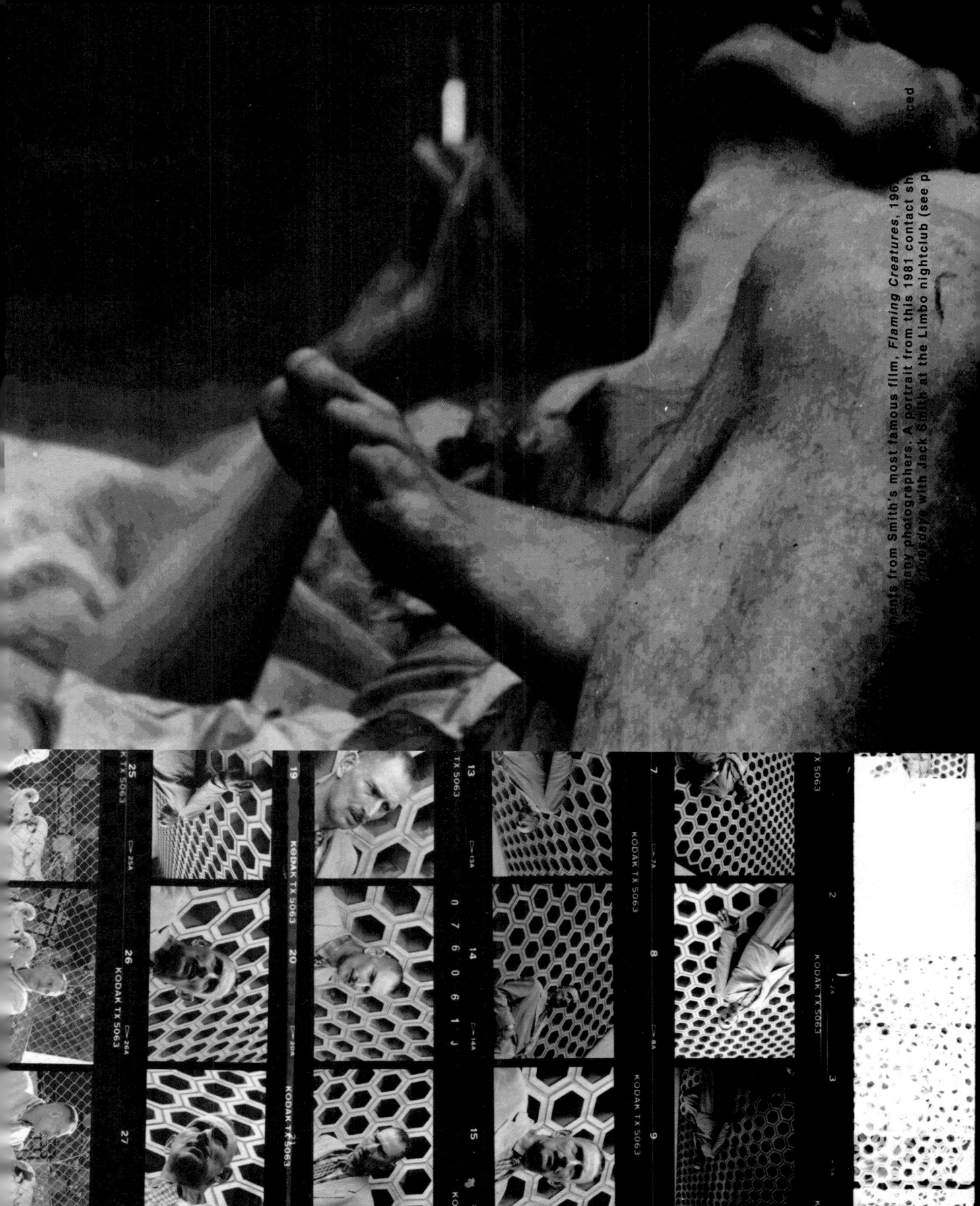

ments from Smith's most famous film, *Flaming Creatures*, 196
many photographers. A portrait from this 1981 contact sh
Tuesday with Jack Smith at the Limbo nightclub (see p

aced

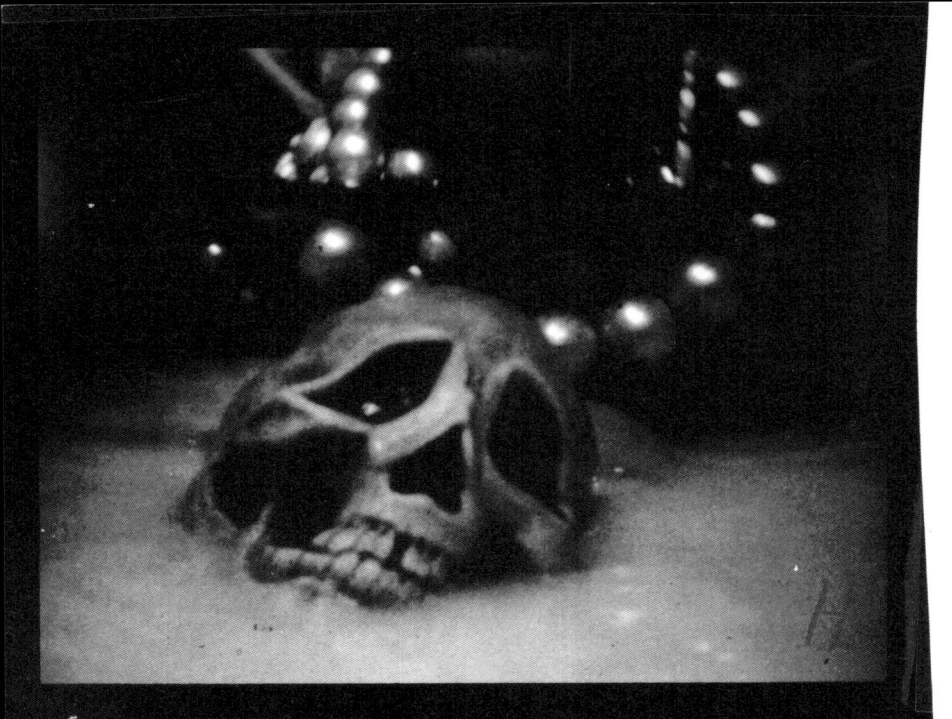

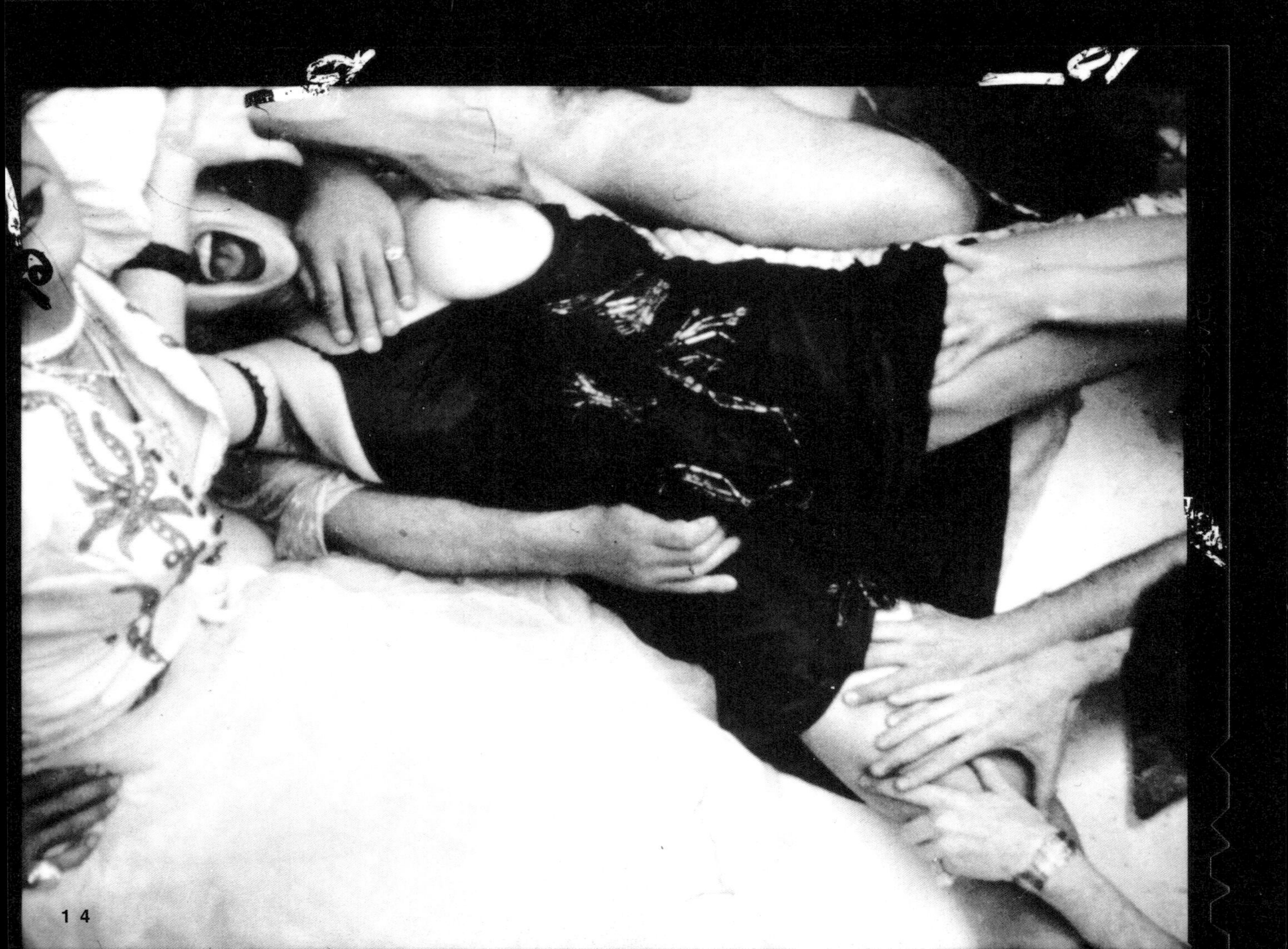

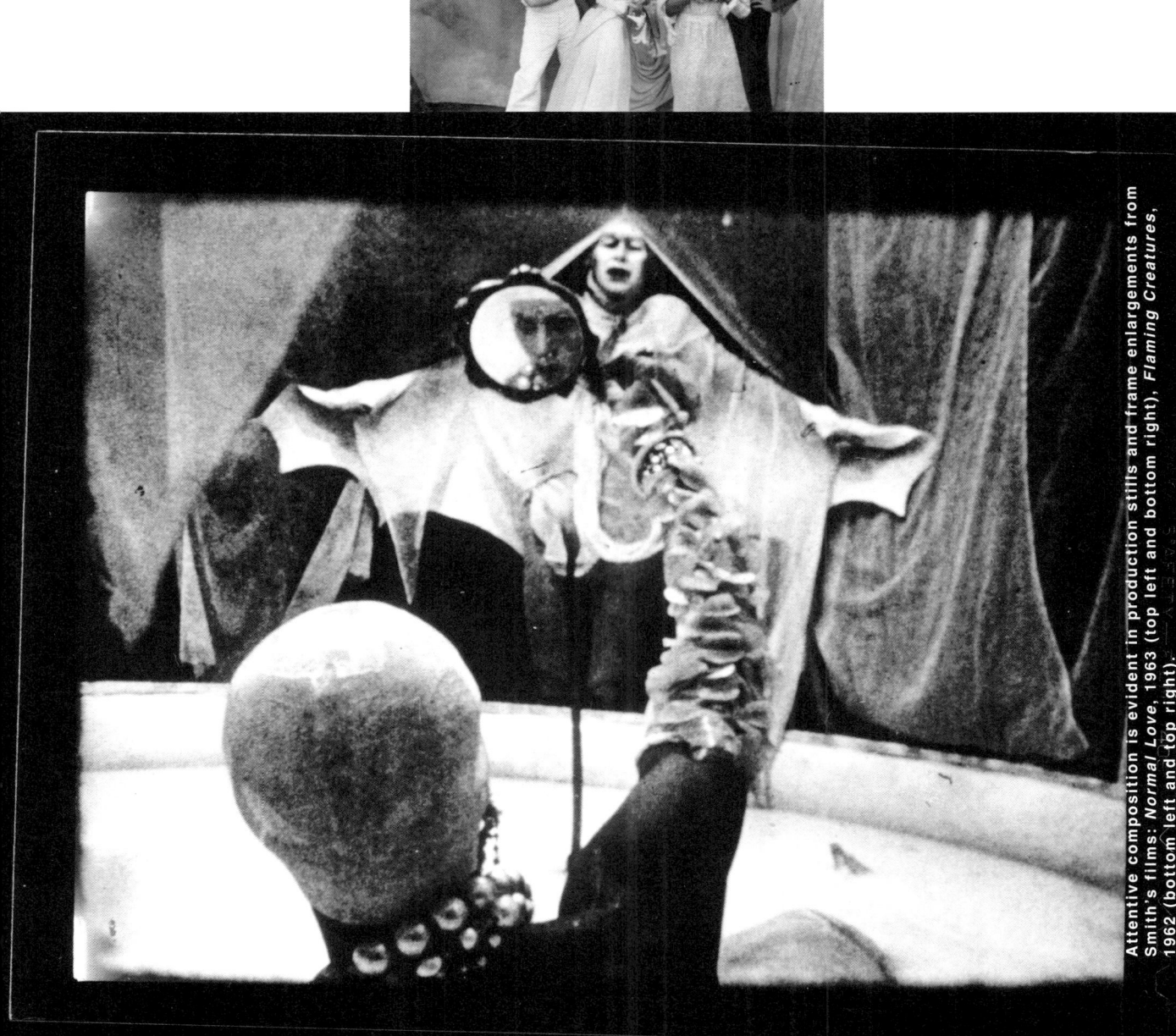

Attentive composition is evident in production stills and frame enlargements from Smith's films: *Normal Love,* 1963 (top left and bottom right), *Flaming Creatures,* 1962 (bottom left and top right).

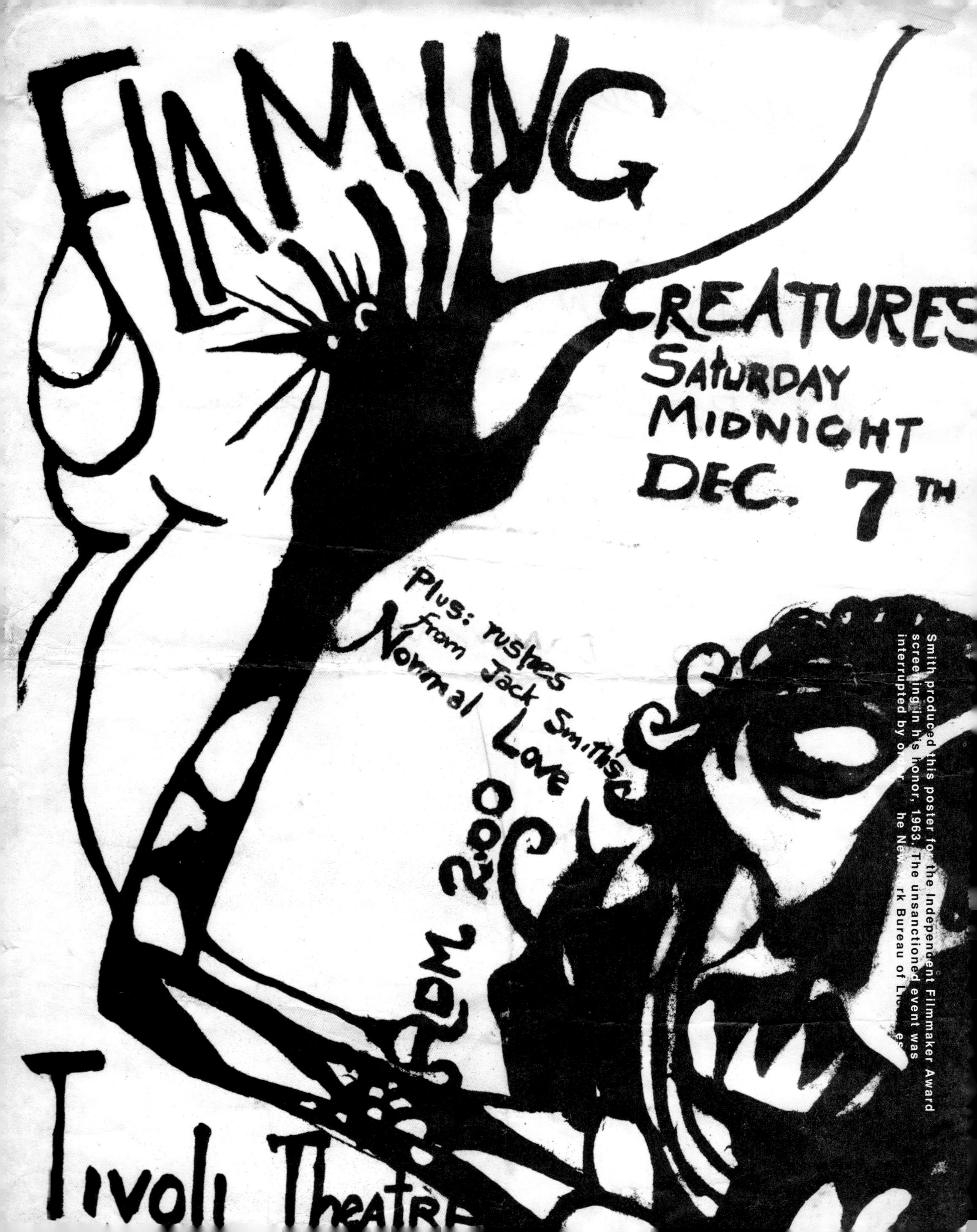

FLAMING CREATURES
SATURDAY MIDNIGHT DEC. 7TH

Plus: rushes from Jack Smith's Normal Love

FILM 200

Tivoli Theatre

Smith produced this poster for the Independent Filmmaker Award screening in his honor, 1963. The unsanctioned event was interrupted by order the New rk Bureau of Lic es

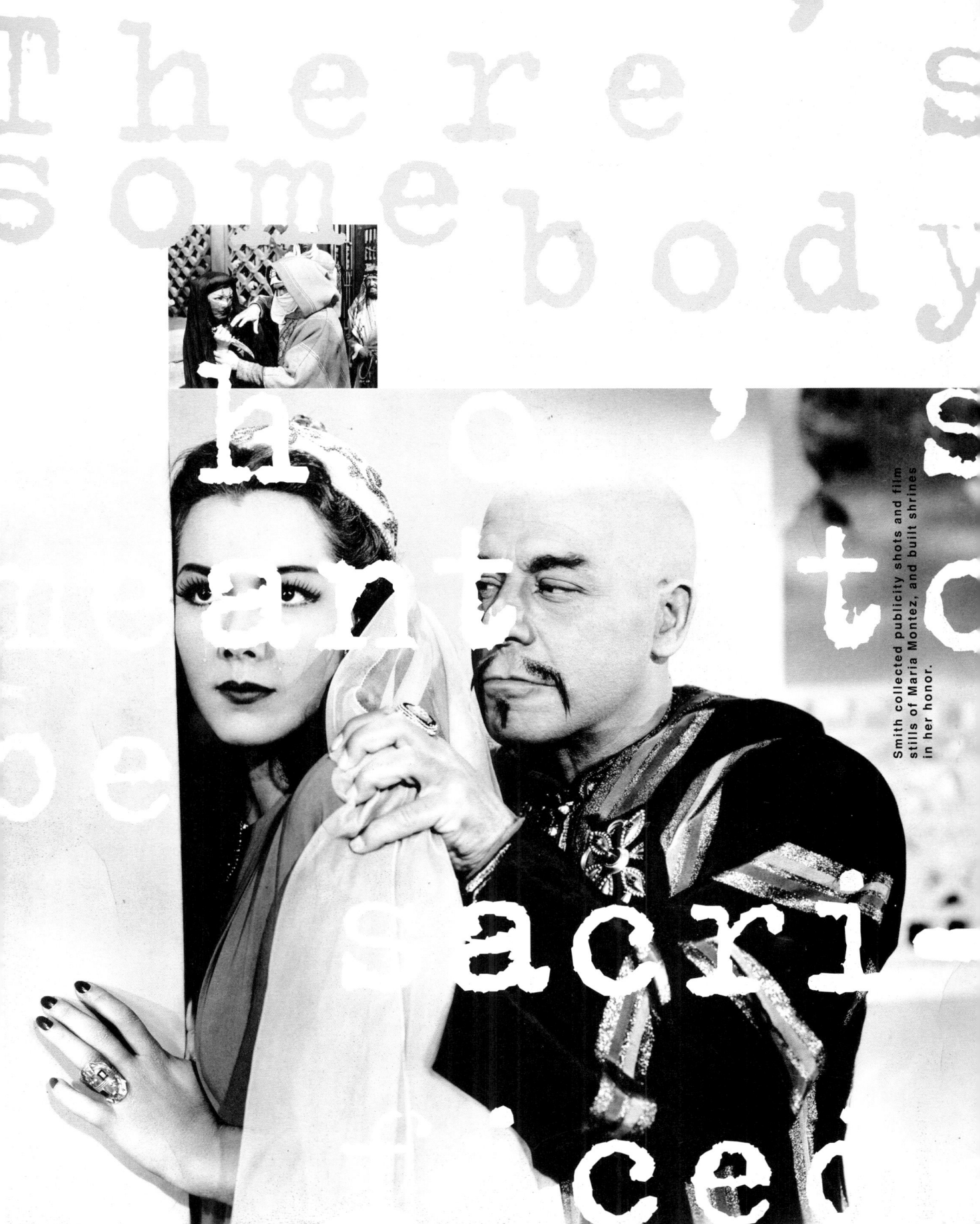

There's somebody he's meant to be sacrificed

Smith collected publicity shots and film stills of Maria Montez, and built shrines in her honor.

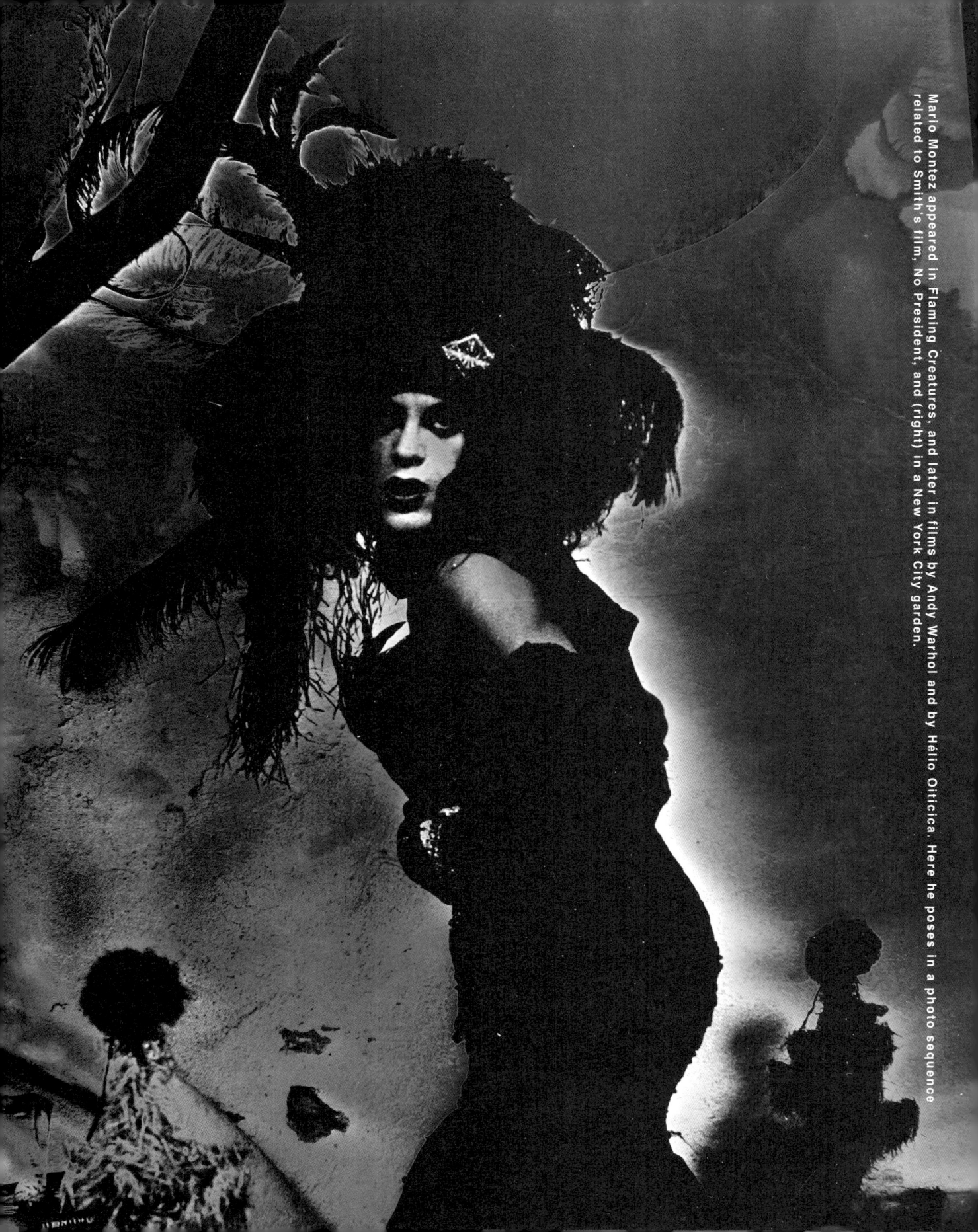

Mario Montez appeared in Flaming Creatures, and later in films by Andy Warhol and by Hélio Oiticica. Here he poses in a photo sequence related to Smith's film, No President, and (right) in a New York City garden.

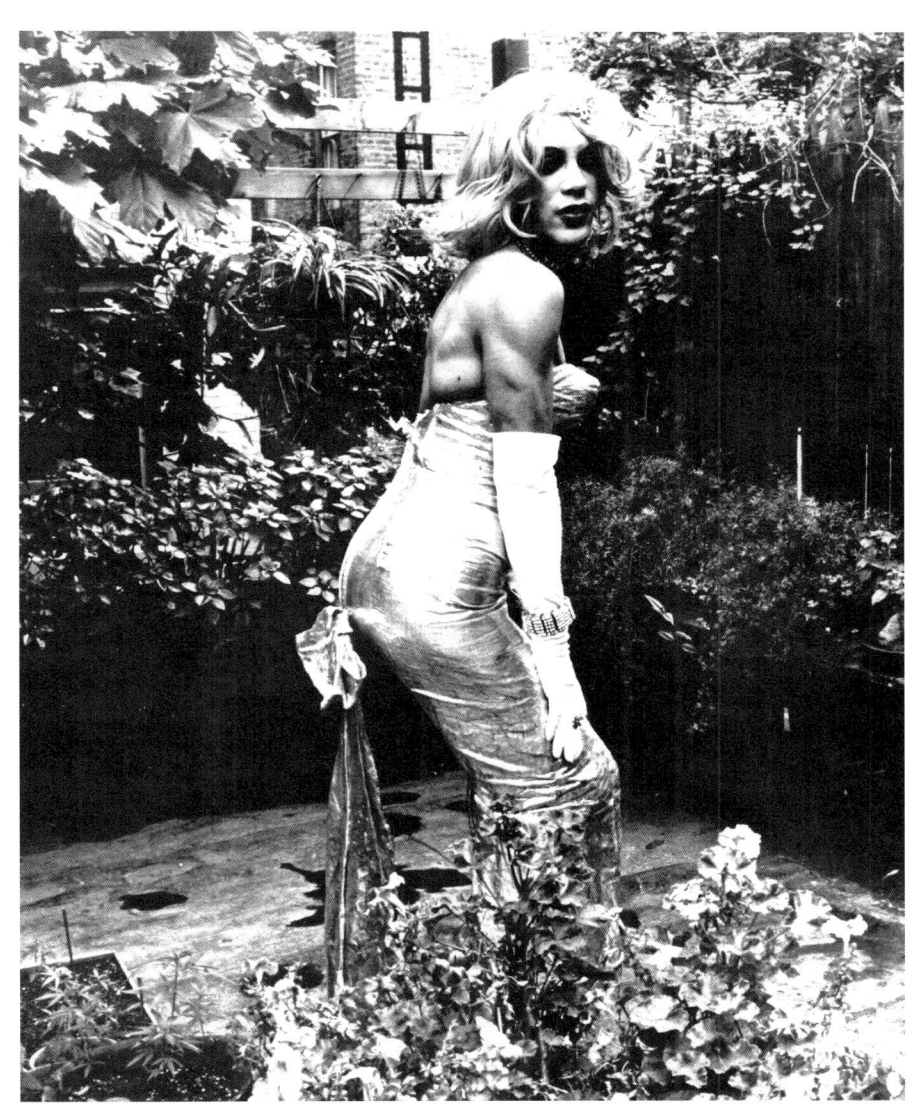

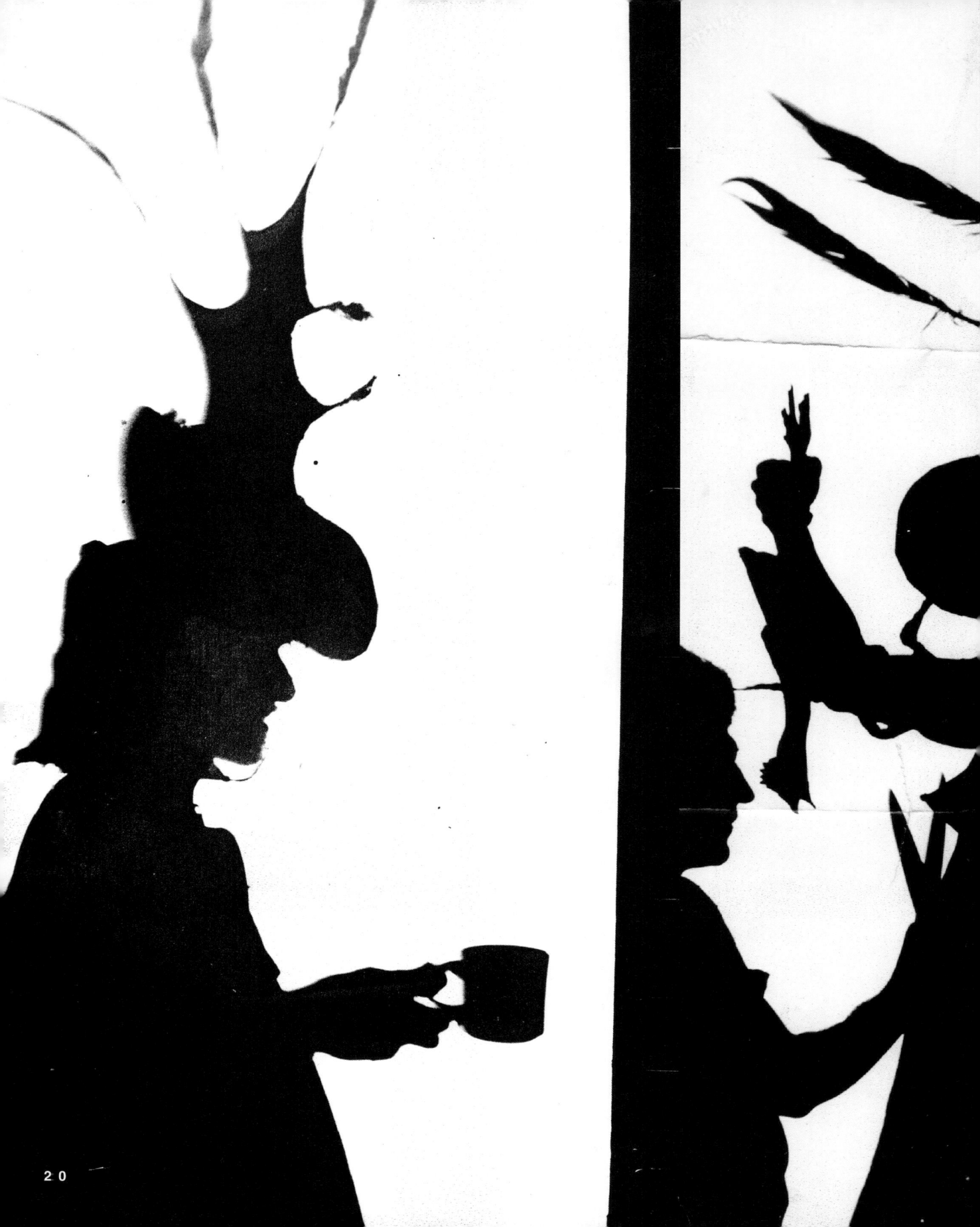

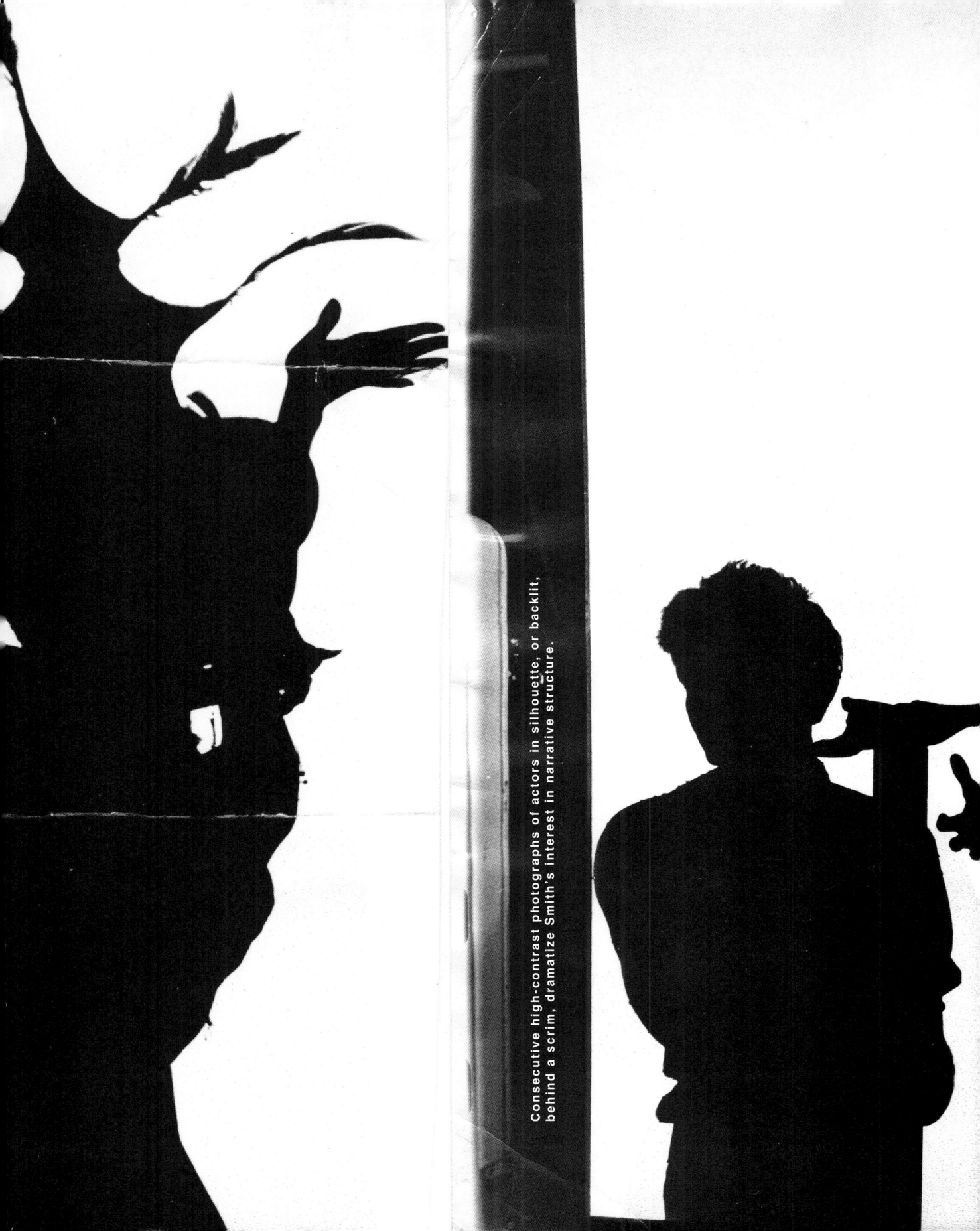

Consecutive high-contrast photographs of actors in silhouette, or backlit, behind a scrim, dramatize Smith's interest in narrative structure.

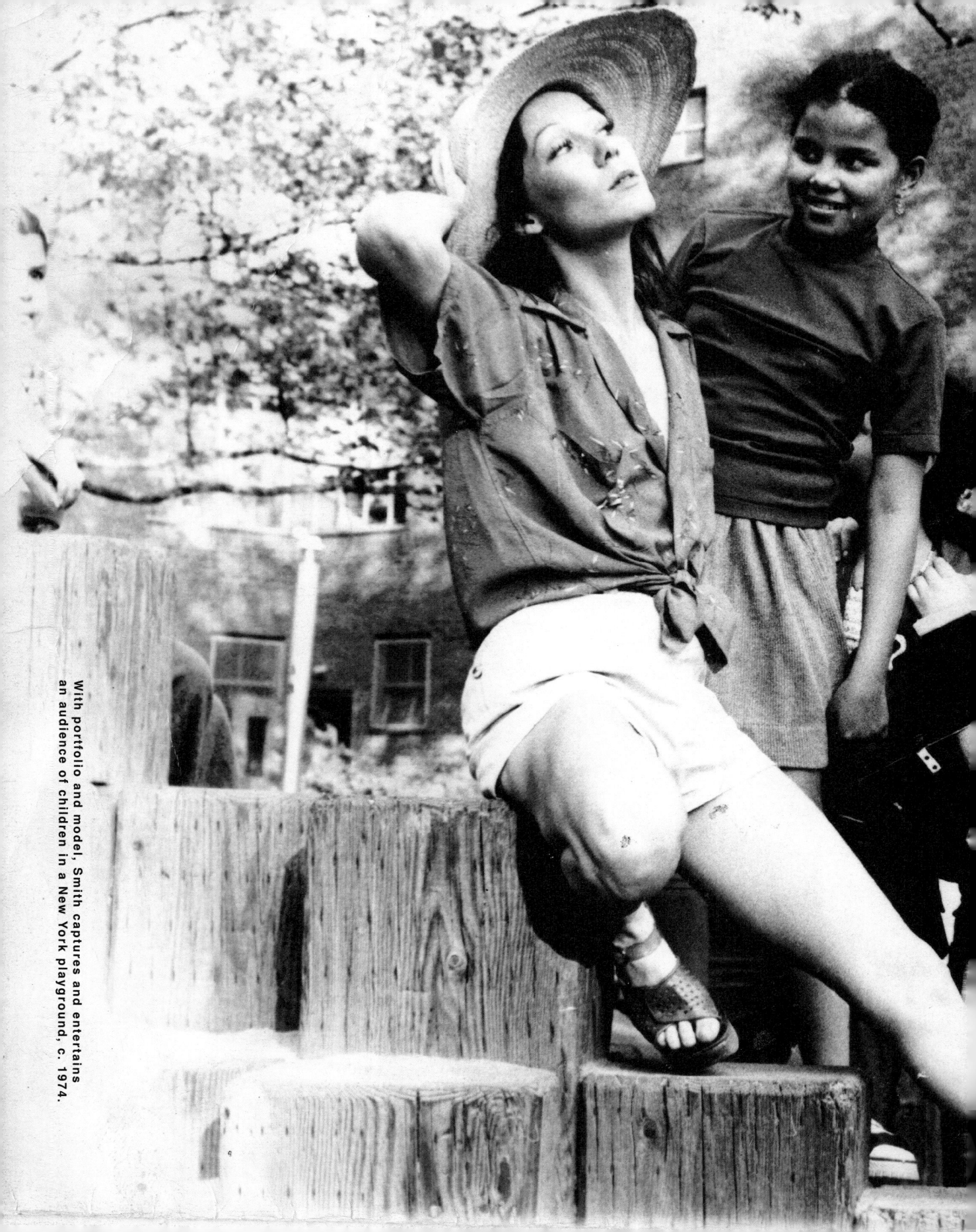

With portfolio and model, Smith captures and entertains an audience of children in a New York playground, c. 1974.

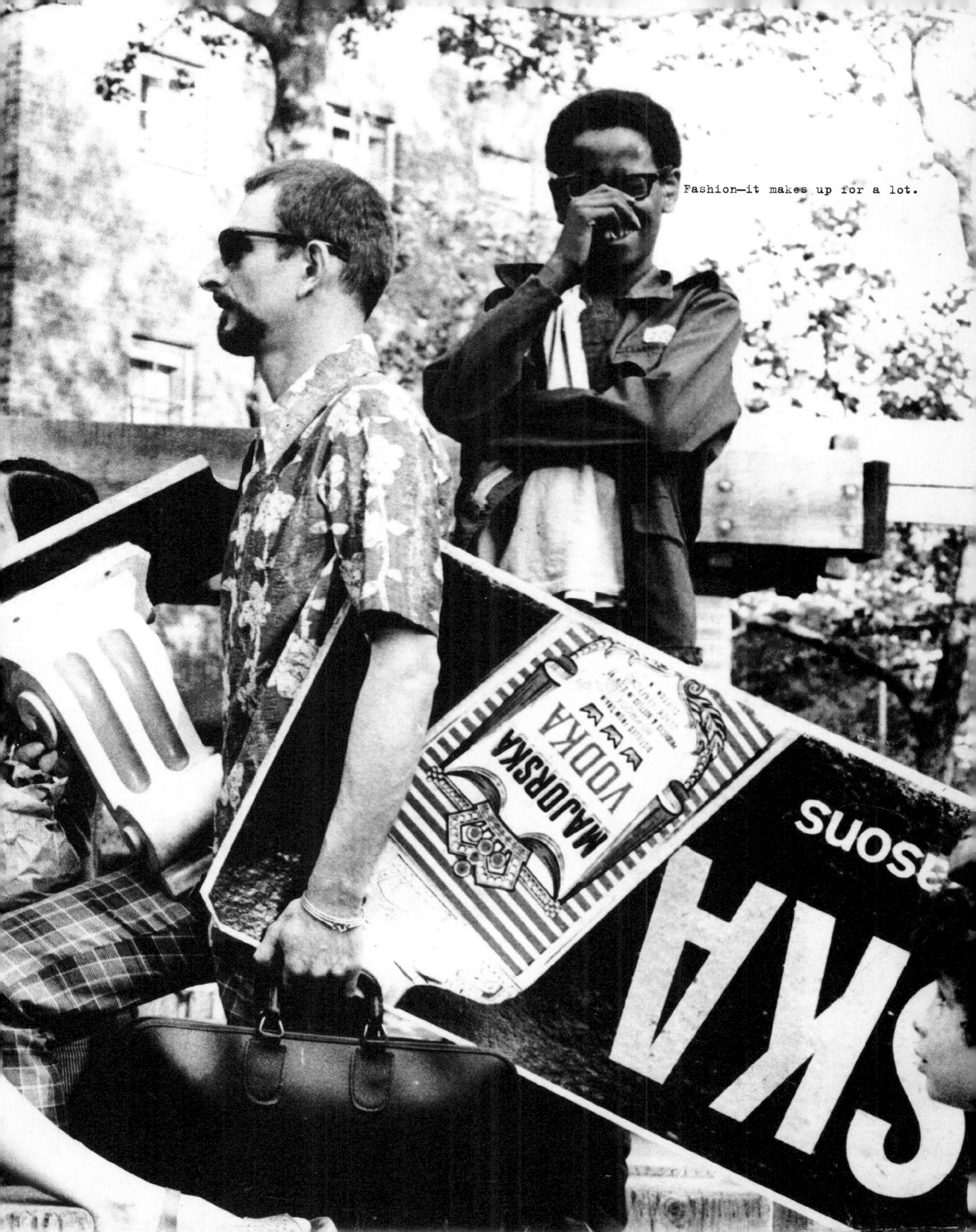

Fashion—it makes up for a lot.

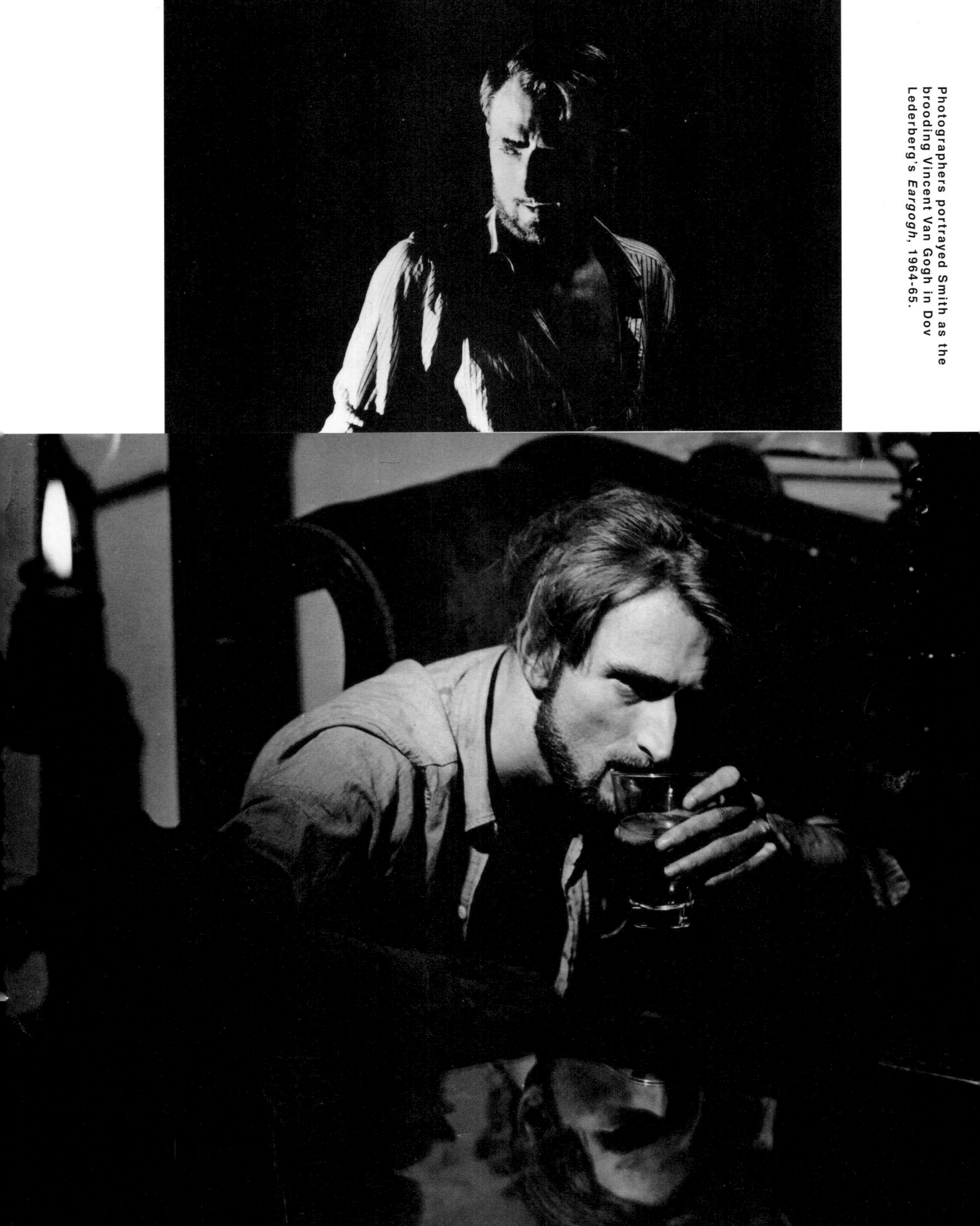

Photographers portrayed Smith as the brooding Vincent Van Gogh in Dov Lederberg's *Eargogh*, 1964-65.

During the Second Half of the Sixties

–Richard Foreman

As has been publicly acknowledged by all concerned, Smith was a major influence on much of the experimental theater that emerged in the seventies. Two strands of the ridiculous—Charles Ludlam and John Vaccaro—as well as the work of Robert Wilson and my own work clearly owe much to Smith's example and inspiration. I suspect that the power of his films probably inclined us all to a consideration of his (at first) more problematic theatrical work. (In my case, the first viewing of *Flaming Creatures* was perhaps the most overwhelming aesthetic experience of my life. I have not seen the film for many years, and have no idea if it would still affect me as it did then, but through fifteen re-viewings over a period of a few months, its impact on me did not lessen. To me, it was a Blakean vision come into three-dimensional, concrete life, and in that same sense "theatrical" in the true sense of the word.)…

I maintain that the theatrical events I experienced at the Cinematheque uniquely introduced me to a world of theater where the issues herein alluded to were clarified in very specific form. These events, which I find much harder to remember than the theater plays I attended during the same epoch, were experienced by me as events of more aesthetic worth, of greater seriousness and human truth, than the Broadway plays of the time. I believe that through the years they have proved hard for me to remember specifically because they dared, as has all important twentieth-century art, to evoke, render, and embody that vast area of our conscious and unconscious experience that the socially given forms in which we live have not named or categorized. The Broadway play arranged ideas and events, moods and sentiments already existing as recognizable gestalts in our mental organization—while the events I saw at the Cinematheque, like all true art, put onstage particular energies that matched no existing mental forms already existing as habit within our consciousness. Society had not preprogrammed us for the stage art on display at the Cinematheque in those days…

Less hard to recall than the Jack Smith play itself {*Rehearsal for the Destruction of Atlantis*} was the Jack Smith performance in an event that

Originally published in David E. James's To Free the Cinema: Jonas Mekas and the New York Underground, *1992.*

was credited to filmmaker Jerry Joffren. Smith was, of course, a performer in many underground films, with a persona quite indescribable, based on the exploration of the ultimate potential within us for allowing human effort, will, and purpose to be deflected and brought to a kind of transcendent, oscillating standstill by the minutiae of every moment lived in the course of "trying to perform." To watch Jack Smith perform was to watch human behavior turn into granular stasis, in which every moment of being seemed, somehow, to contain the seed of unthinkable possibility. It was endlessly fascinating. In the Joffren piece, Jack extended the wait between lines of dialogue to five, ten, twenty, minutes, believe it or not—with a further believe it or not: the wait was exhilarating. Report had it that it was at Jack's urging that the dialogue was extended in this way, something I take on faith since it seems central to the style and aesthetic he manifested in other circumstances. I recall, for instance, an occasion when I had been invited to attend an early rehearsal, of Robert Wilson's *Life and Times of Sigmund Freud*, in certain versions of which Jack appeared, and Wilson, unhappy at the end of the rehearsal, asking Jack for his thoughts, and Jack responding, in the extended nasal drawl that was so much his own, "it has to be…sadder, Bob, it's not saaad enough…make it…slow…er, much slower…er, just much slow…er."

That extended slowness, combined with the continual (and somewhat calculated) going wrong of every performance, brought the audience into a state of present attention that is precisely what other theater avoided in order to affect (i.e., manipulate) its audience. The theater generally hypnotizes; it pulls one into a dream that imitates a place in which the spectator would like to be. (Even Wilson falls into this habit.) The theater of Smith, along with other manifestations that took place in those days of Cinematheque performance, avoided that through building into performance various "confounding" devices—in Smith's case the great slowness informed by a feeling that "everything was going wrong," which made it hard for the audience to remember what was happening at the same time that it was fascinated by what was, indeed, happening in a time rhythm that both spectator and performer were experiencing in sync…

In short, then, I believe that a good number of the theatrical events presented at Mekas's Cinematheque pointed the way to a theater that can only marginally be realized at any historical time, a theater that functions as art functions, directly on the consciousness, and the way that consciousness operates, rather than a theater as illustrative psychology, mythology, or sociology. But it is a theater that nurtures, at all times, the dreams of those few young theater artists who are most insightful and exact in the ability to dredge up from the mind what the social beast has not found useful in its struggle to suppress the real evolution of consciousness and the spirit.

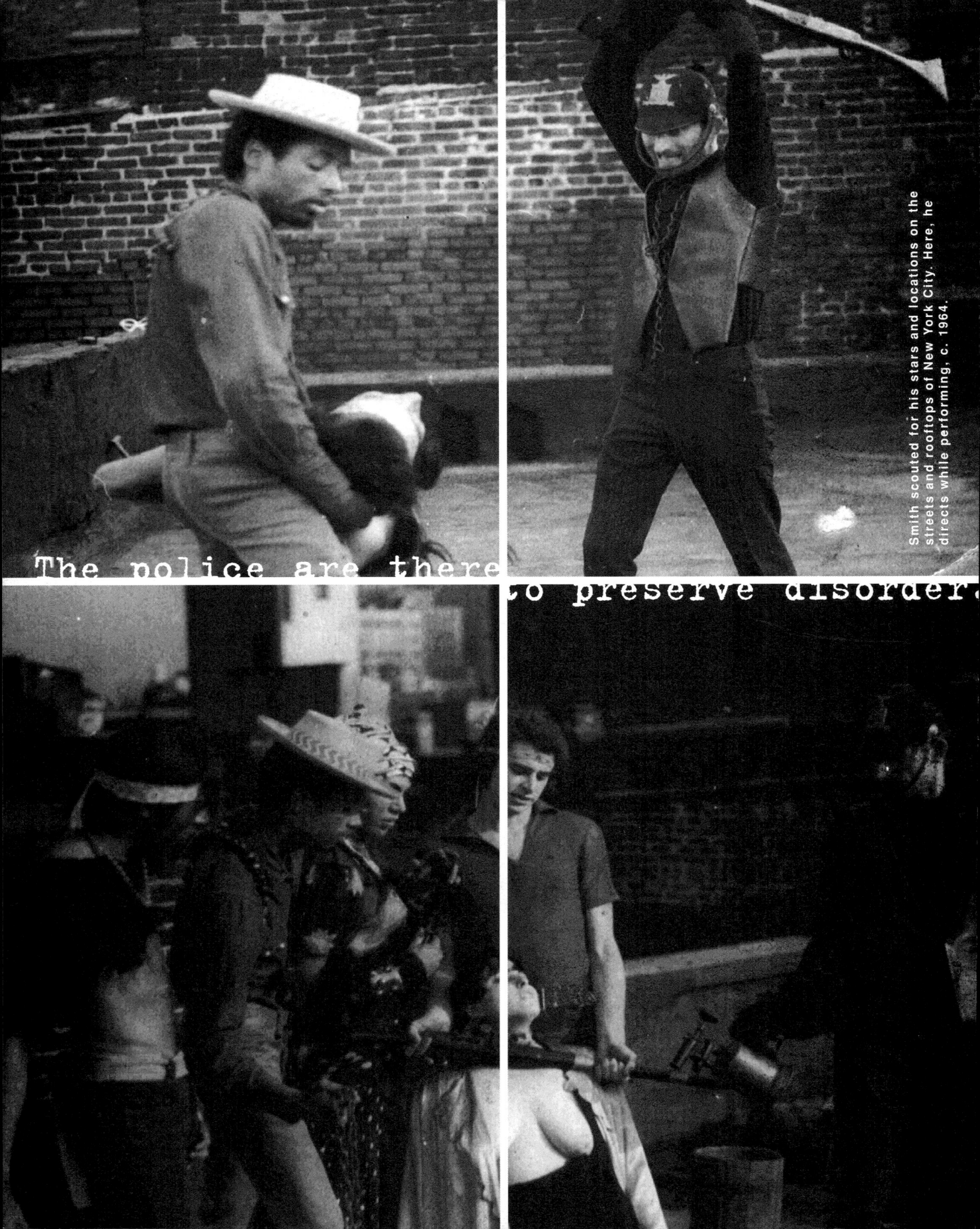

The police are there to preserve disorder.

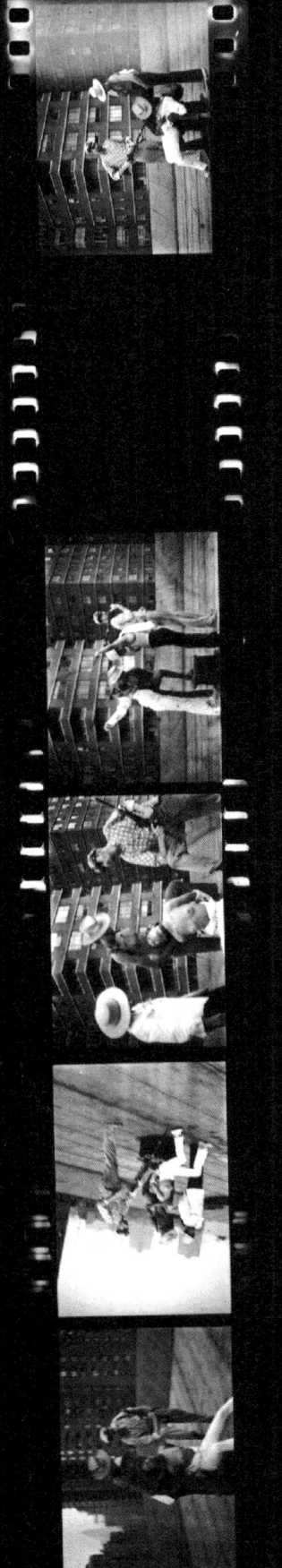
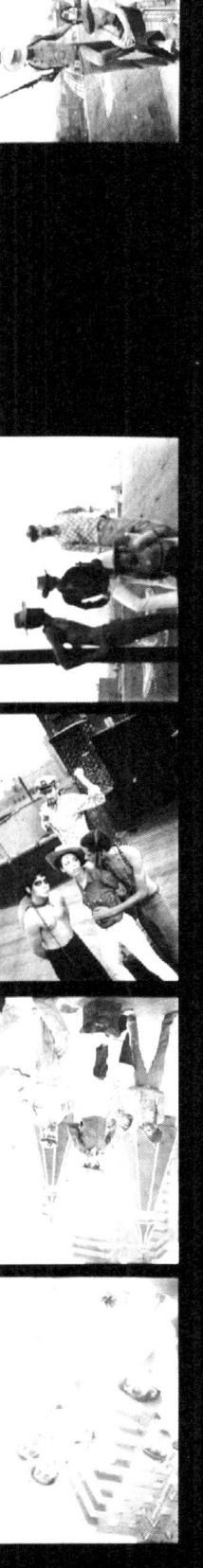
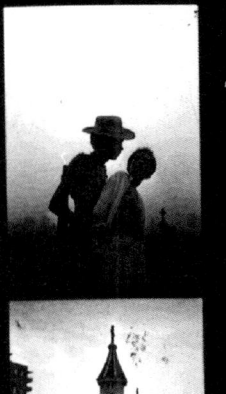
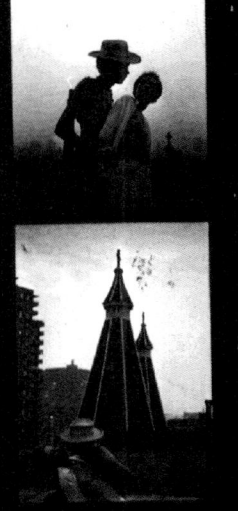
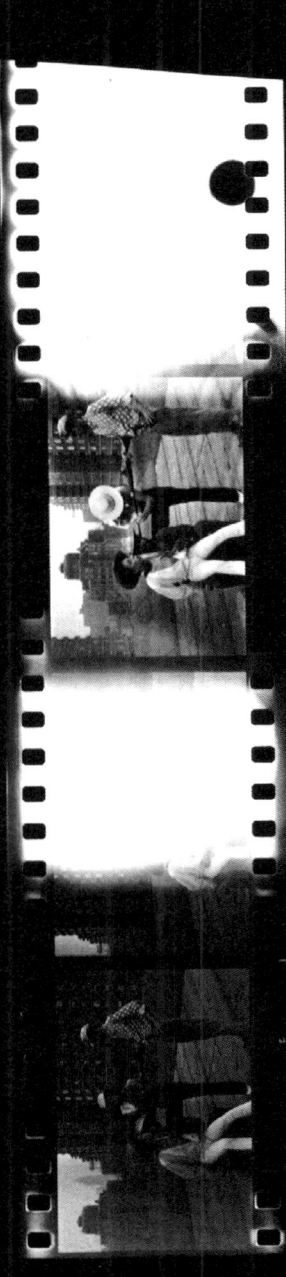

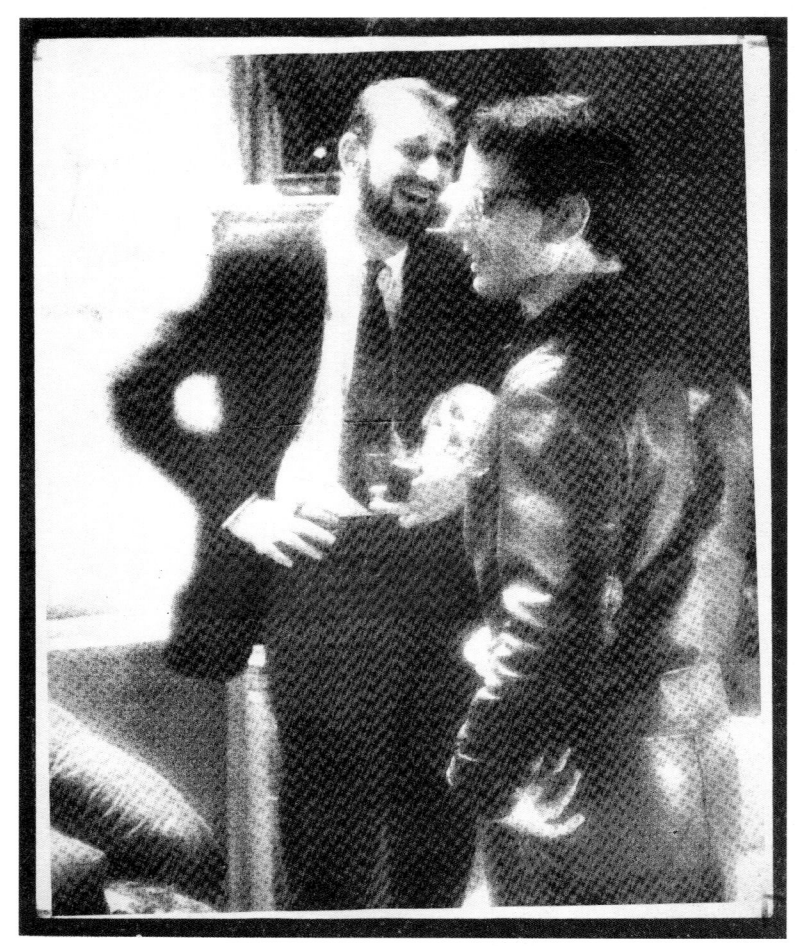

When he wanted to, Smith was an enthusiastic participant in the social mix of his day, and dressed for his role, c. 1965.

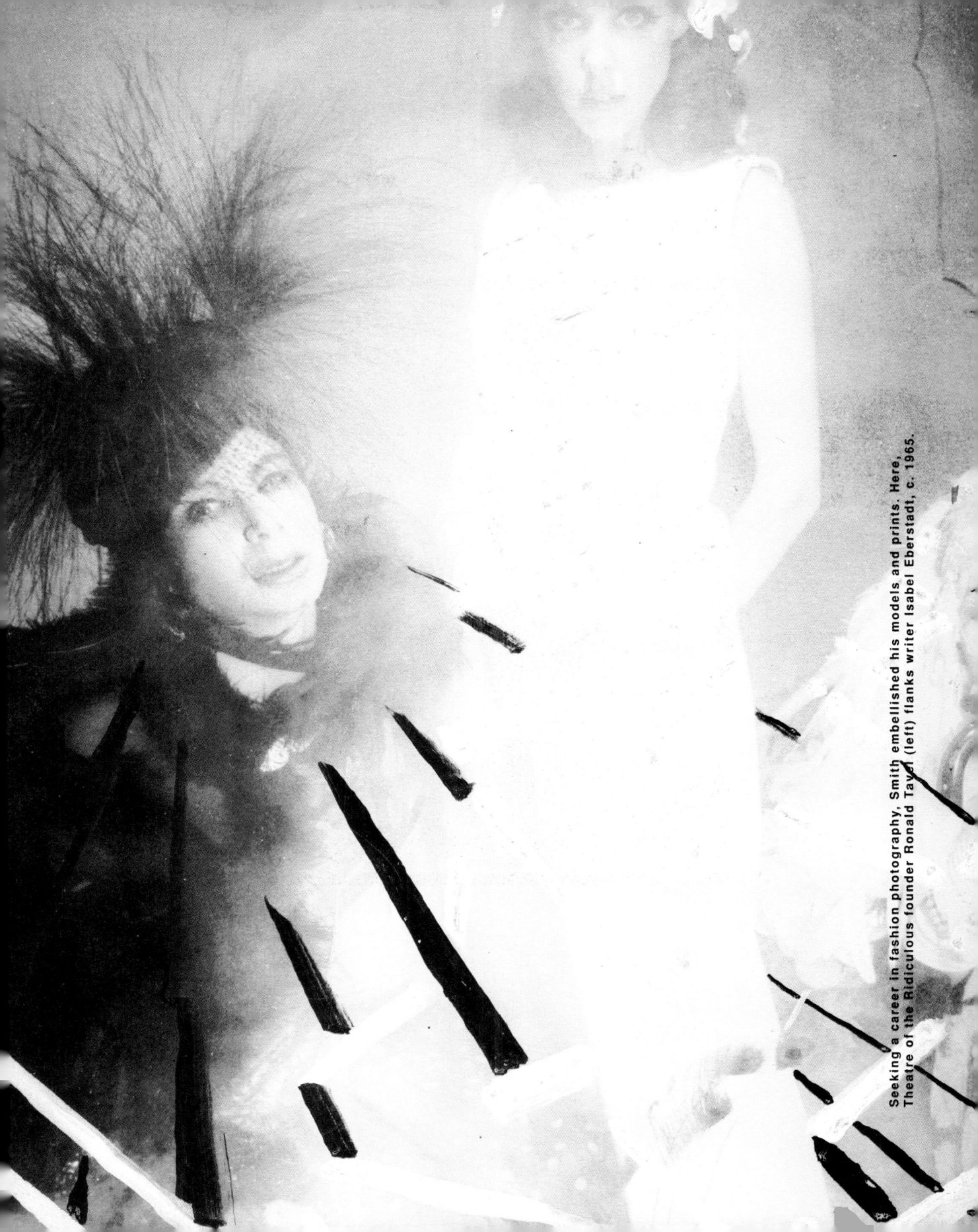

Seeking a career in fashion photography, Smith embellished his models and prints. Here, Theatre of the Ridiculous founder Ronald Tavel (left) flanks writer Isabel Eberstadt, c. 1965.

It's a health food-you simply dr

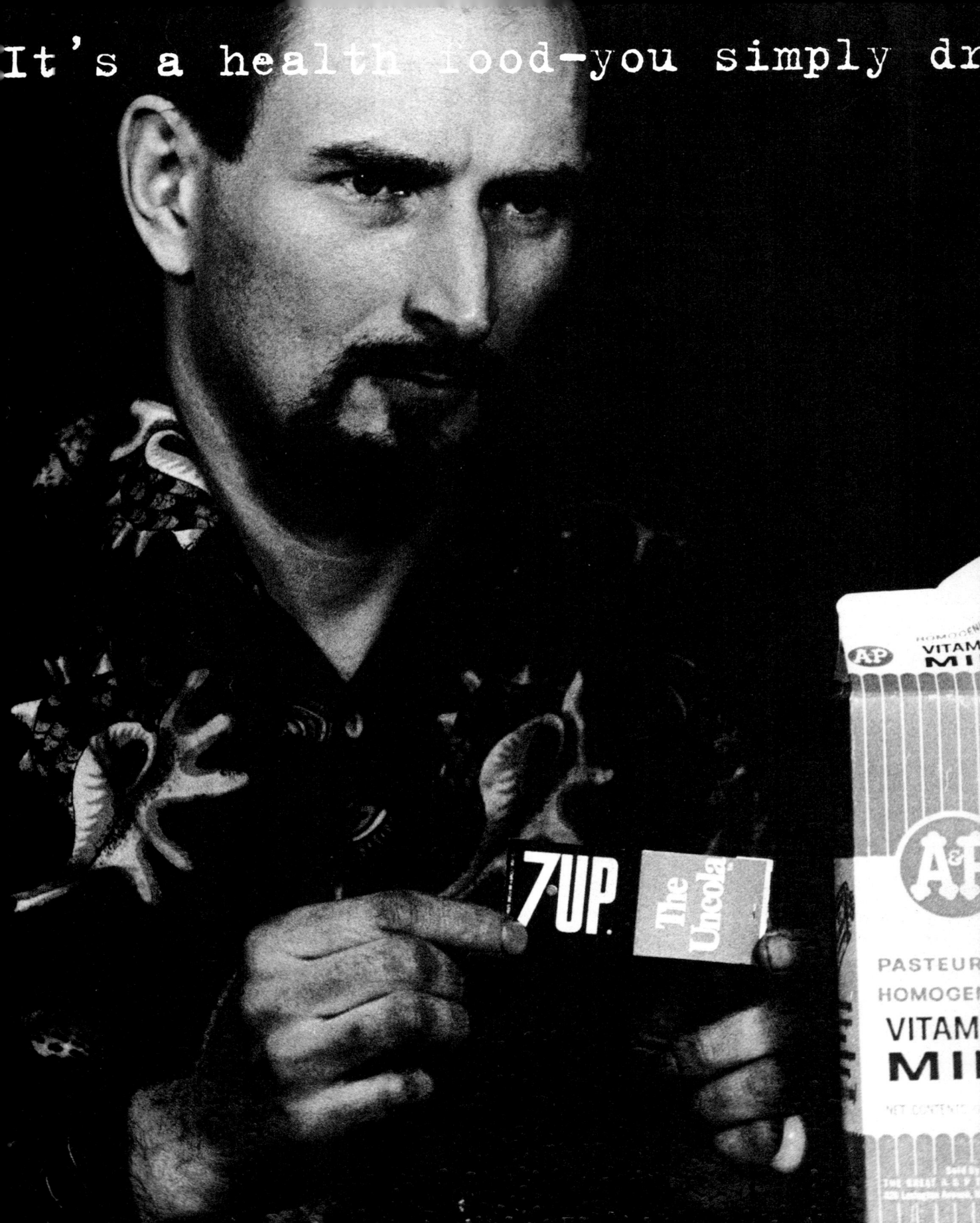

op it directly into the toilet.

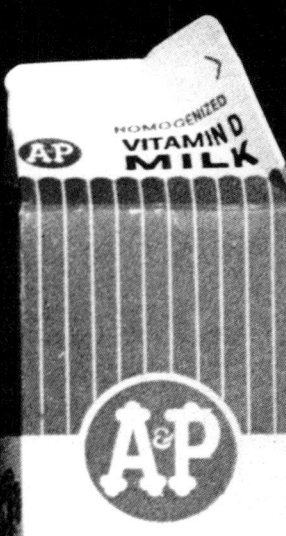

A A 20   A A 20   A A 20   A A 20

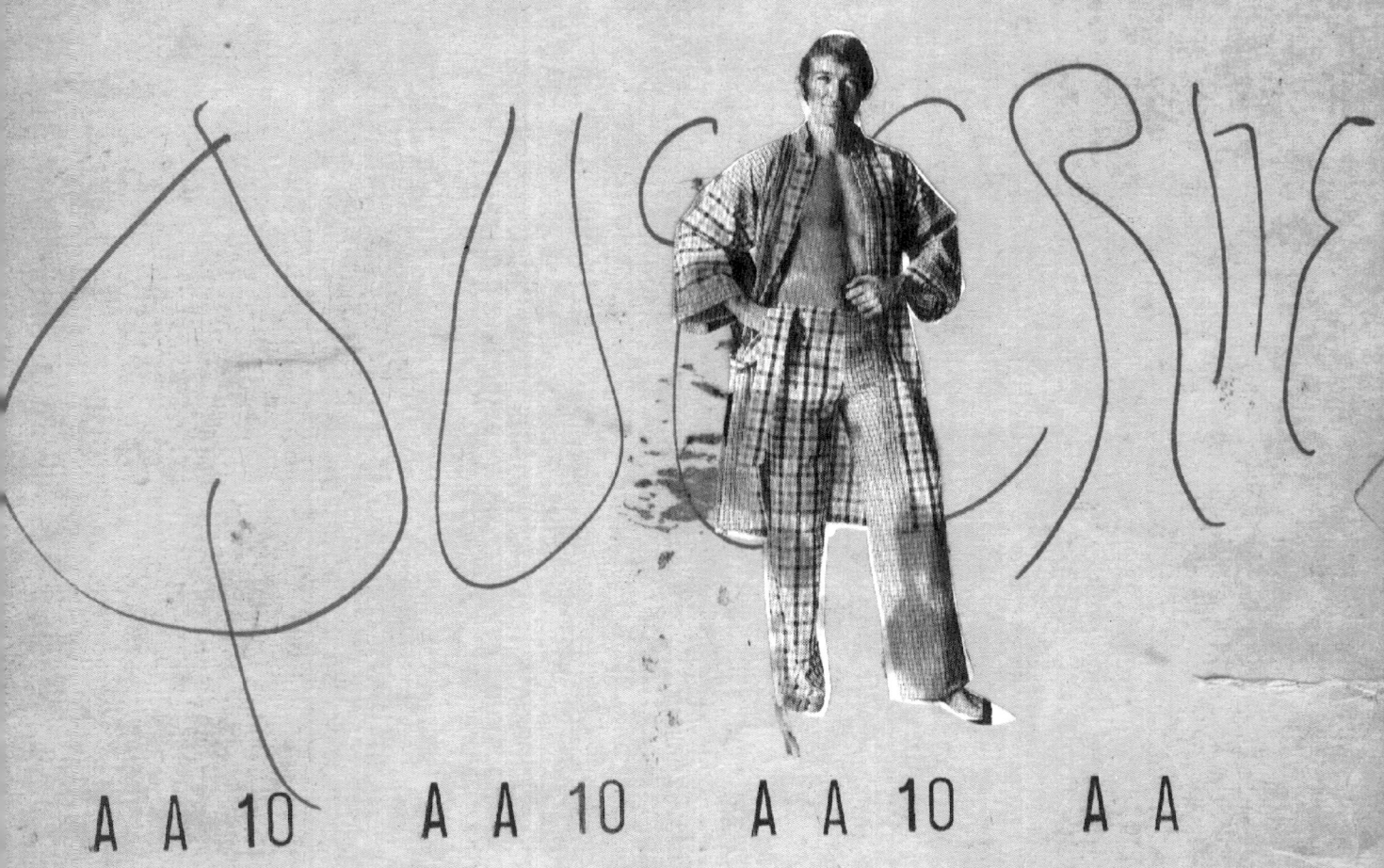

A A 10   A A 10   A A 10   A A

When you have police,

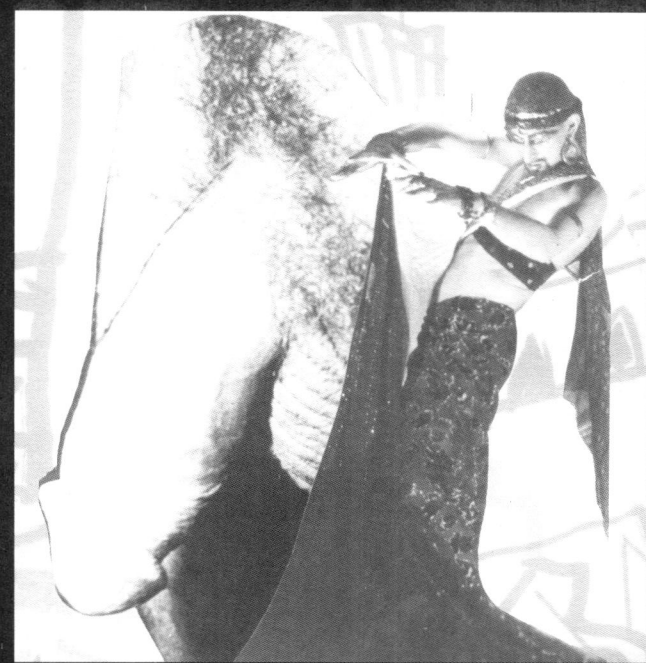

everything looks queer.

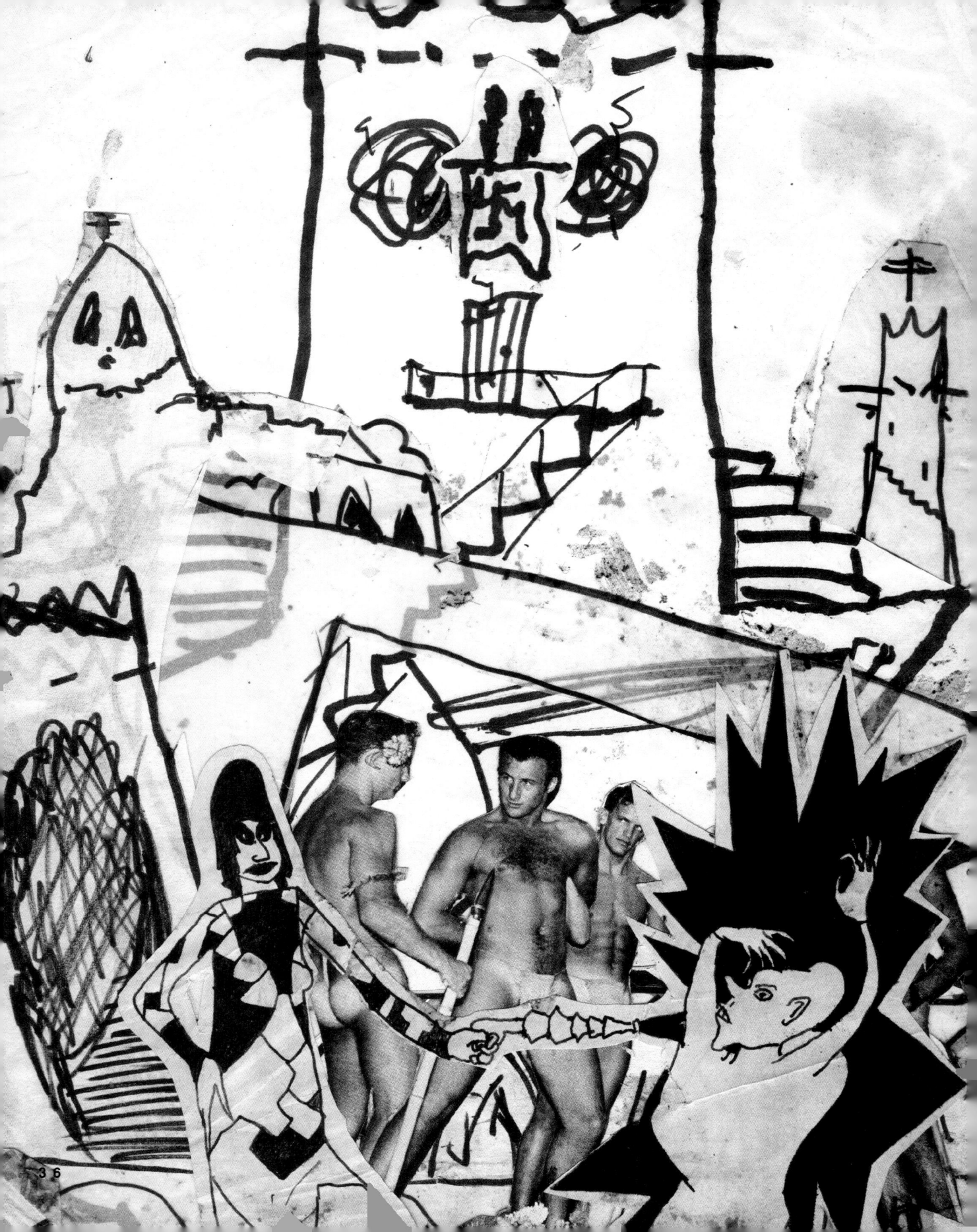

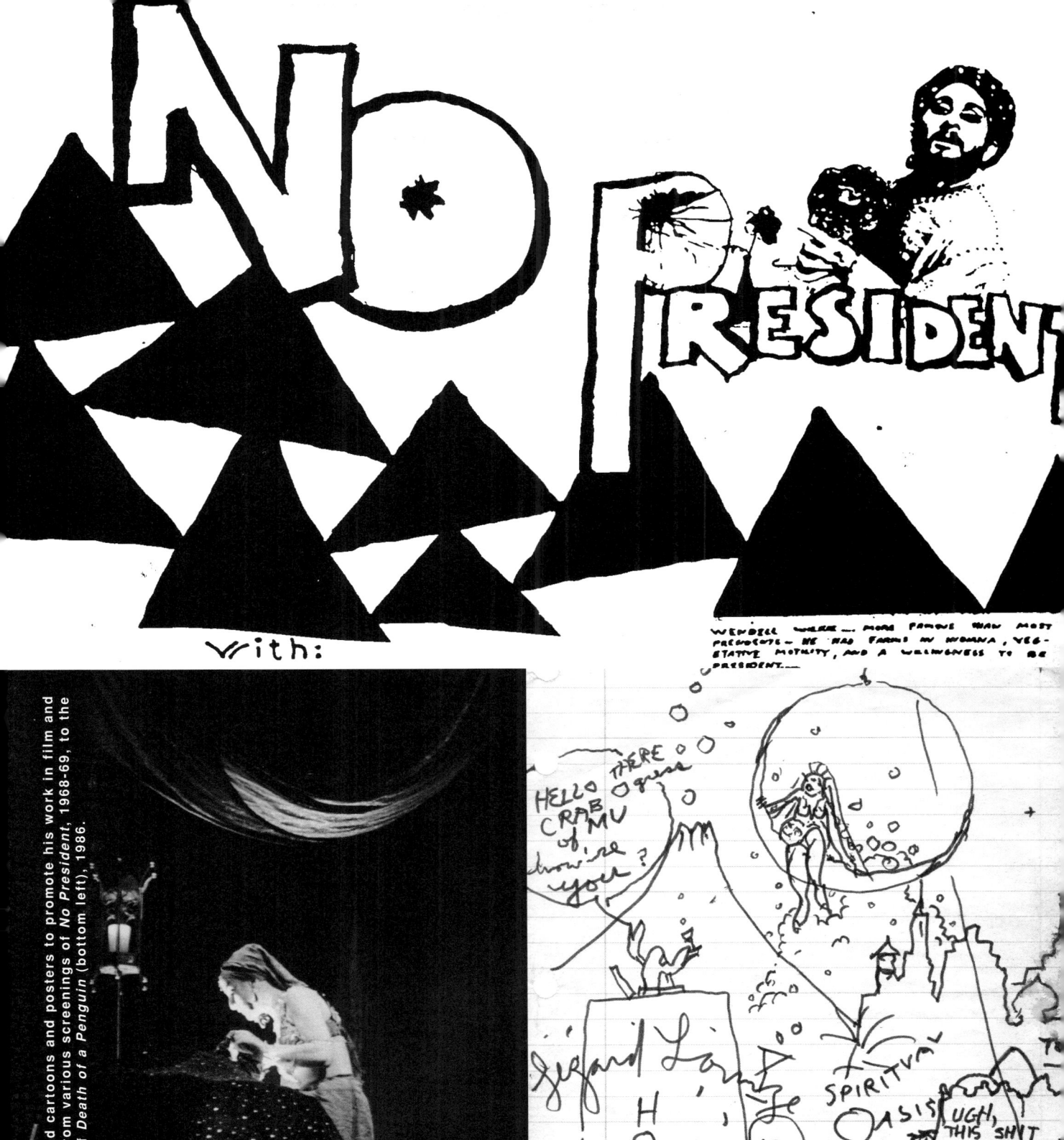

NO PRESIDENT

with:

Smith used cartoons and posters to promote his work in film and theater, from various screenings of *No President*, 1968–69, to the staging of *Death of a Penguin* (bottom left), 1986.

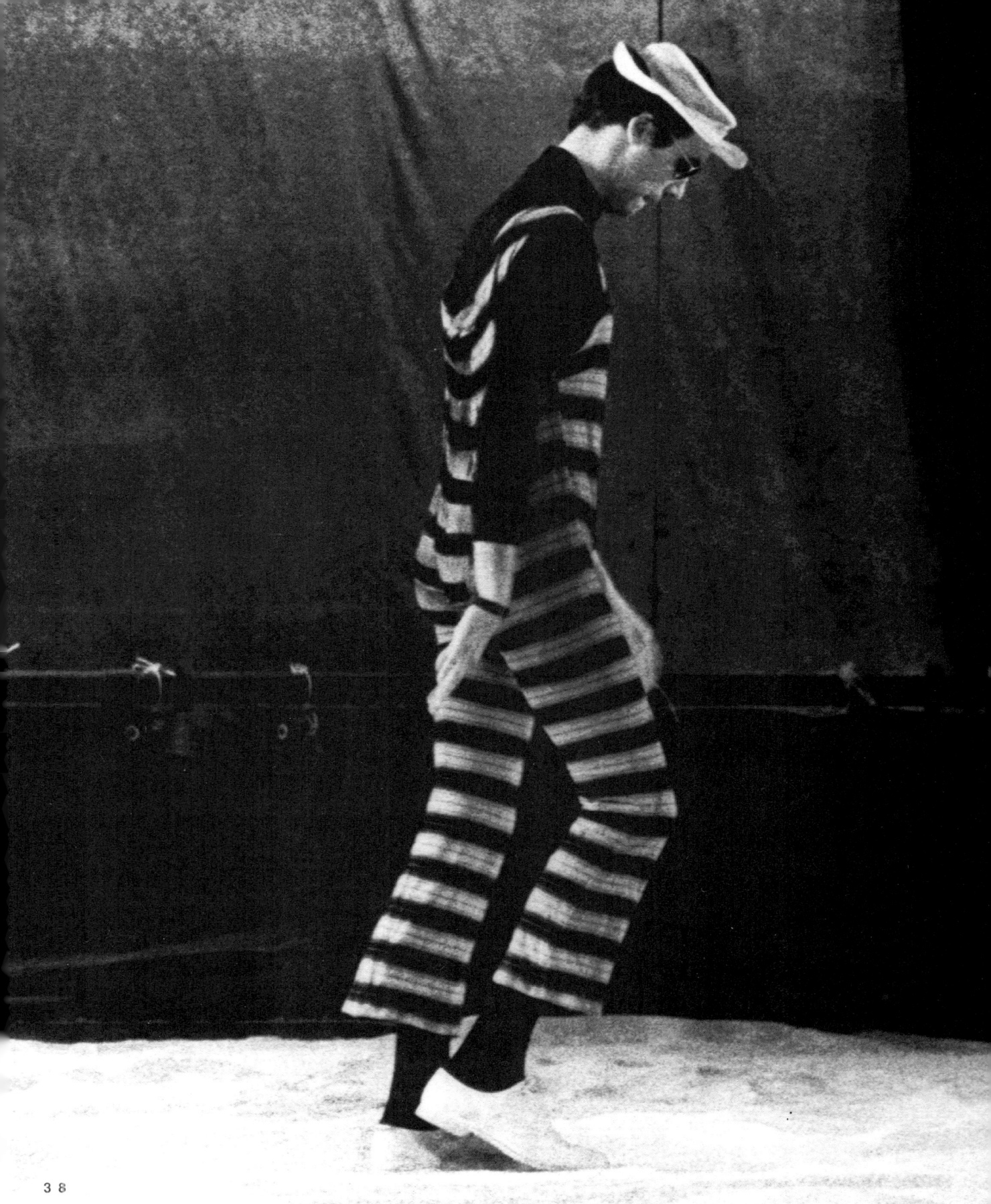

Artists are not helped by seeing what everybody else is boring. Those who make a living by this should not be supported. artists are helped by ~~shame ac~~ ~~watching~~ to work

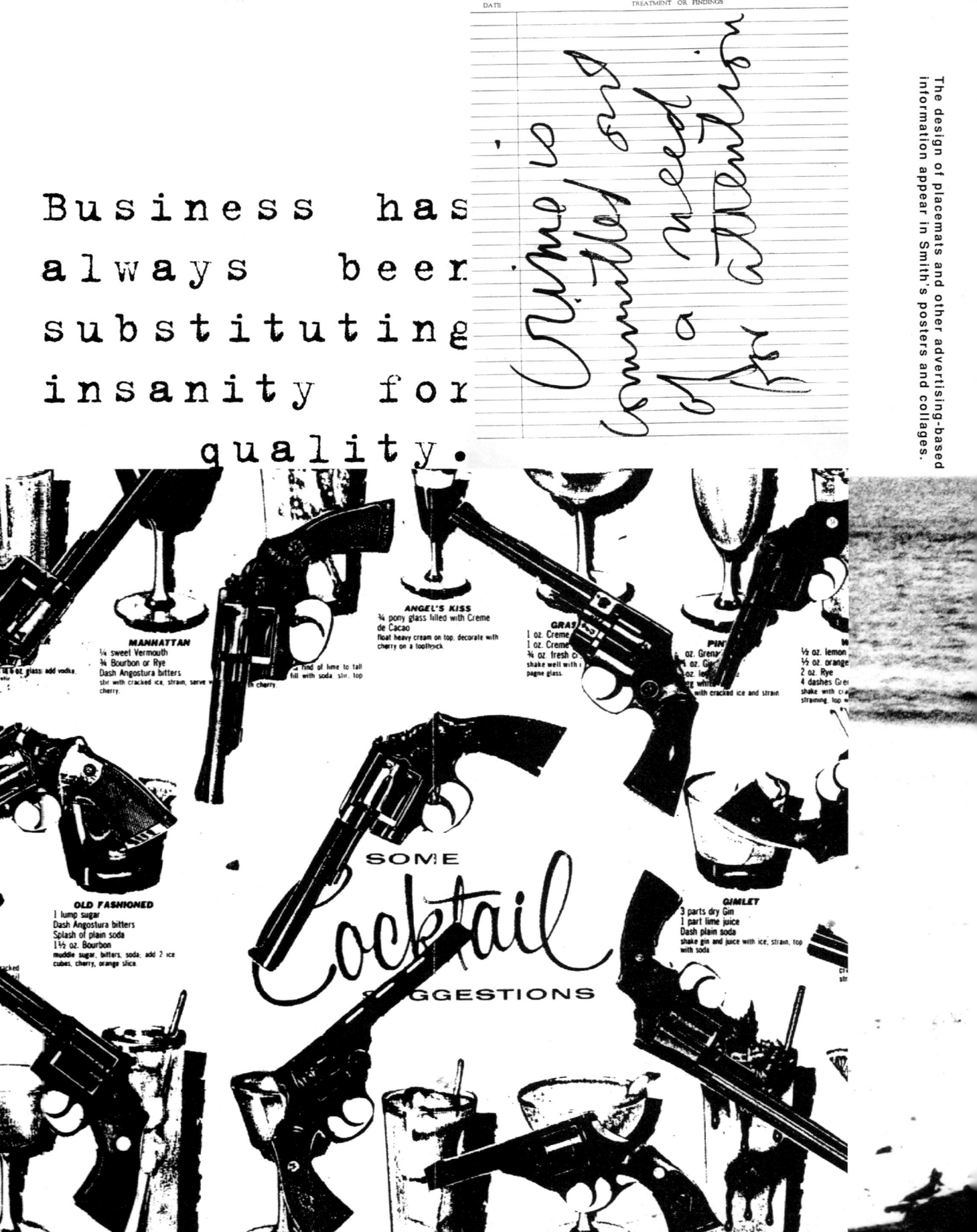

Business has always been substituting insanity for quality.

Crime is committed of a need for attention.

The design of placemats and other advertising-based information appear in Smith's posters and collages.

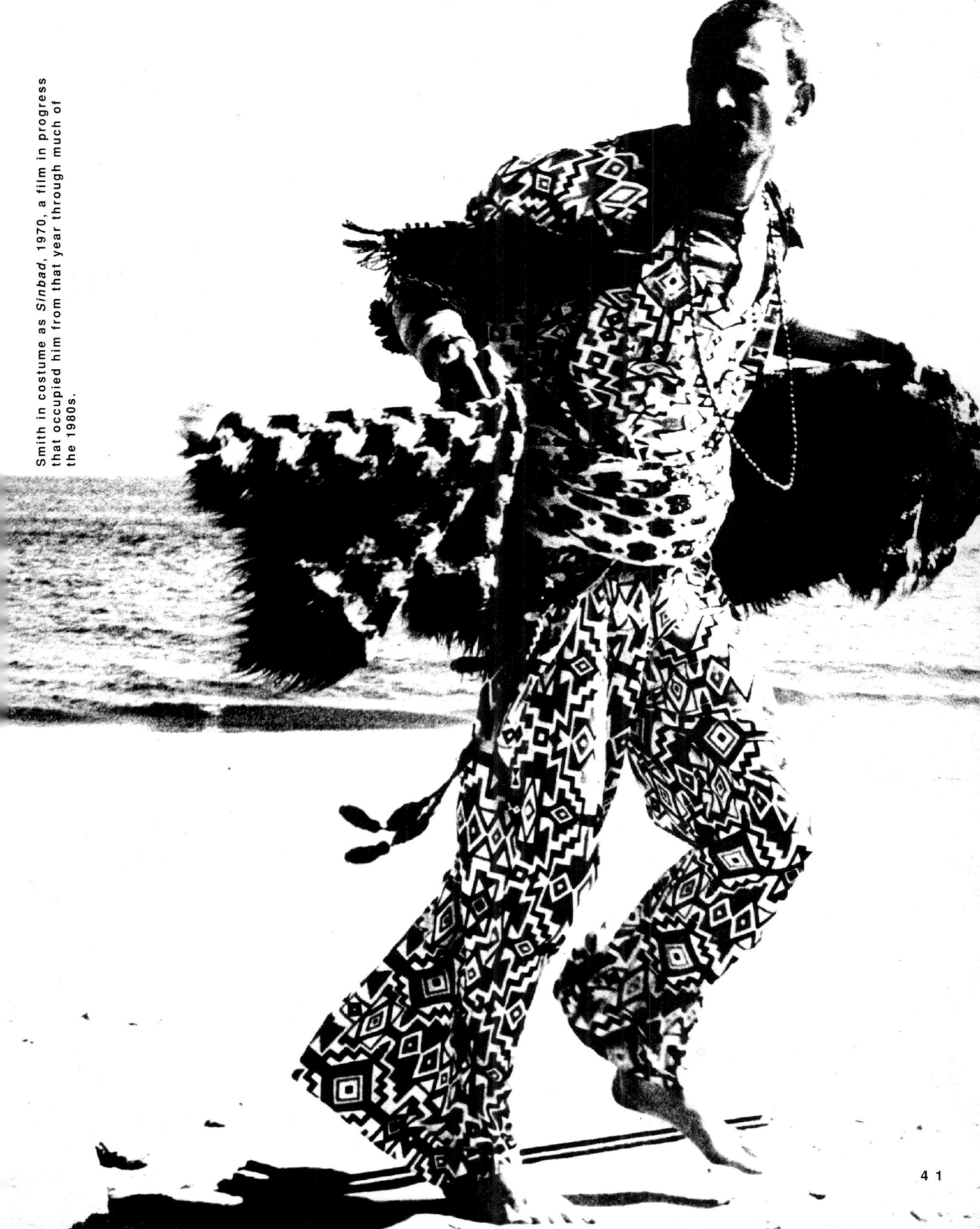

Smith in costume as *Sinbad*, 1970, a film in progress that occupied him from that year through much of the 1980s.

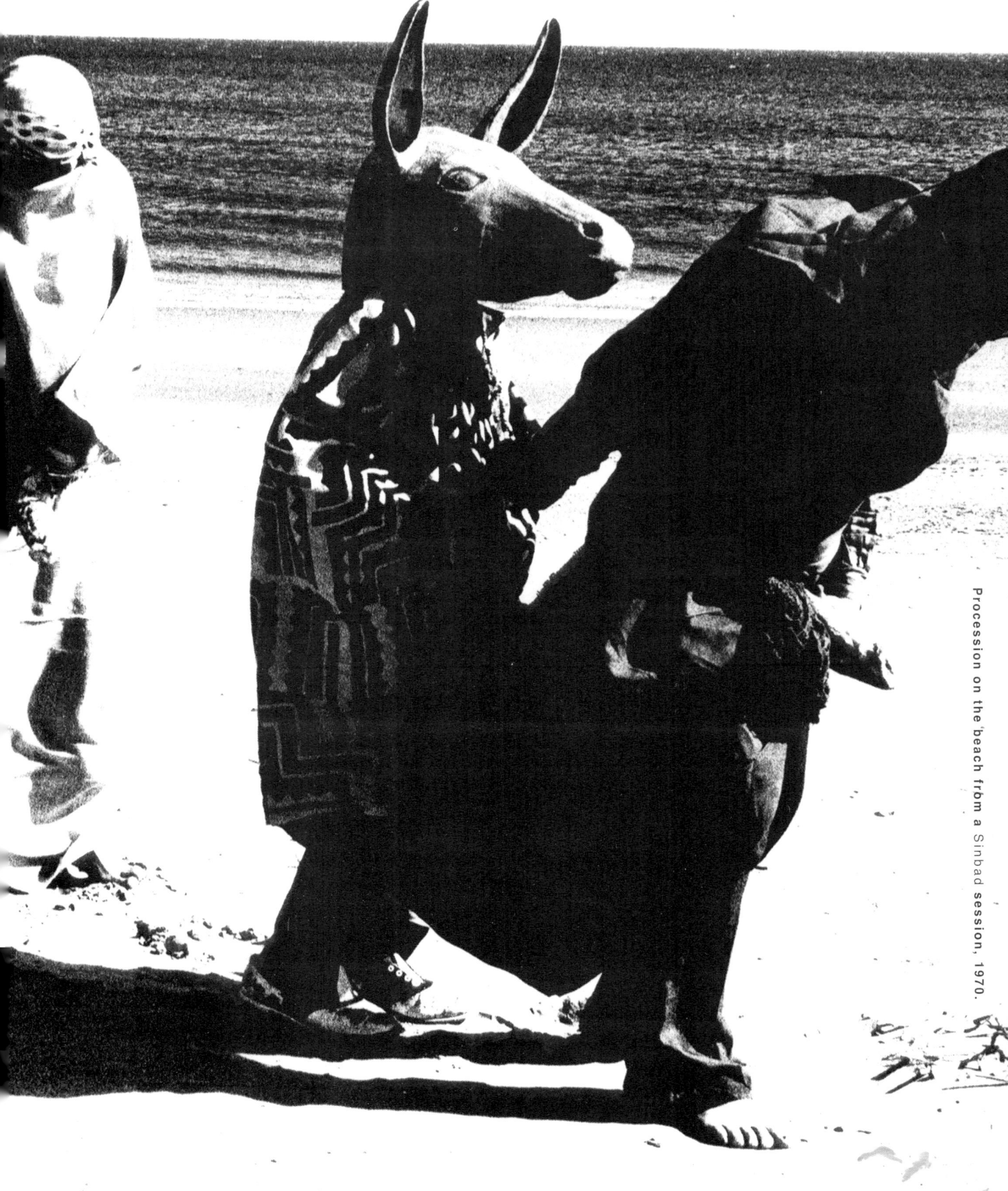

The sheer beauty of junk

—Stefan Brecht

All of Smith's gestures are hesitant. The simplest lifting of an object or securing of a string is a serious task which he will accomplish, but which he does not seem quite to know how to go about. He tries various approaches—in front of you—perhaps gives up some lines of approach too quickly. He is figuring out how to do it while doing it. Changing one slide for another, he stops pulling the first one while a corner of the image is still (dimly) on the screen, then pulls it out. Perhaps he is not sure he is doing the right thing. Any performance of his contains many such episodes of change of approach to a simple practical task. He is continually busy with simple practical tasks. It's not that the show has not been carefully prepared. E.g. the bottles, containers, old Xmas trees, signs, broken toys, baby carriages that compound his stage setting—a central object taking up to 80 percent or more of the area set aside for performance—have all been carefully arranged and this has taken him a long time because many minute rearrangements were needed…

The heap glitters melodiously. It is clearly exotic, a landscape of desire. The fact that the material is with puritanical strictness, in demonic purity junk—in substance, shape and monetarily of absolutely no value—isolates this longing into its form of pure sentiment. But this is no dream world, it is not even the world of daydreams, tho' that is closer: it is the world of art, a formally artificial arrangement. Its artificiality is explicitly part of its form, and that what it is an arrangement of, its matter, doesn't matter, is also part of the form. It is no dream world because the ambiguities between the purity of sentiments that are popular, everybody's and their obvious insane vulgarity (insane because they are far removed from the realities of conceivable pleasure)—an ambiguity operative in Smith's salvaging jetsam infecundated with the big city's desires— and between the maker's 100 percent artistic devotion and the total humor of it are complete. Except where the art elevates that preciousness of material into epiphany of the natural world's capacity for glory, the purity of art is adulterated by precious substances, as those in certain visions of paradise, and by admonitory signs of the work's importance, as where the materials are of good quality. I take leave—he is loathe not to keep working. When I get out on the streets the bars are all closed, there are only late-night people. It is around 4 a.m. I have learned more about art than on any other day or night of my life.

Originally published in Queer Theater, *Frankfurt Germany: Suhrkamp, 1978.*

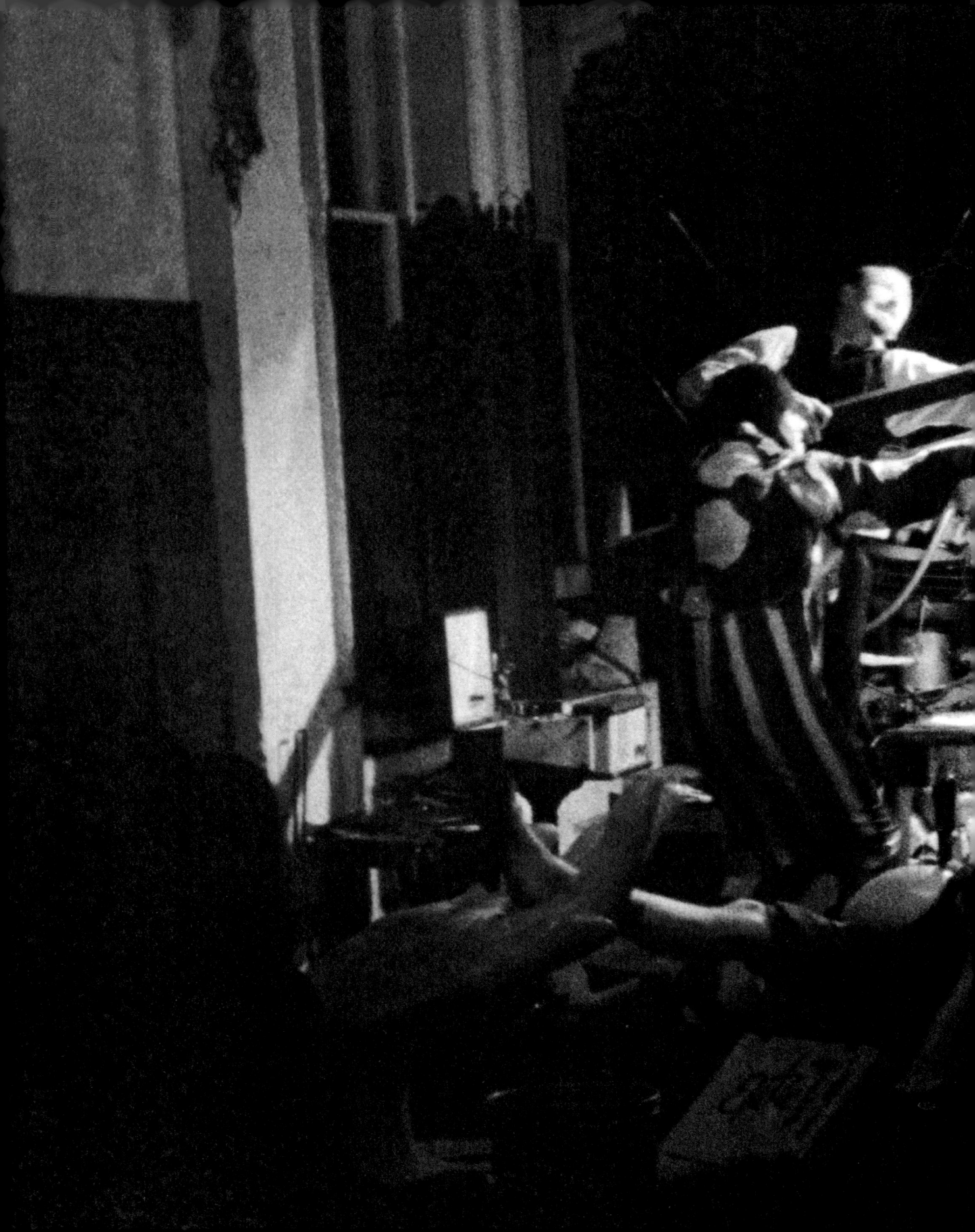

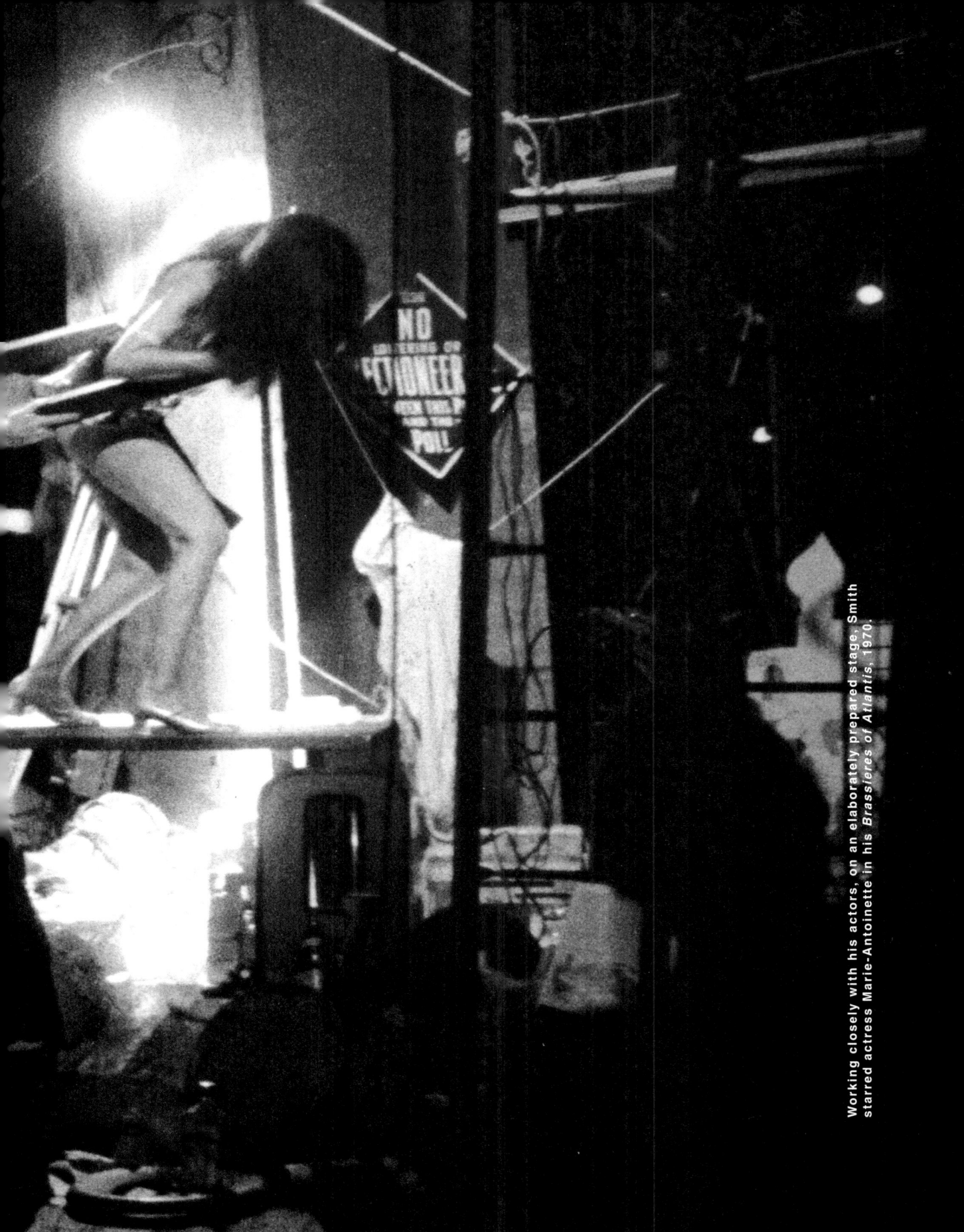

Working closely with his actors, on an elaborately prepared stage, Smith starred actress Marie-Antoinette in his *Brassieres of Atlantis*, 1970.

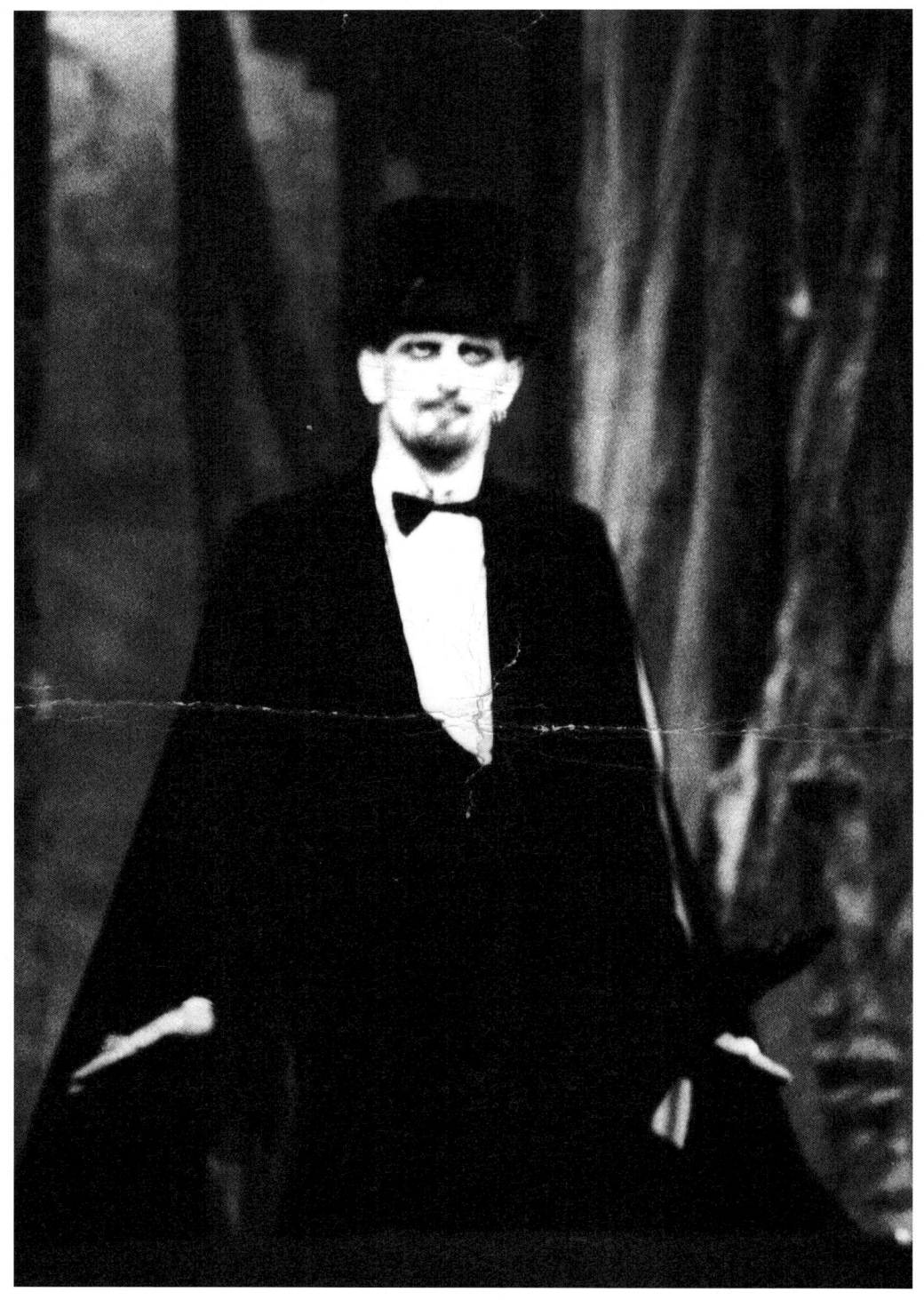

Smith's last association with Robert Wilson was as Man with the Top Hat and Cape in Wilson's *Deafman Glance*, 1971.

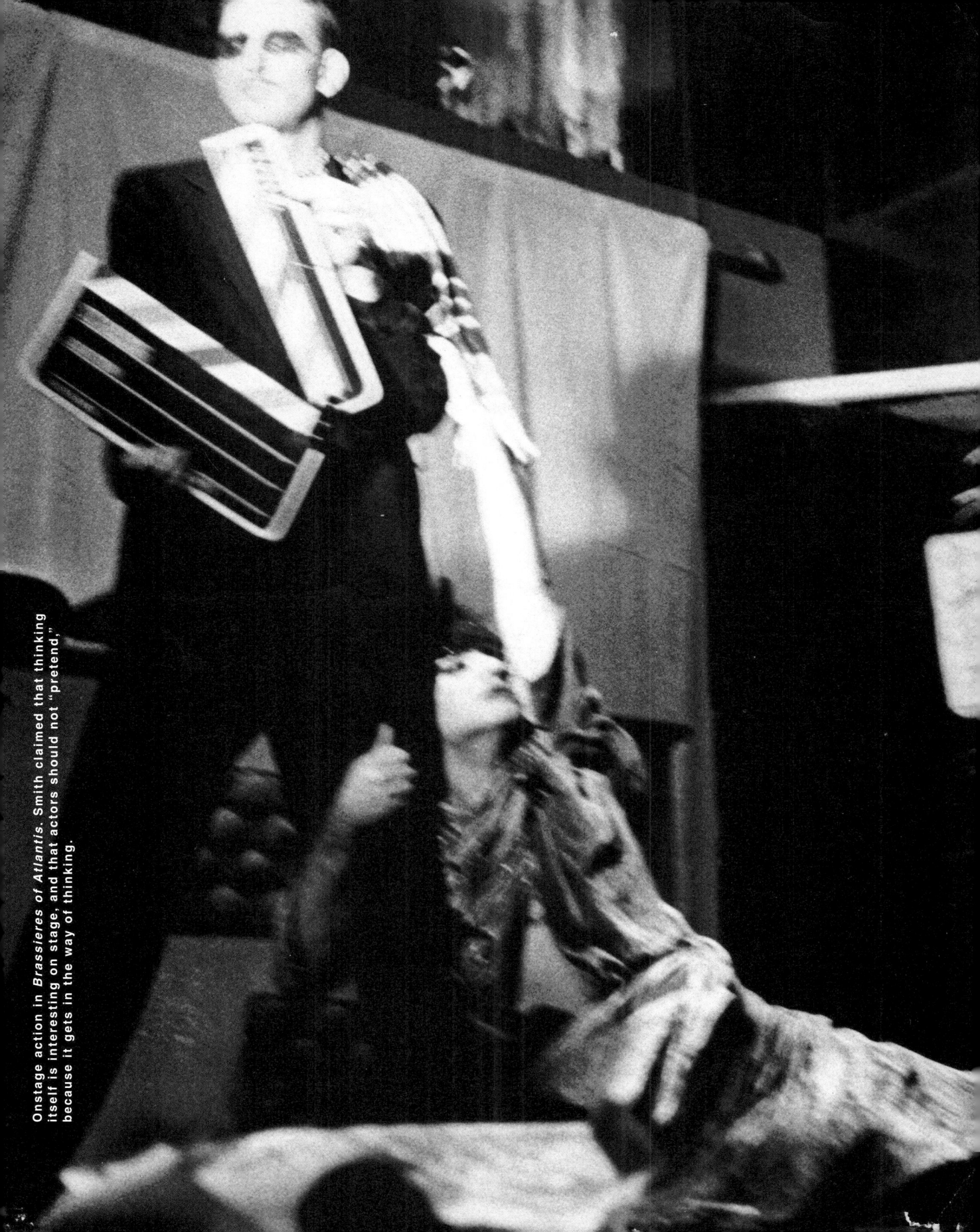

Onstage action in *Brassieres of Atlantis*. Smith claimed that thinking itself is interesting on stage, and that actors should not "pretend," because it gets in the way of thinking.

Jack Smith, or The End of Civilization

—Jonas Mekas

Now it was past 2 a.m., and as I watched, as we watched this fantastic show, I had a feeling, I suddenly was very conscious that it was 2 a.m. in New York, and very late, and most of the city was sleeping, even on Saturday night, and that all the theatres had been closed and over, long ago, all that's called theatre, all the ugly, banal, stupid theatres of the world, and that only here, in this downtown loft, somewhere at the very end of all the empty and dead and gray downtown streets, was this huge junk set and these end-of-civilization activities, these happenings, this theatre. I began getting a feeling, it resembled more and more the final burial ceremonies, the final burial rites of the capitalist civilization, competitive civilization, these were the magic burial grounds and the burial rites of all the corruption, comfort and money and good living, and free gifts of the world that was now asleep, at 2 a.m., only Jack Smith was still alive, a madman, the high priest of the ironical burial grounds, administering last services here alone and by himself, because really the seven or eight people who were now his audience (the other three were on the set) were really no audience at all, Jack didn't need any audience, he would do it anyway, and I had a feeling that he did it anyway, many nights like this, many Saturdays, by himself, audience or no audience, actors or no actors, he reenacted this ceremony, the last man who was still around and above it all and not part of it but at the same time conscious of it all, very painfully conscious of it all, the sadness himself, the essence of sadness itself...

But whatever they did, script or no script, private or instructed, it all fell into the set, into the play, against their won will, hilarious at the moment it all became part of the huge sadness of the burial grounds, the end of civilization sadness, part of the plan, part of the human wreckage, all rearranged by Jack, the Madman of Grand Street, who seemed to know it all, to know the corruption and weaknesses of men, and the problems he'll face with his art, so he preprogrammed it all, so that now whatever anybody does to destroy his art falls into his art, becomes part of the huge collage, no matter what they do. He prearranged the music and the whole set so that it absorbs everything—exactly

Originally published in The Village Voice, *July 23, 1970*

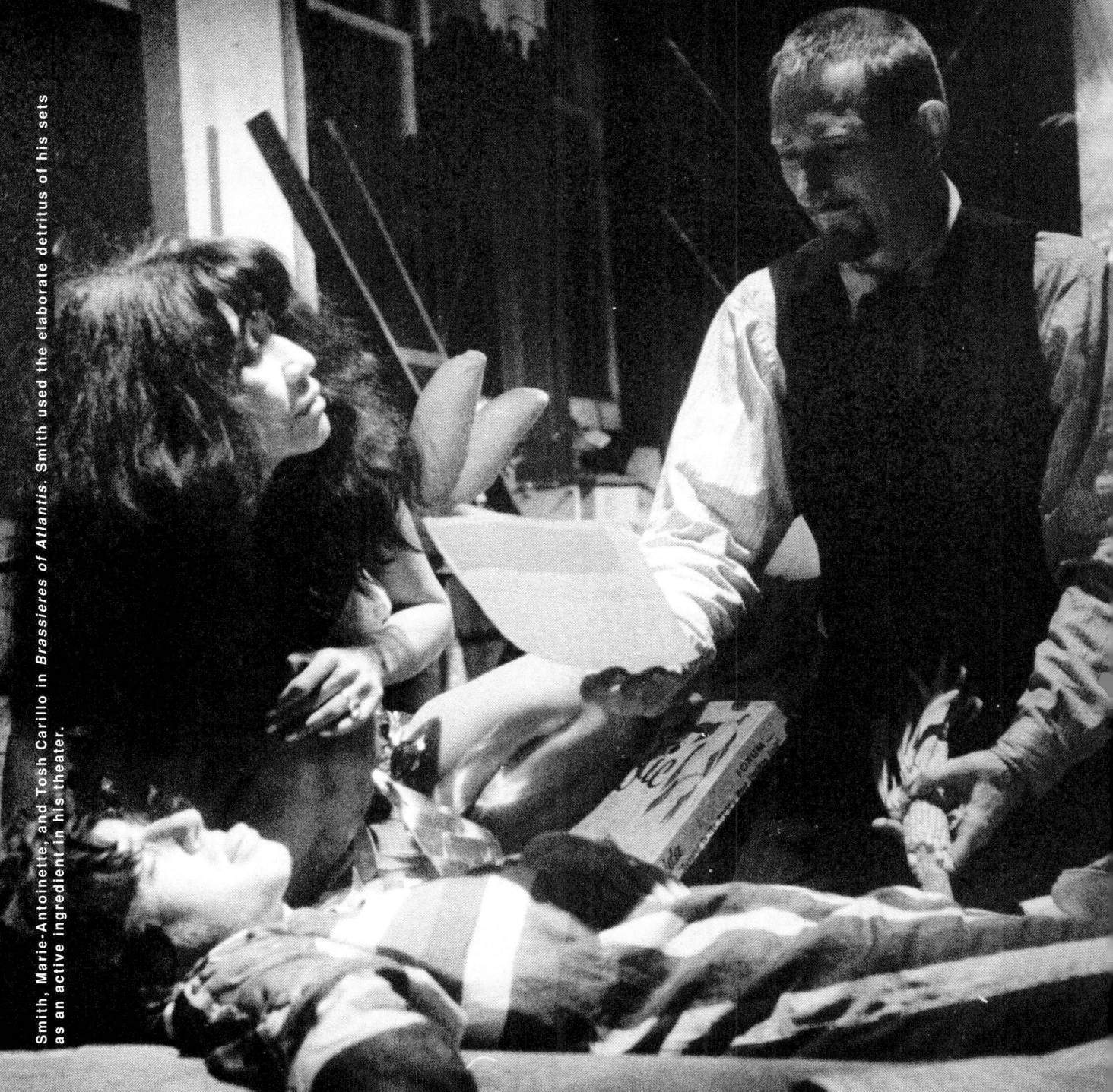

like the end of the civilization itself which it seemed to portray—yes, this set became like this culture that seems to absorb everything and everybody—a huge dumping grounds, an open mouth of graveyards—…

And then Jack said, feigning slight embarrassment, something like "that's it," and he walked across the set, and to the ladder, and he slowly

climbed up the ladder, probably to cut out the spotlights, and we stood there
for a moment, five or six of us, and hesitated, to wait for Jack or not, but we
decided to go, it was close to three o'clock, and we all went down to the street.
I turned around as we left. Jack was still upstairs. The place, the set now was
there by itself, completely empty and alone, the whole place was empty, and I
thought for a moment I should shout to Jack GOOD NIGHT, JACK, but I didn't,
I thought it wouldn't fit in all somehow, and we left—
We walked, five of us, down the long dark Grand Street, without any words,
several blocks, we walked silently and without words, and we knew, we knew
that we had seen one of the greatest and purest theatre evenings of our lives,
and we knew Jack was there alone and by himself in his loft, the keeper of the
graveyard of the end of civilization, and one of the last and uncompromising
great artists our generation had produced, and somehow everything stood
clear inside us, a standard for our lives, and our art was reestablished, for a
moment, this night, in Jack's loft, here, downtown, this late hour, as the city
slept. Somehow there was a new hope and life in the black street again, as
we walked, silently.

(opposite page) Although Smith expressed disdain for contract actress Yvonne De Carlo and her failure to live up to the firey independence of Maria Montez, he identified with both actresses.

glamourize your Messe

THE YUOMME DE CARLO TABERNACL CHOIR IS STANDING AROUND ON THE STAIRWA TO SUCESS, WAVING BLOODT PALM BRANCHES AND WAI TO SING "HYM" TO THE SUN" BY IRVING BERLIN

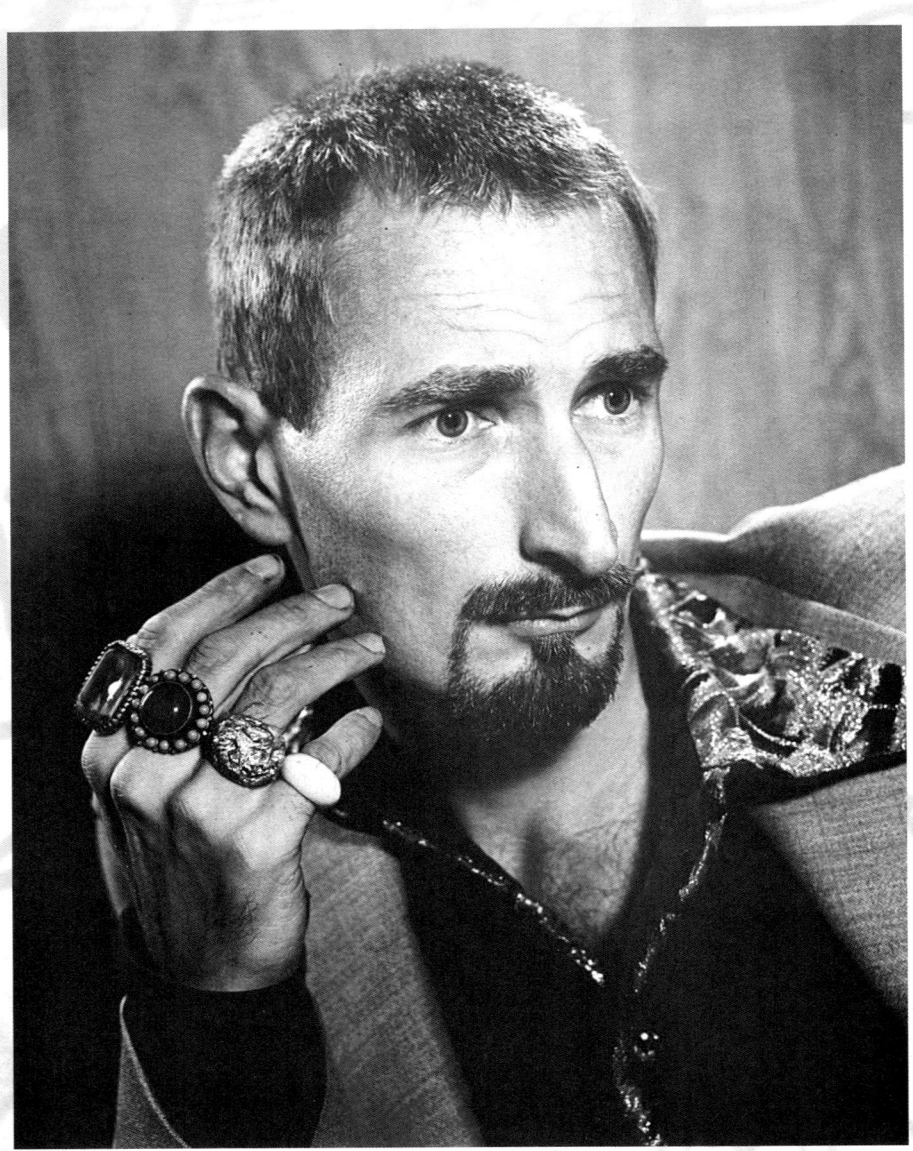

Publicity headshots of Jack Smith by Sal Terra-Cina Photo, c. 1970.

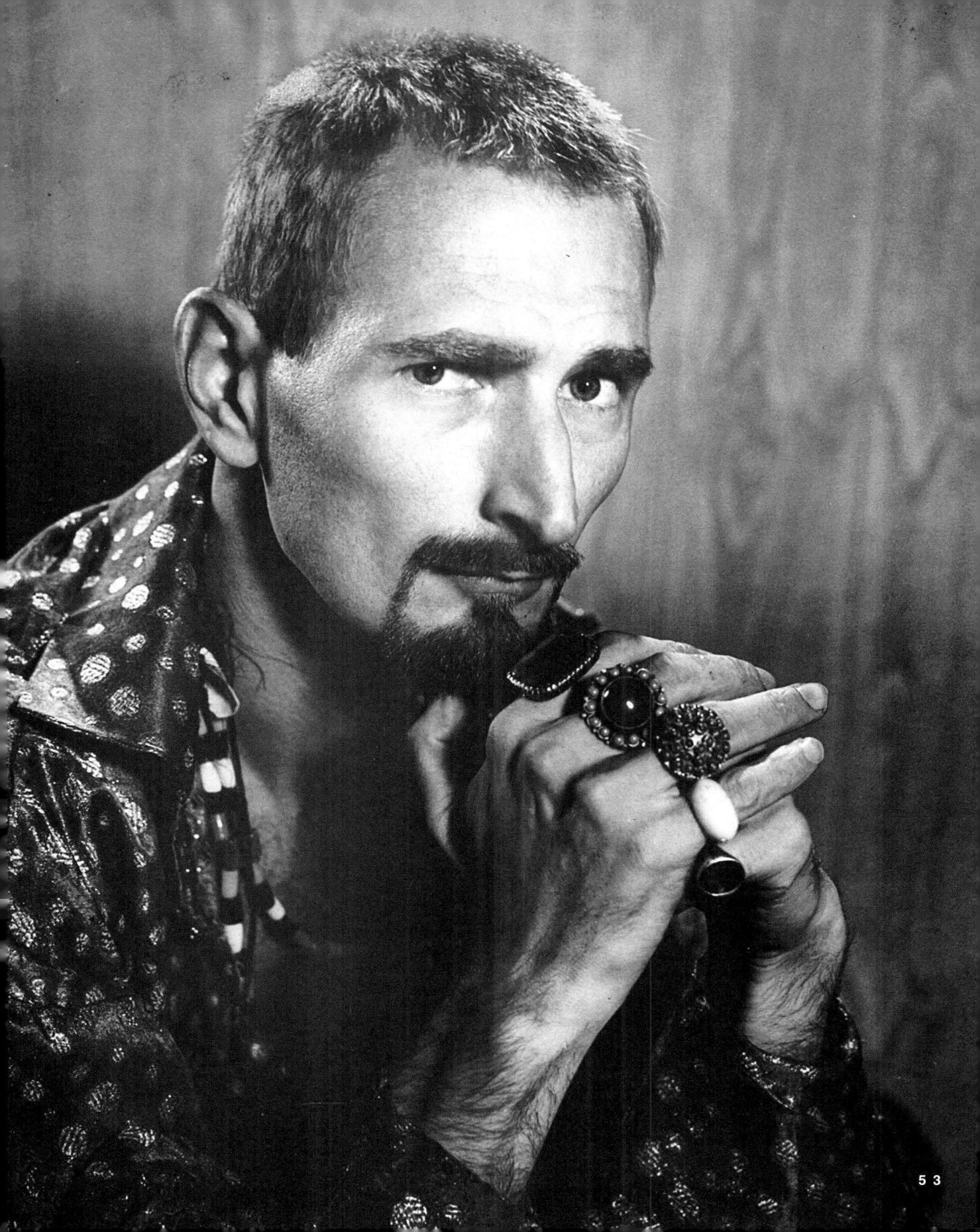

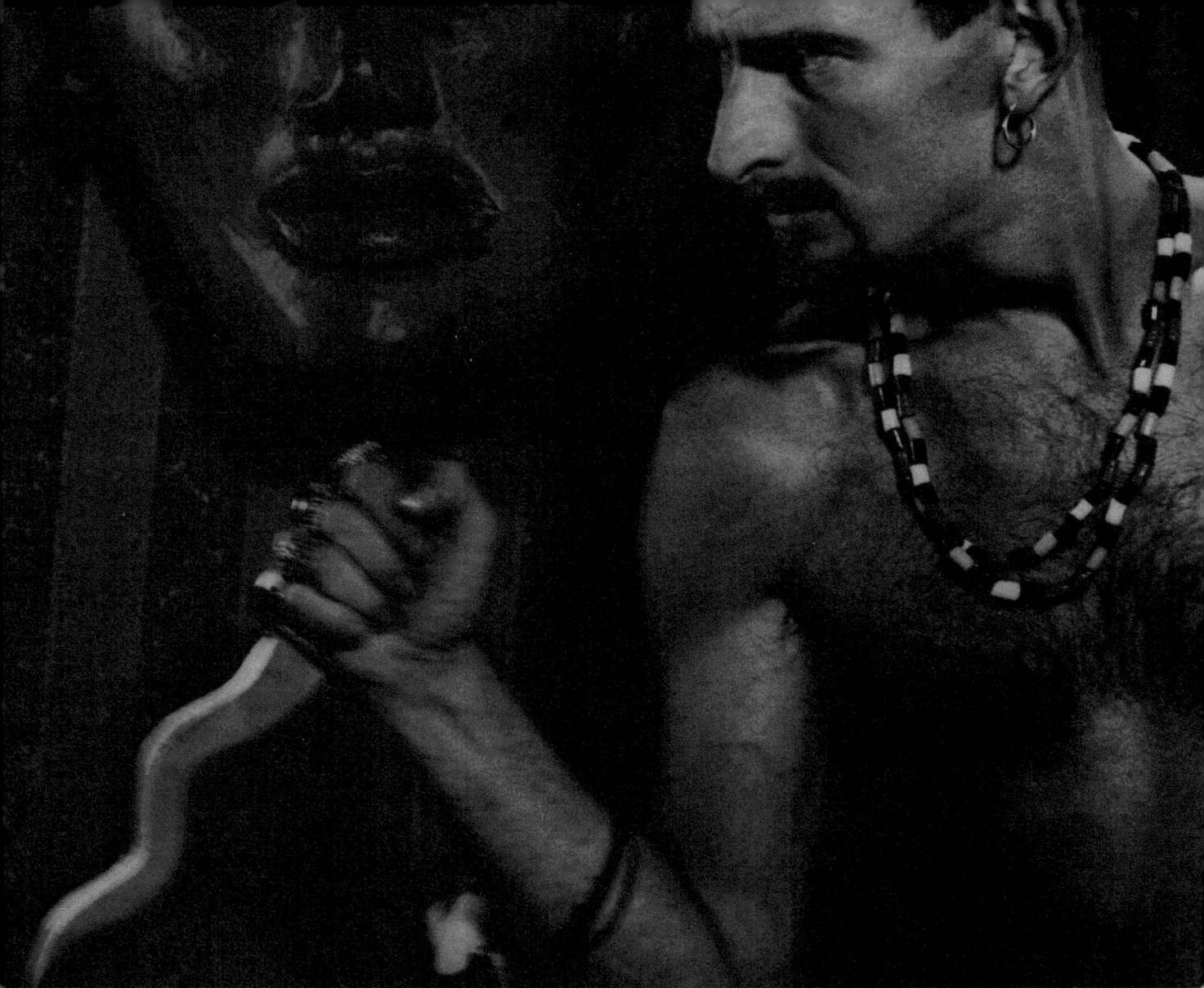

* WARNING: THE ABOVE
LISTED STARS ARE IN BOILED
LOBSTER SUNSET COLOR SLIDES
OF BURNING BEAUTY - (WITH
MUSIC OF ORCHID LAGOON)
NOT IN PERSON!!!

NIGHTLY AT 9:30   18 MERCER ST. $1.50
TIL AUG. 10TH   (OFF CANAL)

Thanks

ED >< 7/08/80 ><16:28   ><F1> PUB <VVI> AD <1910110> CLASS < 335>

SMITH, JACK   > BY <   >

21 1ST AVE   > CITY <NEW YORK   ><NY> <10003>

< 22.00> TYPE<CA> AC#<   > AUTH<   > EXP<   > BOX<   >

<212> START RUNS   STOP   SALES A/R ACCOUNT LINES CODE RATE PRICE

11> <072180> < 2> <072880> <341> <CV> <   > <   > < >< >   >
                                              4   2.75   22.00

ng, gay architecture student sought=QC=
   to share 1/2 expenses, work,=QC=
ticapartment of M/theatrical genius.=QC=
          254-7911=QC=

for

explain-

The City of New York
DEPARTMENT OF SOCIAL SERVICES

26642136

AUTHORIZATION TO PURCHASE FOOD STAMP COUPONS
NOT TRANSFERABLL   NOT VALID WITHOUT IDENTIFICATION CARD

YOU MUST
ENDORSE THE
CERTIFICATE
ON THE BACK
OF THIS CARD

09811-2

SMITH JACK

THIS IS NOT A CHECK

235 E 2 ST
NEW YORK   N.Y. 10009

	CASE NUMBER	FAMILY SIZE
11	3206745	01

NOT VALID AFTER

DATE		
MONTH	DAY	YEAR
05	31	73

AUTHORIZATION NO.

26642136

ing me.

2664213

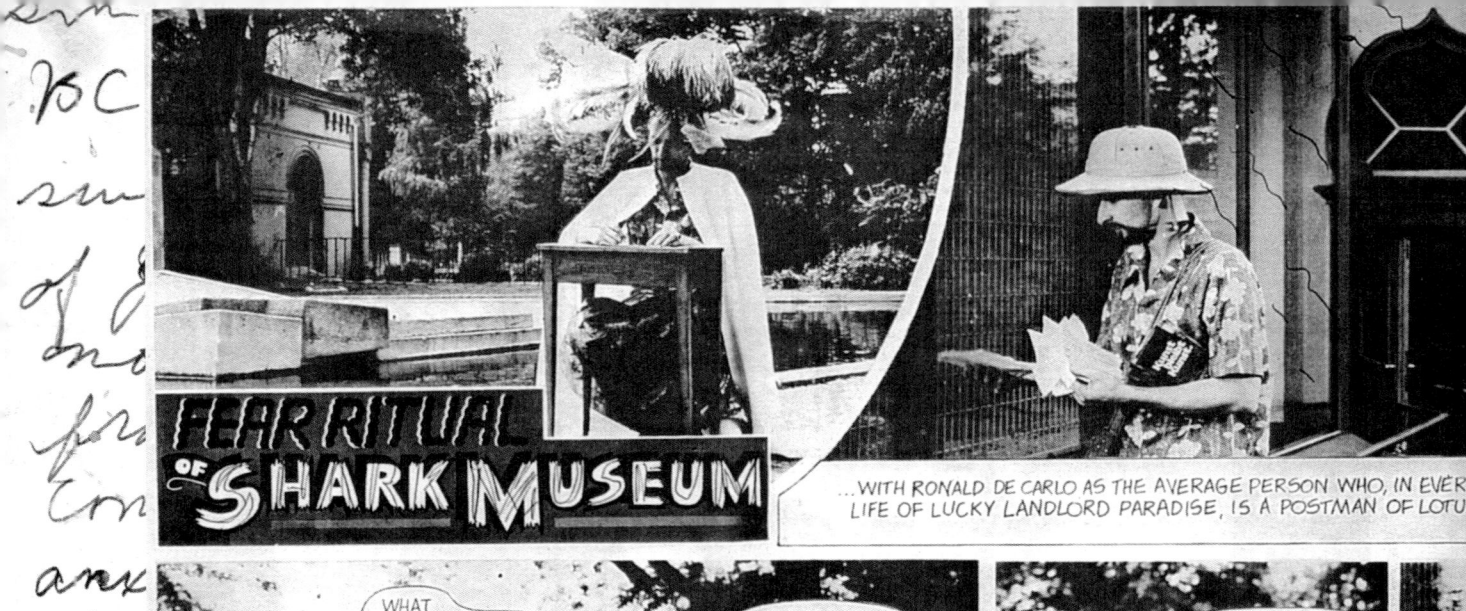

FEAR RITUAL OF SHARK MUSEUM

...WITH RONALD DE CARLO AS THE AVERAGE PERSON WHO, IN EVERY LIFE OF LUCKY LANDLORD PARADISE, IS A POSTMAN OF LOTUS

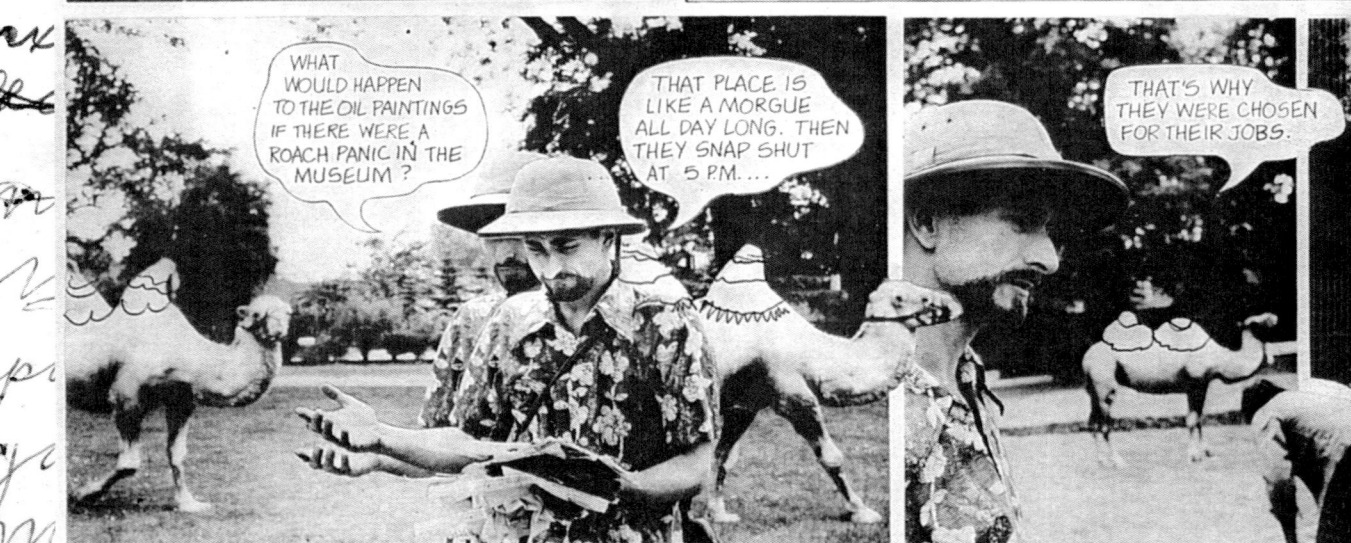

WHAT WOULD HAPPEN TO THE OIL PAINTINGS IF THERE WERE A ROACH PANIC IN THE MUSEUM?

THAT PLACE IS LIKE A MORGUE ALL DAY LONG. THEN THEY SNAP SHUT AT 5 P.M....

THAT'S WHY THEY WERE CHOSEN FOR THEIR JOBS.

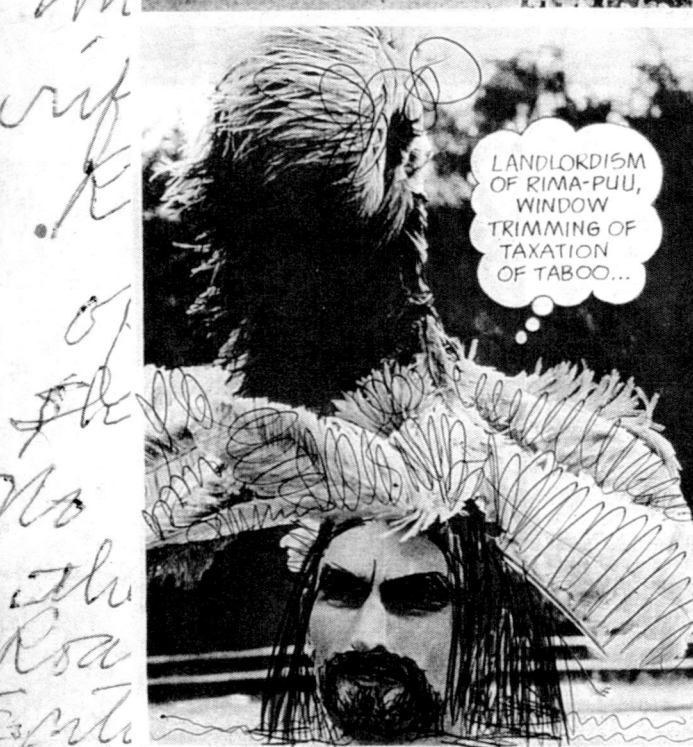

LANDLORDISM OF RIMA-PUU, WINDOW TRIMMING OF TAXATION OF TABOO...

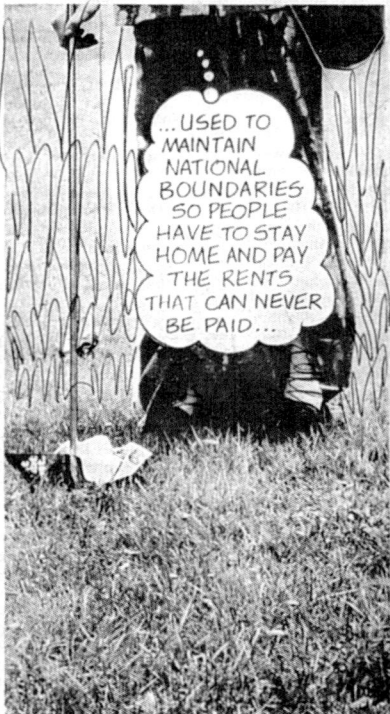

...USED TO MAINTAIN NATIONAL BOUNDARIES SO PEOPLE HAVE TO STAY HOME AND PAY THE RENTS THAT CAN NEVER BE PAID...

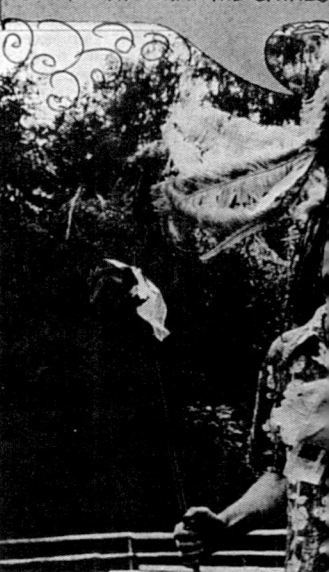

I DON'T WANT TO REVEAL TH OF THE NEIGHBORHOOD, BUT CAUGHT THE COLOGNE MUSE NEGATIVES FROM HIS PIX THE FOR THE CATALOG... FOR THEI ISN'T THAT WHAT THE CATALO

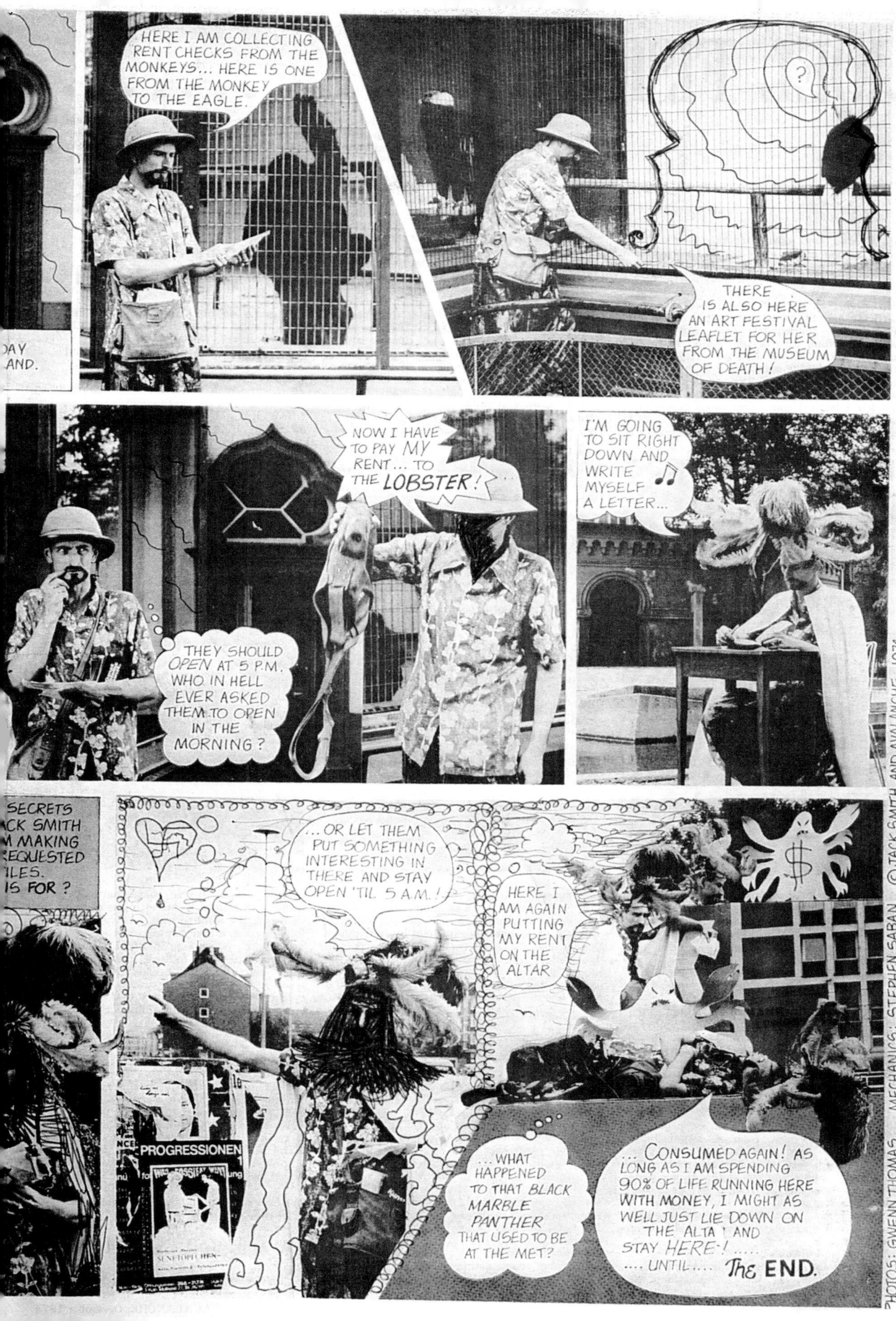

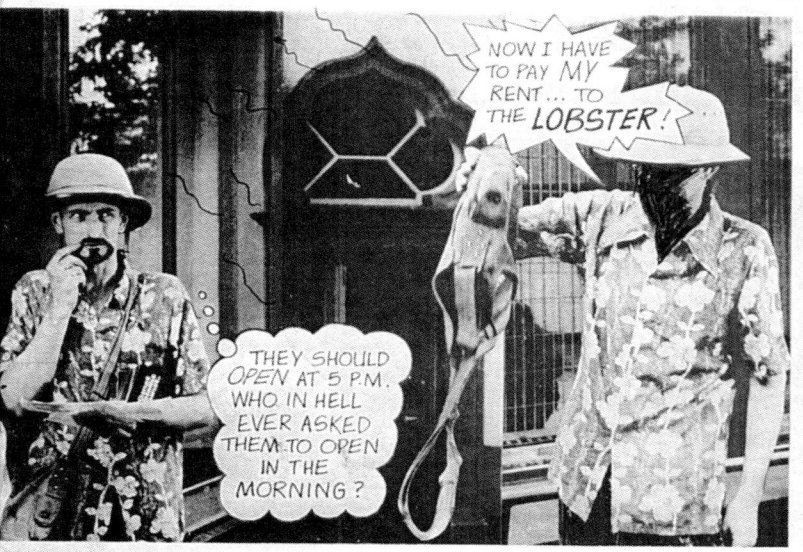
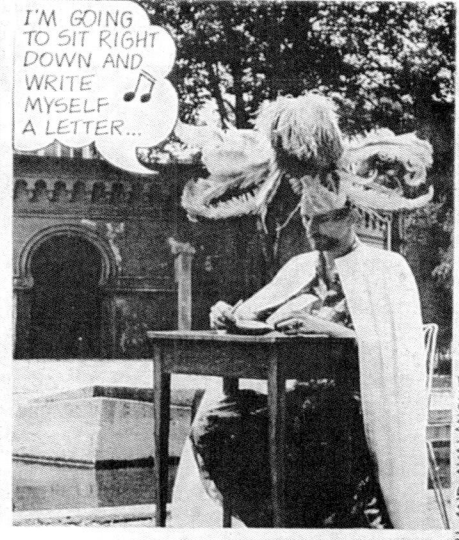
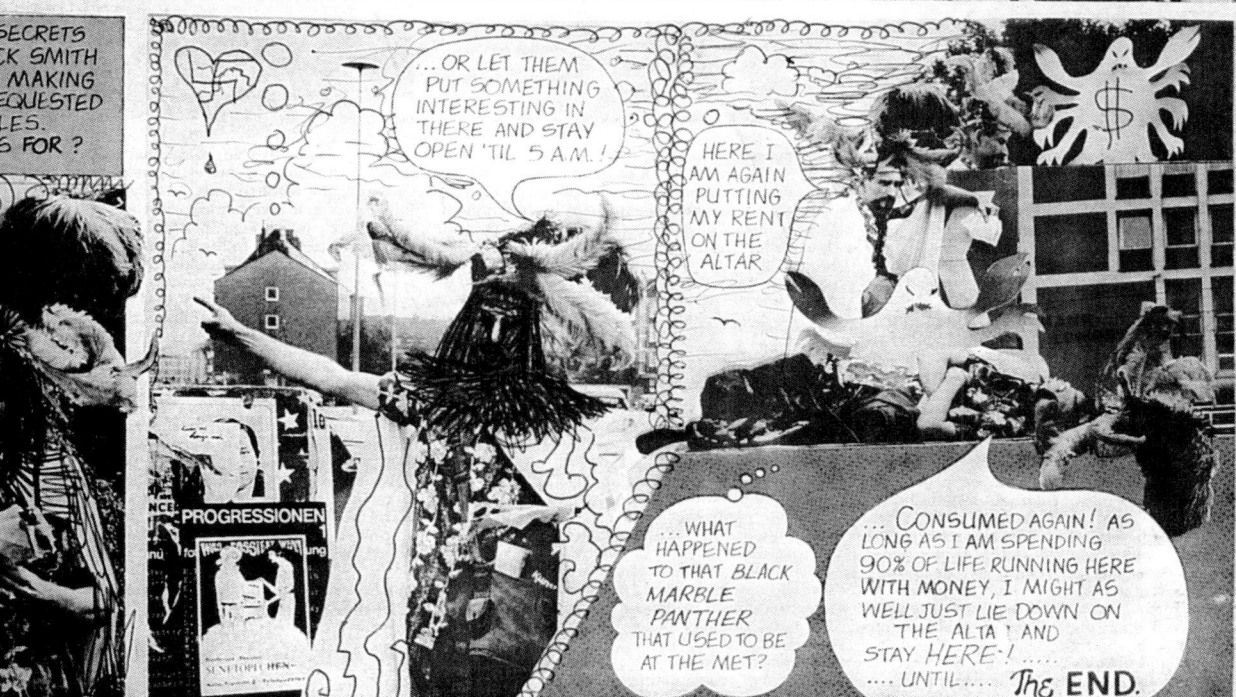

PHOTOS: GWENN THOMAS   MECHANICS: STEPHEN SABAN   ©JACK SMITH AND AVALANCHE 1974

Smith as Ronald De Carlo in this hand-altered copy of *Fear Ritual of Shark Museum,* which appeared in *Avalanche,* December 1974. Photographed in the Cologne zoo, Smith's narrative attacked landlords, museums, and national boundaries.

Canova

"I confess that I don't know much more about ~~Japan~~ film history than you do. I am here ~~of course~~ because of my good looks. All I ~~really~~ My memories of movies only go back to the 40's. ~~But~~

~~of the 40's~~ But ~~I know~~ ~~interested~~ which I am glad to be able to ~~show you~~ remember Judy Canova great days on "the movies along to ~~look you~~ you this in art & LIFE merge Atlantic & on certain days Thief of Bagdad even talk about it immortal after. Judy Canova also movies at movies.

STRUCK OUT AT
VOGUE & ~~sword~~ ETC.
ON A ~~MATCH~~.

~~SHOW~~ PROJECT A
JUDY CANOVA FLIC

58

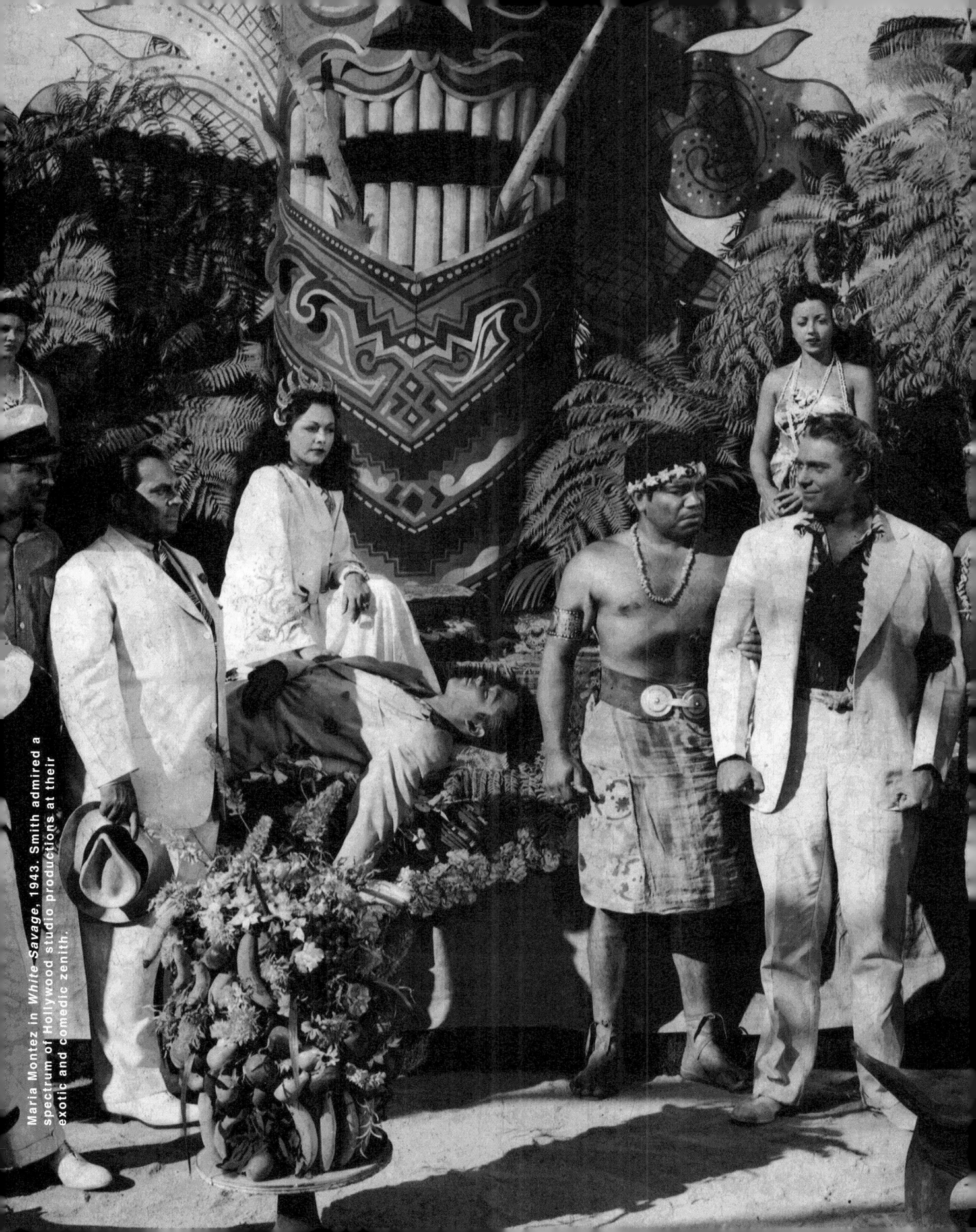

Maria Montez in *White Savage*, 1943. Smith admired a spectrum of Hollywood studio productions at their exotic and comedic zenith.

JUST-TONE - *Electronics Inc.*

MU 4-7573-4

EXPORT IMPORT

CABLE: JUSTURCO
NEW YORK

1235 BROADWAY ● NEW YORK, N. Y. 10001

THE MOVIE TAKES PLACE IN ALOFT THAT WAS DESTROYED
BY A FIRE BUT IS NOW UNDER CONSTRUCTION.

THE ROOM IS ADRK AND YOU CAN BEARLY MAKE OUT A FEW
FIGURES MOVING ABOUT.

ALL OF A SUDDEN THE LIGHT GOES ON AND JACK IS
WHEELED IN BY HIS VALET. HE IS LYEING IN AN
OLD REFRIGARATOR.

HE IS WHEELED UP IN FRONT OF THE PEOPLE

JACK: GOOD EVENING LADIES AND GENTLEMAN DOES
         EVERYONE HAVE SOMETHING TO DRINK?

AUDIENCE: YES

JACK: GOOD; I'LL LET YOU KNOW THE MINUTE THE PARDON
       COMES FROM THE GOVERNOR.

       PERHAPS YOU ARE WONDERING WHY YOUVE ALL BEEN
       CALLED TO THIS LITTLE GATHERING AT THIS LATE
       HOUR ON NEW YEARS EVE?
                 (JACK THEN LOOKS ABOVE AND BEYOND
       HIS AUDIENCE, (over to his left) AND SAYS

         ROCHESTER PLEASE GET ME SOMETHING TO DRINK (PAUSE)
           IS THERE A HARD FROST ON THE MINT JULIP?

JACK THEN LOOKS BACK AT HIS AUDIENCE AND SAYS

       I AM AWARE ~~THAT~~ OF THE FACT THAT YOU HAVE ALL
       BEEN FOLLOWING MY CAREER VERY CLOSELY SO WHAT
       I HAVE TO SAY NOW SHOULD NOT COME AS A GREAT
       SHOCK.
                      PAUSE

       I AM GOING TOBE FROZEN AS A CULTURAL LANDMARK
       SO THAT IN THE FUTURE I AS AN ILLETE FIGURE
       MIGHT BE BROUGT BACK TO LIFE AGAIN AND THROUGH
       MODERN MEDICINE BE REJUVINATED.

             THE AUDIENCE CLAMORS WITH PROFUSE MUMBLING.

avant-garde \(')ä,vän(t)gärd, [F, vanguard] *n-s* **1 :** those who create, produce, or apply new, original, or experimental ideas, designs, and techniques in any field, esp. in the arts **2 :** a group (as of writers or artists) that is unorthodox and un-

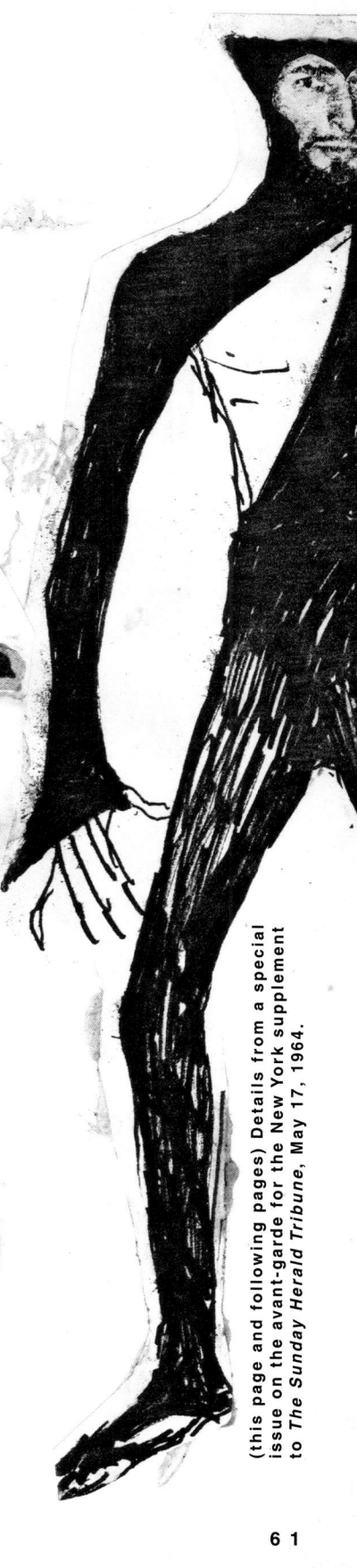

(this page and following pages) Details from a special issue on the avant-garde for the *New York* supplement to *The Sunday Herald Tribune*, May 17, 1964.

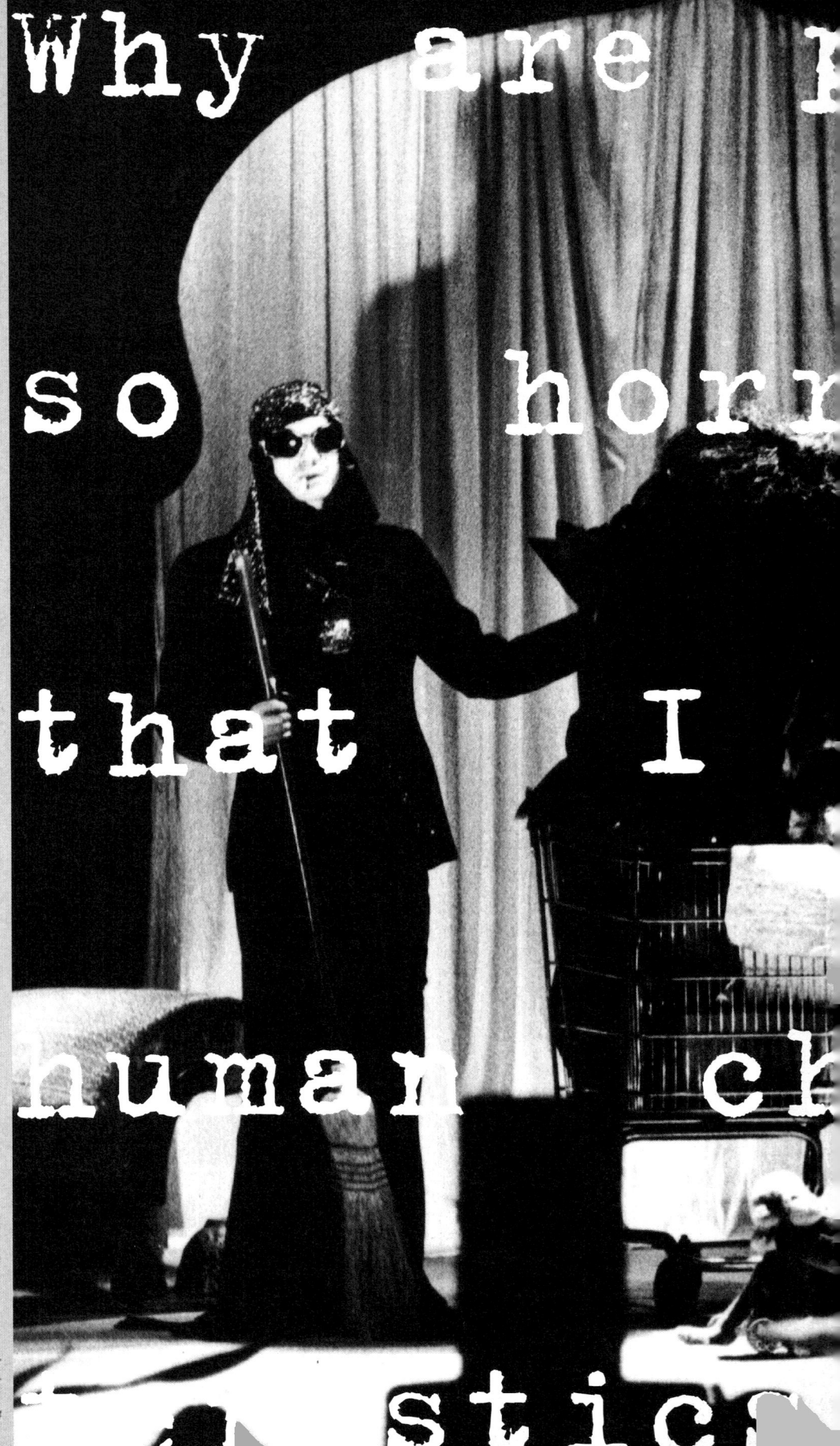

Who's
Who
&
What
to

Make

of

Them:

*An Arbitrary
Assessment*

*As of May 1, 1964; subject to fluctuations in the Dow Jones Industrial Average.

12   New York / Herald Tribune / May 17, 1964

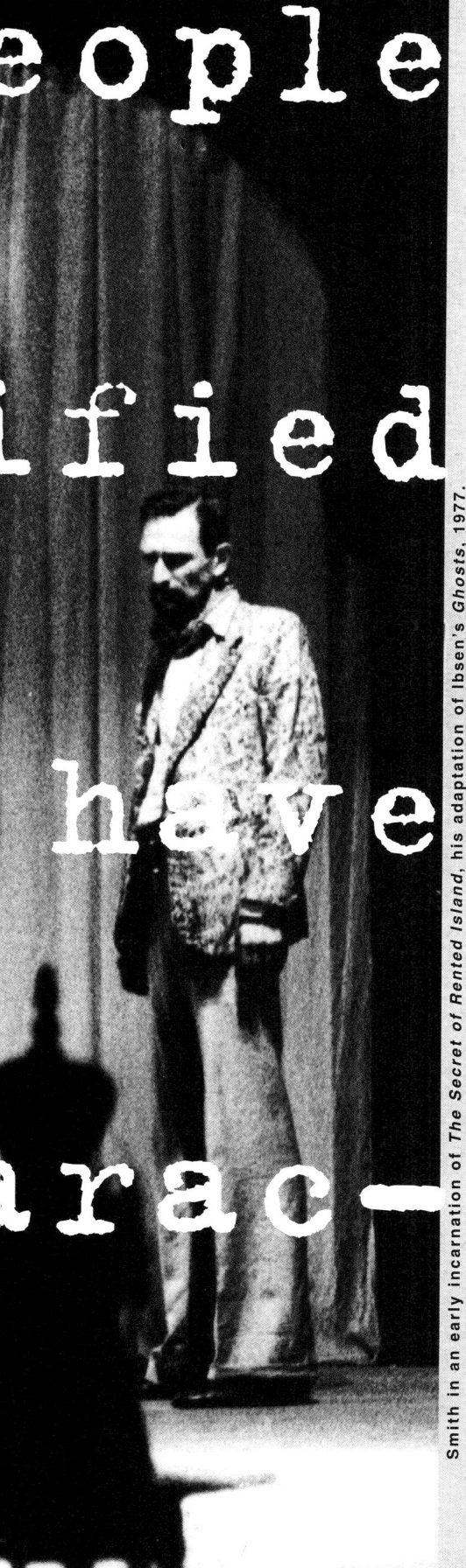

eople
ified
have
arac‒

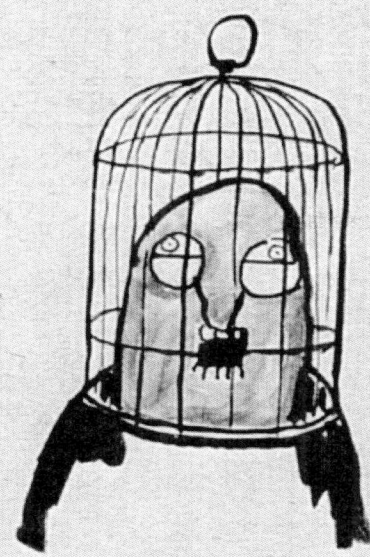

Untouchables

ARTISTS:
  Red Grooms
  Allan Kaprow
MUSICIANS:
  John Cage
WRITERS:
  Allen Ginsberg
  LeRoi Jones
  Peter Orlofsky
  Terry Southern
MOVIEMAKERS:
  Stan Brakhage
  Adolph & Jonas Mekas
  Jack Smith
PUBLICATIONS:
  Magazine *C*
  —*You*, the Magazine
  of the Arts
POETS:
  Peter Orlofsky

Okay Guys

ARTISTS:
  Lee Bontecou
  Jim Dine
  Robert Indiana
  Jasper Johns
  Roy Lichtenstein
  Marisol
  Robert Morris
  Barnett Newman
  Claes Oldenburg
  Robert Rauschenberg
  James Rosenquist
  George Siegal
  Frank Stella
  Andy Warhol

MUSICIANS:
  Milton Babbitt
  Earle Brown
  Ornette Coleman
  Morton Feldman
  Thelonious Monk
  Cecil Taylor
DANCE:
  Merce Cunningham
  Alwin Nikolais
  Yvonne Rainer
  James Waring
MOVIEMAKERS:
  Maysles brothers
  Stanley Van Der Beek
WRITERS:
  Jack Gelber
  Frank O'Hara
  Terry Southern

Nobody Knows
My Name

Lou Harrison
Richard Maxfield
Harry Partch
Charles Wuorinen
La Monte Young

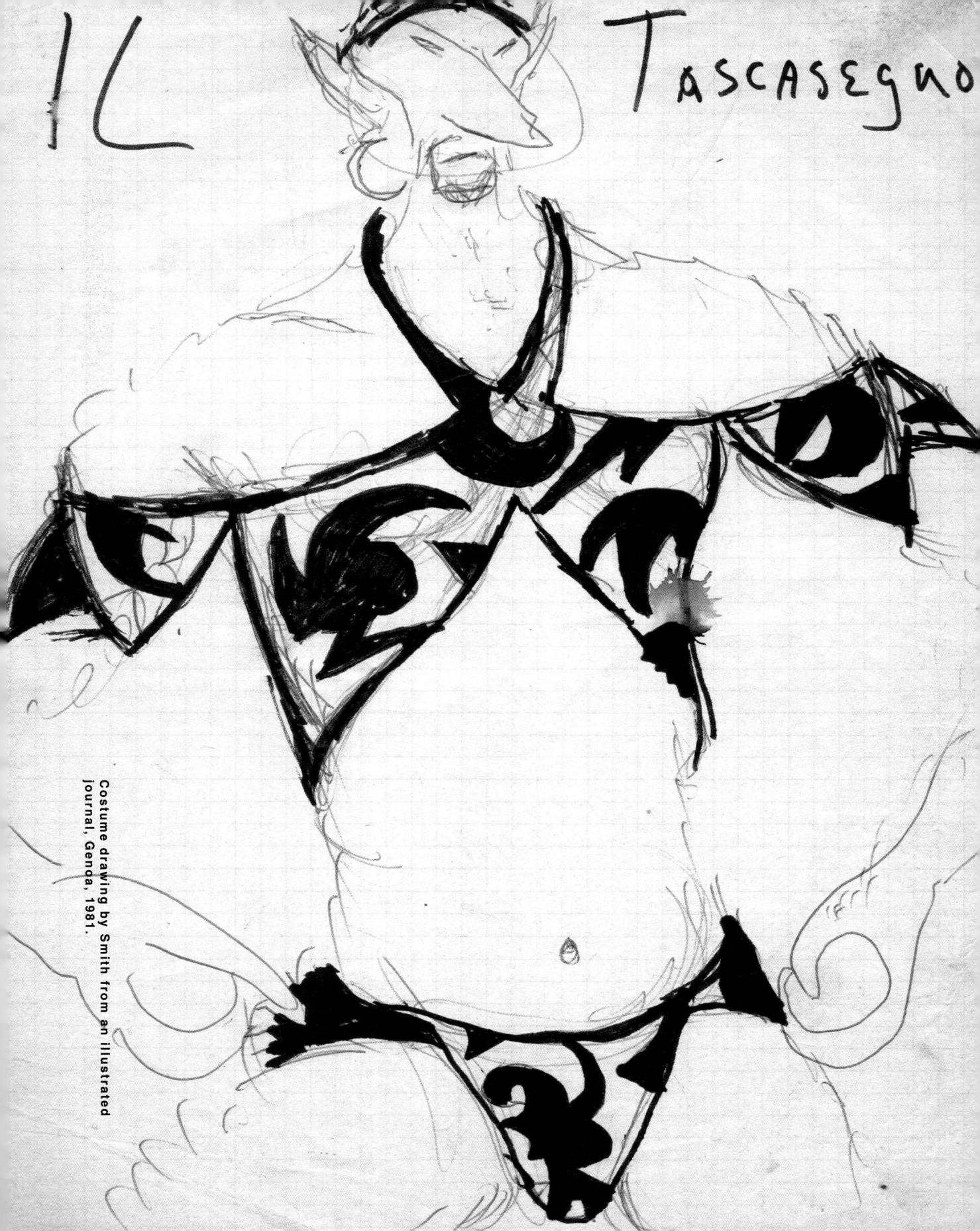

IL   Tascasegno

Costume drawing by Smith from an illustrated
journal, Genda, 1981.

From *Jack Smith's Flaming Creatures*

–Susan Sontag

...Nowhere in the world has the old cliché of European romanticism—the assassin mind versus the spontaneous heart—had such a long career as in America. Here, more than anywhere else, the belief lives on that neatness and carefulness of technique interfere with spontaneity, with truth, with immediacy. Most of the prevailing techniques (for even to be against technique demands a technique) of avant-garde art express this conviction. In music, there is aleatory performance now as well as composition, and new sources of sound and new ways of mutilating the old instruments; in painting and sculpture, there is the favoring of impermanent or found materials, and the transformation of objects into perishable (use-once-and-throw-away) environments or "happenings." In its own way *Flaming Creatures* illustrates this snobbery about the coherence and technical finish of the work of art. There is, of course, no story in *Flaming Creatures*, no development, no necessary order of the seven (as I count them) clearly separable sequences of film. One can easily doubt that a certain piece of footage was indeed intended to be overexposed. Of no sequence is one convinced that it had to last this long, and not longer or shorter. Shots aren't framed in the traditional way; heads are cut off; extraneous figures sometimes appear on the margins of the scene. The camera is hand-held most of the time, and the image often quivers (where this is wholly effective, and no doubt deliberate, is in the orgy sequence.)

But in *Flaming Creatures*, amateurishness of technique is not frustrating, as it is in so many recent "underground" films. For Smith is visually very generous; at practically every moment there is simply a tremendous amount to be seen on the screen. And then, there is an extraordinary change and beauty to his images, even when the effect of the strong ones is weakened by the ineffective ones, the ones that might have been better through planning. Today indifference to technique is often accompanied by bareness; the modern revolt against calculation in art often takes the form of aesthetic asceticism. (Much of Abstract Expressionist painting has this ascetic quality.) *Flaming Creatures*, though, issues from a different aesthetic: it is crowded with visual material. There are no ideas, no symbols, no commentary on or critique of anything in *Flaming Creatures*. Smith's film is strictly a treat for the senses. In that it is the very opposite of the "literary" film (which is what so many French avant-garde films were). It is not in the knowing about, or being able to interpret, what one sees, that the pleasure of *Flaming*

In *Against Interpretation* (Farrar Strauss & Giroux, 1966; originally published in *The Nation*, April 13, 1964).

6 5

Creatures lies; but in the directness, the power, and the lavish quantity of the images themselves. Unlike most serious modern art, this work is not about the frustrations of consciousness, the dead ends of the self. Thus Smith's crude technique serves, beautifully, the sensibility embodied in *Flaming Creatures*—a sensibility which disclaims ideas, which situates itself beyond negation.

Flaming Creatures is that rare modern work of art: it is about joy and innocence. To be sure, this joyousness, this innocence is composed out of themes which are—by ordinary standards—perverse, decadent, at the least highly theatrical and artificial. But this, I think, is precisely how the film comes by its beauty and modernity. *Flaming Creatures* is a lovely specimen of what currently, in one genre, goes by the flippant name of "pop art." Smith's film has the sloppiness, the arbitrariness, the looseness of pop art. It also has pop art's gaiety, its ingenuousness, its exhilarating freedom from moralism. One great virtue of the pop art movement is the way it blasts through the old imperative about taking a *position* toward one's subject matter. (Needless to say, I'm not denying that there are certain events about which it is necessary to take a position. An extreme instance of a work of art dealing with such events is *The Deputy*. All I'm saying is that there are some elements of life—above all, sexual pleasure—about which it isn't necessary to have a position.) The best works among those that are called pop art intend, precisely, that we abandon the old task of always either approving or disapproving of what is depicted in art—or, by extension, experienced in life. (This is why those who dismiss pop art as a symptom of a new conformism, a cult of acceptance of the artifacts of mass civilization, are being obtuse.) Pop art lets in wonderful and new mixtures of attitude, which would before have seemed contradictions. Thus *Flaming Creatures* is a brilliant spoof on sex and at the same time full of the lyricism of erotic impulse. Simply in a visual sense, too, it is full of contradictions. Very studied visual effects (lacy textures, falling flowers, tableaux) are introduced into disorganized, clearly improvised scenes in which bodies, some shapely and convincingly feminine and others scrawny and hairy, tumble, dance, make love.

...*Flaming Creatures* is a triumphant example of an aesthetic vision of the world—and such a vision is perhaps always, at its core, epicene. But this type of art has yet to be understood in this country. The space in which *Flaming Creatures* moves is not the space of moral ideas, which is where American critics have traditionally located art. What I am urging is that there is not only moral space, by whose laws *Flaming Creatures* would indeed come off badly; there is also aesthetic space, the space of pleasure. Here Smith's film moves and has its being.

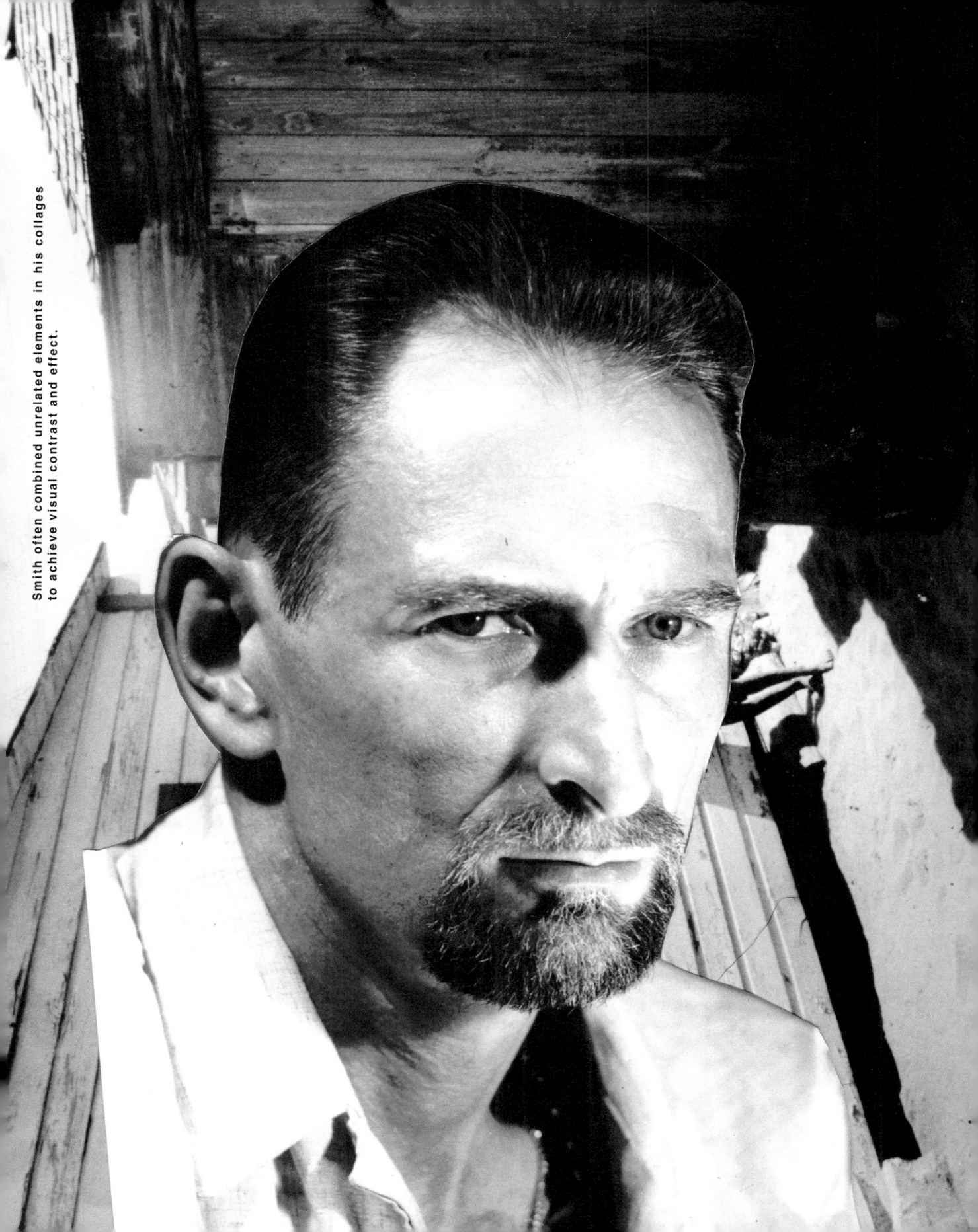

JACK SMITH

THE ONLY NORMAL IN BAGHDAD

EDWARD LEFFINGWELL

H
MAN

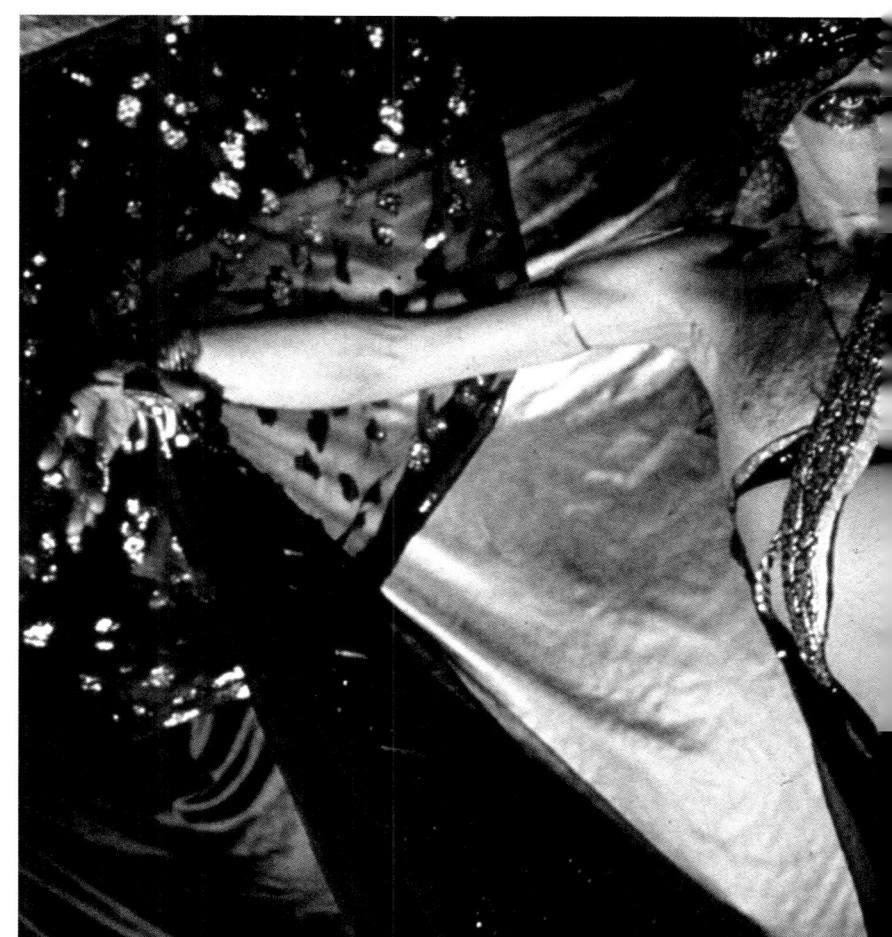

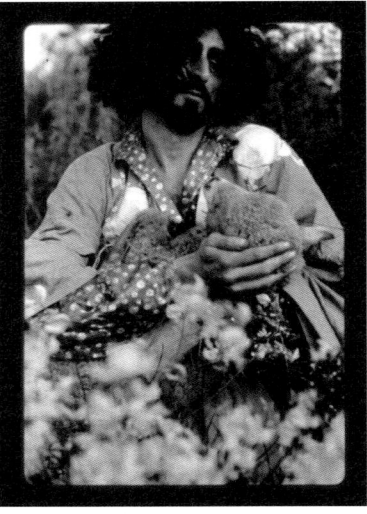

Jack Smith was no fool. He believed that an unholy team of manufacturers, schools, government, and churches had allied to consolidate power and authority none of them could maintain alone. And, that together, this group of makers, teachers, legislators, and priests could shift the blame for social ills from the institution to the individual, enforcing the individual's dependence on the state. Poverty and the inability to transform creative activity into gainful employment, for example, were the consequences of willful dissent, and the failure to recognize and embrace the obvious contributions of capitalism. Smith identified as conspiracy the enforcement of conformity through dependence on the way things were constructed by society for its own preservation.

"A perfect system," he wrote, "whereby if one doesn't, can't work out of fictitious inner strength, then they must pay for help, buy the thing, or marry to be able to work." Because he couldn't afford to pay or buy, and was already wedded to his work, Jack Smith understood that he had to find the strength necessary to accomplish what it was he set out to do: He intended nothing less than the socialization of the function of art. Through the efforts of a cadre of enlightened artists, common needs could be met by the fair distribution of an abundance of goods and services. He imagined a society in which these avatars of culture assisted in that enlightened labor. Because of their stature, movie stars would be called upon to demonstrate their leadership in this enterprise by making yogurt for the people, teaching civil law courses in public schools, legislating the dissolution of national boundaries, abolishing jails, providing community movie sets. With characteristic wit, and a taste for glamour and the ridiculous, and because he was a performer, Jack Smith challenged an undefined segment of an otherwise indifferent public to become an audience, to laugh, and to care.

Consistent with his disregard for formal education, Smith was an autodidact. Demanding of, and also precariously dependent on others because of the collaborative nature of his work, he fashioned new art from the trash heap of what he considered a bankrupt and puritanical culture. As a photographer, he made forays into color at a time when art and fashion were black and white, and then developed a highly original style of composition that he succeeded in translating into motion pictures. Not much to his liking or amazement, he quickly became perhaps the most notorious filmmaker of the flowering of American avant-garde cinema.

With little training as a writer, he re-created himself as a prose stylist, but then dismissed his own efforts when he found little encouragement. More interested in the activity of making and editing film than in the notion of a final product, he ventured increasingly into performance, and in the process directly influenced a generation of filmmakers, photographers, and those who became known as performance artists. As art events and actions of the early 1960s embraced the worlds of dance, cinema, photography, music, and new technology in the gestation of what would be the multidisciplinary vogue known as expanded cinema, Smith combined film and slide projection with performance to produce one of the lively hybrid forms of the genre. And along the way, he collapsed the distinction between the development of an event and its performance.

If his audiences included the simply curious who wandered in from the street, they also numbered a legion of the avant-garde: theater artists Richard Foreman, Robert Wilson, John Vaccaro, Charles Ludlam, and Ronald Tavel; performing artists Lee Breuer, Ron Vawter, and Penny Arcade; pioneering visual artists Walter De Maria, Joan Jonas, Andy Warhol, Richard Serra, Hélio Oiticica, Rebecca Horn, and Nan Goldin; filmmakers Michael Snow, Jonas Mekas, and Ken Jacobs; poet and theater critic Stefan Brecht; film critic J. Hoberman, and many others. A teacher with specific demands, he called his attentive audience the scum of Baghdad and, berating them for their need to be inspired, or "fertilized," ordered them to leave his theater. He could dance. He designed and made costumes, and knew how to wear them. And, finally, he seems to have accepted himself as his own greatest creation, his own surprise, as he directed a succession of photographers to record his artistry in a remarkable series of complex, tightly scripted, and sequenced tableaux vivants.

(previous page) A jeweled and veiled Smith dances in *I Was a Male Yvonne De Carlo for the Lucky Landlord Underground*, 1982. (this page) Smith in a slide sequence as Christ/Abraham/St. John the Baptist, Italy, c. 1975.

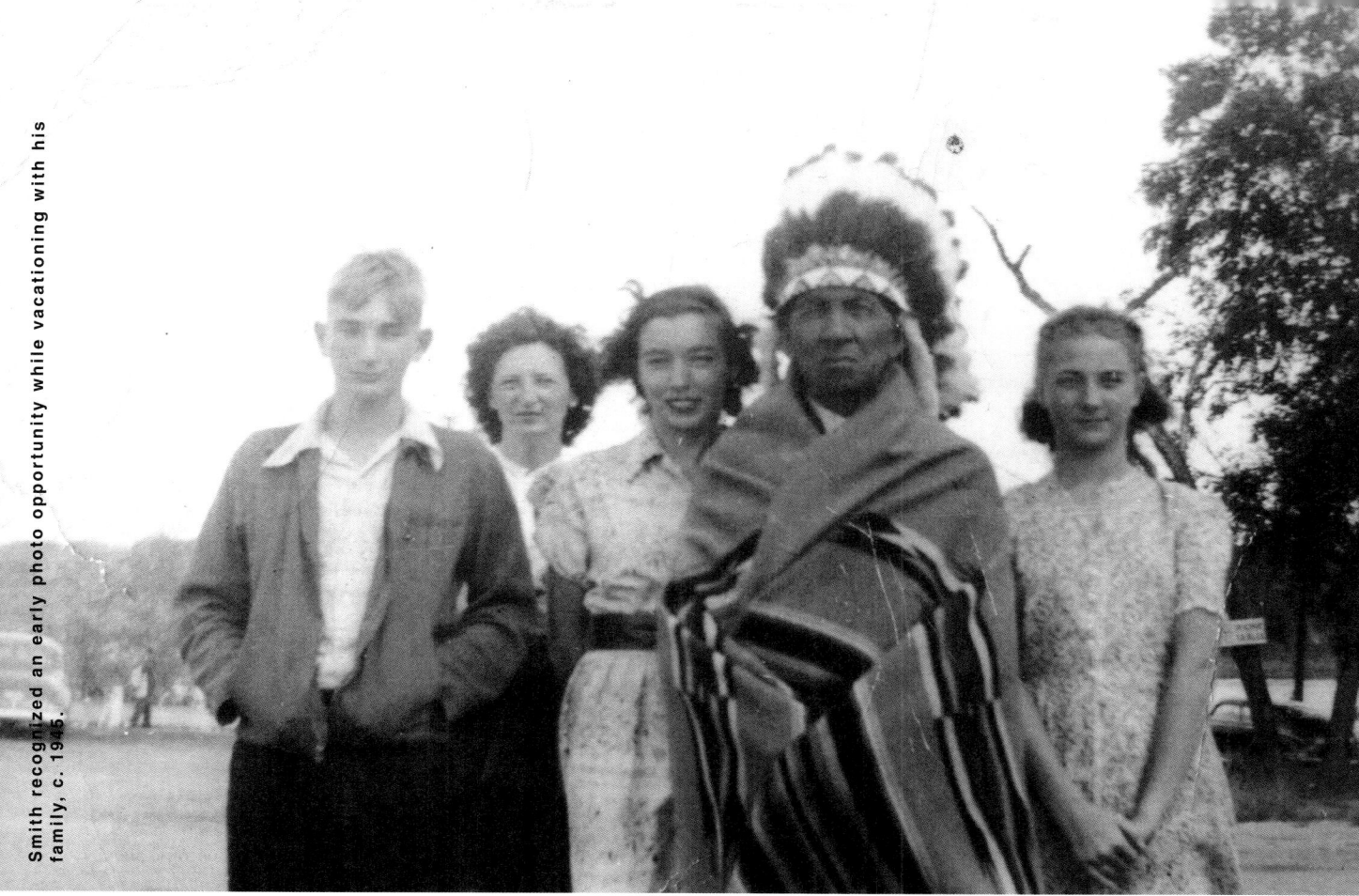

Smith recognized an early photo opportunity while vacationing with his family, c. 1945.

Jack Smith was born in Columbus, Ohio, November 14, 1932, the scion of a hillbilly and a practical nurse. According to his journals, tapes, interviews, and the recollections of associates, Smith left Columbus at the age of seven, moving with his parents and sister as jobs and interests directed. After his father's accidental death on a fishing boat off the gulf coast of Texas, the truncated family established temporary residence in trailer parks, until his mother's remarriage took the family from Texas to Wisconsin.

He was a tall man, six foot three, sometimes stooped, and thin at 150 pounds or so, dark blond, a Scorpio, handsome, with a *Grand Hotel* profile no longer in fashion. It was a long face, artfully composed, with an important dagger of a nose and an intense, commanding gaze, serious cheekbones, eyebrows, hairline. Born to be photographed, he never stopped doing things with his face and hands and body. He was different, graceful, with a resonant voice at a lofty pitch. Often hesitant, but at times specific and direct in his speech, he was both compelling and convincing. Ambivalently sexed, a man who loved women and was obsessed by betrayal, he alternately decried garden-variety homosexuals and pronounced himself a queer.

Jack Smith arrived in New York sometime around 1953. He found part-time work as an errand and office boy and lived in aestheticized film noir style, furnishing his room, as was common practice, with pickings from the invisible department store of the street. In 1956, he met the aspiring underground filmmakers Bob Fleischner and Ken Jacobs while attending classes at City College of New York, and found employment in a photo processing lab. As a principal actor and sometime talent scout, Smith participated in films Fleischner and Jacobs were making and, later on, in those of Ron Rice. He was sympathetic to their considerable wit, improvisational nature, urban ruin locations, posturing, and defiance of conventional standards.

Smith was caught up in the social and aesthetic experiments of the time: communal living; political action; the sharing of food, sex, and other resources (including drugs, at first, asthma cigarettes, psuedoephedrin, and camphor-tainted stimulants from over-the-counter sinus remedies, and then cannabis, amphetamines, cocaine, and hallucinogens.) Thus fueled, Smith and his intimates created and explored their bumpy relationships and attempted to analyze them, trying to understand that there could be different kinds of love that did not necessarily involve sex and were not about the struggle between bodies. There was enough of that anyway. Relationships formed and ended, sometimes bitterly.

Thoroughly poor at this point, without access to a movie camera, Smith transferred his fascination with the exotic image to its expression in photography. Having determined that the achievement of modern art consisted of its engagement with the movement of the eye over a painted surface, he traveled uptown to lectures at the Metropolitan and the Frick museums, learning about composition and how it could be employed to tell a story. Informed by these lectures and by experiment, Smith effected a baroque marriage of content and form in photo sessions, sometimes composing with an exoticism and redundance of mass that was uniquely his, if adapted from Veronese, Poussin, Ingres, Watteau, and Delacroix. He also drew on an existing vocabulary of attitudes found in fashion and among the streetwise, relying on his cast of friends and passersby to assume roles and accept direction. He had a high regard for fashion photography, and entertained hope that he might find some success as a contributor to mainstream magazines.

The periodic *Film Culture* existed as a critical voice for cinema, what and how it could be. Jonas Mekas, its prime mover, also contributed a weekly "Movie Journal" column for *The Village Voice*. The evangelist of new cinema, he believed that however limited the audience, there was a cultural revolution under way in film. Mekas and a few of his colleagues, particularly film theorist P. Adams Sitney, advanced the notion that unknown filmmakers, working in obscurity and penniless, were among the most important artists of the century. In the work of these filmmakers, Mekas hailed the demise of recognizable narrative, the dreamlike suspension of logic, a verisimilitude of daily life, the physical manipulation and deconstruction of the image, and a rupture of decorum. He compared elements of this new cinema to the work of Rimbaud, Baudelaire, Sade, and William Burroughs. He equated the avant-garde with art and, as such, beyond property and status, revolutionary. Nobody knew how far it would go.

A newspaper account in Genoa contrasts Warhol as the microcosm of capitalism and Smith as the banned, lyrical polemicist.

Mercoledì 1 aprile 1981

SPETTACO

Genova: la rassegna «Il gergo inquieto»

Warhol: come fare il noioso e diventare un divo

«Empire», otto ore di grattacielo - Jack Smith, un cineasta bersagliato dalla censura

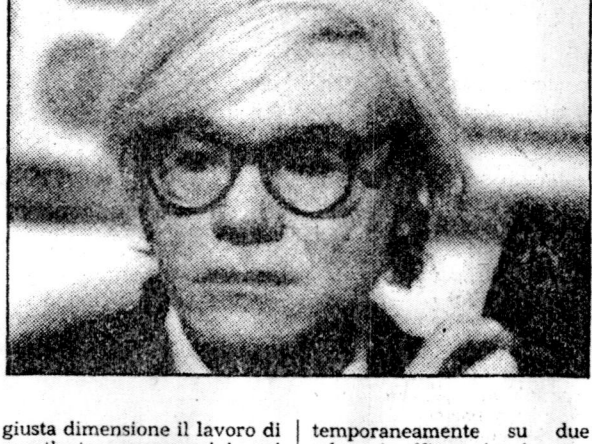

GENOVA — *L'underground classico* e *Andy Warhol Cineasta* sono due titoli del nutrito cartellone del *Gergo inquieto* che, la manifestazione promossa dall'assessorato alla Cultura del Comune di Genova in collaborazione con l'assessorato provinciale, la Regione Liguria, il gruppo ligure del sindacato nazionale critici cinematografici italiani, l'UCCA-ARCI.

Due campi di ricerca che possono essere idealmente uniti in quanto concorrono a formare un quadro sufficientemente completo di uno fra i movimenti che hanno inciso sulla cultura occidentale.

È giusto non isolare i vari aspetti di un fenomeno che, fin dall'origine, ha attraversato più settori; dal cinema all'editoria, dalla pittura agli spettacoli teatrali, dalla musica al videonastro.

Particolarmente opportuna l'attenzione riservata al lavoro di Andy Warhol, cui sono dedicate una personale comprendente una decina di titoli, scelti fra gli oltre cinquanta diretti o prodotti dall'artista newyorkese, e una mostra intitolata *Andy Warhol Enterprise*. Titolo significativo, in quanto Warhol simboleggia una delle strade d'azione e proposta imboccate dall'underground americano: quella rivolta al lavoro «dentro» le strutture dell'industria culturale. Non a caso, nel presentare la sua «sezione», il curatore Germano Celant definisce Warhol «un microcosmo capitalista», sottolineandone la capacità di integrazione consapevole nel sistema al fine di sfruttarne le leggi e violarne i meccanismi. Da questa impostazione nascono l'attenzione per settori della comunicazione che mercificati e mercificanti quali la pubblicità, l'arredamento di empori e ristoranti, la grafica industriale.

Solo partendo da questo dato è possibile collocare nella giusta dimensione il lavoro di quest'autore, compresi i suoi interessi cinematografici. Questi ultimi, ben documentati da alcuni film della metà degli anni Sessanta, da *Empire* (1964 - Impero) a *The Chelsea Girls* (1966 - Le ragazze del Chelsea), poggiano su strutture apparentemente «destabilizzanti» rispetto ai canoni del cinema commerciale, ma fanno leva proprio su di esse per ottenere il medesimo successo, l'identica «fama» a cui aspirano i cineasti «commerciali». Si vedano per esempio le due opere citate: il primo non è altro che l'inquadratura fissa della sommità dell'Empire State Building, colta nella notte del 25 giugno 1964 dal 44° piano del Time-Life Building (nell'edizione originale il film dura otto ore, qui è stata proiettata una versione ridotta a novanta minuti) ed è costituito da una sola inquadratura; il secondo dura più di tre ore ed è formato da due film veri e propri, proiettati contemporaneamente su due schermi affiancati: vi compaiono una serie di piani-sequenza, ciascuno di trentacinque minuti, popolati da omosessuali, sadici, travestiti e da un papa che si proclama protettore di ladri, prostitute ed emarginati vari.

In questo modo la «noia» e l'anticonformismo sparsi a piene mani sullo schermo finiscono per trasformarsi in elemento di richiamo commerciale, in slogan scandalistico-pubblicitario per un'operazione che si muove all'interno delle leggi del mercato culturale. Si ha l'impressione che sin dall'inizio Warhol mirasse più ad un inserimento «clamoroso» nell'industria culturale (al fine di carpirne il midollo e corroderla dall'interno, si dirà poi) che non ad un suo ribaltamento.

Opposto il caso di Jack Smith, un artista che dopo aver ammirato Warhol ed averne interpretato alcuni film ha oggi con lui un rapporto aspra-

mente polemico. Smith nel 1962 *Flaming Crea* (Creature brucianti), pa alle cronache, oltre che uno dei capolavori dell'un ground di quegli anni, a per essere stato il film di sto movimento più bersag dalla censura. Negli Stati ti fu subito sequestrato e potè proiettare solo nel all'estero fu bandito in tutti i Paesi e anche in B ove fu presentato al Fe di Knokke-Le-Zoute, si d te ricorrere alla formula «presentazione fuori con per non incappare nei delle leggi, pur notorian liberali, di quel Paese.

Visto oggi il film ha buona parte della sua car rotica. La posizione di Sn comunque opposta a que Warhol, sia nella sostanz fiuto rigido di ogni con nazione fra arte e indus sia nei modi di fare cir Questi ultimi poggiano s impeto lirico-polemico, l visto nei «materiali in che il regista ha portato nova e fatto proiettare so po essersi assicurato «sensibilità» del pubblic so i suoi primi lavori. In e uno stretto intreccio fra c del sistema (l'America ra sentata come una vecchi renda e semiparalitica ch ne gelosamente stretti i su li del benessere consum e tensione poetica verso tura, il mondo incontan dei «primitivi».

Una visione venata di tismo, ma più toccante e gestiva di quella fornitac l'artista di successo che si piace di essere riuscito a dere (a prezzo vantaggio anima al diavolo.

Umberto R

The civil rights movement was under way, and there were organized protests against the bomb and chemical warfare. Unions still were strong, often fountainheads of belief in cooperation and solidarity and the dignity of the worker, all important notions for an unenfranchised avant-garde. Mekas, who cared deeply about such things, and very much about film, recorded civil defense demonstrations and other protests in his work in film and in his writing. Otherwise intelligent and functional people developed interests that the machinery of religion, defenders of conventional morality, and the government considered not only illegal but a threat to American culture, like pornography and drugs. And, willing to be out in front with them was Jack Smith.

Jack Smith was a performer, and his essential medium was theater. He valued thoughts above words. In an interview published in the journal *Semiotext(e)* in 1978, he elaborated: "Look what I have to do in order to think of thoughts. I have to forget language. All I can do with no education, nothing, no advice, an insane mother I mean, no background, nothing, nothing, and I have to make art, but I know that under these conditions the one thing I had to find out was if I could think of a thought that has never been thought before, then it could be in language that was never read before. If you can think of something, the language will fall into place in the most fantastic way. The language is shit, I mean it's only there to support a thought....Whatever new thoughts you can think of that the world needs will be automatically clothed in the most radiant language imaginable."

During the summer and fall of 1962, Smith shot *Flaming Creatures* on the roof of the Windsor Theater in New York City. Much has been written about the masterful composition of *Flaming Creatures*, Smith's framing of the moving image, the freedom and humor of the film's sexual posturing, and about what this rampant exhibitionism was supposed to mean. But the comparison made to Jean Vigo's classic *Zero de Conduite* is the most apposite, with Vigo's nightgowned, exuberant boys reveling against their masters in a delirious after-hours pillow fight. Both films are linked by the figuratively thematic liberation of inmates taking over the asylum and the celebrations of freedom that ensue.

The guardians of contemporary culture were in agreement about what and how sexual permutations could be represented, but missing among them, even under the categories marked "ridiculousness," "bisexuality," and "polymorphous perversity," was the possibility that Smith could love women and need men, and be amused and saddened and tortured by that human condition. In his film, as well as in his photography, writing, drawings, and collages, Smith dedicated massive amounts of his attention to what he referred to as the moldy hell of men and women, aware of the equal opportunity they had to suffer and experience joy. *Flaming Creatures* is, like Antoine Watteau's early eighteenth-century painting *A Pilgrimage to Cythera*—a *fête galante*, baroque re-creation in art of a theatrical entertainment—ambiguous about everything except the celebration it depicts, poignant because the celebration must end. For Smith, that was life.

Smith remained fiercely concentrated on the project during the months of the film's making, confiding observations, literary fantasies, lists of titles, and drawings to a cloth-bound, leather-cornered ledger marked with the word "journal." In it, he produced several sketches of the painted almond tree backdrop that were used convincingly in the early sequences of *Flaming Creatures*. Summoning the inspiration of his patron saint, Maria Montez, he noted, "I did something quite similar and stuck close to the sketch—I invoke Miss Montez to give it to me to do the same with the script."

The journal context suggests that these otherwise unremarkable drawings date from 1962, the year of the filming, while other drawings represent projects of the following year, including a stick drawing of the sequence that concludes his next film, *Normal Love*. In that film, the cake, designed by sculptor Claes Oldenburg and constructed by Smith's conscripts, became the tiered platform for a truly nutty Busby Berkeley dance routine. Smith's drawing captures the energy of that extended triumphant moment. He notes the signature color of the sequence—pink—and passes judgment on its execution: SUCCESS.

Smith added a few costume drawings to the ledger that sport elements characteristic of his drawings in years to come: gothic horror architecture and landscapes, extravagant attitude, eyebrows, eyelashes, and posturing wrists. Other drawings are scattered throughout the book, including deco mountains with a solitary rickshaw and a downhill sign marked ME; a funny, creepy architectural drawing whose arches become the sockets of a skull; a dozen variations of cursive writing and block lettering, some of it backwards, spelling out "beginnings" and "on and on forever."

In the winter of 1962-63, with the encouragement of Mekas, Smith published "The Perfect Film Appositeness of Maria Montez" in *Film Culture*, accompanied by a series of stills of Montez in *Cobra Woman*, *Arabian Nights*, *Ali Baba*, *White Savage*, and a truly wonderful photo-opportunity shot of Montez with Eleanor Roosevelt. In his first published piece of writing, Smith anticipated the possibilities of the reception of *Flaming Creatures*, writing knowingly, "Film critics are writers and they are hostile and uneasy in the presence of a visual phenomenon." In February, as if to emphasize his defiance of decorum, Smith joined Tony

Conrad and prototypic conceptual artist Henry Flynt, perhaps the father of conceptual art, in picketing the Museum of Modern Art, Lincoln Center, and the Metropolitan Museum with signs bearing slogans: DEMOLISH SERIOUS CULTURE! DEMOL-ISH ART MUSEUMS! NO MORE ART! DEMOLISH CONCERT HALLS! DEMOLISH LINCOLN CENTER! Their protest targeted the exhibition of the Mona Lisa at the Met, and was followed by a Flynt lecture denouncing cultural snobbery the following evening in Walter De Maria's loft.

In March 1964, police confiscated *Flaming Creatures* during a screening, and arrested four of Smith's colleagues in the process. A week or so later, Jean Genet's film *Un Chant d'Amour* was also seized. In a contemporaneous letter to the painter Larry Rivers in London, the poet and curator Frank O'Hara chronicled the events of the moment. He reported the closing of coffee houses and gay bars, the seizure of *Flaming Creatures*, the committees formed in protest, and an account of artists struggling with the city over permits that legalized loft living. Smith himself received little support from beleaguered gay organizations. In a letter to Mekas, the director of the Homosexual League of New York, an advocacy group, admitted a favorable impression of the Genet film, but found *Flaming Creatures* "long, disturbing and psychologically unpleasant....Why don't the filmmakers produce an authentic film about a love affair or something between two boys which takes place in the contemporary homosexual setting."

Whether or not this response troubled, amused, or even reached Smith is unclear. What did reach his attention was the critic Susan Sontag's essay about *Flaming Creatures*, "A Feast for Open Eyes," in the April 13, 1964, issue of the respected liberal weekly *The Nation*, which also included as worthy of consideration a piece on the 1961 Bay of Pigs debacle, the abortive attempt of U.S.-trained guerrilla troops to invade Cuba. Sontag praised Smith's visual generosity, the directness and power of his images, the film's joy and innocence, and went so far as to hail it as a "lovely specimen" of pop art. Damning with faint praise, she concluded: "Apart from the wrongness of censorship itself, there is no need to worry what will be the social consequences if *Flaming Creatures* ever plays at Radio City Music Hall because it won't." Several weeks before, *The Nation* had also published an editorial condemning censorship in general, however distasteful the instance of free expression.

Concerning such unexpected response, Smith wrote of his critics: "Shocked by the seaminess of images of sexpartners not attired in brand new garments moments fresh from the dry cleaners, shocked by images of partners without textureless faces, shocked by the uselessness of anything but cut-out, rigidly self-conscious beings smiling pleasantly, displaying a product and fainting with rapture all at the same moment. And they are shocked by *Flaming Creatures* and have called it obscene."

Smith raised his voice in protest against convention and the suppression of personal liberties, soon broadening the issue to include a cry for the legalization of marijuana, his drug of choice. On August 11, 1965, with filmmakers Piero Heliczer, Stanton Kaye, and others, Smith participated in what was intended as a benefit reading and screening at the Broadway Central Hotel to help raise money for the legal expenses of two men who had been arrested on marijuana possession charges. The audience had been infiltrated by non-paying federal narcotics agents, ridiculously disguised in Hawaiian shirts. Several of the agents surrounded a principal speaker, defendant Jack Martin, and as their identity was disclosed, a fracas ensued. Smith struck one of the agents, and was arrested for assault.

Undaunted, Smith busied himself with another benefit at the Village Gate, this one titled "Young American Beatniks Morally Opposed to Prisons," a "Hallucinatory Colored Light Flip-Out," featuring films of Smith, Heliczer, and Bill Vehr, and appearances by underground stars John Vaccaro, Beverly Grant, and Mario Montez. Smith variously titled the benefit "Grass Busts of the Brassiere World" and "Grass Busts of Narco-Goon Benefit." The court case went into gear, and Smith later observed that if his lawyer had complained about the beating he'd received, the case might have been saved. "Since then my life has become a protracted struggle to remain out of jail—wasteful of money and disruptive of work." He constructed a typescript protest, based on an account of the Broadway Central riot, out of a barrage of notes, and called the essay *Lobotomy in Lobsterland*. Through it, he created one of the key characters in his pantheon of villains, The Lobster, embodiment of the evils of government and private property and, like its namesake, segmented, spineless, cannibalistic.

But Smith was clearly able to channel his outrage at such disturbances, however disruptive, into his work, a technique that provided him with a self-renewing source of material in the years to come. In the winter of 1965, Mekas organized the New or Expanded Cinema Festival, featuring works by Robert Rauschenberg, Claes Oldenburg, Nam June Paik, Robert Whitman, La Monte Young, Marian Zazeela, and others. There were experimental psychedelic light shows and, among them, an Andy Warhol presentation with split-screen projections and a rock band. Smith offered a stage piece, *Rehearsal for the Destruction of Atlantis*, identified as a "Dream Weapon Ritual by Jack Smith Dedicated to Irving Rosenthal."

Directly informed by his recent brush with the law, the work was concerned with police, narcotics agents, and Vietnam, with John Vaccaro brilliantly costumed as The Lobster. While drawing on the event of his recent arrest, *Rehearsal for the Destruction*

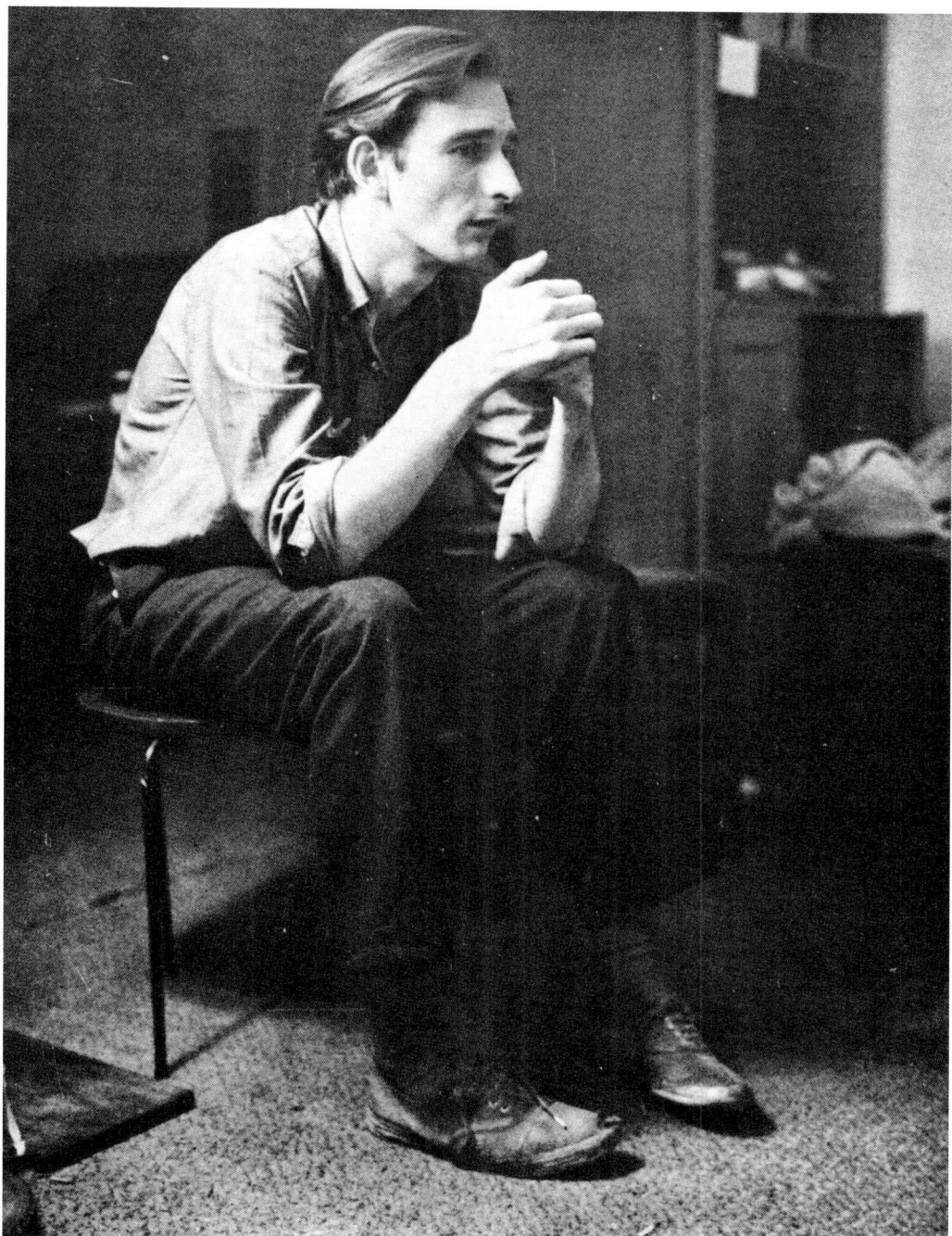

Better to vote for what you want and not get it than to vote for
what you don't want and get it.

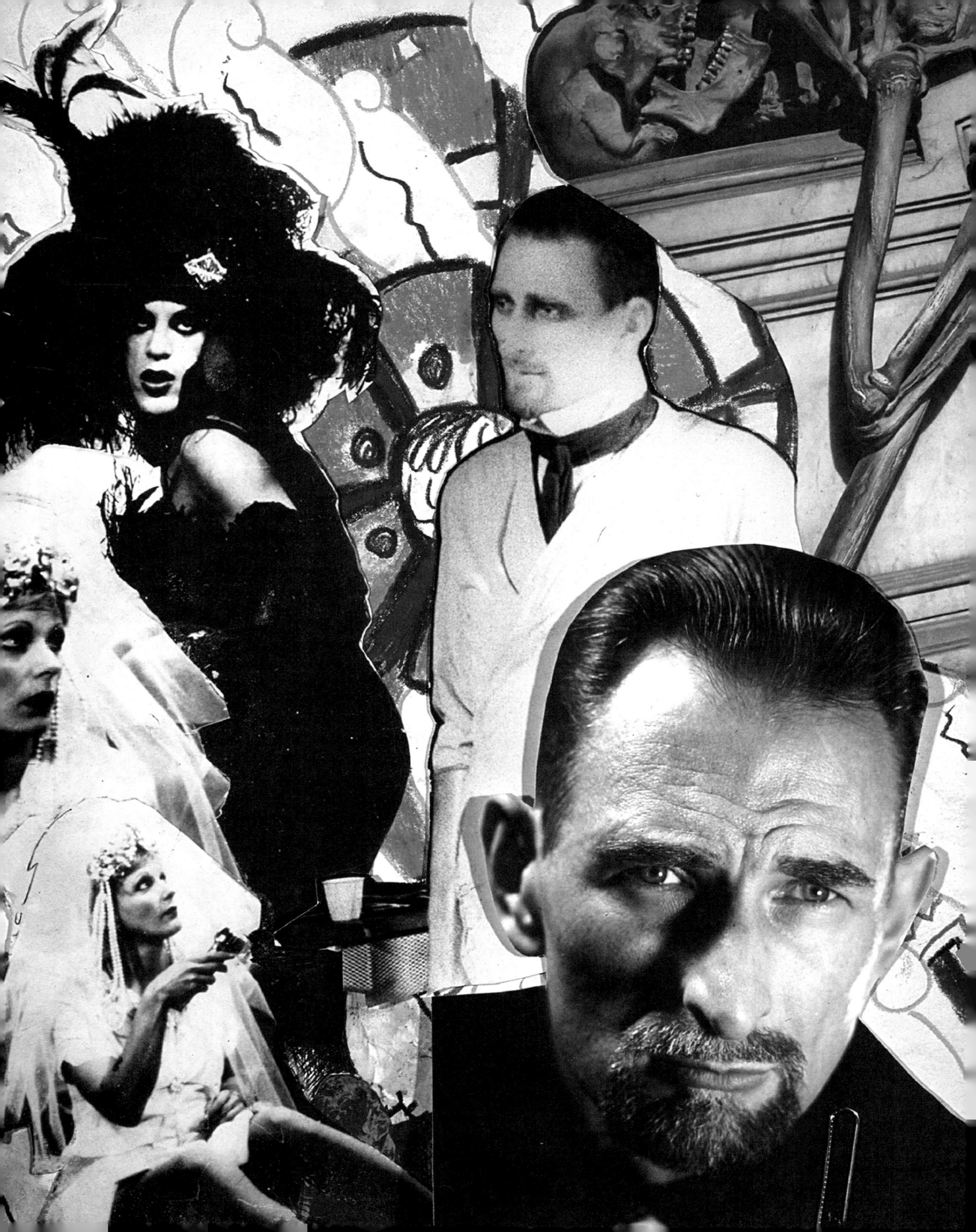

of Atlantis marked a departure from Smith's previous work in film. Richard Foreman observed that this performance came together in such a way that the temporal activity of its creation and its witnessing, rather than the performance as a crafted result, became the objective.

Foreman's recollection as a member of the audience is evocative in spite of, or because of, the fact that he does not recall much of the performance. He admitted that he was inclined to consider Smith's first endeavors in theater production seriously on the basis of his admiration for *Flaming Creatures* alone. But, on reflection, he realized that his experience was "of greater seriousness and human truth" than anything available in the theater at that time. What Foreman recognized early on was Jack Smith's ability to transport an audience to a state of consciousness and awareness otherwise unavailable, and that this was an accomplishment of a very high order.

The following February, composer Jerry Leiber and his then wife, actress Gaby Rodgers, staked Smith to a filming visit to Carnival in Rio, where he met some interesting, not quite famous people, "a very high-strung bunch of people, each nervous about something." They included an American parachutist who lived to jump with red, white, and blue parachutes and with flares on each foot; an American journalist working as the night editor of the *Brazil Herald*; and the model Nena von Schlebrugge, who was in the process of divorcing Timothy Leary. He intended to work a proposed film-in-progress around this somewhat exotic trio, but mostly succeeded in filming samba schools. He also managed to lose his passport, got dragged out of the path of television camera crews, and fell and broke his leg. On his return to New York, he appropriated a wheelchair during a hospital check-up, and headed home (wheelchairs were somewhat in demand among impoverished filmmakers for dolly and tracking shots). Later, he removed his cast himself.

Despite the modest support of a few uptown patrons, Smith was often unable to pay his rent, at that time $150 a month. He judged the paying of rent a fruitless, endless, and enslaving enterprise that could never end. His tactics were various, and at one point he wrote to his landlady in Yonkers: "After all these years of seeing that you always got money I now find that you do not appreciate it. I'm afraid I must ask you to either stop praying for me or else present the building to me as a gift. This I think you will find is all you can do and will be the cheapest thing for you to do. And it should be done graciously." On another occasion, he wrote: "But let me say to you in a friendly way, I know that you know that we all either have to become lawyers or go into show business. What if it turned out that I was a saint."

While both Smith and Andy Warhol branched out in many areas, Warhol, who styled himself "director, The Plastic Inevitable," made an apparent breakthrough with the split-screen, randomly associated *Chelsea Girls*, which became, to general astonishment, a commercial success. Warhol achieved both money and unimaginable notoriety instead of scandal and litigation. Of Warhol's success, Smith observed, in an interview in a column published by his colleague in film, Dick Preston: "They're all hypnotized by the blandness...the smoothness of the finish. Critically you can't deal with Warhol any more than you can deal with the plaster....What Warhol uses is icing instead of plaster...and the sparkle on top of the icing is amphetamine. There's nothing underneath. He himself has been terribly bruised by commercialism. He's the product of unarrested commercial intrusion into our daily lives. His films are not much different from all the plaster that's showing on 42nd Street. His main contribution lies in the truth of his sound track which underlines the phony nature of the commercial movie. But there's still nothing underneath. And yet, in the long run he may be doing something good for the medium."

In fact, Smith hoped for recognition for his work as actor, at one point writing to Warhol to suggest alternate titles for Warhol's unfinished *Batman/Dracula*, venturing that its release would fuel his acting career. Following his early appearances in Ken Jacobs's films, Smith had, to that end, actively participated in the work of his colleagues, appearing, for example, in Ron Rice's *The Queen of Sheba Meets the Atom Man* and *Chumlum* (1963). He appeared as Orpheus in Gregory Markopoulos's *Illiac Passion*, filmed for the most part in 1964, but not released until 1968; as Vincent van Gogh in Dov Lederberg's *Eargogh* (1964-65); Carl Linders's *Skin* (1964); and Bill Vehr's *Brothel* (1966); and in a number of Piero Heliczer's films.

Smith's interests as writer, draftsman, and designer also flourished, and in 1966, at Ron Tavel's invitation, he produced highly detailed costume designs for the Play-House of the Ridiculous Repertory Club presentation of Tavel's *The Life of Lady Godiva*. The crayon-bright drawings, bristling with attitude, eyelashes, and serious shoes, are signed and dated, an indication of his regard for them. By the end of that year, he also wrote a signed, but apparently unpublished, essay praising an exhibition of the sculpture of Walter De Maria.

In 1967, he appeared in Mike Sullivan's *No Smoking*; played Starveling the Tailor in a production of *A Midsummer Night's Dream* at the Theatre de Lys; and starred as the slow-motion "Mr. X" in Charles Ludlam's *Big Hotel* (1967), which the actor and poet

Taylor Mead described as "one of the greatest things in the theater I've ever seen. But I think the next day Jack stabbed somebody or something in rehearsal for some reason, and that ended the play." However accurate an account, Mead's characterization of Smith as prone to violent behavior is consistent with his conduct during the Broadway Central riot, and his reputation for acting out caused real concern among otherwise likely collaborators and friends.

Smith christened his loft as home to "The Plaster Foundation," a "free" theater, in 1968. He obsessively rearranged the sequences of *Normal Love*, and arranged screenings of the unfinished project *Kidnapping and Auctioning of Wendell Willkie by the Love Bandit*, eventually known as *No President*, incorporating found footage and filmed sequences. He was increasingly committed to live theater and the staging of performances to be photographed and then projected as slides. Beginning in 1968, Smith presented variously titled works: *Brassieres of Atlantis*, *10 Million B.C.*, *Boiled Lobster Easter Pageant*, *Miracle of Farblonjet*, and *Withdrawal from Orchid Lagoon*.

From the time of Smith's *Rehearsal for the Destruction of Atlantis*, his performances were attended by an often small but distinguished following, including Foreman, Robert Wilson, and the poet and critic Stefan Brecht. In 1969, Smith appeared, tusks and all, as the Walrus in Wilson's *Life and Times of Sigmund Freud*, where his influence on Wilson was apparent in gestures and movement. Foreman observed: "To watch Jack Smith perform was to watch human behavior turn into granular stasis, in which every moment of being seemed, somehow, to contain the seed of unthinkable possibility....Wilson was unhappy at the end of the rehearsal, asking Jack for his thoughts, and Jack responding, in the extended nasal drawl that was so much his own, 'it has to be...sadder, Bob, it's not saaad enough...make it...slow...er, much slow...er, just much slow...er'"

Other theatrical presentations followed, including *Claptailism of Palmola Christmas Spectacle* and *Gas Stations of the Cross Religious Spectacle*, performances that were variations on a theme of personal relationships, perceived wrongs, and riffs on movie and radio drama of the 1940s, often featuring slide projection. Stefan Brecht, a chronicler of Smith's work from 1970 through 1977, recalls several performances in his book *Queer Theatre*, vividly describing the mise-en-scène as a careful arrangement of junk:
"...metallic and plastic street refuse measuring in the inches and feet, broken, and bottles. A minor votive screen in the background, with empty bottles in the niches. A toilet with junk in it, including a crippled, perhaps headless doll. Old, small Christmas trees with hardly any needles left. Feathers, wire netting, a string of colored lights...a sensitively restrained encroachment on a chance disorder which has been allowed to affirm itself. Smith seems to have picked up these things by an attraction to the definitely squalid, a sentiment for orphanage among the merest means. The disruption of function defines the heap."

In 1971, Smith appeared as "the magician," or the Man with the Top Hat and Cape, in Wilson's *Deafman Glance*, using the stage name of Sharkbait Starflesh. Wilson posted a note to him: "Jack, you being there is so important." It was his last appearance with Wilson, although he later received a written invitation from him to appear as the eponymous figure in *The Life and Times of Joseph Stalin*. Wilson wrote: "I know you feel I have done you wrong. Anyway the play is for you. The part is really glorious. Stalin as a father, as a priest, as a movie star, as on a telephone a lot....It is the perfect part for you—no doubt about it. How are you? I think about your friendship despite what you may feel and that means a great deal to me—you are the best actor I know—anyway I would like for you to play Stalin—I can pay you this time....The last scene is incredible with 100's people rushing towards Stalin (he's all in white)

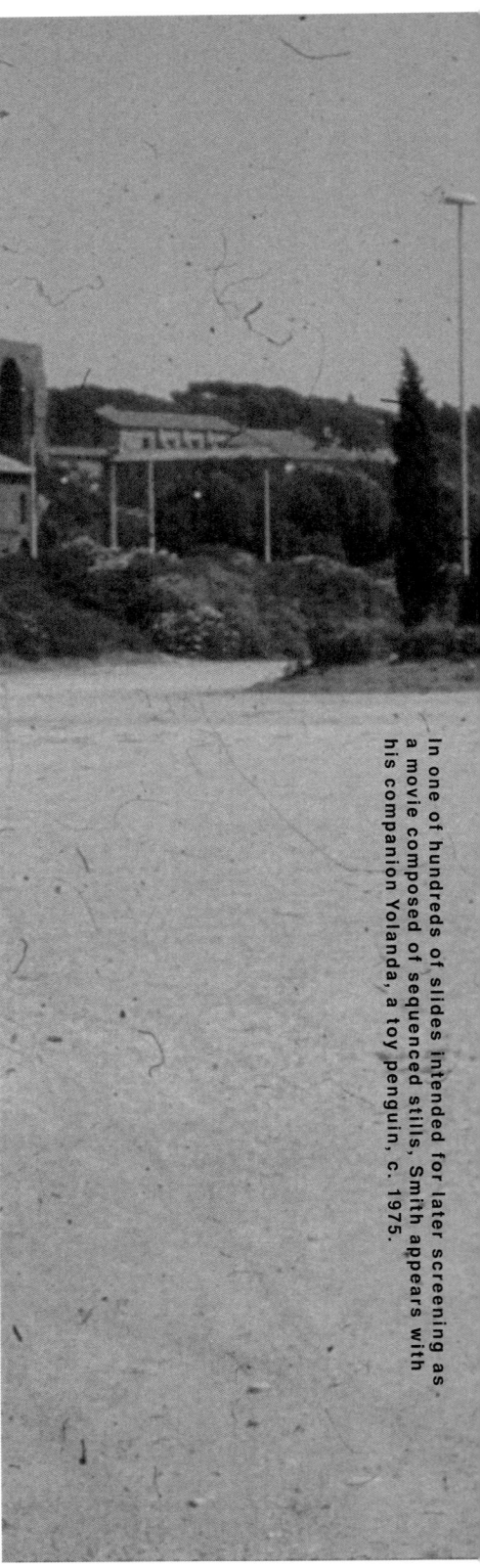

In one of hundreds of slides intended for later screening as a movie composed of sequenced stills, Smith appears with his companion Yolanda, a toy penguin, c. 1975.

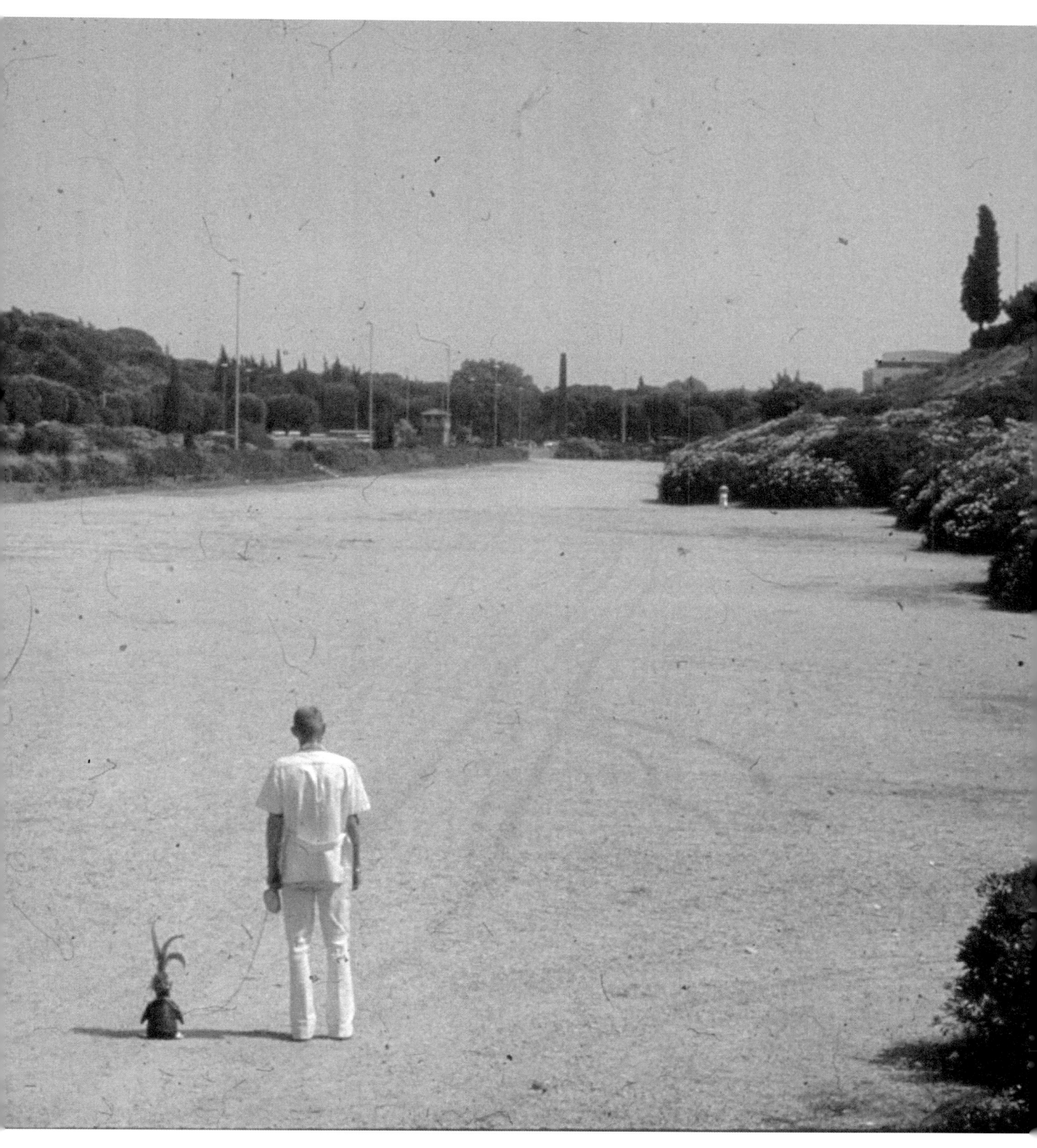

December 1974

Avalanche

$1

Editor:
Artist-in-Residence:
Production:

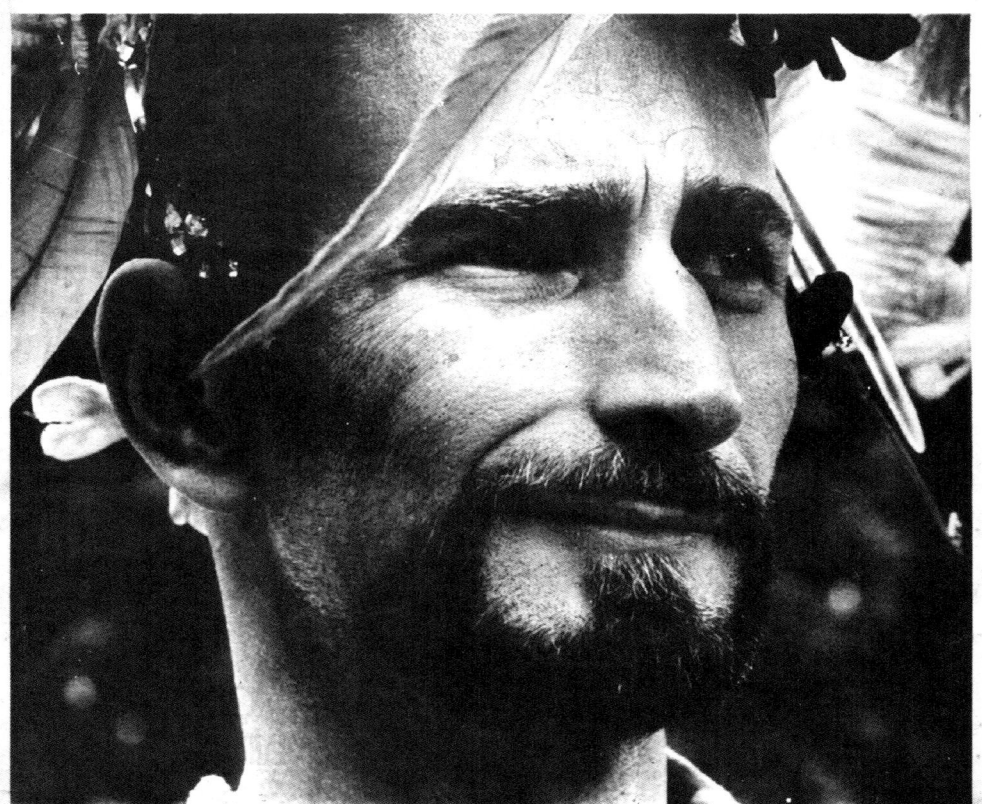

JACK SMITH

Joel Fisher	Terry Fox
Daniel Buren	Simone Forti
Hans Haacke	Stephen Laub
Gordon Matta-Clark	Phil Glass Ensemble

Smith on the cover of *Avalanche*, in costume as Ronald De Carlo, 1974.

ready to get into an airplane and he stops the crowd with slight gestures of his hands—If you would consider the part—and this time there is $ to pay you—please let me know."

Wilson signed off with a drawing for stage movements. Smith was convinced that Wilson, like Foreman, Mekas, and others, had followed his work to be fertilized, to receive the inspiration they lacked in order to do their own work. He refused Wilson's invitation. To this day, Wilson refers to what has become his signature technique as "this long, slow, Robert Wilson movement," although the patent, perhaps, belonged to Smith.

Smith's charges concerning Mekas's collusion and corruption ran deeper than such accounts might warrant. He had previously condemned Mekas for sacrificing *Flaming Creatures* to the courts, and insisted that as the film's champion, Mekas had opposed censorship only because it was a radically chic thing to do at the time: It made Mekas appear a saint while enhancing his own career. Further, he claimed Mekas had hypnotized Susan Sontag with his vision of free cinema, while diverting her attention from the socialistic commitment implicit in the organization of the Film-Makers Co-op. He also charged Mekas with stealing the careers of young filmmakers by imprisoning them in his vaults, only letting them out at night, and then only rarely. He indicted Mekas for the alleged theft of the original of *Flaming Creatures*, and when the missing film was found by filmmaker Jerry Tartaglia, quite by accident, a few years later, he believed that Mekas had determined that it was the right time for the film to resurface. He claimed that Mekas had sullied his reputation by making it seem as though he, Smith, was trying to destroy himself and all his work. He enshrined Mekas in his "Mausoleum" of Anthology, next to The Lobster and the Lucky Landlord, as Uncle Fishhook, Uncle Roachcrust, Jonas Mecrust.

Mercifully, Smith was able to tame his beasts by incorporating them into his work, providing them with costumes, scripting their performances, transforming them into cartoon characters in a modern day morality play. He used costumes and tableaux as his structure, and slides, along with live performance and selections from a vast arsenal of music and tapes, as his medium. In 1974, Smith met the German art impresario Hildegarde Lutze, then living in New York, a key player in the Germany-New York art axis of the time. Abundant, blonde, extravagant, into clothes, a scenester, she was a professional catalyst and something of a match for Jack Smith. Lutze, as she was known, invited Smith to present *Sacred Landlordism of Lucky Paradise* at the New York gallery of German dealer Rheinhard Onnasch, and sought to represent him in Europe. That summer, Smith constructed a script (starring himself) for still photographs taken by Gwenn Thomas on the grounds of the Cologne zoo at the time of Projekt 74, organized by the Kölner Kunstverein. A selection of images corresponding to the narrative, laid out in fumetti, with cartoon balloons, appeared in the hip avant-garde magazine Avalanche as "Horror of Shark Museum." Smith starred, with a supporting cast of camels, monkeys, and an eagle, as Ronald De Carlo, "the average person who, in everyday life of Lucky Landlord Paradise, is a postman of Lotusland."

During the Cologne visit, Smith also staged a narrative photo shoot, titled "Moses," intended for slide sequencing and projection. Elaborately costumed, Smith accentuated his eyes with iridescent blue glitter and donned a pharaonic headdress. Posing in angular, hieroglyphic attitudes, he makes his way through the paths of a bosky setting to the edge of a pond, and encounters his exotically beautiful collaborator, Babeth, in desert tribal dress, major makeup. Much in the manner of Ruth St. Denis, Smith strikes prayerful attitudes and gathers bits of detritus into his basket, the surrogate Moses found in the bullrush trash heap of civilization.

The photographs, by avant-garde German filmmaker Wilhelm Hein, are elegantly framed, but are clearly the result of Smith's direction, with their emphasis on chiaroscuro, framing, and camera angles. In this highly choreographed session, and in those that followed in future years, Smith became the author of the script, director, star, and cinematographer, exercising complete control of the production. The slides themselves were to be projected as part of a growing, changing slide show, incorporated into the layered mise-en-scène of future plays and performances, and used in the production of handbills and posters.

Months later, in Rome, Smith introduced an ongoing figure into his performances, a toy penguin, surrogate for himself and Maria Montez, both, in his eyes, the victims of studio politics. As Smith scripted these stories, the glamorous Yolanda la Pinguina, or Inez the Penguin as she was also known, was a creature of the studio system, and subject to its demands. In Rome, Smith staged a number of these scenarios, starring the penguin and himself, in photographs taken by his collaborator, the young talent Ivan Galietti, and others.

Smith took Yolanda everywhere, more or less, and wrote her into his performances. She joined him as the star of *I Danced with a Penguin*, and appeared in that role on German television, with Smith partnering as a solemn Fred Astaire. Kept in a box while waiting for her next role, or a comeback, Yolanda eventually, gloriously expired, then rose from the dead (real trouper that she was) in the elegiacal performances of *Death of a Penguin*, photographed by Peter Schönherr in the ruins of a bombed-out church in Hamburg. (In October 1975, Smith scheduled *Horror of the Rented World*, "a Slide Show in Boiled Lobster Color," at the Collective for Living Cinema, to formally introduce the penguin in his New York repertory.)

Pursuing material for his work with slides, Smith intensified his exploration of the great roles in the canon of Western culture. Having addressed the story of Moses, Smith took on the biblical role of Christ, a part that had intrigued him for years. He had once told poet, photographer, and Warhol associate Gerard Malanga, in a riotous interview for *Film Culture*, "…I think a pretty good role would be Christ. But that is too much related to the Dracula thing anyway, so maybe I never will—maybe the interest has all gone out of that, or maybe it would be too repetitious of Dracula. But anyway the world could use a new idea—a new Christ image, and it would be fun to sort of work that out." In working out his new role, Smith created a character that joined attributes of both Abraham and Christ.

Smith's ambitions for theater expanded, and at the Collation Center, in January of 1977, he opened *Secret of Rented Island*, an adaptation of Ibsen's *Ghosts*, alternately known as *Orchid Rot of Rented Lagoon*. He explained the play as "a catalogue of wrecked lives-what people have done because they were afraid of what other people would say." Of all Smith's performances, *Rented Island* produced the most attentive audiences. Brecht, J. Hoberman, and others took notes and reported the protean nature of the production on different nights. Foreman was there, as were Robert Wilson and his entourage. "It was a sympathetic audience," Foreman observed, "an audience with the patience and tolerance of a supportive therapist."

With *Rented Island*, Smith brought together aspects of his work beyond film that would allow him total artistic control. Depending on the performance, his cast consisted of one or more live actors, including himself, and a mannequin's leg, high-heeled and protruding through a scrim, but mostly of stuffed toy animals—little costumed monkeys that could embrace each other with Velcro, and an elaborately outfitted pink hippopotamus in the role of Regina. Smith played most or all of the parts by producing several tapes of dialogue to accompany the action, while he maneuvered the toys into various positions on the stage by pulling a string. In an article by Gaby Rodgers, Smith announced that Mrs. Alving was to have "twenty breasts in diagonals on her front and back….Oswald will be a style parade. The part will glamorously degenerate into a style parade. It is timely doing *Ghosts*," he continued. "There are new strains of VD which will not respond to penicillin, you know." The climactic final scene replaced Ibsen's "Mother, give me the sun," with a request for Doris Day singing "Once I Had a Secret Love." Smith carefully documented various performances, and at one point included a time-lapse movie camera to record both a performance and the activities of a photographer and assistants engaged in documenting the performance.

Smith always put great store in the willingness and ability of his associates to serve him as "slaves." Performance artist Penny Arcade recalls telling Smith that she had always loved his work, and wanted to do something with him. "And he leaned forward, with a very surprised look on his face…looked at me and he says, 'Oh! Do you sew?' 'Sew? I was thinking about acting.' 'Everybody wants to act. Nobody wants to sew. You can't create theater if you don't do the sewing. That's the real creativity, not the acting. That's easy.'"

The next year he moved from Second Street to First Avenue, a six-floor walk-up he thought of as a film studio: The pantry was Stage A; the kitchen, Sound Stage B. "Sound Stage C is the bathroom. The refrigerator is a tomb for food." Filled with his signature mass of exotic detritus, the bathroom a jungle of plastic palms, Smith found the apartment "glorious." It became a dream of Baghdad and an experiment in architecture, as he created pavilions of fabric, exotic niches of blue-painted plaster, arches, and sconces. It also served as a theater, and those in attendance recall having a hard time finding the bathroom and, that accomplished, difficulty locating the toilet.

In 1981, Smith visited Genoa for the Restless Language (Il Gergo Inquieto) Film Festival, organized by Italian curator Germano Celant, critical voice of the arte povera movement. He was invited to screen his films, including *Flaming Creatures*, at a time of his choice, and to participate in a seminar dedicated to the underground films of the sixties. With the aid of photographer Nanda Lanfranco and others, he broadened the range of his activities to include photo shoots, a lecture, and performance, and stayed on as Lanfranco's guest for three months.

To the astonishment of the Genovese, Smith attempted to introduce brassieres for men into the cultural fabric of the city. He told his gallery audience that he was not much interested in the differences between women and men, and announced that this glamorous innovation, lost in development since the demise

Portrait of Smith mirrored in Mylar by poet Ira Cohen, 1966.

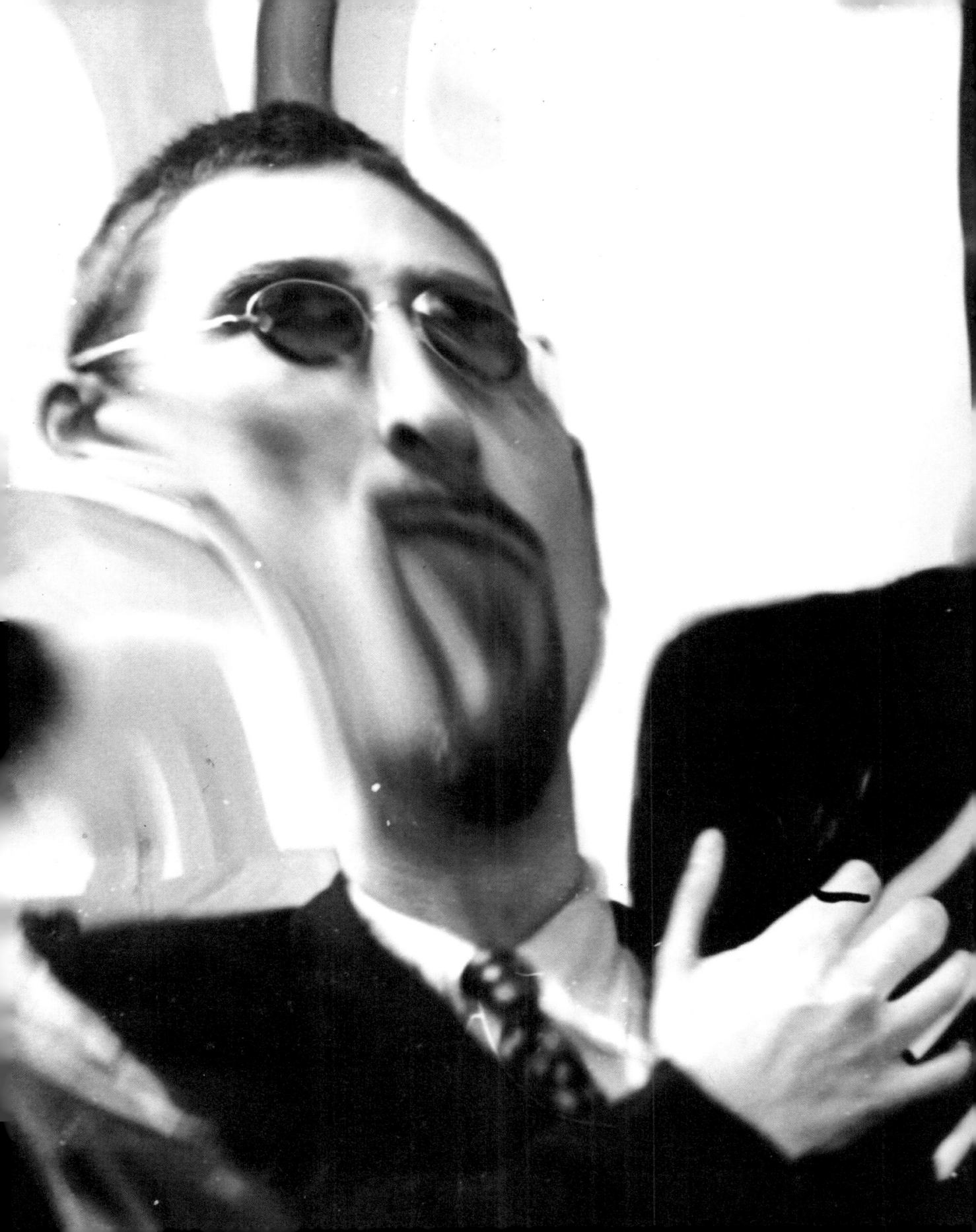

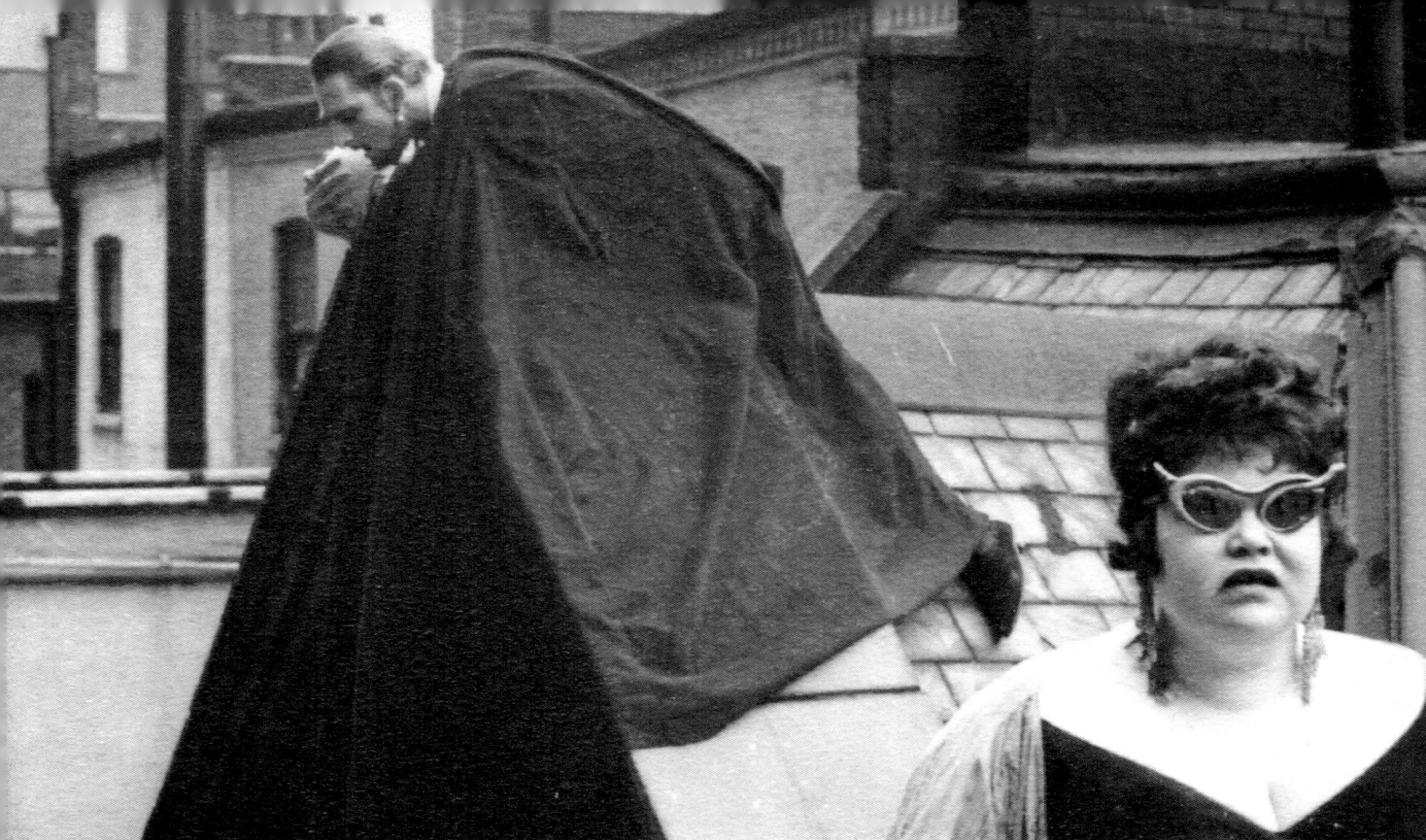

Smith and actress Tally Brown on location for Andy Warhol's *Batman/Dracula*, 1964.

of the codpiece during the Renaissance, would add glamour and healthful androgyny to the fashion problem of pockets: their irrational placement along the hip. He observed, as if in proof that the brassiere as contemporary codpiece replacement was a rational advancement in design: "Would God put a pocket on a leg?"

During his visit, he railed against a newly opened art school, blaming it and the university for justifying their judgments by teaching students that creativity is a glandular disturbance. He then attempted to clarify a point concerning the difference between uncommercialism and noncommercialism, something of importance to him. "Alora," he wrote, "I too must pay for the passage of time and intestines in the form of paying for food and in the form of the rent that can never be paid. The exact word to describe this is UN-commercial.... Everything you see here tonight is not LIKE commercial art, though I do expect to make money with it-just as any sane person expects to make money from their work. To recapitulate-Yes, to make money but NO, not like commercial theatre! For example, in the commercial theatre you never saw a depiction of an artist being paid in advance for his work...so tonight we are not being noncommercial but we are being very UN-commercial. Is there a question remaining about this?"

Returning to New York, he produced drafts of a letter to Joseph Papp at the Public Theater, offering the director a production called *The Pirate and the Penguin*. Among other things, he told Papp: "My method of working has been evolved over the years and is not based on the usual rehearsals of a perfected piece of writing. There would be such a piece of writing but only AFTER the run of the play and then typically would never be referred to again. I have an outline of course, which by the way is in place to the extent that I could meet with you and describe I think to your satisfaction, but there are long passages of improvisation as the perfection of the story is sought for in front of the audience in a very living manner, and when a chunk of the play is perfected it is kept and the actors will go after another section on other nights."

Smith continued to perform at the Millennium, and at downtown clubs, the Limbo and the Pyramid among them, as younger artists developed interest in his work. The clubs were renegade, drag-friendly, hip. He appeared as the Bubble Goddess in Ela Troyano's film *Bubble People* (or *UUlua*), and in 1984, at the Pyramid, he began an extended, two-year "cabaret performance" of *Clash of the Brassiere Goddesses*, with such permutations as *Clash of the Brassiere Maidens* and *Brassieres of Uranus*. Tavel, who had survived twenty-two years of friendship with Smith by this time, appeared in the production in 1984, and recalls the work structured as a play, with costumes, dialogue, and stage directions, but also as a study in chaos.

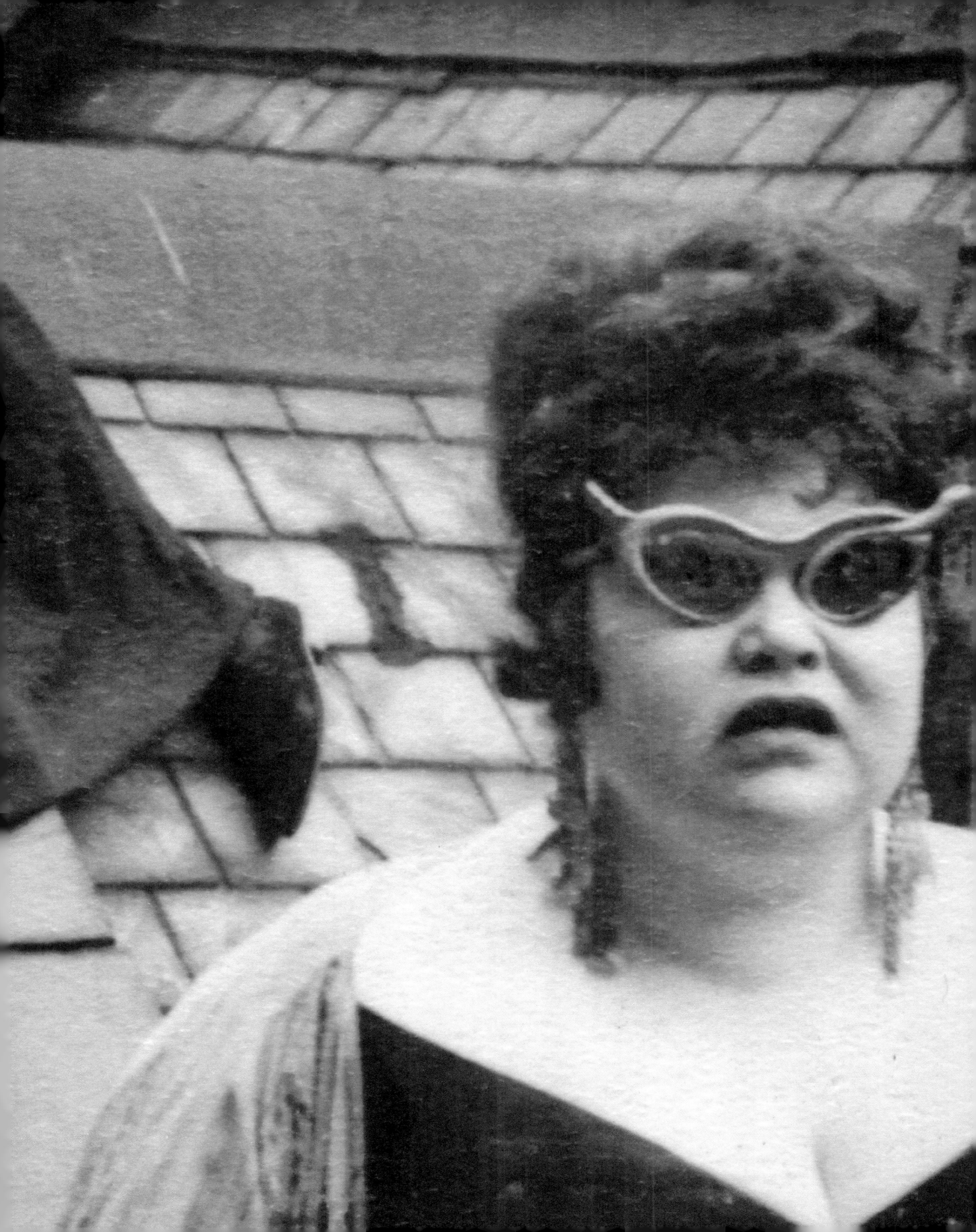

As there were to be no rehearsals, Smith intended Tavel to read, rather than memorize, the script. Among the props was an exoticized rocket ship, with curtains, and to the costumes, Tavel added a discarded lampshade, an incredible thing, huge, tasseled, transformed into an exotic hat. The performance unfolded in the bowels of the back room of the Pyramid, on Avenue A in the heart of the Lower East Side, on a makeshift stage of crates, before a very young and wildly enthusiastic assembly of tough, moshing, and slam-dancing club kids. Unable to see the script very well, Tavel felt humiliated and lost, and feared he would fall as the platform wobbled and the crates began to separate. Finally, the script called for Tavel to appear to mount Smith from behind, which somehow appalled the young audience, who, in any case, cheered, loving every moment even though they couldn't possibly have followed anything that was going on. To this day, Tavel remains puzzled that Smith seemed so satisfied with the production.

Smith successfully developed a routine of lectures and performances for the college and art school circuit, where he explained how the "basic proposition" of *Sinbad in the Rented World* "is that the ancient and Arab is one of the best means we have left now to show us the way out of an ugly, rectangular, machine-dictated architecture....I have turned an apartment in an old building, built by Italian workmen, into 'Basra' the Arabian Nights apartment. Here, art has been put back into architecture, where it belongs, as in ancient times....The shooting script is finished, the apartment is finished (and may be visited), and the Sinbad costumes are finished."

In Toronto, Smith substituted a performance of *Brassieres of Uranus*, featuring the "Dance of the Sacred Foundation Application," for the requested screening of *Flaming Creatures*, which he refused to submit to the Canadian Film Board for inspection. In a lecture to students, he put his concerns less obliquely: "Art is not something to superimpose over everyday life. If it's any good it has always come from everyday life. But our ideas about art are so perverted that it's become a guessing game. One year it's confused with Katharine Hepburn's jaw line....Making art never was supposed to be easy. It really has to be very boring. How on earth do you think any of the masterpieces of the past were produced? In continuous fits of ecstasy? No it must become very, very boring, no matter what they say about the ecstasy. It must become not only boring, but really, really, deadly boring. And it's the person that can live with that boredom and continue to go on doing things that has the resources to deal with that boredom. That's what it takes to make art."

In March 1985, Smith presented a program for the Visiting Filmmakers Series at the School of the Art Institute of Chicago, and a performance of *The Death of a Penguin* at Randolph Street Gallery. He screened *Flaming Creatures* and *Exotic Landlordism of the World*, his latest version of *Normal Love*. Smith told John Luther Schofill, who interviewed him for the program notes: "Right now, I just need an agent. I'm past the point where I need a manager. If you ever hear that I've got a manager, you'll know he's decayed."

Smith kept working, and in 1987, he staged performances at the Limbo Cafe on the Lower East Side. People entered his life and left again as friendships began and failed, and as his health failed. Identified as medically disabled and immune compromised,

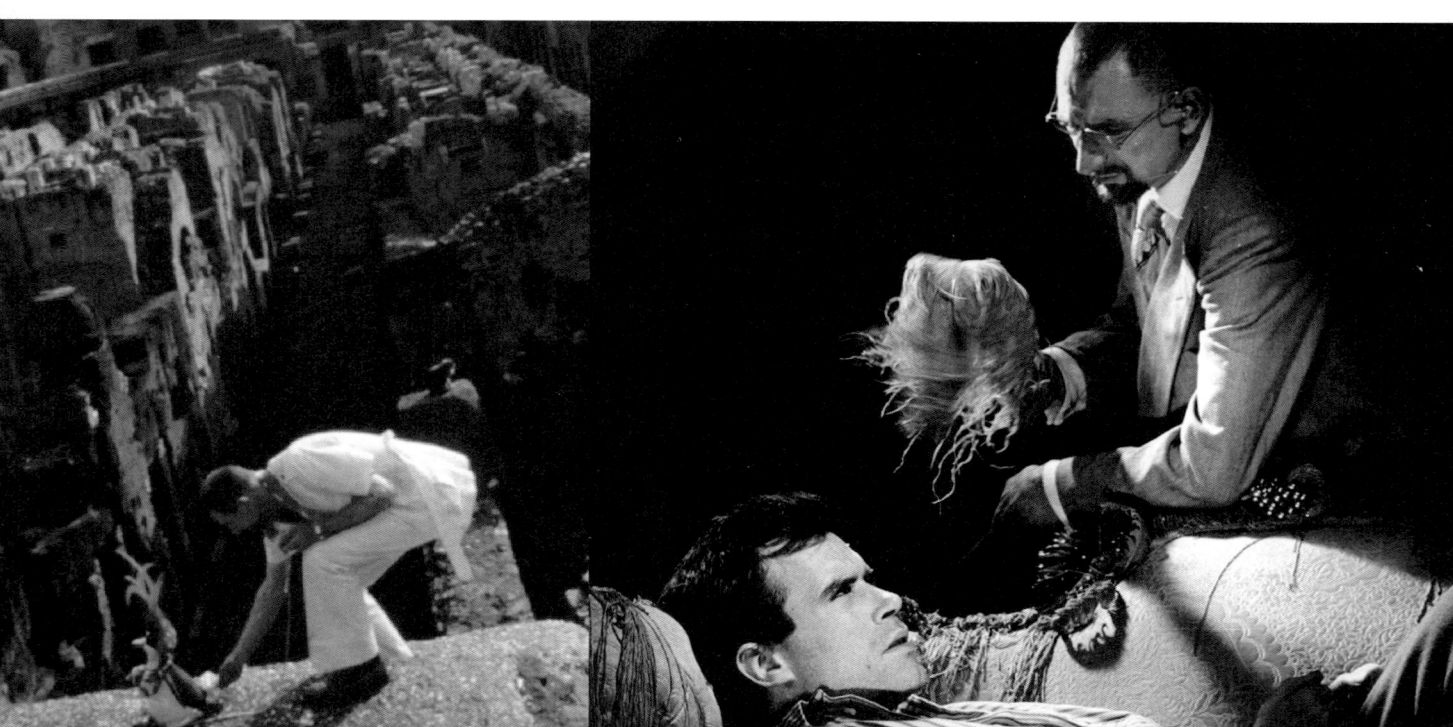

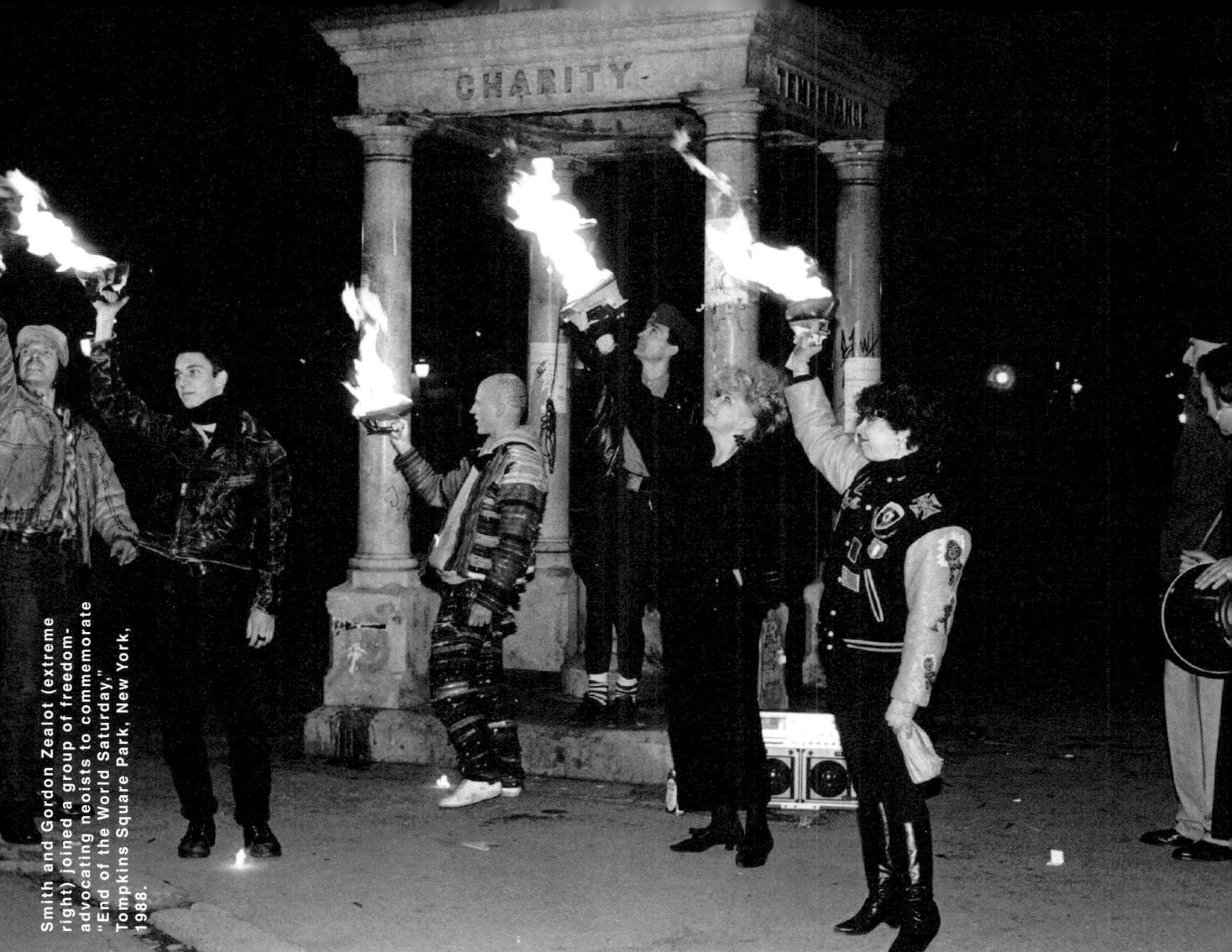

Smith and Gordon Zealot (extreme right) joined a group of freedom-advocating neoists to commemorate "End of the World Saturday," Tompkins Square Park, New York, 1988.

he was awarded SSI benefits. A few months later, he participated as a panelist on "The Artist Versus the Hippopotamus" at the True Comedy Theater, and began rehearsals for his role as Upton Sinclair in theater director William Niederkorn's *The Chaplin Acts* at La Mama E.T.C., appearing in cast photos. He withdrew before the opening.

Among the photographs that document the last year of his life, there is one that includes Smith at the edge of a group of half a dozen young "neoists," street radicals with a taste for performance. They are assembled near the pathetic neoclassical monument to the virtues in Tompkins Square Park on the Lower East Side, at the conclusion of a neoist event called "End of the World Saturday." Smith watches from a few feet away, as the marchers raise burning torches into the night air, held aloft like Liberty's lamp. But the torches are laundry irons whose flat plates had been coated with rubber cement and set ablaze. Smith wears a look he sometimes assumed in situations like these, social sorts of gatherings, uptown or downtown. A look of concentration, slightly distanced, observing, as if he had been drawn, out of curiosity or perhaps because of a moment's loneliness, to the periphery of the circle of their activity, and thought about who they were, and wondered what they wanted, or intended. And if they, too, were Flaming Creatures.

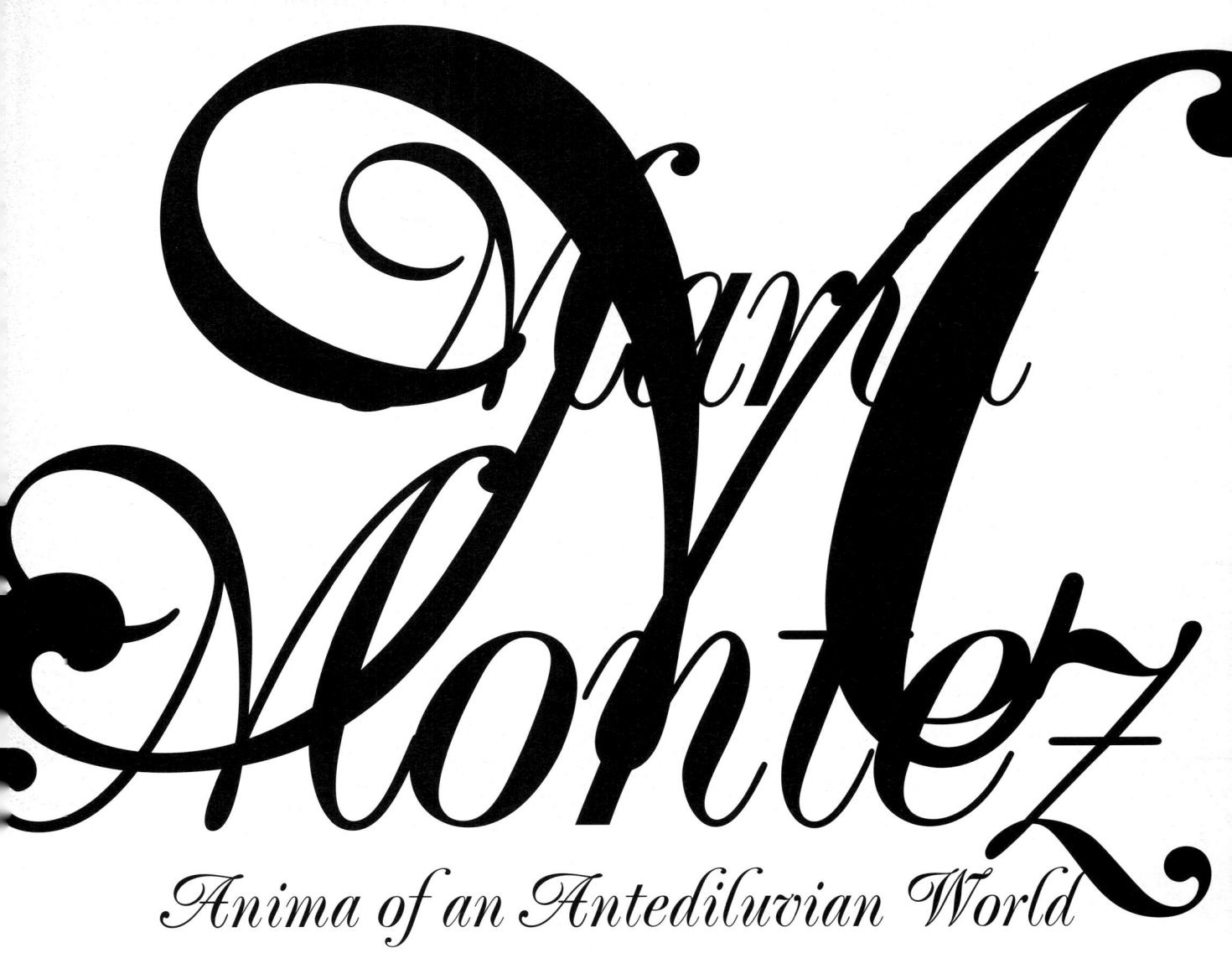

Maria Montez

Anima of an Antediluvian World

By Ronald Tavel

Enact anger, hauteur, and disappointment was what she *could* do. That anger that perhaps is the most accessible platform for the amateur actor, but which contributed so promotionally much to her fiery image. That riveting brand of Spanish hauteur, imperial and insolent, which would cast her more often than not as royalty, nobility, or gentry. And that disappointment—which she knew so well, obstructing her brief, somewhat underrealized life in the guise of colleagues with a congenital failure of imagination—that lent depth and dignity to her touching screentale moments.

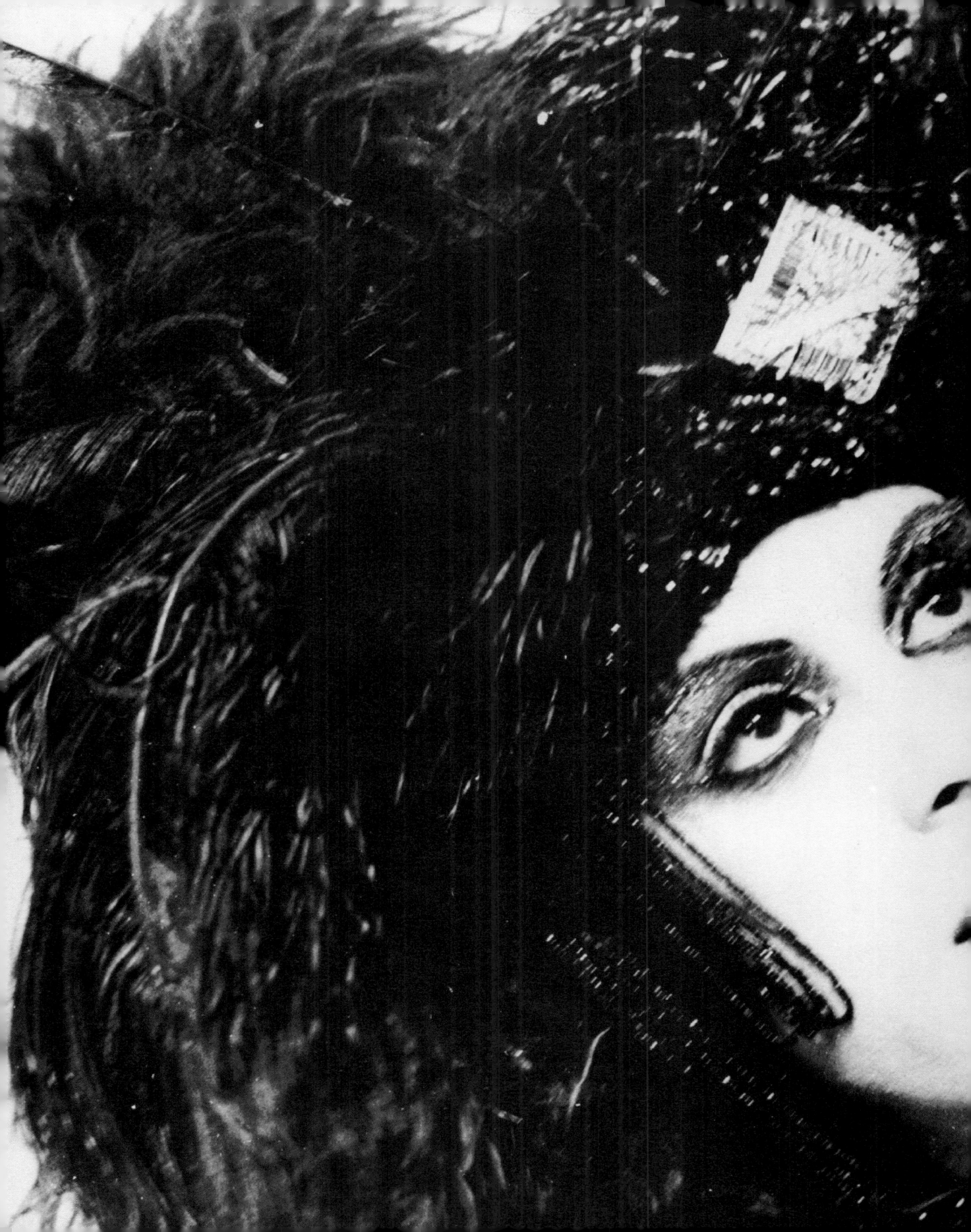

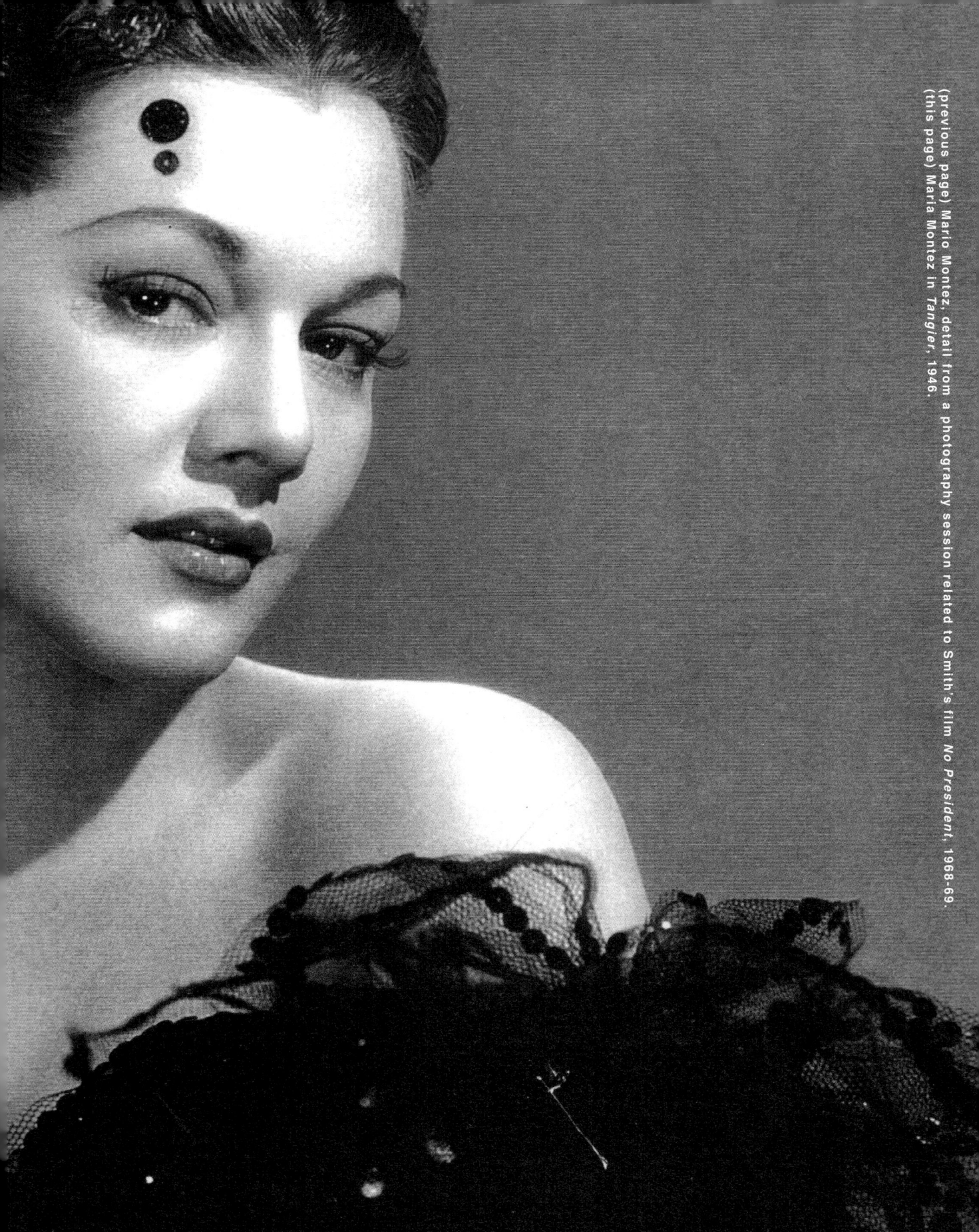

(previous page) Mario Montez, detail from a photography session related to Smith's film *No President*, 1968–69. (this page) Maria Montez in *Tangier*, 1946.

The anger:

She flies into a fit at a perceived slight on the parts of cowboy Johnny Mack Brown of Boullion City and gunrunner Rod Cameron in *Pirates of Monterey*, and at Billy Gilbert for merely "calling time" in her first, but long-built-up-to, star-making minute in *Arabian Nights*. She unleashes her wrath at Robert Barron, a bearer of evil tidings, and Mary Nash, a matriarch pulling rank on her in *Cobra Woman*, and at a drunk, love-sick Jean-Pierre Aumont testing her patience with his naiveté in *Hans le Marin*. And she kicks off one of filmdom's furniture-smashing, all-time epic tantrums on learning of Turhan Bey, her regal brother's debt-mounting and face-diminishing debauchery on Coral Island's white trash waterfront, to mark her tempestuous, barge-borne entrance in *White Savage*.

The hauteur:

Not our peer, she peers disdainfully down at us and her fellow players from the topless tower of her unshakable, photogenic self-confidence, whether that distance is measured by a throne, as in all the island idylls, or as a climb to the throne through her five desert Aeneids, or by Castilian, French or Rumanian title in *La Donna del Corsaro*, *Pirates of Monterey*, *The Exile*, and *Gypsy Wildcat*. Speculating on this persistent impression, director Robert Siodmak observed: "She believed completely in her roles. If she was to play a princess I had to treat her like one all through lunch… was twenty-four hour method acting before its time." But even as a displaced war orphan (*Tangier*), taverner in the clutches of the Grand Inquisitor (*Il Ladro di Venezia*), or duplicitous prostitute (*Hans le Marin*), hers is still majestic mettle being tested, and we're assured that terror, torture, execution itself must leave it intact.

The disappointment:

Her stare stark with silent bitterness, as a dancer who thought she would be queen the day before (in *Arabian Nights*), she descends from the slave pens to mount the auction block into an all but unreachable, irreversible despair…Her realization that the lives including her own which she jeopardized and/or lost to win the titular rogue, Paul Christian, in *Il Ladro di Venezia*, was all for naught, is given in the last sad take a disturbingly detailed close and deliberate zoom to final frame by a possibly guilt-ridden John Brahm atoning in the cut for posthumous release. Guided by Max Ophuls, she delivers the definitive interpretation of the Feldmarschallin character in *The Exile*: A great court beauty who makes her last pitch and loses, to take it on the chin in an ineffably extended scene of grace, gallantry, and then letting go.

Behind that grace was the experience of the inability of Walter Wanger, then president of the Academy of Motion Picture Arts and Sciences, Jean Cocteau, and even Orson Welles, who one after one second thought themselves in a failure of nerve to find the art equivalent for the pristine magic she placed at their disposals.

Having said all this, that is, what as a performer she *could* make memorable, we have to add that her thespian accomplishments are perhaps only of secondary interest in an account of her impact on the arts, dramatic and plastic, of the American sixties-seventies; and of her fascination for a number of the ground-breaking artists of that period, among them Jack Smith, fascination that crossed over and beyond the obsessional into the *literally* continuous preoccupation with the woman on all but a religious and mega-adulatory level. Mantling himself in her, laying claim to her in fandom's name and nature of both wholly identifying and being violently possessive, Smith saw her as the maker of all art and, in a process of projection, revisited her in the series of women and men he was to love and all the beauty he intended to create in his life. Thus at times, metaphorically, every pertinent phenomenon was screened through her. And yet, this *was* entirely the result of her work in film. That being so, the precise character of her work needs a language aimed at least at the beginning of demystifying her cult, the altar-building, and her creative legacy. That any consensus thus far has been academically calcified by so often referring to the work of Maria Montez as a logical impasse, inaccessible to the uninitiable who, born with scales on their eyes, must go through movie-viewing icon-blinded, a prevailing no little contributed by Smith himself — forces the attempt to navigate from as well as out of this impasse to resort to one's sense of the rapturous as much as the rational.

Still, we must return to, or dispense with, the question of her acting ability — or inability as tiresome, lowbrow mainstream as observers would have it — for, emphatically enough, her inoculative influence may be coaxed from the shadowed corners of her period, tropic, or medieval sets if *that* impression, her inability is scrutinized.

Impressively, it was *this* photogenic quality, i.e., her lensable belief, that triggered Smith's ambition in film. Again, precisely, that the woman's belief, and exactly what that belief embraced, was filmable. What, then, did it embrace? A world as fantastical, dazzling, lush, surprising, and crowded with beauty as some children find it to be. And that her's was a central role in that kaleidoscopic daydream—importantly, this, too, filmable—as the princess *for* whom it all exists and *by* whom, i.e., by whose imagination, it all does. And that this passion, he contended—this painterly ecstasy, the Delacroix and Chateaubriandian of her soul could register on film, *could be recorded* on stock—was what made her a star.

In overnight twelve-hour sessions that date back to 1962, Jack Smith and I often sat up together enjoying her occurrence. We speculated on why and how she made the glittering chimera mirrorland that enveloped her available for lens-+ing, the neurological aura of her body heat, her custom-made, Kirlian cobra headdress. Her thought is film. Within a decade, Jack would say, "Thinking on stage is interesting."

The consensus, even among screenasts with small professional stake in her determination, is that she is mesmeric: "smol-dering," "bizarre," "hallucinatory," "fabulous and unique." At times, so distracting she prevents one from following the plot (a complaint during her Hollywood days, an obvious priority now). Just how, just why? And through which chan-+nels does she make available her salability? What is her salability? To an extent her appeal is psychological—to escapism, cross-dressing and transvestitism, and exoticism; her enfranchising, specifically, the disfranchised; and her compelling ability to bring an abstraction of self to an epiphanal symbol—Antinea as Destiny, Fate.

The escapism is of a timeless, universal sort, which is why it was so readily encased in timeless fairy tales, and not just of that period repeatedly cited (World War II) that magnified that antecedent in her appeal. And, crucially was to the always second-class citizen, to those who, watching a cowboy and indian movie, identified with the indians, and with third-world persons, be they Islander, Arab, or Asian; with women, blacks, Jews, Gypsies, Armenians and Amerindians, and Aborigines of every unspoiled track in mercifully distant places. Of those, who in their soul—in the center of their earliest memories—felt different, their memories unbroken pain: not of a majority, not of they who say what shall be.

This injured gathering's largest group, women in history, identifies the cross-dressing, for the escape involves a game of triumphant women, as in the eventually, sexually solvent cobra twins, Tollea and Nadja. It is images for a temporary enigma created by men, hence created, unreal to a certain extent, and which Montez pretends at being; therefore, also always gaming and a fantasy level of living. And in her jocularity, her pretend, her seventeenth century, Arabian, or flung-far-as-Java garment and gown ineluctably become "pass-on" costumes: If and since she could don them to key into or kick off the hajj, she does so to show you how. And Smith understood that perfectly: "What worked for her, could for you," being an important part of the message for him. And so, his lifelong attention to the meticulous in costumes, the costumes that are your ticket or comp to victoryland, not just which and how many sequins, but the which and how many fold in the gown when you sat posed for the still camera, and poised for the moving one. He could be fanatical about such things.

Inescapable in this escapism, or, if you will, the unbearability of this, your time and place, is the marriage of the sexual and exotic, for it is the escape of the (secretly) Sexual Other to the other-than-this. And here there is universal agree-ment about the diva's double qualification: "Voilá! Avec l'exotique Maria Montez!" as the voiceover in a French docu-mentary on Albert Camus has it, explaining that in the immediate postwar years he spent time in Paris, "much of it in the company of the world's most *glamorous* people."

She was poster-copy marketed, above all "Tempting, tempestuous…Daughter of Eve with the soul of Satan," "Temptress of the tropics…Ravaging the souls of men with the lash of primitive hate…and the call of pagan love," "Primeval priest-ess in a temple of terror!" "Wicked in the wilds! Pagan witch, no man could tame—or resist!"—as an exotic treat. And the thrust of her own real life, repeated attempts to escape through the use of her sultry allure, so inherently and unavoidably filmable, played neatly into Hollywood's hands.

Inevitably, to West Indians, her mystique stretched even beyond poster-copy promises. As the Dominican Republic's only international spokesperson, she was honored with the Order of Juan Pablo Duarte, and the order of Trujillo, the highest awards for furthering United States-Dominican Republic relations and for outstanding feminine achievement (that nation's first). Dominican dictator Raphael Trujillo turned her birthplace into a museum and named streets and avenues in several cities after her. In Martinique and Puerto Rico, she was believed to have medicinal powers: her films could cure the children of diphtheria, depression, and rickets.

Enfranchising the minorities, the loner, the sexual outlaw: In the seven epics for which she is most remembered by Americans, as well as in the generation-spanning show-biz yarn Universal wedged midway into these (she is charming

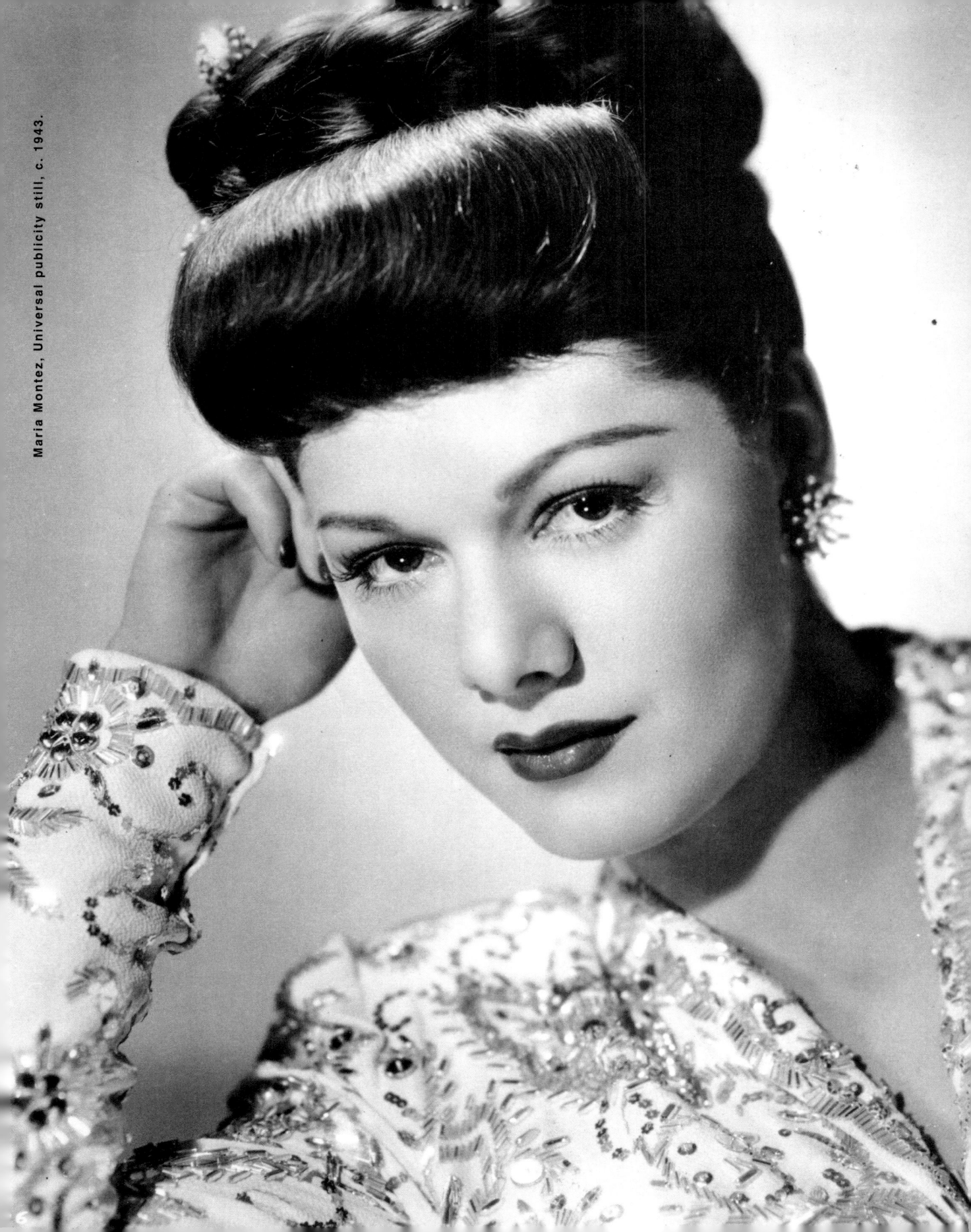

Maria Montez, Universal publicity still, c. 1943.

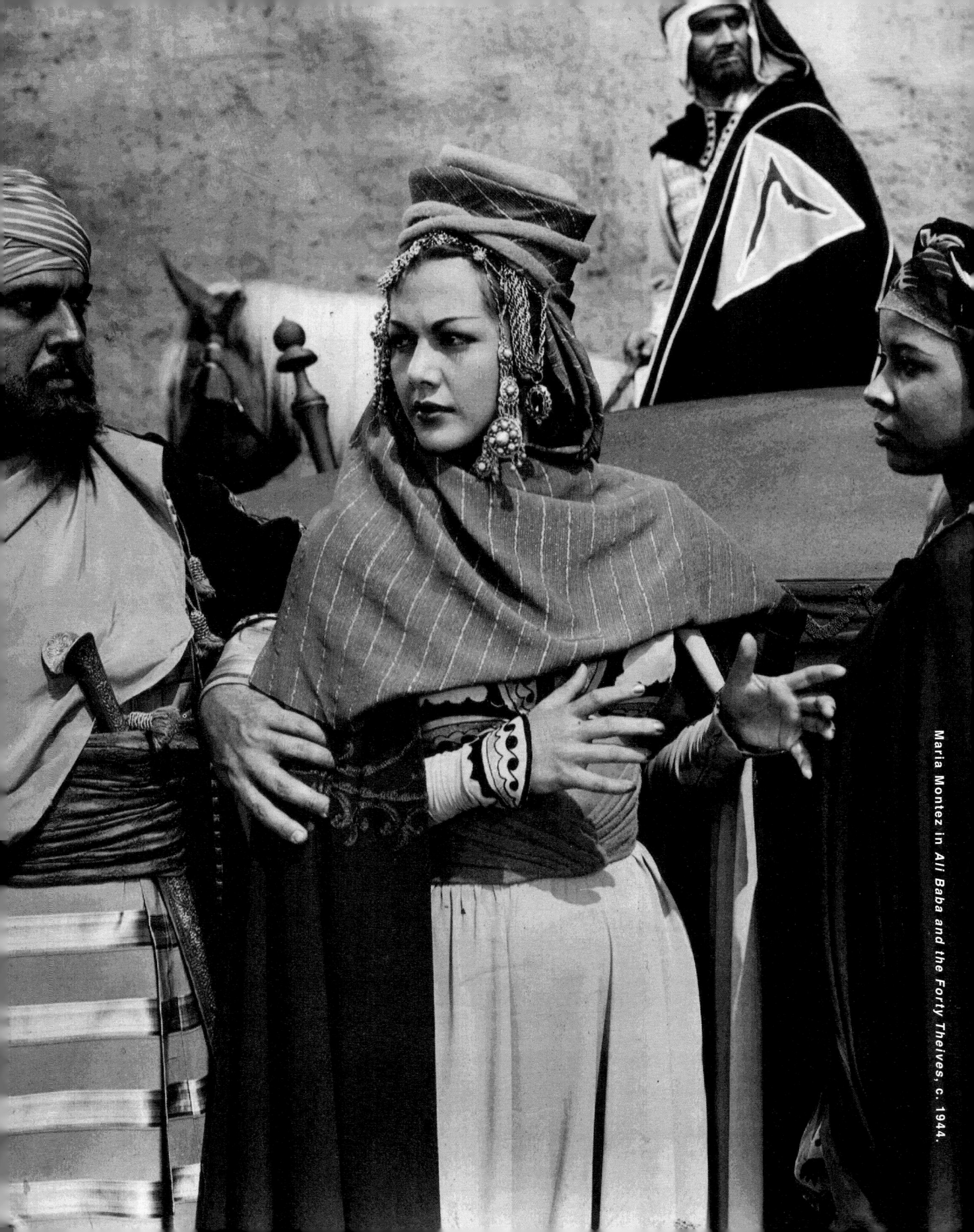

as a European stage star in *Bowery to Broadway*), the white male powermonger comes into his own, e.g., discards the shackles of slavery, ascends the throne, or succeeds in business — from shark fishing to producing musicals — only when and if he paints his own parameter by winning her as wife. True, she then must transfer the power natal to the all-desirable object to the male, but there's been a term as corporation president for her/us. And a term, or tentative taste, of power is all we think we're entitled to/can get.

Empowering the powerless is the psychology behind her most famous scene: The ritual dance in *Cobra Woman*. At an attendance-required, ophiolatry ceremony, she upbraids the cowering populace for tithe-defaulting, is divested of blood-red, Quetzalcoatl-feathered cloak and cobrahood headdress by her half dozen blue chiffoned handmaidens and, after completing the initiation mysteries — mesmerizing (phallically immobilizing) the cult's mascot King Cobra — rushes out onto a ramp in an orgiastically choreographed delirium to point, furiously-ecstatically-sadistically, at the spellbound, lapsed-worshippers, one after one. And the luckless witnesses at the wrong end of her finger are then lifted up screaming and hauled off to a holding pen to await their thousand-step climb to the mouth of Cobra Island's smoking volcano and "the fire of everlasting life"! Decked out in every imaginable, thrill-packed pulp fiction, comic book and strip, and kid's adventure trip from H. Rider Haggard and Dumas to Edgar Rice Burroughs, Kipling, Stevenson, De Foe, Malraux, and Stan Lee you can shake an Aaron stick at, and hence finger-lickin' good down to her ophidian, form-fitting S-M costume. What's going on here is ultimate power to the disfranchised: we've no more than to point to our enemy by the scores, 200 in a single shot to be precise, and they instantly dematerialize. It's matched only by the common dream of suddenly rising like an eagle and gliding low over the rooftops when attacked by one's foes, and is ever so more colorful and sexual than that.

It was inventors seeking filmic symbol for their metaphysical concerns like Sirk, Brahm, Cocteau, and Ophuls, who were most impressed by Montez's accomplishment, her success in concretizing illusive abstraction with her lovely, flickering image. The work was my own first encounter with art and sponsored my decision to spend a lifetime in its service; and Smith agreed that *Siren of Atlantis* was Maria's primary achievement. His evaluation: "Stunning." And, in the early eighties, in an expedious mood, he stated that, despite the commercialism of her films, Maria Montez was able to deal with both intellectual and aesthetic issues.

But for Smith personally, the ends of art were less heady. In 1965 he told me he was fascinated by my study of her as a human being, because his study, he proclaimed, was purely visual. He wasn't taken with how she revealed in shot to unprotected shot her anxiety (*Bowery to Broadway*) or carelessness (*Gypsy Wildcat*) or unhappiness (*Sudan*) or joy (*White Savage*); how few hours of sleep she'd had (*Arabian Nights*) or how few hours had passed since an argument with studio heads, a publicist, or director (*Tangier*). He thought that as sculpture seeks the perfect three-dimensional object, and presumably found it in the Venus de Milo, film must seek the perfect two dimensional object in motion, and finds it in Maria Montez: The warm butterfat of her shoulders, the swaying generosity of her unrestricted breasts, her ever narrating features, her complexion exemplary for Technicolor, her walk that turns a tacky, trodden track (in *Cobra Woman*) into a mnemonically primordial garden.

Jack was altogether innocent of the lore of her day encoding tantalizing, and especially foreign, brunettes as Free Sex, (i.e., "You don't have to marry 'em"), not very curious about Roosevelt's Good Neighbor Policy that played no little part in promoting her career, nor particularly traumatized by her record-breaking number of film baths eerily adumbrating her demise. He was not interested in seeing my freshly taken photo of her tomb. Rather, his attention was concentrated on how her enfeelinged contour or aural silhouette ignited the composition in which you placed her, whether it was the above mentioned park, or a city of tents (*Arabian Nights*), or woodland lakes (*Gypsy Wildcat*, *Pirates of Monterey*), desert pools (*Ali Baba*), island pools (*White Savage*, *Cobra Woman*), port-polluted channels (*Hans le Marin*, Marie Roget), or Baghdad or Bhasra or Marseille, Palermo or Venice: where-imaginary-ever you set her, the physical force of her fantasy life caused its soundstage or on-location to sparkle — like the iceland in the yard in *Curse of the Cat People* — caused it to come into a celluloid habitat of the individual's, the artist's, the common man's mind. A Midas of the Imagination. That she as a movie house object was a wand that touched a steel-grey, hostile world into a shelter for the sensitive, a bearability. He called it "Montezland."

And, in a sense, Montezland was the Lower East Side Jack lived in, when we walked-a-nightaway SoHo before it was called that, silhouette-wet and deserted, or to the abandoned synagogue below Houston and beyond Norfolk, a Levantine carpet-borne enticement unbelievably there, with minaret window niches, gilt crescent arches, blue mosaic walls with artfully domed, empty recesses. He took me there when the moon was full, and he'd rush ecstatically down and up the dark, broken staircases into the breathless romance of its shattered towers.

But it was all in a state of decomposition by the 1980s, that East Village, a Samarkand untended, and fraught with doorstep-lurking danger from the Caribbean monkey people who had "a tenuous connection with reality" and absolutely no idea of what New York was about. So he referred to it as the realm of "Yvonne De Craploads, Queen of Monkeyland." Yvonne De Carlo, of course, was The Wonderful One's replacement in Hollywood; she had cherished no secret "art" ambitions and gave the studio few headaches. And, if she had no magic, no tangible passion, no legendary superstructure, well, that was the age Hollywood was moving into. But at a point even before then, sometime in the mid-seventies, following the Great Underground Diaspora, Jack felt Manhattan had stepped down into that De Carlo age and was stuck in the gummy cobwebs covering the real thing. I also had the feeling that he said Miss De Carlo as one says "Gee" rather that Jesus, or "Gosh" and "Golly" rather than God. And when I'd confront the neologist with that suspicion, he'd shyly, even humbly agree. It was not wise to tempt the minatory gods with continual familiarity.

Finally, when he named even himself Jack De Carlo or Uncle De Carlo, as in his photo-comics that depict his willing sacrifice of himself upon the altar of landlords, he not only appeared to come to terms with a second-rate America, but actually to relish the inferior De Carlo product, "whose early films have the fluidity wanting in the dead-on confrontation of those knee-to-head midshots in Miss Montez movies." So in time, 21 First Avenue, gagged or repetitious and more self-conscious, the golden age of his singular imagination indeed did seem distant, always in some other room of that railroad apartment, a space beyond the cobwebby one where we, stuck, waited for the giant, salivating arachnid like a diminutive Johnny Sheffield in *Tarzan's Desert Mystery*. I could become uncomfortable then. My father walked in his sleep on a roof's low railing in that very neighborhood, and I have a fear of somnambulism.

It is easy to point to *Normal Love* as a work that draws its look, its feel, its colors, images, and backyard fairy moth sheen directly from *White Savage. Buzzards Over Baghdad*, some of the earliest footage we have from Jack, retells the climactic sequence Ford Beebe helmed for *Arabian Nights. Flaming Creatures* alludes to the earthquake in both color island epics, the processional in *Ali Baba*, MM's personal Nubian slave in *Arabian Nights*, the juxtapositional idea of what he confessed he adored, etc. And, when he took on the persona of dagger savvy Jungle Jack, he was rear-projecting Johnny Weismuller's "Jungle Jim" (a B-series based on the comic book) as another De Carlo-like spin-off on MM. The numerous, languorously posed ladies and gents posing as ladies in *Flaming Creatures* are lesser printouts of the poster art for her films, and in particular of the most popular ones for which she invariably modeled, whether painted or photoed, in alluring recumbent positions. "Nobody could recline like Maria Montez," Jack observed. And, of course, her non-acting of characters in place of yet another perfectly adequate, pointless performance was paramount in his thoughts: it stoked up crucial energy for his countercapitalistic impulses, is the inspiration for some of the more breathtaking urges in the live one-madman shows especially — urges that would impel Jack to self-critique under his breath, "Gilded, gilded…" Why should a camera trained on persons inclusively mean it is persons acting? Waxing near distraught after a New Yorker Theater screening of *Cobra Woman*, he exclaimed, "Those reviewers always spoke about her bad acting. Yet, you cannot rip your eyes off her! What she's doing is what acting is substituting for!"

Jack confided that her husband, Jean-Pierre Aumont, informed an interviewer once that Maria had a private chapel built in 1100 Tower Road, Beverly Hills, to safekeep a statue of her patron saint, San Antonio, to whom she spoke daily, admonishing him to give her countless things: furs, hats, honors, the adoration of L.A. and all Europe. So, in imitation Jack built an altar to her, his Christian Science saint, on which he set her photo to oversee and share his confidential life; and he literally prayed to her daily for artistic inspiration, and claimed it was she who instructed him to place her altar itself at the center of *Normal Love*… "Hearing is obeying," he intoned.

Other stars have provided an image in which to live: Maria Montez provided a vocabulary in which to robe and narrate the more memorably vanguard and radical art of our time. But her ultimate influence on Smith, and his ultimate tribute to her was the rebuilding of Baghdad/Babylonia into his apartments, a city, a world, a wall, a building. He had duplex lofts in SoHo and removed the floor between them to construct, virtually by himself, and ostensibly for a projected picture called *Sinbad*, a cathedraling set that reminded me of Fairbanks, Sr.'s silent, *Thief of Baghdad*, but which got its seed from Maria's *Raiders of the Desert, Arabian Nights, Ali Baba and the Forty Thieves*, and *Tangier*. And, later, in his sixth-floor walk-up on First Avenue, he reworked each of the five consecutive cubicles into a different realm, among them, the Egyptian room inspired by *Sudan*, a nouveau sci-fi/pre-ark Vale of Euphrates reimagined from Atlantis, and a most incredible bathroom with a cabriole antique tub (i.e., palace pool-size in *Ali Baba* or hooded iron hand-pour, as in *The Exile* or, to be sure, deathset for Miss Montez), and space for just enough potted palms and succulents to allow him to squeeze-set them into an impenetrable Melanesian jungle tipping its hat to *Moonlight in Hawaii, South of Tahiti, White Savage, Cobra Woman*, and *La Donna del Corsaro*. An open Arabian niche cut into the wall that the bathroom shared with the (Persian) sitting room provided an unavoidable view from the latter into the sacred pool bath. But, this, Jack explained would enable him to excuse himself at propitious moments, leave his company, and spy on them from inside the bath. Conversely, one might peer through the niche from the Persian room and through buttonholes in the tropical density beyond, to where some (hopefully, tempestuous) beauty might well be bathing. His dwelling reconstructions or devotion to architecture consumed years of his life, and were of application and seriousness that would appear to have utilized his concerns and obsession with the "late lovely" more than any other of his many and wonderful outlets, whether film, criticism, collage, sketching, set designing and building, or performance. And, they were most directly related to his political thinking as well, and in a way so straightforward as to make recent commentary on Smith from the left seemed forced and dishonest.

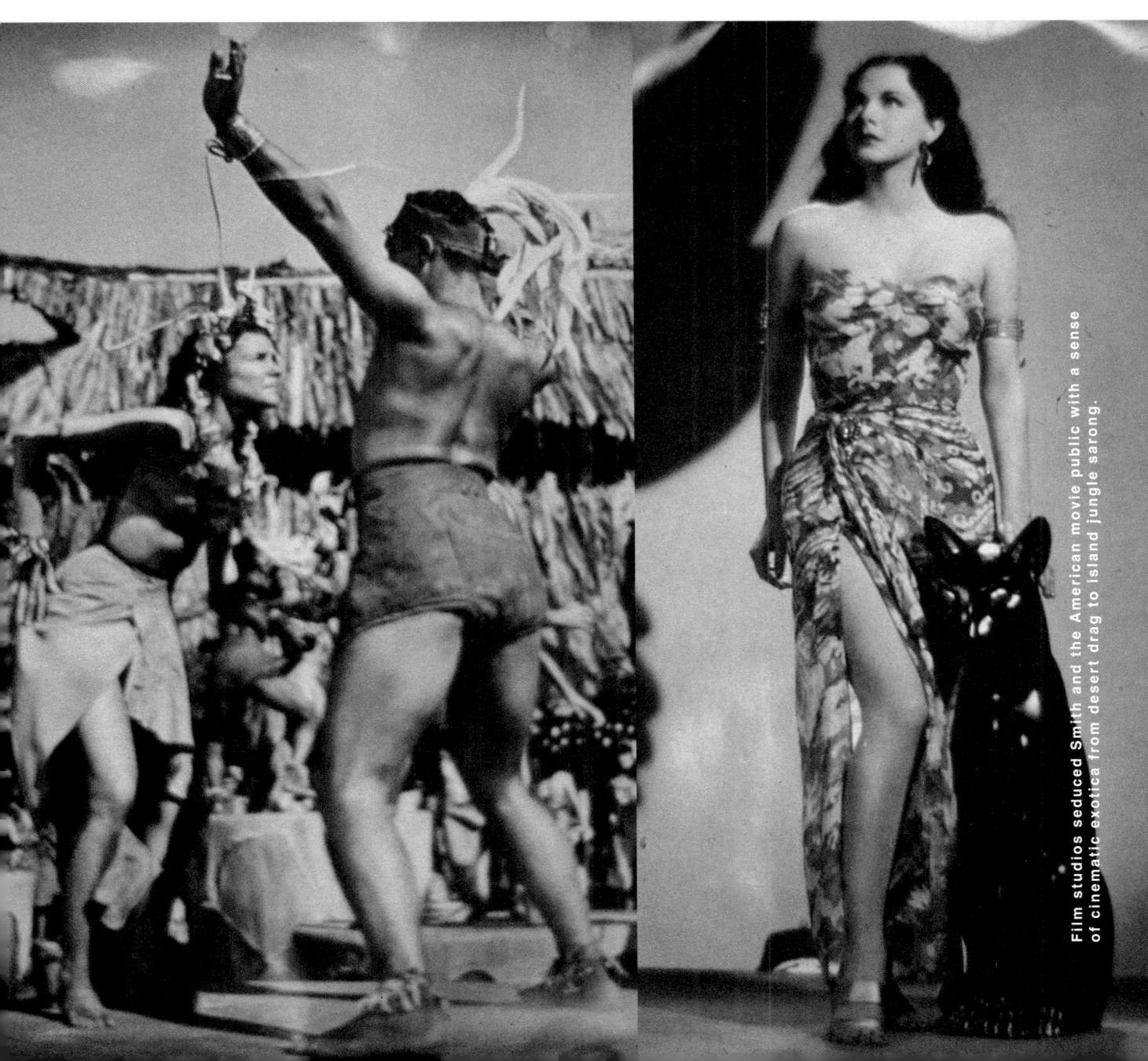

Film studios seduced Smith and the American movie public with a sense of cinematic exotica from desert drag to island jungle sarong.

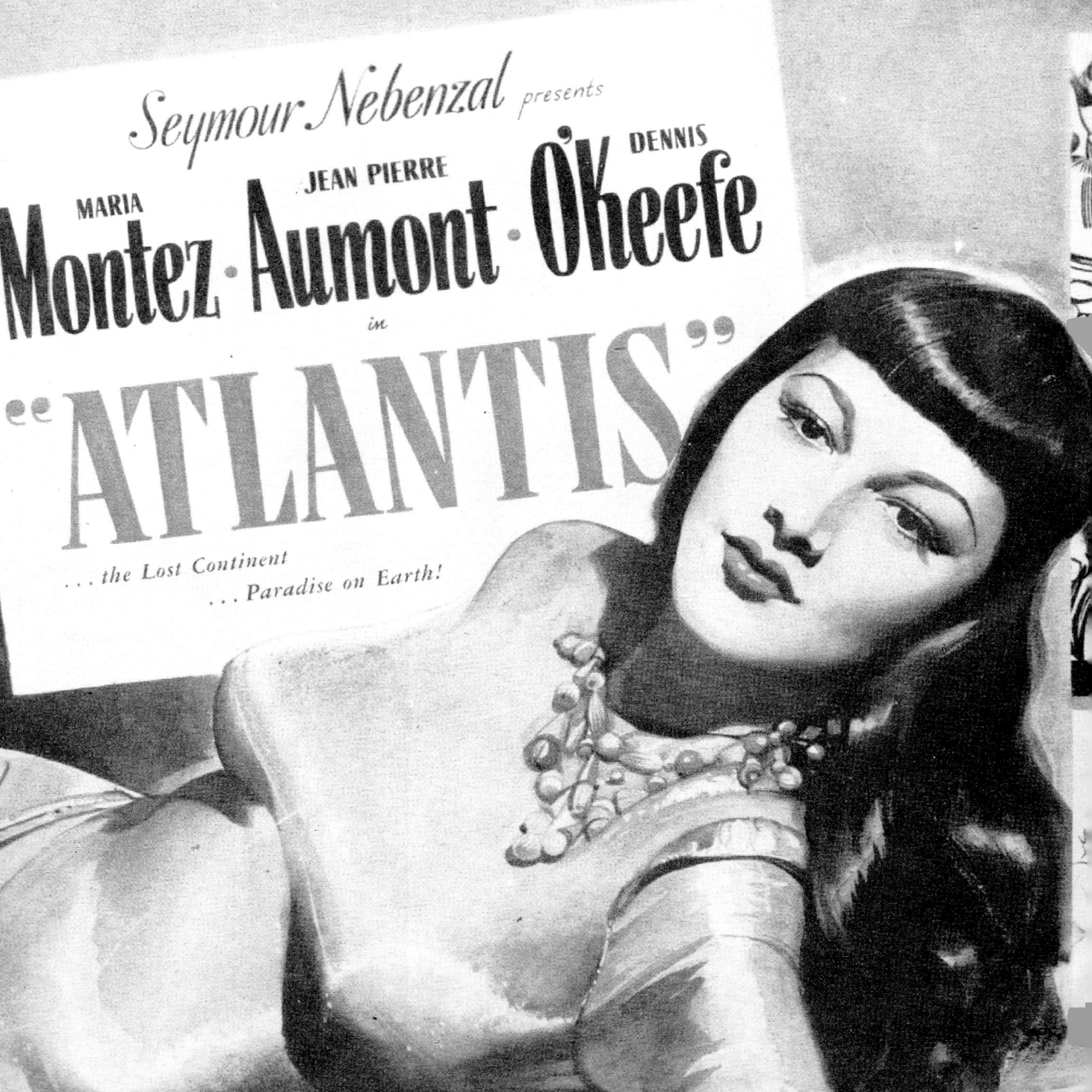

Smith on Montez:

I met Jack Smith through Joel Markman and René Rivera, and served as a set engineer for *Flaming Creatures* and still-model for many an s.s. ("shooting session"). He in turn constructed the sets for my first two plays and designed the costumes for the third. Only his erraticness stood in the way of his becoming my official director, but I appeared opposite him in his own play, *Clash of the Brassiere Maidens* (1984). He hoped I would develop the writing of intertitles into an art form and so engaged me to create a set of them for *Buzzards Over Bagdad*, which he intended to plate elaborately, but alas never did. Appropriately, the last time I saw him we attended together a Film Millennium screening of *The Exile*.

At the time of the star's death, Jack was nearly twenty and an usher at the Orpheum Theatre in Chicago, which took advantage of the headlines to cash in on a festival of her films. This was his introduction to the woman who, "flaming and raging," would guide his future creativity. Below, some of his observations on her; in quotes are what I remember verbatim.

"People who say Maria Montez couldn't act are the same people who say Marilyn Monroe can't sing."

"The difference between *Arabian Nights* and *Gypsy Wildcat* is the difference between art and camp. I keep telling you people that Miss Montez has a great sense of humor."

"Those myna (minor) birds they always had doing her Lochinvar! Didn't even know how to comb their hair."

"Turhan Bey was the only man she ever seemed to see. The others were mere pasty novelties on her charm bracelet. Ever notice how when he's in a scene, she gets smaller, more feminine?"

"Art is one big thrift shop."

"The Miraculous One was raging and flaming. Those are the standards for art."

"Shall we seek the sanctuary of my den of cutthroats and thieves, and see how much mileage we can get off a dead star tonight?"

"The scores of the Marvelous One's movies are symphonies. But you know that."

"*Ali Baba* is the worst!"

"The sets for *Ali Baba* are my favorite. The processionals—when I was a kid I loved processionals."

"That tent set for her seduction in the stronghold of the slaves (*Sudan*)—God! Cowhide thongs and cardboard. Universal was the cheapest!"

(*Sudan*) "She should have been more involved in the climax."

(*Cobra Woman*) "She isn't in it enough. That twenty minute prologue is Hollywood at its worst. It's the best and worst Hollywood movie ever made."

In *The Mystery of Marie Roget*, cameraman Elwood Brendel editorializes on MM's o.s. murder a few minutes further on in the film by shooting her extended arms while waltzing from behind with a gold candlestick in the foreground: "Did you catch that crucifixion image of Miss Montez at the ball? She drew cameras to her."

(Referring to the dairy restaurant on Delancey) "Ratner's is done in *Sudan*-deco."

On stars: "The average life span of a star is 5 years. A star is someone who produces delight. They produce delight by being continuously interesting on screen. Someone is interesting when they reveal a truth about human nature. And they never repeat themselves. Giving a good performance isn't the safest way to do that."

Suddenly standing up in a moviehouse to upbraid those in the audience laughing at an outrageous moment in *Cobra Woman*: "I suppose you'd like it better if her performance was plastic!"

On models: "A model is someone who always has a specific idea on their face. That's what you shoot."

"Her flicks always had to have a scene with someone up on the torture rack. In *Thief of Venice*, they strung her up on it. Such bad taste."

Recalling an unintentionally funny moment in the climax of *Ali Baba*, when Turhan Bey begs MM to "open the gates for your people, my Lady!": "Did you see her open the gates for your scum of Baghdad? They nearly ran her over!" There-inafter, Jack would refer to the public at his live shows as "the scum of Baghdad." The phrase actually is spoken by Kurt Katch midway in the intrigues: "...and he will rally the scum of Baghdad to his cause!"

We'd gotten the Cinematheque to agree to screen some MM films (June '67), but all they could rent was *Tangier*. As soon as the credits rolled for the last feature on the program that night, the audience rose as a man and filed out. Jack rushed to the exit as if to stop them somehow and, furrowing his brow at me, he wrung his hands and cried out: "You can count the scum in New York by the number of people leaving this theater now! Come, let's go sit down in the front row, and watch in delirious solitude!"

After the screening ended:

"In one way of looking at it, it's a bad movie; and in another way, it's very good."

And as if she were a pair of glasses, sometimes all things were seen through her:

"O Maria Montez, give socialist answers to a rented world!"

"Well, Ronnie, we accomplished one thing in our lifetimes...Took twenty years, but we rescued The Holy One from oblivion."

And on my informing him that her daughter Tina was born on St. Valentine's Day, and that she herself is buried in Montparnasse:

"Everything about her was a poem."

Enough has been said about the Theatre of The Ridiculous for me not to have to note that the paradigm she breathed breath into by being, in no conventional reading of the phrase, a professional performer, was crucial to my decision to come to theater, and to what I'd have of it. What makes her so obsession-fomenting, and so the wellspring of icono-*clastic and humanistic speculation is what she can do, display, and reveal in the "surround" of acting; it held and still holds whatever interest I have in theatre, or need to have in film.

Nor to note the disappointment I felt all Jack's life in his fixation on backtracking to a brilliant decade, and in our many incompleted projects. Complaining steals from creativity. So does envy, paranoia, and the cultivation of ill-will toward others. The ungrateful Apple and the narrow-minded who made it their trap fostered a great deal of his negativism, but we are meant then to use that—as when we tell an uneasy actor to "use" his stage fright, and insecurities and misgivings, to make them "work" for him, for his performance. But, taking to New York like the proverbial fish to (Atlantis) water, Jack berated fate all his life, acknowledged but indulged his madness, ate up his energies in poison-pen letters, poison telephone messages, and fury at every runaway hit and arts grant on the grapevine as his private, paranoic mythology well implies—tombstoned with minor birds and panders ("Andy-Panda"), landlords and vampires and crustaceans insatiably snatching up his "pasty" concepts and "moldy" notions in their firehouse-orange and boiled-red chela.

But, on sufficient occasion he saw and let us see those greedy crustaceans shuttle through the cerulean gaze of gilled Lamurians; he let us glimpse all that "gilded" gimcrackery as the anima and animus of his antediluvian recall.

I was living in New Orleans and trying to rouse a roommate too dissolute to go out on the street and get a job when Penny Arcade called me to tell me Jack had died. I dropped the phone, and ran away from it, sobbing and jabbering, "No! No! No!"

And, I was a kid in Coney Island gathering my courage to conquer a fearful fantasy by getting on the cloud-topped Wonder Wheel, when its loudspeaker, tuned to a radio station, blasted a news bulletin: the death of Maria Montez, she'd drowned in her bath in far-off France. It made no sense. Like every little boy on my block, I was set on growing up to marry her. What would happen now? I couldn't process the information. I decided to dismiss it. By then no one had spoken about her for a while, anyhow. I boarded a car on the Wheel and it took me up haltingly farther off the ground than I'd ever been in my life. From the windows of the car when it reached it's height, the quarter-million people on the beach, the great gray Atlantic beyond them, and the world's largest amusement park seemed small.

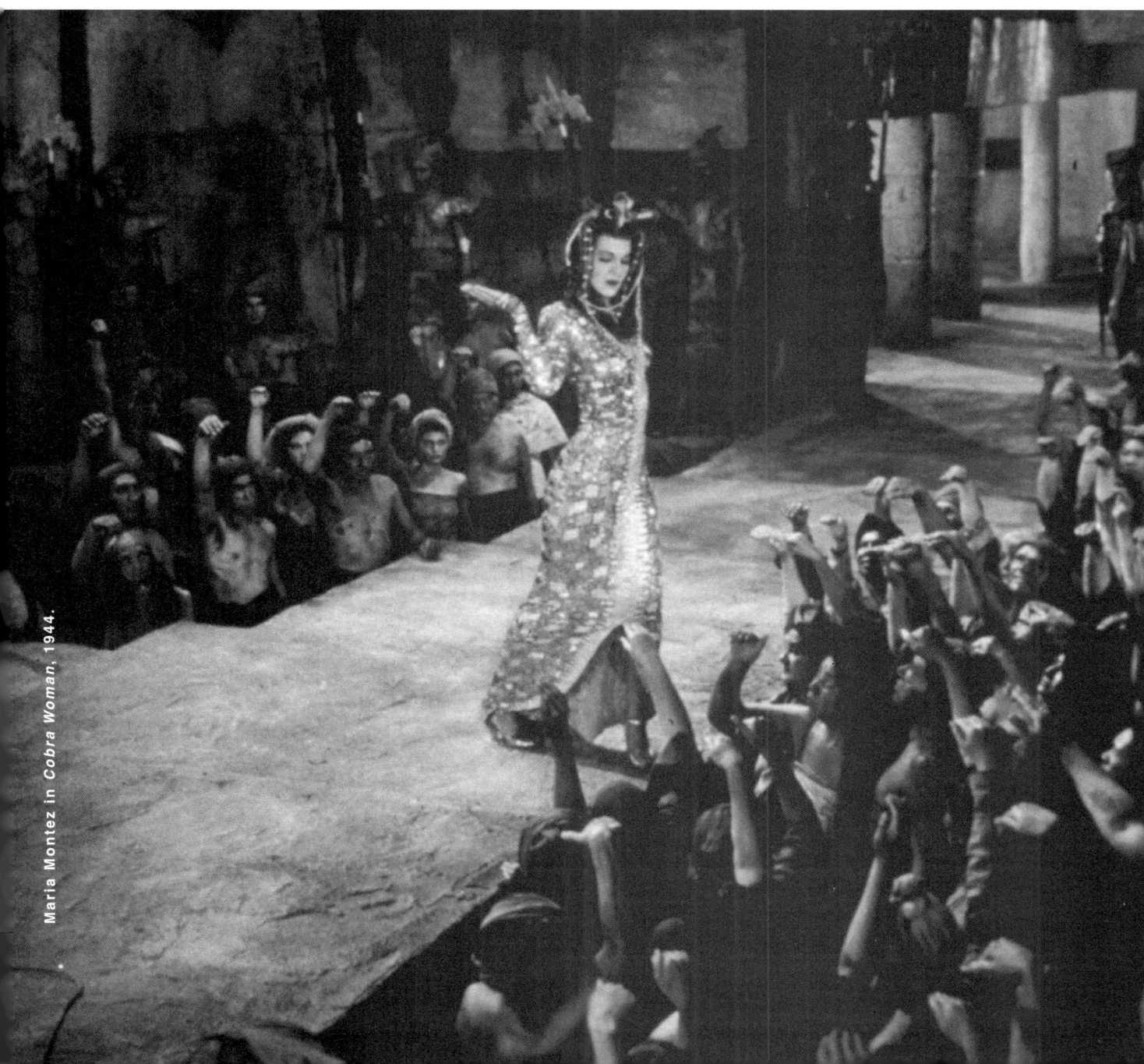

Maria Montez in *Cobra Woman*, 1944.

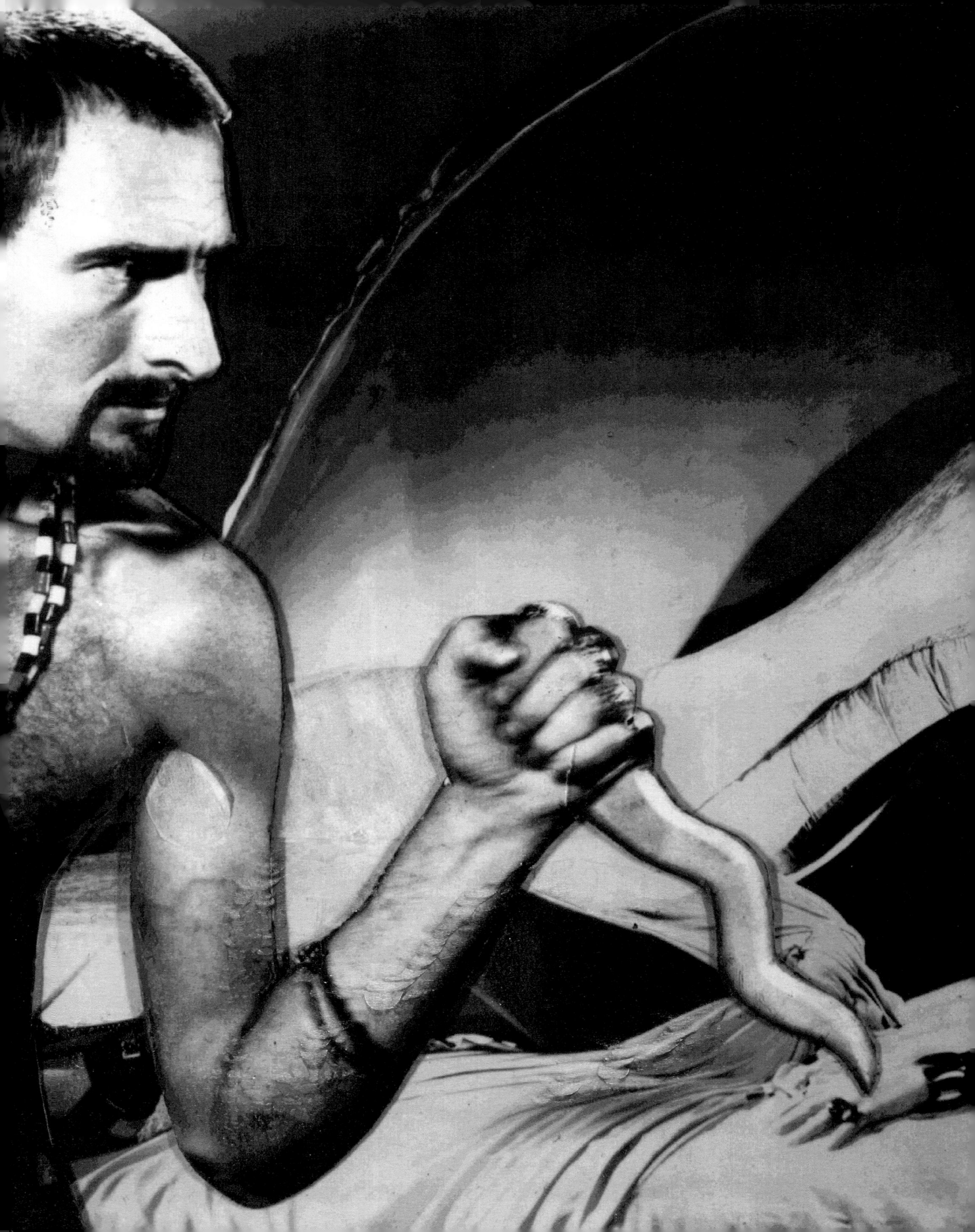

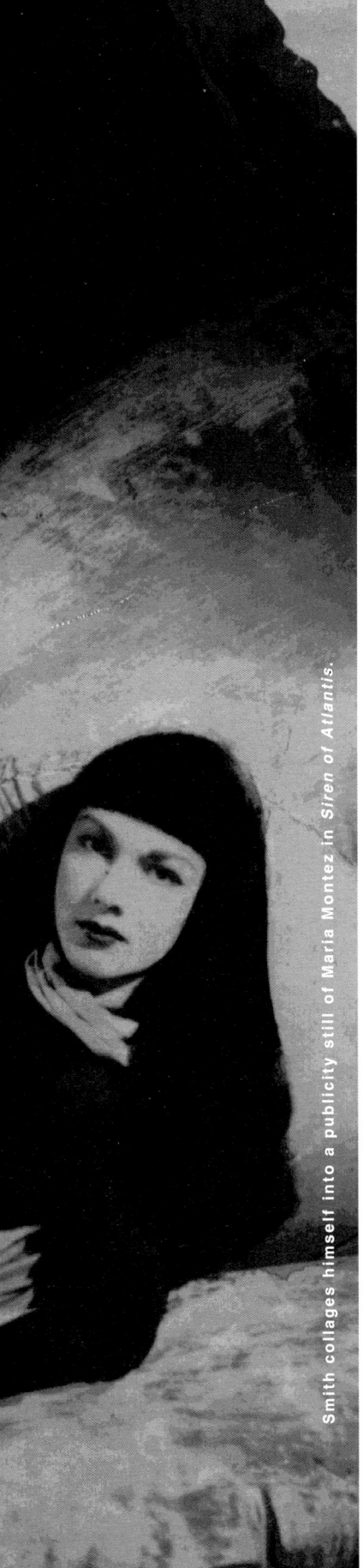

Smith collages himself into a publicity still of Maria Montez in *Siren of Atlantis*.

Filmography

LUCKY DEVILS
(Univ., 1941. Small role. Dir., Lew Landers. Adventure. BW.)
THE INVISIBLE WOMAN
(Univ., 1941. Walk-on. Dir., A. Edward Sutherland. Mystery. BW.)
BOSS OF BULLION CITY
(Univ., 1941. Female Lead. Dir., Ray Taylor. Western. BW.)
THAT NIGHT IN RIO
(Fox, 1941. Bit role. Dir., Irving Cummings. Musical. C.)
RAIDERS OF THE DESERT
(Univ., 1941. Supporting Role. Dir., John Rawlins. Adventure. BW.)
MOONLIGHT IN HAWAII
(Univ., 1941. Supporting role. Dir., Charles Lamont. Comedy. BW.)
SOUTH OF TAHITI
(Univ., 1941. Lead. Dir., George Waggner. Adventure. BW.)
BOMBAY CLIPPER
(Univ., 1942. Feature role., Dir., John Rawlins. Espionage. BW.)
THE MYSTERY OF MARIE ROGET
(Univ., 1942. Feature role. Dir., Phil Rosen. Period mystery. BW.)
ARABIAN NIGHTS
(Univ., 1942. Lead. Dirs., Walter Wanger, John Rawlins, Ford Beebe. Adventure. C.)
WHITE SAVAGE
(Univ., 1943. Lead. Dir., Arthur Lubin. Adventure. C.)
ALI BABA AND THE FORTY THIEVES
(Univ., 1944. lead. Dir., Arthur Lubin. Adventure. C.)
FOLLOW THE BOYS
(Univ., 1944. Guest appearance. Dir., A. Edward Sutherland. Musical. BW.)
COBRA WOMAN
(Univ., 1944. Lead. Dir., Robert Siodmak. Adventure. C.)
GYPSY WILDCAT
(Univ., 1944. Lead. Dir., Roy William Neill. Adventure. C.)
BOWERY TO BROADWAY
(Univ., 1944. Feature role. Dir., Charles Lamont. Musical. BW.)
SUDAN
(Univ., 1945. Lead. Dir., John Rawlins. Adventure. C.)
TANGIER
(Univ., 1946. Lead. Dir., George Waggner. Espionage. BW.)
THE EXILE
(Univ., 1947. Feature role. Dir., Max Ophuls. Historical. Sepia.)
PIRATES OF MONTERY
(Univ., 1947. Lead. Dir., Alfred Werker. Adventure. C.)
SIREN OF ATLANTIS
(Independent., United Artists release 1949, filmed Spring 1947. Lead. Dirs.: There is no directing credit on the film, but participants claim the honors were shared by Douglas Sirk, John Brahm, Arthur Ripley and Miss Montez herself. Adventure. BW.)
HANS LE MARIN
(Discina, 1948. Female lead. Dir., Francois Villiers. Film Noir. BW. In French.)
PORTRAIT D'UN ASSASSIN
(S.E.L.F., 1949. Female lead. Dirs., Bernard Roland, Orson Welles. Drama. BW. In French.)
IL LADRO DI VENEZIA
(Fox, 1950. Lead. Dir., John Brahm. Historical. BW. In Italian.)
AMORE E SANGUE
(A.B. La Querica, 1951. Lead. Dirs., John Wolff, Marimo Girolami. Drama. BW. In Italian.)
LA DONNA DEL COSARO (LA VENDETTA DEL COSARO)
(Athena Cinematografica, 1951. Female lead. Dir., Primo Zeglio. Adventure. In Italian.)

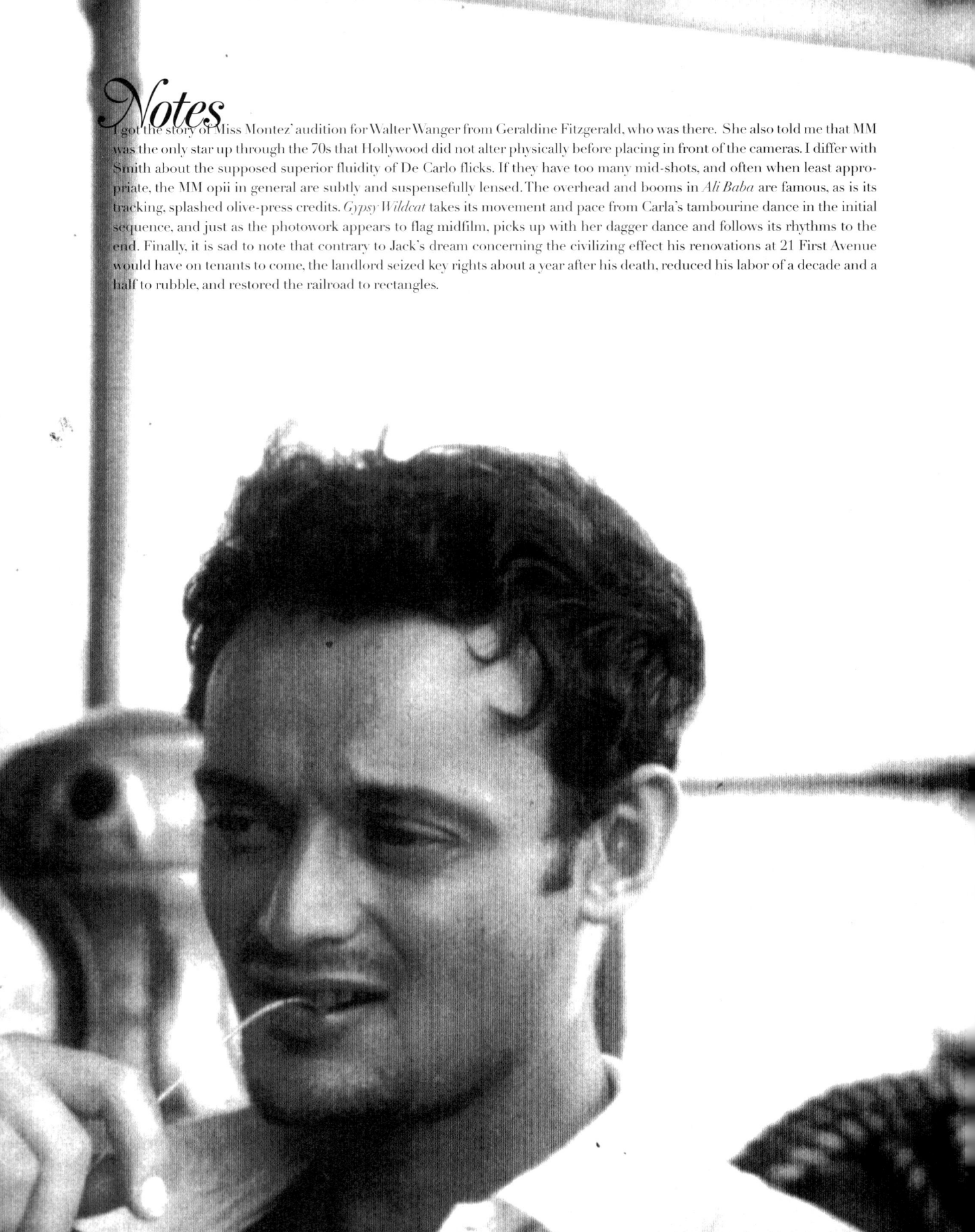

Notes

I got the story of Miss Montez' audition for Walter Wanger from Geraldine Fitzgerald, who was there. She also told me that MM was the only star up through the 70s that Hollywood did not alter physically before placing in front of the cameras. I differ with Smith about the supposed superior fluidity of De Carlo flicks. If they have too many mid-shots, and often when least appropriate, the MM opii in general are subtly and suspensefully lensed. The overhead and booms in *Ali Baba* are famous, as is its tracking, splashed olive-press credits. *Gypsy Wildcat* takes its movement and pace from Carla's tambourine dance in the initial sequence, and just as the photowork appears to flag midfilm, picks up with her dagger dance and follows its rhythms to the end. Finally, it is sad to note that contrary to Jack's dream concerning the civilizing effect his renovations at 21 First Avenue would have on tenants to come, the landlord seized key rights about a year after his death, reduced his labor of a decade and a half to rubble, and restored the railroad to rectangles.

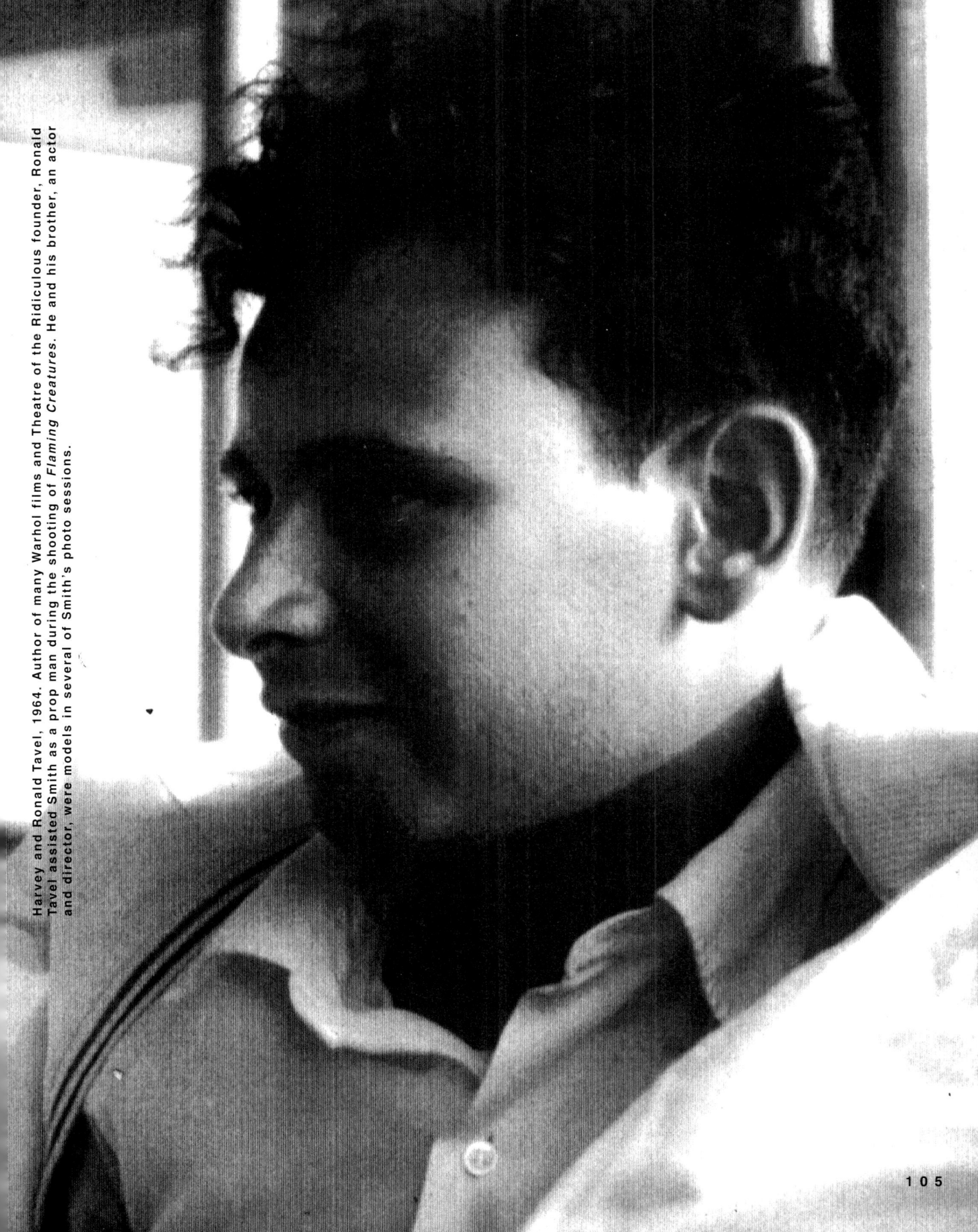

Harvey and Ronald Tavel, 1964. Author of many Warhol films and Theatre of the Ridiculous founder, Ronald Tavel assisted Smith as a prop man during the shooting of *Flaming Creatures*. He and his brother, an actor and director, were models in several of Smith's photo sessions.

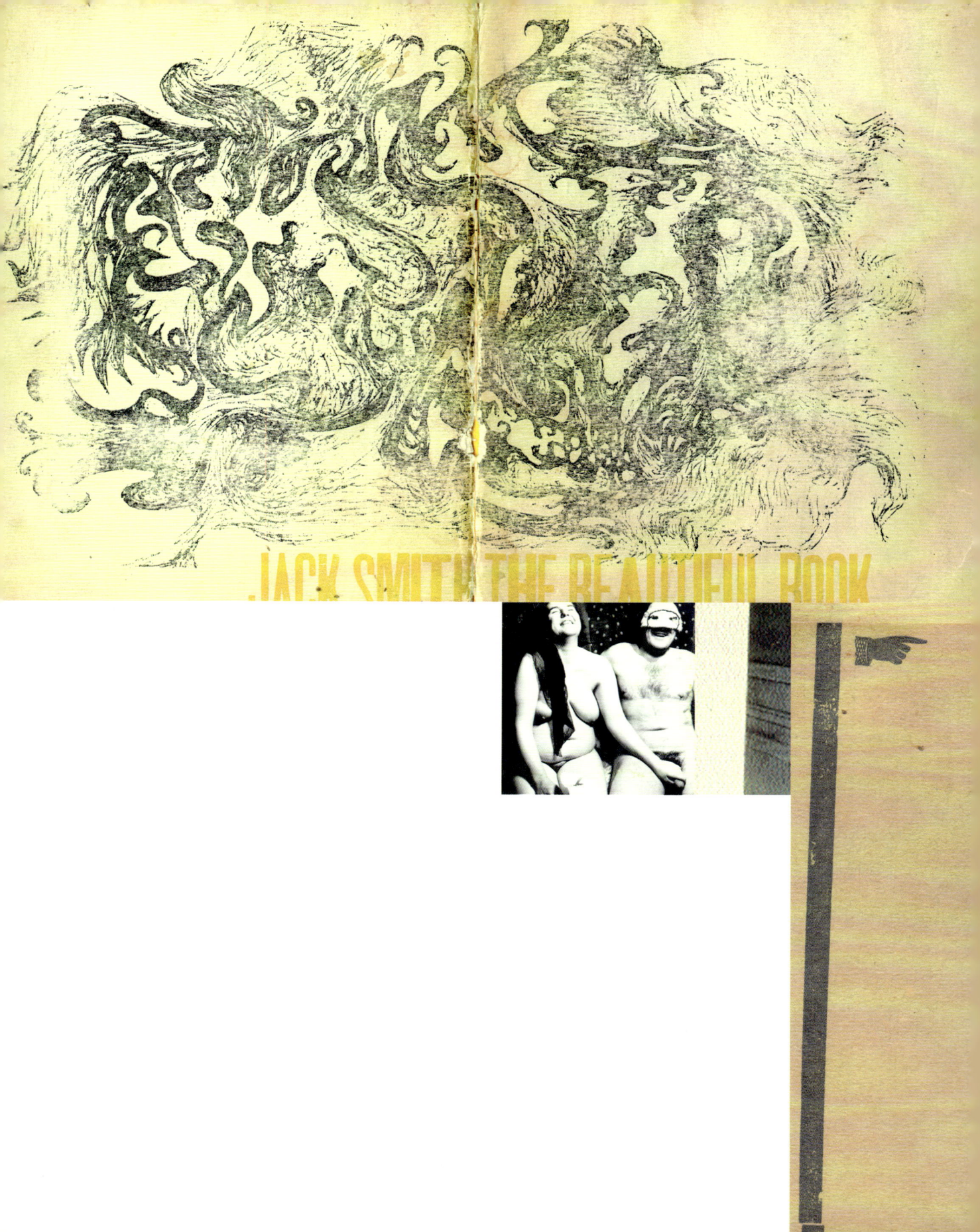

JACK SMITH THE BEAUTIFUL BOOK

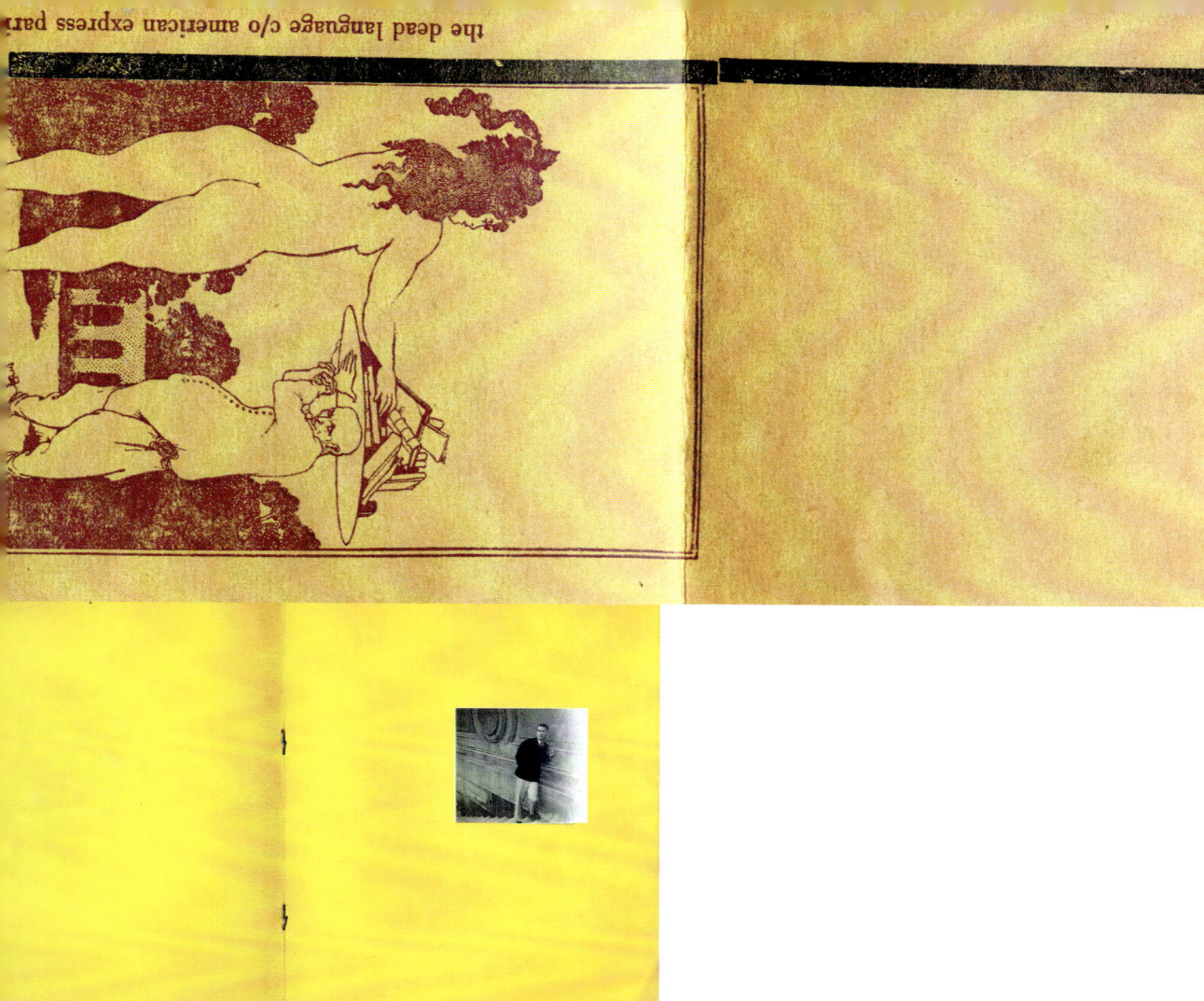

(this page and following pages) Elements of *The Beautiful Book* published by Piero Heliczer, New York, 1962. This artist's book included tipped in photographs by Smith, a cover design by Marian Zazeela, and a bookmark with Beardsley drawing promoting the publications of Heliczer's the dead language press.

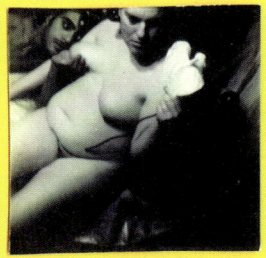

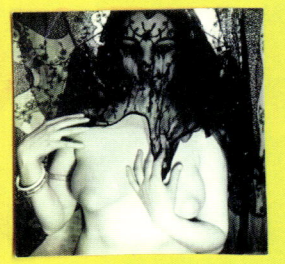

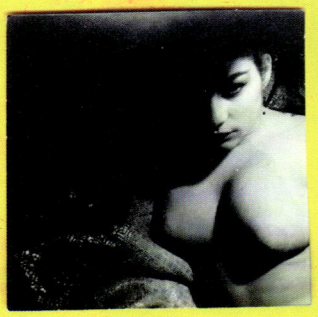

the beautiful book

xviii stills · by jack smith with a drawing
by marian zazeela new york 1962
4 dollars or 16 nouveaux francs or 24
shillings
"we studied these photographs with keen
eye discovering new & more beautiful
images hidden in every dissolve & curve of
the draperies & silks which ran through
these masterpieces like some long lost
mysterious fume from byzantium,, ron rice

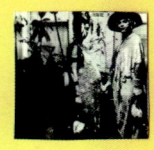

the first battle of the marne

six poems by piero heliczer new york 1962
2 dollars 8 nouveaux francs or 12 shillings
"i see him through his poems & i see
danger,, fielding dawson

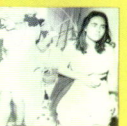 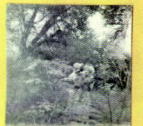

loverman

a very free translation of the lemminkainen
cantos of the kalevala by anselm hollo new
york 1963
1 dollar or 4 nouveaux francs or 6 shillings

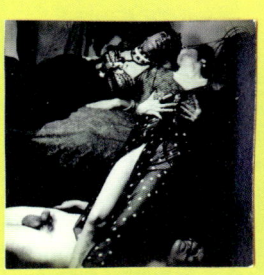

make checks payable to piero heliczer

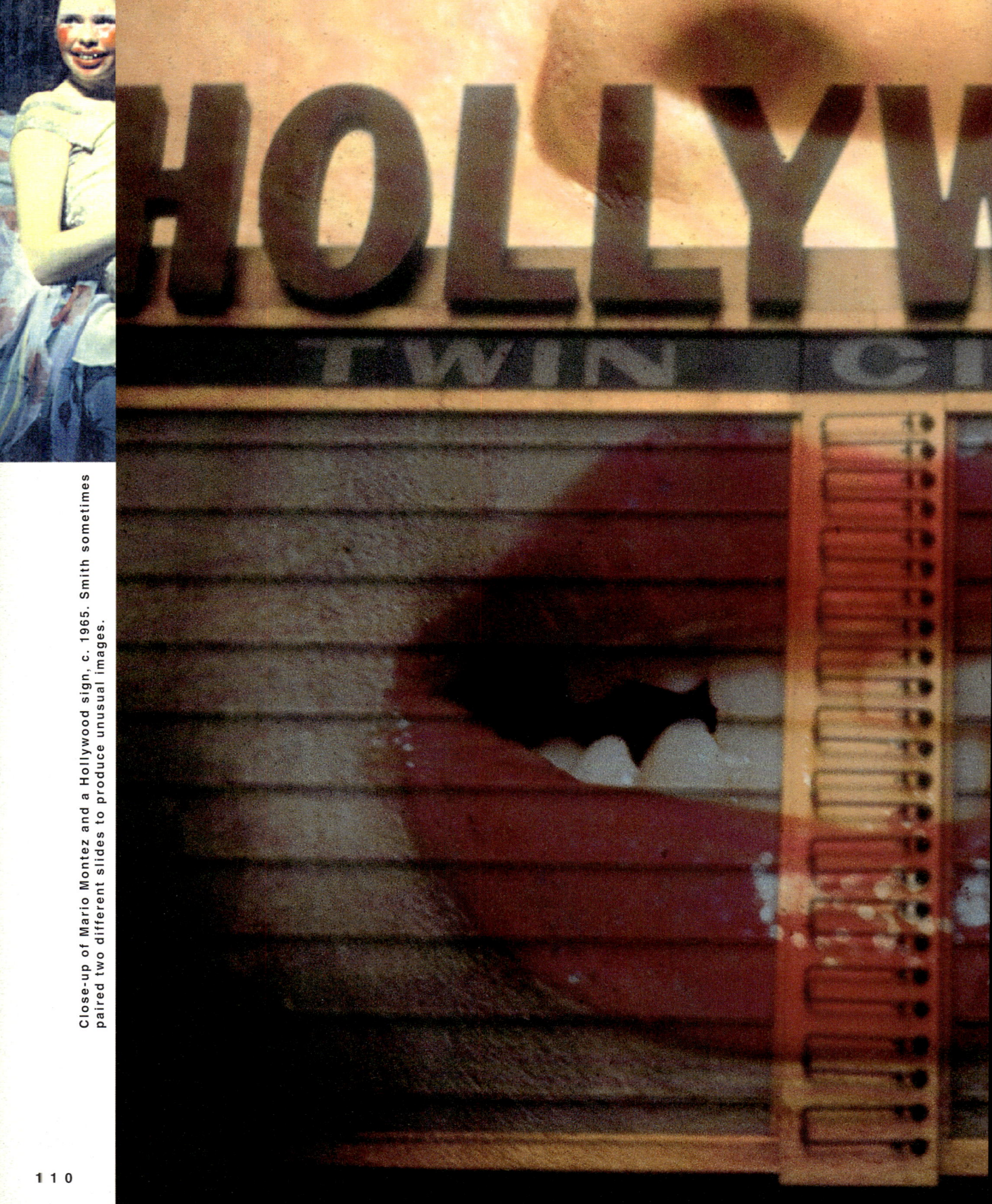

Close-up of Mario Montez and a Hollywood sign, c. 1965. Smith sometimes paired two different slides to produce unusual images.

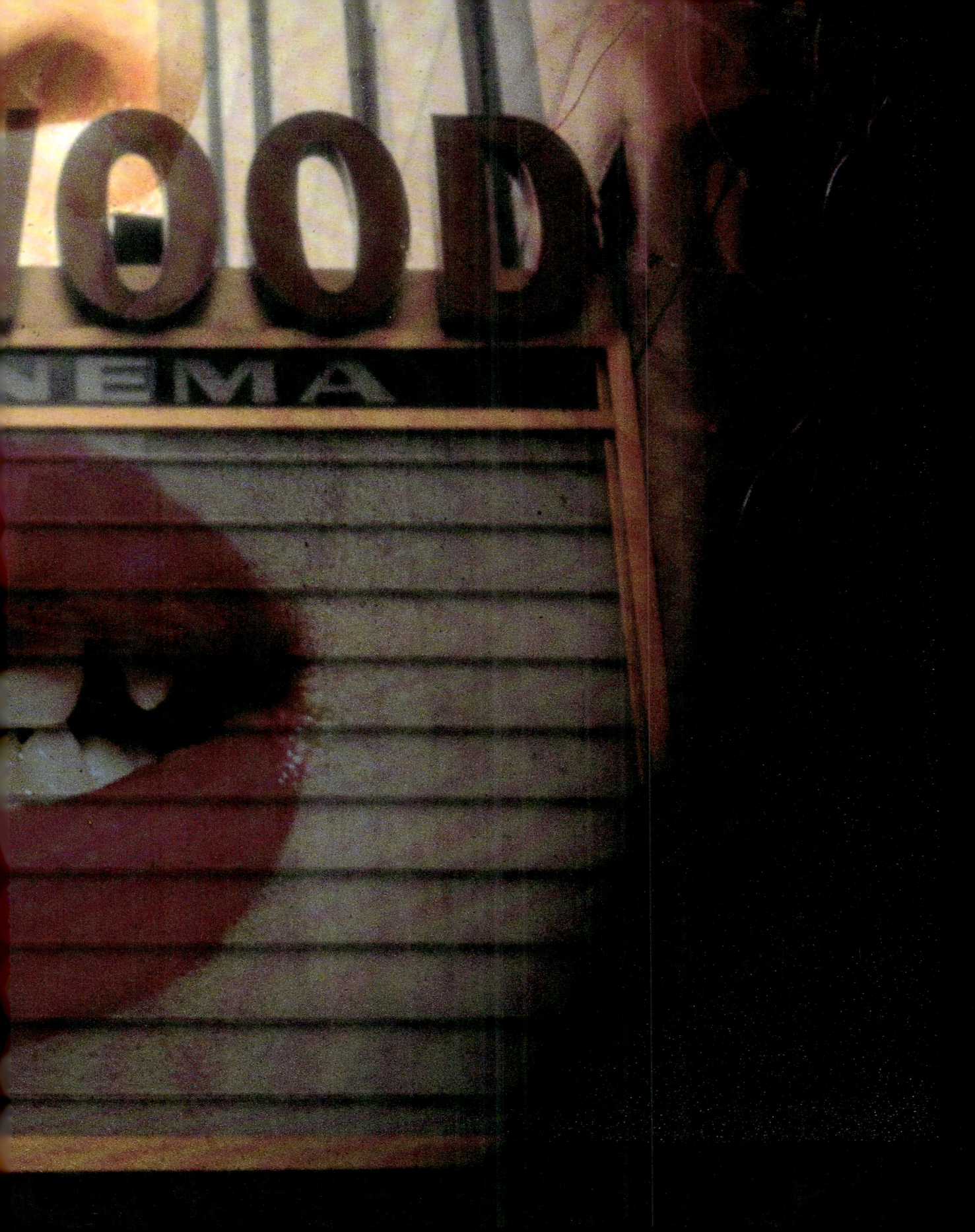

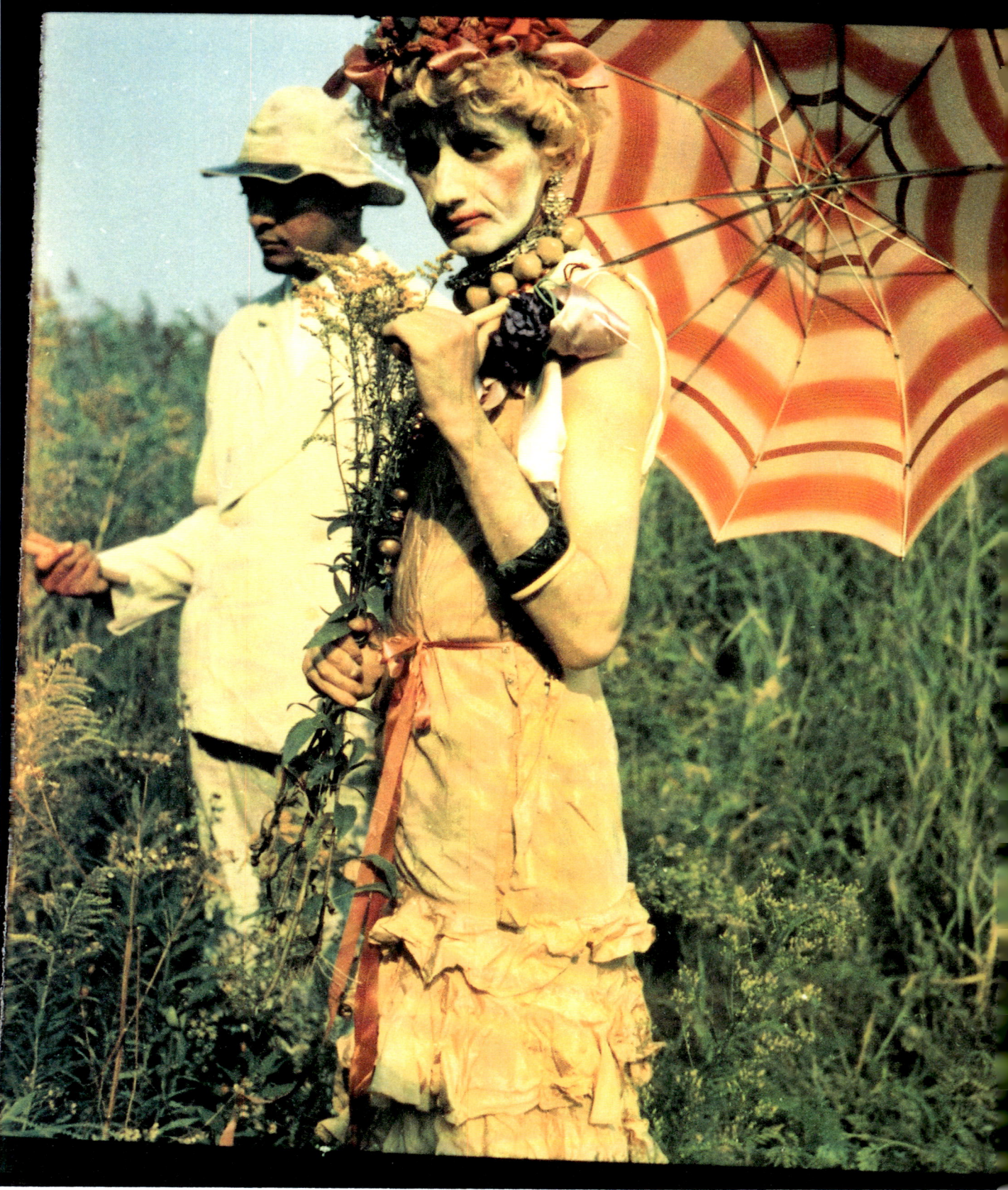

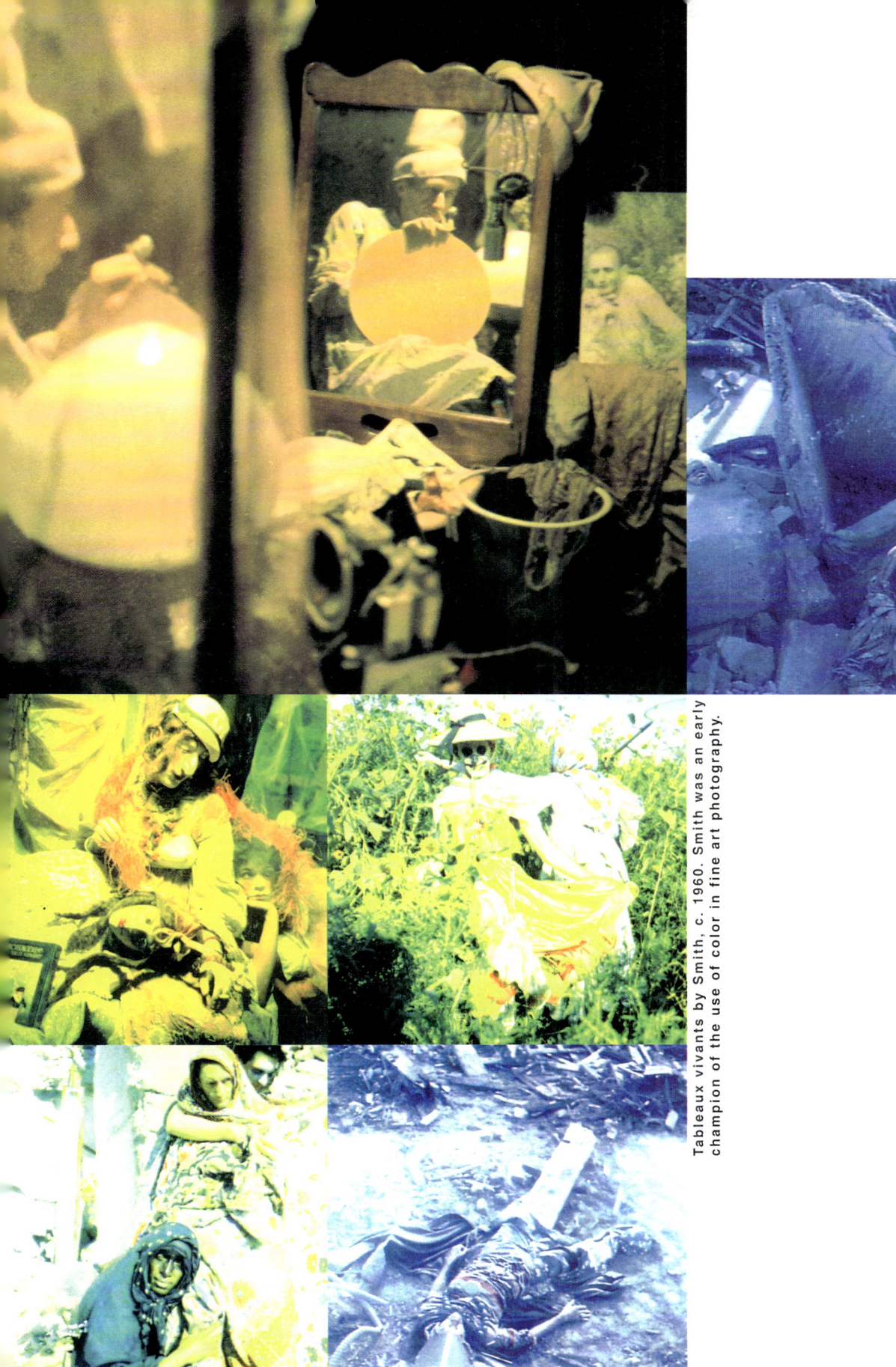

Tableaux vivants by Smith, c. 1960. Smith was an early champion of the use of color in fine art photography.

113

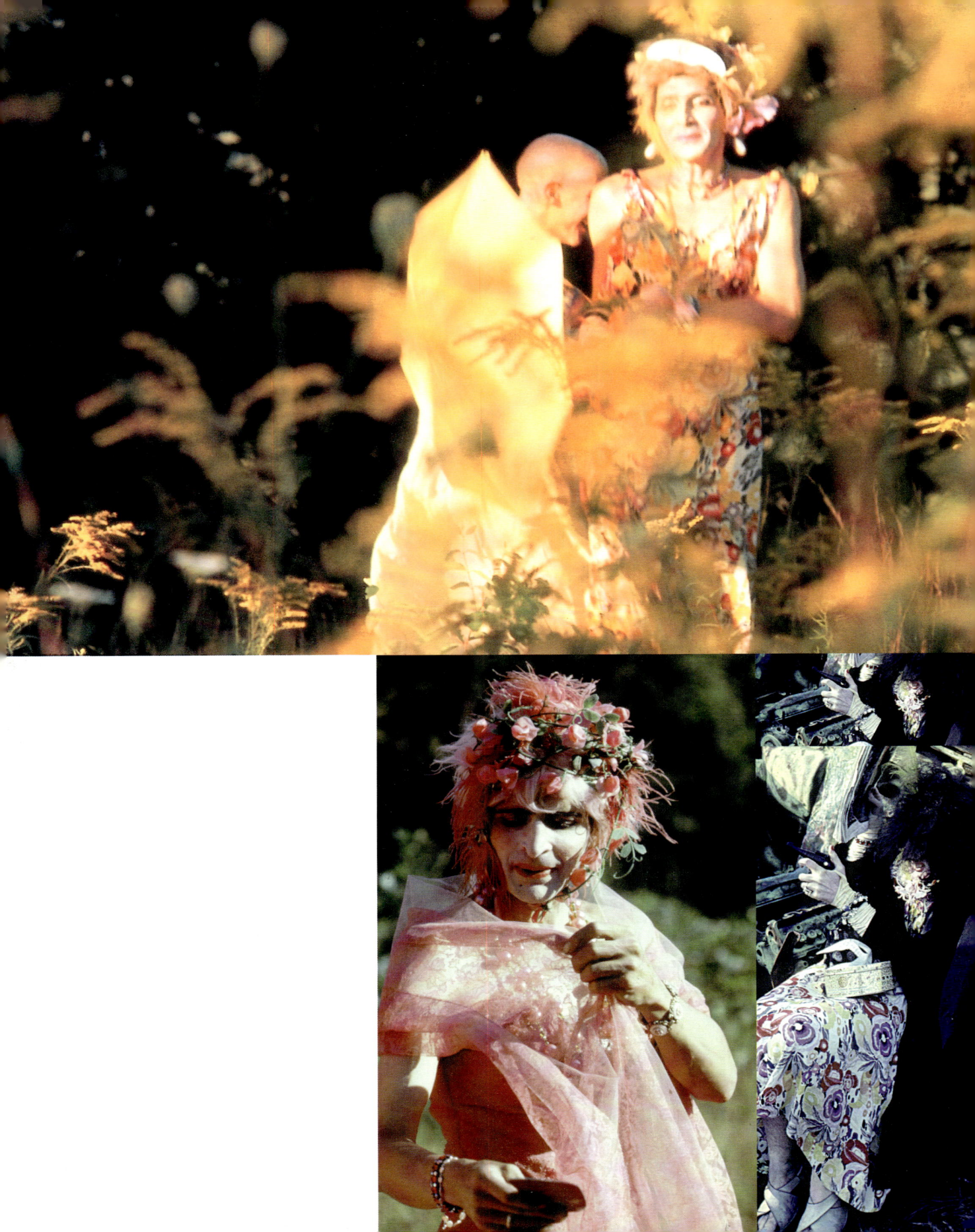

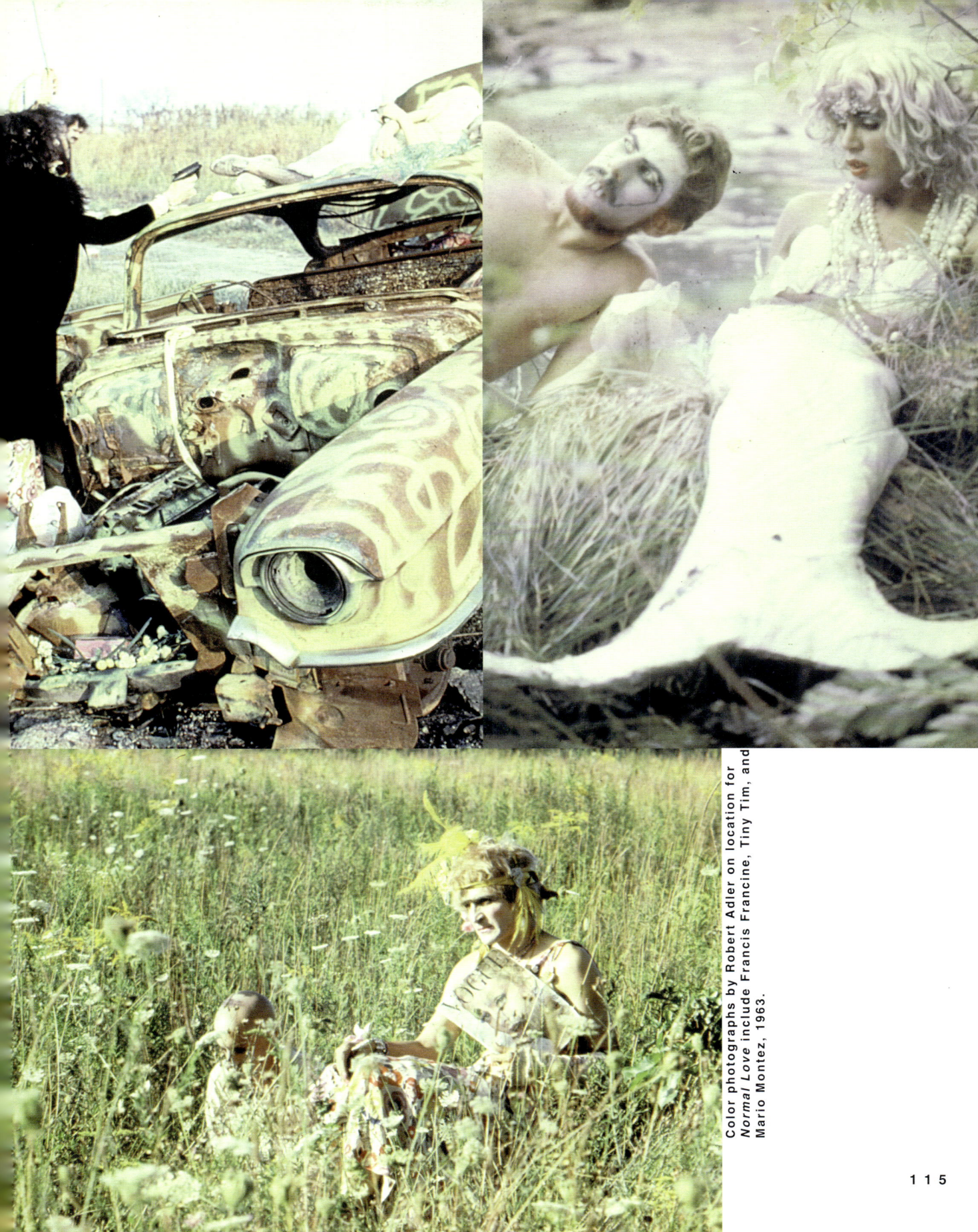

Color photographs by Robert Adler on location for *Normal Love* include Francis Francine, Tiny Tim, and Mario Montez, 1963.

115

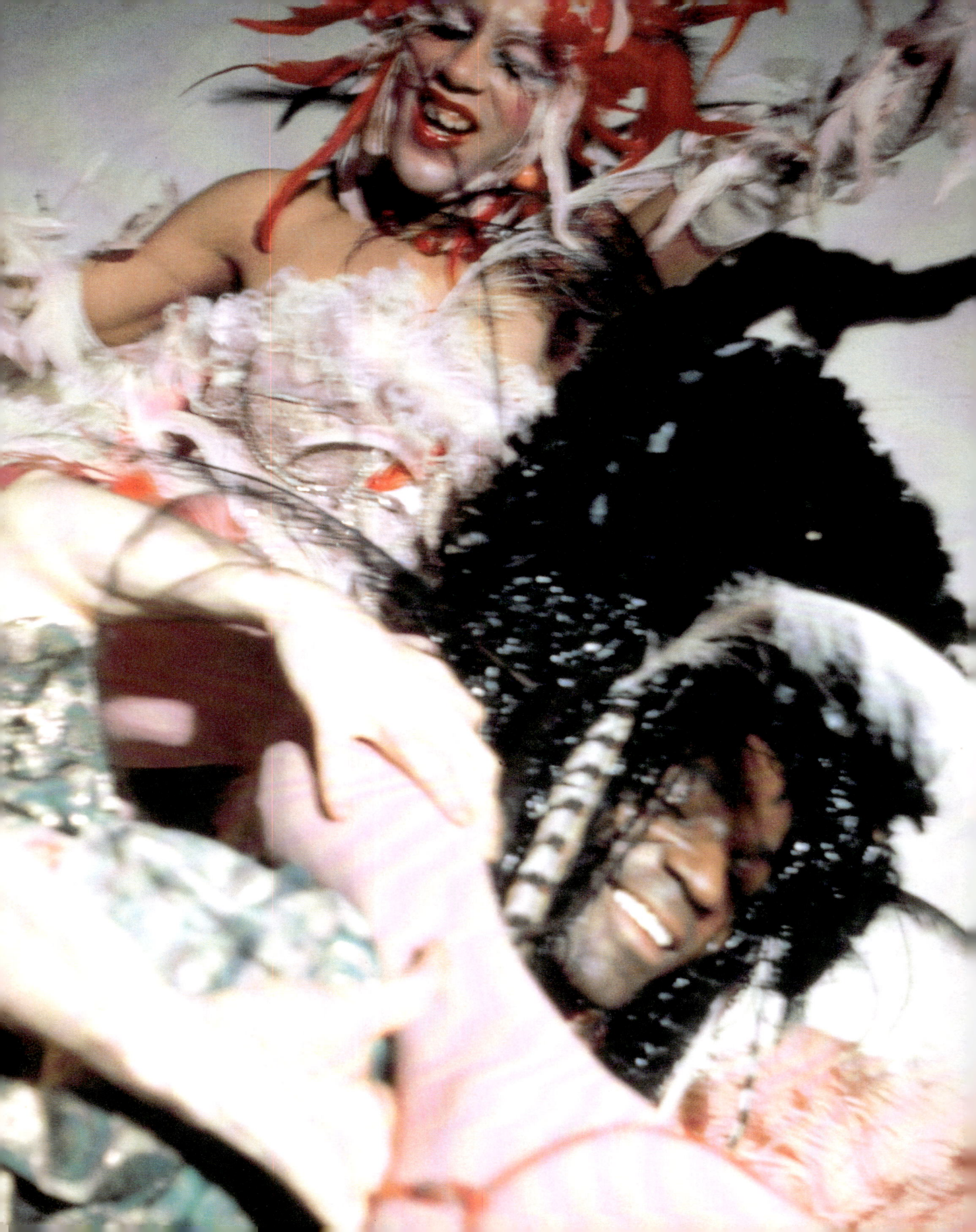

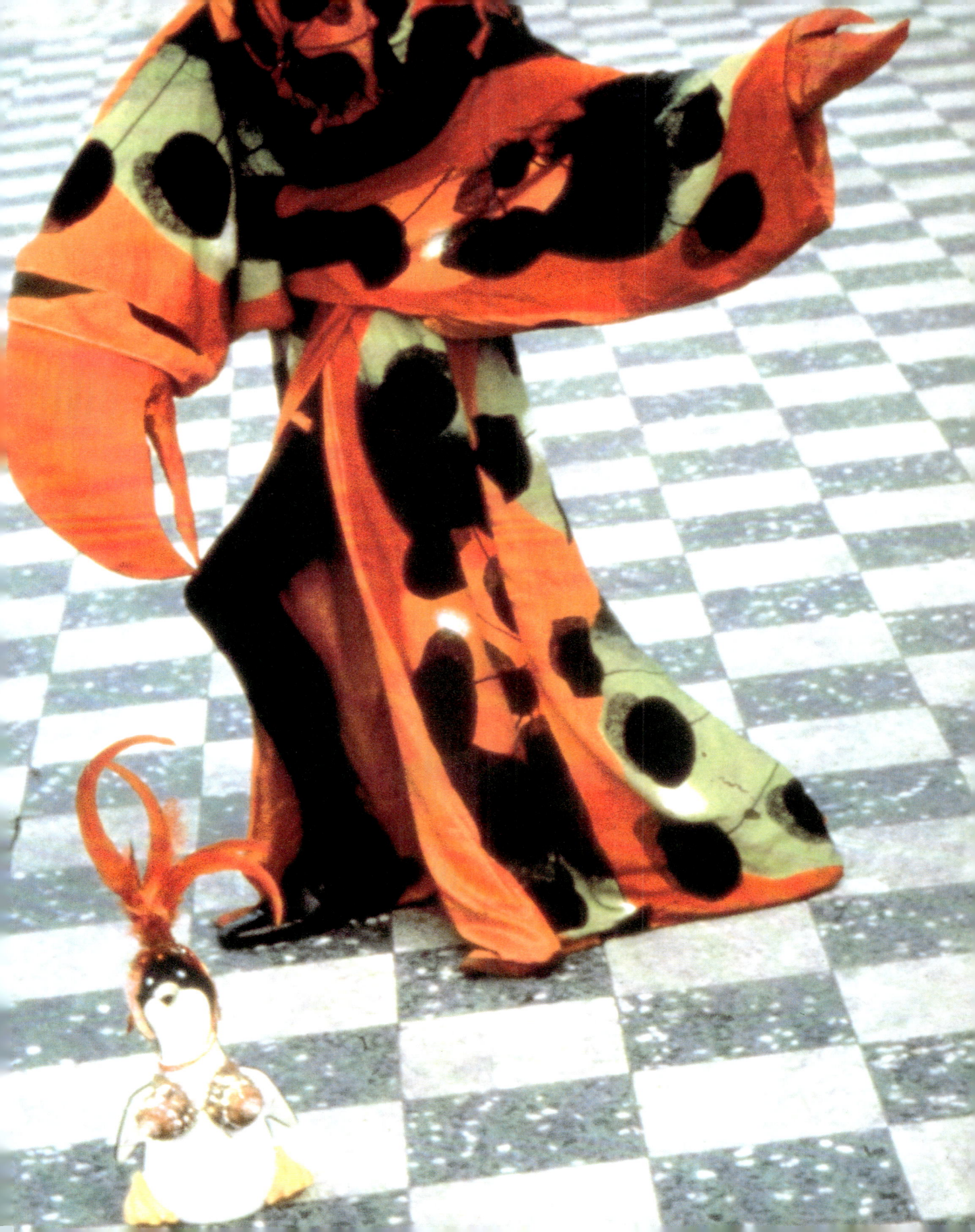

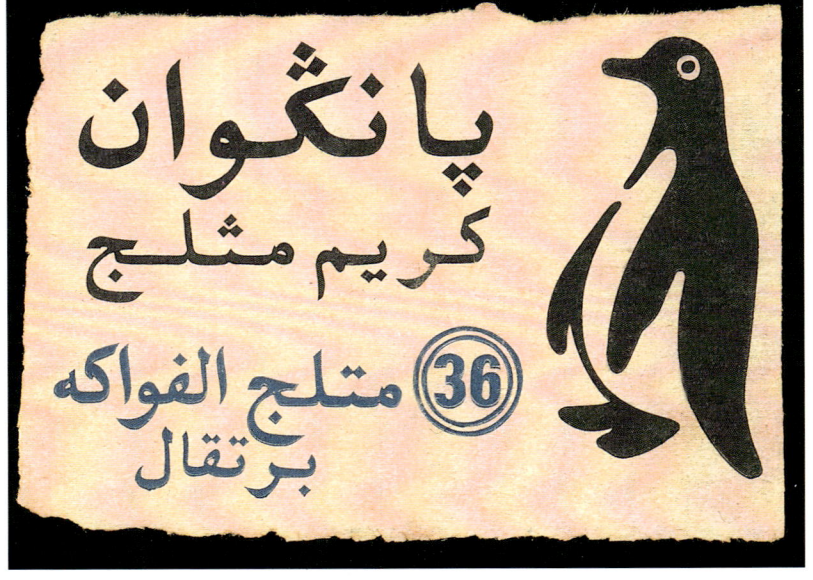

118

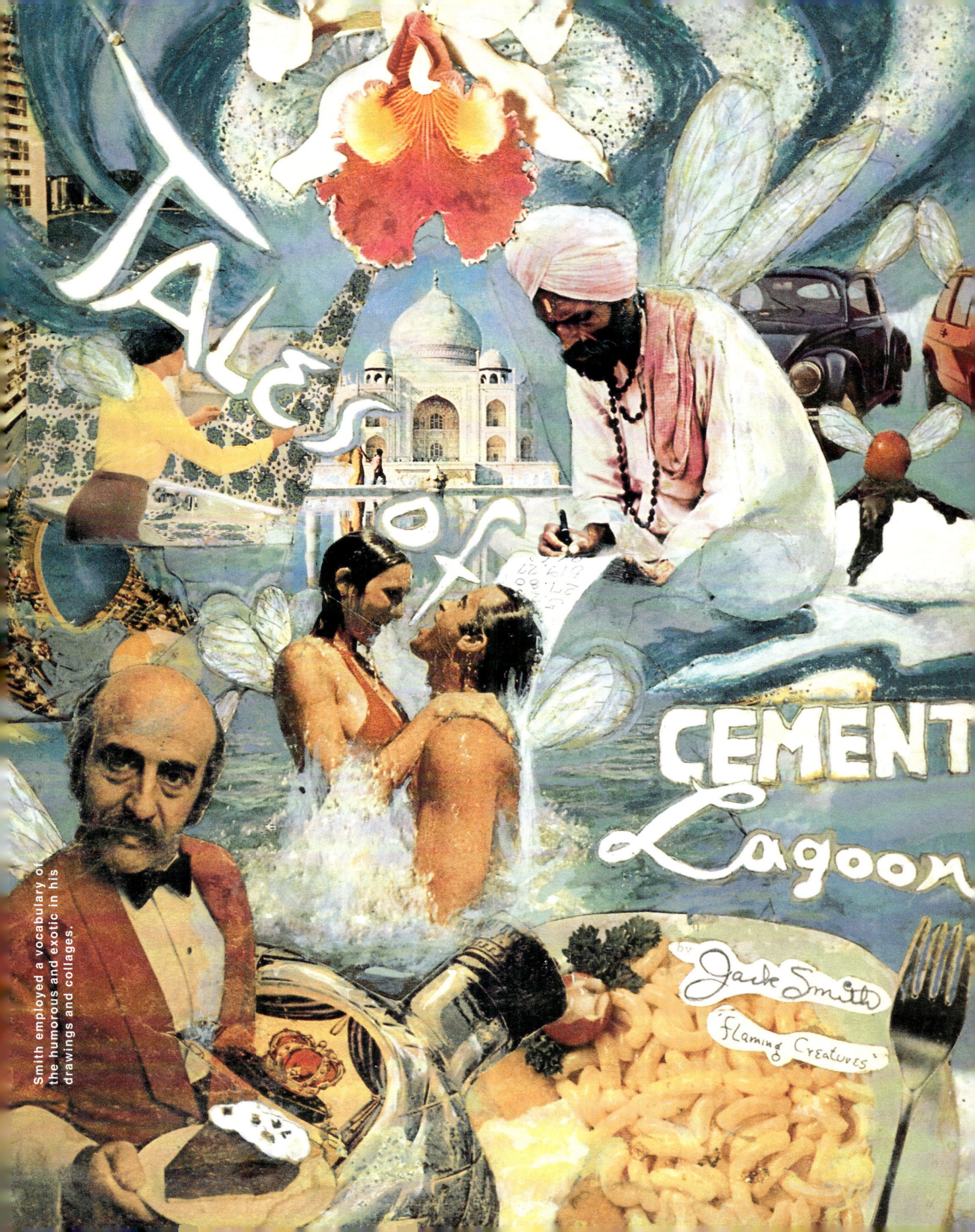

Tales of

CEMENT

Lagoon

by *Jack Smith*
"Flaming Creatures"

Hello, I'm Rose Laverty,

Deep down inside of me (laff) I'm a very patriotic girl. Last night on the Celebrity Beanbag program I was given the humility award for my (with mongolian pride).

NINETEENTH PLANE CRASH!!! you may have noticed my plastic pan - and as you can see my dancing boys are ~~~ ~~~ ~~~ Aren't these roses beautiful? Roses have always been identified with me as all my fans know - ~~~ real fans that is ~~~ that is my real fans, not just bloodsuckers - here's my identified with roses. ~~~ who are ~~~ Real fans that is ~~~ not bloodsuckers.

~~~ ~~~ ~~~ Let me tell ~~~ of my plane crashes. I've had quite a few plane crashes - ~~~ The last one I was going to entertain our boys their LIVES DEPEND ON

Keeping the war going! Their lives depend on it ... actually my song was ended by a few bad roles — but (thoughtful, ser my career was finally undoubt ended when a sightseeing bus I was on was smashed in by a helicopter on the New Jersey TURNPIKE!

I'm going to sing a song for you......

SONG

that bottle - oh let me ~~~ Oh - it fell - Oh let me pick it it - oh SHIT COCK ~~~ - fuck you!! mothering OH SHIT - GOD BLESS ~~~

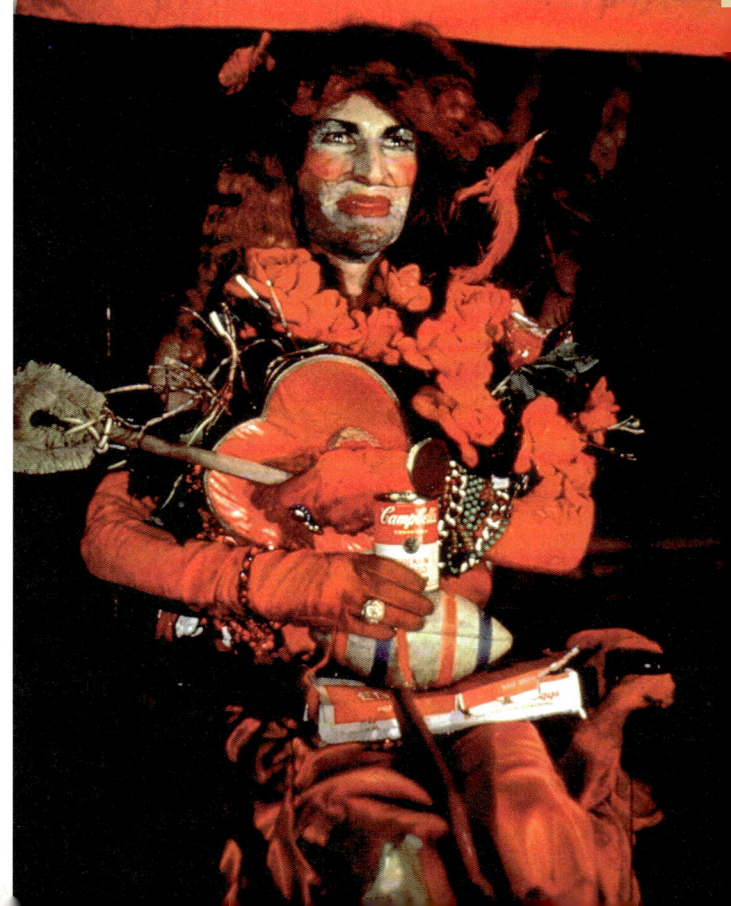

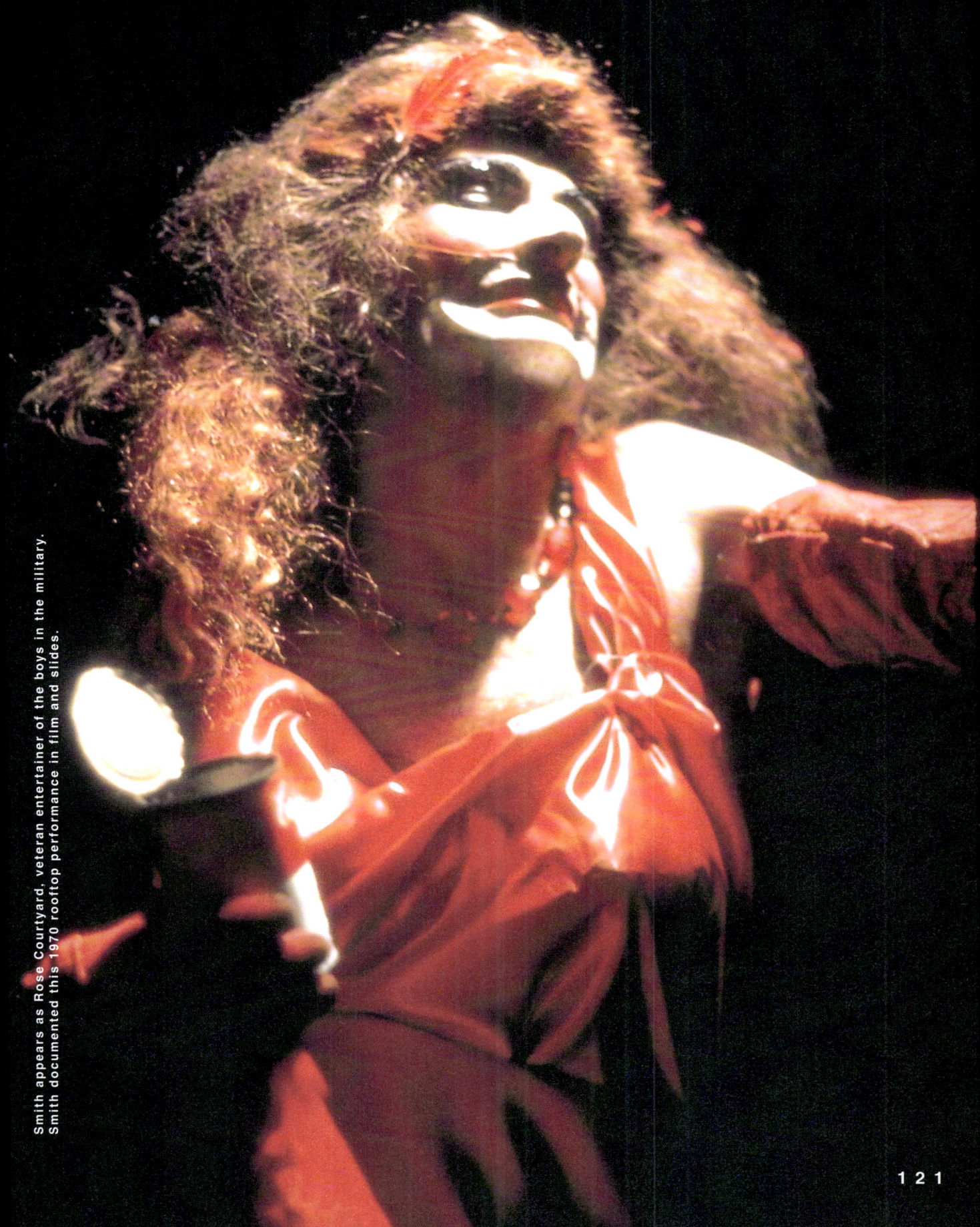

Smith appears as Rose Courtyard, veteran entertainer of the boys in the military. Smith documented this 1970 rooftop performance in film and slides.

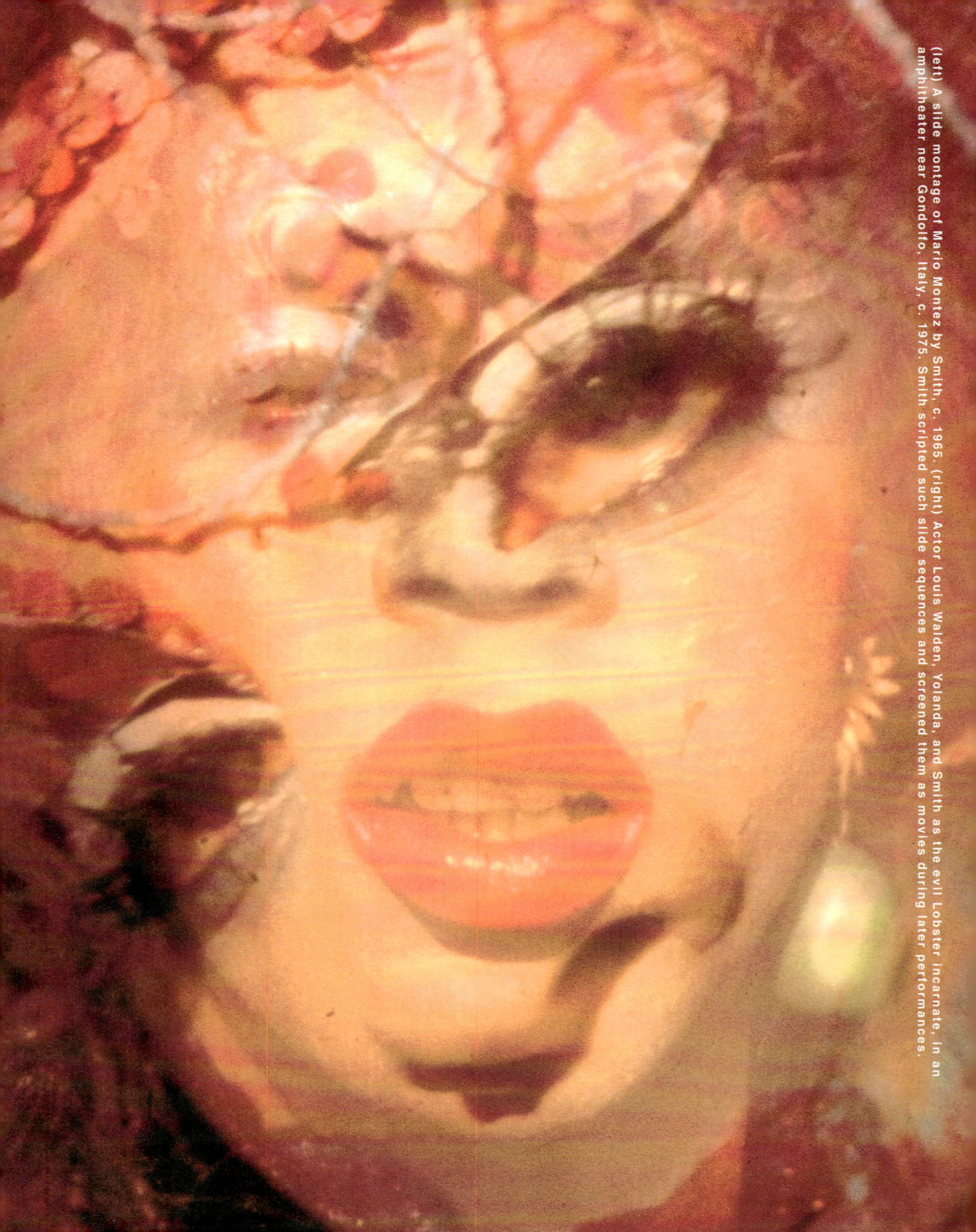

(left) A slide montage of Mario Montez by Smith, c. 1965. (right) Actor Louis Walden, Yolanda, and Smith as the evil Lobster Incarnate, in an amphitheater near Gondolfo, Italy, c. 1975. Smith scripted such slide sequences and screened them as movies during later performances.

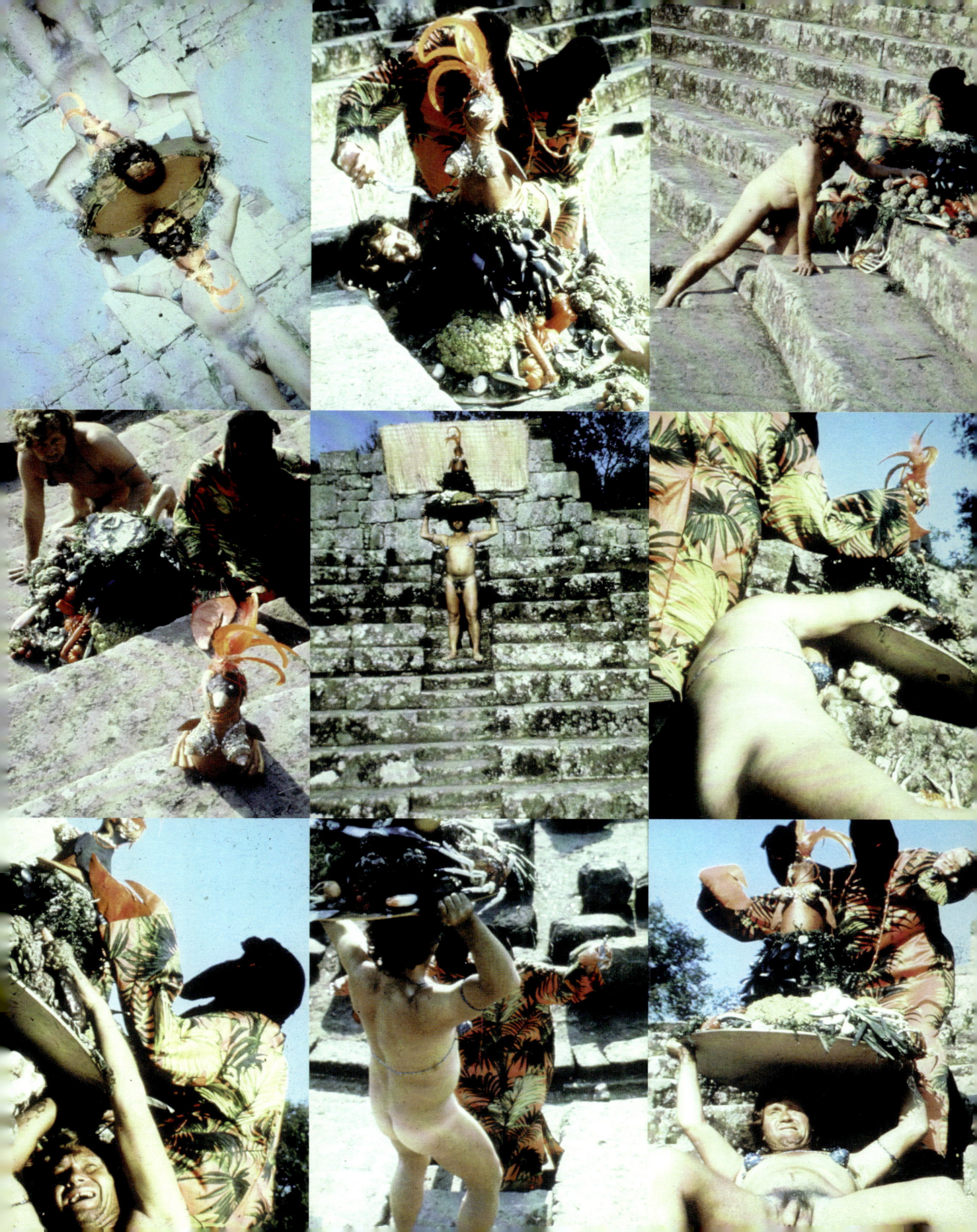

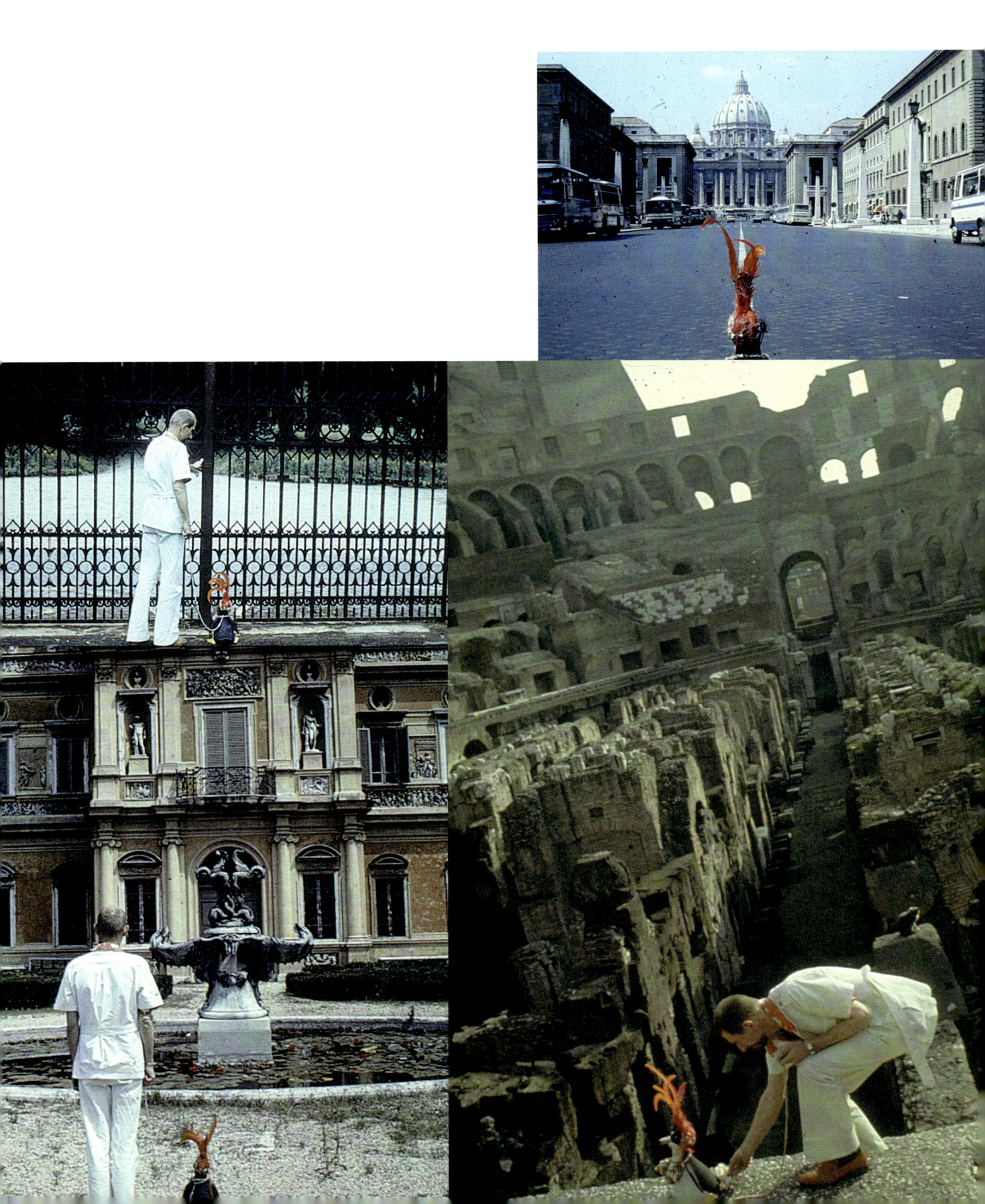

Yolanda, with feathered topnot, jeweled brassiere and rhinestone leash, takes in the sights, Rome, 1975.

People who are de-
humanized can't help
etc.
in
sermon of CHRIST?

126

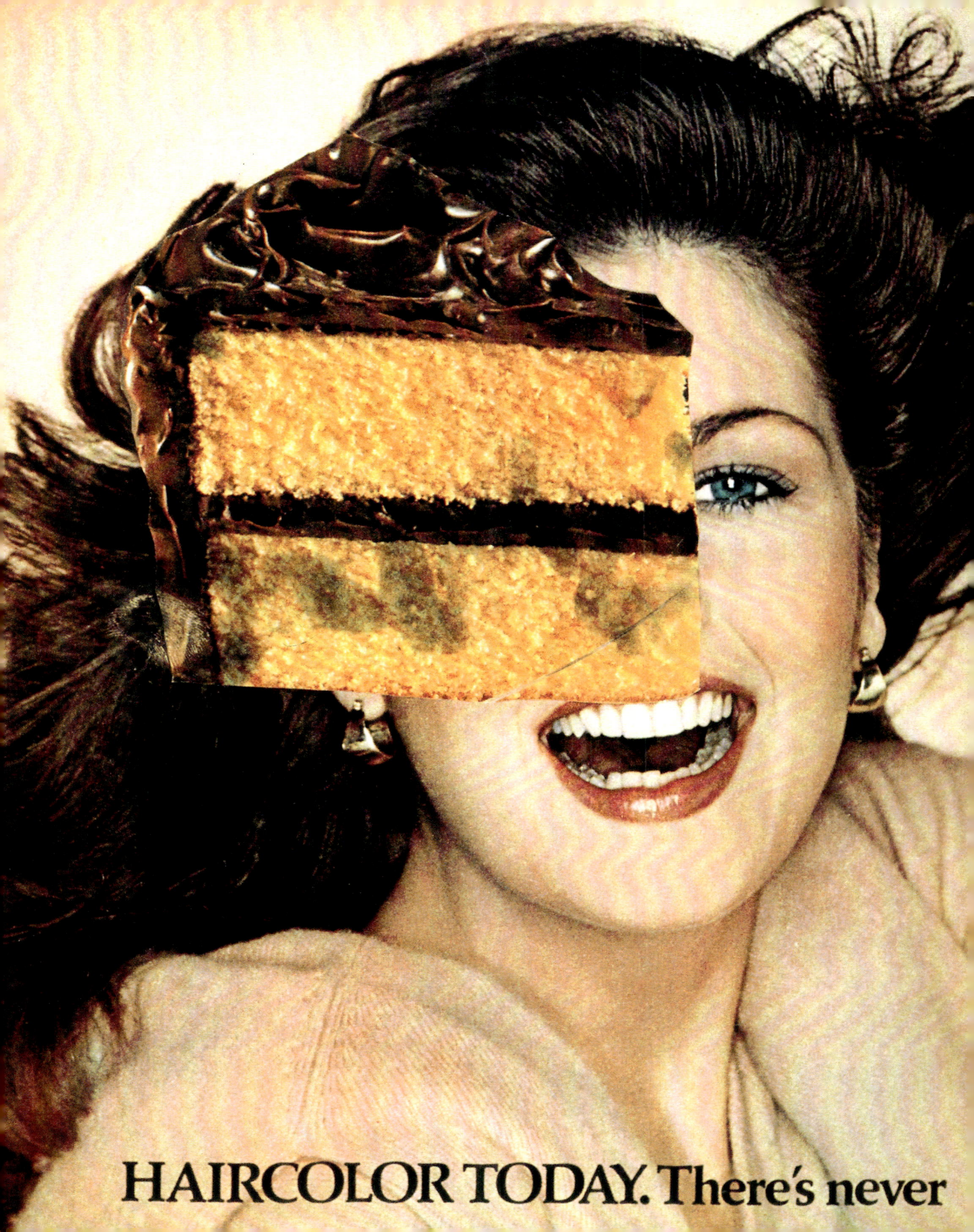

HAIRCOLOR TODAY. There's never

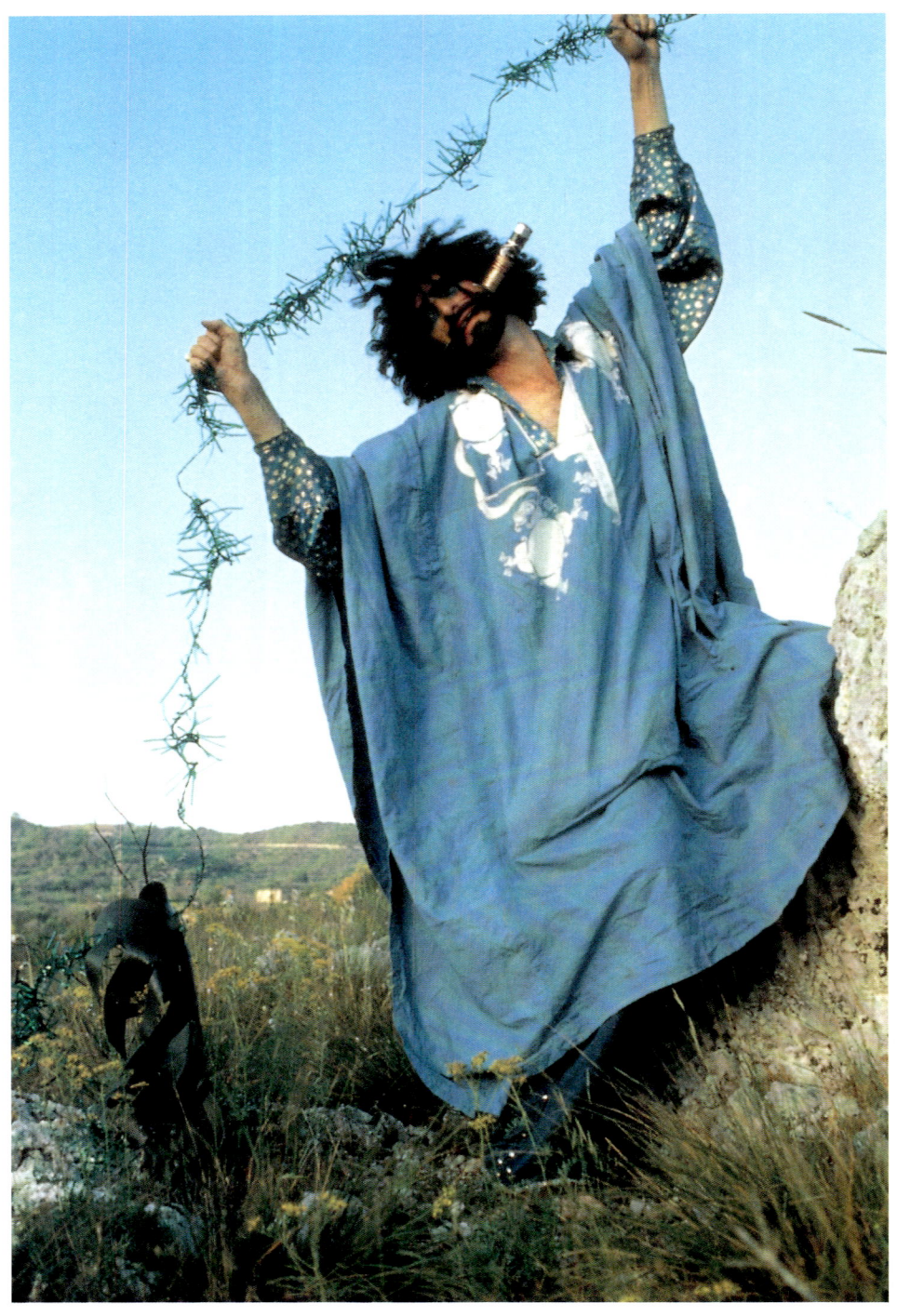

Smith in an ahistorical biblical role as Abraham, Christ, and John the Baptist in scenes for a slide movie, c. 1975. (detail, right) Smith places false eyelashes on a dead sheep.

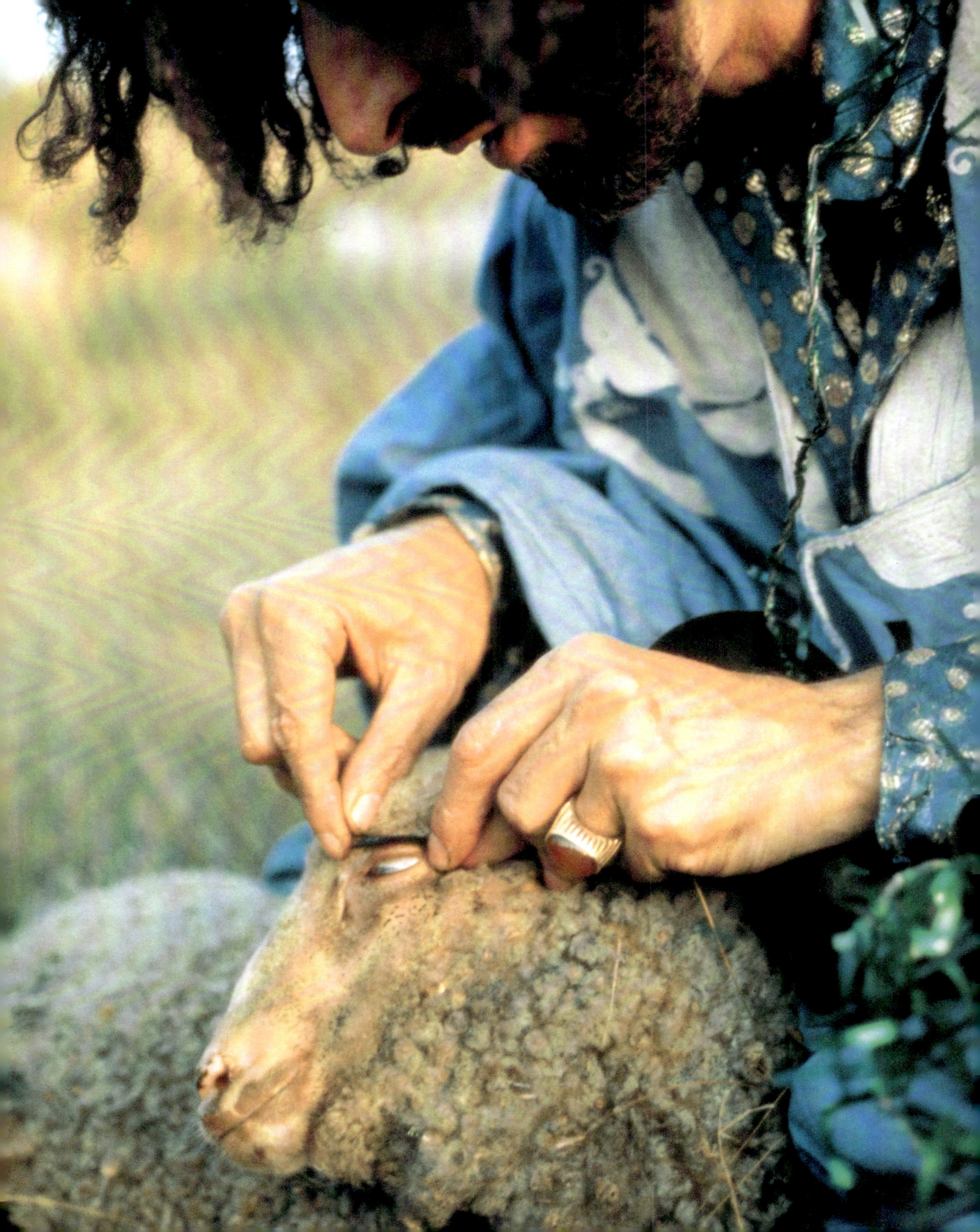

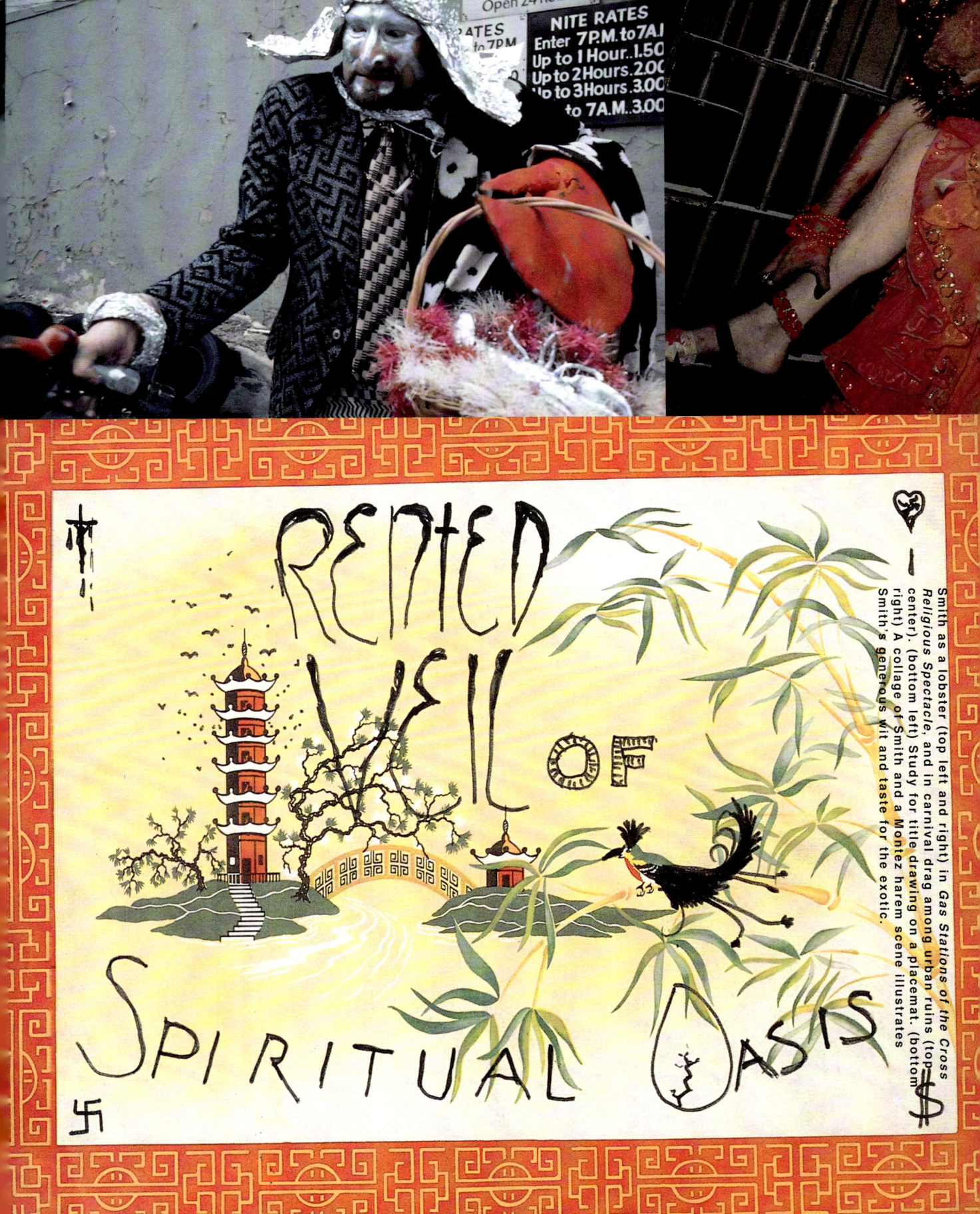

RENTED VEIL OF SPIRITUAL OASIS

Smith as a lobster (top left and right) in *Gas Stations of the Cross Religious Spectacle*, and in carnival drag among urban ruins (top center). (bottom left) Study for title drawing on a placemat. (bottom right) A collage of Smith and a Montez harem scene illustrates Smith's generous wit and taste for the exotic.

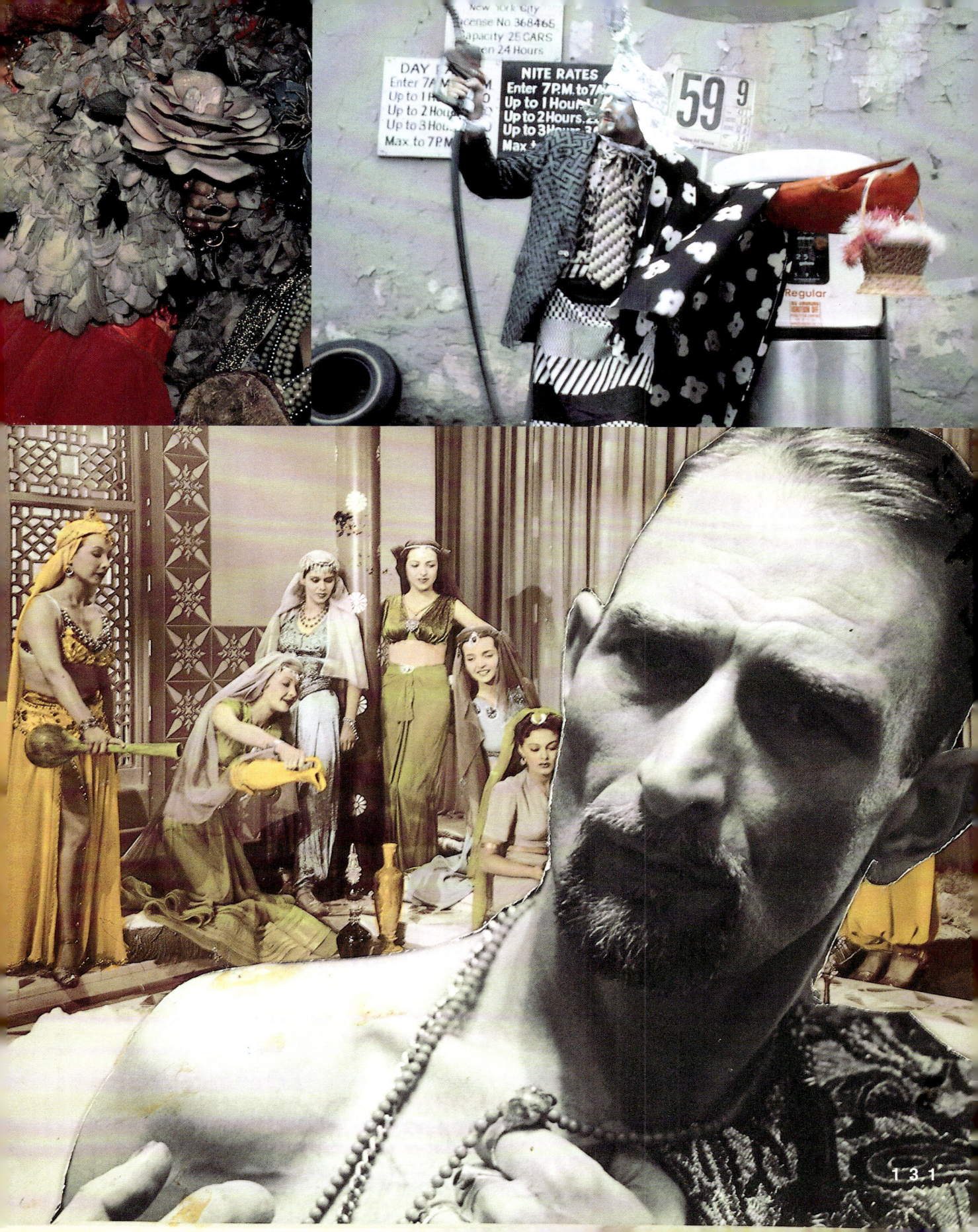

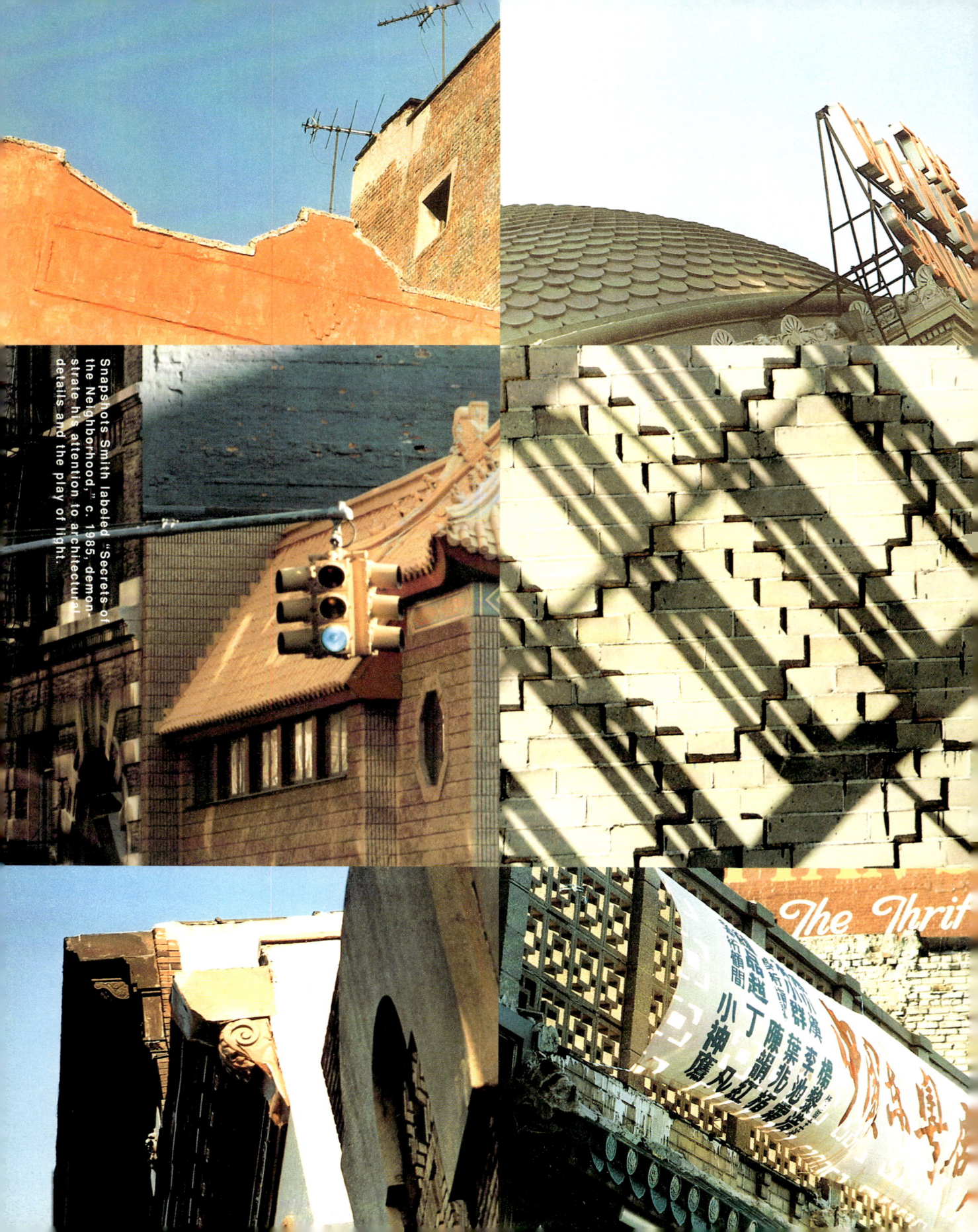

Snapshots Smith labeled "Secrets of the Neighborhood," c. 1985, demonstrate his attention to architectural details and the play of light.

Portrait studies of Smith in later years, and a costume drawing by Smith for *Sinbad in the Rented World*, 1983.

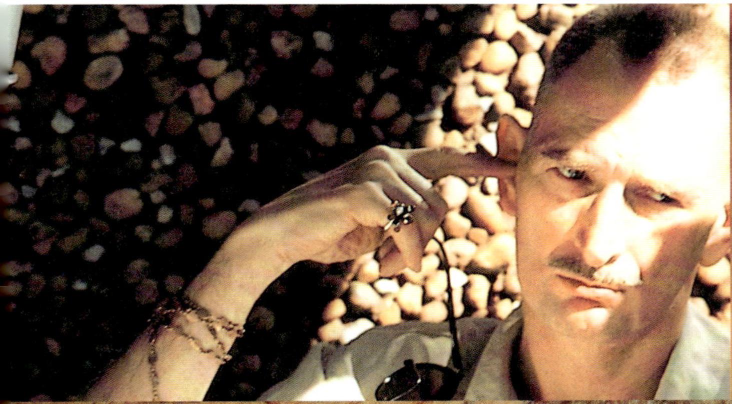

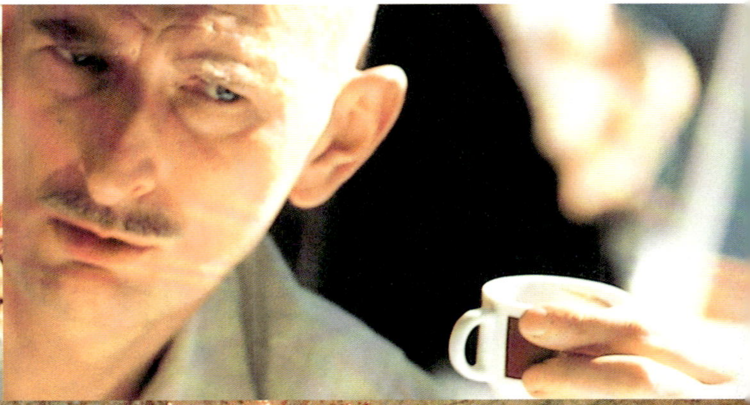

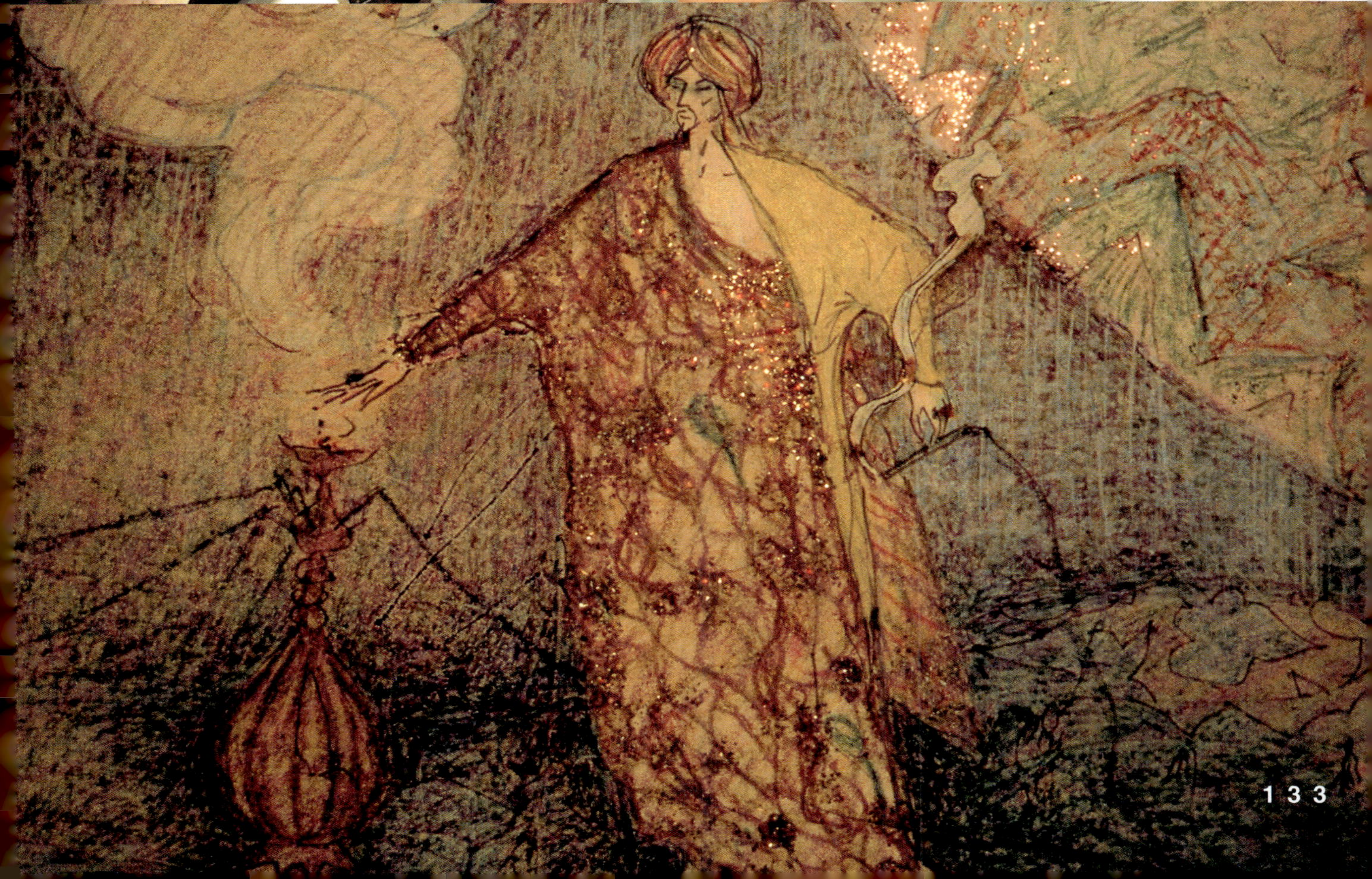

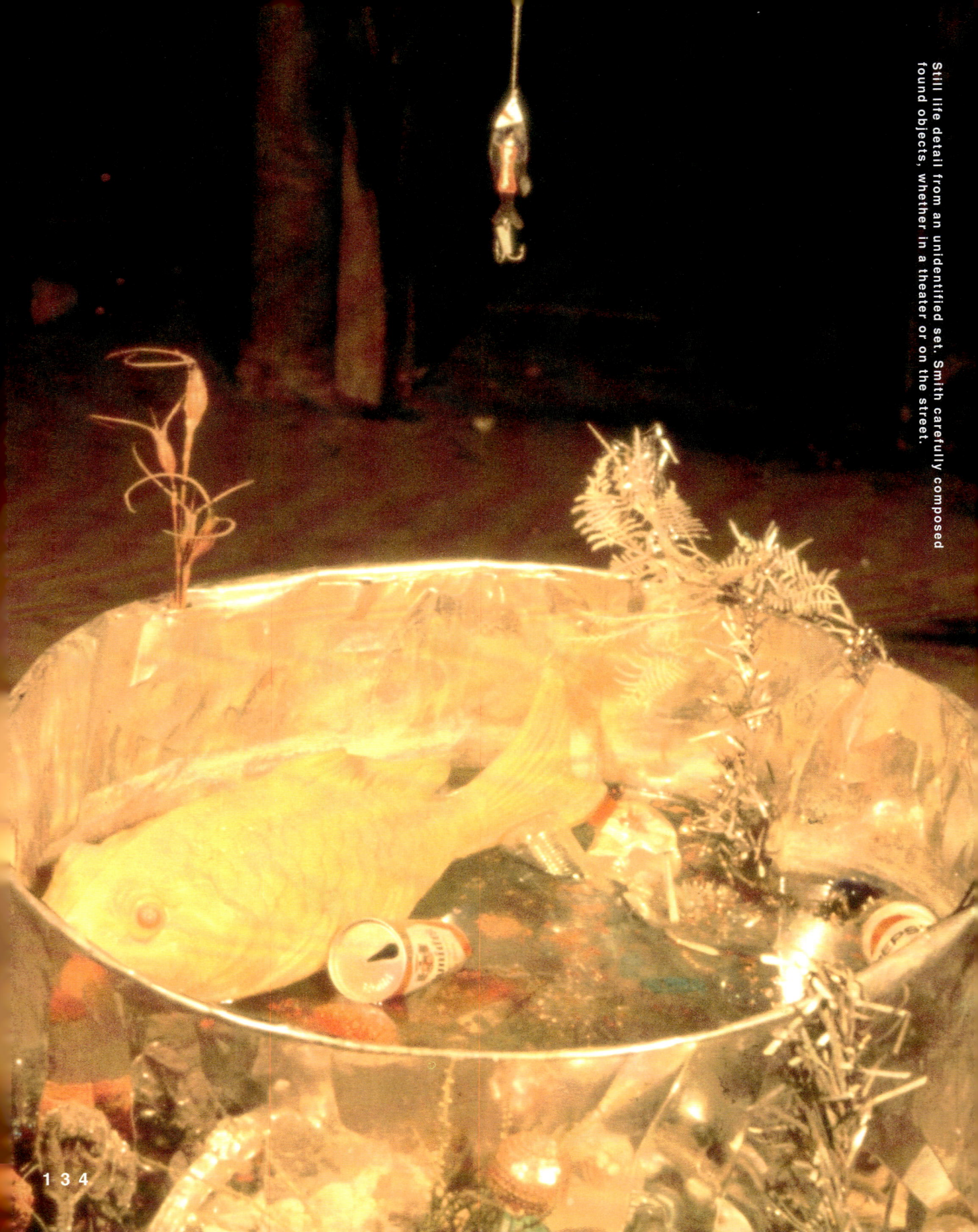

Still life detail from an unidentified set. Smith carefully composed found objects, whether in a theater or on the street.

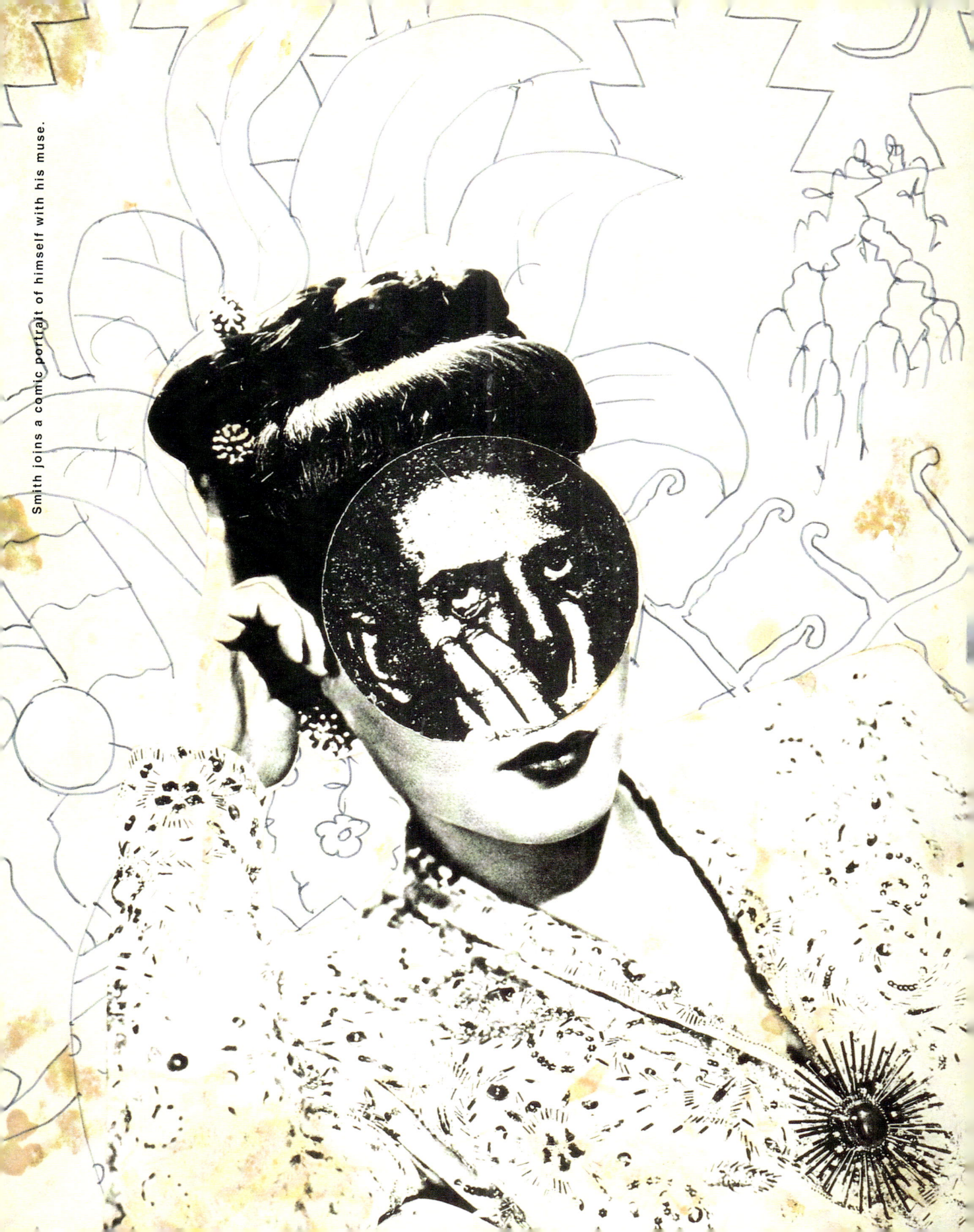

Smith joins a comic portrait of himself with his muse.

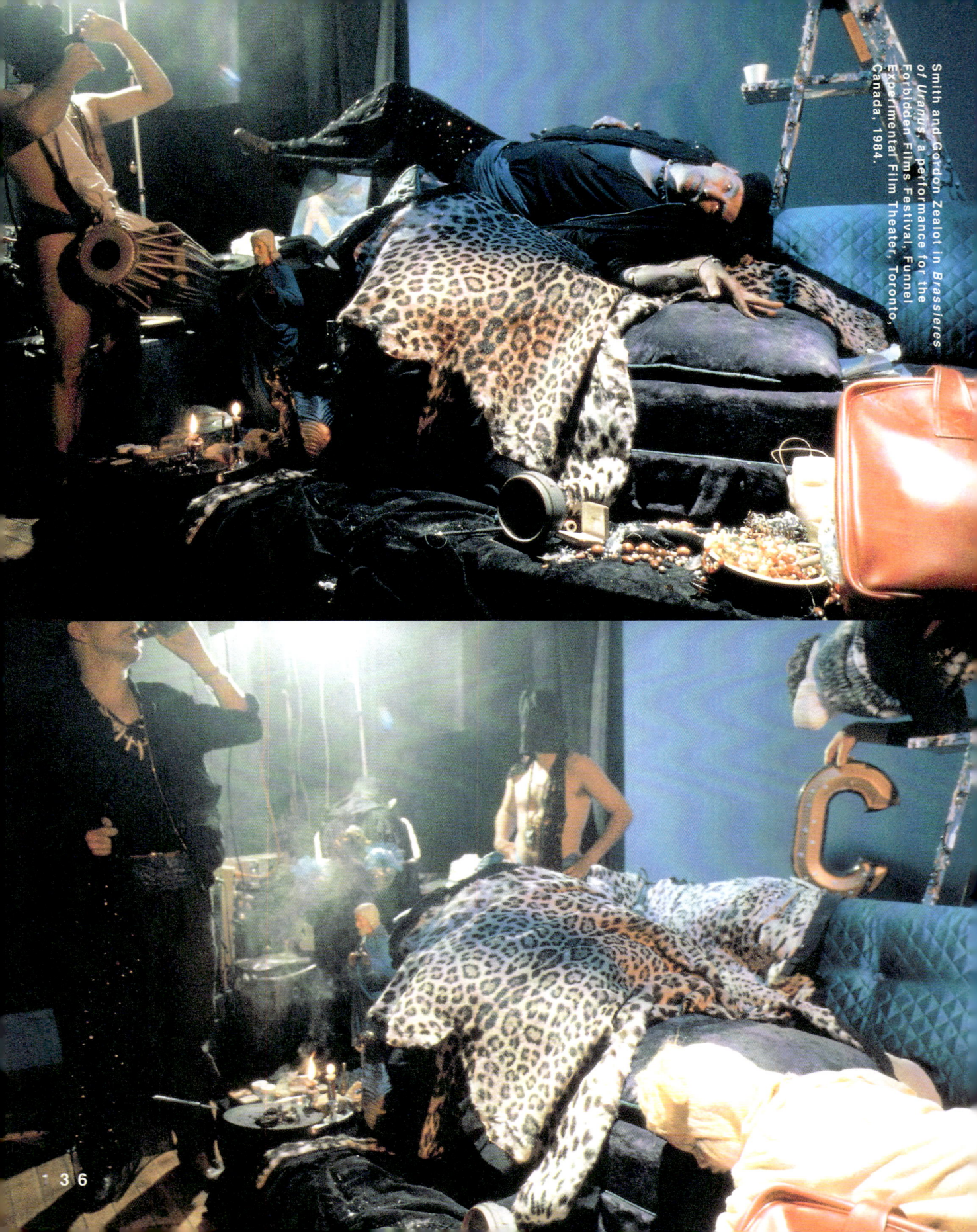

Smith and Gordon Zealot in *Brassieres of Uranus*, a performance for the Forbidden Films Festival. Funnel Experimental Film Theater, Toronto, Canada. 1984.

In my last program I was a

male Yvonne de Carlo for

the Lucky Landlord Underground.

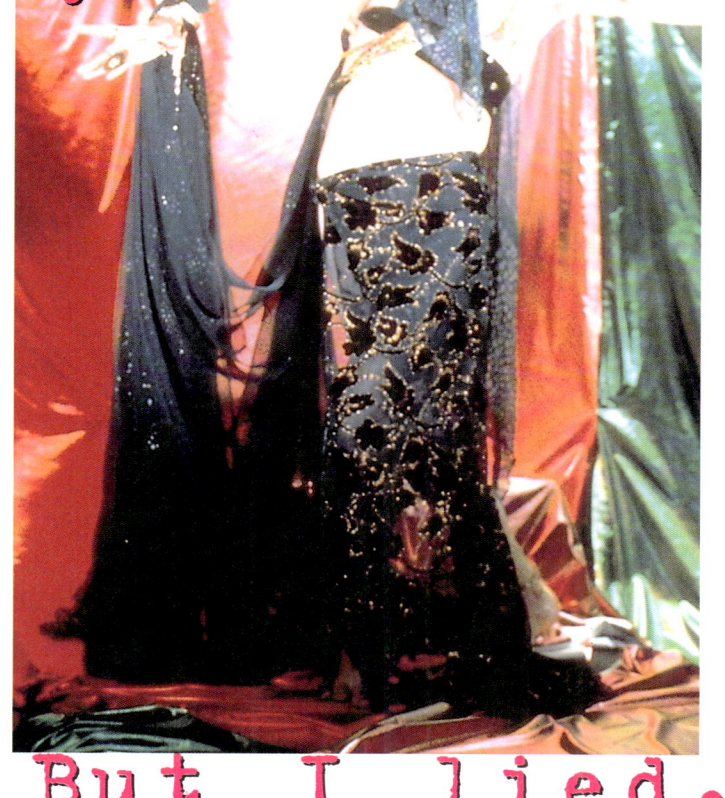

But I lied.

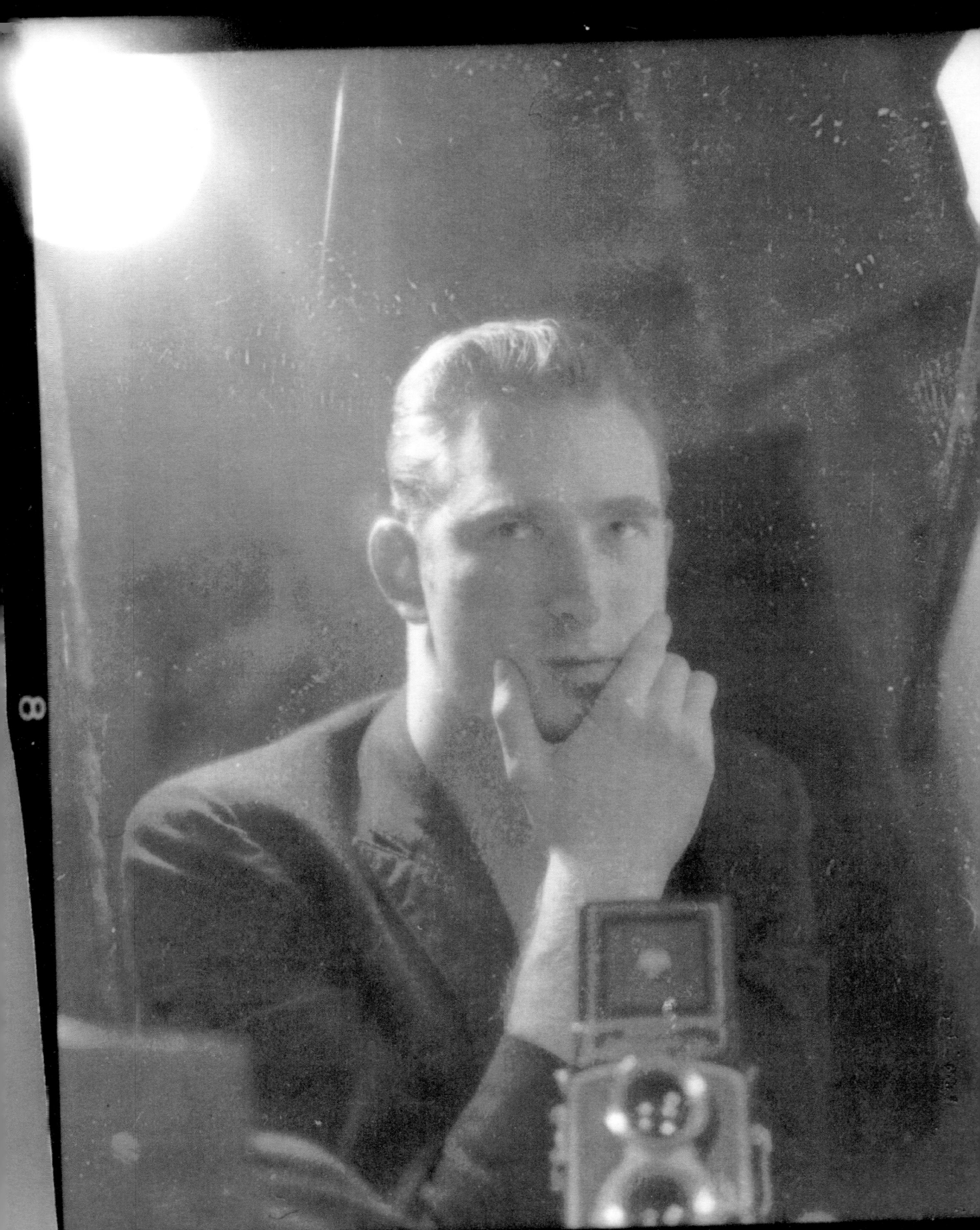

Anywhere Out of the World: The Photography of Jack Smith
-Lawrence Rinder

"The public doesn't want modern art.
The public has never wanted it and they never will."[1]

— Jack Smith, 1988

Jack Smith's photography, film, and performance conjure a world of flagrant passion, campy humor, and morbid beauty. Going against the formalist grain of modern art, Smith was a storyteller, a fabulist. He relished the complexities of human character and the peculiarities of human form, especially when that form was languorously posed, draped in chiffon, or transformed by mascara and rouge. His devotion to art was total and, though no political activist, he insisted that art be an antidote to the spiritually and aesthetically deadening effects of American capitalist society.

Smith's photographs have the rare ability to evoke in a single image an entire world, an epoch, and an ethos. Deftly composing figures, costumes, and settings, he created complex images that are as emotional, allegorical, and strange as the baroque and symbolist art he so admired. He was inspired, in particular, by Aubrey Beardsley's languid and grotesque fin de siècle caricatures and by the paintings of Fragonard and Veronese, whose "Venus and Mars United by Love" (c. 1576) was his favorite destination at the Metropolitan Museum.[2] Remarkably, Smith's sumptuous images were achieved using an extraordinary poverty of means. He photographed primarily in the confines of his own East Fourth Street apartment and used as props only materials he found on the street, purchased in thrift stores, or which were given to him by equally destitute friends. His models were not professional actors, but rather were drawn from the eccentric company of New York City's underground Bohemia. Whoever they were though—drag queen, hustler, artist, or errant Park Avenue matron—once captured on film by Smith, they were transformed into fantastic exemplars of his strange, other-worldly vision of humanity.

In the early 1950s, Smith moved from Los Angeles to New York City, where he ultimately settled in the East Village, a Manhattan neighborhood of warren-like tenements that had been sheltering immigrants of various kinds for a century. The East Village was still home to poor immigrants, mostly Italians, Puerto Ricans, and Ukrainians. Vestiges of various folk cultures survived in the strange displays of bric-a-brac in the old storefront windows, in the summer street festivals, and in the music and conversation of the ubiquitous stoop gatherings. Caribbean, Mediterranean, and Eastern European cultures combined into a rich and peculiar accumulation of smells, sounds, and images.

Smith was another kind of immigrant, an immigrant from middle America. He was raised in Ohio, Texas, and Wisconsin, spending the formative years of his youth in the dark, magical realm of American movie houses. He was entranced by the exoticism and Technicolor splendor of 1930s and 1940s Hollywood movies from the cheesy, low-budget variety to the all-out extravaganzas.

Smith found salvation from the banality of postwar American mainstream culture in the sheer artifice and ingenuity of these celluloid dreams. For him, the East Village must have seemed like an unselfconscious, impoverished version of the glamorous Hollywood studios, in which each culture ingeniously re-created a simulacrum of its distant origin. It was a tremendously fertile environment for Smith, and one that provided him with imagery, materials, and inspiration for nearly thirty years.

Around 1957, Smith opened the Hyperbole Photography Studio in a storefront space on Eighth Street near Cooper Square. Like Claes Oldenburg's "The Store," which opened nearby in 1961, Smith's studio was less a commercial enterprise than a kind of ongoing performance/installation. The unsuspecting customer who came in expecting to have a portrait taken usually ended up posing instead for one of Smith's bizarre tableaux.

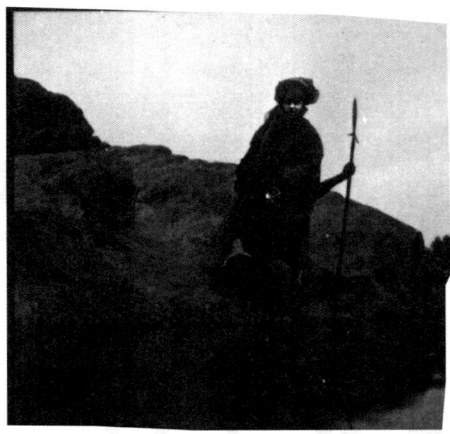
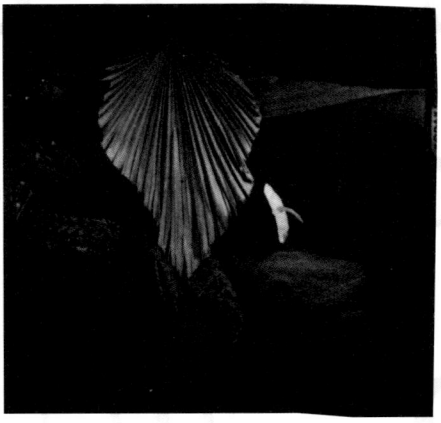

There is a distinct morbidity to many of the photographs taken at Hyperbole. Models are often shown lying in state or in ambiguous recumbent positions that suggest relaxation, sleep, or death. Certain sequences allude to suicide, ritual murder, and necrophilia; yet, despite the gruesome themes, Smith's models are often grinning.

Smith relied on the innate expressiveness of the human form, the symbolic richness latent in the poses of, and relationships between, figures. In addition, he, like many of his contemporaries, was fascinated by the poetic and visual richness of found objects and informal props. In many of his early photographs, these elements visually combine with the models to convey an allegorical meaning that remains obscure, perhaps calculatedly so, even as the images offer purely visual appeal. In some images, the relationship between figures is quite abstract, to the extent that the colors and textures of the various fabrics become as important as the people who wear them. The sheer richness of color, texture, light, and shadow combines to create a highly sensual, almost hallucinatory effect.

The avant-garde filmmaker Ken Jacobs, who was one of Smith's closest friends and collaborators between 1955 and 1961, recalls Smith's early photo sessions: "People were made to look like they were in a scene from a movie. It was Jack's movie. The most important thing was to bring the actors into connection with each other and then you could imagine the play from their attitudes toward each other. It would be redundant actually to act out. More was possible if things were left indefinite. The eccentricity in this work is the architectonics of the dramatis personae."[3]

In the late 1950s, besides shooting at Hyperbole and in his apartment, Smith made numerous forays to outdoor locations. The rubble-strewn lot of what was to become Lincoln Center at Broadway and 65th Street was a favorite site. The photographs taken there present expanses of broken concrete and twisted metal bars in which the orientation of gravity and scale is almost completely lost. The dour, costumed figures in other outdoor photographs of the period have a mythic, archetypal gravity, more evocative of a grim Northern European sensibility than of the exotic Middle Eastern scenarios with which Smith is usually associated.

In an interesting counterpoint to his otherworldly fantasy images, Smith also took a limited number of photographs of the East Village that have the straightforward, documentary quality of work by contemporary photographers such as Weegee, Helen Levitt, and Diane Arbus.[4] The April 1962 issue of *Scene*, a short-lived culture magazine, contains Smith's photo essay "new york—the underworld people" and includes candid street photographs juxtaposed with posed images. The editor's introduction reads, in part: "Jack Smith has chosen the fringe world of the subconscious as the subject for his photographic art. He depicts the shadow area between the normal and the perverse with extraordinary sensitivity to symbol and nuance. Roaming through the odd corners of the city, Jack Smith captures those rare moments when the subconscious erupts close to the surface. A scene in a cemetery becomes a necrophilic nightmare; Central Park is transformed into a surrealist vision; a Greenwich Village party, haunted by transvestites, is made uncomfortably visual. Smith's vision is strange, but no one who examines these pages can doubt its power."[5]

Rather than encountering a "real" world on the street, Smith simply found an extension of the exotic dynamics of pose, expression, and costume that he constructed for himself in his studio or posed in other outdoor settings. Among Smith's photographs from around 1958-59, some of the most original works are those shot in the cramped space of his apartment. These color photographs are extraordinary puzzles of bodies, bedclothes, and a host of other seemingly unrelated items: a frozen chicken, an old radio, a chart of the stars, drapes, veils, books, and photos clipped from newspapers. Smith additionally used mirrors to further fracture and complicate perspective and identity. As if to allude to one of the inspirations for his complex, synthetic compositions, Smith has one of his models hold a book of paintings by the master of visual and thematic paradox, Edouard Manet. Perhaps the most profound influence on Smith's early photography, however, was the film director Joseph von Sternberg.

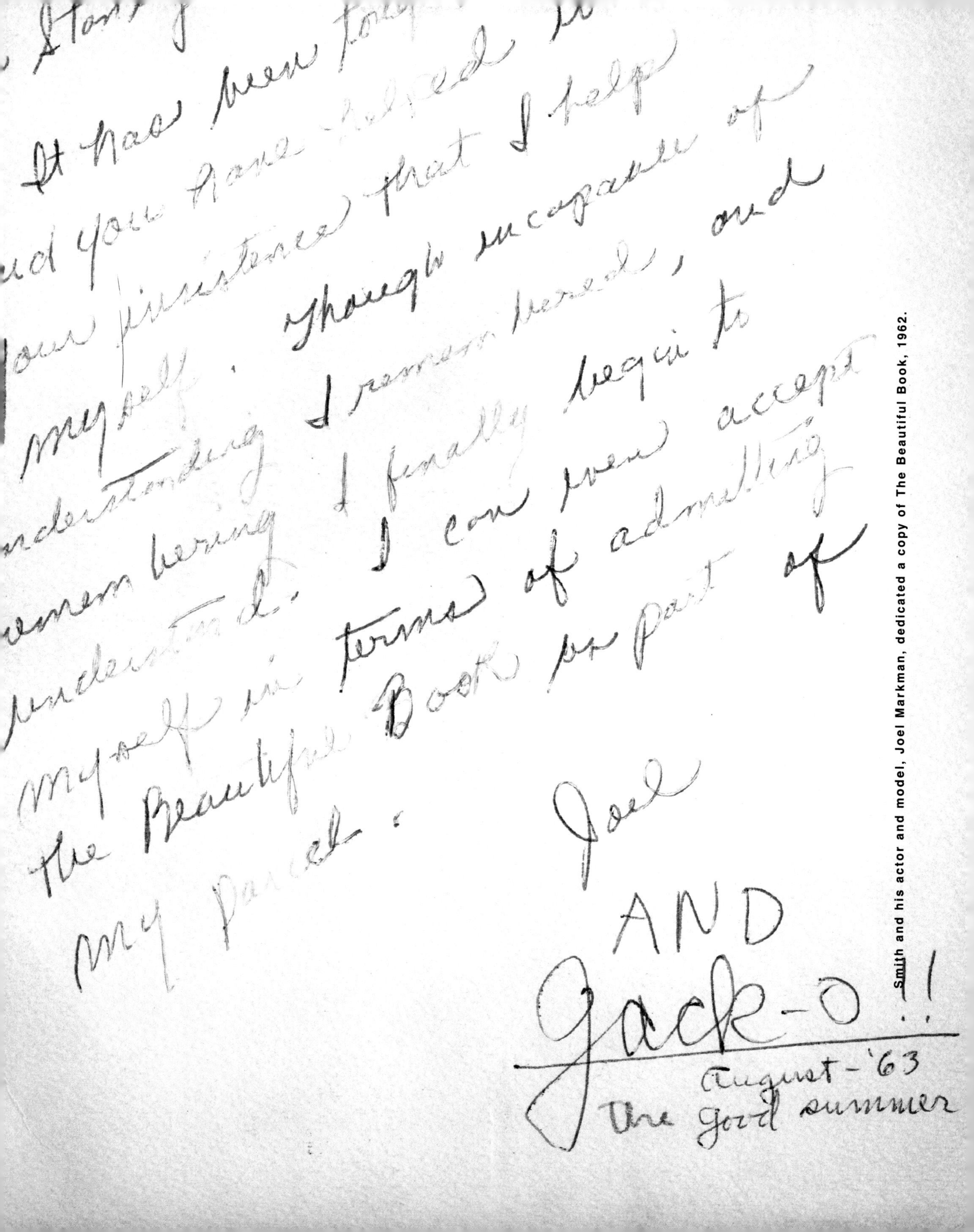

..., Stone J

It had been long ...
...d you have helped to
...our insistence that I help

myself. Though incapable of
understanding I remember therself, and
remembering I finally begin to
understand. I can even accept
myself in terms of admitting
the Beautiful Book or part of
my parcel.

Joel

AND
Jack-o !!
August - '63
The good summer

Smith and his actor and model, Joel Markman, dedicated a copy of The Beautiful Book, 1962.

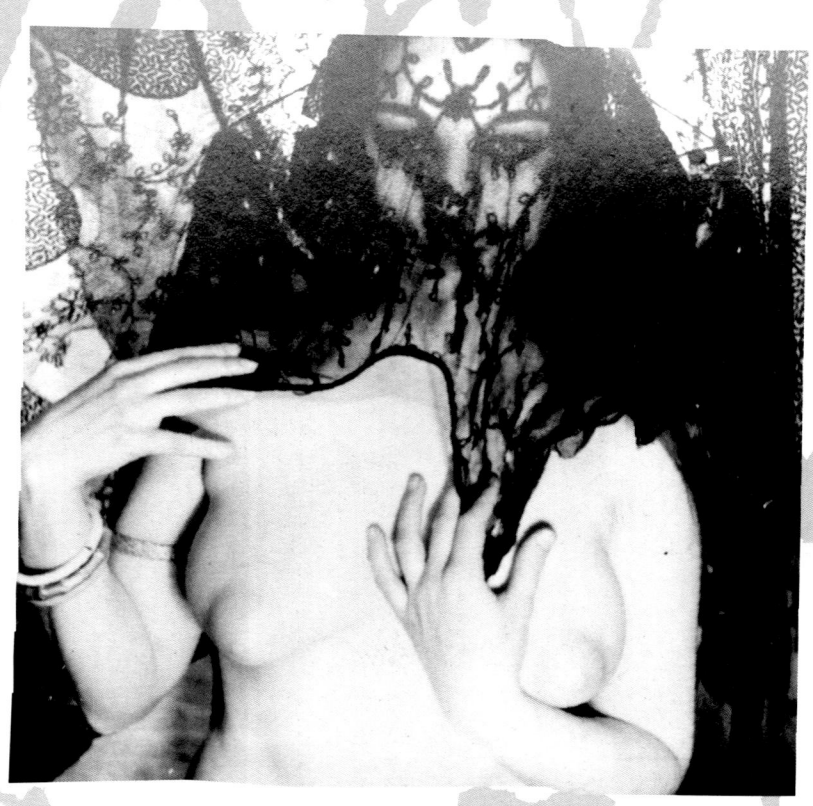
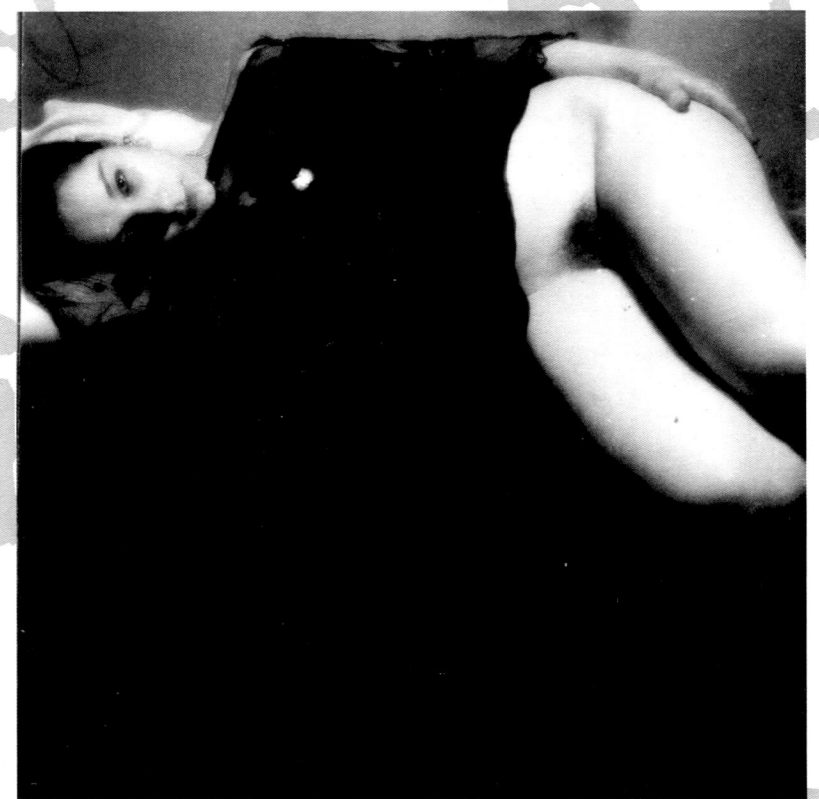

Smith's muse Marian Zazeela in tableaux photographs by Smith, c. 1961.

Smith greatly admired Sternberg's total devotion to visual effect, at the expense of plot, acting, or whatever else might get in the way of a compelling *visual* image. In his 1963 essay, "Belated Appreciation of V.S.," Smith wrote: "His expression was of the erotic realm—the neurotic gothic deviated sex-colored world and it was a turning inside out of himself and magnificent. You had to use your eyes to know this because the soundtrack babbled inanities—it alleged [Marlene] Dietrich was an honest jewel thief, noble floosie [sic], fallen woman, etc. to cover up the visuals. In the visuals she was none of those. She was V.S. himself. A flaming neurotic—nothing more nothing less—no need to know she was rich, poor, innocent, guilty, etc. Your eye if you could use it told you more interesting things (facts?) than those. Dietrich was his visual projection—a brilliant transvestite in a world of delirious unreal adventures. Thrilled by his/her own movement—by superb taste in light, costumery, textures, movement, subject and camera, subject/camera/revealing faces—in fact all revelation but *visual* revelation."[6]

In Smith's interior images from 1958-59, there is a strong flavor of Sternberg's cluttered, shallow space, his veils and mirrors, his chiaroscuro and dramatic overhead lighting, and his sense of theatrical body language and gesture. The space of Smith's images is literally heaped with people and props, and the only relief from the clutter is in the shadows cast from one object onto another. Film theorist Carole Zucker's observation on Sternberg's compositional technique applies equally to Smith: "In his films we become 'crowded out'; we are not invited in to look, but only to look in on the events....He disposes lines and shapes in the frame in a way that deprives human figures of their individuality and organic forms of their naturalness."[7]

In these photographs, too, Smith embraced the "trash" aesthetic that was to re-emerge to great effect in his later film and performance work. Jacobs, who claims to have awakened the previously fastidious Smith to the richness of this aesthetic of impoverishment, observed: "You see the actual, the banal, you see what you're stuck with and you also see the ideal. The humiliation of what you are and what you aspire to be makes the aspiration all the more glorious because there you are earthbound, and you don't have an open check-book like you would on a Hollywood set where everything you do becomes vapid and nothing. You actually get real drama."[8] Similarly, Irving Rosenthal, Smith's close friend and model, recalls: "All of us had an aesthetic at that time. It was that we didn't need Hollywood, the mass media, the academic poets; we didn't need any of that. We were all capable of producing art for each other, without any money, or without much money. We were really poor and it was alright to be poor. It was our aesthetic to use whatever was at hand. Everybody went out 'junking.'"[9]

Smith shared Jacobs and Rosenthal's appreciation for a culture of impoverishment and for the necessity to expose the sham conditions of the bourgeois cultural establishment. However, for Smith, the transformation of detritus into art was almost an alchemical ritual. The passion of his attraction to kitsch and trash is revealed in his adoration of the sets and decor of 1930s and 1940s Hollywood B-grade films, most importantly those starring the Dominican Republic-born actress, Maria Montez. "To admit of Maria Montez validities," Smith wrote, "would be to turn on to moldiness, glamorous rapture, schizophrenic delight, hopeless näiveté, and glittering technicolor trash!"[10]

Besides creating fantasies from assemblages of bodies and props, Smith also exploited the extreme close-up as a means of blocking out the coarse reality that might surround an otherwise exotic face. One photograph of Jacobs shot in Smith's apartment bathtub has all the watery mystery of an Odilon Redon pastel. *Ouled Naiel*, acquired by the Museum of Modern Art in 1960 and subsequently shown there in the exhibition "Recent Acquisitions 1960-61," is a tightly cropped image of a model costumed and made up to look like a North African dancing girl.[11] In another series of close-up portraits of the same model, and probably shot in the same session, Smith orchestrates pale yellow, magenta, bone white, and blue to create an effect of great subtlety, freshness, and allure.

Smith was a pioneer in the use of color in art photography. Certainly, a number of fashion photographers including Horst P. Horst, Irving Penn, and Cecil Beaton had been publishing successful color photographs for more than a decade; however, until the introduction of the type-c print in 1956, exhibitions of color photographs were virtually nonexistent. The type-c print transformed color photography from a specialized and expensive endeavor to one available to amateurs, artists, and large-scale commercial production. In the inaugural 1956 issue of *Popular Photography* magazine's Color Annual, the publisher and editor Bruce Downes wrote: "The age of color has shaken off its swaddling clothes and is on the verge of maturity."[12] Smith's first one-person exhibition, held in 1960, consisted of thirty large-scale color photographs.[13] In a remarkable debut for an unknown artist, this exhibition was held at the Limelight Gallery, one of the most prestigious photographic venues at the time, where such luminaries as Eugene Atget, Berenice Abbott, Henri-Cartier Bresson, Ansel Adams, and Paul Strand were regularly exhibited.[14]

Despite his early success with color, after 1961 virtually all of Smith's photography, with the exception of the photos used in his 1970s and 1980s slide shows, were black and white. This change may have been due to the termination of his employment at the Medo photo laboratory where he had been able to do his own color printing after hours. Smith continued to develop black and white prints in his apartment and, on occasion, had commercial prints made from color negatives.

Smith staged a series of photo sessions from late 1961 through the filming of *Flaming Creatures* in the summer of 1962 that resulted in many beautiful and evocative black and white images. He made numerous small-format prints from these sessions—most of them no larger than contact prints—which are among the few vintage Smith photographs to have survived. In 1962, Smith and Zazeela developed a layout of sixteen of these small prints intended for publication as an artist's project, *16 Immortal Photographs*, in Jonas Mekas's avant-garde film magazine, *Film Culture*. *16 Immortal Photographs* was intended to be a four-page magazine layout, each page containing four square black and white images abutted to one another to form a composite square centered on the page. Since Zazeela and Smith chose to reproduce a number of the photographs sideways, the overall composition on each page is extremely jumbled, forming a kind of abstract visual poem. Even in advance of the release of *Flaming Creatures* in 1963 and its resulting infamy, Smith and Zazeela were concerned enough with issues of decency and indecency to submit to *Film Culture* three additional pages of layouts that could be substituted, "in case you are afraid to print any of the pages with cocks cunts or other censorabilia."[15]

While *Film Culture* declined to publish *16 Immortal Photographs*, Smith successfully produced, with the poet Piero Heliczer's the dead language press, an artist's book titled *The Beautiful Book* in a limited edition of two hundred copies in late 1962.[16] *The Beautiful Book* consists of nineteen tipped-in black and white photographs. Among other precedents and possible influences are La Monte Young's *An Anthology*, a book collection of proto-Fluxus artists' projects that, according to Young, Smith helped to collate, and Wallace Berman's art and poetry magazine, *Semina*, the 1957 edition of which included hand-mounted black and white photographic images.

Roughly half of the photographs in *The Beautiful Book* feature the artist Marian Zazeela, and the cover design is based on one of her sketches. Smith, who met Zazeela through Rosenthal in the fall of 1961, quickly developed a passionate attachment to her, consciously modeling their relationship on that of Sternberg and Dietrich.[17] Indeed, there is a striking resemblance between Smith's photographs of Zazeela and Sternberg's film images of Dietrich. Whether seen in reflection, half hidden in shadow, covered by a veil or the fronds of a plant, Zazeela, like Dietrich, is often only partially revealed, an emblem of unattainable desire.

The Beautiful Book features a number of other models, including Mario Montez, Francis Francine, Joel Markman, and Arnold Rockwood (a.k.a. Pasty Arnold), who appear frequently in Smith's early 1960s photographs as well as in his films. From his earliest photo sessions in New York, Smith depended on this faithful coterie of models as well as on people he seduced or paid to participate for one shooting session only. The creatures, though, came and went, in part due to the vagaries of their own lives and in part due to Smith's notoriously harsh temper and demanding work ethic.[18] By the mid-1960s, many of Smith's models, whom he labeled as a group, the "Superstars of Cinemaroc" (his own imagined film studio), went on to become the superstars of Andy Warhol's Factory. Even Smith himself fell into Warhol's orbit, acting in an unreleased early film, *Batman/Dracula*. The term "superstar" as well as the very idea of Warhol's Factory—an avant-garde, Bohemian simulacrum of the traditional Hollywood studio, consisting of an ensemble of essentially replaceable stars and starlets presided over by a charismatic auteur—were appropriated by Warhol from Smith's Cinemaroc.

But unlike the archly passive and often invisible Warhol, who might make a film simply by turning on the camera and letting it run in front of some hapless subject, Smith's relationship to his models was highly engaged. Rosenthal, who, like Zazeela, began posing for Smith in 1961, recalls: "Jack's shooting sessions were transformative. He was a transformer of people who got the artistic effects that he got because he had the power of transforming, like a guru. Yes, he was creating works of art ... some of us at the shooting sessions understood that. But others came just because of his transformative power. The sessions were extremely arduous. Jack was always after the essence of his models. Kind of like a shrink. People would sometimes leave crying. You couldn't trust him. He was very cruel."[19]

While the psychological dynamics evident in Smith's photographs may appear hermetic, Smith himself seems to have enjoyed reading into his images and sequences his own idiosyncratic analyses. On the verso of a 1961 sequence of color photographs, Zazeela handwrote explanatory captions developed in collaboration with Smith. These brief texts provide fascinating clues into Smith's subtle reading of his own art. Titles provide

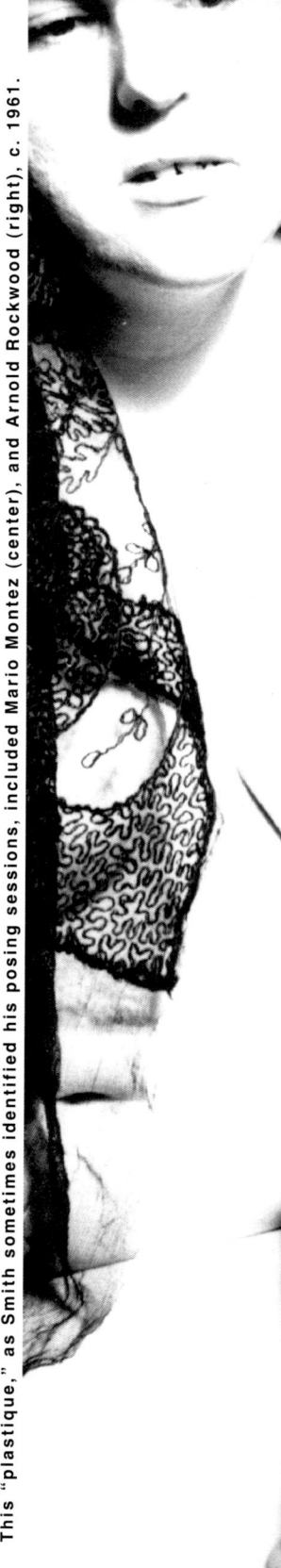

This "plastique," as Smith sometimes identified his posing sessions, included Mario Montez (center), and Arnold Rockwood (right), c. 1961.

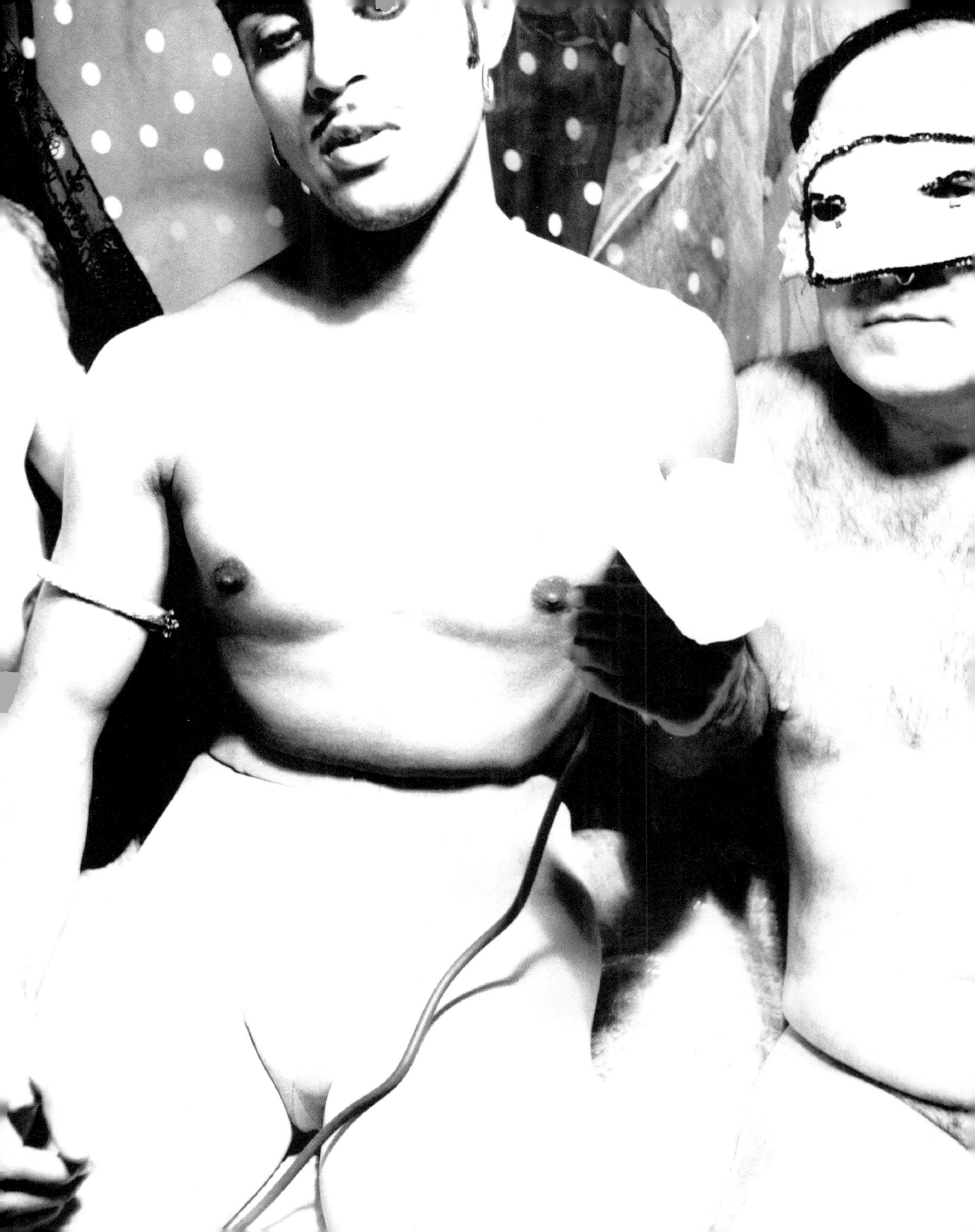

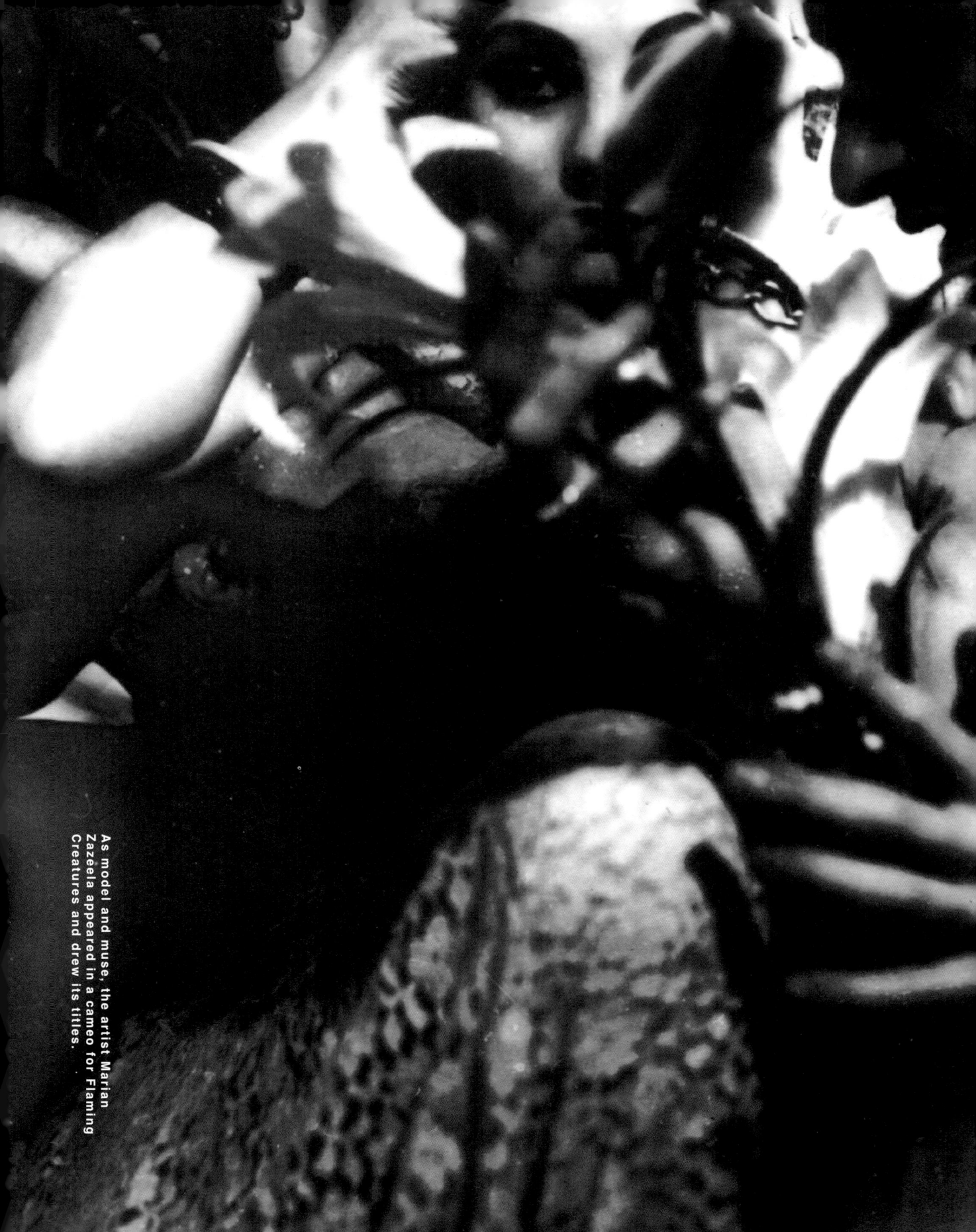

As model and muse, the artist Marian Zazeela appeared in a cameo for Flaming Creatures and drew its titles.

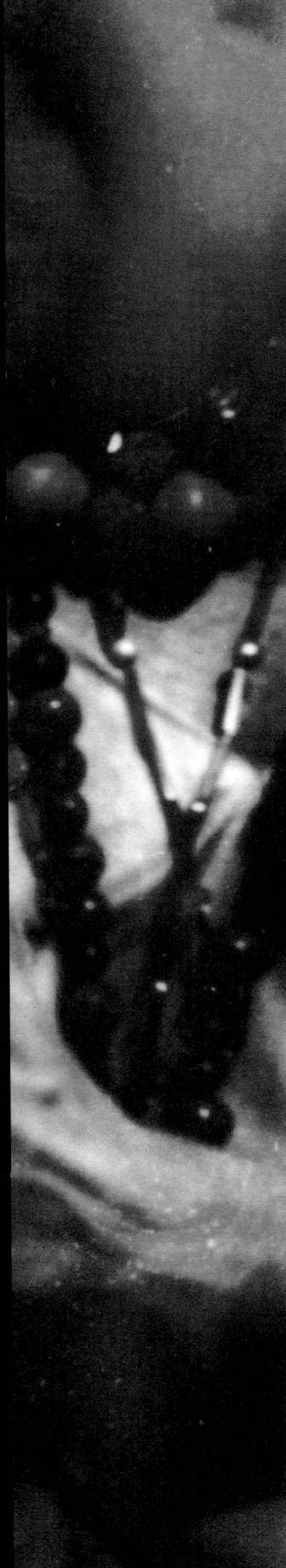

further access to his nuanced psychological sensibility, as in a layout of five photographs titled "Superstars of Cinemaroc," which Smith put together for Ira Cohen's literary magazine *Gnaoua #1* in early 1964. One image, for example, is given the rather baroque title *Mavis Davis at the moment she heard of her sister's spiral staircase miscarriage in a girls' school in Switzerland.*[20] Smith's creative textual glossing applied not only to his own work, but extended to found images as well: A glossy 8 x 10 publicity shot for the Maria Montez film, *The Arabian Nights*, was inscribed by Smith on the verso, "Surrounded by Stanleys Dreaming of Becoming Blanche," alluding both to characters in Tennessee William's play *A Streetcar Named Desire* as well as to Smith's own one-time lover who was named Stanley. Through Smith's eyes, the sheiks's mean scowls are transformed into the jealous yearnings of brassiere envy.

Smith's interest in the relationship between image and text extended to a project that appeared in the December 1974 issue of the art magazine *Avalanche*. This piece, titled "Fear Ritual of Shark Museum," is composed of photographs of Smith by Gwenn Thomas shot at the Cologne Zoo. Smith plays "Ronald De Carlo...the average person who, in everyday life of Lucky Landlord Paradise, is a postman of Lotusland."[21] While De Carlo delivers mail—"an art festival leaflet from the Museum of Death"— to an eagle and collects a rent check from a monkey, his cartoon-style thought bubbles muse on the corruption of establishment culture and the inequities of rent. Dressed in a Hawaiian shirt, cape, and ostrich feather hat, De Carlo is hardly your everyday Marxist ideologue but, rather, a character that suggests the ironic, flamboyant strategies of recent queer radicalism.

In 1966, Smith adapted his photographs to yet another interesting format, in this instance an "underground movie flip-book" titled "Buzzards over Bagdad," produced as a multiple for inclusion in a 1966 issue of *Aspen*. Known as "the magazine in a box," each issue of *Aspen* was designed by a different guest editor. The December issue was designed by Andy Warhol and David Dalton and resembles a box of Fab detergent. The flip-book can be flipped in either direction: in one direction is Smith's piece, "Buzzards," in the other is "Kiss" by Andy Warhol. On the first page of "Buzzards," Smith writes: "Meboubeh, the slave woman, lifts the artificial elephant off the love bandit's chair...and creates a pasty novelty." The sequence of images begins with a close-up of a rotating table fan. Then the camera moves back to reveal, standing on the right, The Love Bandit, and walking across from the left, Meboubeh. The camera zooms in as Meboubeh reaches down to lift an elephant tusk off a chair beside The Love Bandit.

The stark presentation of figures against a plain white background in "Buzzards over Bagdad" is characteristic of Smith's mid-1960s photography and represents a departure from the complex and densely detailed compositions he had been exploring since 1957. The dust jacket of Irving Rosenthal's *Sheeper*, for example, features a photograph by Smith of the author, in which the arabesque curves of Rosenthal's caftan and turban provide a simple counterpoint to the strange organic forms arrayed on and above his dressing table. Another image from the period shows a group of exotically garbed figures whose eccentric, high-contrast outlines echo the style of high-fashion photographers such as Cecil Beaton and Richard Avedon. Indeed, the writer Isabel Eberstadt recalls that around 1965 Smith greatly admired and was desperate to meet Avedon. She introduced the two at a party given by Truman Capote; Eberstadt recalls, however, that nothing came of it because Avedon found Smith to be unnervingly intense.[22]

The metamorphosis in Smith's photographic style parallels changes in his social and financial circumstances. By 1965, he had become "famous," in part due to the legal controversy surrounding *Flaming Creatures*, and was receiving a stipend from Eberstadt. Although he had always been interested in fashion photography, it was only as a foil against which to develop his own idiosyncratic style. By 1965, however, according to Eberstadt, Smith had become obsessed with the idea of publishing his fashion photographs in *Vogue*. Receiving no response to his submissions of material, Smith, in a final desperate move, marched into *Vogue's* offices to confront the magazine's editor, Priscilla Peck. Rebuffed, Smith followed Peck into the ladies room and barraged her with insults. He was not offered a contract. According to Eberstadt, it was Smith's mysterious, fog-shrouded full-length portraits of her with which he had hoped to catch the interest of *Vogue*. While Eberstadt looks conventionally fashionable in these photographs, Smith has nonetheless populated their peripheries with an assortment of his typically outrageous drag queens.[23]

Despite the changes in his style, when Smith was given a one-person photography exhibition in 1965, which he titled "The Great Pasty Triumph," at the Ferewhon Gallery on East First Street, he chose to include a large group of color images shot exclusively before 1962. Printed commercially at the time of the exhibition, approximately eighty of these 3 ¼" square photographs were mounted on 3 ½" white wooden cubes. According to an unpublished review of the show by critic Barney McCaffrey, they were "grouped in several series—each series in itself making an interesting geometric design. The groupings were based on subject matter—usually a group of shots taken at the same time in the same environment. Transition between the various series was based on several premises—philosophical (life to death), emotional (light to strong), personal (relationships of people in the photos to each other and to the photographer) and others such as color range, composition, etc."[24]

After 1965, Smith ceased creating photographs for display as artworks in themselves, but photography continued to play an important role in other aspects of his work. From the early 1970s through 1987, for example, Smith presented his photographs in the form of slide shows. These events, like his so-called expanded cinema screenings, were, in effect, multi-media performance pieces. They were remarkable for Smith's unique projection method and performance style. As the Brazilian artist Hélio Oiticica remembered: "the slides displaced ambience by a non-specific time duration and by the continuous relocation of the projector framing and re-framing the projection on the wall-ceiling-floor: random juxtaposition of soundtrack (records)."[25] Although others recall the relationship between the images and music to be much less random, all agree that these events were peppered with spontaneous interruptions and adjustments.

Another dimension of Smith's late photographic work is the large number of self-portraits, including conventional Hollywood-style head shots, costumed full-length poses, and collaged images in the style of film publicity shots. Jacobs recalls that in the late 1950s Smith considered trying to get work as a model, and the early portraits (some of which were shot by Jacobs) of a screen-idol-handsome Smith may derive from this abortive attempt at gainful employment. It is interesting, though, that Smith continued to have conventional head

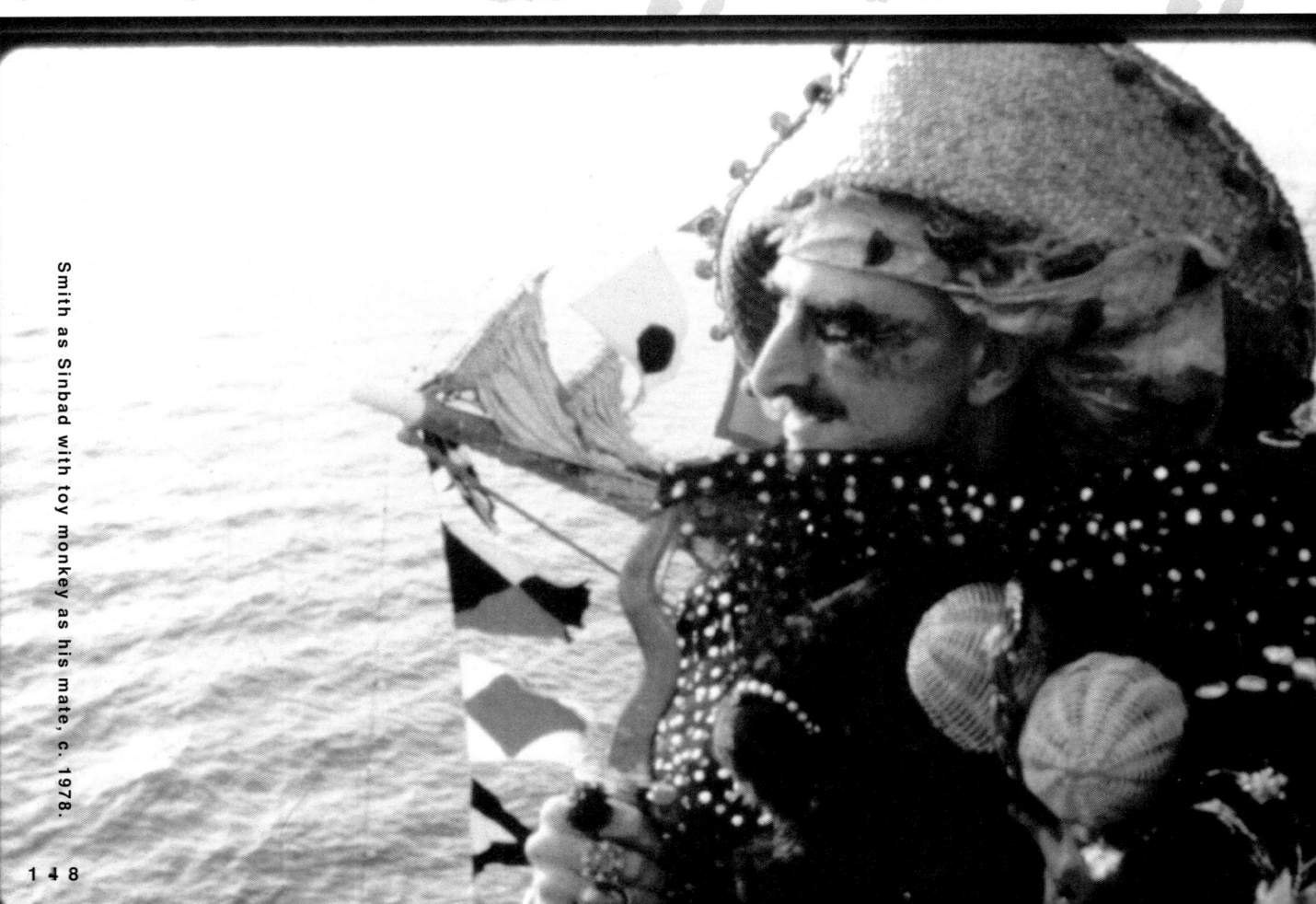

Smith as Sinbad with toy monkey as his mate, c. 1978.

shots of himself taken even into the 1980s, long after he had stopped scouting out modeling agencies.[26] Throughout the 1980s, however, he was more likely to invite friends to meet him for extended photo sessions in which he would pose in costume, in fabric-draped interiors or in outdoor locations.[27] Smith used these self-portraits primarily for publicity purposes, composing and re-composing them for various formats: flyers, posters, press prints, and newspaper ads. A number of the images were collaged onto backgrounds taken from stills or publicity shots from his favorite films. Re-photographing these collages, Smith was able to create an almost seamless impression of himself transported into various exotic fantasy realms.

Smith's photography was appreciated by few people during his lifetime. Rather, his reputation is based almost exclusively on his films and performances. Certainly his work in these media was profoundly influential, whereas his rarely shown photographs exerted little, if any, influence on other photographers. Today, exceedingly few vintage prints of Smith's photographs survive, the victims of loss, fire, and Smith's own predilection for con-

stant transformation and reuse of his materials. Luckily, many of his negatives do still exist, and, while we can generally only guess which images he would have chosen to print, how large he would have printed them, how—or if—they would have been cropped, and how the original color would have appeared, these negatives give us a fascinating view of the world as seen through by Smith's singular vision. His was a world of poverty and depravity suffused with glamour, sensuality, and drama, a debased world redeemed by art. Smith's belief in the power of art to counteract the evils of American society could be dismissed as naïve, romantic, and, indeed, maybe it was in social and political terms. Yet, the better world he imagined was not just an eccentric escapist fantasy. It was a reality that he brought into being with each click of the shutter. His images are object lessons in the survival of the creative spirit. Smith was one of those rare figures in the history of art in whom boundless imagination and originality is coupled with tremendous aesthetic refinement. And, it is above all in his photographs that the critical tension between flamboyance and precision is most profoundly achieved.

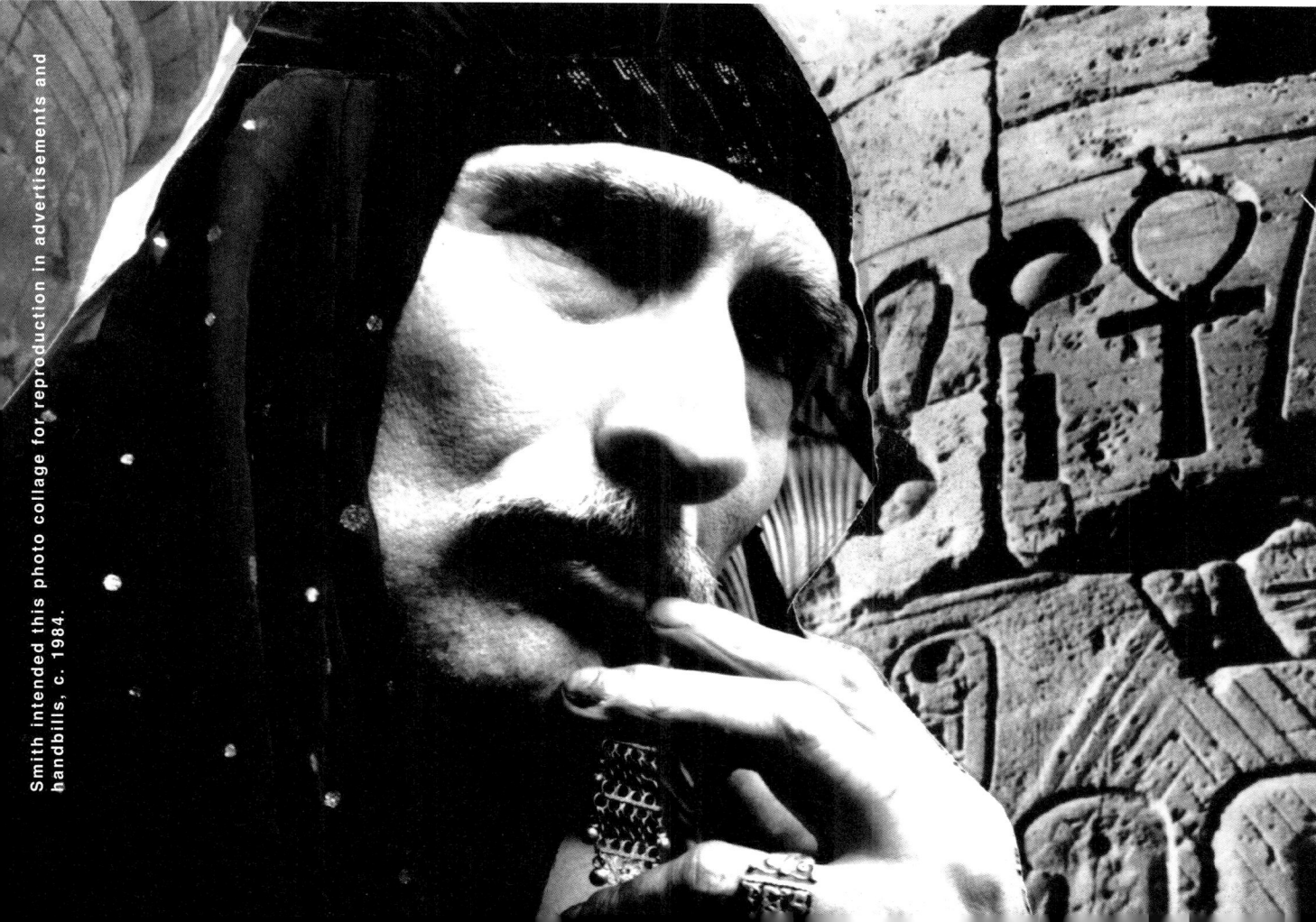

Smith intended this photo collage for reproduction in advertisements and handbills, c. 1984.

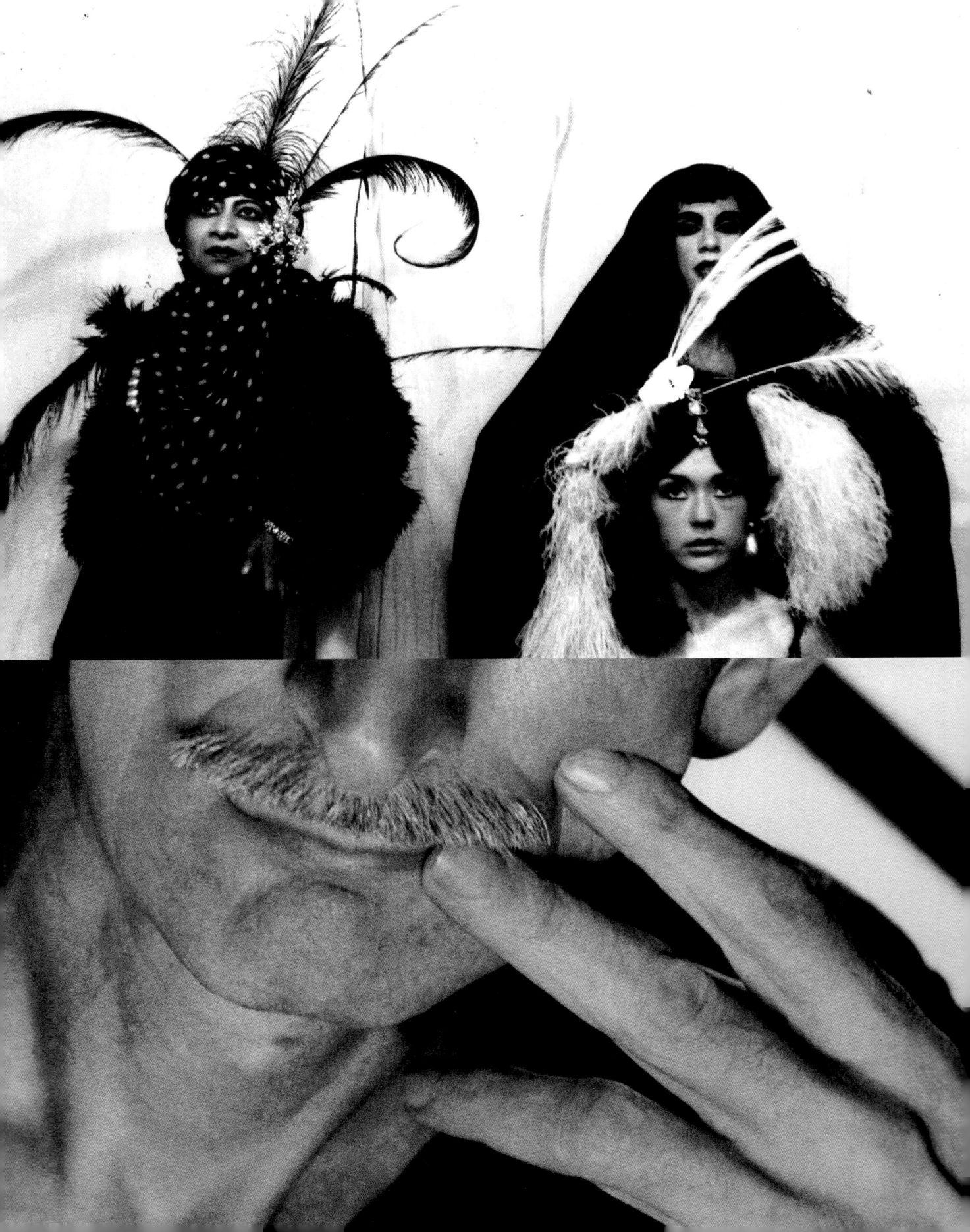

1. Jack Smith, "The Artist Versus the Hippopotamus," in *The True Comedy Planet*, no. 2 (December 20, 1988), pp. 3-4.

2. For Smith's explanation of his attraction to baroque art, see "The Artist Versus the Hippopotamus," in *The True Comedy Planet*, 1, no. 1, (September 20, 1988) and no. 2, (December 20, 1988).

3. Ken Jacobs, unpublished interview with the author, November 1, 1995.

4. In an unpublished November 1, 1995 interview with the author, Ken Jacobs recalled that Smith greatly admired Weegee's work. And in Patricia Bosworth's *Diane Arbus: A Biography* (New York: Alfred A. Knopf, 1984), p. 179, the author notes that "Jack Smith said he kicked Arbus out of his apartment when she persisted in taking his picture and pictures of his various costumes."

5. *Scene*, no. 2 (April 1962(pp.12-13. This issue of *Scene*, subtitled "Entertainments for Men," also includes reprints of articles by Art Buchwald, Evan Hunter, Ted Joans, and Steve Allen.

6. Jack Smith, "Belated Appreciation of V.S.," in *Film Culture*, no. 3 (Winter 1963-64), pp. 4-5.

7. Carole Zucker, *The Idea of the Image: Josef von Sternberg's Dietrich Films* (Rutherford, New Jersey: Fairleigh Dickinson University Press, 1988), pp. 26,40.

8. Jacobs, unpublished interview with the author, November 1, 1995.

9. Rosenthal, unpublished interview with the author, June 22, 1996.

10. Jack Smith, "The Perfect Filmic Appositeness of Maria Montez," in *Film Culture*, no.27 (Winter 1962-63), p. 28.

11. The Arabic term "*ouled naiel*" literally means a person from the Naiel tribe of Algeria; however, its most common usage is slang for a dancing girl or female prostitute.

12. Bruce Downes, "An Introduction to the World's First Color Photography Annual," in *Color Photography Annual* (New York: Ziff-Davis Publishing Co., 1956), p. 11.

13. Two of these works, mounted on cardboard and roughly 24" x 20", are in the collection of Irving Rosenthal.

14. The Limelight Gallery exhibition was organized by Lew Parrella, a part-time assistant to gallery director Helen Gee. The press release for the exhibition reads, in part: "Although Mr. Smith deals with recognizable subjects, his work represents a kind of photographic projection of an inverted eye. The viewer is at first shocked by the seeming incongruity of the objective aspects of the pictures: close-up exaggerations of mysterious-looking faces, trappings that smack of Moroccan motifs, exotic juxtapositions of figures and gestures surrounded by drapes and debris, all in particular and unnatural casts of color. Further contemplation of these strange images, however, and their effective communication with the viewer on a specific emotional level, testify to the surrealistic potential of the photographic medium when the medium is skillfully guided by a surrealistic imagination and artistry. Mr. Smith is quite successful in achieving his individualistic aims...Undoubtedly this show will stir up a little commotion among the so-called avant-garde in photography. But if Jack Smith's work is really appreciated, it will show up the great percentage of conservative and even dead imaginations that lurk under the guise of modern photography in this presumably mature era of the medium."

15. Marian Zazeela and Jack Smith, "16 Immortal Photographs by Jack Smith," project proposal (one-page xerox copy of type-written original, 1962).

16. A later, pirated edition of *The Beautiful Book* has a black cover and contains only eight prints.

17. Marian Zazeela, unpublished interview with the author, August 17, 1995.

18. Among the models Smith worked with from 1957 to 1961, were Francis Francine (a.k.a. Frank di Giovanni), Reese Haire, Louise Hines, Ken Jacobs, Ted Joans, Mario Montez (a.k.a. Rene Rivera), Linda Sheehan, Jerry Sims, Cecelia Swann, Linda Talbot, and Jimmy Walsh. After 1961, many of these dropped away and were replaced by others including Pasty Arnold (a.k.a. Arnold Rockwood), Susanna De Maria, Isabel Eberstadt, David Gurin, Piero Heliczer, Joel Markman, Doris Nieder, Jeanne Philips, Irving Rosenthal, and Marian Zazeela. Smith's intensely creative relationship with Ken Jacobs came to a halt in the summer of 1961 in Provincetown due to friction and misunderstanding following Smith's announcement of his homosexuality.

19. Rosenthal, unpublished interview with the author, June 22, 1996.

20. Jack Smith, photocopy of one-page holograph addressed to Ira Cohen, dated by Smith "Eighth Ocean," circa 1963.

21. Jack Smith, Gwenn Thomas (photographs) and Stephen Saban (mechanicals), "Fear Ritual of Shark Museum," in *Avalanche* (December 1974), pp. 26-27.

22. Isabel Eberstadt, unpublished interview with the author, April 22, 1996.

23. Ibid.

24. Barney McCaffrey, photocopy of "Review of the Jack Smith Photo Show 'The Great Pasty Triumph,'" March 8, 1965, p. 1.

25. Hélio Oiticica, *Hélio Oiticica* (Rotterdam: Witte de With, 1992), p. 180.

26. "He was into old," Jacobs recalls, "He was into the ravages of time on people's faces ... all the things they'd gone through. He would forever regret that people were trying to hide the effects of time on their face. He said that when he was old he was going to make himself available to photographers to use him however they wanted to use him." Unpublished interview with the author, November 1, 1995.

27. Among those who assisted Smith with his photography in the 1980s were Uzi Parnes, Ela Troyano, Michael Oppedisano, Charles Allcroft, Ivan Galietti, and Sheyla Baykal. Oppedisano recalls that on more than one occasion he responded to Smith's invitation to photograph him only to realize that Smith had not loaded the camera with film. Nevertheless, Smith insisted that they proceed with the shoot.

26. Unpublished interview with the author, June 17, 1996. Perhaps, it was not accidental that virtually all of the people Smith invited to photograph him during this period were involved in some way with performance art.

Mehboubeh (Jeanne Phillips), Susanna De Maria, and Mario Montez in an image related to Smith's No President used in the film's advertising, 1968-69.

the BIG HEAT

MAKING and UnMaking FLAMING CREATURES

- J. Hoberman

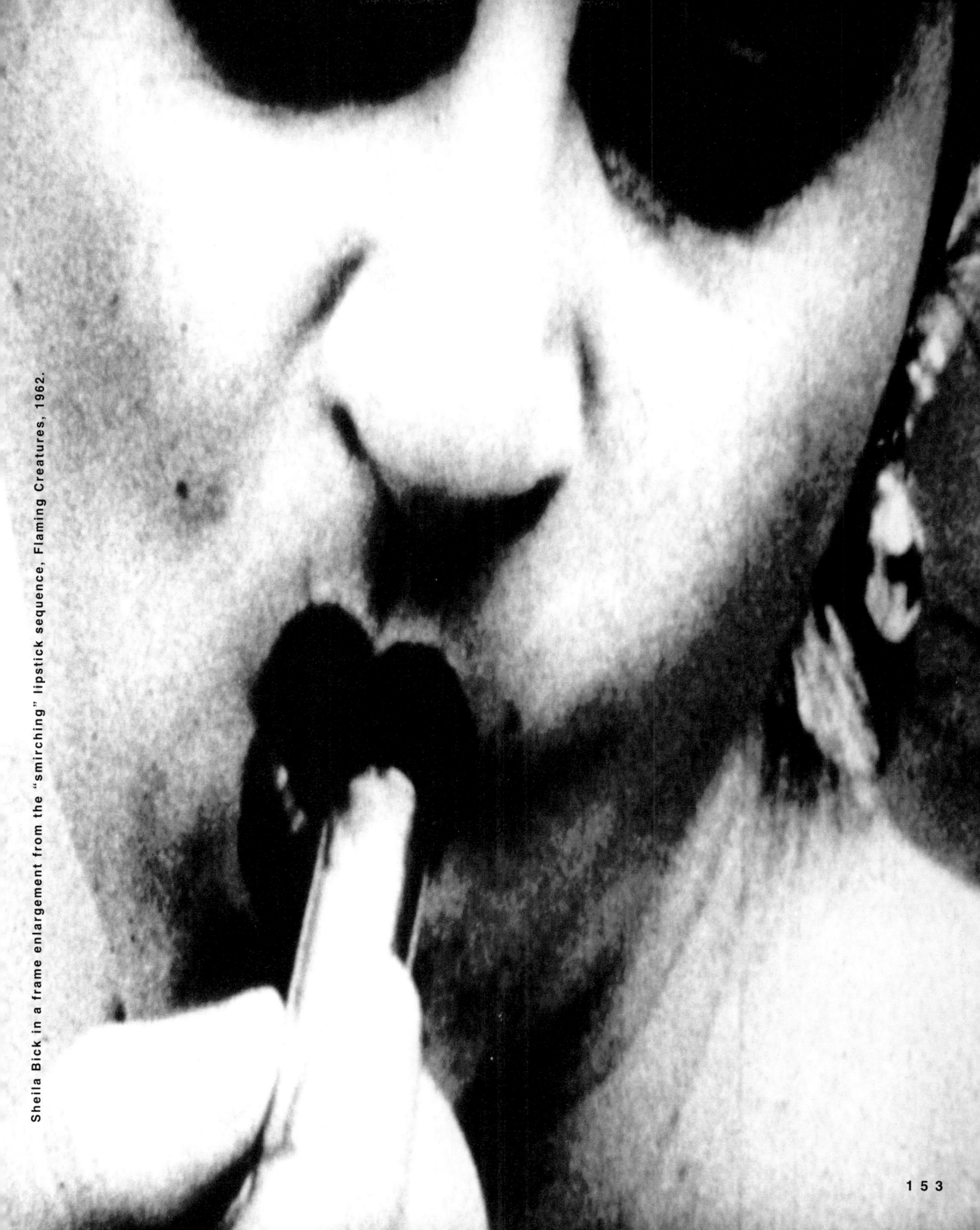

Sheila Bick in a frame enlargement from the "smirching" lipstick sequence, Flaming Creatures, 1962.

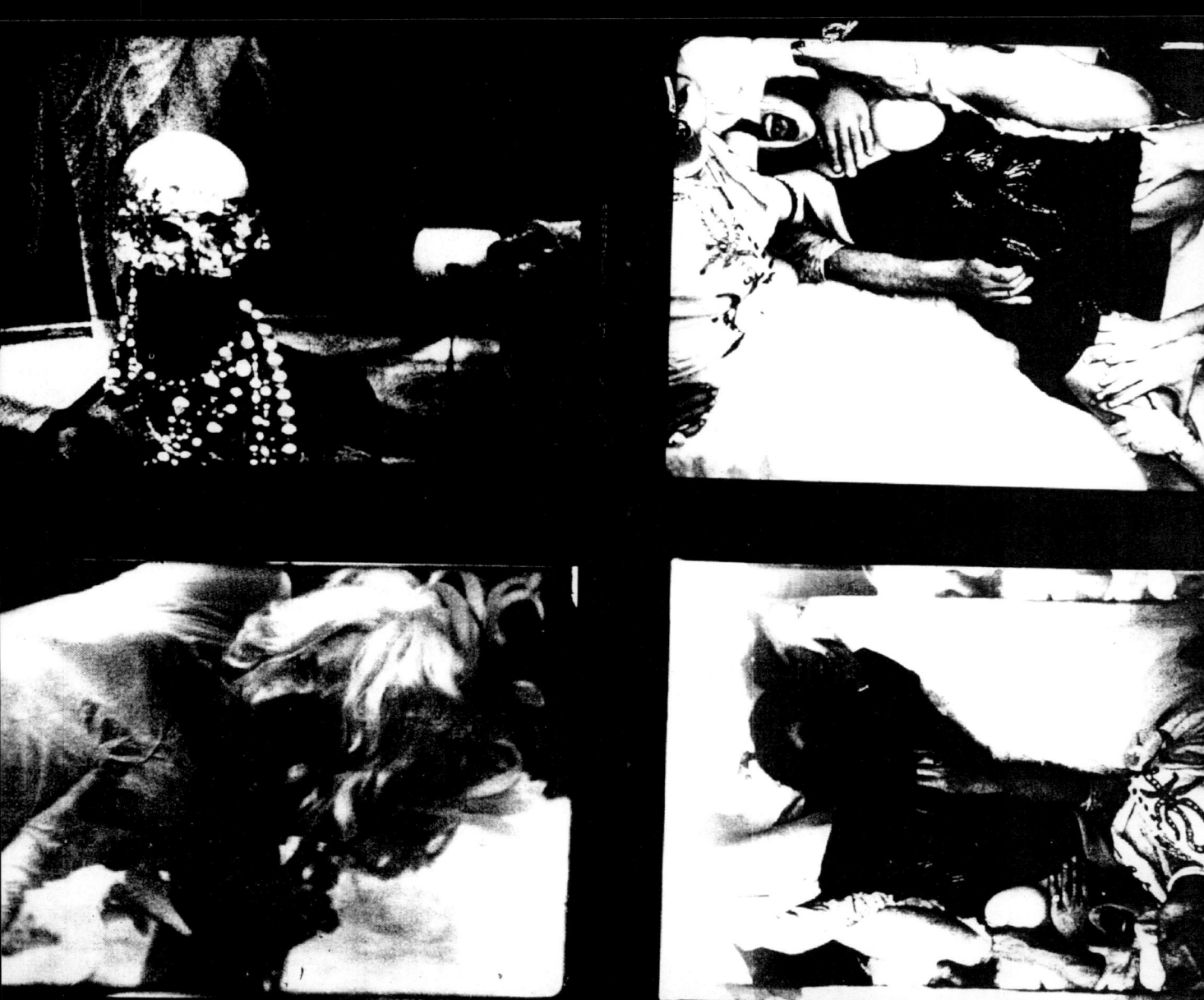

If you do not have an official intern-work program, would you please post this letter and the enclosed material on a bulletin board, so that interested students may apply to me personally.

Sincerely

Jack Smith

Summer 1962: Early intimations of the Orgy to come. Lee Harvey Oswald has returned to America from the Soviet Union. Students for a Democratic Society draft their Port Huron Statement. JFK sends troops to Ole Miss. The French leave Algeria.

That season as well, Jack Smith shoots the movie eventually known as *Flaming Creatures*—populating the roof of an ancient Lower East Side movie house with an assortment of neighborhood poets, painters, vanguard composers, communists, druggies, wild women, and homosexual men such as no Hollywood orgy-master, neither D. W. Griffith nor Erich von Stroheim, would ever use.

At once primitive and sophisticated, hilarious and poignant, spontaneous and studied, frenzied and languid, crude and delicate, avant and nostalgic, gritty and fanciful, fresh and faded, innocent and jaded, high and low, raw and cooked, underground and camp, black and white and white on white, composed and decomposed, richly perverse and gloriously impoverished, *Flaming Creatures* was something new under the sun. Had Jack Smith produced nothing other than this amazing artifice, he would still rank among the great visionaries of American film.

Flaming Creatures proposed an entirely new form of cine-glamour—one that owed everything and nothing to Hollywood's. This discontinuous, forty-two-minute succession of "exotic" tableaux, served with a rich stew of (mainly) dated pop music, is a cross between Josef von Sternberg at his most studiedly artistic (*The Scarlet Empress* or *The Devil is a Woman*) and a delirious home movie of a transvestite bacchanal—except that "transvestite" is not precisely the word for Smith's gang of Arabian odalisques, Spanish dancers, blonde vampires, and sultry beatniks (half naked, some actual women). Nor would Sternberg have had the radically pragmatic aesthetic daring to use grossly outdated black and white film stock and thus give his images the flickering ethereality of a world half-consumed in the heat of its own desire.

A burst of thrilling, pseudo-Oriental pageant music and a mysterious silvery screen: *Flaming Creatures* begins with an oblique evocation of Jack Smith's muse, the actress Maria Montez. The film's leisurely credit sequence is underscored by a three-and-a-half minute chunk of soundtrack lifted from the 1944 Montez vehicle *Ali Baba and the 40 Thieves*, replete with sonorous gongs and portentous drum rolls, and the hissed promise that "Today. . .Ali Baba comes today!"

As in the Montez movie, there is a sense of anticipatory tumult in the harem that, like all harems, implies the possibility of unlimited erotic pleasures. Amid light-struck close-ups of puckered mouths, wagging tongues, and—without any warning—a fondled penis, a variety of creatures rear up before the ornately-lettered titles, rendering these credits even more difficult to read. Performers dart back and forth. A masked man, burly and bare-chested, enfolds a woman in his cloak and—in reference to a similar move in Sternberg's *Shanghai Gesture*—ducks out of camera range to reveal the barely decipherable cast names for the third time.[1]

False starts are one of *Flaming Creatures*'s recurring formal devices. Having playfully delayed the action through the extension of the credits, Smith cuts to a middle shot of his star Francis Francine in brocaded turban and matching white gown rapturously sniffing a lily. A somewhat longer shot introduces Delicious Dolores, a dark and zoftig young woman in a clingy black slip and floppy hat (Sheila Bick), who is leaning back, hand on her head, before the

movie's single backdrop—a Whistleresque painting of an outsized white vase containing a generous sprig of what could be almond blossoms.

A 78 rpm recording of a soprano trilling the popular 1930s rhumba "Amapola (Pretty Little Poppy)" provides the accompaniment for Dolores's slow shimmy, her exposed back and ample backside turned to the camera. Francine waves and enters the frame. Suddenly lady-like, the pair flutter their fans, air kiss, and insincerely pinch each other's cheeks, turning away and back in synchronized disdain: which of the two is the "dainty little flower" celebrated by the song?

The record's end signals what Smith's journals term the "Smirching Sequence." Overhead shots showcase various creatures—including Francine, Dolores, and skinny, angular Joel Markman, here wearing a false nose and a ragged negligee—as they apply lipstick, sometimes in close-up, to the accompaniment of a convincing mock radio advertisement, complete with corny music, for a "new heart-shaped lipstick [that] shapes your lips as you color them." The illusion of an actual commercial is, however, shattered when Smith himself interrupts the genteel pitch-artist (Francis Francine) to wonder, "Is there a lipstick that doesn't come off when you suck cocks?"

This question (and Francine's prim answer, "indelible lipstick") precipitates a festive montage of hairy legs, waving penises, and rolling eyes. The background music continues, punctuated by the sound of amplified lip-smacks. All manner of unshaven mugs (photographed on a variety of film stocks) are seen, heads thrown back, studiously painting their smirched lips. Markman is concentrating with such intensity that he doesn't seem to notice the cock that coyly peeks over his shoulder. A brief tableau of half-naked bodies is followed by a somewhat longer shot of creatures collapsing in slow motion. After a static composition carefully framed to present us with the sole of someone's dirty foot, Francine is reintroduced in close-up, glaring at the camera as the high-pitched Japanese ballad, "China Nights," wells up on the track.[2]

In a paroxysm of jealousy or lust, Francine begins chasing Dolores. The cartoon quality of this undercranked (hence fast and blurry) pursuit is accentuated by being staged and cut to suggest several impossible vectors as the rival stars pass back and forth before the great vase. At last, Francine seizes Dolores from behind and hurls her to the ground. Dolores cries out or, perhaps, she only pretends to. Faintly dubbed screams are heard as her breast, rendered even more generous by the camera's proximity, bounces out of her gown. As a kind of visual joke, Smith here inserts a close-up in which Dolores more decorously undoes her strap, then cuts back as she is overwhelmed by a horde of amorous creatures.

As "China Nights" disappears mid-phrase, the cacophonous shrieks grow louder, mixing with an ominous thunder roll. The glass-paneled black lantern, another exotic knickknack that dresses the otherwise austere set, begins to sway as if in the first tremors of an earthquake. Dolores struggles. She beats her fan on the gang of creatures pinning her down, jiggling her breasts, poking their noses into her armpit, and otherwise exploring her person. She may even be screaming in earnest as her gown hikes up and the masked man of the credits (Arnold Rockwood) slithers forward on his stomach to work his head between her thighs. Orgy time! At this point, approximately halfway through the movie, the overhead camera begins to take part, flailing over a tangle of writhing bodies. A second creature—a skinny male, with a black wig and tatty slip—is held down beside Dolores and, feigning a campy panic, similarly ravished. The camera shakes; the earth moves; the lantern sways precipitously. Plaster dust cascades over the entwined creatures. Any single frame of the sequence is a dense arrangement of eyes, legs, hands, and genitalia. By way of a climax, Smith contrives a hyperkinetic close-up of one creature's furtive attempt to lick another's toe.

The debris seems real enough, although, as the writer David Packman has observed, the persistent, disembodied screams suggest the "grisly effect" of a Coney Island spookhouse. Abruptly, there is silence. The orgy is spent. Dolores staggers dramatically to her feet, accompanied by the austerely distorted strains of Bartok's "Concerto for Solo Violin," and promptly swoons backwards into the solicitous arms of the lithe and smiling Fascinating Woman (Judith Malina) who wears pearls around her neck and has a flower clenched between her teeth.

Petals rain upon the women as they kiss. A veil drifts idly in the breeze. For several minutes, the camera considers the empty space and a fly crawling on the wall. Presently, as if in response to country singer Kitty Wells's plaintive declaration that "It Wasn't God Who Made Honky-Tonk Angels," a wooden coffin is seen to open and Our Lady of the Docks (Joel Markman), a bewigged transvestite vampire clutching a lily in each hand, awakes and emerges. Picking her way through the wreckage—which includes the fallen lantern—and prowling among the comatose creatures, Our Lady kneels over Francis Francine's neck to feast. She attacks her victim, rolling her eyes back in sated delight. Church bells toll. Other eyes open in extreme close-up. It might almost be a moment from Sergei Eisenstein's *Ivan the Terrible*. Then, Our Lady lifts her dress and idly plays with her penis.

This resurgence of carnal interest, accompanied by the genteel strains of the Cuban bolero "Siboney," another 1930s standard, has a restorative effect. The creatures rise. The seraglio stages a carnival. Our Lady foxtrots with Francine—charmingly, neither seems certain which one of them should lead. This sequence, which, at seven minutes, is the movie's longest, is extensively edited and certainly combines several shooting sessions. As the camera whirls overhead, Our Lady can be seen dancing with at least two other people—one, the poet Ed Marshall; the other, an actual woman. Both are wearing Francine's distinctive turban and matching dress. (The costume, Smith often said, was the character. The actor only brings it to life.)

Like a Busby Berkeley musical, *Flaming Creatures* ends with an extended series of ensemble and solo dance numbers. Here, as throughout, the participants are cropped by Smith's hand held camera in unexpected ways. A sailor, apparently picked up that day and brought to the set, looks on bemused as a creature in a flat-brimmed hat and blackface (Piero Heliczer) skips from side to side in a sort of capering hornpipe. Our Lady is transfixed by a lily. The camera, similarly fascinated, investigates an armpit. Then, with a blast of bullfight music, and after one false start, the regal, giggling Spanish Girl (Mario Montez) twirls across the set.
As the bullfight music mixes with "Siboney" and an Italian aria, the screen is packed with all manner of dancing creatures, dappled by moving shadows and cascading streamers to suggest the Mardi Gras revelers in Sternberg's campiest Dietrich vehicle, *The Devil is a Woman*. This cavorting is intercut with a mock Delacroix tableau displaying an impassive odalisque (Marian Zazeela), her arm languidly resting on her head and one breast exposed. She is surrounded and cushioned by a cluster of mock Arabs (Irving Rosenthal, Marc Schleifer, La MonteYoung), one of whom solemnly points to her nipple.

Ending as leisurely as it began, *Flaming Creatures* offers several minutes of curtain calls. In poignant silence, the Spanish Girl spins like a dervish and Our Lady extravagantly smokes a cigarette. Then, one final surprise: an incongruous burst of the Everly Brother's version of the teen-anthem "Be-Bop-a-Lula" as a flurry of last-minute kisses and swoons gives way to a shot of a leg dangling a high-heeled pump, the image of Our Lady being groped, an inverted flower, the end title, and a final close-up of a jiggling breast.

Flaming Creatures is both placeless and timeless. The setting could be anywhere. The action might have erupted at any previous moment in movie history from *Intolerance*'s 1916 Hollywood Babylon through Busby Berkeley's closed slave-market set in *Roman Scandals* (1932) to the pad upstairs from the cold-water studio in Robert Frank and Alfred Leslie's *Pull My Daisy* (1959). Nevertheless, like Jean-Luc Godard's more conventionally macho *Breathless* (1959) or Bruce Conner's found-footage assemblage *A Movie By Bruce Conner* (1958), Smith's film, which he later described as taking place in a haunted Hollywood studio, was evidence of a new cinematic self-consciousness.

Smith himself was a movie cultist. His aesthetic manifesto, "The Perfect Filmic Appositeness of Maria Montez," written as he was shooting *Flaming Creatures* and published in the winter 1962-63 issue of *Film Culture* while he edited the movie, proposes a realm of "secret-flix." Drawn almost entirely from the period of Smith's youth, this personal canon mixes horror films and mysteries (Bela Lugosi vehicles, the Bob Hope spookhouse comedy *The Cat and the Canary*, Gale Sondergaard as the Spider Woman), with musicals (Busby Berkeley's *Hollywood Hotel*, Vincente Minelli's *The Pirate*, and anything with a production number set in Rio de Janeiro), swashbuckling "Spanish Galleon flix" and exotic "Dorothy Lamour sarong flix," singling out two utterly dissimilar stars, hillbilly comedienne Judy Canova and Universal's "Queen of Technicolor" Maria Montez.

Having absorbed this Hollywood poetry as a child, Smith had tried, since his adolescence, to bring it back to life. Ken Jacobs, Smith's most crucial aesthetic cohort during the late 1950s, recalls seeing "the charming, all-heart 8mm movie [Jack] shot in his early teens, *The Saracens*, for which his mother had sewn costumes for the neighborhood kids and in which the roofs of neighboring suburban homes loom clearly over the strung cloths penning in his Bagdad." *The Saracens*' inadvertent documentary aspect naturally appealed to Jacobs. Indeed, it was largely through his association with Jacobs, who was similarly fascinated by mass culture detritus, that Smith came to appreciate the pathos of the Hollywood illusions which obsessed him.[3]

Throughout 1958 and 1959, Smith appeared as the primary figure in Jacobs's still-unfinished epic, *Star Spangled to Death*, and in its unedited (or rather, edited-in-camera) spinoff, *Little Stabs at Happiness*. Both films were shot on the roof and in the courtyard of the West 75th Street apartment building where Jacobs was employed as superintendent—as well as in various New York junkyards and construction sites. In early 1959, Smith collaborated with Bob Fleischner, the City College student who had introduced him to Jacobs, on a "comic horror film." This abandoned project, edited by Jacobs the following winter into a portrait of Smith,

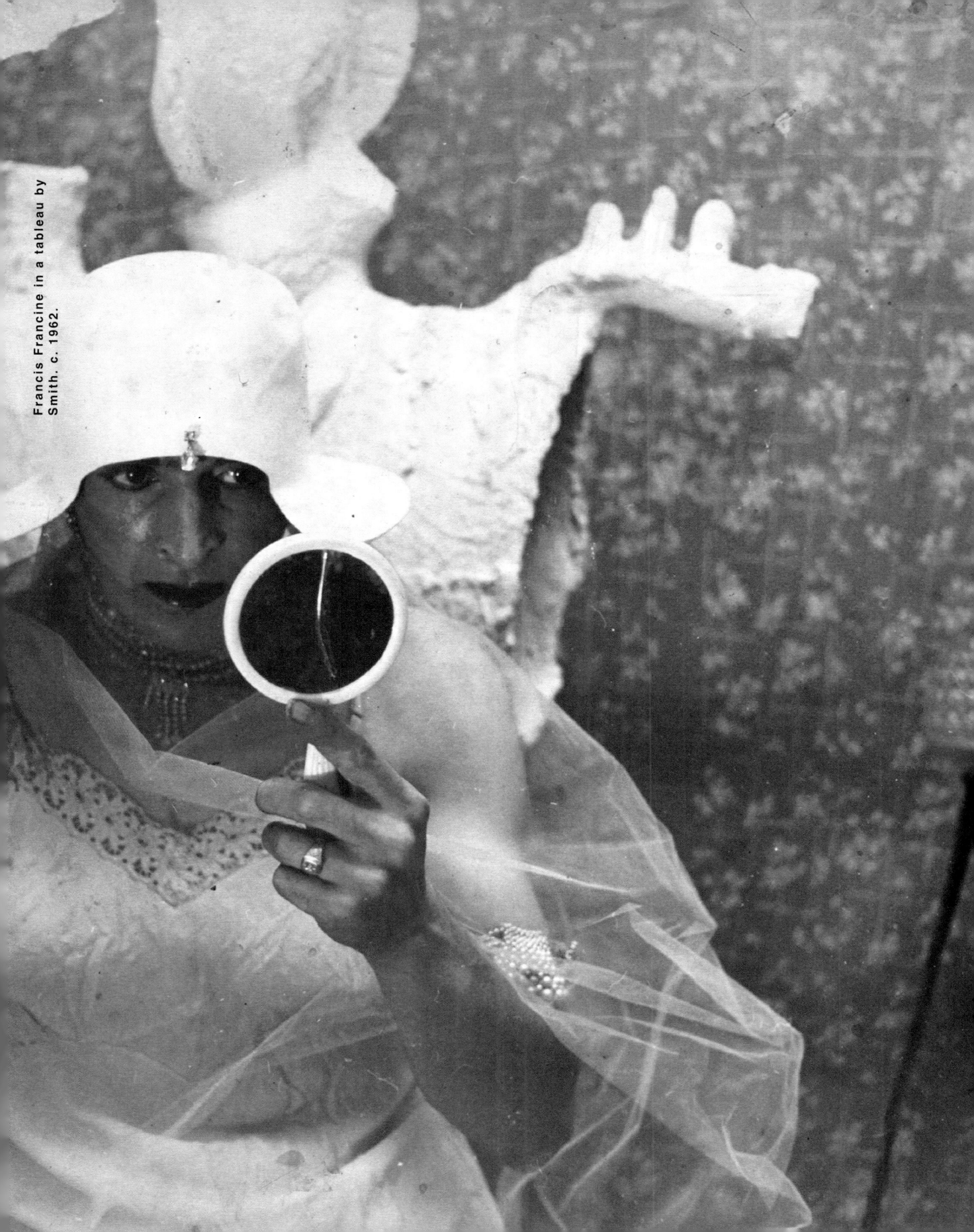

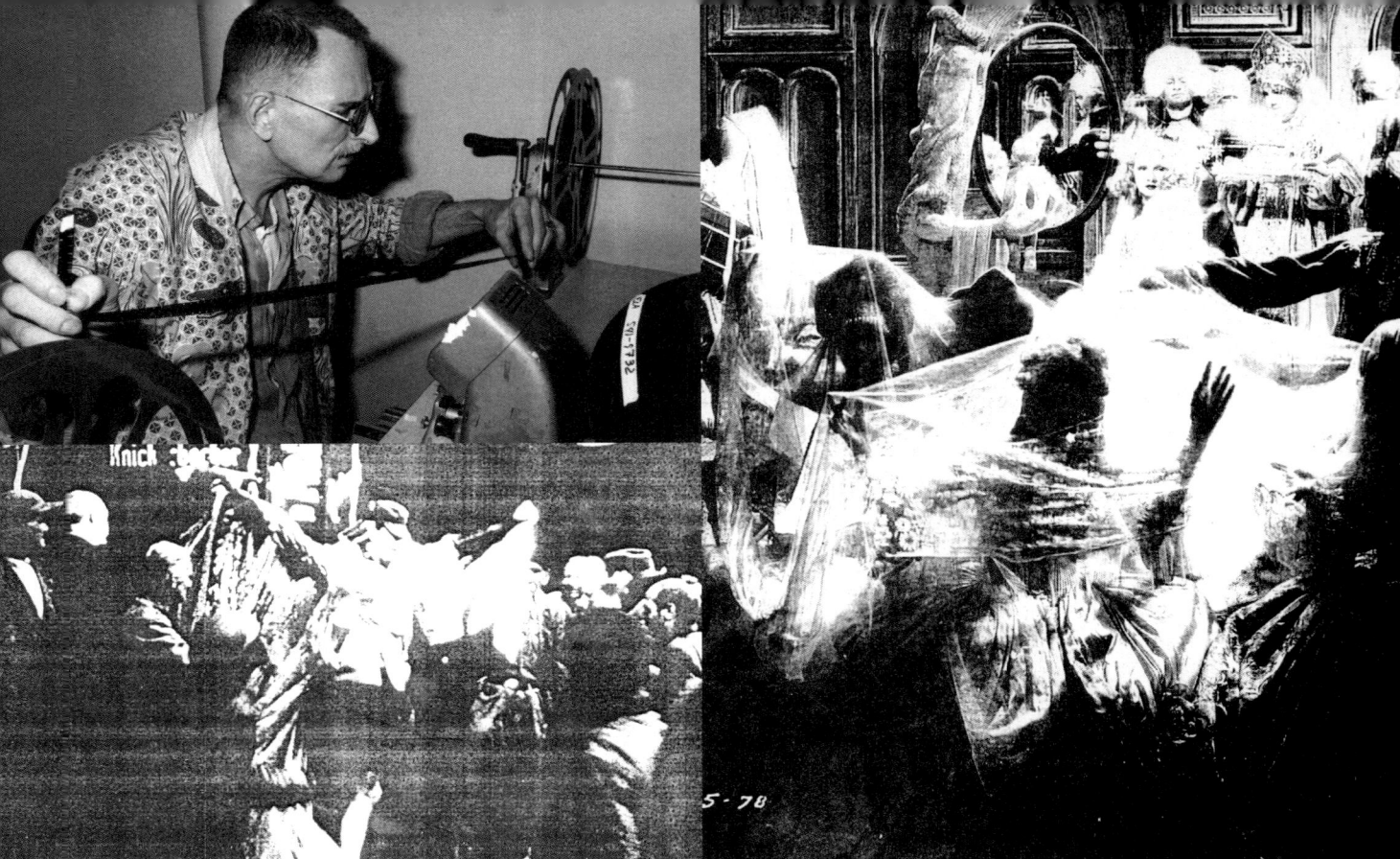

would be known as *Blonde Cobra*, conflating the titles and the divas of two favorite Smith movies, Sternberg's *Blonde Venus* and the Montez vehicle *Cobra Woman*.

Although Smith was then primarily preoccupied with photography, he also made two short 16mm films. The first, *Scotch Tape*, was a single hundred-foot roll of Kodachrome shot in 1959, using Jacobs's Bell & Howell at one of Jacobs's locations—the rubble-strewn site of the future Lincoln Center. The movie was titled after the dirty piece of stickum that had wedged itself inside the camera gate and was thus printed in one corner of the frame throughout the film.) *Overstimulated*, Smith's second, somewhat longer film, shot in black and white in his Lower East Side apartment, features Fleischner and Jerry Sims (a favorite Smith model, also prominent in *Star Spangled to Death*) wearing long, filmy dresses and jumping up and down in front of a flickering television set.

It was during this period that Smith saw the artist Joseph Cornell's brilliantly fetishistic transformation of one of Cornell's secret-flix. To make *Rose Hobart*, Cornell had distilled and reshuffled footage from the 1931 exotic adventure *East of Borneo* into a new and non-linear film which he titled after *East of Borneo*'s female star. Jacobs, working sporadically as Cornell's studio assistant, borrowed *Rose Hobart*'s spliced original as well as the "Holiday in Brazil" record album that served as musical accompaniment. Jacobs held onto the Cornell film, which had not been publicly screened since its December 1936 premiere at Julien Levy's gallery, for over a year while he and Smith subjected it to careful study. "We looked at it in every possible way: on the ceiling, in mirrors, bouncing it all over the room, in corners, in focus, out of focus, with a blue filter that Cornell had given me,

without it, backwards. It was just like an eruption of energy." As film critic and historian P. Adams Sitney was the first to point out, *Flaming Creatures* can be seen as a version of *Rose Hobart*, in which Hollywood secret-flix fantasies are restaged rather than re-edited.[4]

Jacobs and Smith made their last film together, *The Death of P'Town* and had their final falling out during the summer of 1961. That fall, Smith met the young painter and recent Bennington graduate Marian Zazeela through his friend, writer Irving Rosenthal. Zazeela was the most important female model in the series of photography sessions Smith staged weekends from late 1961 through June 1962 at his Lower East Side apartment—tableaux that featured a number of *Flaming Creatures*'s subsequent participants (including Francis Francine, Mario Montez, Joel Markman, Ronald Tavel, and David Gurin).

Elsewhere in the neighborhood, a pair of young film buffs—Walter Langsford and Ed Stein—had assumed the lease on the Charles, a moldering 700-seat movie house on Avenue B, a few blocks north of Tompkins Square Park. Langsford and Stein recruited Jonas Mekas, *Film Culture* editor, *Village Voice* film critic, and Film-Makers Cooperative cofounder, to organize a series of one-person shows for avant-garde filmmakers. In addition to these, Mekas suggested that the Charles begin monthly open screenings where young and unknown artists might show their work. Admission to these shows, which was ninety-five cents for one movie, began in early 1962 with a crowd of hungry filmmakers lined up around the block and culminated in July with a grand competitive festival.

Smith recalled this time as a Golden Age that ended only "when the ecstasy got out of hand and it became difficult to

baroque compositions, costumes, and excessive effects of Hollywood's glittering productions, such as Joseph von Sternberg's The Scarlet Empress, 1934 (left), and Erich von Stroheim's The Wedding March, 1928 (right).

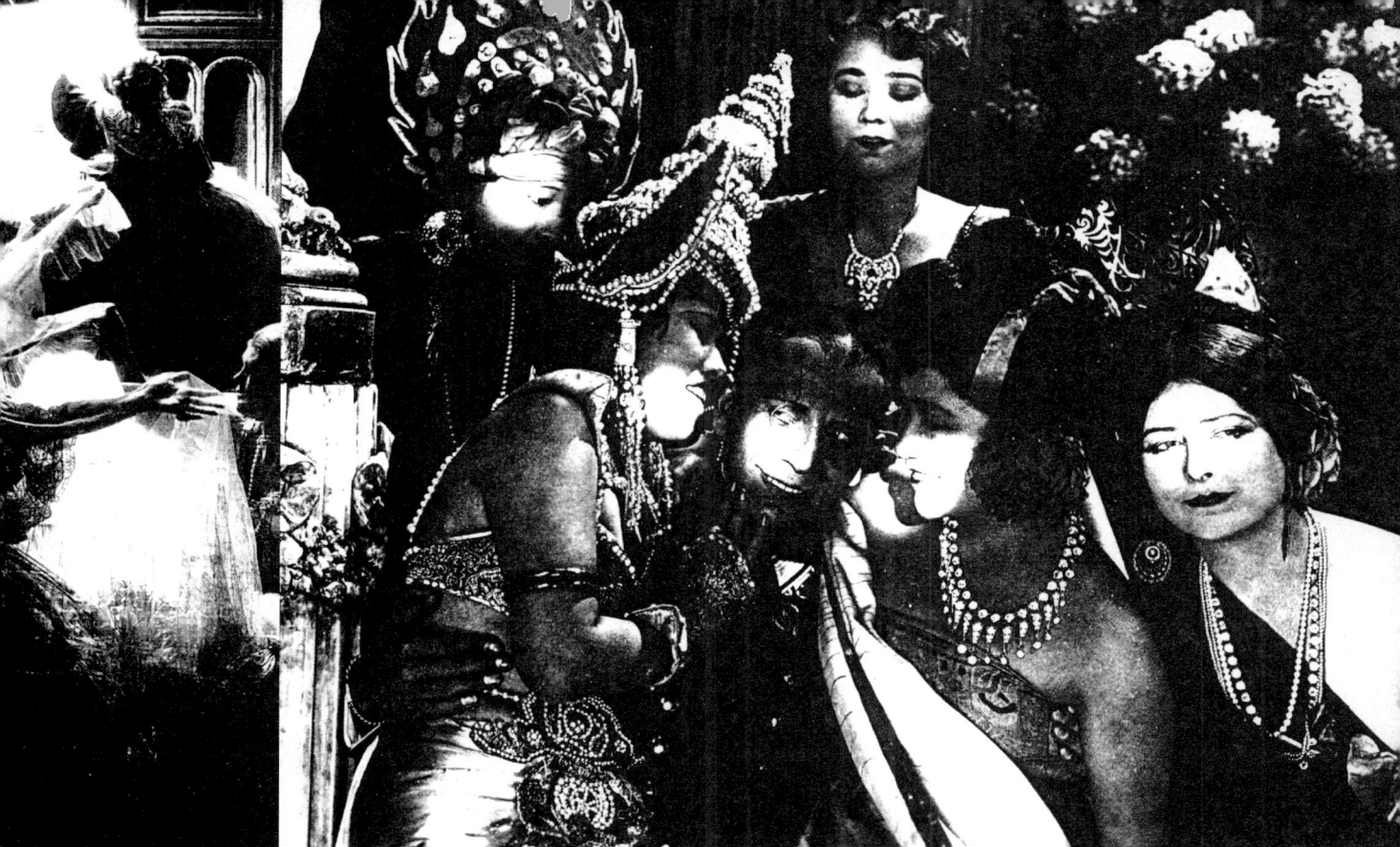

Smith's passion for film carried him from appearances as an actor, here in scenes from Ken Jacobs's Star Spangled to Death, 1957–60 (bottom left), to editing on the movieola at Millennium, c. 1984 (top left). He admired the

collect admissions because of the confusion between film-makers and audience." Jacobs's *Little Stabs at Happiness*, shown anonymously at the Charles to the accompaniment of several ancient 78 rpm records, attracted Mekas's attention, as did *Scotch Tape*. Indeed, Smith later wrote that *Flaming Creatures*'s polymorphous spectacle was specifically made for the Charles, a kindred exercise in ecstatic confusion, intended to be projected on the big movie screen for the delectation of the hip and rowdy Lower East Side audience that frequented the theater.

A synthesis of Smith's photographs, fantasies, and recent film experiences, *Flaming Creatures* was initially conceived as a vehicle for Marian Zazeela. However, Zazeela's meeting and subsequent involvement with the composer La Monte Young precluded her participation: "I had to spend night and day with La Monte," she later explained. Thus, "La gran estrella Maria [sic] Zazeela," as she is known in Smith's journal, was replaced by another Lower East Side ingenue, Sheila Bick.

The musician and future filmmaker Tony Conrad, a disciple of Young's who had just graduated from Harvard, was invited to stay at Zazeela's vacated East 9th Street studio. There, in the early summer, he discovered Smith installed and in the process of assembling *The Beautiful Book*, a collection of photographs which Conrad deemed "some kind of bizarre, contemptible New York art pornography."

By his own account, Conrad initially regarded his eccentric roommate with some condescension. "I found Jack one day working on a gigantic gray painting of a vase of flowers, maybe nine feet square. "How marvelous," thought I, ironically, "a vase of flowers" "Oh, uh, Jack, what is this?"

Jack said, "'It's the set for my new movie.'"

Although "still at this point quite unimpressed," Conrad, nevertheless, offered to help Smith transport the painting to his movie's location, shlepping it a dozen or more blocks to the leaky, tar paper roof of the Windsor Theater at 412 Grand Street, where *Flaming Creatures* was staged and shot over the course of eight or so weekend afternoons throughout the late summer and early fall.

Having established the Charles as an ongoing concern, Walter Langsford had acquired the venerable Windsor (said to be the city's oldest movie house) with an eye to expanding his Lower East Side exhibition empire. Photographer/filmmaker Dick Preston, who produced some animated collage trailers for the Charles, took the unfinished loft above the theater as his studio. This space, which overlooked and opened onto the Windsor's roof, served as *Flaming Creatures*'s dressing room and prop department, as well as providing a physical support for the painted backdrop Conrad helped carry to the set.

On his first visit to the Windsor roof, Conrad discovered that "there were lots of weird substances being consumed and strange people arriving on the scene…And boy, was I surprised when it turned out that people took three hours to put on their makeup; I was very more surprised when people took several more hours to put on their costumes." Conrad's ultimate surprise came when, after assigning him a dress to wear, Smith "ripped it down the back to expose my ass and turned my back to the camera.."

When, in "The Perfect Filmic Appositeness of Maria Montez," Smith wrote that film is "a place where it is possible to clown, to pose, to act out fantasies, to not be seen while one gives (Movie sets are sheltered, exclusive places where nobody who doesn't belong can go)," he was, in a sense, describing the making of *Flaming Creatures*. The two-story Windsor was flanked by higher buildings which, as old-law tenements, had no side windows. Thus, the lengthy preparations and riotous goings on involved in the production of the movie were only visible from an adjacent roof, several stories up. (Preston remembers sporadic complaints, but no actual disturbances.)

Production photographs reveal *Flaming Creatures*'s sheltered, if not shaded, open-air set to be a secluded, surprisingly small space—marked by a painter's dropcloth estimated by one participant as only ten by fourteen feet—not unlike the courtyard used by Ken Jacobs for *Star Spangled to Death*. A ladder, supported at a slight angle by a seven-foot step ladder and the roof of Preston's loft, provided a hook for the glass lantern and served as a rickety catwalk for overhead shooting. Smith not only directed *Flaming Creatures* but, using available light (if not a light meter), filmed the action himself. His sole credit is "Photographer" and he can be seen, in one of the photos, holding a 16mm Bolex with three lenses.[5]

Conrad's recollections suggest that *Flaming Creatures*'s lengthy Mardi Gras sequence was, in fact, the first section of the film to be shot, although, by all accounts, Smith took great care in preparing for each shooting session. Preston, an observant non-participant, was surprised at how "orderly" and "businesslike" the production actually was. Although he could not imagine a finished film emerging from such primitive conditions, he recalls being struck by the actors' "reverence" for Smith.[6]

Ronald Tavel, who crouched on the catwalk pouring plaster dust down on the actors while Smith filmed the rape-earthquake-orgy, cites the solemnity with which one of the women was filmed partially nude. Other participants remember an altogether more delirious environment. By Joan Adler's account, the orgy was shot "in broiling sunlight with the set falling all over [the performers] high as kites, Jack pouring ceiling plaster all over them (a large chunk bruised Frankie, who got mad telling about those sufferings too) and careening dangerously above on some swinging, homemade contraption."[7]

While it would surely be an exaggeration to describe *Flaming Creatures* as having been created in a state of stoned ecstasy, the participants were scarcely innocent of New York's still underground drug culture. Marijuana, cocaine, and methamphetamine were at various times used on the set; one participant recalls that the husband of a leading actress was arrested for cocaine manufacture at the time of the filming.

According to Tavel, *Flaming Creatures* was originally to be called *Pasty Thighs and Moldy Midriffs*. (Alternate titles gleaned from Smith's journal include *Flaking Moldy Almond Petals*, *Moldy Rapture*, and *Horora Femina*.) By summer's end, the title was definitely *Flaming Creatures*. Zazeela, who painted the film's spidery credits, consented to pose for one sequence. In late September, after the Mardi Gras and rape-earthquake-orgy scenes were filmed, she arrived at the Windsor accompanied by La Monte Young and Irving Rosenthal.

The *Flaming Creatures* shoot extended well into October. Judith Malina, the co-founder of the Living Theater, remembers filming her scene with Sheila Bick on the afternoon of Yom Kippur. Malina, fasting in observance of the day, recalls that Smith positioned the two actresses on

"a heap of flower petals and garbage" with "absolutely no preparation." Smith's letter to his friend, David Gurin, suggests that, a week or so later, *Flaming Creatures* was still in production: "Instead of finishing the movie according to the script I shot some pure psychotic footage of Sheila SINGING. . .singing mind you—I was reeling I was so zonked that morning behind that c. . .Now I spend my days wondering where to insert that footage." Smith further notes that "the movie's expenses are mounting" and there was difficulty getting the footage processed: "We have to send it to Colorado to Stanley Brakhage."[8]

That only fifteen minutes of *Flaming Creatures* out-takes are known to remain suggests a frugal shooting ratio, all the more impressive in that Smith evidently filmed many

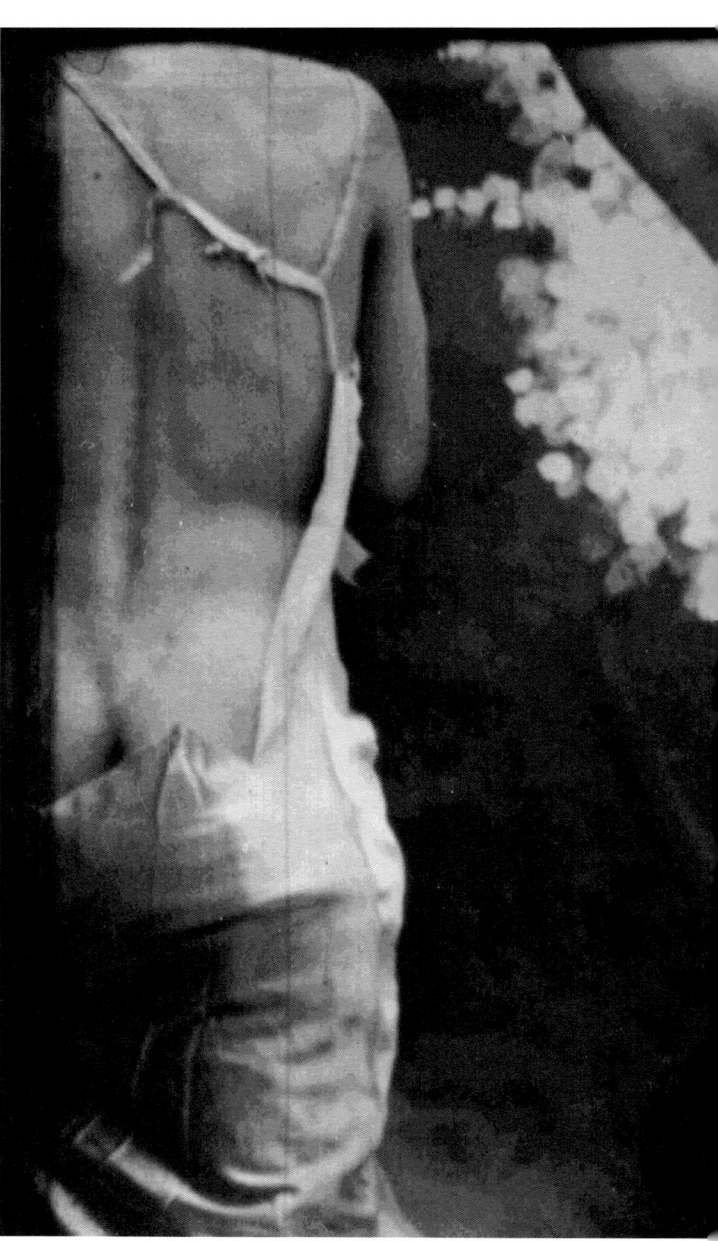

crucial scenes without benefit of seeing his earlier rushes. Gregory Markopoulos would write that Smith needed only a week to cut *Flaming Creatures*. Given the density of the montage (and the other events of the fall, which included Smith's arrest for shoplifting), this seems highly unlikely. In any case, several months were required for the closely synchronized sound accompaniment that Conrad assembled on ¼" magnetic tape in the winter of 1962-63.[9]

Smith screened the unfinished *Flaming Creatures* for friends and associates throughout the winter, with one publicized benefit organized by Piero Heliczer's dead language press at painter Jerry Joffen's cavernous West 20th Street loft—a space which, among other things, had a reputation

among heroin users as a shooting gallery. (In addition to Conrad's tape, the movie was accompanied by Taylor Mead on the violin.)

News of *Flaming Creatures* broke into print in mid-April when Jonas Mekas wrote in his *Village Voice* column that Smith had just completed "a great movie." *Flaming Creatures*, Mekas maintained "is so beautiful that I feel ashamed even to sit through the current Hollywood and European movies. I saw it privately and there is little hope that Smith's movie will ever reach the movie theatre screens. But I tell you, it is a most luxurious outpouring of imagination, of imagery, of poetry, of movie artistry, comparable only to the work of the greatest, like von Sternberg." Not two weeks later and accompanied by a second version of Tony Conrad's soundtrack, a further revised *Flaming Creatures* received its theatrical premiere, midnight, April 29, at the Bleecker Street Cinema on a bill with *Blonde Cobra*. "The audience burst forth and roared," Gregory Markopoulos wrote, "while the walls of censorship began to crack."

That summer, Mekas relocated his underground screenings to the Gramercy Arts, a small theater in the East 20s, off Lexington Avenue. Meanwhile, Smith—funded largely by Mekas (himself funded by filmmaker philanthropist Jerome Hill)—was now filming a "commercial" color follow-up to *Flaming Creatures*, *The Great Pasty Triumph*, known briefly as *The Pink and Green Horrors* and eventually retitled *Normal Love*.

The Gramercy hosted a number of notable premieres that fall, including Kenneth Anger's *Scorpio Rising* and Andy Warhol's six-hour *Sleep*, while police harassment became a regular feature of the show. Because the films exhibited were not submitted to the New York State Board of Regents for licensing, it was deemed illegal to charge admission. Mekas's strategy was to present the films free and to solicit contributions for the Love and Kisses to Censors Film Society. When *Flaming Creatures* was shown, it was prudently advertised as "a film praised by Allen Ginsberg, Andy Warhol, Jean-Luc Godard, Diane di Prima, Peter Beard, John Fles, Walter Guttman, Gregory Corso, Ron Rice, Storm De Hirsch, and everybody else."

By then *Flaming Creatures*'s first reviews had also appeared. Arthur Knight, Playboy's resident expert on "sex and the cinema," saw the movie at the Cinema Theater in Los Angeles on a bill with Stan Brakhage's *Dog Star Man* and, describing it for the readers of *The Saturday Review*, was appalled: "A faggoty stag-reel, it comes as close to hardcore pornography as anything ever presented in a theater.... Everything is shown in sickening detail, defiling at once both sex and cinema."

Drawing ever more attention to *Flaming Creatures*, Mekas rented the midtown Tivoli Theatre, a seedy venue known for sex exploitation films, to present Smith with *Film Culture*'s annual Independent Filmmaker Award. *Flaming Creatures* "has graced the anarchic liberation of new American cinema. Jack Smith has attained for the first time in motion pictures a high level of art which is absolutely lacking in decorum; and a treatment of sex which makes us aware of the restraint of all previous film-makers."

December 7, moments before the ceremonial midnight screening was to begin, the theater management buckled under the pressure from the city's Bureau of Licenses and canceled the show. Outraged, Mekas gave Smith his award outside, using the roofs of the cars parked along Eighth Avenue as his stage. Then, a few hundred New American Cinema partisans led by Barbara Rubin, one of the young firebrands of the Film-makers Cooperative, occupied the Tivoli until evacuated by the police. In a statement printed in the next issue of *The Village Voice*, *Film Culture* spoke for all filmmakers: "We'll find places to show our work. We'll screen our movies in public places, on the highway billboards and in the streets, if necessary."

Less than a month later, the *Flaming Creatures* crusade went international. Mekas had been invited to judge an experimental film festival in Knokke-le-Zout, Belgium. When *Flaming Creatures* was refused a screening, he resigned from the jury, threatened to withdraw the entries of other American filmmakers (including Kenneth Anger, Stan Brakhage, Robert Breer, and Gregory Markopoulos), and organized special showings in his hotel room. Among those present, perched on the bathtub or bed, were Jean-Luc Godard, Agnes Varda, and Roman Polanski. The word-of-mouth was sensational. "Two minutes after I met Federico Fellini in Rome," Stanley Kauffmann reported in *The New Republic* later that winter, "he asked me whether I'd seen Jack Smith's *Flaming Creatures*."

With the irrepressible Barbara Rubin as his confederate, Mekas chose New Year's Eve to commandeer the projection booth of the festival theater. Pretending to tie up the projectionist, filmmaker Jean-Marie Bouchet, and planting a print of *Flaming Creatures* between the reels of Warhol's six-hour *Sleep*, Mekas provoked a disturbance that was widely reported in Europe. A small riot broke out, and as the Belgian Minister of Justice (and honorary head of the festival) arrived to quell it, Mekas projected the film on the minister's face until all power was cut off. Ultimately, the jury awarded *Flaming Creatures* a special "damned" film prize. According to Mekas, most of the jurors thought it was a documentary. "A wild image of America we left in Knokke-le-Zout, I tell you," he noted in *The Village Voice* . "No wonder a State Department man was sitting next to our table wherever we went."

Thus, *Flaming Creatures* made *Variety*'s front page—and not for the last time. But, if, as the show-biz bible reported, "Belgians Balk N.Y. 'Creatures,'" New York itself was cleaning up for the 1964 World's Fair. Village coffee houses and off-off Broadway theaters were shuttered; Times Square tango palaces and taxi dance halls were closed; Lenny Bruce was arrested for obscenity at the Cafe A-Go-Go. Unlicensed screenings of underground movies were hounded from venue to venue. On February 3, *Flaming Creatures* was shown with *Normal Love* rushes at the Gramercy Arts. Two weeks later, the theater was shut down.

The next screenings were at the New Bowery Theater at 4 St. Marks Place where, on February 20, Smith had projected *Normal Love* production slides to the accompaniment of a taped radio speech by Antonin Artaud. *Flaming Creatures* was shown, together with Warhol's newsreel *Jack Smith Filming Normal Love*, on Monday, March 2, with an undercover policeman in the audience. The following night, two NYPD detectives broke up a near-capacity showing attended by some ninety spectators. "It was hot enough to burn up the screen," one cop would tell the press. The police impounded both films, the projector, and the screen, arresting Mekas, the theater manager, Jacobs, the projectionist, and ticket-taker Florence Karpf.

The case, *People of the State of New York vs. Kenneth Jacobs, Florence Karpf and Jonas Mekas*, was taken by the prominent civil rights lawyer Emile Zola Berman who, according to newspaper accounts, at times thought he was representing the exhibitors of a film entitled *Crimson Creatures*.

Nevertheless, according to Judge David Trager, then a young lawyer working on the case, Berman (whose most notorious subsequent client would be Sirhan Sirhan, the assassin of Robert Kennedy) believed that *New York vs. Jacobs* had the potential to go to the United States Supreme Court.

Defending *Flaming Creatures* in the April 13 issue of *The Nation*, Susan Sontag scored "the indifference, the squeamishness, the downright hostility to the film evinced by almost everyone in the mature intellectual and artistic community." Although this squeamishness extended to *The Nation* (Sontag recalls that the editor who assigned her the piece was fired as a result) and beyond (on April 7, the Modern Museum in Stockholm canceled a New American Cinema series that might have included *Flaming Creatures*), "mature" support may not have mattered. The three-judge Criminal Court panel, which included former New York City Mayor Vincent Impellitteri, refused to allow expert testimony, with the single exception of Sontag's, on either *Flaming Creatures*'s artistic merit or its alleged pornography.

Film historian Herman Weinberg, producer Lewis Allen, poet Allen Ginsberg, and filmmakers Shirley Clarke and Willard Van Dyke took the stand in vain; the prosecution case rested entirely on treating the judges to a screening. "Two of them munching cigars, watched impassively as the movie was shown in chambers," one daily reported. According to Jacobs, "Jack bothered just once to observe a court session. He left without a word but clearly disdainful, as if we were fools for involving ourselves in this, like we had a choice."

On June 12, Jacobs and Mekas were convicted and sentenced to sixty days in the New York City workhouse. The trial was followed, four days later, and to some extent upstaged by *People of the State of New York vs. Lenny Bruce*, which ran for months in the same Criminal Courts Building and resulted in Bruce's conviction for giving an "indecent performance." Jacobs and Mekas's sentences were suspended, as was Karpf's, but the court ruling has never been reversed. (Technically, *Flaming Creatures* remains obscene, at least in the boroughs of Manhattan and the Bronx.)

Smith's filmmaking activities were also suspended, or rather, he joined forces that summer with Andy Warhol, performing (and, by some accounts, directing) for the one underground filmmaker in New York with sufficient financial resources to keep his movie machine in constant operation.

As *New York vs. Jacobs* worked its way through the courts, *Flaming Creatures* rocked the film societies of the nation's universities. On April 1, 1965 (a week after the first teach-in against the war in Vietnam was held at the University of Michigan in Ann Arbor), Albuquerque police broke up an off-campus screening arranged by students at the University of New Mexico, who claimed that the film's star was a UNM graduate, and confiscated the print.[10]

Another screening—organized by the local chapter of Students for a Democratic Society, the largest organization of campus radicals in America, a month after the *Flaming Creatures* case reached the United States Supreme Court—was broken up on November 9, 1966, at the University of Texas in Austin. SDS, which recognized a hot issue when it saw one, was also involved in an incident at the University of Michigan two months later.

The evening of January 18, acting on a professor's complaint, an Ann Arbor police officer halted the screening at the Architecture School auditorium just as the rape-earthquake-orgy sequence commences, fifteen minutes and thir-

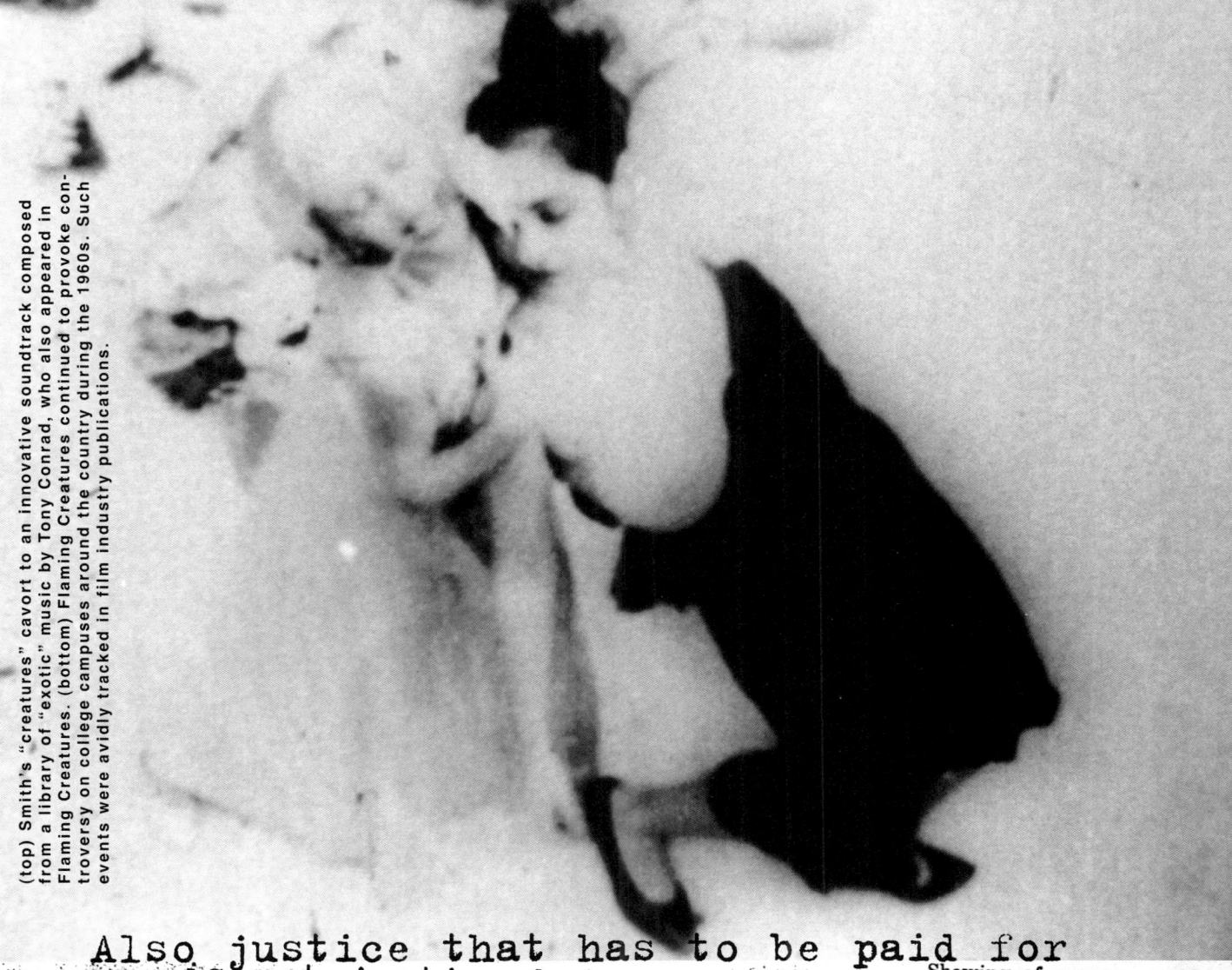

Also justice that has to be paid for
is not justice but oppression.

VARIETY DAILY _____ **Tues, Feb. 11, 1969**

Police Mace Notre Dame Students, Seize Pic As Obscenity On Campus

By Joseph Klein

South Bend, Feb. 10 — Sheriff's deputies used Mace Friday in a confrontation with students protesting seizure of a film at a Notre Dame conference on censorship and pornography. Several students and two deputies suffered minor injuries in the melee. The conference, to run through today, was also a casualty — terminated on orders of the school administration.

Never before, according to officials, was the Notre Dame campus marred by a student-police collision.

Showing of a pornographic film at a Thursday session provided the spark for Friday's outburst.

A rep of St. Joseph County prosecutor's office and members of the South Bend Citizens for Decent Literature were in the audience Thursday when the film, "Flaming Creatures," was projected and withdrawn after recognition of the error two minutes later. Student leaders of the conference explained the can containing the film was mislabeled. "Flaming Creatures" has been ruled obscene by the U.S. Supreme Court.

Responding to the complaints of the citizens group and the prosecutor's representative, the university ordered the conference to proceed without two of its features —

UPROAR AT NOT

n under a girl's coat.
w of resistance, the depu-
ntered with Mace. Four

The
preside
confere

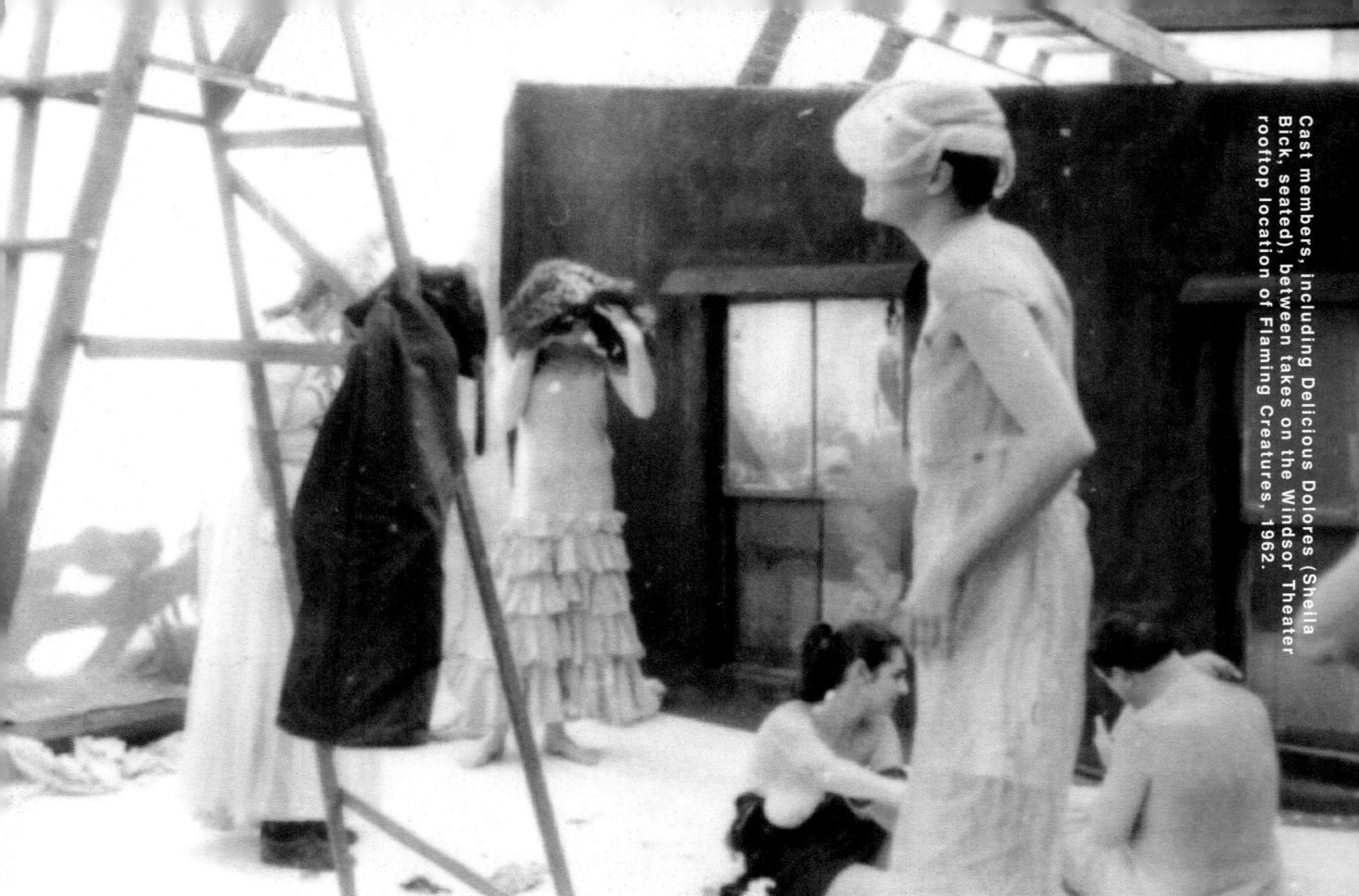

ty seconds into the movie. A group of irate students initially blocked the officer's exit from the booth. Later, a hundred or so marched downtown to stage a four-hour sit-in at the station house, demanding the film's return. Three student members of the Cinema Guild and their faculty advisor were arraigned on charges of showing an obscene motion picture.

The subsequent hearings, laws suits, and trial preoccupied Ann Arbor for the remainder of the year when, unmoved by history professor Robert Sklar's defense testimony, a municipal judge ruled *Flaming Creatures* "a smutty purveyance of filth [that] borders on the razor's edge of hard-core pornography." By that time, the *Flaming Creatures* appeal had been dismissed as moot by five of the nine justices of the United States Supreme Court. The four dissenting justices were split: Chief Justice Warren and Justice Brennan affirmed the judgment of the lower court while Justices Fortas and Douglas voted to reverse the judgment.

In the waning days of the Johnson administration, *Flaming Creatures* became an organizing tool for the right as well as for the left—thanks to Justice Fortas's stated opinion that he favored reversing the original Criminal Court decision. This footnote became a political football when, in the summer of 1968, lame duck President Johnson put forth Fortas for Chief Justice. In the Fortas nomination, Senate conservatives found a way to attack the civil libertarian position of the Warren court. Their weapon would be Fortas's liberal rulings on pornography.

The print of *Flaming Creatures*, confiscated in Ann Arbor, was flown to Washington, D.C. In late July, the ranking Republican on the Senate Judiciary Committee, Strom Thurmond, organized a "Fortas Film Festival" in Room 2228 of the Senate office building, where a fourteen-minute filmed striptease, two other skin flicks, and *Flaming Creatures* were projected on the wood-paneled wall. Members of Congress were invited, as was the press, and Thurmond, who claimed that he had "shocked Washington's hardened press corps," thoughtfully furnished glossy frame enlargements from the movie.

The anti-Fortas forces announced plans to send prints of *Flaming Creatures* to women's groups and civic clubs in hopes of triggering further outrage. Before the Fortas nomination collapsed in September, there was talk of showing the film on the Senate floor. Although that screening never came to pass, *Flaming Creatures* is likely the only American avant-garde movie ever described in the *Congressional Record*. This "home-made film," the September 4, 1968 record reads: "has gained a notorious reputation for its homosexual content. [It] presents five unrelated, badly filmed sequences, which are studded with sexual symbolisms. . .a mass rape scene involving two females and many males, which lasts for 7 minutes, showing the female pubic area, the male penis, males massaging the female vagina and breasts, cunnilingus, masturbation of the male organ, and other sexual symbolisms. . .lesbian activity between two women. . .homosexual acts between a man dressed as a female, who emerges from a casket, and other males, including masturbation of the visible male organ. . .homosexuals dancing together and other disconnected erotic activity, such

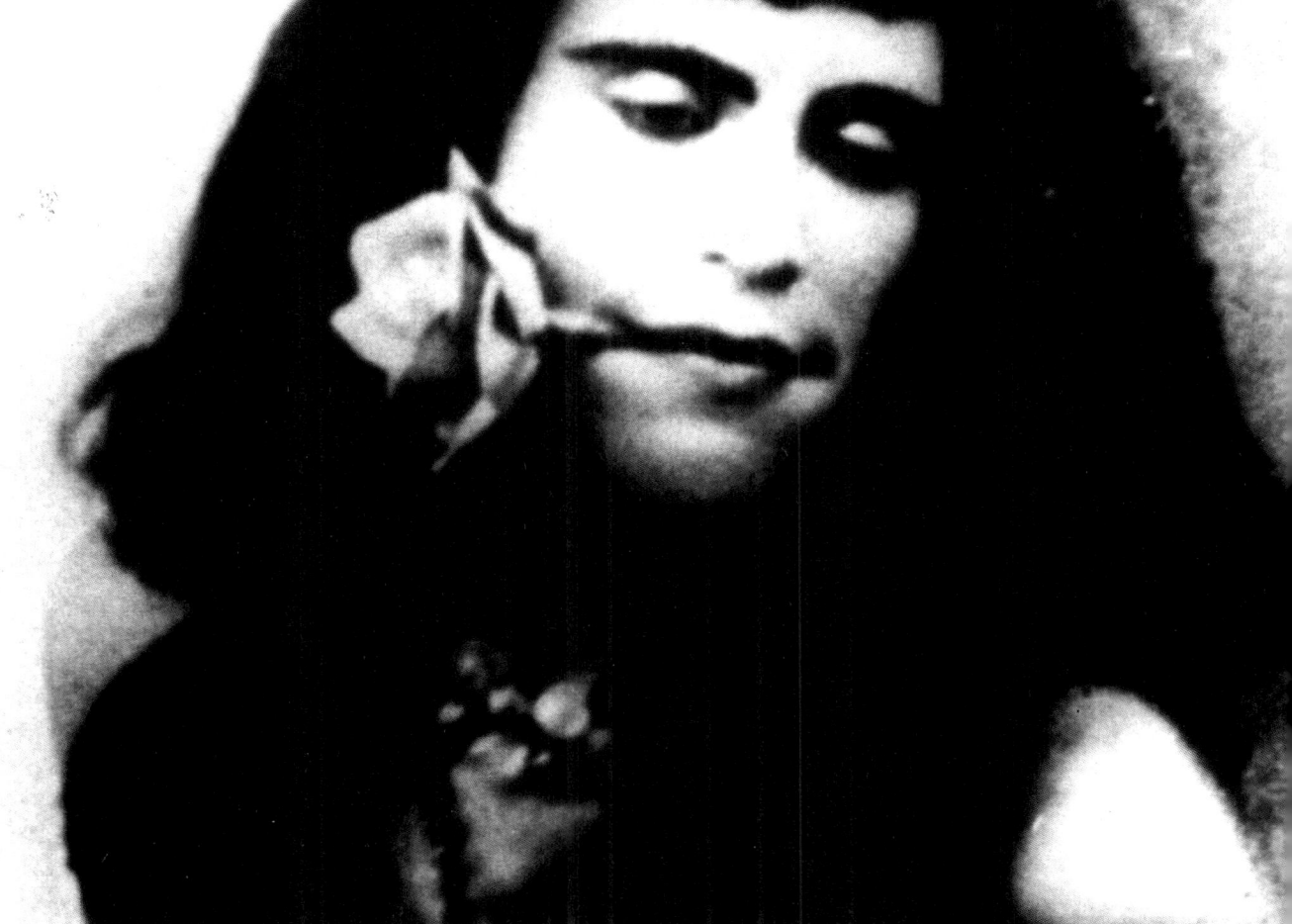

Dolores Flores (later Mario Montez) as the
Spanish dancer, Flaming Creatures, 1962.

as massaging the female breasts and group sexual activity."

This earnest testimony, as hopeless as it is graphic, was supplied by the founder of Citizens for Decent Literature, Cincinnati lawyer Charles Keating (convicted, twenty-five summers later of seventy-three counts of fraud, racketeering, and conspiracy in defrauding Lincoln Savings and Loan Association and its investors). More suggestive was the account of *Flaming Creatures* an anonymous senator offered a Newsweek correspondent: "That movie was so sick," the senator explained, "I couldn't even get aroused."

While *Flaming Creatures* was scarcely the only explicit movie produced by the early 1960s underground, it triggered a rage that far exceeded the hostility directed at such candidates for martyrdom as Stan Brakhage's *Window Water Baby Moving*, Carolee Schneeman's *Fuses*, or Barbara Rubin's *Christmas on Earth*. These movies were merely explicit, or, in the case of Jean Genet's venerable *Un Chant d'Amour* and Kenneth Anger's *Scorpio Rising*, blatantly homoerotic. The behavior in *Flaming Creatures* is something else—extravagantly queer to be sure but even queerer than that.

The anonymous senator's response suggests that *Flaming Creatures*'s failure as pornography was something worse than pornography itself. At once splendidly visionary and startlingly anti-illusionist, Smith's movie offered a liberation from "good" technique as well as every sort of "proper" behavior, including the despotic fantasy conjured by the notion of an orgy in the harem. (Smith's journal notes that the orgy-earthquake-rape scene ends with the revelation of Francine's "erection under his dress." Yet, as virtually every

commentator has noted, the movie is notable for its absence of tumescence.)

"The shaken breast and the shaken penis become interchangeable," Susan Sontag wrote. Those rudely brandished dicks, neither wholly erect nor entirely flaccid, are ultimately, only penises. Thus, *Flaming Creatures* was guilty of a criminal disrespect more serious than burning the flag. In so casually representing the male organ, it desecrated the underlying symbol of all power structures—the United States Senate, not the least.

Flaming Creatures is all dress-up and over-exposure, at once calculated and inadvertent. The seraglio is filled with secrets—disguised faces, painted lips, every manner of veils and gossamers, casually blurred genders, and abstract body tangles. There's a spatial ambiguity that goes beyond the visual, a serious lack of gravity, an absence of perspective. Are we inside or out? What are the rules? Senators search for authority in vain.[11]

Smith's aesthetic revelation is founded on the revelation of artifice—the discrepancy between sound and image, the transvestites who flaunt their cocks, the camera that seems to participate in the filmed orgy, and the democracy of desire. Projecting intersexuality, monosexuality, homosexuality, no sexuality, just sexuality, it is a spectacle inspired by the utopian confusion between filmmaker and audience. Ali Baba never arrives. Photographed rather than directed by its maker, *Flaming Creatures* is a movie with no master in the harem.

The literature on *Flaming Creatures* is scant but distinguished. Susan Sontag's lucid, impassioned, and widely-anthologized *Nation* defense became the cornerstone of the movie's critical edifice, further developed (with superb description) by P. Adams Sitney in his *Visionary Filmmakers*. David Packman's appreciation in *Film Culture* 63-64 links *Flaming Creatures* to the earliest movie attractions; more recently, Michael Moon's persuasive and erudite analysis in *October* 51 locates *Flaming Creatures* in the tradition of gay male performance.

[1] The *Flaming Creatures* credits are:

Francis Francine	Himself
Delicious Dolores	Sheila Bick
Our Lady of the Docks	Joel Markman
The Spanish Girl	Dolores Flores [Mario Montez]
Arnold	Arnold [Rockwood]
The Fascinating Woman	Judith Malina

[According to Marian Zazeela, who created the credits, Malina declined Smith's offer to reconfigure her name as "Judith Medina."] and

Maria Zazeela	Marian Zazeela

The numerous uncredited participants include Tony Conrad; David Gurin; Piero and Kate Heliczer; Ray Johnson; Angus MacLise; Ed Marshall; Henry Proach; Jerry Raphael; Irving Rosenthal; Mark Schleifer; Ronald Tavel; John Wieners; La MonteYoung; the granddaughter of the owner of the neighborhood kosher Chinese restaurant, Bernstein-on-Essex; and a sailor who (according to Zazeela) Smith had "plucked off the street."

A second poster gives the movie's technical credits:

Photography	Jack Smith
Assistant Director	Marc Schleifer

[Marian Zazeela's amicably estranged husband, Schleifer's major role was described by one participant as "roaming around town trying to get a coffin."]

Recording	Tony Conrad
Special Assistant	Dick Preston
Facilities	The Windsor Theater

[2] "China Night," taken from a 78 rpm record supplied by the ex-merchant marine Arnold Rockwood, is the title song from the 1940 Japanese movie(one of several "Chinese continental friendship films" starring Yoshiko Yamaguchi a/k/a Li Zianglang, an actress born to a Japanese family in Manchuria, and thus perfectly bilingual. (In *China Night*, she typically plays a poor Chinese girl who hates the Japanese who killed her family but nevertheless falls in love with a Japanese sailor.)

[3] The extant footage of the 16mm *Buzzards over Bagdad*, on which Smith was apparently working when he first met Jacobs in 1956, suggests a relatively straight-forward gloss on the Maria Montez vehicle, *The Arabian Nights*. Jacobs regarded Smith's intentions as devoid of irony although that was certainly not the case a decade or more later when Smith intercut *Buzzards over Bagdad* with documentary footage taken, in February 1966, of the Rio de Janiero carnival.

[4] A copy of *The Beautiful Book* Smith annotated for Marian Zazeela makes reference to "the previously greatest movie on earth, Joseph Cornell's Rose Hobart film." *Rose Hobart* subsequently evinced itself as an influence on Jacobs' oeuvre with his re-filmed 1905 short, *Tom, Tom, the Piper's Son* (1969) as well as in his numerous projection pieces.

Flaming Creatures was shot on a variety of black-and-white reversal film stocks, including such exotic brands as Agfa-Ferra-nia and Dupont, stolen from the out-dated film bin at Camera Barn. According to Tony Conrad, Smith made particular use of Perutz Tropical film(a specialized German stock designed for shooting at high temperatures(because, thanks to the counter location, it was the easiest to shoplift. Dick Preston noted that the late-afternoon lack of direct sunlight contributed to the ethereal, distinctively low-contrast quality of the imagery.

[6] Various participants assumed Smith's direction was improvised and spontaneous. In fact, his journal notes are fairly detailed. *Flaming Creatures* was intended to open with a "Smirching Sequence: Marion [sic] & Francine applying lipstick." The scenario continues: "Marion and Francine pose about envying each others lips…F.F. grabs at M. The chase. Marion strikes with purse. The clinch. F.F. pulls out her tit. (E.Q. [earthquake] builds up) …C.U. of F.F. bouncing M's tit. Marion screaming and struggling. Final shot of many people holding M down as F. bobbles her tit. F's erection under his dress."

With the exception of the final filip and the substitution of Sheila Bick for Marion Zazeela, the film plays much as written. The screams are written into the script as are the tolling bells which accompany "Marion recovery." (There is, however, an unfilmed twist: "Mary [the part taken by Judith Malina in the movie] puts Marion on a camel and they ride off across the desert (Mary's burnoose flowing (chorus of religious music swells)."

[7] The source of this falling plaster may be deduced from an anecdote related by Walter Lansford who recalled that *Flaming Creatures* was in production while he and a crew were renovating the Windsor Theater below. Smith "went up on the roof with what equipment he had and what friends he had. And we went on about our business. Half an hour or so later we heard this tremendous crashing noise from the roof, and I ran up and Jack had a sledgehammer, and he was banging away at one of the main support beams." In a journal entry dated August 11, Smith refers to "the incident on the Windsor Roof" and expresses an unfounded concern that Langsford might prevent subsequent filming. In September, Langsford and Stein announced plans to reopen Windsor as a sister theater to the Charles; both movie houses went dark the end of the year.

[8] Brakhage, who was experienced in processing problematic footage, had a close working relationship with Western Cine-Lab in Denver. On Halloween 1962, Smith wrote David Gurin that, although *Flaming Creatures* was completely shot, "I've been waiting 3 weeks now for it to be sent to Colorado to be developed. Due to Dick Preston's farting around."

Flaming Creatures' total budget, Jonas Mekas would later report in *The Village Voice* (6/13/63), was $300. While this unverifiable figure was likely devoted to film processing, some was spent on props. Smith's October 6 letter to Gurin complains of being "double-crossed by funeral home turds" who charged him "$10 rental for Joel's coffin."

[9] Before working with Smith on the *Flaming Creatures* soundtrack, Tony Conrad created *Scotch Tape*'s audio accompaniment by matching Peter Duchin's rhumba "Carinhoso" to the footage. The result, Conrad would recall, inspiring him to become a filmmaker. "All of a sudden, a commitment emerged, a kind of special pleasure that reached out and grabbed the whole scene in a way that was inhabited by a very very special comic presence. And it was on the way to ecstasy, and in fact, it was ecstasy. And at that point, I was won over to be a filmmaker; it was such an extraordinary thing to see, what happened to sound in the presence of a moving image." Conrad remembers this screening as happening at the Charles, which would mean the summer of

IN THE

SUPREME COURT OF THE UNITED STATES

OCTOBER TERM, 1966

No. 660

KENNETH JACOBS, FLORENCE KARPF AND JONAS MEKAS, *Appellants,*

vs.

PEOPLE OF THE STATE OF NEW YORK, *Appellee.*

ON APPEAL FROM THE SUPREME COURT OF THE STATE OF NEW YORK, APPELLATE TERM, FIRST JUDICIAL DEPARTMENT

BRIEF OF AMICUS CURIAE IN SUPPORT OF JURISDICTIONAL STATEMENT

Interest of Amicus

Amicus submits this brief (with the consent of the parties, which is on file in the Clerk's office) because of its support, since its inception in 1947, of free expression in the arts and, in particular, its dedication to the encouragement of

(1)

1962. On February 11, 1963, *Scotch Tape* was programmed by Jonas Mekas, along with *Little Stabs at Happiness*, *Blonde Cobra*, Ron Rice's *Senseless*, and films by Bhob Stewart and Ray Wisniewski, at the Bleecker Street Cinema under the rubric "Newest Absurd and Zen Poetry." Smith's records indicate a check for the composite *Scotch Tape* print, provided by Mekas, and dated April 22, a week before the *Flaming Creatures* premiere.

[10] By the end of 1965, Smith had removed both the *Flaming Creatures* and *Overstimulated* original negatives from the Filmmakers Cooperative. At some point in the late sixties, he produced a new high contrast print of *Flaming Creatures*. The edit-ed camera original was subsequently lost until discovered in 1978 by filmmaker Jerry Tartaglia among a mass of lab-discarded 16mm footage.

[11] The gender confusion had been compounded by early commentators. Smith told Ken Kelman that the movie's female star Sheila Bick was, in fact, a hermaphrodite. Kelman duly reported this in his review of *Flaming Creatures* (*Film Culture* 28) and it has been repeated elsewhere. Similarly, Judith Malina, who wears a masculine blond wig from the Living Theater production of William Carlos Williams's *Many Loves*, was mistakenly described by P. Adams Sitney as a transvestite.

The Message from Atlantis

— Nayland Blake

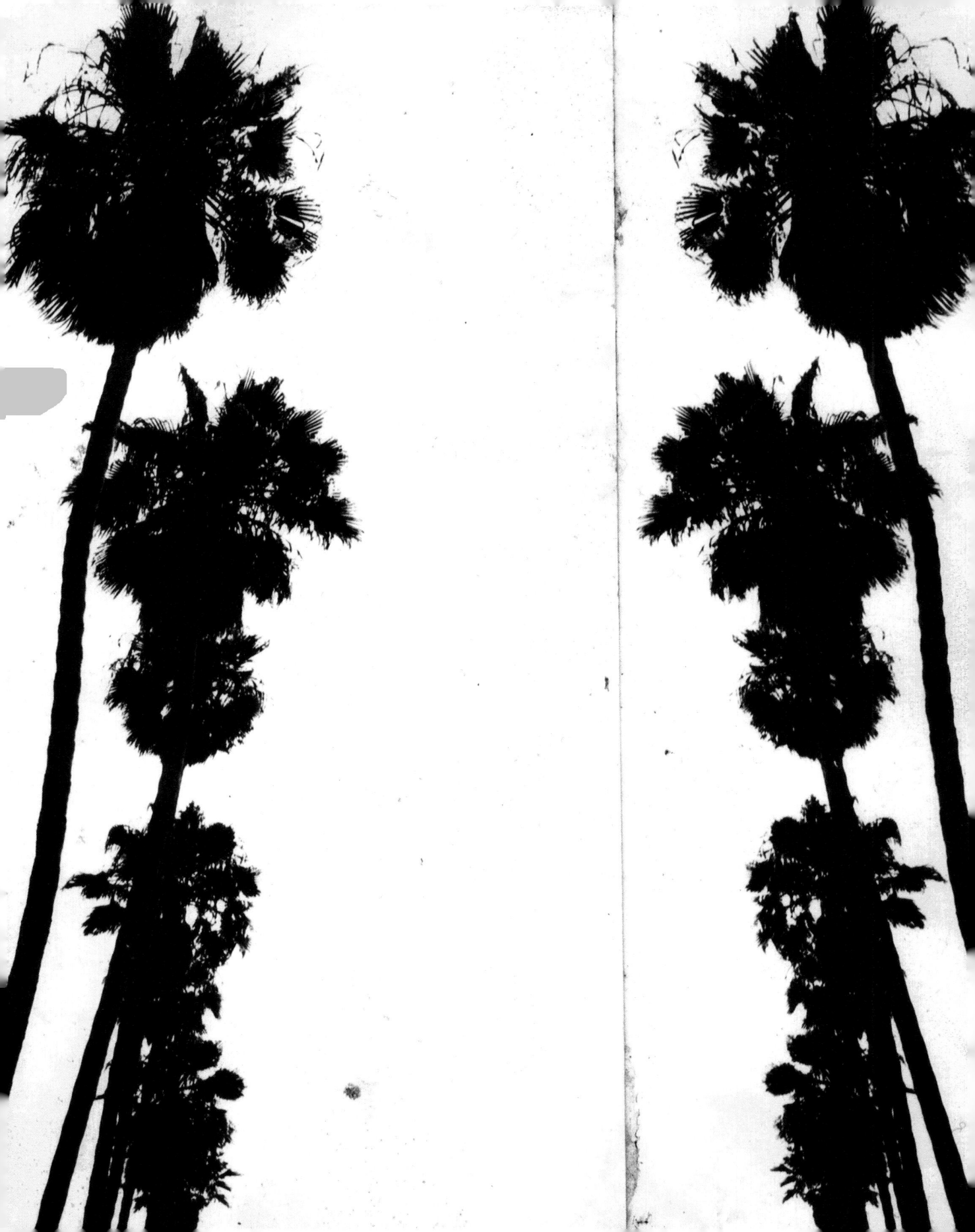

Jack Smith's work was like a powerful essence dispersed during his lifetime throughout the worlds of theater, film, writing, and art; a time bomb that continues to explode; a submerged continent whose artifacts—gifts from nearly forgotten gods—wash up on our mundane shores. The effects of his work appear everywhere today, and yet most people in the arts—practitioners and spectators alike—have little, if any knowledge of the man who originated them. As Smith's work enters into history, the danger is that his essential difference will be lost, that he will be made to fit into the polite parody pantheon that American culture reserves for those it posthumously defangs.

How does one do honor to the achievements of past artists without also enacting a kind of violence to their memory? Our use of the past ultimately says more about us than it does about the past. We queers especially are always constructing our forebears in retrospect, feeding on a distortion of the dead, granting ourselves permission to move forward by reading (and often misreading) the works of those who went before us. Even the resurrection of the recent past can produce archaeological aberrations, distortions that betray their subject more often than not. Both Smith's life and work were, and are, difficult, demanding in the best sense of the word. It is important to understand and preserve that difficulty as we try to unravel the legacy of that life and work.

Like many people, my own path to Jack Smith was circuitous. I grew up in Manhattan during the sixties, and by my early teens had become an art nerd—a social misfit who, along with a group of friends, used a glue of science fiction, free jazz, avant-garde art, and film to cement a "superior" outsider status. I had also become a homo, which meant that I spent the mid-seventies doing things like bluffing my way into the Adonis Theater to watch porn movies and to give and receive furtive hand jobs, leafing secretly through issues of *Michael's Thing* at out-of-the-way newsstands, and wandering around Christopher Street looking at clones and feeling like a freak. Gay culture was coming into being in the West Village, and I was desperately looking for something that corresponded to my interior emotional experience. But, there was something mismatched, a discrepancy between the bourgeois consumerism of the emerging gay market and the iconoclastic aestheticism I valued. I didn't know then that there was more than one way of being gay, and I felt irrevocably split.

Those two sides of my life—the art nerd and the homo—came together in 1976, when at the age of sixteen I first saw Jack Smith's *Flaming Creatures* and *Scotch Tape* at the Anthology Film Archives. My friends and I had been seeing whatever was being shown there: Robert Breer animations, Paul Sharits flickers, Maya Deren, Stan Brakhage—all of which fed our sense of superiority, of being in the know. But *Flaming Creatures* was an entirely different order of experience. For the first time, I saw art that spoke to both halves of me. What was on the screen was at once intimate, ludicrous, and ravishingly beautiful: A bunch of queers cavorting

It's good—
if it weren't
Bloomingdales
it would be
better.

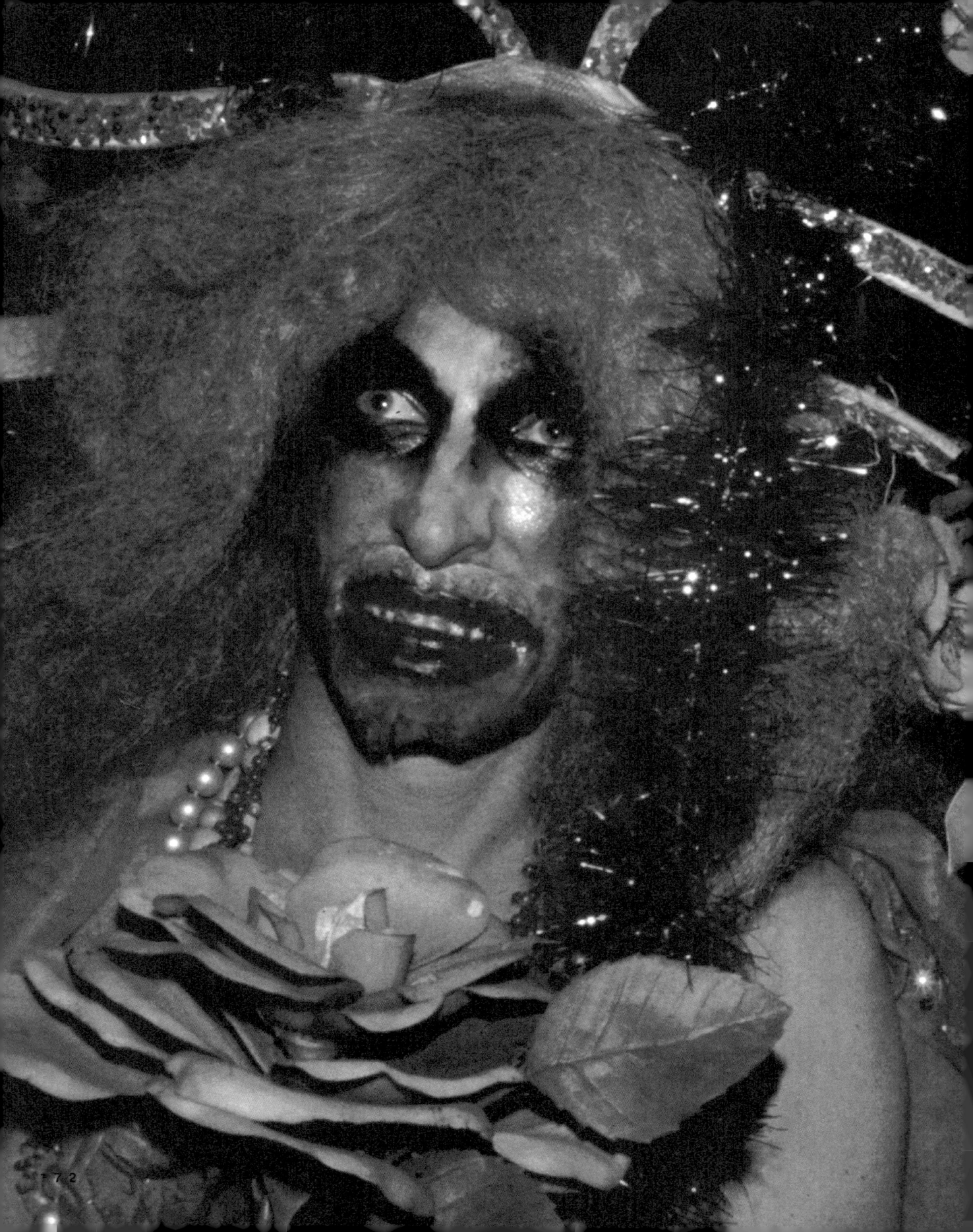

in front of a barely discernible painting of a vase of flowers; mincing drag queens putting on lipstick as if it were a sacrament; a vampire and a Spanish dancer flickering in and out of existence through the veils of flaring, overexposed film. Something peculiar was animating these elements, something that was fagotty, smart, and fun; something that left its mark on me—a message from Atlantis. I knew then that Christopher Street was not the whole story of gay life.

In the summer of 1980, I read an article in *The Village Voice* called "The First Radical Art Show of the Eighties." It described "The Times Square Show," an exhibition of the work of dozens of artists installed in an abandoned massage parlor not far from where I lived. I saw that Jack Smith was billed to perform at the show one Saturday at midnight. I showed up and waited with a bunch of other devotees for about an hour. Having had no previous experience with Jack's audience "winnowing," I finally gave up, baffled, and went home. "The Times Square Show" changed my ambitions for my work. Just as I had seen that I didn't need to settle for the middlebrow aesthetic of the gay mainstream, I also saw that my work didn't have to fit in with the sterile white boxes in SoHo or in stiff, distant museums.

In 1984, after art school, I moved to San Francisco. While it was filled with gay people, San Francisco's cultural universe had no overlap between the art world and the gay community. Paradoxically, I was reliving my adolescent split between identifying as a gay man on one hand and as a poststructurally theorized artist on the other. I was casting about for another way of working, another sort of paradigm. Luckily, I came across Stefan Brecht's book *Queer Theatre*, with its sympathetic descriptions of Jack's performances in the sixties. I remembered *Flaming Creatures*, heard that Jack was showing up at the San Francisco Cinematheque to screen it, and off I went. Of course, he didn't show. But, I began thinking about Jack and remembering what my experience of his films had been. I re-read Brecht's book often in the years that followed. I recalled my surprise and delight in the sexuality and buffoonery and drop-dead glamour of *Flaming Creatures*. I understood that that spirit was what was missing from my work. I also understood that it was what was missing from both the gay and art worlds of my time.

For much of my artistic life I had fumbled towards queerness, towards "queer art," and my fumblings kept leading me back to Jack Smith. Even his no-shows were calculated statements of value and elusiveness. My points of connection/non-connection with Jack and his work, are exemplary of the ways artistic influence works. We imagine that artist X sees the work of artist Y, or studies with, or works for, them, becoming the bearer of a seed of influence that germinates and is passed on successively. But, often influence proceeds fitfully and piecemeal. Often, all we have to lead us on as artists is our hunger for a type of experience or information, or our own dissatisfaction. Part of us senses what we don't know, what we need to know, and we fumble for it. Sometimes we are left with secondary texts, apocrypha, or only with absences.

What are the lessons and qualities of Smith's art? Smith asserted that seriousness and dedication, not production value, created artistic worth. In all mediums, his art is one of fragmentation and transformation, often conducted at an incremental pace. He favored compositions that were overwrought, knotted together, difficult to decipher. In his images, we are always looking through something—veils, bodies, encrusted junk. These all-over compositions are then contrasted with eccentric details that leap out at us. There is mess and occlusion, and then there is a flash of naked insight. Disarray and hierarchy battle each other, illustrating how commonplace it has become in the twentieth century to see art in the arrangement of objects as well as in their creation. Smith believed this so deeply that many of his performances were little more than opportunities for the audience to watch him arrange things. His impromptu deflated the twinned pomposities of performer and spectator.

Smith reveled in images of decay, death, humidity. In his work, rot is often presented as a desirable state, a condition in which boundaries break down and rebirth becomes possible. Rot is contrasted in Smith's work with encrustation, a process that he continually derides, linking it to plaster, falseness, icing, sugar. The wet and crumbling fecundity that brings forth orchids is set against the dry, powdery scabbed crust, the "black roachcrust" that covers over our everyday lives. Smith's villains are creatures with exoskeletons, lobsters, roaches, crabs, scorpions—animals covered with crusts.

Rot and decay are the result of death, of course, and Smith, like many artists, was haunted by images of death. But for him, death and decay exist as the positive pole opposed to undeath—vampirism and zombification. Smith exploited this dynamic in film, which, like all photographic mediums, is inherently vampiric: It freezes its subjects in time on the screen while the actors and audience continue to age. The moving picture image thus mocks the body's frailty. Stories of resurrection, death, and vampirism have always sprung from cinema's dark heart. Sharing in this thematic bloodline, *Flaming Creatures* contains a literal vampire story. The film seems haunted by the ghosts of film's earliest images. Mario Montez's charming dance underneath a lamp could have been lifted from an experiment by Edison or a Melies magic film. It seems to contain some irreducible nugget of pure cinema-ism.

In addition to its formal and thematic complexity, Smith's work is also politically challenging. But, when Smith is talked about at all, it is rarely as a political artist. His political ideas are treated as ludicrous and secondary, but in fact they are the crux of his work. Smith's politics were the only kind of politics that matter—utterly utopian, visionary, and grounded in his everyday experience, something he shared with many artists of his generation. But, Smith also shares in the scorn that is now heaped on the political ambitions of that generation.

His work rests on two aesthetic assertions: first, that art is being made around us all the time—every time we arrange something—and that everyone is acting all the time; and second, that the organizations supposedly dedicated to presenting, preserving, and fostering art are actually engaged in endless attempts to stamp it out and bury it beneath layers of plaster and crust. It thus be-

Smith, appearing in exotic costumes and wild makeup, took glamour to an outrageous extreme. c. 1965.

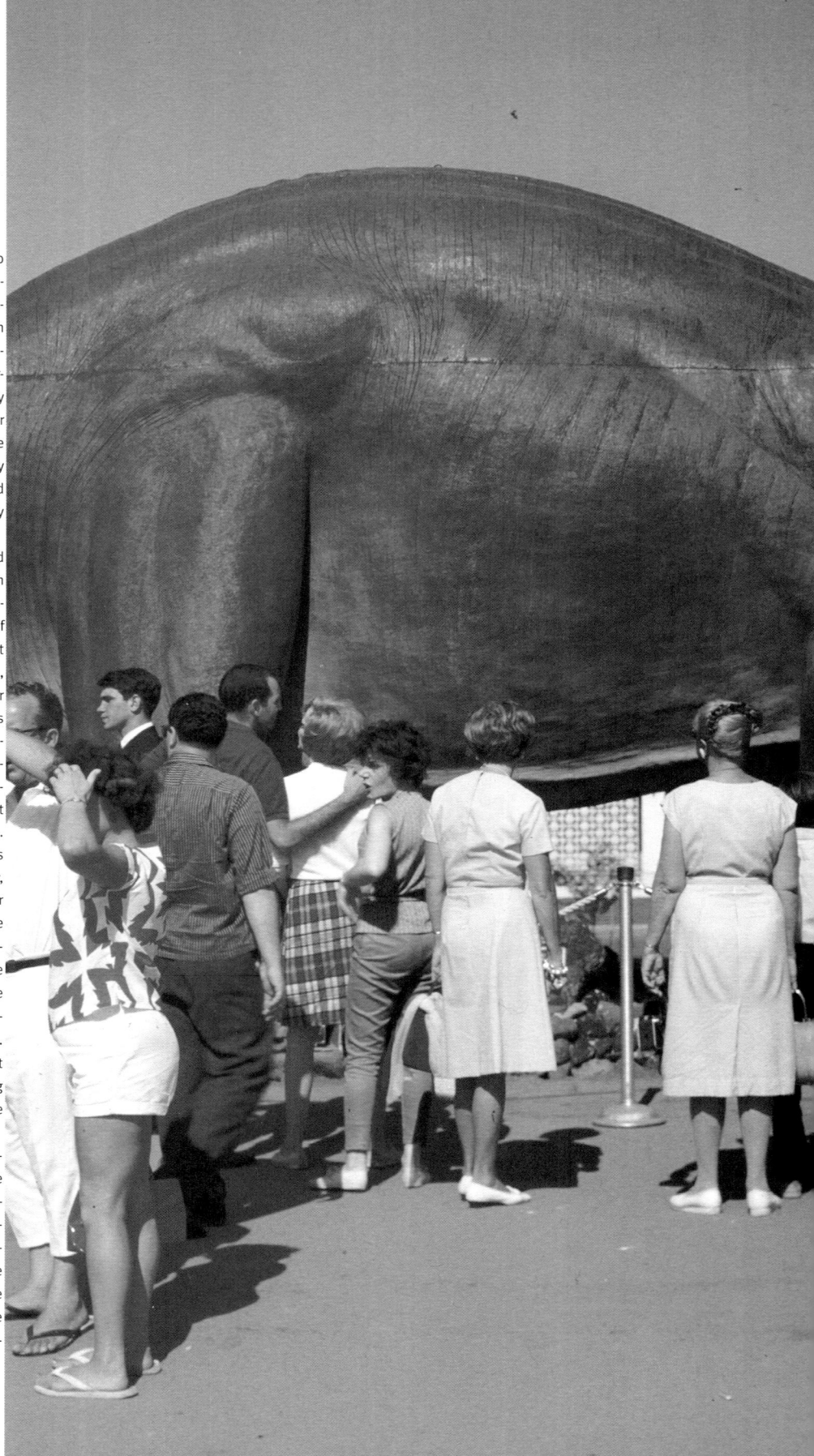

comes essential for artists to refuse to make art in the old-fashioned manner and to refute and resist the art establishment, even in its most benign forms. Smith's cancellations and no-shows underlined the point that while art may be all around us, it is not at our disposal, not something to be picked up like a Kleenex and airily disposed of. Art has to be worked for, even if that work is of a highly eccentric nature.

Smith's activities also included a sustained and spirited attack on the injustice of capitalism, an injustice exemplified in the notion of rent. Smith continually pointed out the fundamental absurdity of rent, the idea of paying over and over again for what one already owns (obviously, this was not an opinion that endeared him to his various landlords). This view extended into his criticism of the nascent underground film scene as well. Smith's endless embittered attacks on Jonas Mekas pointed out how, the moment we begin to codify our experience of art, and to manage it, we become yet another muse-+um, another landlord. Unlike the pageantry, the queerness, and the play in Smith's work, this uncomfortable assertion is hard to digest. It is Smith's version of the leftist political rhetoric that was floating through the art world in the late fifties and early sixties.

His assertions about social issues seem fresh today because they are grounded in the experience of capitalism's everyday boredoms and frustrations. Smith's politics were those of the downtrodden as opposed to the academic; he hated rent because he was a hapless renter; he dis-

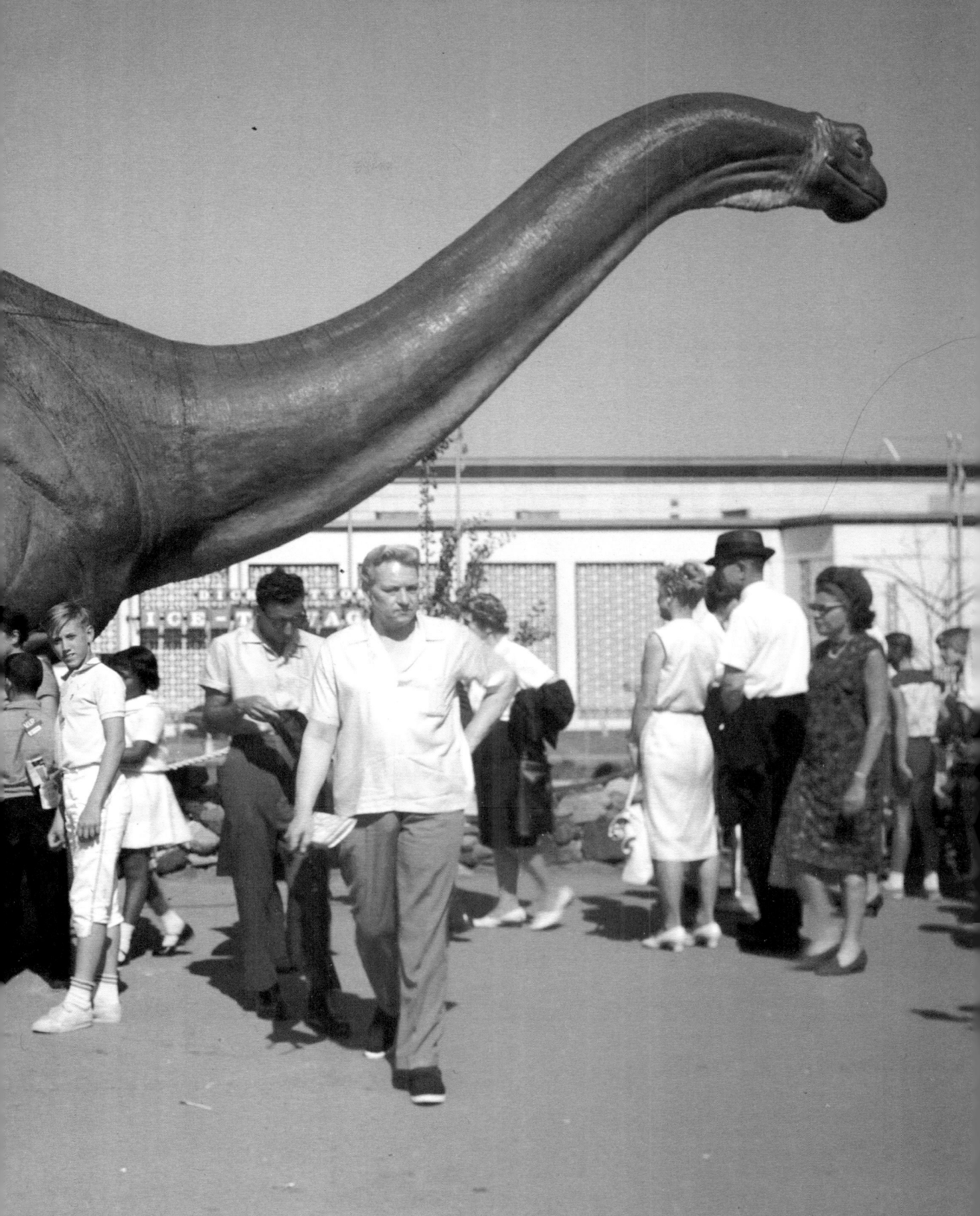

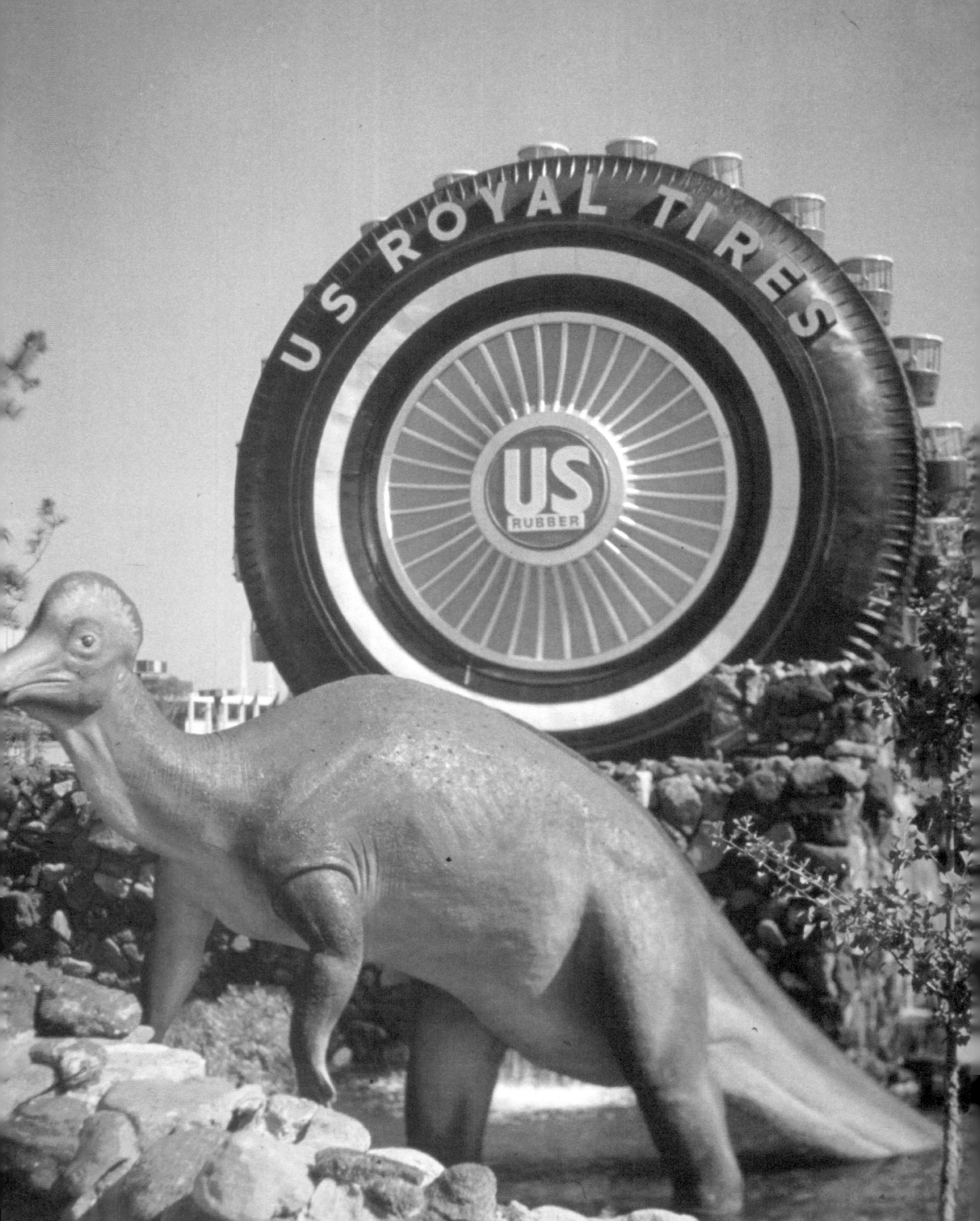

trusted critics, curators, and academics because he saw them as continually prospering at the ex-pense of artists. All of Smith's work, in one way or another, pointed to the real purpose of the art establishment: The domestication and trivialization of art itself, as part of capitalism's relentless trampling of the humane.

It is difficult to place Smith in relation to other artists. Certainly there are points of overlap between his work and the work of people around him (for example, the relationship between Smith's settings and the elaborate interiors of Alan Kaprow's Happenings or the chaotic environment of Claes Oldenberg's store). But these similarities do little to illuminate what was, and remains, important about Smith and his work today. His connection to other artists is less one of visual similarity than it is of type. Smith was a visionary, an outsider artist. Even though he functioned at the center of a sophisticated art scene, the tone of his work was closer to folk art than to contemporary art.

More particularly, Smith's work has much in common with that of religious visionaries like James Hampton and Georgia's St EOM (Eddie Owens Martin). Hampton is the constructor of the "Throne of the Third Heaven of the Nation's General Assembly," a work composed of 180 objects (chairs, cabinets, frames, and other bric-a-brac) covered in foil and purple paper and dedicated to the Second Coming of Christ. He began working on the piece around 1950 when he was in his late forties, and he continued for over twenty years, eventually filling the obscure garage he had rented to house it. The throne is at once an elaborate altar, a physicalization of scriptural teaching, and a model of an earthly paradise. Like much modern art, the "Throne" is a transfiguration of mundane materials into glittering powerful objects, but this metamorphosis is the result of Hampton's prophetic vision of himself as the herald of Christ, not the result of a rhetorical point about high and low culture.

St EOM's major work was the "Land of Pasaquan," a house and sculpture garden that celebrated his spiritual awakening. EOM had been a gay hustler, a drug runner, and a fortune teller in New York in the twenties. He eventually developed his own elaborate religion and returned to his home in rural Georgia to build a sacred temple to it. "Pasaquan" ended up being more than a temple, however. It grew into a compound of stucco-and-adobe pagodas, linked with brightly decorated walls. The garden is punctuated with totemic columns depicting faces of the enlightened. The constant use of bright color, scalloped edging, and ziggurat shapes evokes Mayan pyramids and Bavarian gingerbread, all at once. The walls are covered with murals of landscapes, erotically entwined figures, and religious geometry, derived from EOM's attempts to achieve a spiritual synthesis, a depiction of utopia and an evocation of the lost cultures of Atlantis and Mu.

One major difference between Smith and other visionary artists is that he talked back to the art establishment. For the most part, visionary and folk artists are relegated to the role of idiot savant and assumed to be unable or unwilling to defend or explicate their work. Smith, on the other hand, was eloquent if elliptical in his statements about his work and its place in the world. His knowledge, coupled with his unwillingness to play any of the roles laid out for artists by the art world, doomed him to an unjust obscurity.

In both its forms and its politics, Smith's work was difficult, if not impossible, for the critical establishment to manage. Like much of history, art history is written by the victors, and current attempts to reassess the art of the sixties betray this. Those figures most opposed to the workings of art history have been conveniently "disappeared" by art historians. Perhaps, it is fairer to say that they have successfully escaped the system they opposed, but the price of escape has been eventual anonymity. Today, we are left with secondary sources, with traces sometimes thrice removed. The disappearance of the political dimension of much sixties art is certainly part of the larger cultural tendency to jettison historical veracity in favor of academia's overreaching interest in historical style. Smith's activities left him in the paradoxical position of exerting great influence on a cultural scene that he was largely written out of; he was both insider and outsider.

Another artist who had a similar insider/outsider relationship to the mainstream art world and who could be called a spiritual father to Smith was Joseph Cornell. Like Smith, Cornell had little formal art education. Both were eccentric visual stylists who were entranced by the abundance of New York's streets and cobbled together the detritus of the city into fantastic worlds of their own invention. Cornell clipped and filed obsessively, compiling extensive dossiers on his favorite stars. Smith built an altar to Maria Montez in his apartment. While many other artists are drawn to the look of their pieces (what Jack would call the icing), few plumb their spirit.

Both Smith and Cornell were artists of arrangement, rather than invention. They worked with existing materials and forms, creating something new from their juxtapositions. This montage method is obviously filmic, and both artists loved silent film. Cornell's *Rose Hobart* is a re-edited silent one-reeler that turns a few moments from a hokey jungle adventure into an aching meditation on dreams and longing. Its wistful romance is a far cry from *Flaming Creatures*'s disorienting frenzy, but Smith was clearly influenced by it. He and his collaborator Ken Jacobs screened a print of *Rose Hobart* over and over, when Jacobs worked as an assistant to Cornell. *Flaming Creatures* occupies a temporally suspended place in film history that is analogous to the sense of timelessness of Cornell's boxes, which look as though they could have been made in the mid-nineteenth century.

More than an individual artist, Smith was an emblematic cultural figure. In this sense, he resembled another cultural trickster and genius, jazz musician Sun Ra. Starting in the late fifties, Sun Ra forged an identity as a bandleader, pianist, and bricoleur that has inspired artists like George Clinton and David Hammonds. Sun Ra's stage shows combined big band jazz with modern dance, loopy tribalism, psychedelia, group singalongs, Egyptology, and science fiction. He claimed to be a descendant of Egyptian gods who were visiting Earth from his home planet Saturn. Previous leaders might have asserted that the future of black people was in Africa; Sun Ra asserted that it was in outer space. His musical sets ranged from the bop arrangements he had grown up playing to extended improvisations that evoked European composers like Stockhausen and Xenakis. He dressed his band in elaborate, glittery costumes and strange plastic turbans of obscure religious significance.

Like Smith, Sun Ra took ordinary artistic rules and roles and utterly transformed them, combining artistry and travesty. A quick glance at the Sun Ra discography yields albums with titles such as: *Holiday for Soul Dance*, *Outer Space Incorporated*, *Pathways to Unknown Worlds*, *Cosmo Omnibus Imaginable Illusion: Live at Pit Inn*, *Cosmic Tones for Mental Therapy*, and *Other Planets of There*. His records are miracles of the unexpected, veering from extended percussion jams into soapy renditions of gay chestnuts like "Over the Rainbow." Both Smith and Sun Ra queered the traditions they grew out of. Both used the metaphor of the lost continent of Atlantis as a place of escape, a location their projections of utopian fantasies. Both invented lost continents at a time when their culture was extremely homophobic and racist, constructing fantastic worlds as defenses against the intolerable conditions around them.

Visionaries do not have heirs, they have disciples. While much of today's art world seems influenced by Smith's innovations, he cannot be said to have founded a school. Echoes of his work are evident, however, in the art of Jessica Stockholder, Mike Kelley, Nichole Isenmann, Cindy Sherman, Jerome Caja, Judy Pfaff, Cady Noland, Lucas Samaras, Vincent Fecteau, the performance artist Collette, Ethyl Eichenberger, to name but a few.

Certainly Mike Kelley, an artist omnivorous in his use of devalued icons of working class culture, uses many of the same visual and performative devices as Smith. His references to scatology, the pathetic, and queer culture bring him further into Smith's orbit. Before Kelley worked seriously as an object-maker, he was a performer who combined props, images, autobiography, and theoretical musings into vaudevillian tableaux. His best objects, like brilliant pop songs, retain that performative spirit. Kelley's "Arena" series presents pairs of thrift store stuffed animals confronting each other on blankets and afghans. Within the confines of these simplified "stages," the animals appear to be acting out mock philosophical dialogs that play on audiotapes. These pieces contain many parallels to Smith's *Secret of Rented Island*—from the stuffed animals, as surrogate actors, to Kelley's attenuated, overstylized voices on the tapes. But, the guiding principle of Kelley's work has always been a kind of morphology, particularly evident in his performances, where the narrative thread is preserved by one object or statement of a transformative nature. Kelley seems to be continually saying, "This is like this," a statement quite different from the obscure and more magical transformation in Smith's work.

Karen Kilimnik also echoes Smith's work in her seemingly haphazard arrangements and installations. Since the late eighties, Kilimnik has used everything from flour to pop songs to live horses in her sculptures, which are often moody meditations on media figures or loving evocations of romantic pasts. Kilimnik's works seem barely organized, recalling Smith's tenuous settings, but they are underlaid with a punkish anger that surfaces in surprising ways. Her 1995 exhibition at the Jack Hanley gallery in San Francisco brought together Smith's method and some of his subject matter. In a space filled with sepulchral, reddish light, the viewer found a dozen flimsy, tiny cardboard coffins, covered in felt and cheap plush, surrounded by framed photographs of the interior of burial vaults and pencil drawings of fashion models. Inside some of the coffins were candles in the shape of cherubs, cosmetics, and a Barbie doll made into a dual bride/vampire figure. With a sense of self-parody, Kilimnik melded expressions of her lesbian sexuality with notions of social, sexual, and psychic vampirism.

In 1993, Cindy Sherman produced a body of work that evokes the elegant rot of Smith's cosmos. Sherman photographed the contents of a bag of festering garbage over a period of months, using saturated colored lighting and extreme close-ups. The resulting images are post-apocalyptic landscapes, seductive and nauseating in their moistness. The original forms of the individual components are impossible to make out. Instead, the heaps of trash merge in a spectacle of decay. While some of Sherman's earlier work may remind one of the careful posing and seduction of Smith's *The Beautiful Book*, this series of pictures possesses the deepest affinity with Smith's orchestrated piles of refuse.

The differences between Jack Smith's work and that of young artists today are striking. The political, disruptive dimension of Smith's work—its utopian ambitions—is often absent from today's work, much of which is predicated on an assumption of inadequacy and failure. The use of pathetic materials, the slipshod, provisional gestures all point to an inability to imagine a single way in which this unredeemed world might be different. Contemporary artists cluster around garbage cans in New York hoping to find something thrown out by real people, so that its new utilization might reinvigorate the dying twitches of the commercial art world. Thus, much of today's funky, slim art trades on the energy of previous innovations.

The good thing about today's ephemera is that it falls apart so fast that in ten years you can try the same thing again, and it looks fresh. On the surface, this seems to be part of Smith's legacy, but in actuality his work was concerned with success. Smith's hesitations, dislocations, and dysfunctions are not images of inability, but the breaking through of an entirely new order of thinking into the self-congratulatory world of American culture. His romance of rot, for example, denounces the banalities of capitalism and attacks the American consciousness much as the extremes of Butoh were an attack on the postwar Japanese consciousness. Smith realized that when art has been converted into another sideshow of the rented lagoon, the most powerful thing it can do is to NOT SHOW UP. Slack they may be, but today's artists (god save us) are punctual: The show opens, the audience gets what it came for—all is made easy.

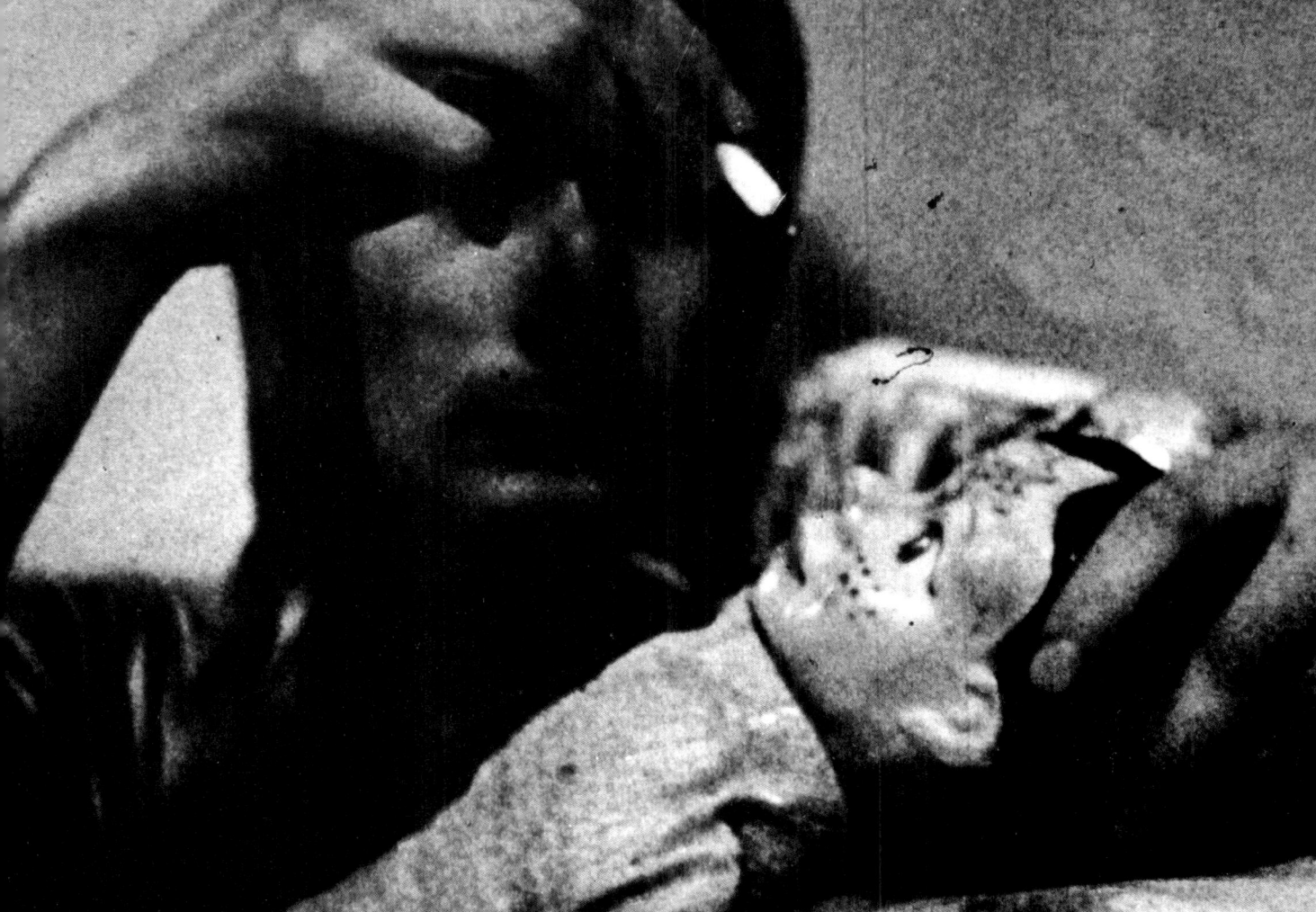

Smith in Ken Jacobs's *Little Stabs at Happiness*, 1958-60.

This earnestness and punctuality reinforce the assumption that pervades today's art practice, namely, that artists, dealers, critics, collectors, and the public are all on the same side. This illusion gained currency in the 1980s as the art world grew increasingly fascinated by the spectacle of its own success. These various constituencies, which coincidentally circulate around art objects and events, came to see themselves as slightly varied parts of the same system, each with its own place and function. To question this notion is to risk accusations of footdragging, sour grapes, or näiveté, but such shallow, soporific coziness immediately raised Smith's indignation and scorn. That anger underlies the demands he placed on his audience and his friends—an anger that looks as quaint to today's art milieu as pilgrim probity or medieval chivalry.

The thing that finally sets Jack apart is the time he lived in—a time when it was still possible to conceive of a past. Today we are continually haunted by the husks of our trends and fads, as our culture presents the past as a parade of styles offered to us on a dessert tray. Today's artists also have had their expertise made easy for them; the undead past swirls around in our heads all the time. Want to get into baroque art? Fluxus? Dixieland? Japanese manga? Santeria? The "Mary Tyler Moore Show?" Just turn on the tap. Maria Montez's films are more available than ever before. P. S. 1's exhibition and publication almost ensure that Smith's films will finally find their place in the marketplace of ideas. The expansion and development of information storage and transmission technologies like the VCR and the PC in the eighties have produced an enormous content shortage, a gap that is now being filled with everything from music and movies from around the world to enormous compilations of previous material. In the late fifties and early sixties, just seeing movies from the thirties and forties required a surprising amount of diligence. The underground at that time was not a foyer. It was, like most ghettos, part prison and part refuge—but definitely not what it is today, a term designating a market niche.

Irony has become the crucial methodology for getting young people to buy old stuff; nostalgia is the selling point for old consumers. Combined with a cynical collapse of belief in a viable future, this phenomenon has spelled the end of the past as past. Contemporary art functions in the same fashion as other sectors of the retail market. Young artists peddle various retreads of work from thirty years ago, which helps their profile, and reopens areas of profitability in the secondary market. We see the soul-less transformation of trash into art and the outside visionary turn into the insider huckster so often that we can't imagine a situation where it wouldn't happen.

Instant access to data destroys the uniqueness of events just as modern architecture, urban planning, and commercial development have conspired to destroy the uniqueness of place. Insofar as revolutions are events, the death of the event means that for artists today, the revolutionary dimension of artistic practice has become even more elusive; indeed, the "revolutionary" has simply been co-opted as yet another style. Society at large has become in fact more vehement in its assertion that the revolutionary dimension doesn't even exist, that it is impossible to transform the essential conditions of one's existence. From now until eternity, there is only rent, the endless paying out for things one already owns.

Given today's context of ubiquitous, commerce-driven information, difference is quickly subsumed by the marketplace. Communities, which come together through shared oppression, struggle for self-definition in the face of dissolving identities and trivialized meanings. Queer art runs the risk of becoming just another channel for viewers to flip past.

The queer contribution to cultural discourse is often discussed in terms of camp. Contemporary culture is seen to be pervaded by camp attitudes, and camp itself is portrayed as an outsider's action of cultural resistance. Camp is a thorny subject, a cultural gesture that both subverts and reinforces convention, but one thing is true: Camp has become an impossibility today. Camp, as Jack Smith practiced it, is an attitude of profound seriousness and connoisseurship directed at an inappropriate subject. Thus, it parodies notions of scholarship and cultural value. The subjects of camp are not fit for the type of study and veneration applied to them. By indulging in recondite social fetishisms, camp carves out a place of cultural refuge, if not resistance. The crucial component of this formulation is the seriousness and scrupulousness that underlies camp, an attitude of mind that has wholly escaped us as a culture, only to be replaced by a defanged, ubiquitous irony. This is presented in some circles as evidence of a widespread queer sensibility, but the difference is that irony, requiring no work, never presents a challenge to its practitioner, nor does it provide the possibility of cultural resistance. Unlike irony, true camp is not waiting to tear aside the mask and agree that we are all on the same

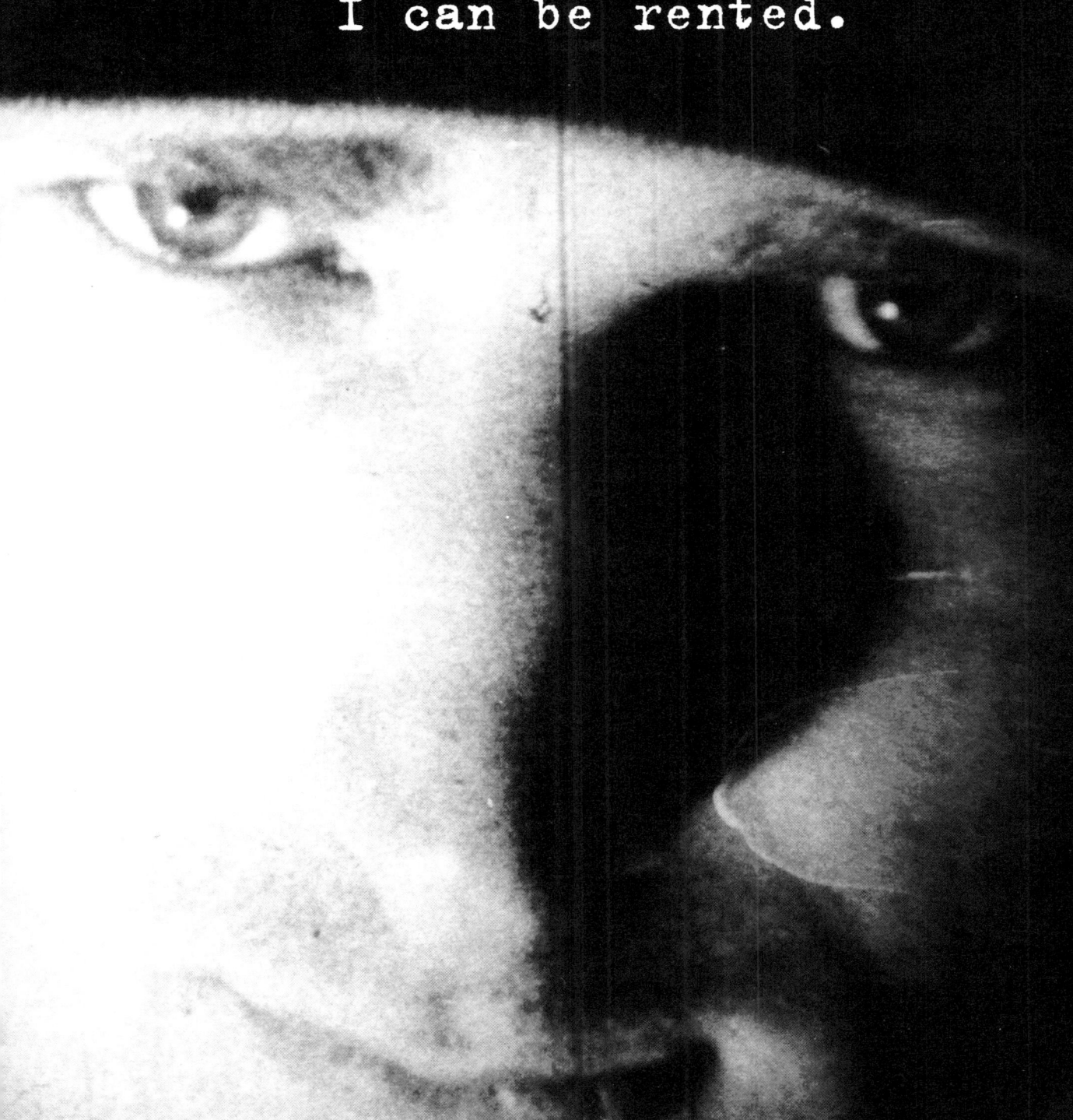

I can be rented.

side after all. But to practice camp, one must be in earnest. In the arts, the era of the late fifties and early sixties was one of great public play, but it was play conducted with steely determination. For queer artists, camp was a prime tool in that play.

In 1963 and 1964, in anticipation of its role as host for the World's Fair, New York began to clean up the ragged fringe of its brilliant tapestry. The city closed gay bars, cracked down on prostitution, began to use health and obscenity laws to harass the artistic avant-garde, and grouped the left; queers and artists were considered equally dangerous. The underground of the early sixties was indeed a melange of people who identified with groups that put their own spins on what it might mean to be queer, leftist, or an artist.

For homosexuals, the rash of obscenity prosecutions provoked a class split, driving the aesthetically advanced queer world further underground and clearing the way for the bourgeois gay movement to become the dominant voice. The West Village triumphed over the East. The gay culture that grew up after Stonewall aspired to assimilate, leaving little room for those freaks who, like Jack, were beyond the pale and could never conceive of—much less hope for—assimilation. The aesthetic sense of this group was bounded on the left by socialist realism (affirmative images of gay people) and on the right by beefcake (affirmative images of dick). This may go some distance in explaining the emergence and subsequent popularity of Robert Mapplethorpe. By the mid-seventies, porn theaters were showing gay sex infinitely more prurient and explicit than anything that had been made by underground filmmakers (whose legal travails had done much to ease censorship). Indeed it was not the explicit sexual acts but the art itself that had troubled the authorities. The early sixties also marked the point at which the art world began to distance itself from queer content and identity, moving from a garrulous, ambisexual representation toward an increasingly formalist abstraction. As the avant-garde art scene began to repress its queerness, the gay scene began to repress its avant-garde-ness.

If one were to view Jack Smith's work as a precursor to today's explosion of drag performance and mass media drag imagers, it would not only be a gross oversimplification of his work but a misreading of the genealogy of contemporary drag. For Jack's drag was about neither passing, nor clowning: It was an evocation of travesty, of the carnivalesque. His costumes do not play on gender roles but subsume gender into a fetishistic celebration of societal confusion. While *Flaming Creatures*'s cast appears to be composed mainly of drag queens, many of the actors are simply heavily made-up women. And, in Smith's later works, extravagant costuming replaces cross-dressing almost entirely. The drag in his work consequently is far from the legacy that has given us today's battalions of Ru Pauls and Lypsinkas. Much of the performing tradition of today's drag is derived from vaudeville and ultimately from minstrelsy, working class forms of gender and racial anxiety. In the same way that donning blackface allowed whites to illustrate both their desire for, and difference from, black bodies and black cultural expression, most drag allows men the luxury of playing at female identification without losing phallic power. Thus, drag is a sanctioned, temporary crossing of boundaries, rather than an elimination of those boundaries. Indeed, in the nineties, drag queens have been trotted out as happy-go-lucky window dressing on the periphery of modern life; as outrageous-looking (is there a more boring emotion than outrage?) men who still care about straight folks—papas and mamas and kinder on the inside; and, as fairies who, like the fairies in Disney's world, just want folks to love and tolerate each other. In the gay community, drag has become so accepted that notions of its transgression scarcely ever occur.

Mainstream artists are obsessively searching for the true outsider spirit that used to exist within the hidden margins of American society. But, they search for that spirit only to make it perform tricks of a special effects dummy (r.i.p., Ed Wood). They want a past whose revival has no consequences for the present. The marginal has ceased to exist as a real cultural category; it has been replaced by the underdeveloped. Official culture has always had a vampiric relationship to real vision, transforming primal power into undead commodity. The excitement we experience in relation to true works of art is the knowledge that anything can happen, that we don't know where a narrative line, or note is taking us. In works like *Jurassic Park*, that notion is dangled in front of us, only to be replaced by the deadening certainty of knowing exactly what will happen. The knowledge of infinite possibility is perhaps the only thing that art can teach us and the only thing it need teach us. The brilliance of Jack Smith's work is that it constantly proceeds in unexpected directions, making unexpected connections, startling us with its newness.

Like the hired-gun scientists in *Jurassic Park*, I have been trying, as an artist, to reconstruct a dead titan. And, like them, I've used secondary sources, blood from a mosquito trapped in amber, a written description of a performance, a funerary reminiscence. Like every other artist, I take my nourishment from past efforts, a fly on the corpse. But how can we sustain ourselves without betraying those who came before? How do we honor a body of work without destroying its spirit? This exhibition and book are ways of honoring Jack Smith. But, it is a half measure at best, one that treads perilously close to the institutions that Smith so mistrusted.

Why Jack Smith today? What is the importance of looking at his work? Perhaps, because we need it so much. As we look around,

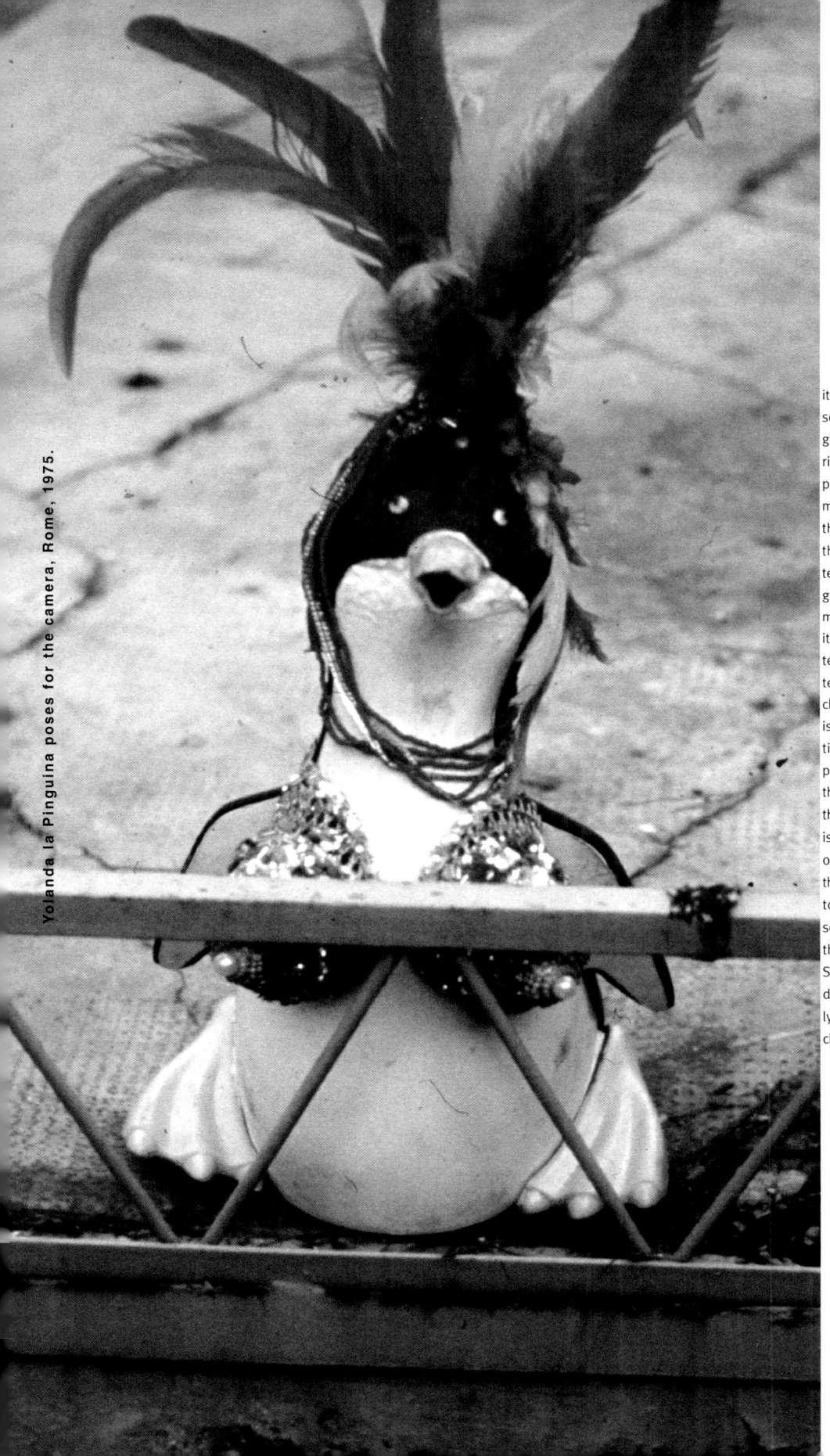

Yolanda la Pinguina poses for the camera, Rome, 1975.

it is clear that we have given so much up that we have forgotten that we even had the right to ask for things that previous generations demanded without qualm, like the utter transformation of the conditions of our existence. To understand the true genius of Smith's work, we must take it whole, not chop it up into highlights and masterpieces. Much of Smith's interaction with the public was characterized by deep dissatisfaction, scorn, and frustration on both sides. It's important not to lose sight of that fact. It may well be that the legacy of prophetic artists is not to give us specific ways of doing something but, by their example, the permission to be fearless in our own search for a way to do something. Viewed in that spirit, Smith's vision is far from understood, but still enormously potent in its potential to change our lives.

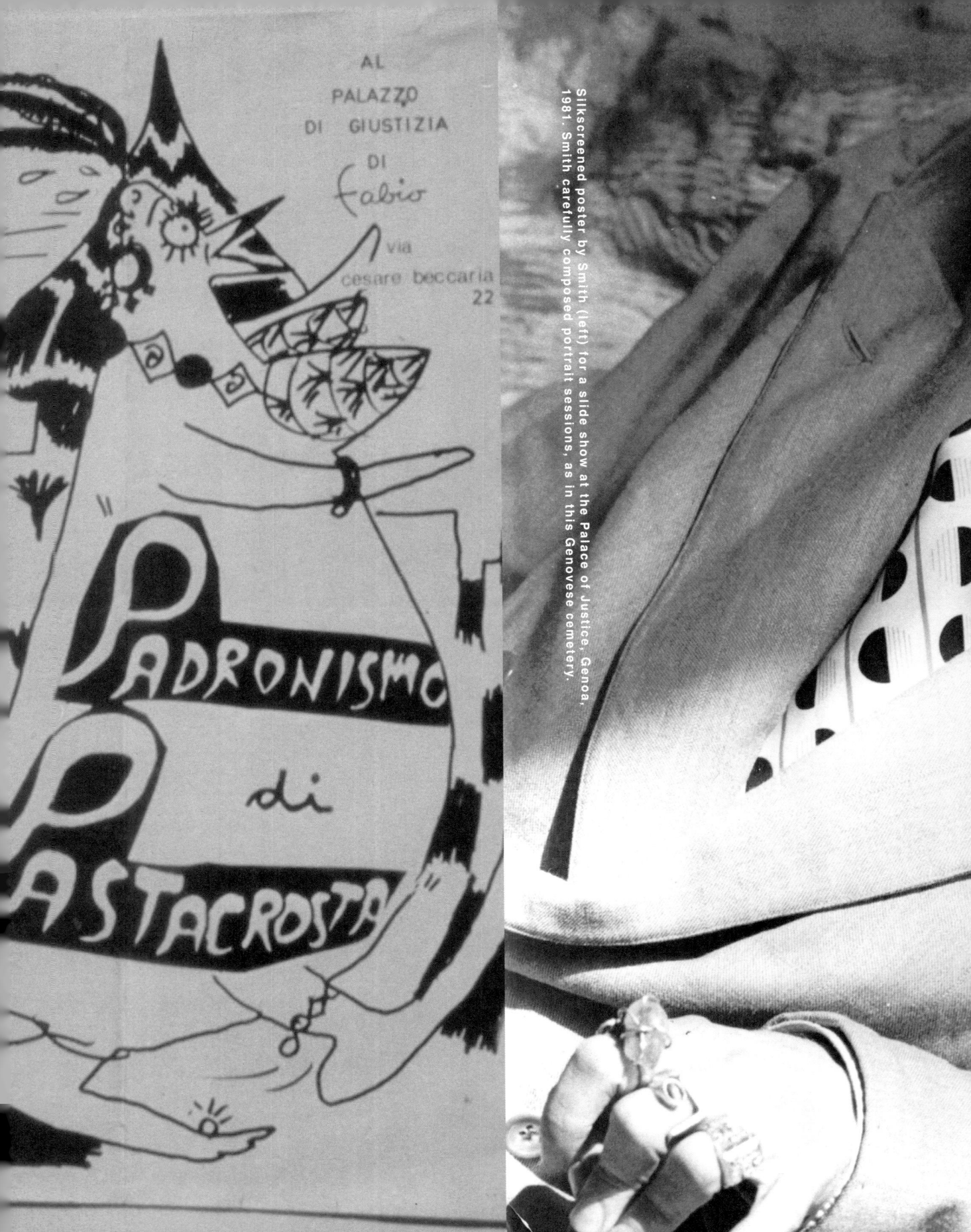

Silkscreened poster by Smith (left) for a slide show at the Palace of Justice, Genoa, 1981. Smith carefully composed portrait sessions, as in this Genovese cemetery.

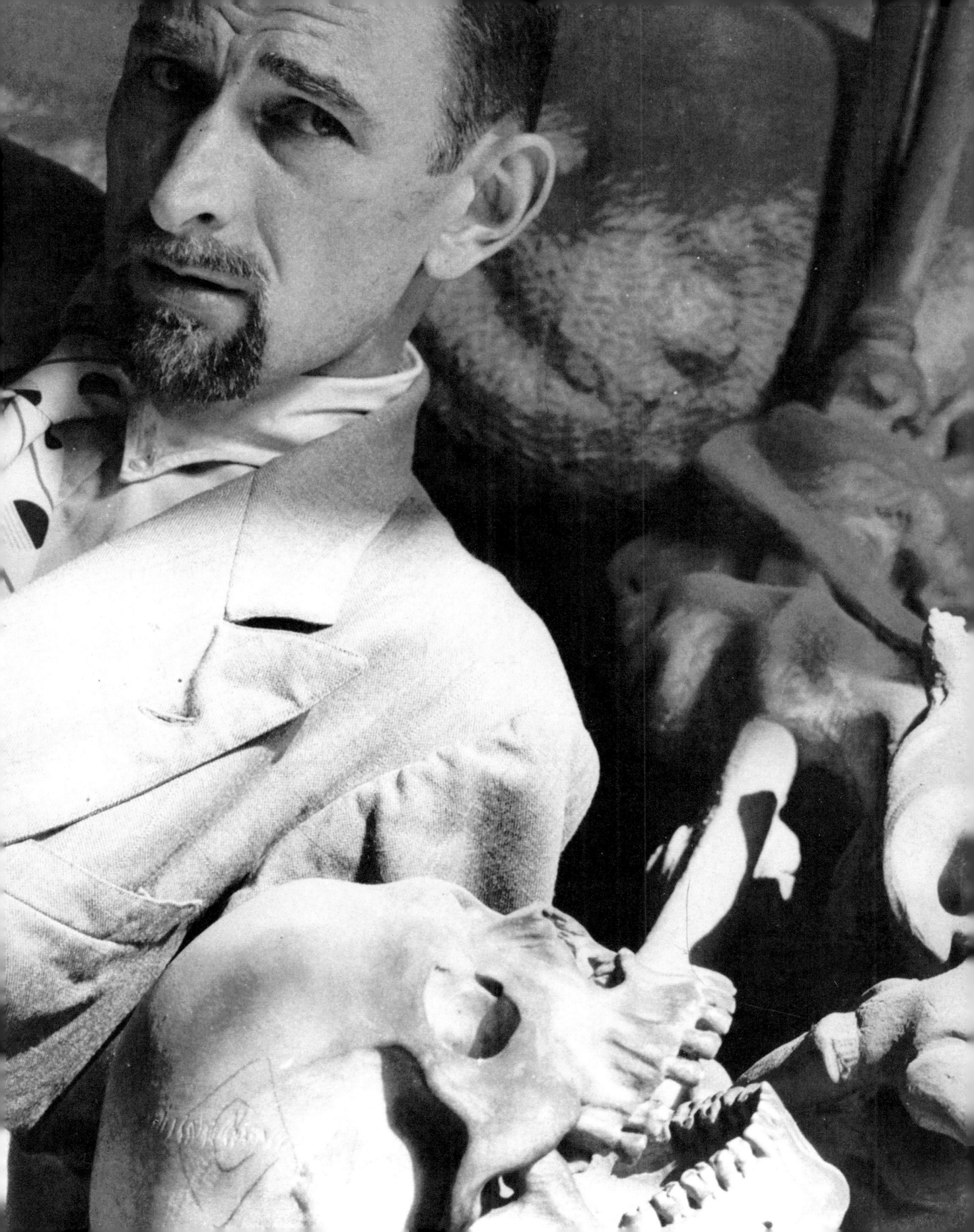

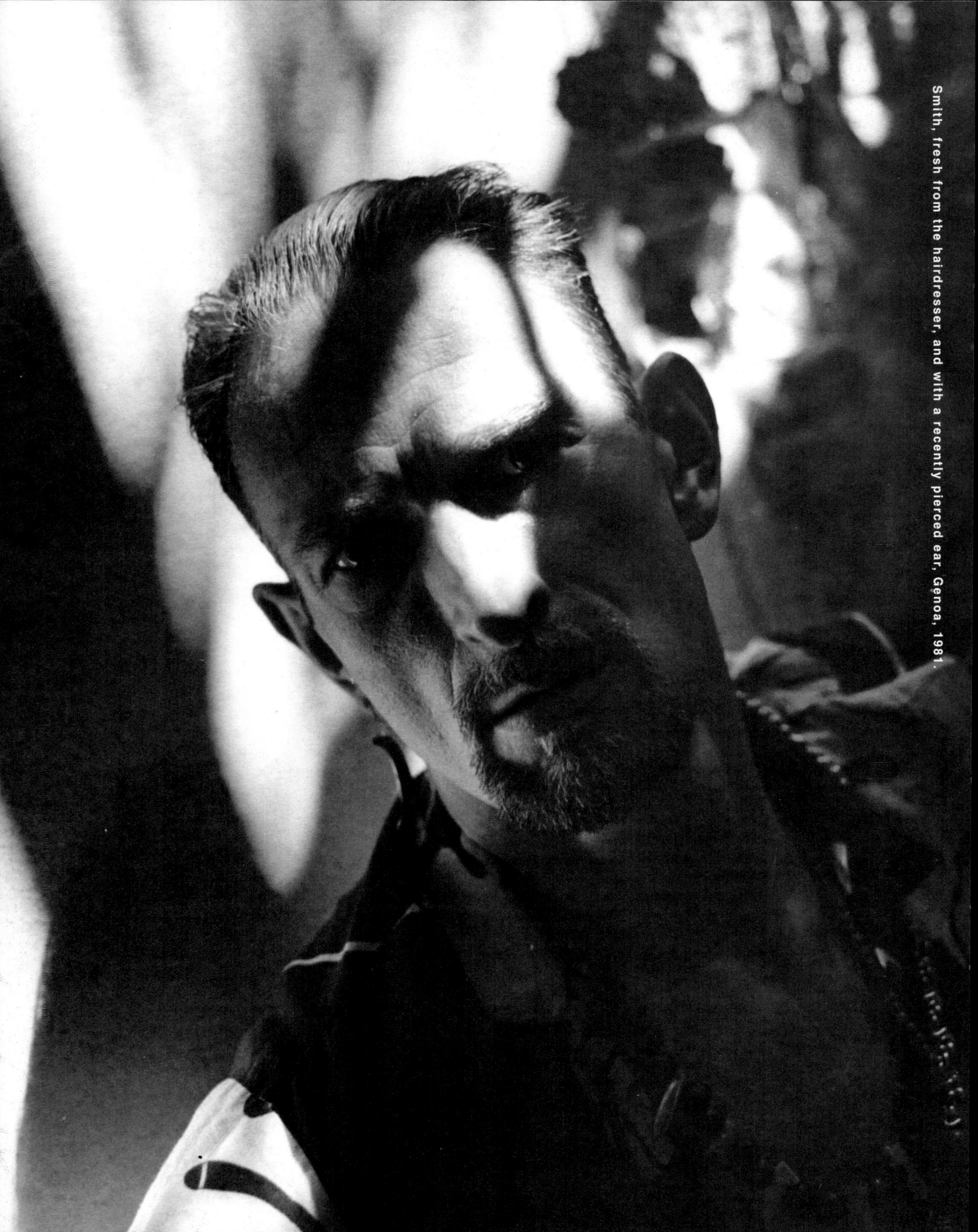

Smith, fresh from the hairdresser, and with a recently pierced ear, Genoa, 1981.

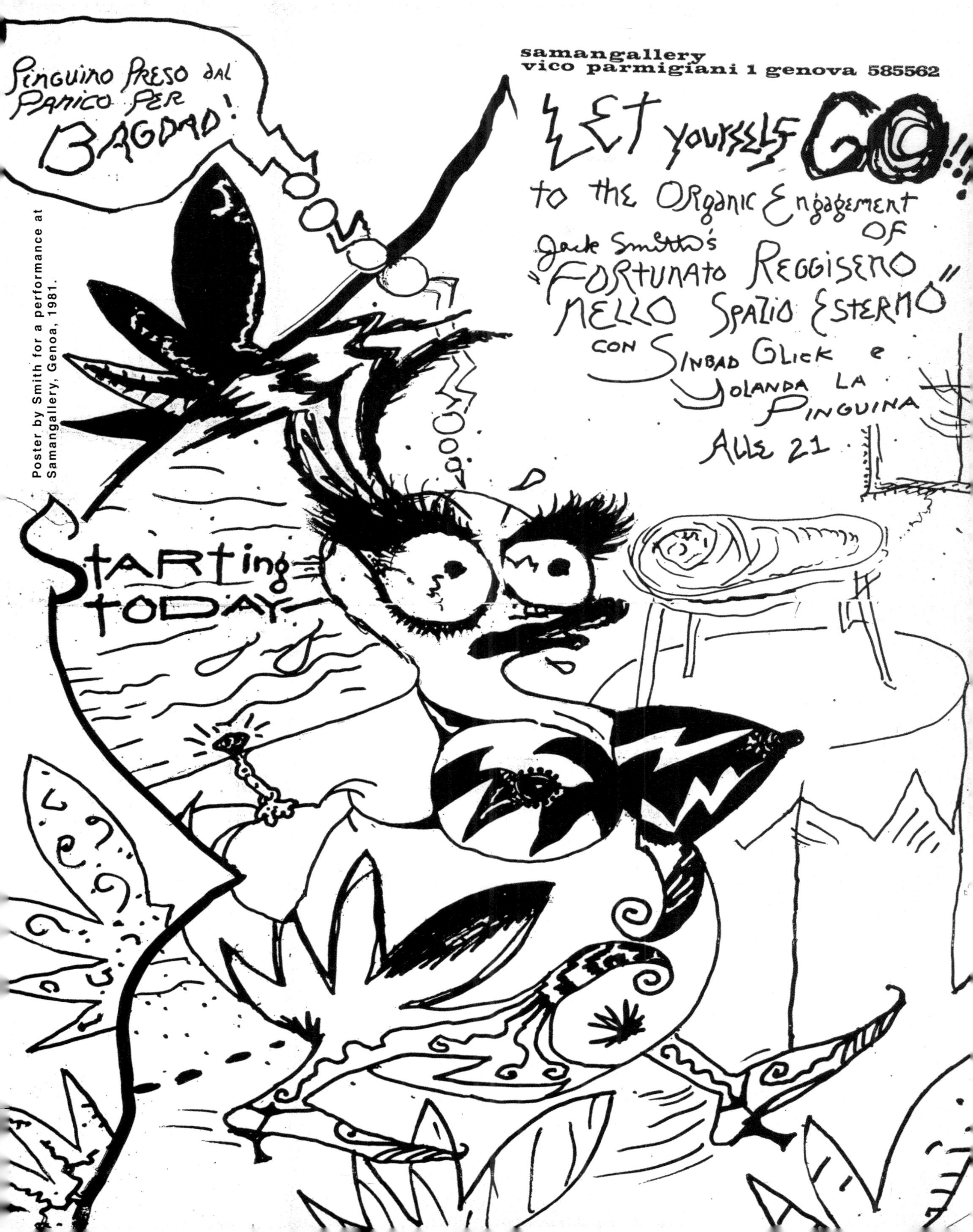

Poster by Smith for a performance at Samangallery, Genoa, 1981.

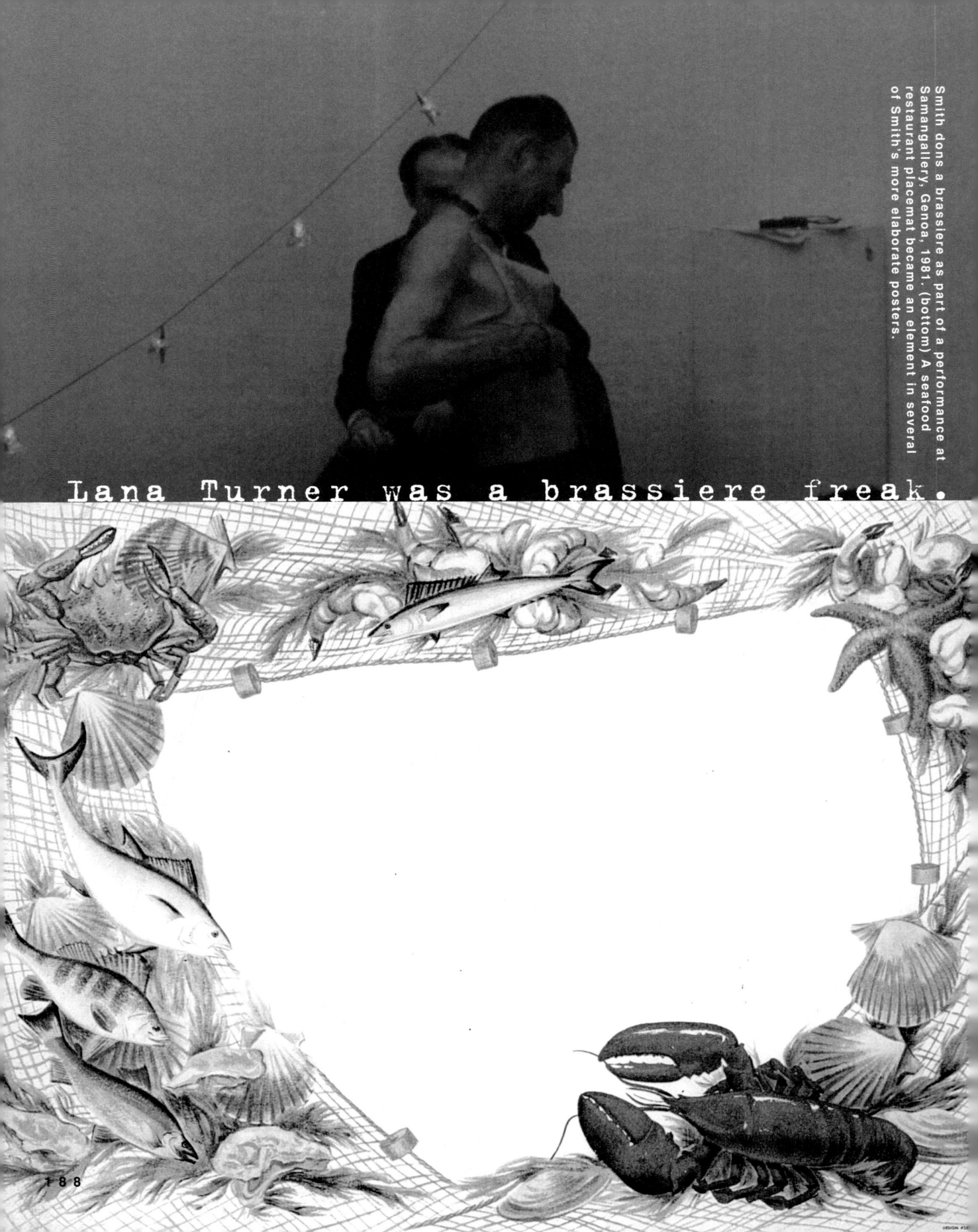

Smith dons a brassiere as part of a performance at Samangallery, Genoa, 1981. (bottom) A seafood restaurant placemat became an element in several of Smith's more elaborate posters.

Lana Turner was a brassiere freak.

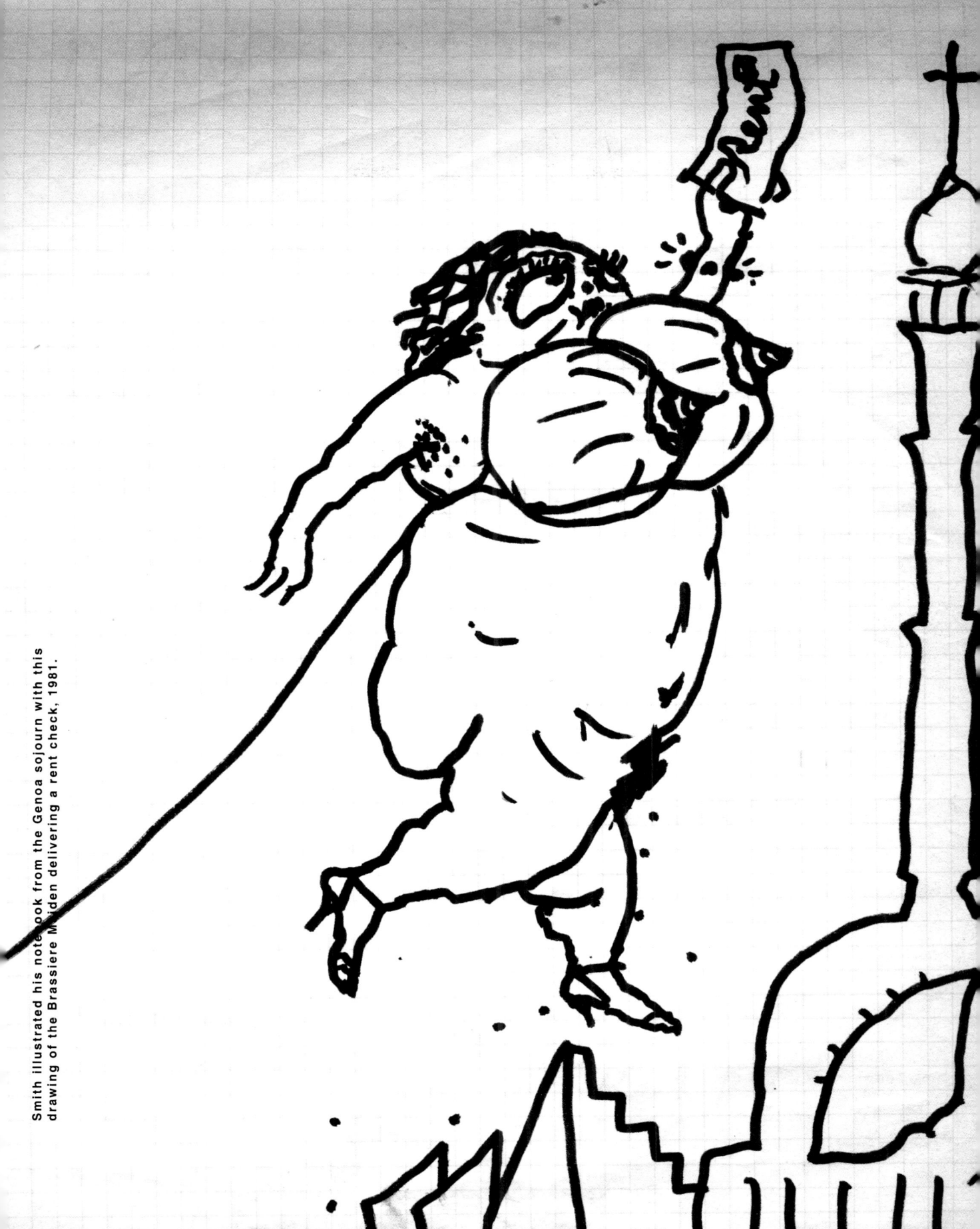

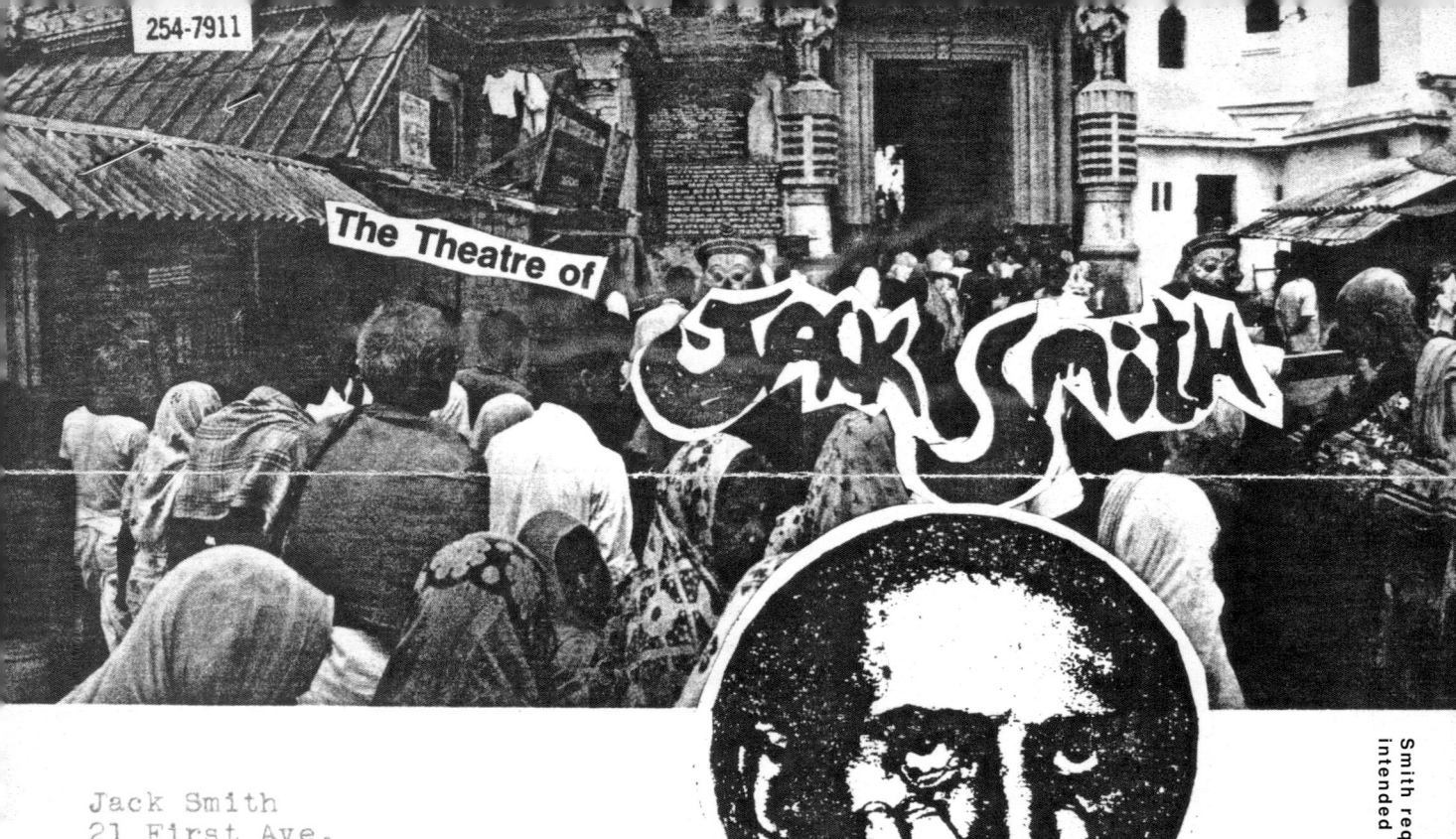

The Theatre of Jack Smith

Smith requested and received an extension for a National Endowment for the Arts grant intended for his Sinbad film project, 1982.

Jack Smith
21 First Ave.
New York, New York
10003
June 6, 1982

Dear Sir,

 I am requesting a time extention on my grant. It was never my intention to finish this film project in less than four years. I would like a new ending date of a year and a half from now. I am starting the actual filming of the project this summer. I would be happy to come to Washington to show you scenes of the film as production begins.

 Thank you for your assistance. If there are any questions please contact me.

 Very Sincerely

 Jack Smith

 Jack Smith
 Tel #: (212) 254-7911

NEA
APPROVED
...w ending date
...cember 31, 1983
D.DiLico 7/8
...thorized
GRANT NO.: R81-34-34M
NEW END DATE: 12/31/83
APPROVED: C.M.W./MEDIA
 6/22/82

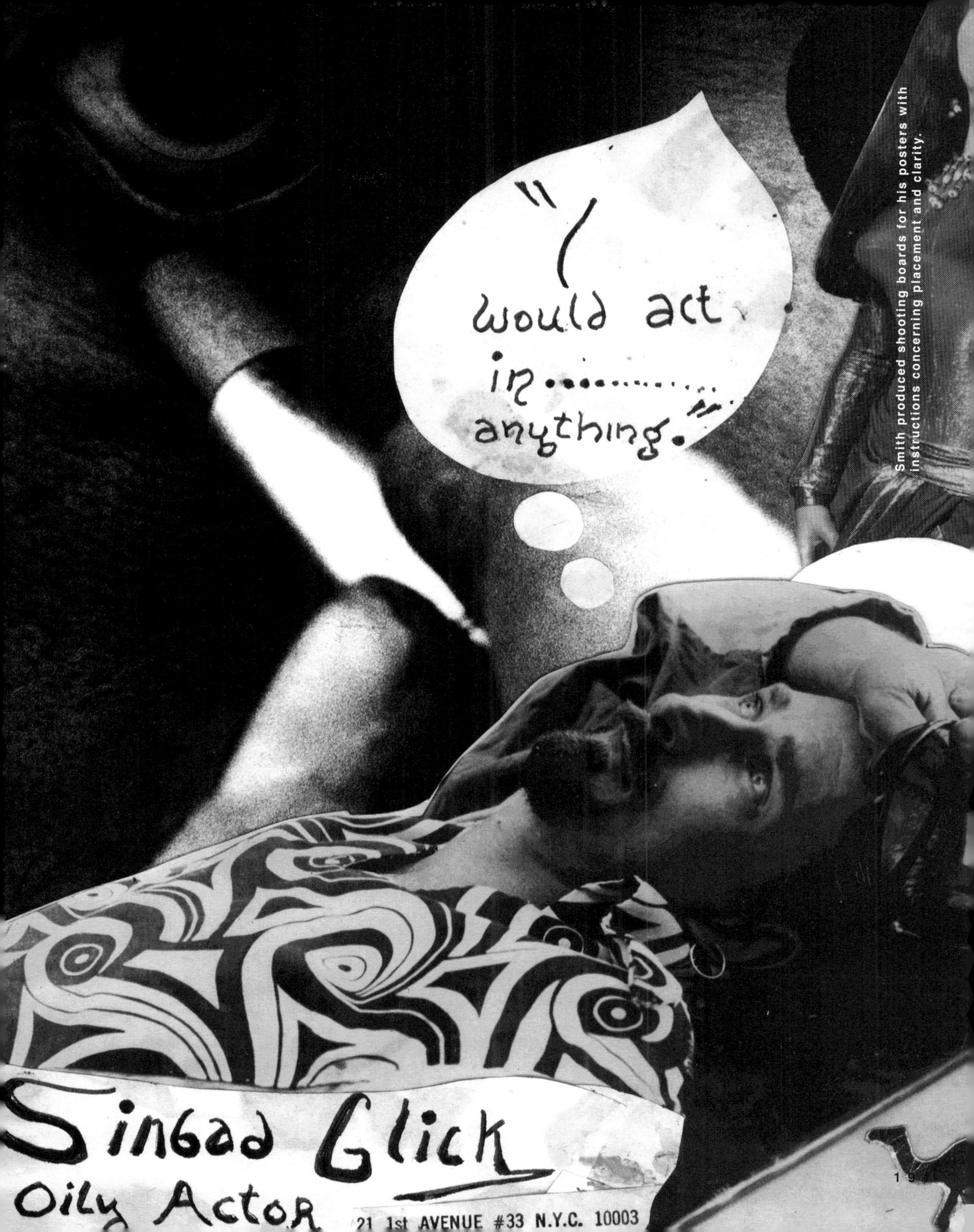

Smith produced shooting boards for his posters with instructions concerning placement and clarity.

The Last Days and Last Moments of Jack Smith

–Penny Arcade a.k.a. Susana Ventura

It took Jack minutes to walk down the six flights from his apartment to the street where Ivan Galietti and I waited by my car. Six flights that he used to lope down in less than a few seconds. "Bring the car," Jack had commanded on the phone. "I want you to take me to the hospital." Ivan and I stood on the street, glancing at the doorway, waiting for Jack's great slouching form to emerge. "Jack will never climb those stairs again," I said to Ivan. "No," Ivan replied, nodding at the still empty doorway. "No, I don't think so. He's too weak. This is it."

Suddenly, Jack lunged through the door, his grey wool coat flapping wildly around his emaciated form. His head was thrown back, slightly cocked to the left, while the rest of his body seemed to be veering to the right. There was chaotic motion, yet he was standing still. His eyes raking the sky, arms flying heavenward, he addressed the top floors of First Avenue, crying out, "Now I know why we cannot have bowls of gravy!"

Jack, covered in cheap gold and silver chains from midnight binges on home shopper's network, looked out of place in the August light. "Oh! I look like a wino!" Jack said, catching his reflection in the jewelry store window. "That's why I have to encrust myself in jewels! When people see you're sick or poor, they just ignore you. They treat you like shit." Kurt Lavine, Jack's upstairs neighbor, helped Jack into the car and slipped into the back seat. We said goodbye to Ivan. As we pulled away from the curb, Jack turned to me and said, earnestly, "We have to find a malted before we do anything else. I've almost completely given up on finding a banana split in this god forsaken town." As I pulled up in front of Veselka's on Second Avenue, I turned to Jack and suggested he order some "real" food. "I've been dazzled by ice cream my entire life!" he replied. Kurt ran in, quickly returning with the malted. Jack took his first sip, moaning, "I can't believe this! You can't get a malted in this town. America is finished! They don't know how to make a malted in this country anymore! There's syrup in this malted! Syrup!" He ranted and slurped the malted as he gave the exact recipe for a genuine malted. As he finished, we pulled up in front of Beth Israel Hospital. He threw his head against the car window and shrieked, "I've fought a battle against bad food my entire life, and I'm losing!" As soon as Jack was admitted to his room, they put him on IV Bactrin. He was suffering from an advanced stage of pneumocystis. Jack fought with the doctors and nurses, "They want to turn me into a human pincushion! I don't want to stay here! I just want to die! Why can't I just die? I contacted the Hemlock Society, but it takes months to die by their system!" Turning to me he said, "I want you to bring me something to kill myself with." "O.K. Jack," I said, "but don't you think you should wait to kill yourself at home? I mean, killing yourself in a hospital seems redundant. Why don't you just take the medicine and get better, and then you can kill yourself at home!" Jack turned to the nurse allowing her to place the IV in his arm. "I suppose you have a point there," he said.

Three days later, my phone rang at 2:30 am. It was Ira Cohen. "The hospital just called. They said Jack's in a bad way. Meet me at the hospital." I stumbled out of

Excerpted from the original published in Film Culture 76, *June 1992*

bed, pulled on clothes, and went out into the street, bumping into Mitch Markowitz, who I lived with then. He was coming home from his film courier job. "What's up?" he asked when he saw me. "It's Jack," I said. "Ira called. I'm going to the hospital." Without another word, we headed for Beth Israel. Arriving in Jack's room, we found him unconscious. A very young doctor came into the room. "Look, your friend is in pretty bad shape. He won't live till 7 a.m." Ira, Mitch, and I were dumbfounded. "You can remove his oxygen mask," the doctor continued, "I'll just close the door." "I don't think so," I said. "We're not removing his oxygen." "Suit yourself," the doctor shrugged, "but there's no way he's going to survive till morning, his case is very advanced." The doctor left, and Ira, Mitch, and I began to massage various parts of Jack's body, talking to him as we did. We kept up the massage and talk, encouraging each other and encouraging Jack. At 6:30 a.m., my hand entwined in Jack's cold claw, Jack suddenly tightened his grip. "My God!" I thought, "this must be rigor mortis!" I found myself pinned to Jack's chest by his action. "They're going to have to saw his arm off to release me," came the panicked thought. Suddenly Jack lurched, pulling himself up to a sitting position, braced by my hand in his vice-like grip. Opening his eyes, he glanced around at our faces, "What's going on?," he murmured. "You're back, Jack! You're back!" We all jumped up and down shrieking, to Jack's bemused bewilderment. The doctor entered the room, shrugging his shoulders, gave us the *hi sign*, and left.

The next few days were a jumbled reprieve, filled with friends, uneaten food, Jack's request for drugs to kill himself with, and Ira Cohen's and my attempt to get Jack to make a will to protect his work. "Burn everything," he said over and over. "I've lived my life in obscurity, now I'm dying in obscurity." "But Jack! What about all the people who never hurt you? What about the future?" I countered. "The future? The future? It will only get worse!" he moaned. That stopped me cold. Often when Jack spoke, he cracked the psychic treadmill I unconsciously run on, and a flare would light the murky corners up. This was one of those moments. Jack was a visionary who could make you see what he saw. 'Well," I stumbled, "what, what if your work is sealed for two hundred years, then all the people who stole from you will have a heyday showing your work, and then your work will be sealed up again." "My god! You're right! I hadn't thought of that!" Jack screeched, bolting upright. "First I have to get back home," he said, "and organize everything properly. A lot of stuff has to be given away; other stuff has to be thrown out." I spent hours naming institutions that might be homes for his work. He hated them all equally for one reason or another till I mentioned the Smithsonian. "Ah! The Smith-sonian," he murmured...

Late that night I returned for the nightshift. Michael Oppedisano was at the bedside. We exchanged some tense words over Jack's bed. Jack was unconscious. Suddenly Jack glided to a sitting position, his arms raising. "See!" Michael said, "he's doing his dance of the seven veils." Jack's eyes were open now, fixed on some distant ecstatic point. His movements were deliberate, ritualistic. Whatever he saw was so powerful a vision, so achingly beautiful, that the feeling streamed through the room. Slowly it abated, and he lay back. Earlier in the day, Jack had given me his keys to get his mail and water his pot bush, one of the lushest I'd ever seen on the Lower East Side. I had suggested bringing back some of Jack's favorite things, but he balked. He didn't want anything of his in the hospital. He wanted to go home.

The next day Jack stayed unconscious, breathing fitfully. I heard he had visitors, Bill Niederkorn, Agosto Machado, Uzi Parnes, Ela Troyano. Ginsberg returned to photograph Jack on the IV, which infuriated me, since Jack had stopped him from taking pictures the day before. I heard Ken Jacobs had come, seeing his old partner for the first time in years after a bitter separation…

Hours passed. Jack's skin surface felt colder and colder, denser somehow. Ira Cohen and Mickey Meyers, a professional psychic and ìghost buster,î smoked cigarettes in the lounge. I stood by Jack's bed, talking to him non-stop about what I could remember from the *Tibetan Book of he Dead*…

The nurses liked that we, Jack's friends, worked with them, so they were always willing to come and help change the sheets, whenever there was an accident, even several times in one day. I held Jack in my arms on one side of the bed so the nurse could make up the other side, and I remembered what Sheyla Baykal, who had cared for several dying friends, had said to me two nights before, when she came to sit by Jack. "It's close to the end, Penny. You can't do anything for Jack now but help him die as comfortably and with as much dignity as possible."

But somehow I didn't believe it was the end. The end of Jack? Impossible. "You have a lot of experience with this," I said to the nurse. "Jack's body temperature keeps getting colder. Can you tell how much time he has before he dies?" The nurse glanced from me to Jack and said, "No, I couldn't make a prediction like that. It's different in each case, but I never worry about the hour of my death because Jesus is my personal savior." "Christ!" I thought, "this is the last thing I need! Someone witnessing for Jesus." But I kept my mouth shut. The nurse spoke again as we switched places to make up the other side of the bed. "Does your friend believe in God?" he continued, nodding toward Jack, who lay against my chest like a crumpled Pieta. I was a little dazed. I hadn't slept in three or more days. I was surprised to hear him speak. "Does Jack Smith believe in God?" I repeated. "No. No, Jack Smith doesn't believe in God. God, however, believes in Jack Smith!" Suddenly Jack's body shook with a rattling cough, accompanied by what sounded like laughter. The nurse was horrified. The coughing went on for several minutes. "My God!" I thought. "Is Jack laughing?"

Mickey came into the room. Suddenly I felt a huge urge to go to Jack's house. Mickey said she would stay in the room while I did. I ran to my car. Arriving at Jack's, it felt spooky and empty. Jack kept the lightbulbs in his house unscrewed—an eclectic form of burglar proofing—so unless you knew where the lamps were, you couldn't get the lights on. I gathered up beautiful cloths and scarves—blue nile incense, a few tapes, early Arabic music that Bill Niederkorn had made for him, and a Marlene Dietrich tape. Whatever struck me.

I hurried back to Jack's room. We decorated the room and Jack's bed with lush scarves and drapings. We lit incense and put on music. We took turns staying and talking to Jack. I held Jack's hand and stroked his forehead, saying to him, "You can go anytime you want, but it would be so lovely if you would wake up one more time so I could see you, and we could have a laugh or else you can just let go. Whichever you want is fine." I said this over and over as Jack's regular breath came and went with his oxygen mask. He had fought the mask for days, but now he rarely brushed it from his nose. Time passed slowly with me stroking Jack's forehead, repeating and repeating every instruction on dying I ever heard. Calling him "Jackie" over and over.

In one moment, as I said, "You can just exhale and let go," I heard Jack exhale. I watched and watched for the inhale. I couldn't tell if seconds or minutes had passed. "My God!" I said out loud. "You did it. You're dead!" I was struck that the feeling in the room hadn't changed. Jack didn't feel gone. I ran out of the room to

Smith poster (left) for *I Was a Male Yvonne De Carlo for the Lucky Landlord Underground*, 1982. Writer Irving Rosenthal used this film-related photograph (right) by Smith for the jacket of his 1967 "memoir," *Sheeper*.

get Mickey and Ira, nearly knocking over the nurse who was entering the room for her rounds. Running back with Ira and Mickey, I found the nurse trying to find Jack's pulse. "I think he's dead," I said quietly to her, and then jumped joyously up and down saying out loud, "You did it, Jack! You did it! You're dead!" The room was filled with the huge presence of Jack. A presence that was the same minutes before he was dead, but now, without the constraint of his body, loomed large, expanding, filling every corner. I glanced at Ira, Mickey, the nurse. They all felt it too. It was magnificent! Royal! Luminous! All that Jack was, and more. We all swooned under the power of it. An extraordinary force of love, nearly physical, like in the greatest lovemaking. The nurses came into the room to check Jack. The doctor was called, the incense burned, the music played, and we stood around, loving Jack. The doctor entered the room, the same young resident from the week before. He asked me how Jack died. I repeated that he had just quietly exhaled and died. "That's extraordinary," the young doctor mused. "No trauma? No thrashing? A man this sick would normally convulse."

We helped wash Jack's body. Ira anointed Jack's head, feet, and hands with musk oil from a great Moroccan perfumer. We watched as they bound Jack's hands and feet with white cloth, as they tied his jaw up, a look Jack had affected in many performances, that look we know as Marley's ghost. Jack's face looked ecstatic, as if he had seen the most beautiful sight of his life, or had just had an extraordinary orgasm. "Ira, Ira," I said, "take out you camera. Photograph Jack now. He looks so beautiful! So magnificent! Evangelical!" Ira stood on a chair and took four photos. They placed Jack in a body sack. The nurse who had been Jack's constant attendant approached us with the doctor. "I just want to tell you that no one has ever died on this floor like this before. It's so beautiful." The doctor pressed forward: "Your friend was so lucky, so many people who are as far gone as he was would die alone, without friends. There's rarely anyone when the end comes. Who was he? He must have been a very important person." "He was Jack Smith," I explained, "one of the greatest artists who ever lived." "Jack Smith," the doctor repeated as if it was the most exotic of names. It was 6:35 a.m., September 16, 1989. As they waited for the orderlies to come remove Jack's body to the hospital morgue, I went to the phone and called everyone who had left his or her number. We cleaned the room and left in the early morning sun. The pain, the sorrow, and loss hadn't hit yet.

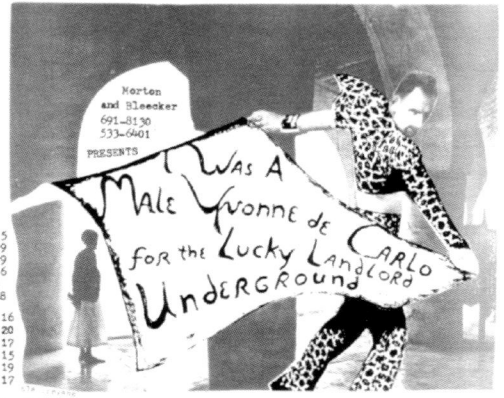

The Theatre of Exotic Aquatics

Morton
and Bleecker
691-8130
533-6401
PRESENTS

I Was A Male Yvonne de Carlo for the Lucky Landlord Underground

On the third Friday of every month...
at 8 & 11 pm   tickets $7.00

FLAME OF CEMENT LAGOON PERFORMANCE
by
Jack Smith

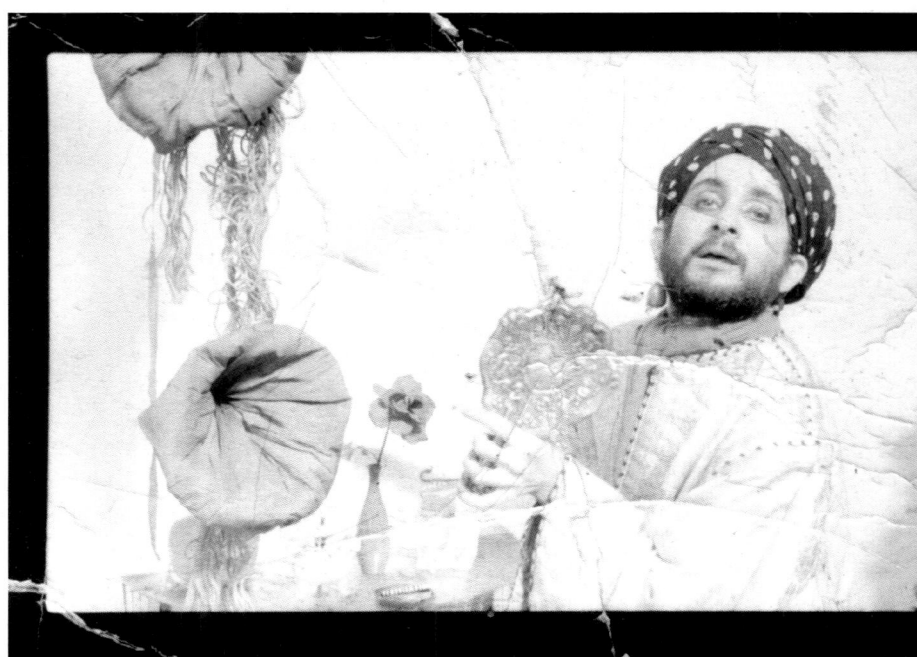

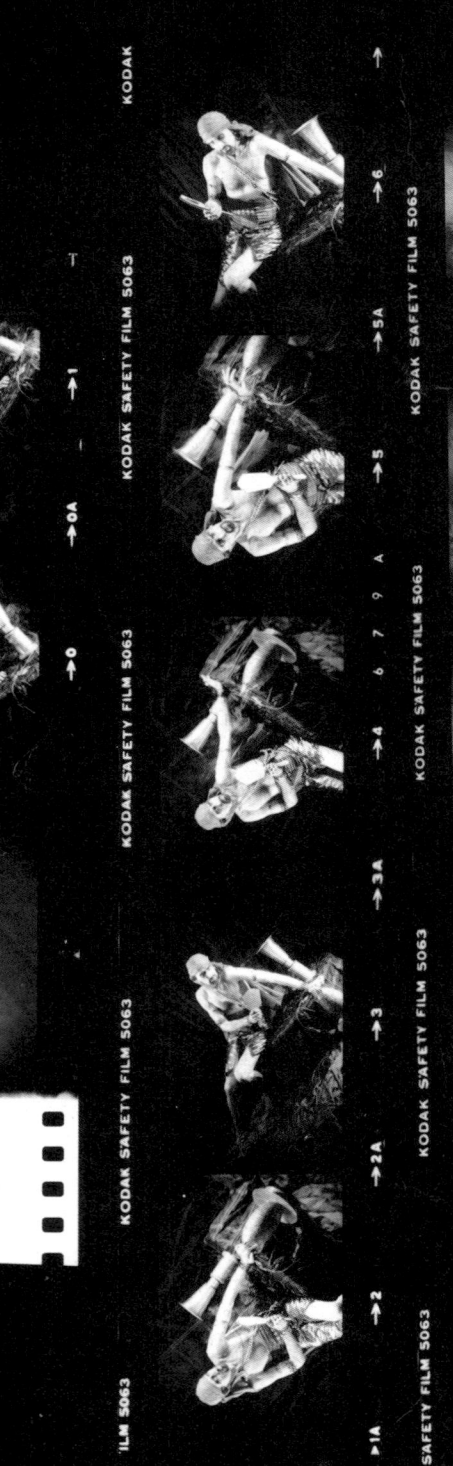

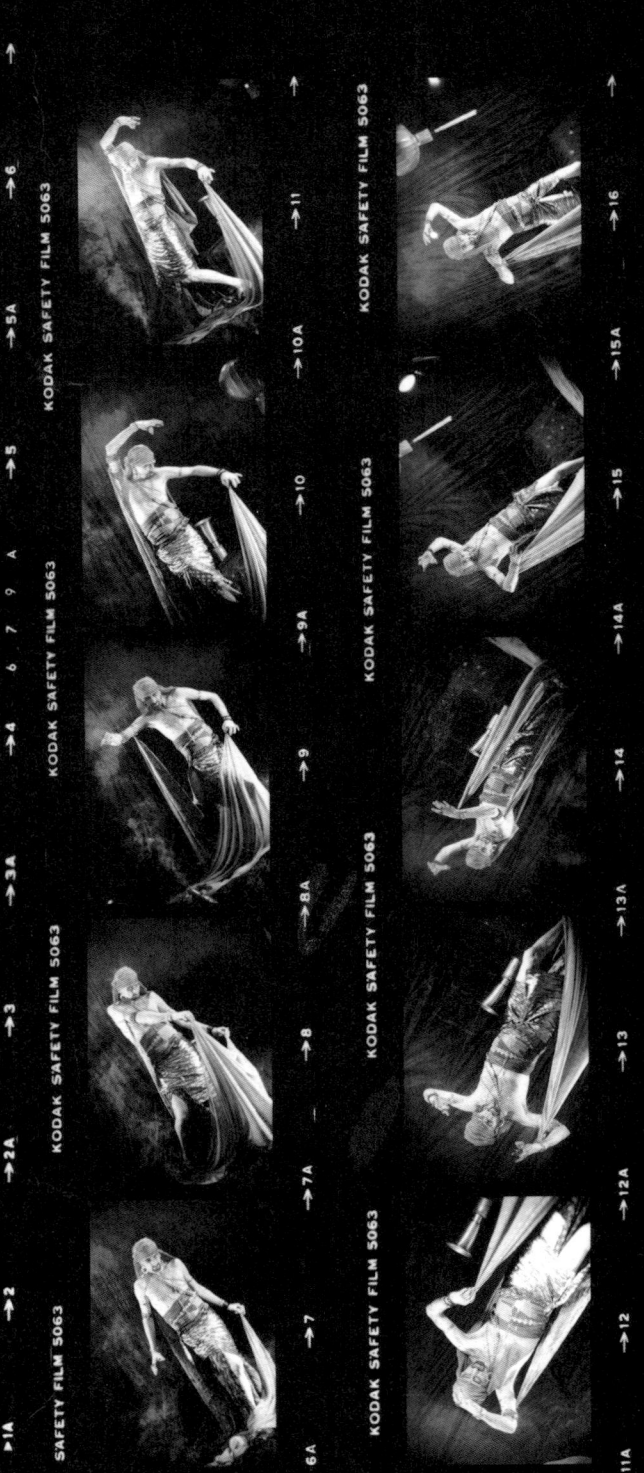

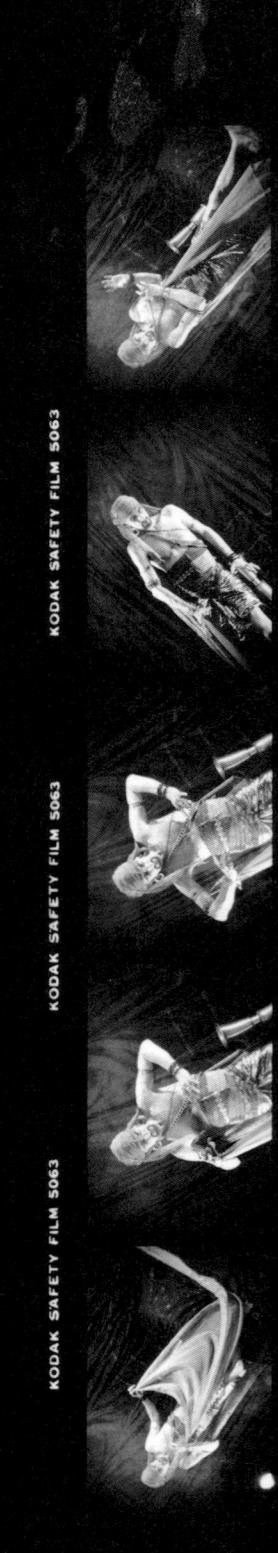

Smith in exotic motion, 1982.

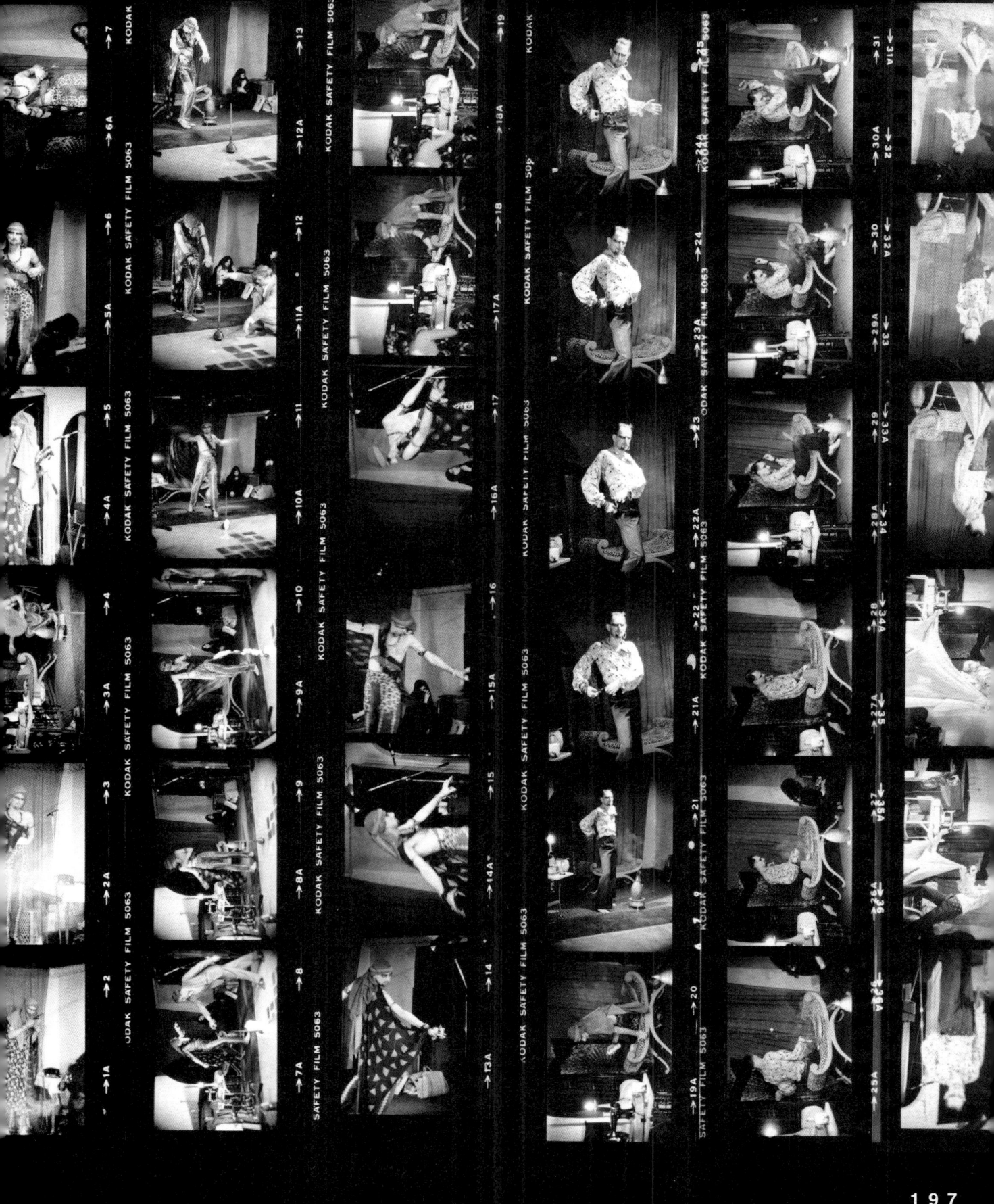

197

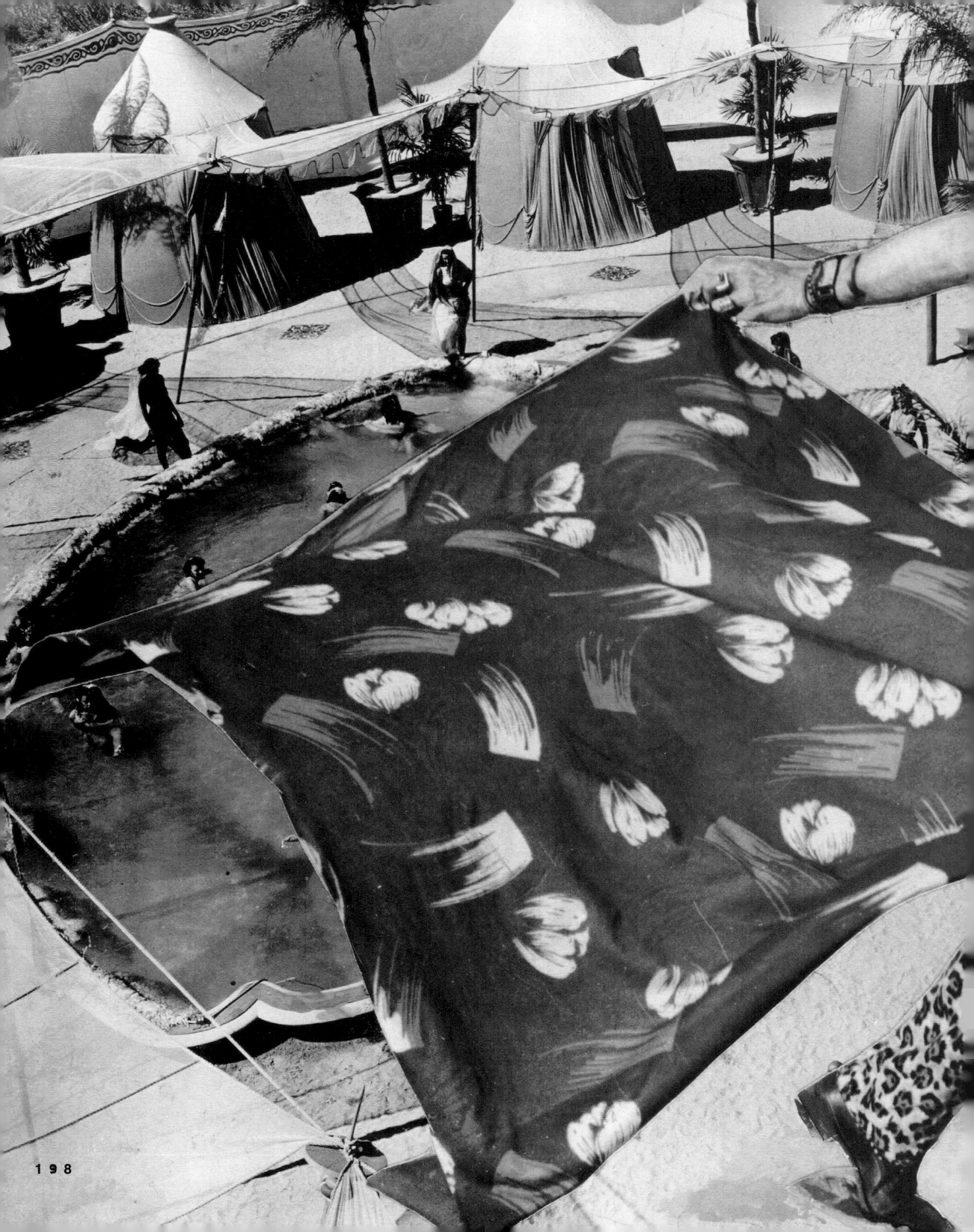

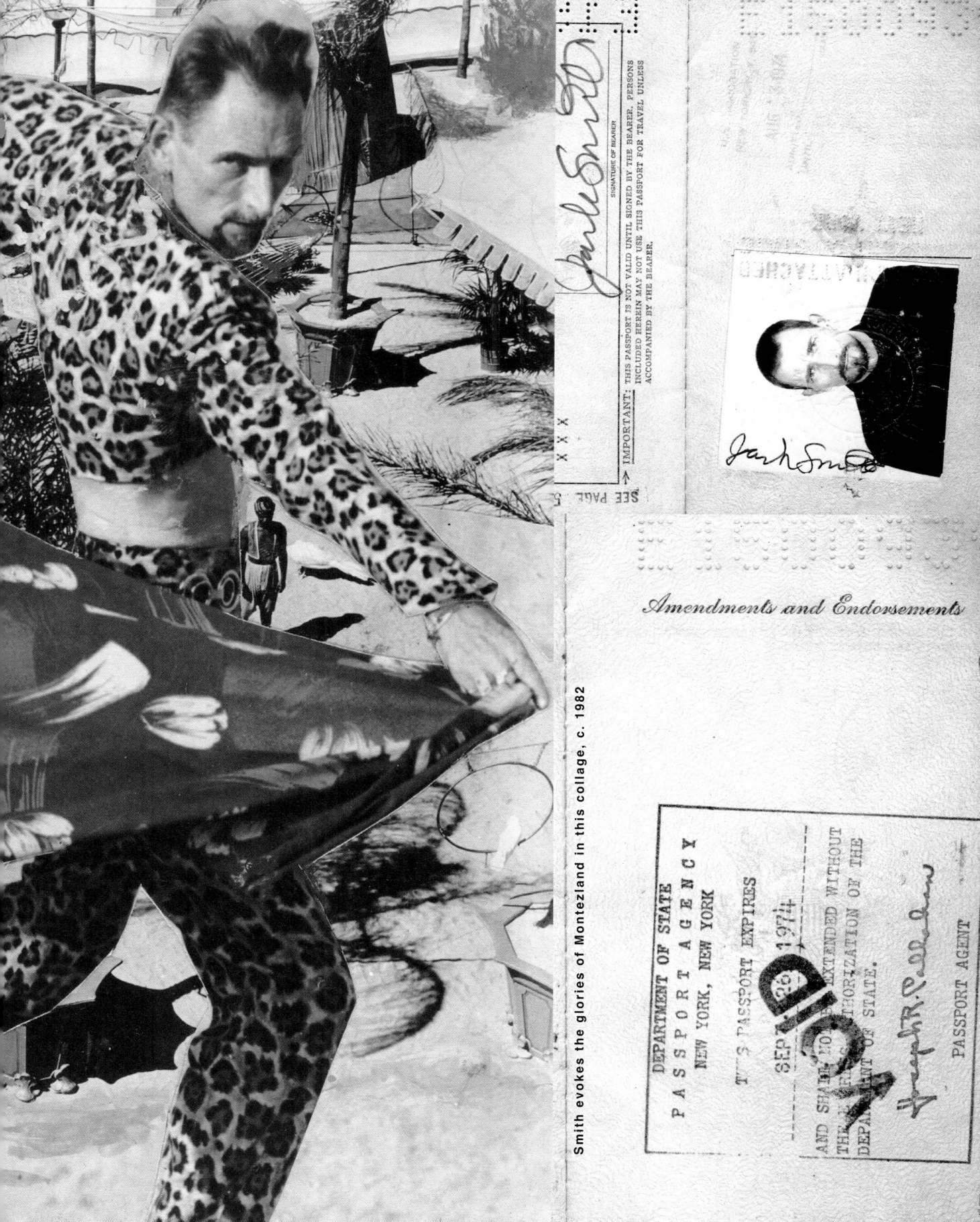

Smith evokes the glories of Montezland in this collage, c. 1982

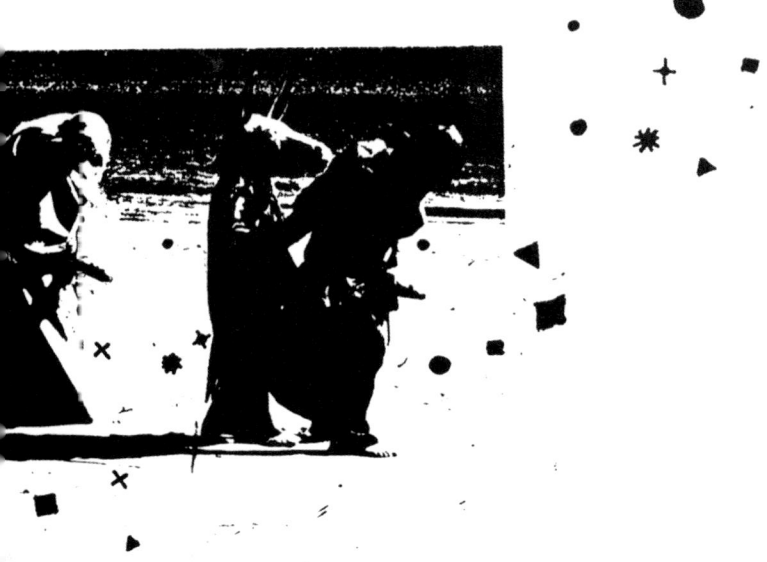

Intended as an all-purpose brochure for Smith programs, this handout incorporated "greatest hits" moments from his career.

From the mid-1960's on, Jack Smith—best-known as the director of *Flaming Creatures* (1962-63), a key work in the American avant-garde film—has astonished New York audiences with a series of highly influential performance pieces. Although Smith's theatre, which is even more fugitive and underground than his film production, has attracted little critical writing, it has made itself felt in the work of artists as otherwise disparate as Ronald Tavel, John Vaccaro, Richard Foreman and Robert Wilson. At the same time, Smith's refusal to separate his persona from his art presaged the gallery-based "performance artists" of the mid-1970's. His presentations include the ongoing

"SCHEDULE THE SCUM OF BAGDAD MIDNIGHT SHOW IN YOUR THEATRE"!

Jack Smith

"He is the hidden source of practicall everything that's of any interest in t so-called experimental American theate today. Absolutely. And I mean everybod from Wilson to myself to Ludlam to Vac and many other people, owe a great dea Jack Smith." Richard Forman

THE DEATH IN UNCLE ARCHIVE'S VA

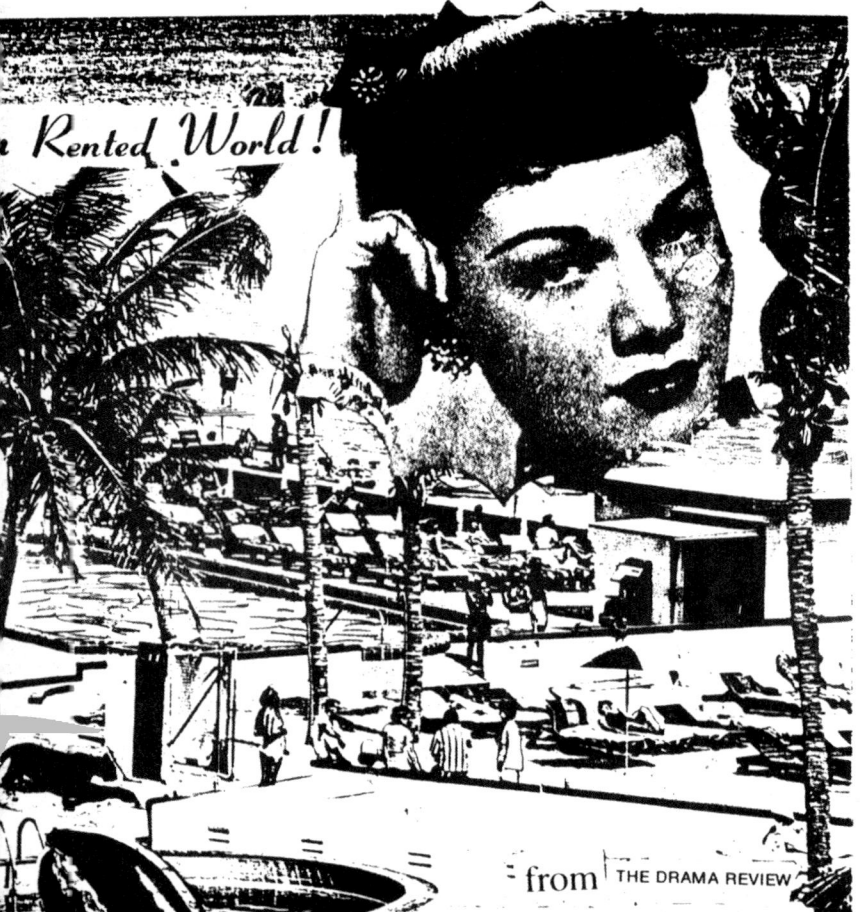

Rented World!

from THE DRAMA REVIEW

program

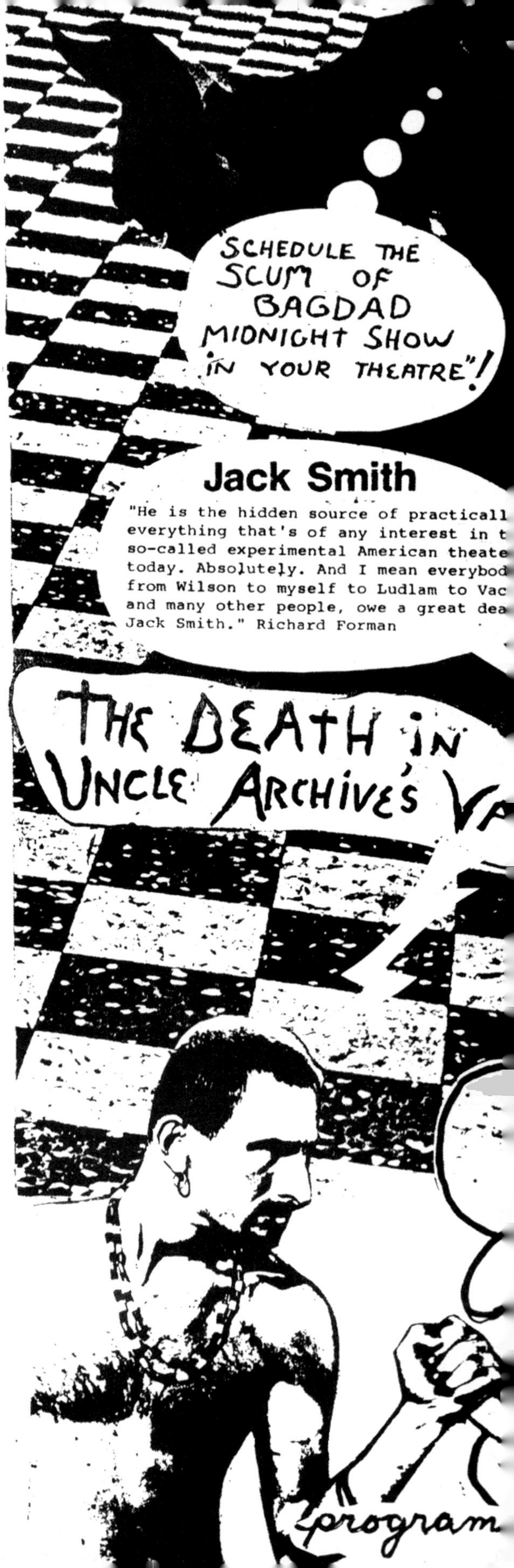

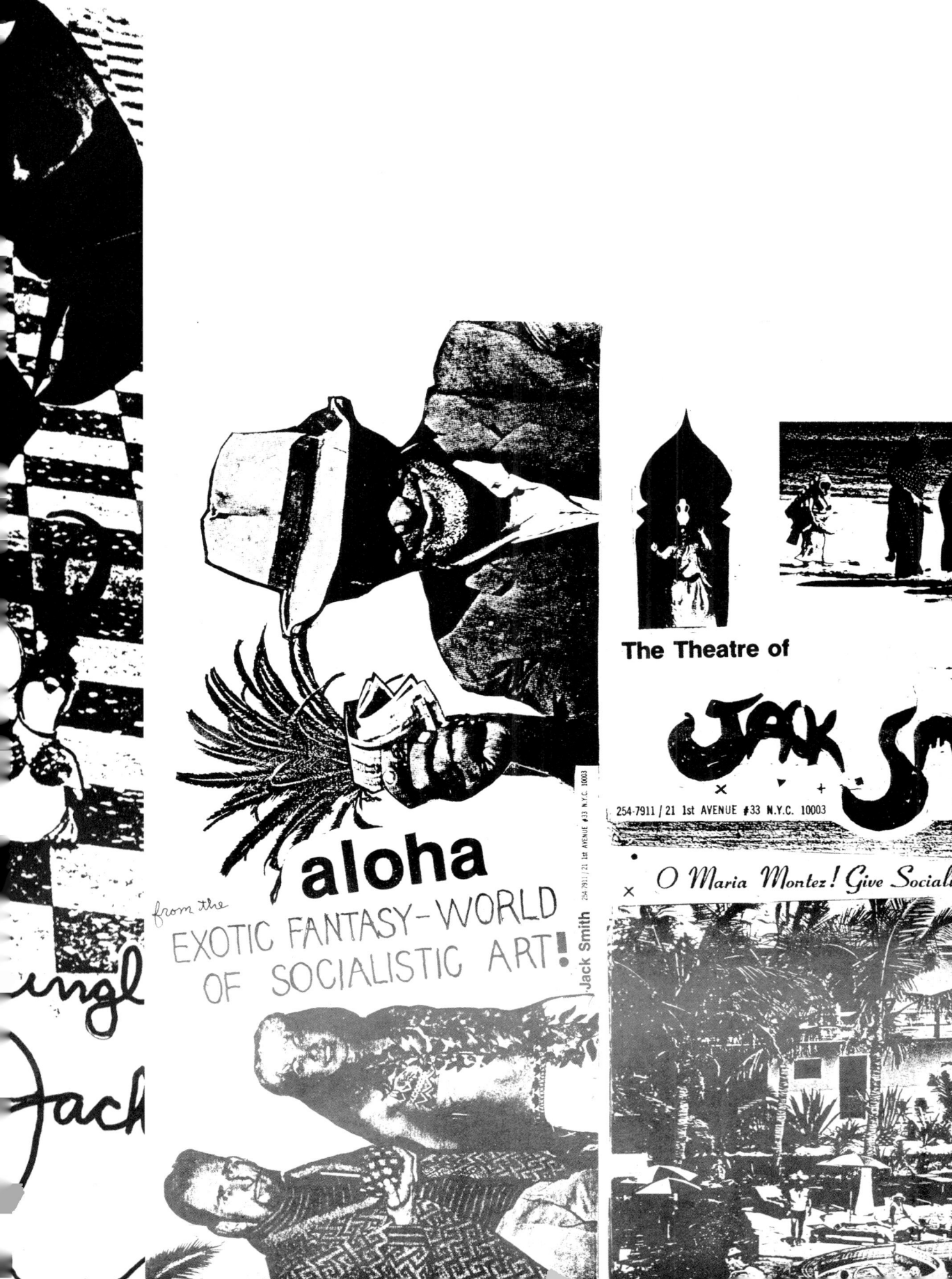

aloha

from the

EXOTIC FANTASY-WORLD
OF SOCIALISTIC ART!

Jack Smith   254-7911 / 21 1st AVENUE #33 N.Y.C. 10003

The Theatre of

Jack Smith

254-7911 / 21 1st AVENUE #33 N.Y.C. 10003

O Maria Montez! Give Socialistic An

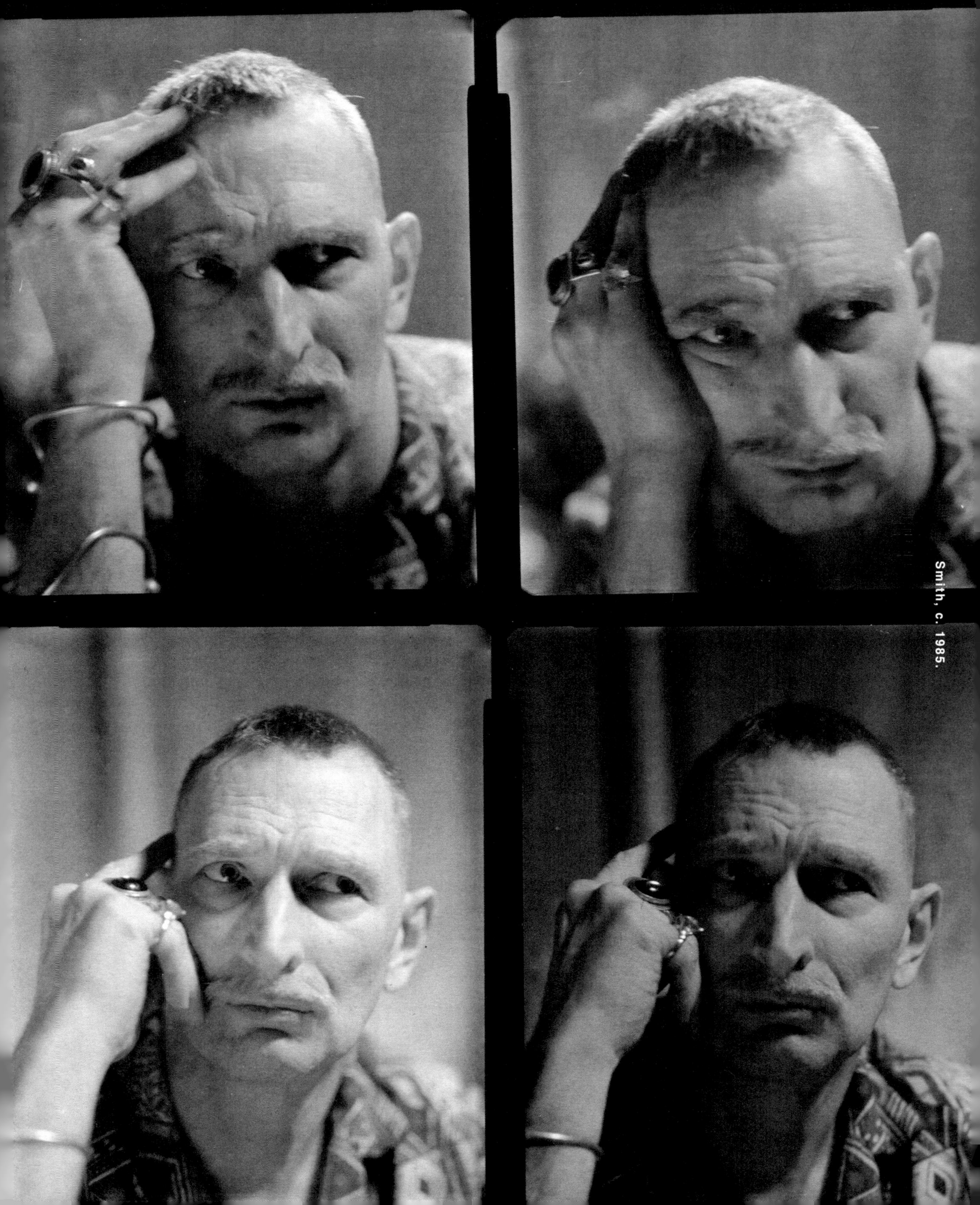

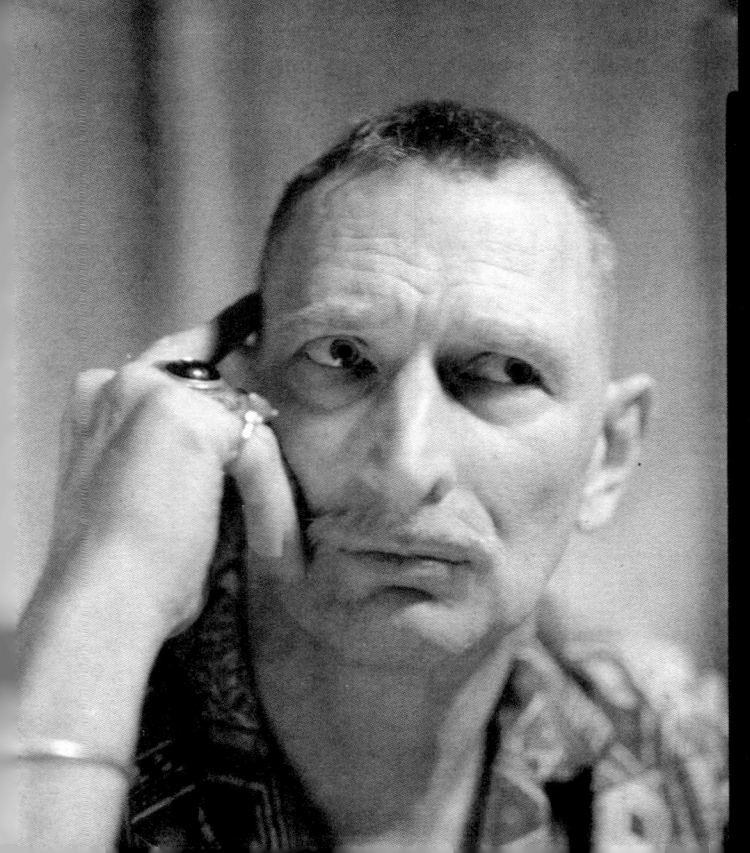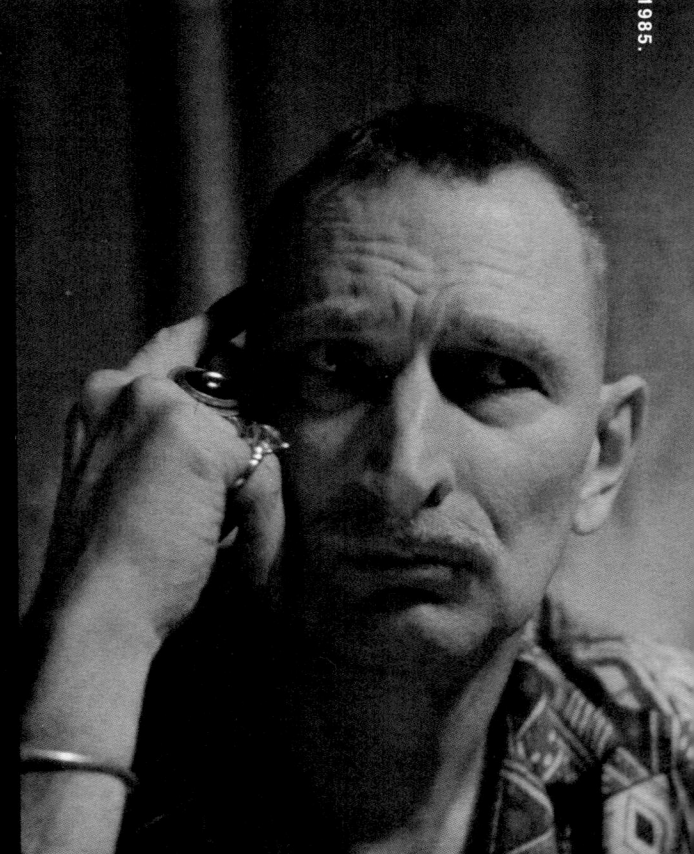

Smith, c. 1985.

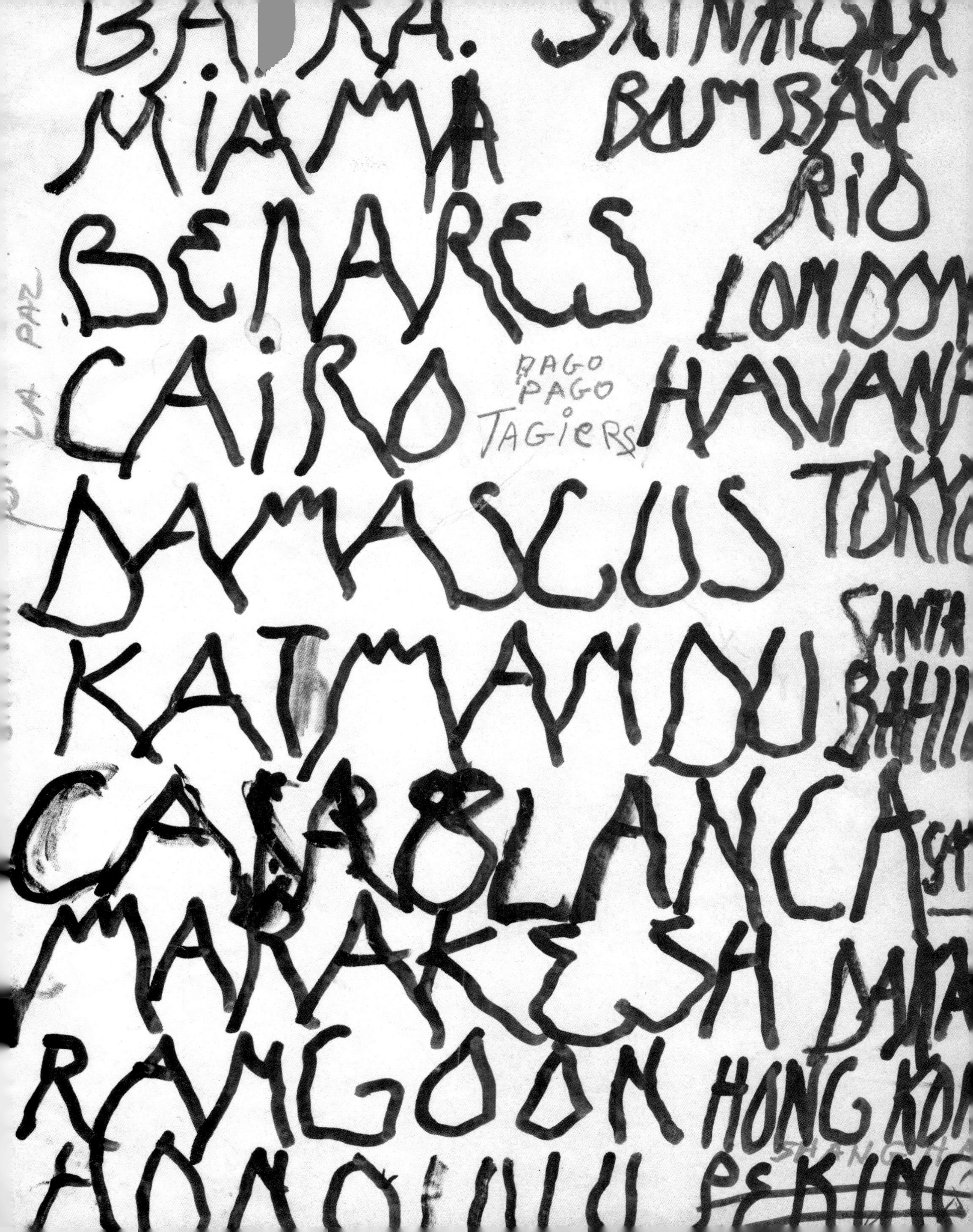

BARA. SRINAGAR

MIAMA BOMBAY

RIO

BENARES LONDON

CAIRO PAGO PAGO TAGIERS HAVANA

TOKYO

DAMASCUS

KATMANDU SANTA BAHIA

CASABLANCA

MARAKESH

RANGOON HONG KONG

HONOLULU PEKING

LA PAZ

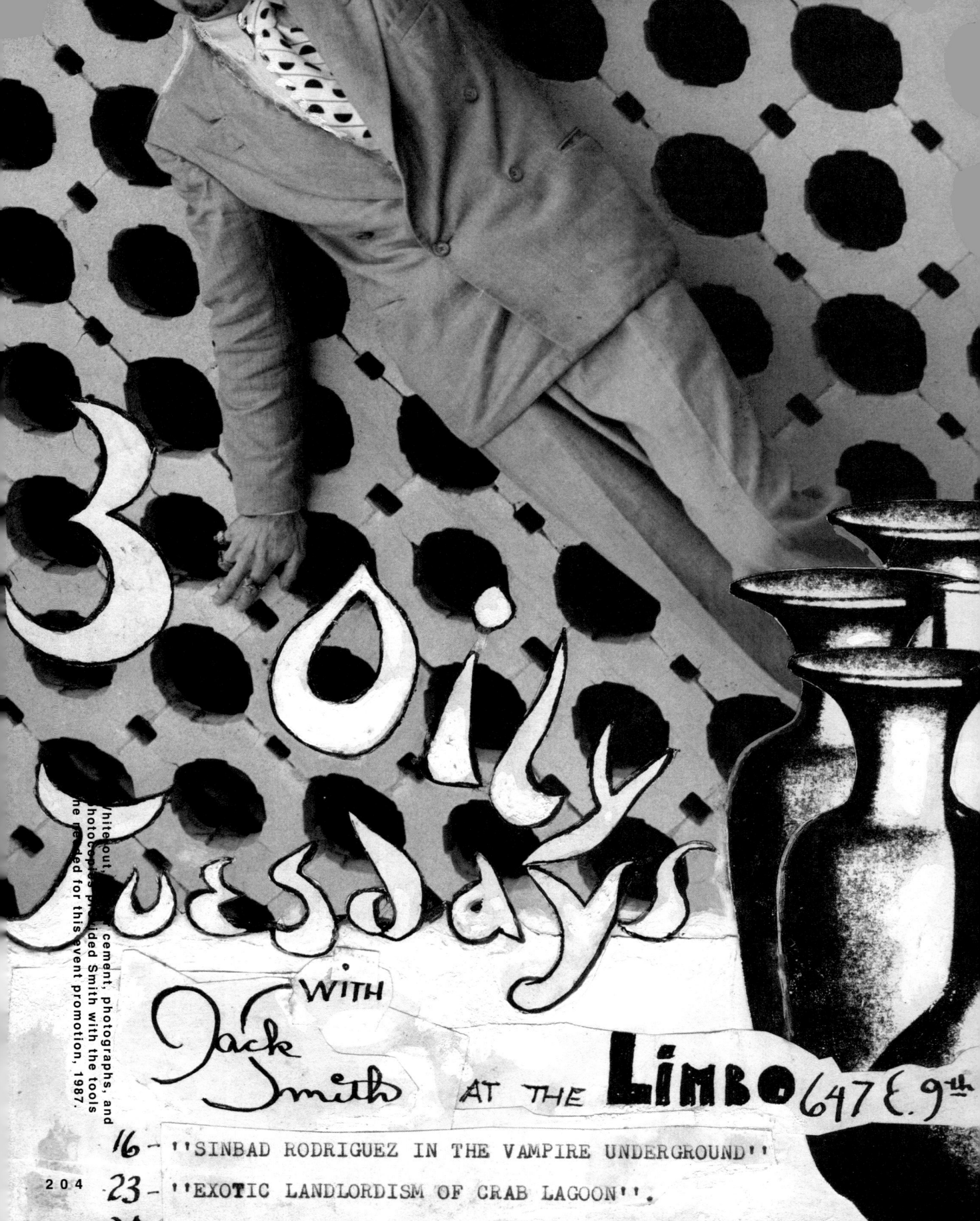

3 oily Tuesdays

with Jack Smith at the LIMBO 647 E. 9th

16 - "SINBAD RODRIGUEZ IN THE VAMPIRE UNDERGROUND"

204   23 - "EXOTIC LANDLORDISM OF CRAB LAGOON".

30 - "DEATH OF A PENGUIN"

Contact sheet from a portrait session, c. 1970.

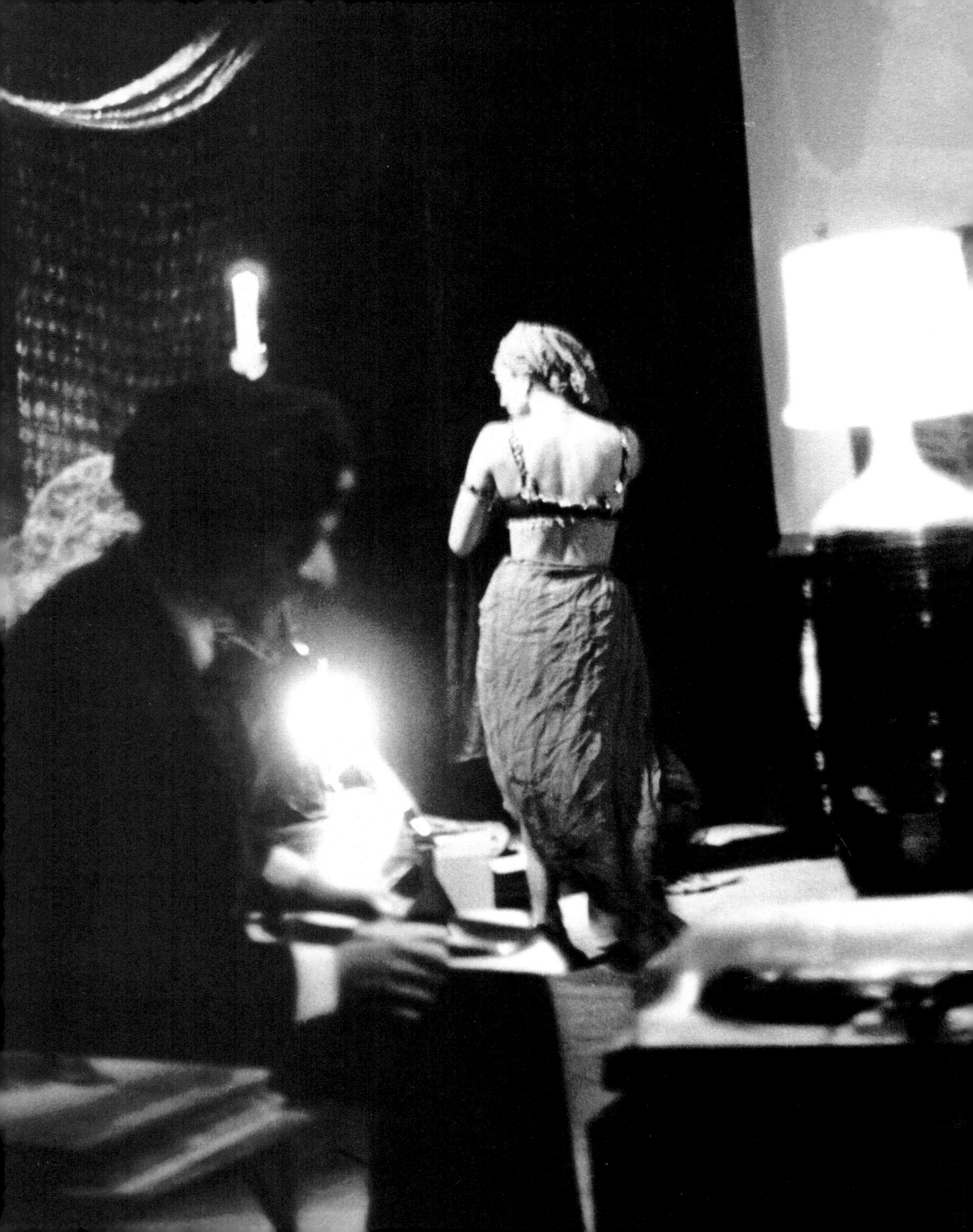

Even tho peo-
ple are treat-
ing me as
I were, I have
be careful
to think
of myself as
insane.

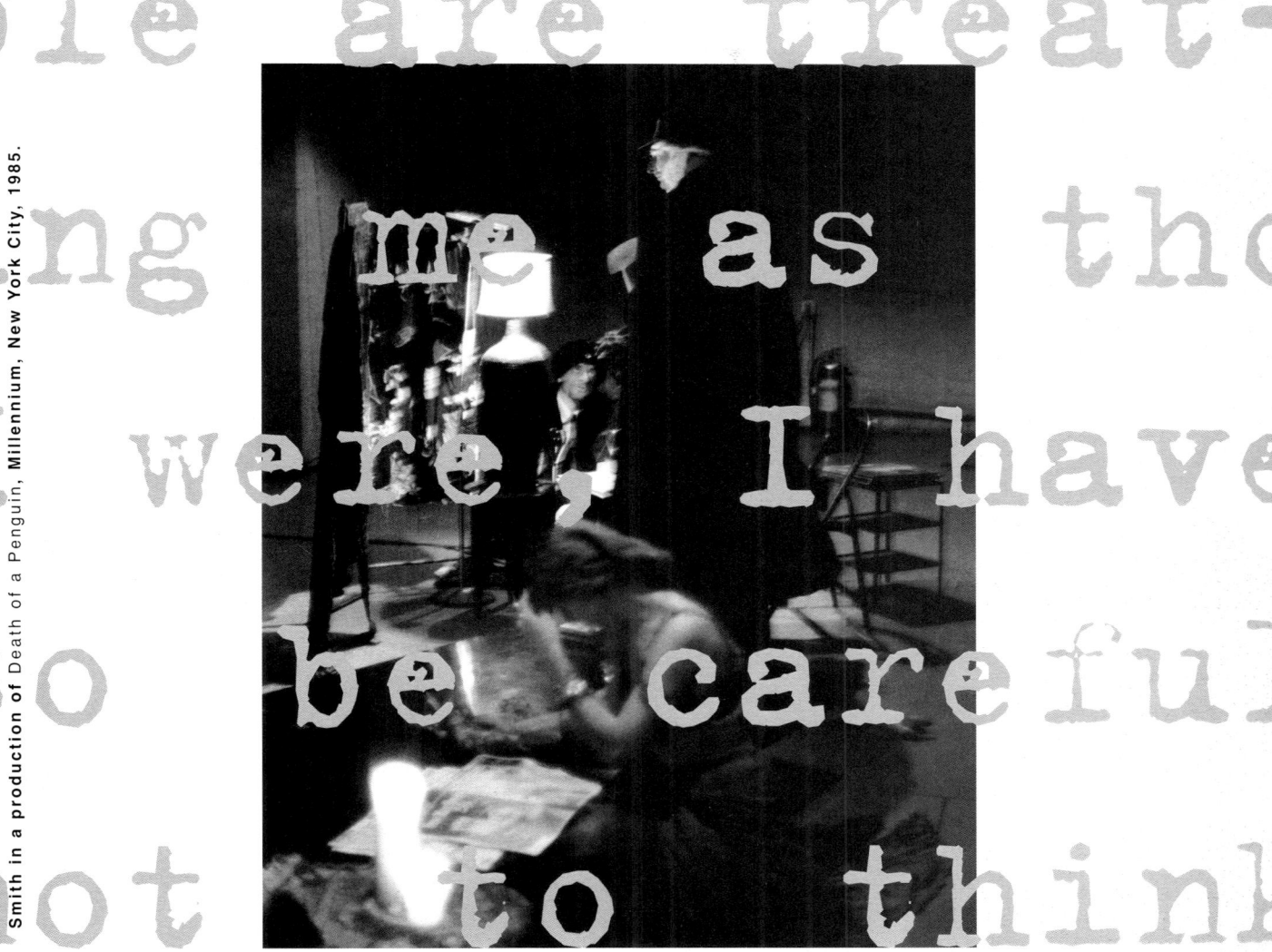

Smith in a production of *Death of a Penguin*, Millennium, New York City, 1985.

Restoration and Slavery

—Jerry Tartaglia

"At first I thought the creature was sent by Fishhook." Jack would not believe that the camera original material of *Flaming Creatures*, which I had just returned to him, had simply been lost for thirteen years and found by accident. He seemed intent upon spinning a tale in which the film had been stolen by Fishhook, hidden away in the "Safe," and for some unrevealed reason, was now being returned to him, by me, an agent of Roachcrust. By the end of our evening together, spent over a cup of lukewarm-tapwater-instant coffee, he came to accept the bizarre truth that I had simply found the film stuck in a pile of sound fill which had been discarded by a lab. He projected some slides for me, talked to me about being queer, and promoted his theory of voluntary slavery. When I was ready to leave, he said that this story of the finding of *Flaming Creatures* was "very Baghdadian." As I walked out, he quipped, "I guess I owe you one." That was 1978.

Jack had many voluntary "slaves" over the years. I have heard of people who spent hours painting and re-painting a single corner in his loft, or endlessly rearranging props and materials in seemingly eternal preparation for a film shoot. Though Jack died in 1989, his system of voluntary slavery lives on in the restoration of his work. In choosing to work on the preserving and restoring of the films of one of the great filmmakers of our time, I discovered that the only will to which I can be subjected is that of Jack Smith. The fact that he isn't here to dictate the exact execution of the details requires of me an internalized task master. This discipline requires that traditional filmmaking and restoration practices be set aside. The reason is simple. In the collected body of work by Jack Smith, we are dealing not with a straightforward film auteur, but with a theatrical and cinematic genius who prescribed his own parameters in film and performance. The task of restoration and preservation of this enormous body of work demands that we begin with the utmost respect for the processes which brought him to produce this work.

Excerpted from the original

In his time, Jack was both a filmmaker and what was later to be called a performance artist. In many ways, he was the grand daddy of performance art. His events involved people, objects, projected slide images, film, and lots of time. The film material was projected with music which he selected on the spot from his large and eclectic collection of LP's. Some of the material was workprint from his "completed" feature films like *No President* or *Normal Love*, some if it was new material, and some of it was comprised of other of his short films, inserted in their entirety into the "performance" reels.

To a restorer, this set of circumstances is enough of a challenge. However, Jack added a small twist to his performances. Oftentimes, while the film was screening, he would remove the take-up reel and begin re-splicing the material into a new arrangement. Obviously, this had to be accomplished quickly, before the remaining material had run through the projector. Jack developed an ingenious way of re-editing during a performance. He used tape splices. Sometimes the tape was conventional film splicing tape, most of the time it was cheap masking tape, paper tapes, even duct tape. The bits of tapes were just large enough to hold the film strips together, and small enough to pass through the projector gate. The visual result of this method was astonishing. The splices were visible, of course, but the material was re-woven into a new tapestry of visual excess with each screening. One hour of film material, in this way, could be transformed into a three-hour film experience.

Twenty years later, those same splices turned brittle, leaving a hardened adhesive residue and projection gate dirt at each joint. The restoration of *Normal Love* was particularly encumbered by this problem. Each splice had to be disconnected. The celluloid had to be gently scrubbed free of the residue, and a new hot splice had to be done. In some situations, the bond was too tight and the film too brittle, so the masking tape splice had to be entirely excised. When possible, I left some of those splices intact. I wanted today's viewers of the work to have some inkling of the visual effect which punctuates the film through the surface activity created by masking tape passing through a projector gate. Fortunately, the lab which did the internegative understood the challenges which we faced in this restoration work, and accommodated the peculiar needs of the project.

Since the objective of the restoration is to preserve Jack's work, a new print had to be struck of all the film. Jack had shot all of his work on 16mm reversal filmstock. Smith often used outdated stock because he had no money. This frequently produced very beautiful color. At the time of his death in 1989, color reversal film in 16mm was almost completely phased out as a viable medium. Therefore, the work had to be prepared for an internegative from which prints could be struck. It certainly allowed for the preservation of the work in all of its luscious and vibrant color, but it also prompted serious aesthetic questions about the restoration process itself.

If Jack had been only a filmmaker, the restoration would have been rather straightforward. But, since he, himself, had recut *Normal Love* into new versions for performances, the restoration of the original film version could actually destroy the performance reels which themselves were legitimate work. Some filmmakers advised that Jack had cut up his films for these per- formances, and that this somehow reflected a deterioration of his creative abilities. Others claimed that his high-strung temperament had gone over the edge, and he was "destroying" his own films. Neither of these asser- tions reflects the truth about Jack Smith's art. My responsibility as restora- tionist is to preserve the work as Jack created it, and not according to the dictates of the various factions of his many friends and even more former friends, all of whom insist that their particular experience and memory of him and his work reflects the sum total of his oeuvre. Likewise, I bear a responsibility to preserve the performance reels as they constitute a major portion of his lifetime of work in film.

The solution thankfully came in the form of a music cue sheet from Tony Conrad, who had created the soundtrack for *Flaming Creatures*. Jack had asked him to do the same for *Normal Love*, so Tony began by preparing a cue sheet. Apparently, that was as far as he was able to go. Jack's person- ality intervened and Tony left the project, although Jack left his name in the credits. The cue sheet provided the order for the scenes in *Normal Love*.

My task was to identify and locate those scenes and reassemble the film. I spent a good deal of time looking at the reels of film, over and over again. I had to familiarize myself with Jack. I had to understand what he had done. I did not believe that he was insane, nor that he was a cinematic nihilist who had randomly cut up his movies. Surely, an artist who had created the beauty and humor of *Flaming Creatures* knew what he was doing. I kept watching and reviewing the tens of thousands of feet of film. Some of it I clearly identified and put aside for the *No President* restoration. Some of it I recognized from the verbal accounts given to me by Jack's closer friends, and by people who had seen many of his performances and had taken notes. These performance reels were also put aside, even though some of them contained images from *Normal Love*. But, Jack knew what he was doing, after all. These images were mostly duplications of the images on the reels which he had labeled "Normal Love." Some scenes were clearly part of *Normal Love* but were not listed on the cue sheet, and therefore were apparently not intended for inclusion in the original version of the film. Those scenes comprise the "Addendum" to *Normal Love*. The only extant material from the film, which is not included in either the restored version nor in the addendum, are some shots which Jack himself put into the performance reels entitled: "Exotic Landlordism" and "Cement Lagoon." I decided to leave them where they were. Those performance reels are edited by Jack Smith, and I did not want to impose my interpretation upon the chronology which he himself created.

These performance reels actually comprise the bulk of the oeuvre. They include a number of completed films, as well as material which appears to be intended only for inclusion in his performances. Many of them include Jack in various roles, or should I say "costumes," since he worked on the assumption that a costume created a role. *I Was A Male Yvonne De Carlo*, *Jungle Jack in Cologne Zoo*, *Bald Mountain*, *Love Thing*, *Abortion Pit Nightmare*, *Wino*, *Cement Lagoon*, and *Hamlet* are some of the performance reels in which Jack appears. These reels have not been as widely screened as the more infamous "completed" films: *Flaming Creatures*, *Normal Love*, *No President*, *Scotch Tape*, and *Overstimulated*. Sometimes, when Jack screened them, he gave the performances themselves different titles. In anycase, I leave that jigsaw puzzle to some other preservationist. I do believe, however, that these performance reels will, in time, elucidate the genius of this artist, and clarify his role in influencing a generation of filmmakers, photographers, theater artists, and erstwhile volunteer slaves.

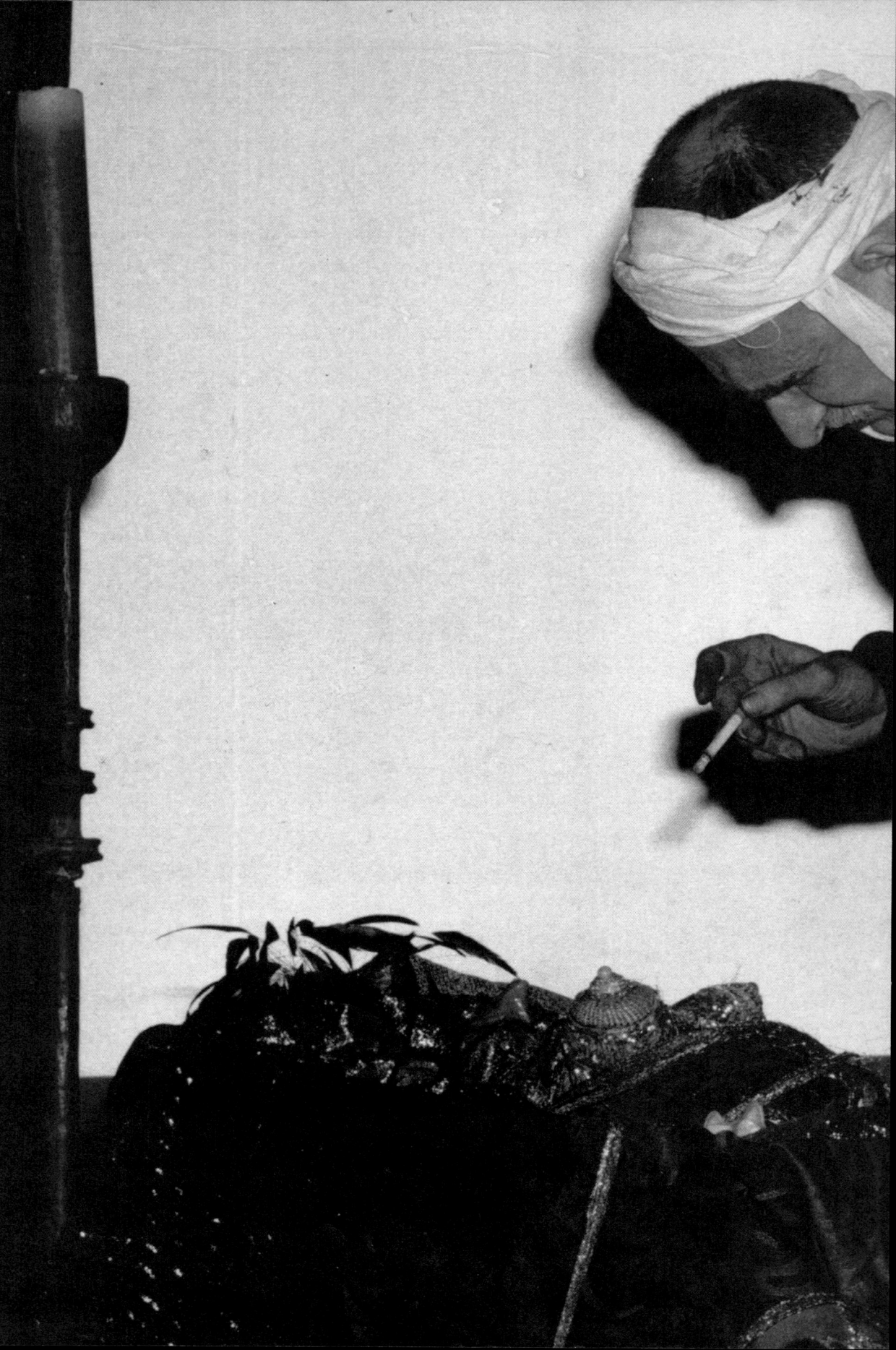

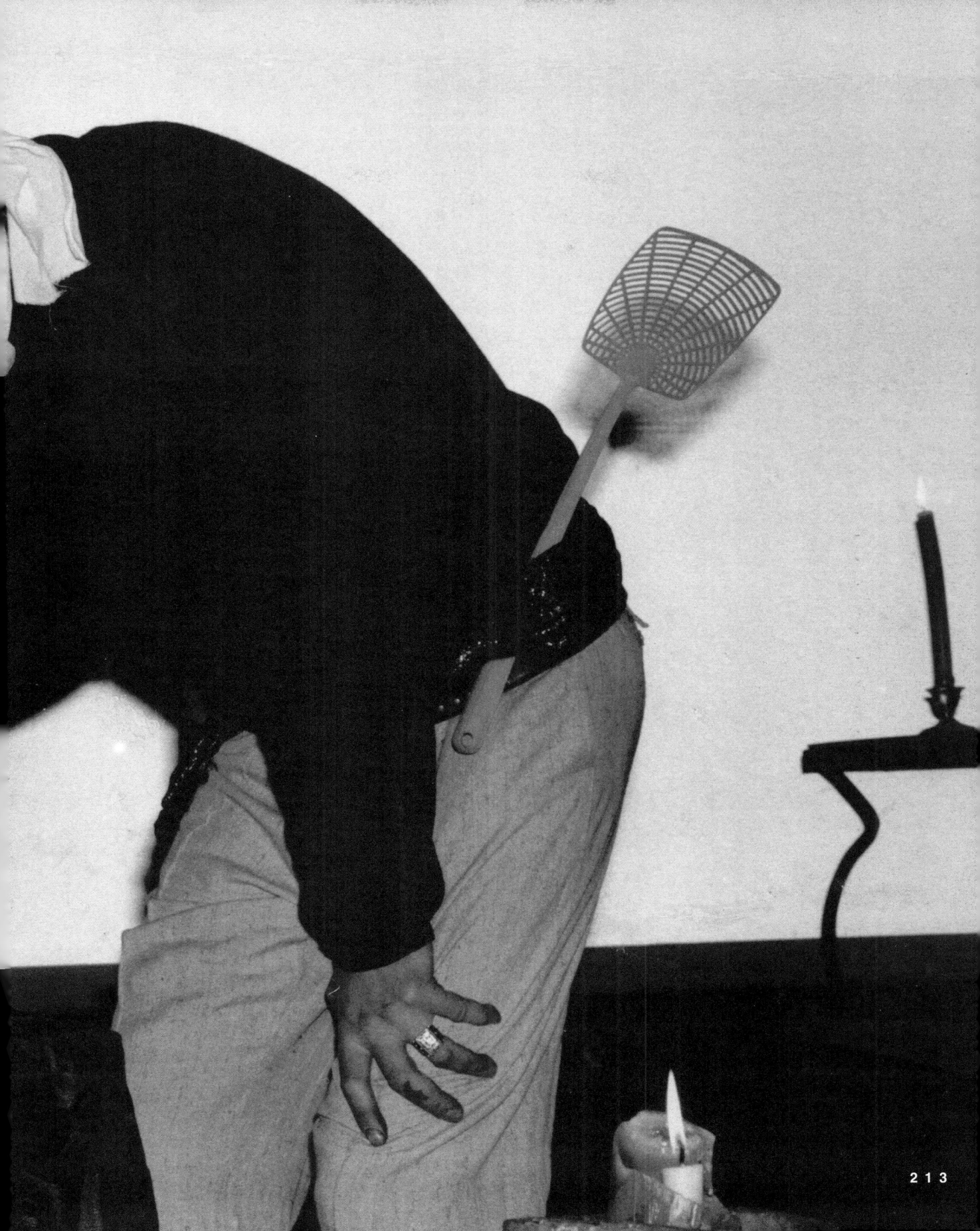

If there
thing go

thing

Rome it

Rome it

baths, r

courts.

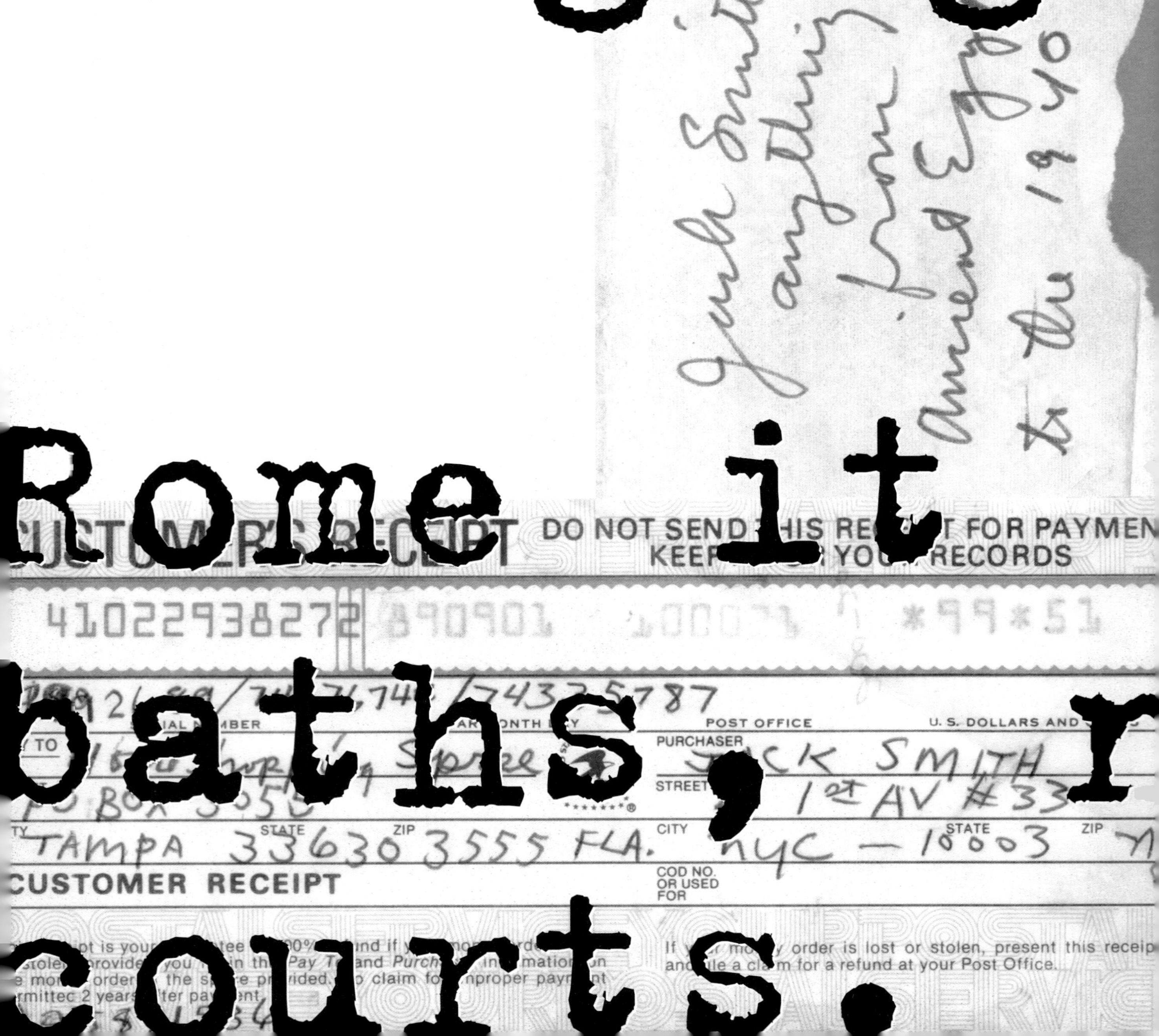

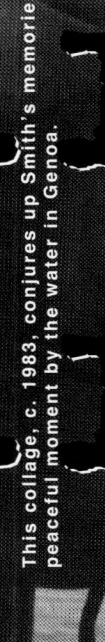

was any-
od about

as thei
ot thei

This collage, c. 1983, conjures up Smith's memories of a peaceful moment by the water in Genoa.

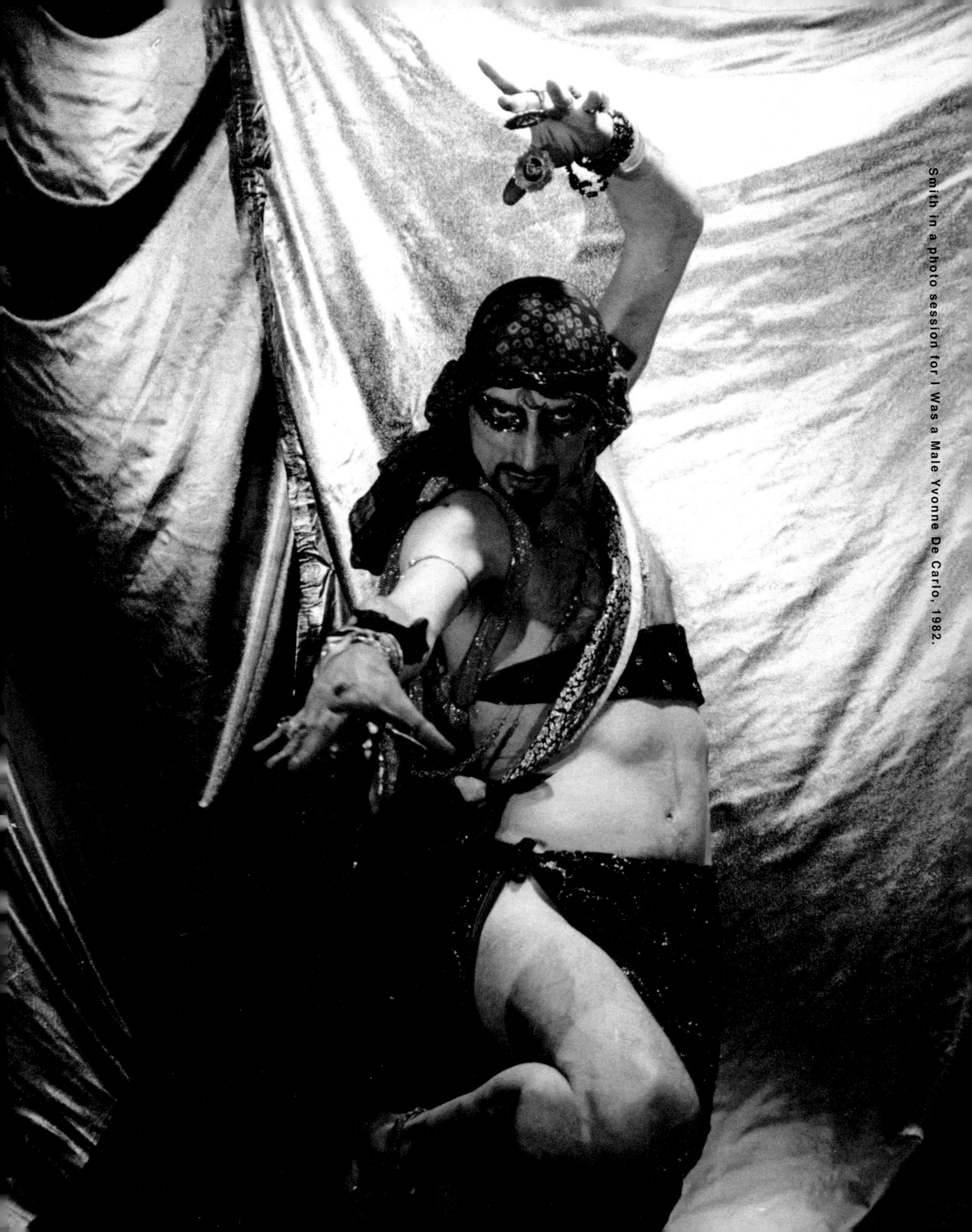

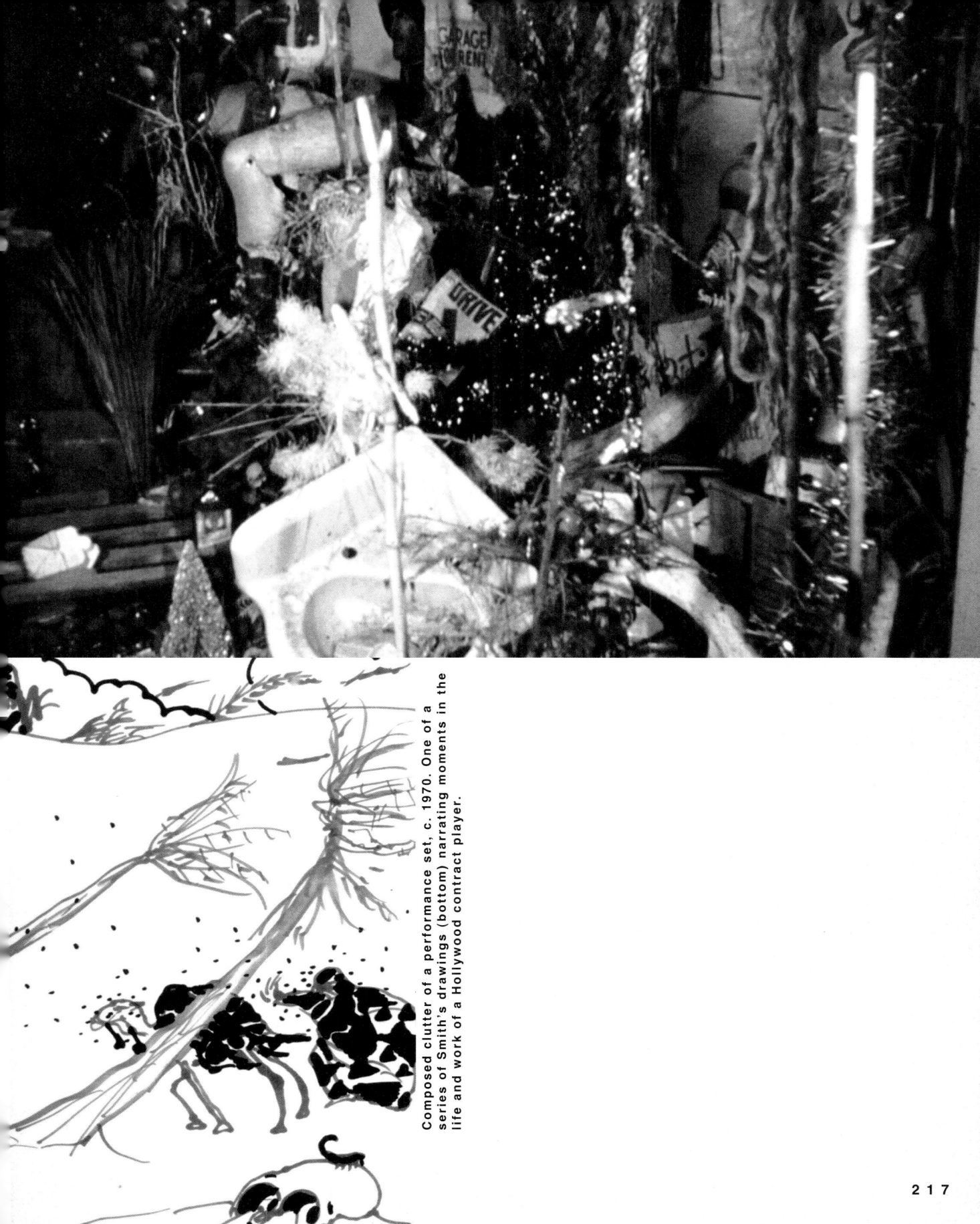

Composed clutter of a performance set, c. 1970. One of a series of Smith's drawings (bottom) narrating moments in the life and work of a Hollywood contract player.

What is more fairy-like than normals with their

spirituality of miracles and super naturalism?

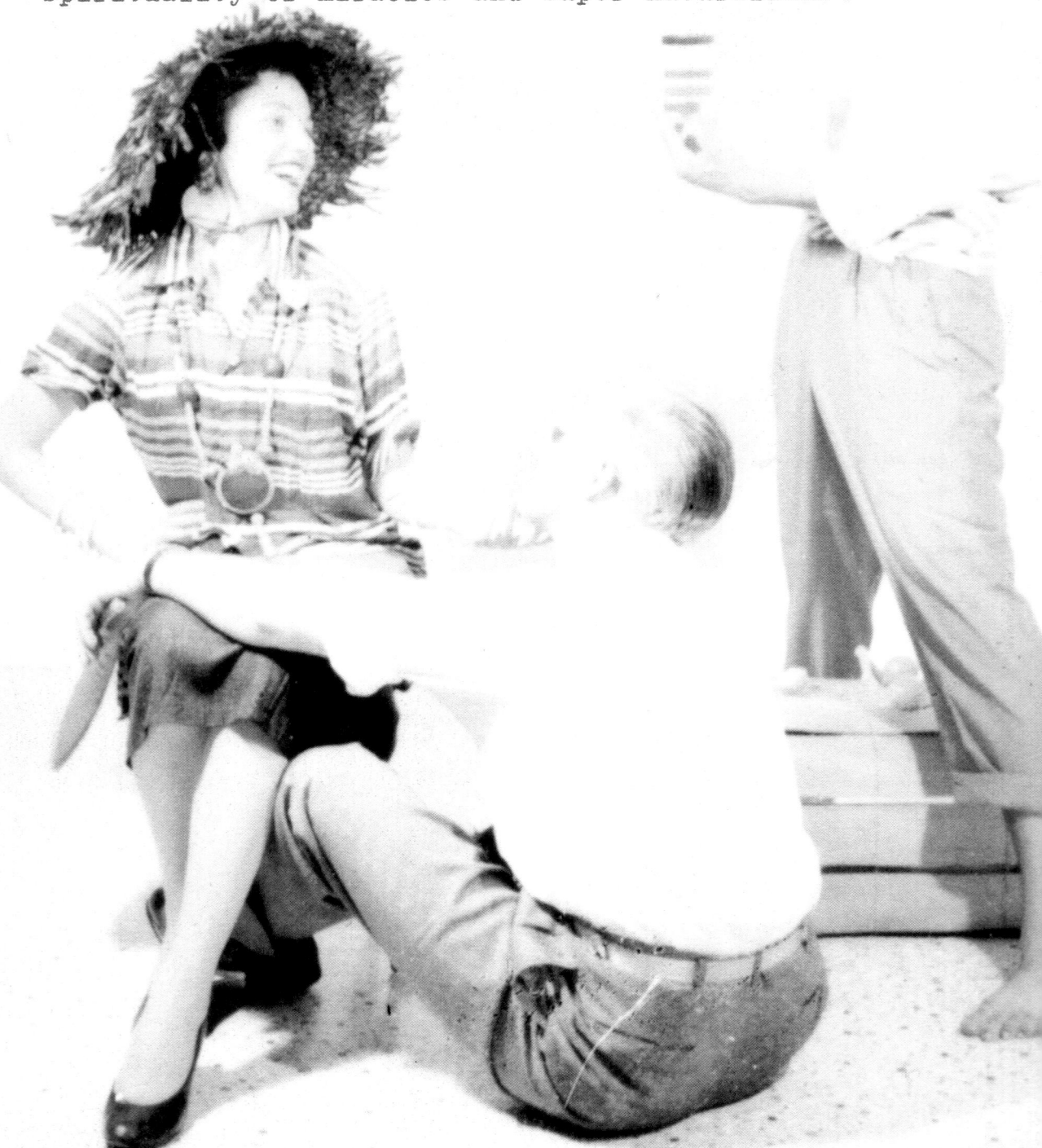

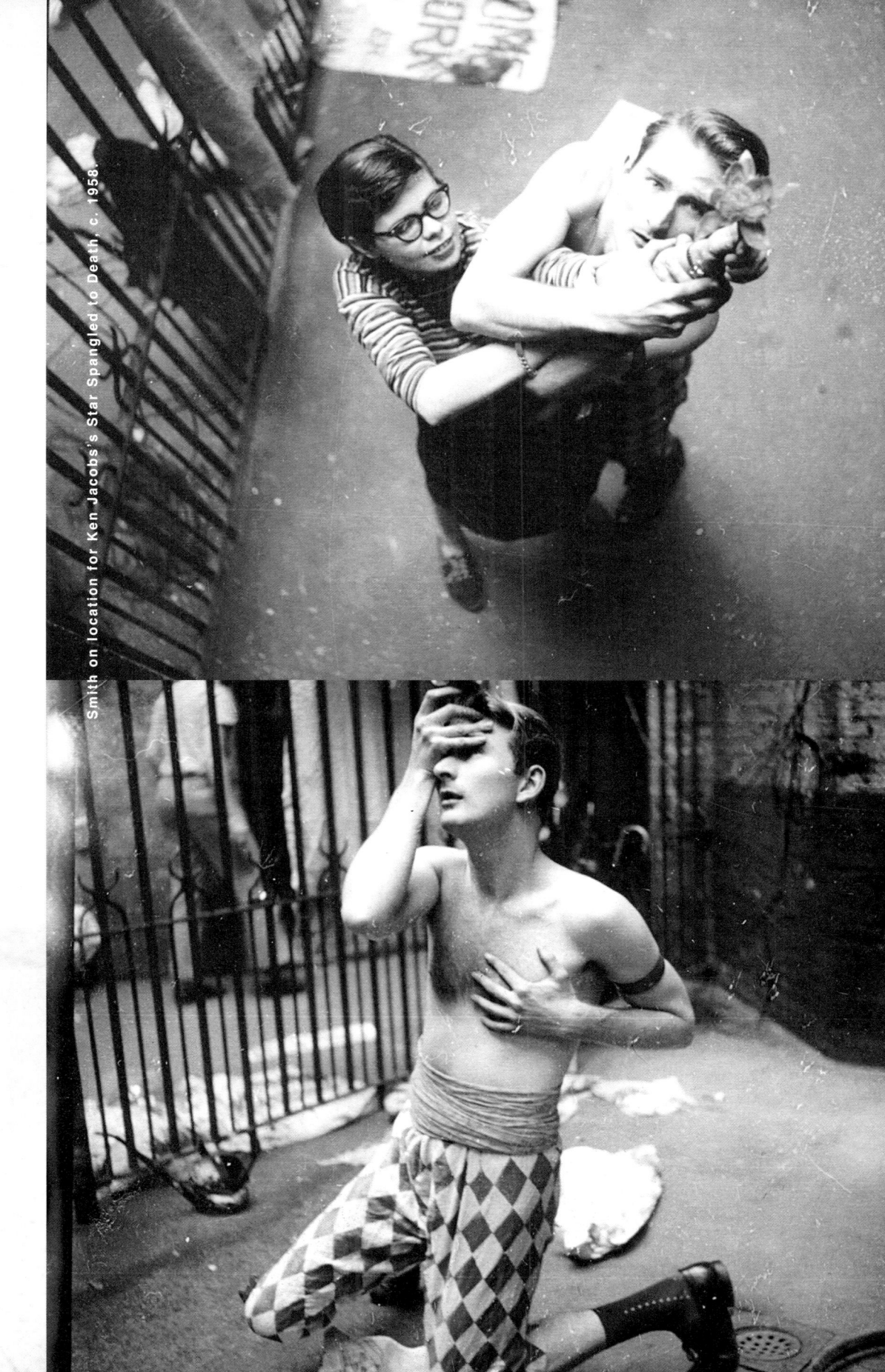

Smith on location for Ken Jacobs's Star Spangled to Death. c. 1958.

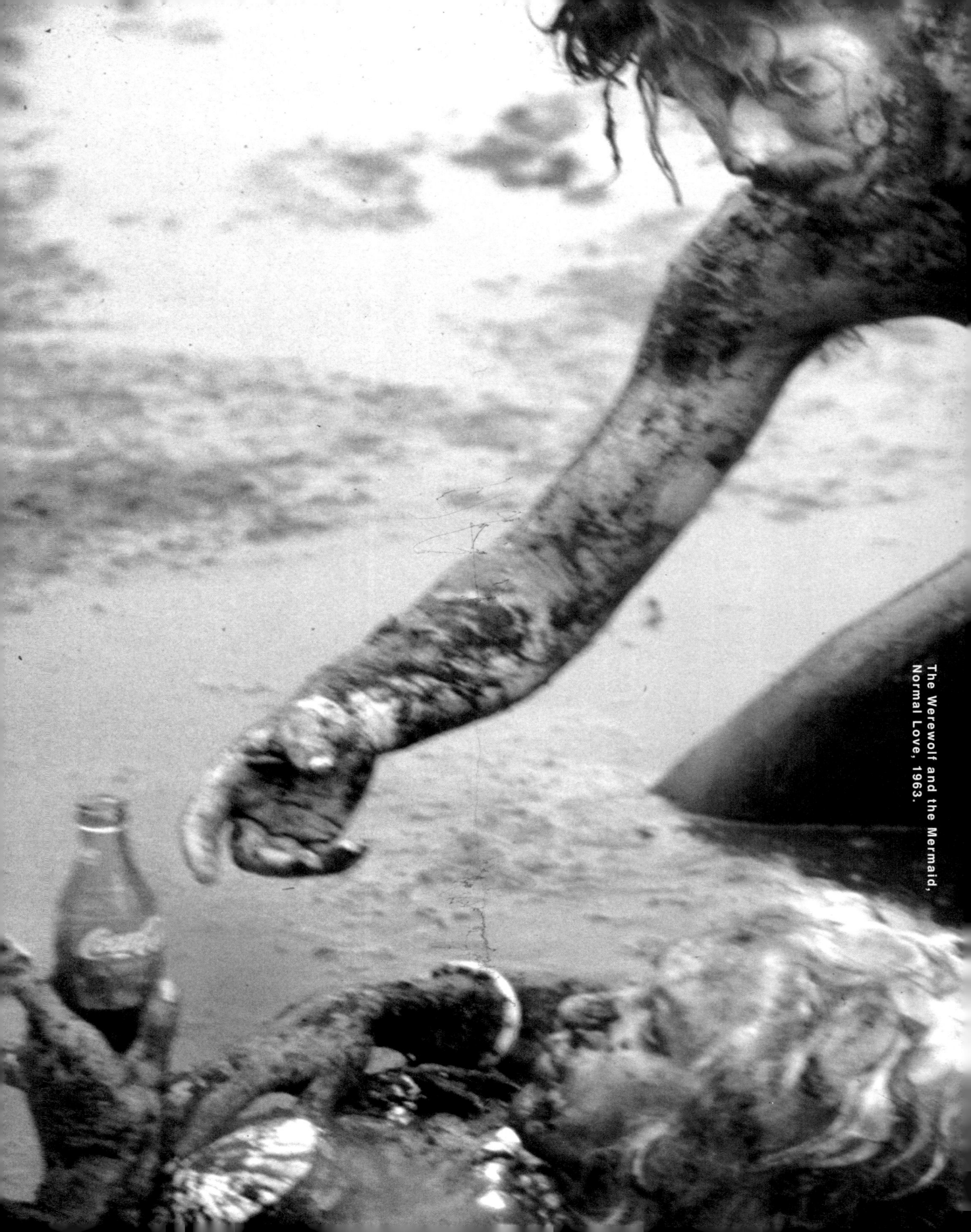

The Werewolf and the Mermaid,
Normal Love, 1963.

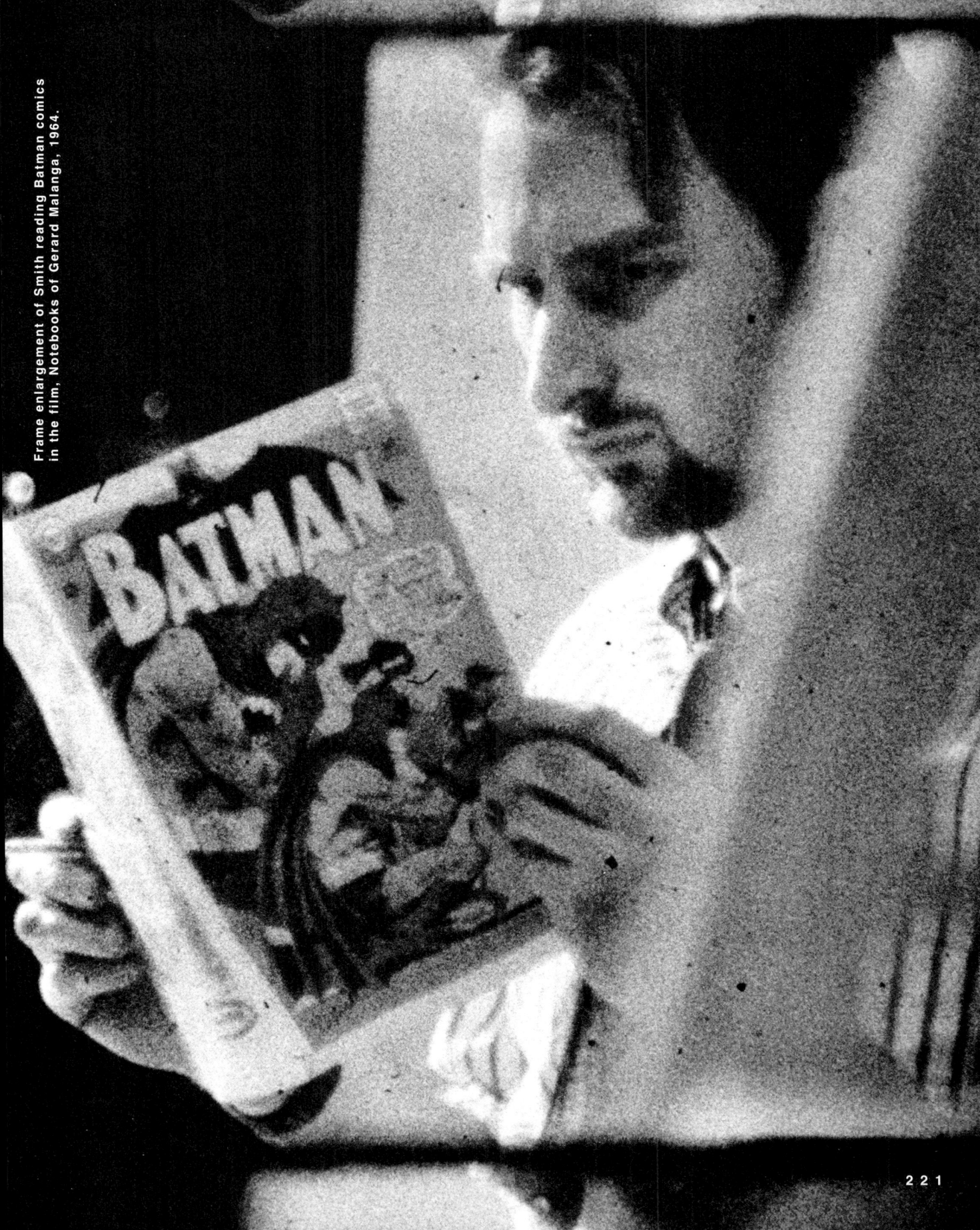

Frame enlargement of Smith reading Batman comics in the film, Notebooks of Gerard Malanga, 1964.

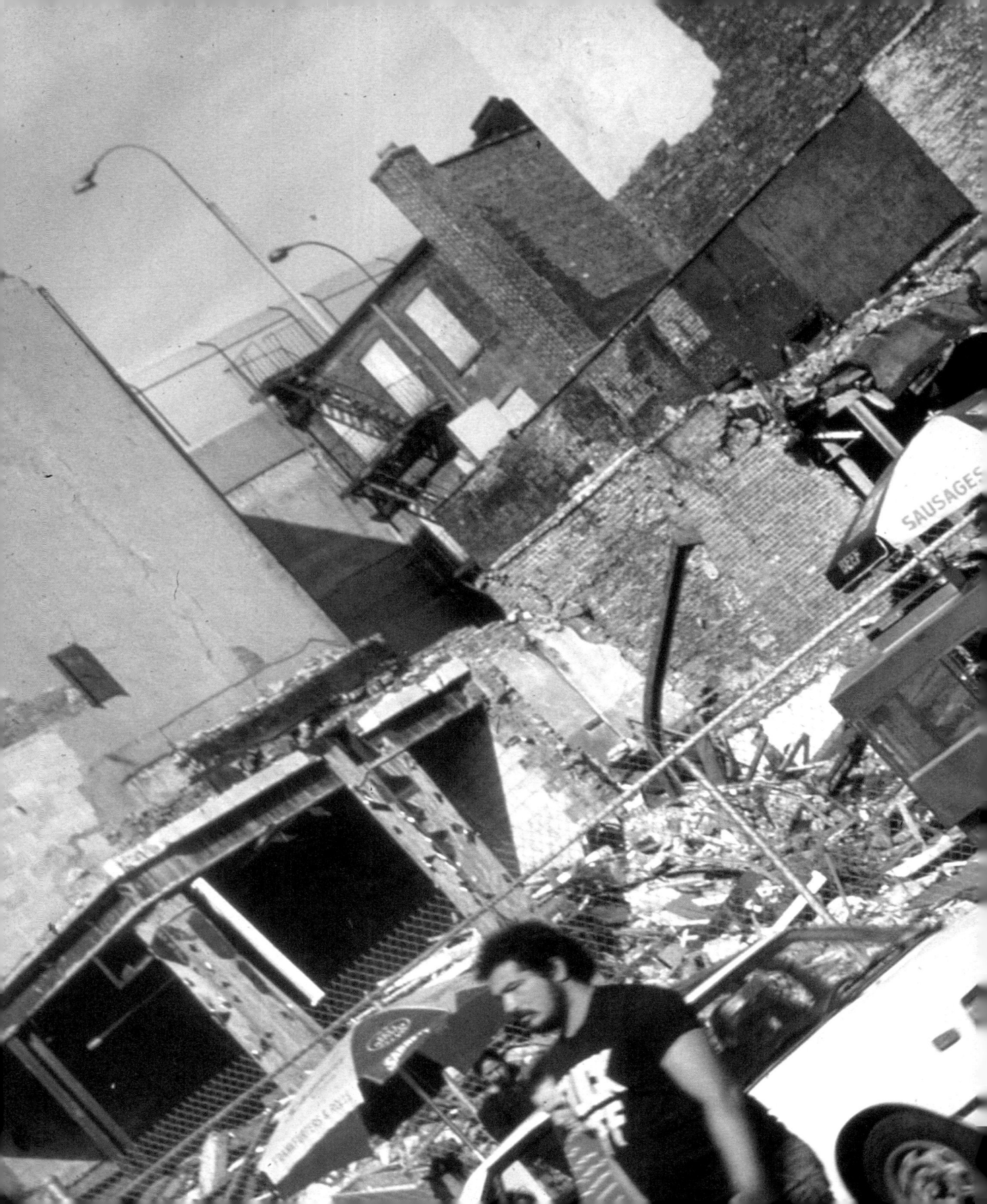

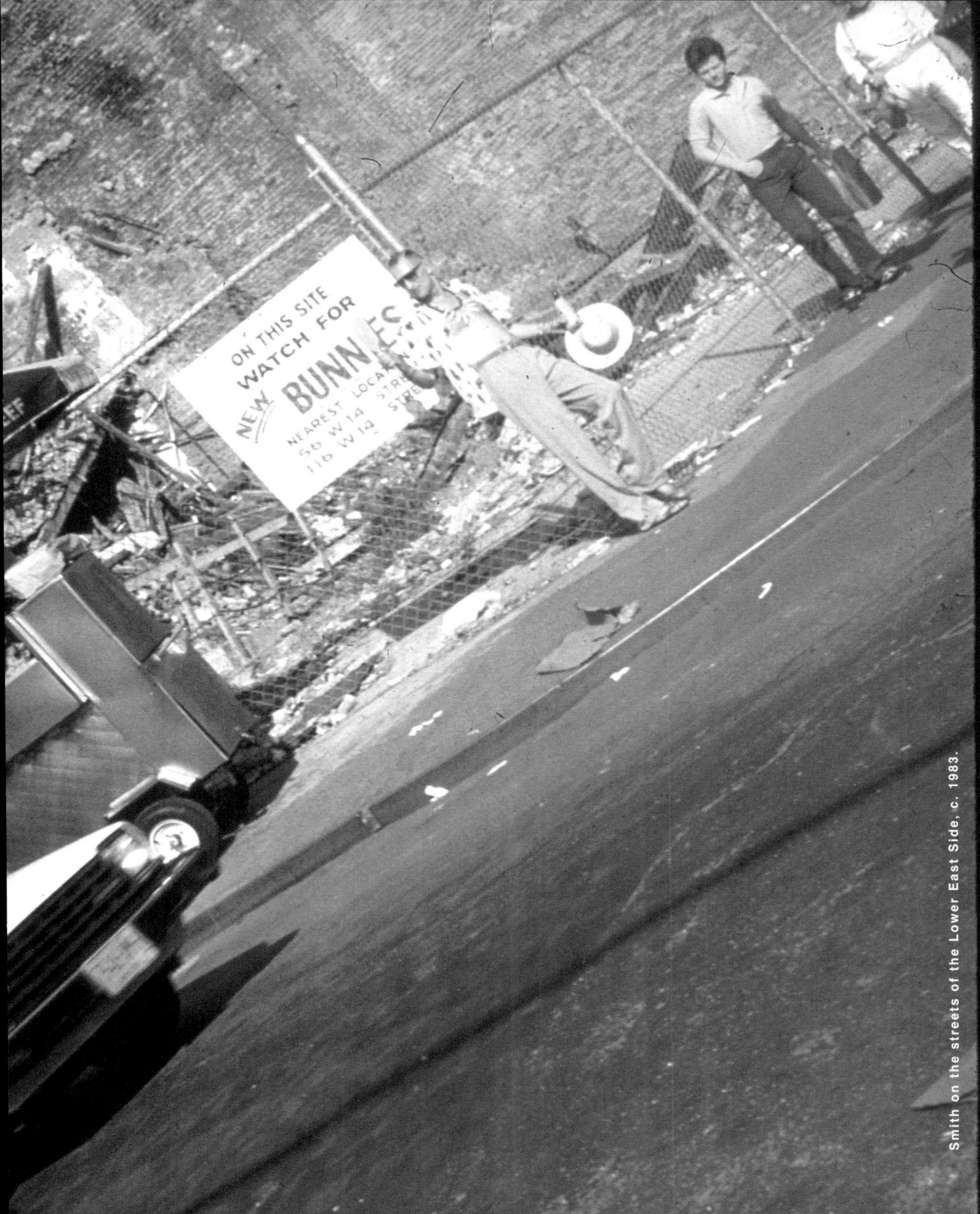

ON THIS SITE
WATCH FOR
NEW BUNNIES
NEAREST LOCATION
56 W 14 STREET
116 W 14 STREET

Smith on the streets of the Lower East Side, c. 1983.

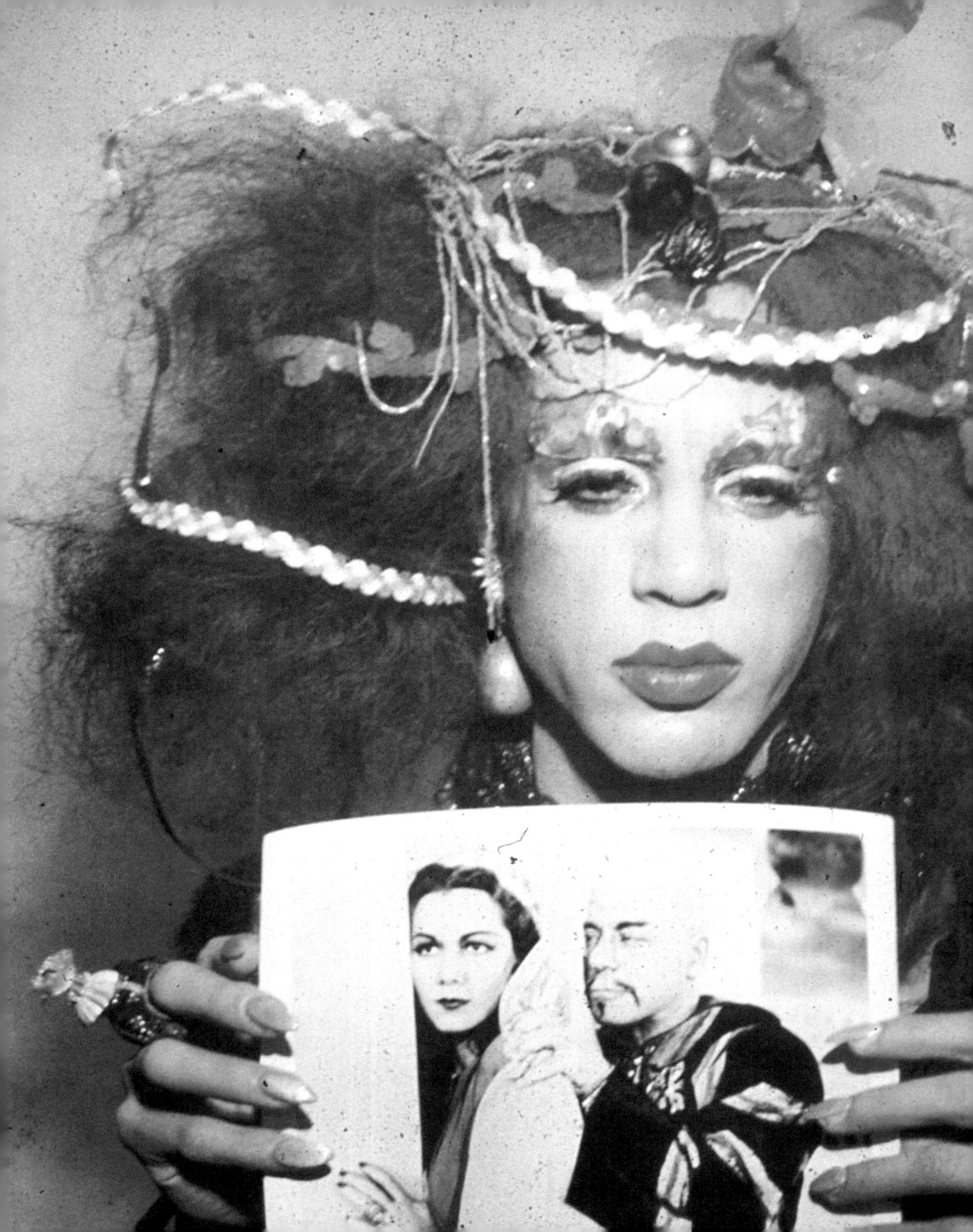

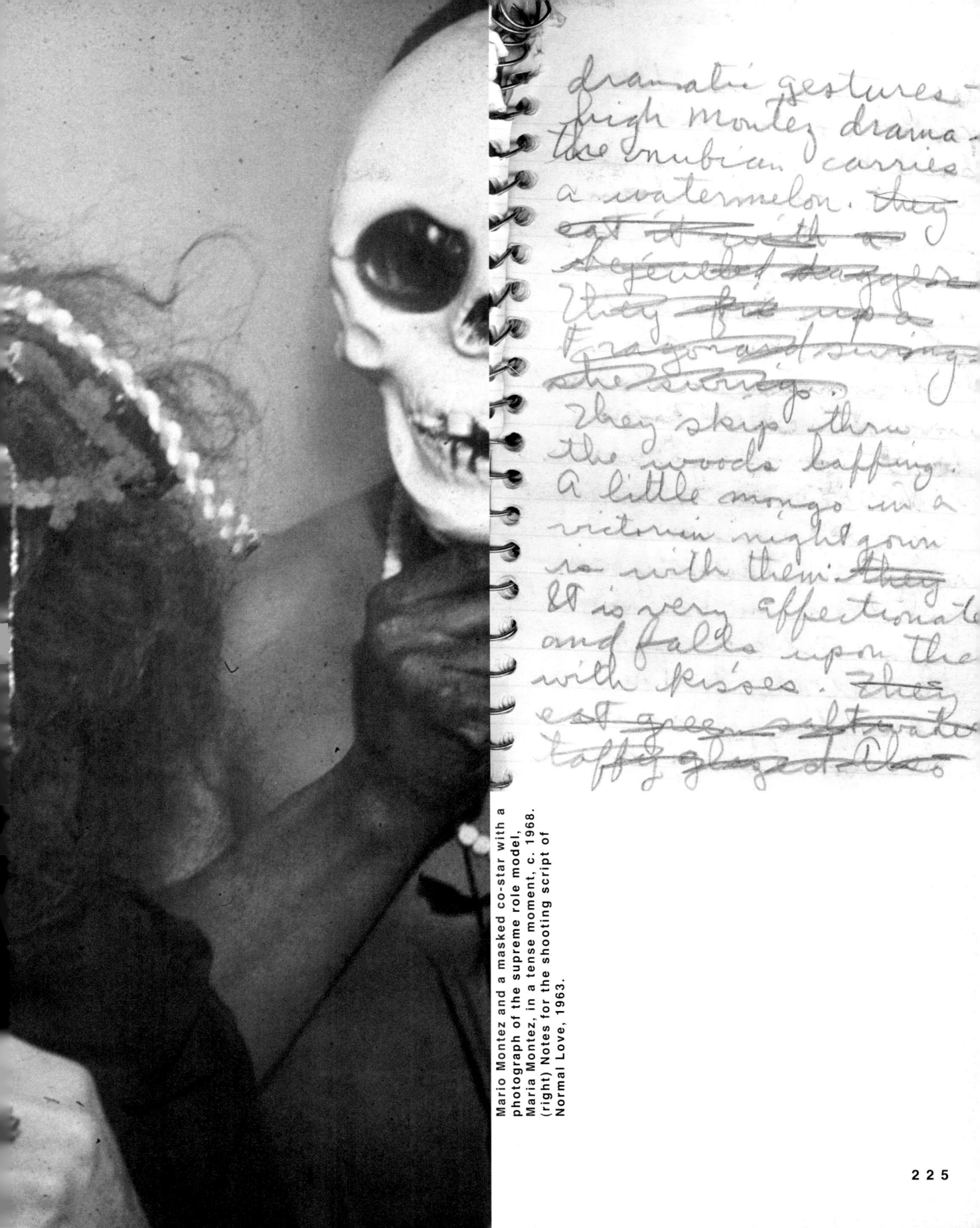

dramatic gestures – high Montez drama – the nubian carries a watermelon. they ~~eat it with a serrated dagger~~ ~~they fix up a~~ ~~fragrant swing~~ ~~the swing.~~ They skips thru the woods laffing. A little mongo in a victorian night gown is with them. ~~they~~ It is very affectionate and falls upon the with kisses. ~~they~~ ~~eat green salt water~~ ~~taffy glazed~~

Mario Montez and a masked co-star with a photograph of the supreme role model, Maria Montez, in a tense moment, c. 1968. (right) Notes for the shooting script of Normal Love, 1963.

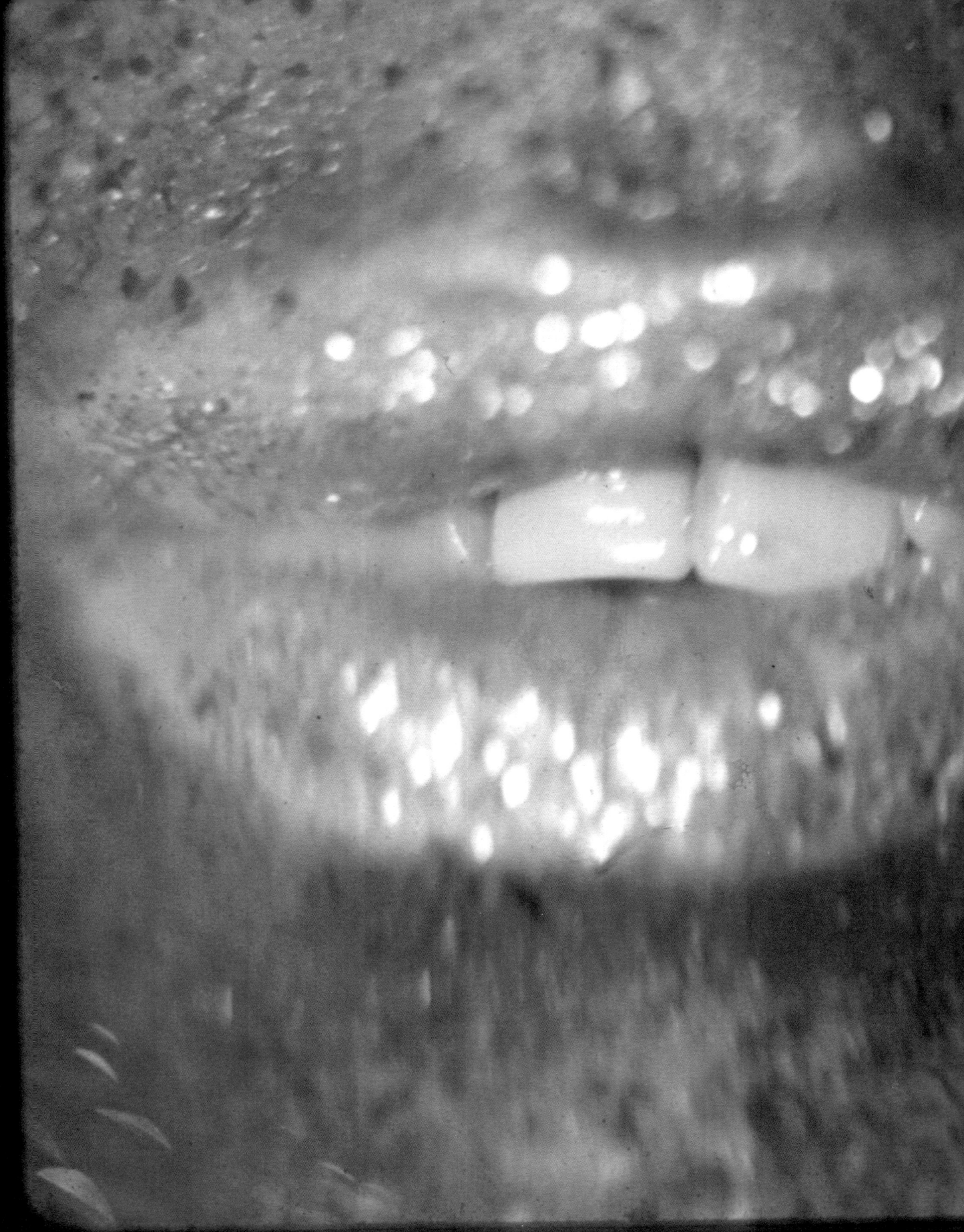

Close-up of John Vaccaro as the Frog, 1965.

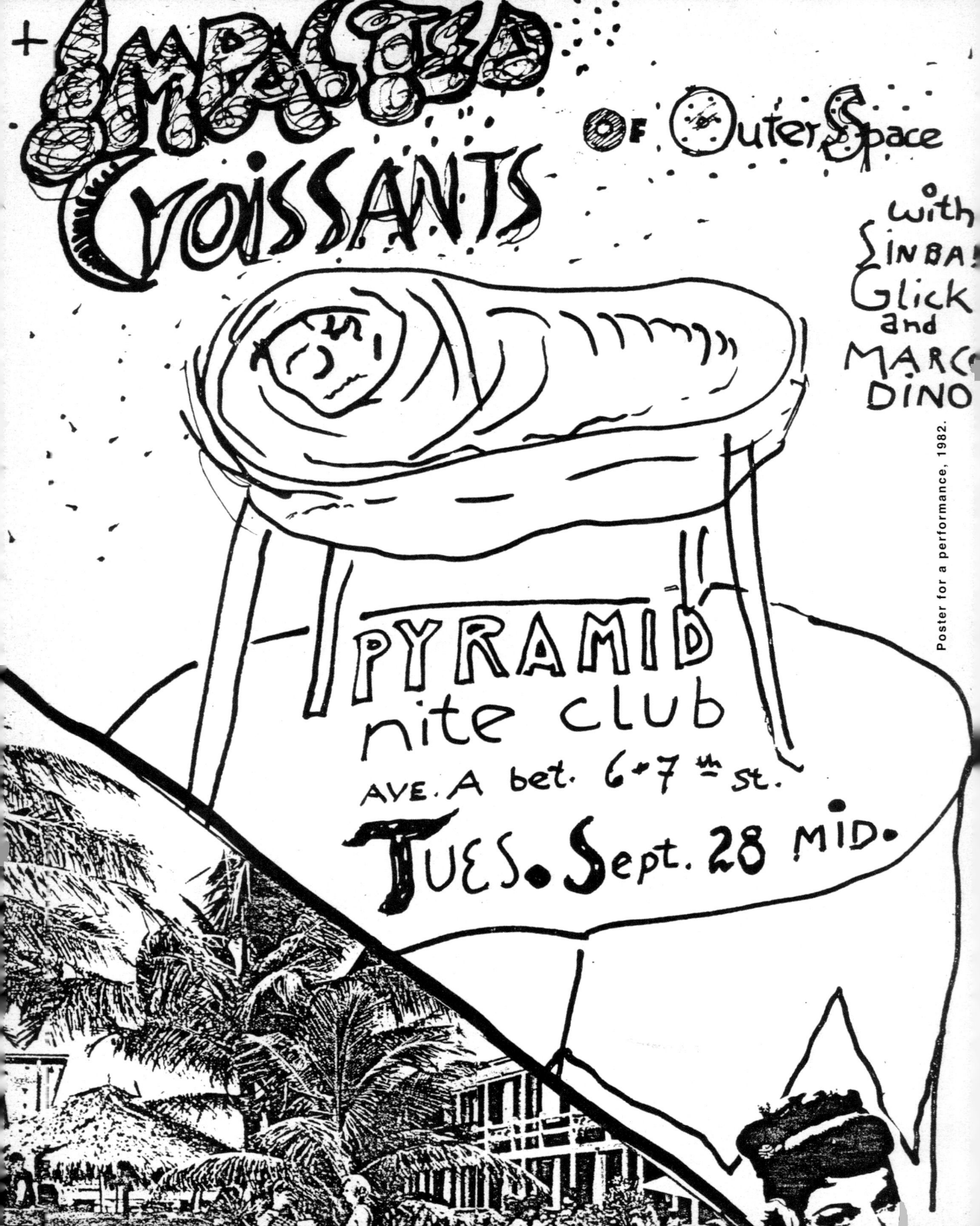

IMPACTED CROISSANTS OF OuterSpace

with SINBA! Glick and MARC DINO

PYRAMID nite club
AVE. A bet. 6+7th st.
TUES. Sept. 28 MID.

Poster for a performance, 1982.

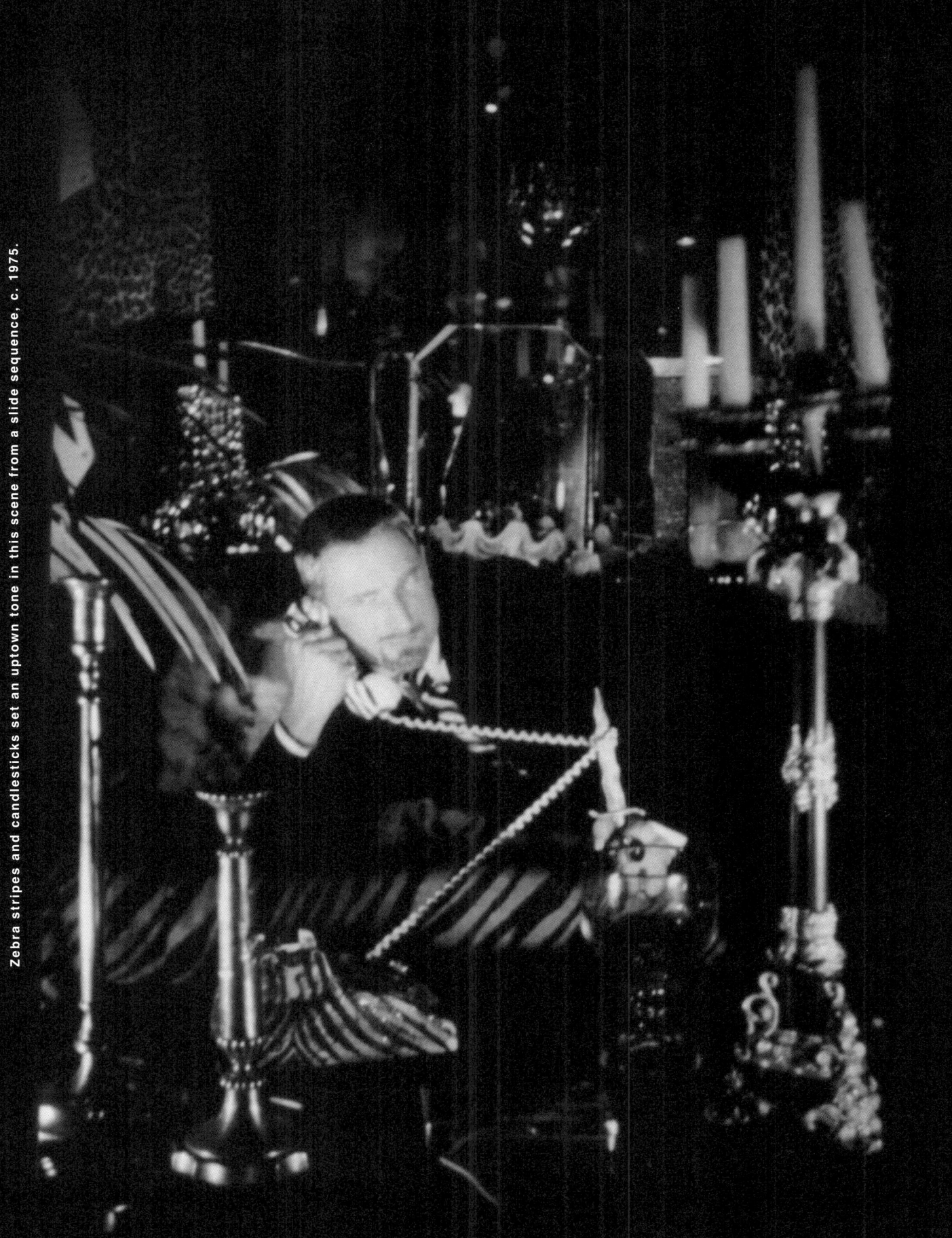

Zebra stripes and candlesticks set an uptown tone in this scene from a slide sequence, c. 1975.

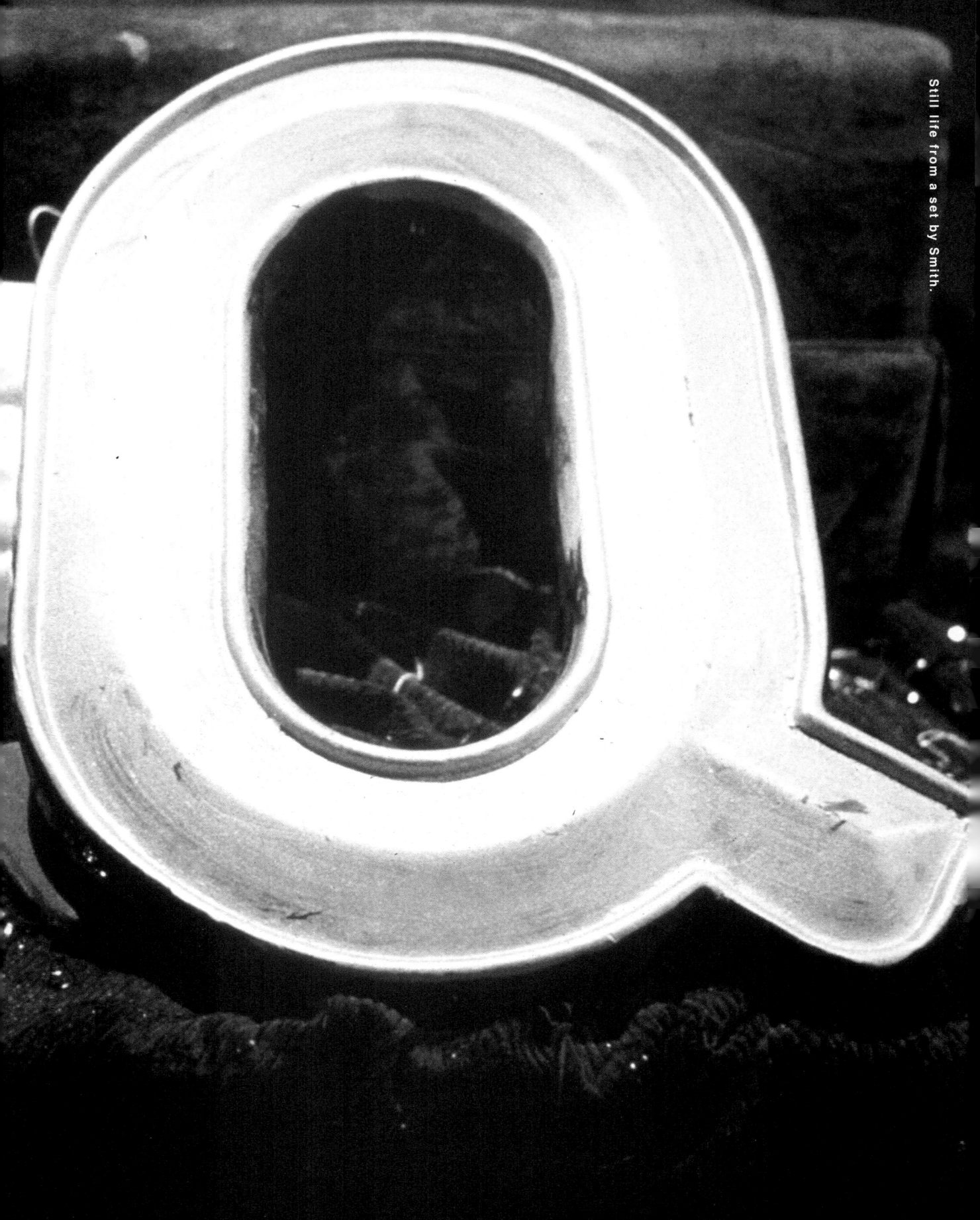

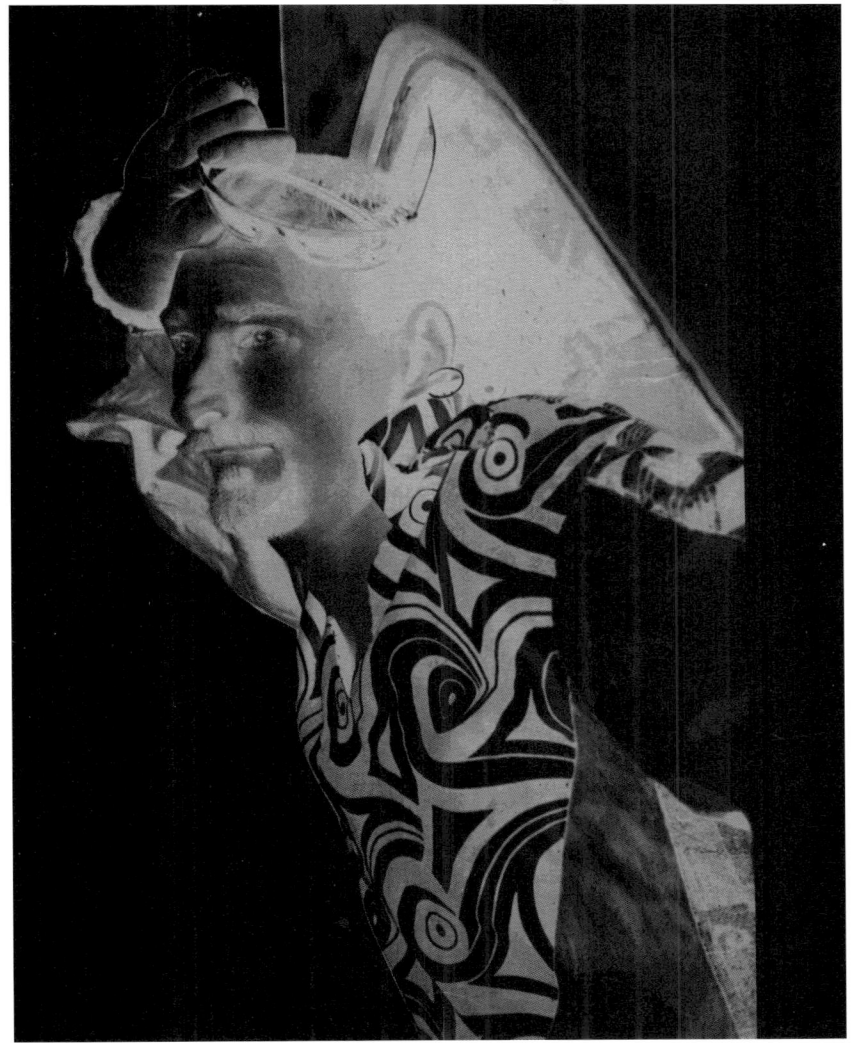

Using a favorite photograph, Smith experiments with solarization effects in the darkroom.

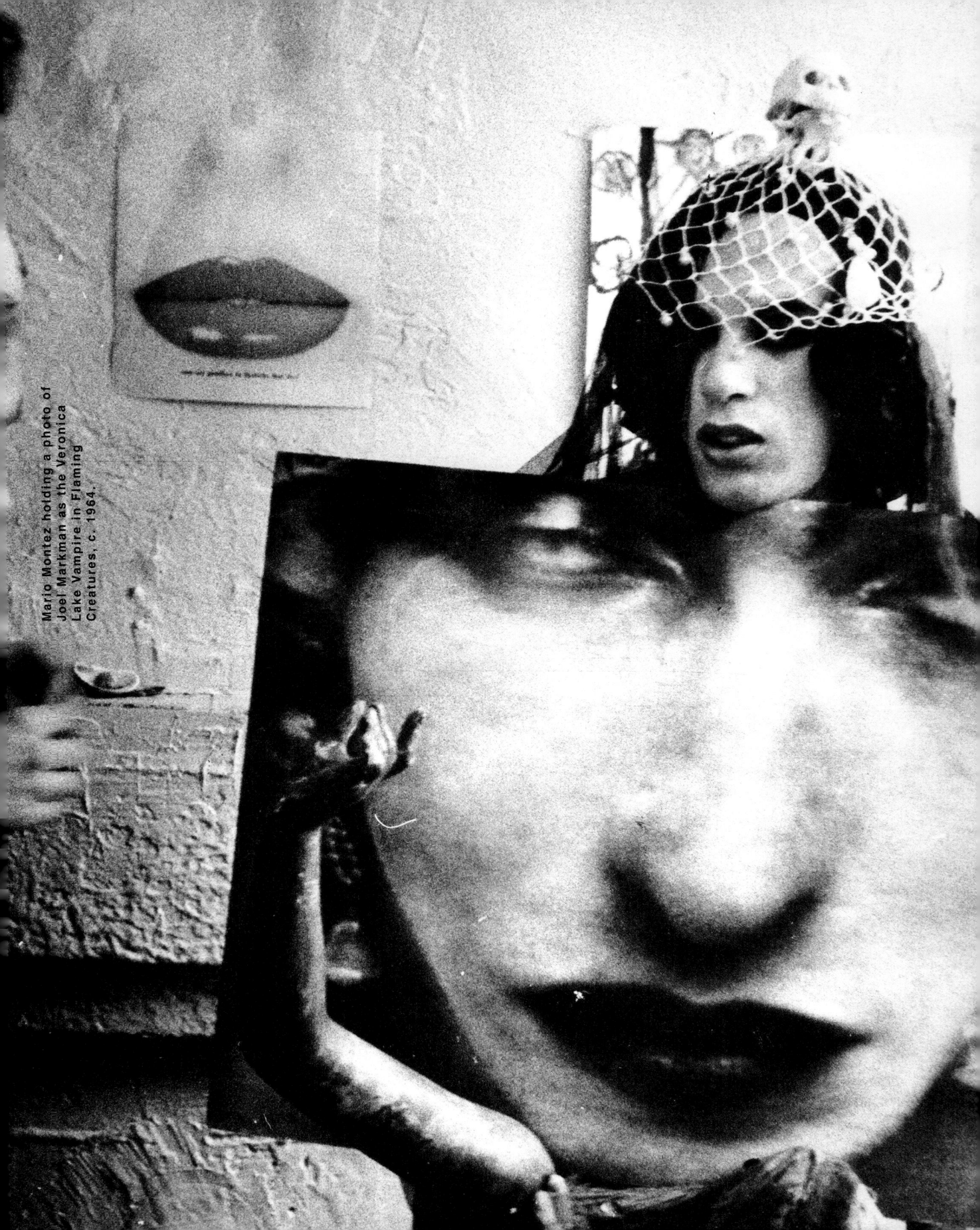

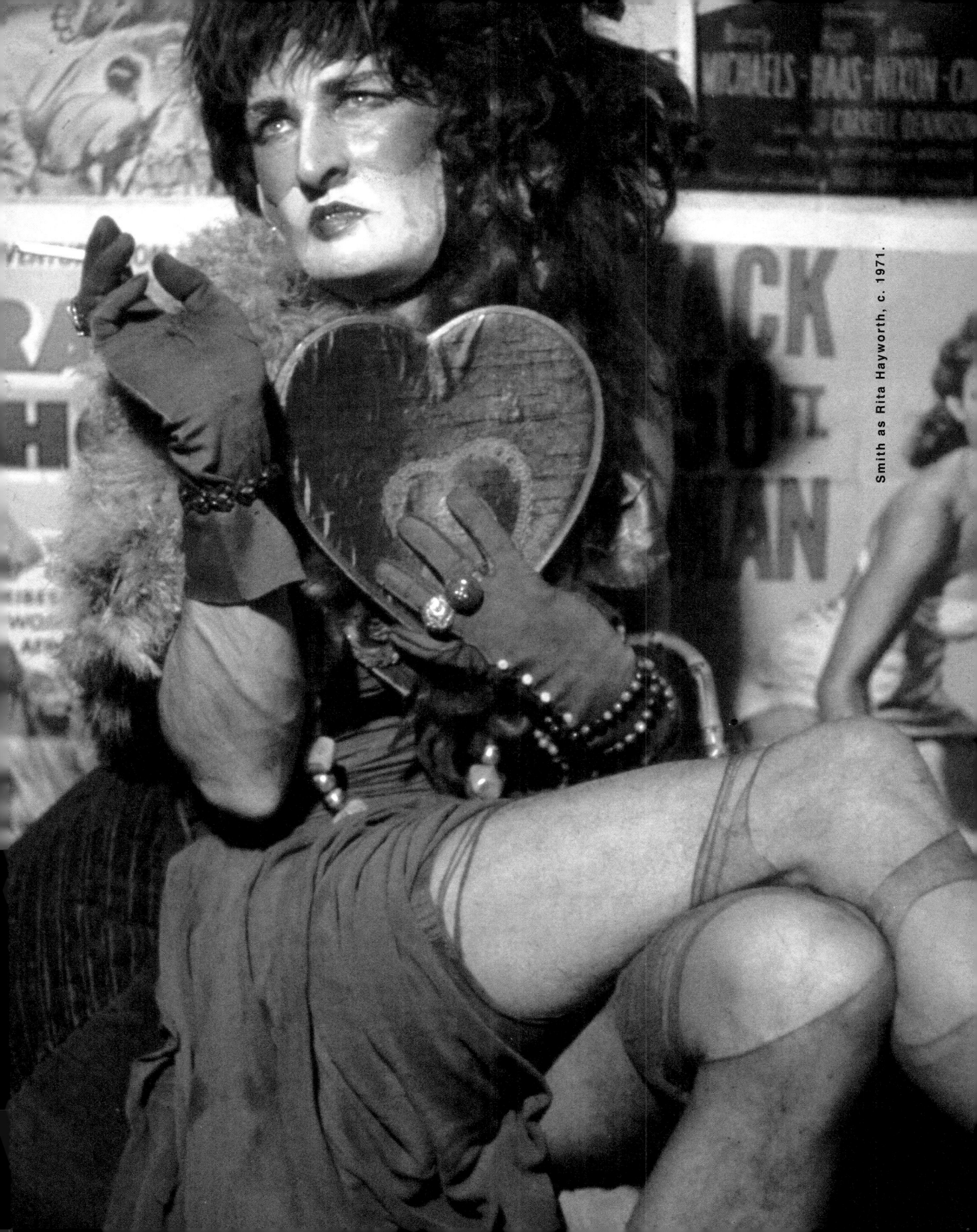

Smith as Rita Hayworth, c. 1971.

Next stage of life
needs that weren't ~~apparent~~ before

Money for expanding - money
~~of~~ teeth - hair - gymn -

Provide for Old Age

What you HAVE and THANK GOD

(1.) a glorious past.

(2.) a life of inspirational achievement & learning in ARTS

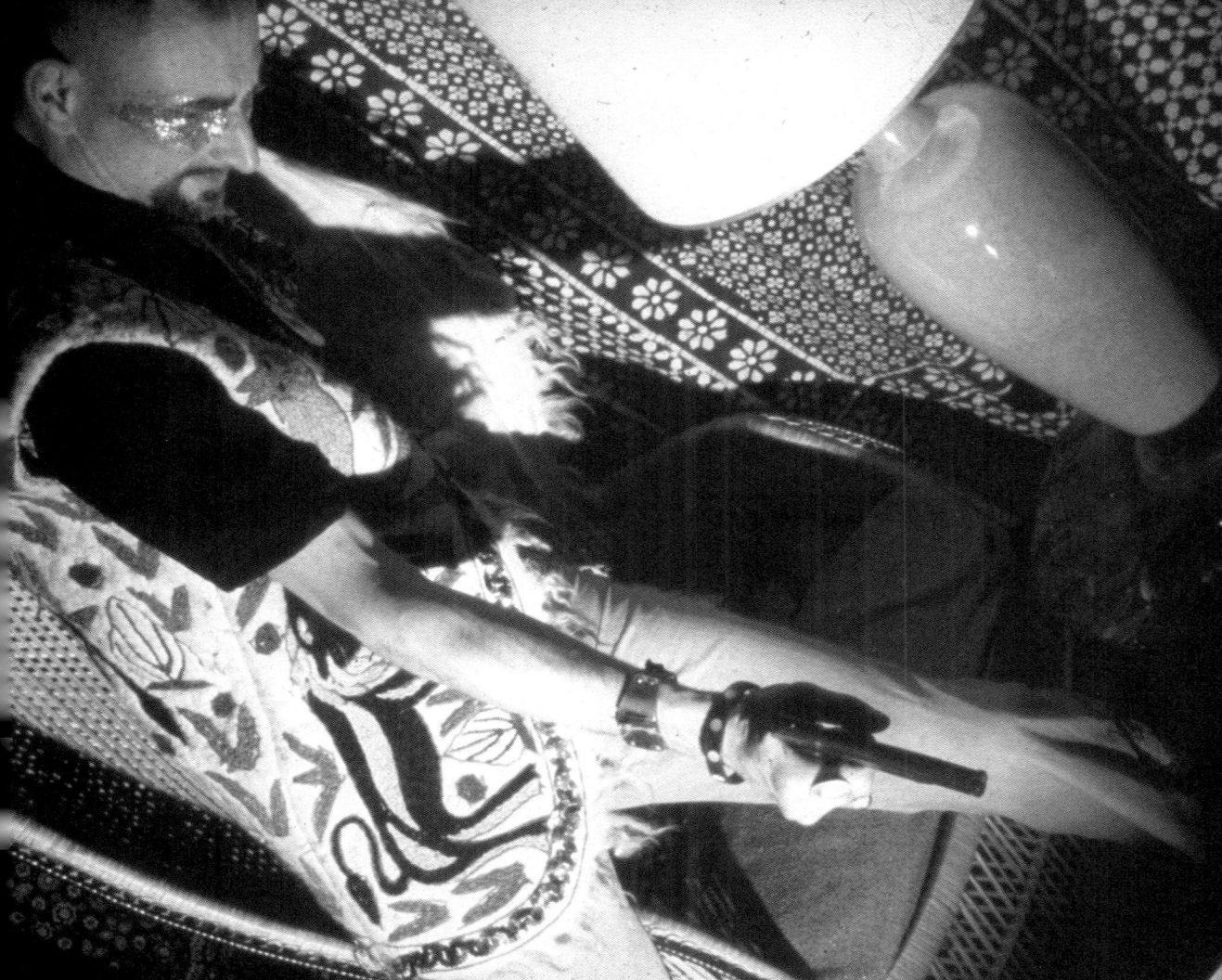

Smith at home on the Lower East Side. Smith listed his First Avenue apartment as one of his lifetime achievements.

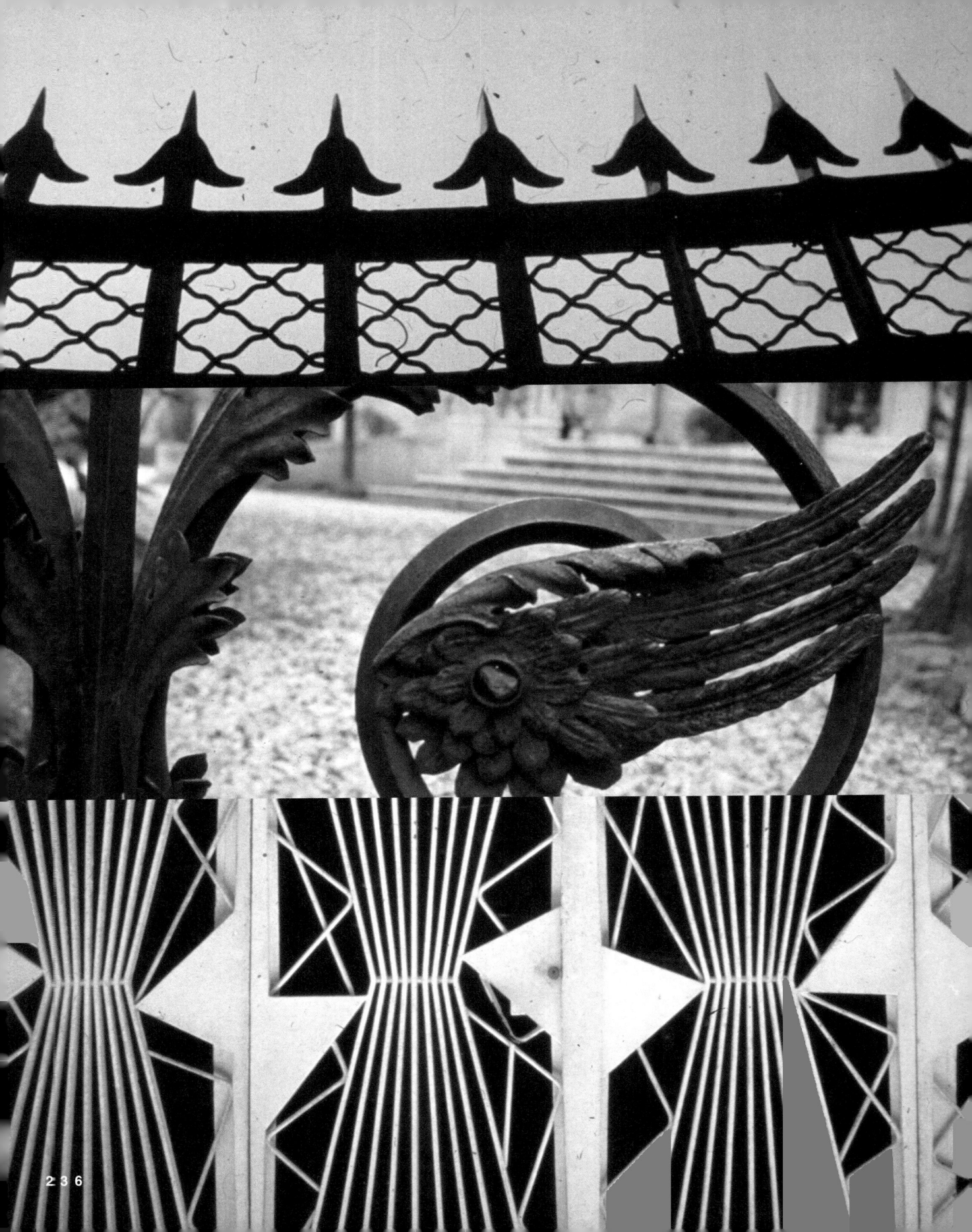

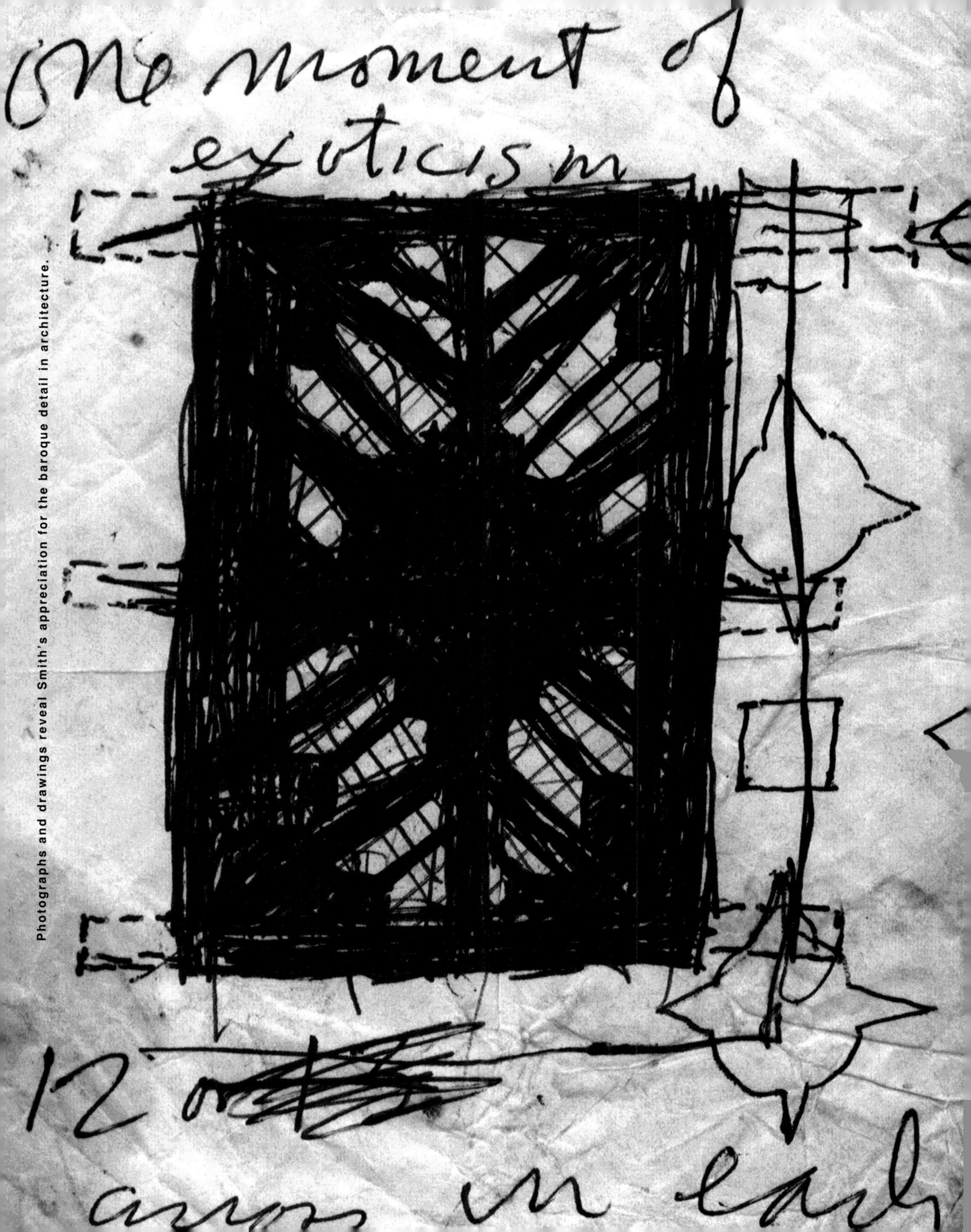

No moment of exoticism

12 or

arms in early

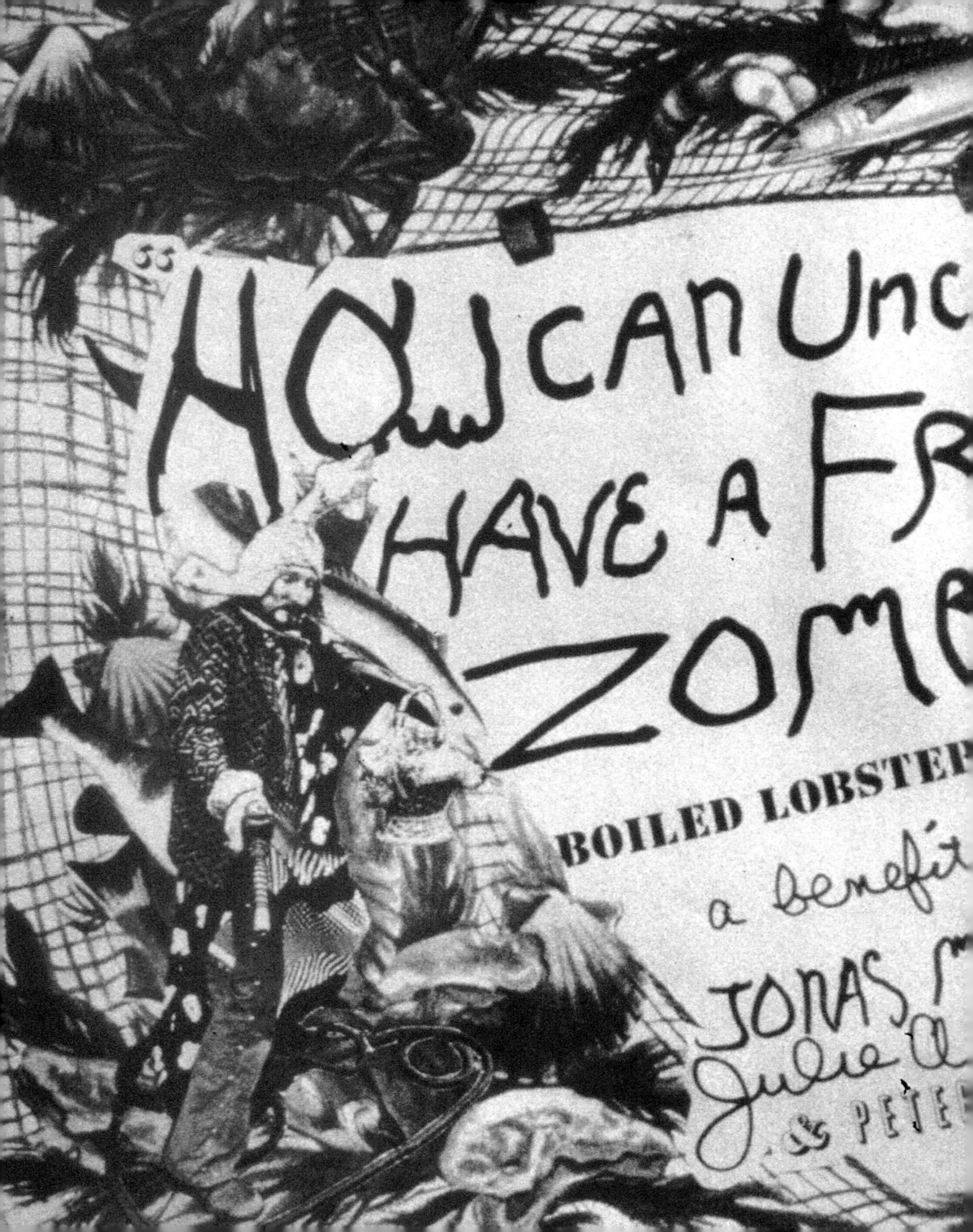
HOW CAN UNC
HAVE A FR
ZOME
BOILED LOBSTE
a benefit
JONAS
Julie
& PETE

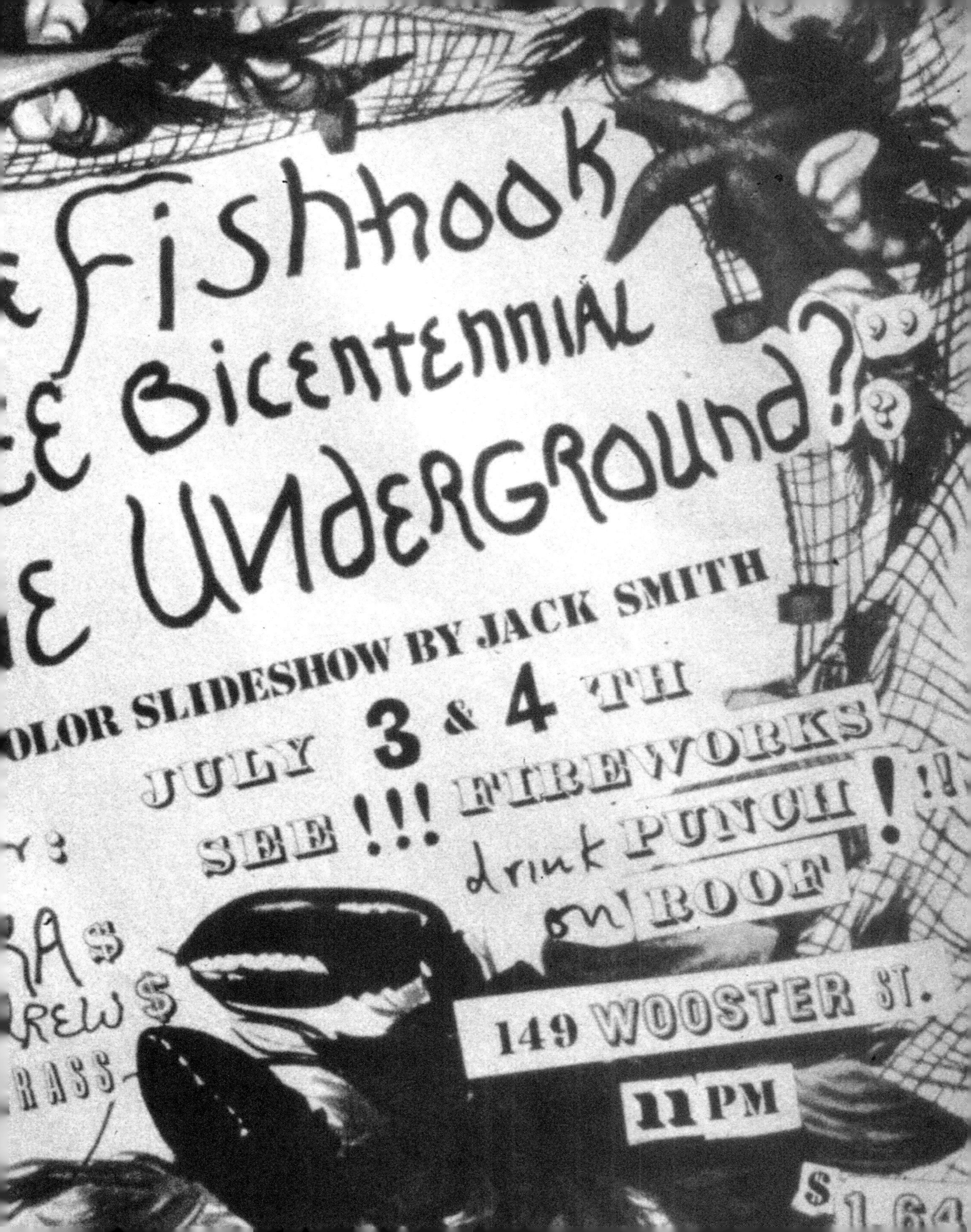

Fishhook
Bicentennial
Underground?"??

COLOR SLIDESHOW BY JACK SMITH

JULY 3 & 4 TH

SEE !!! FIREWORKS

drink **PUNCH** ! !!!

on **ROOF** !

149 WOOSTER ST.

11 PM

$1.6

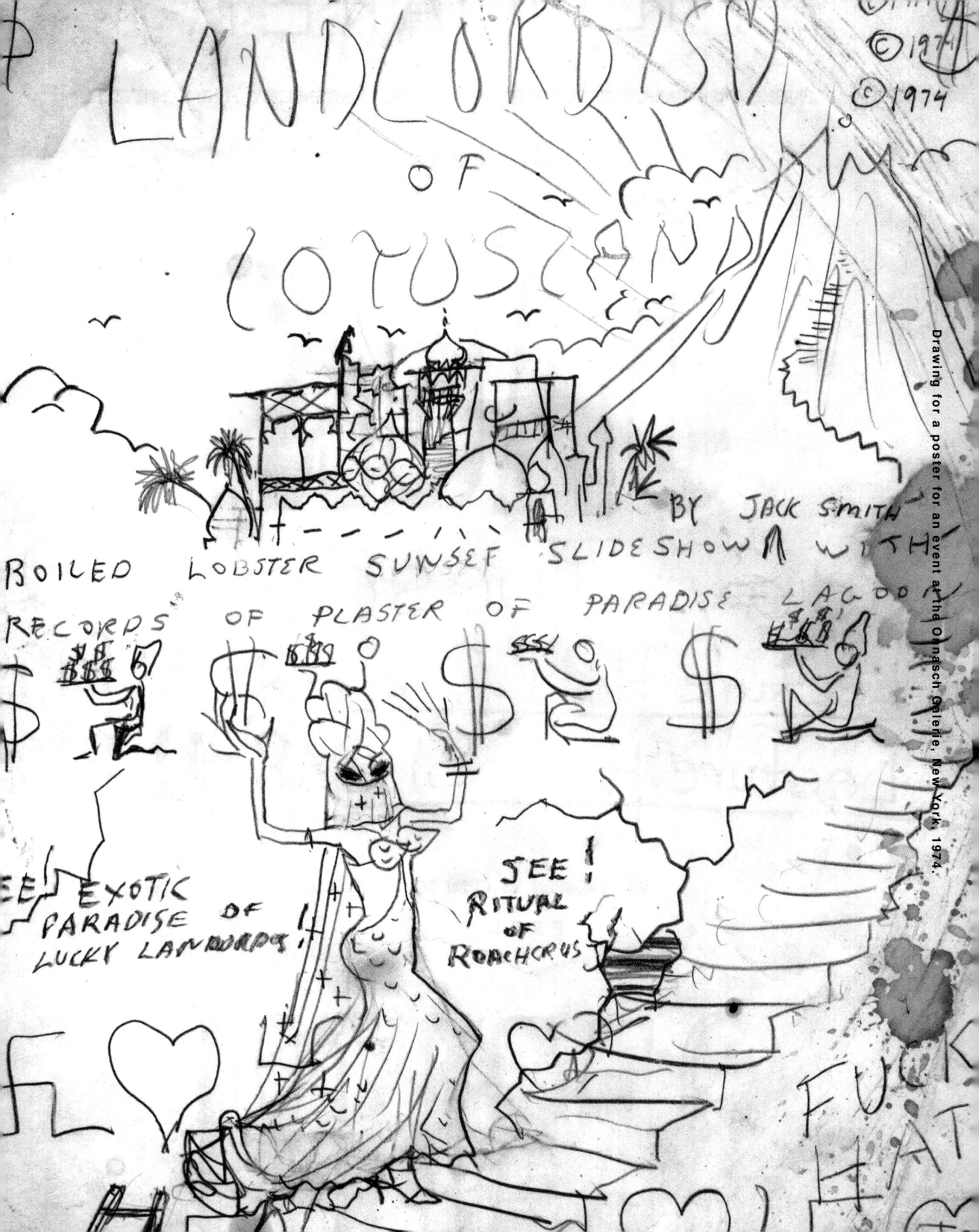

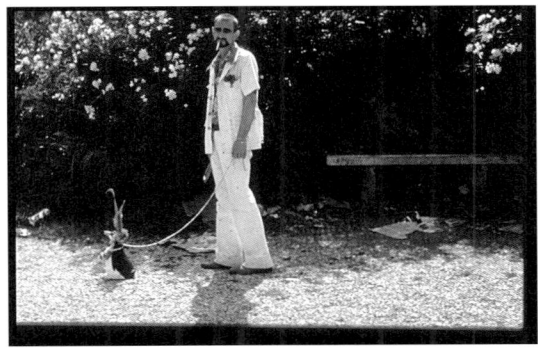

Smith and Yolanda in Rome, 1975.

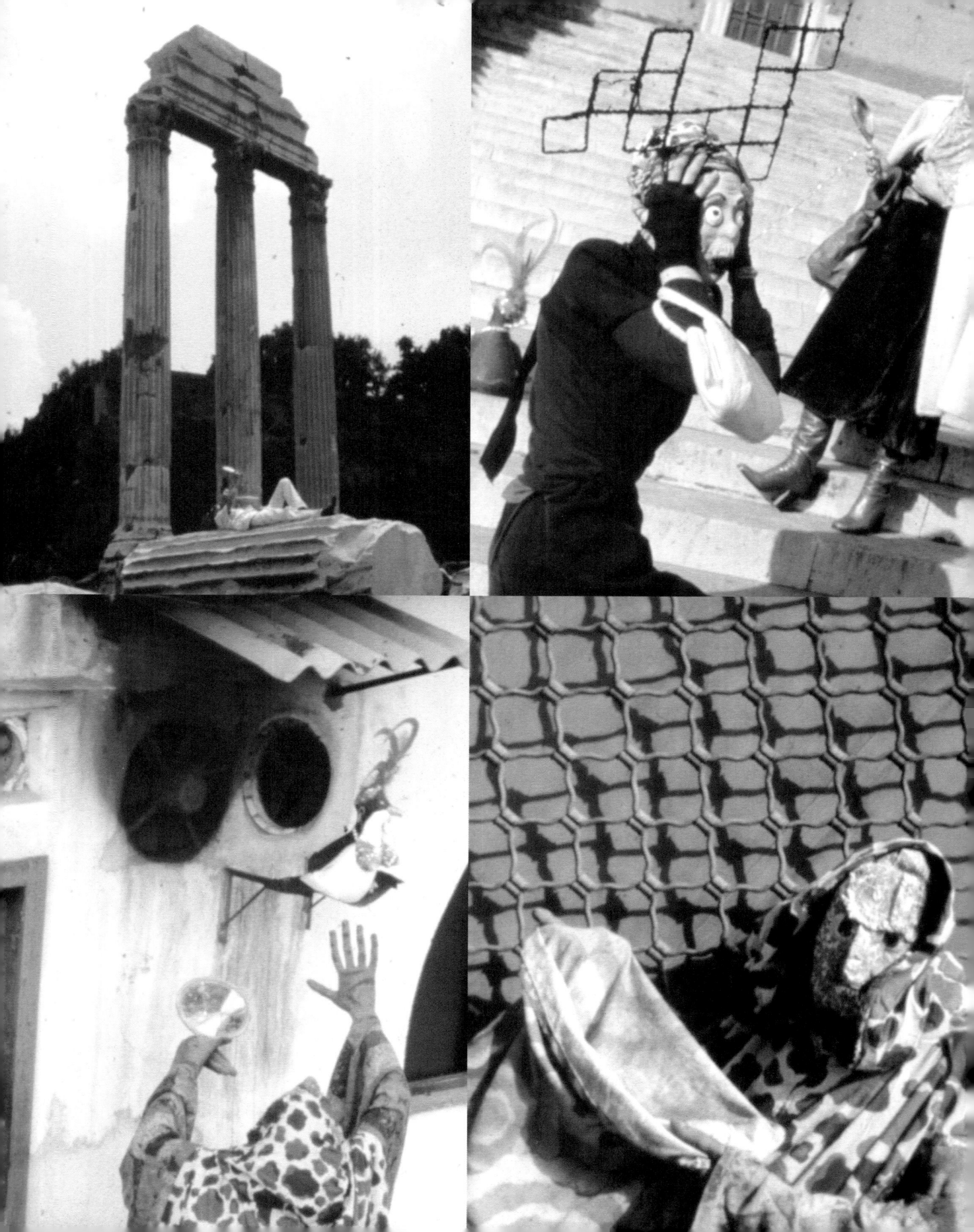

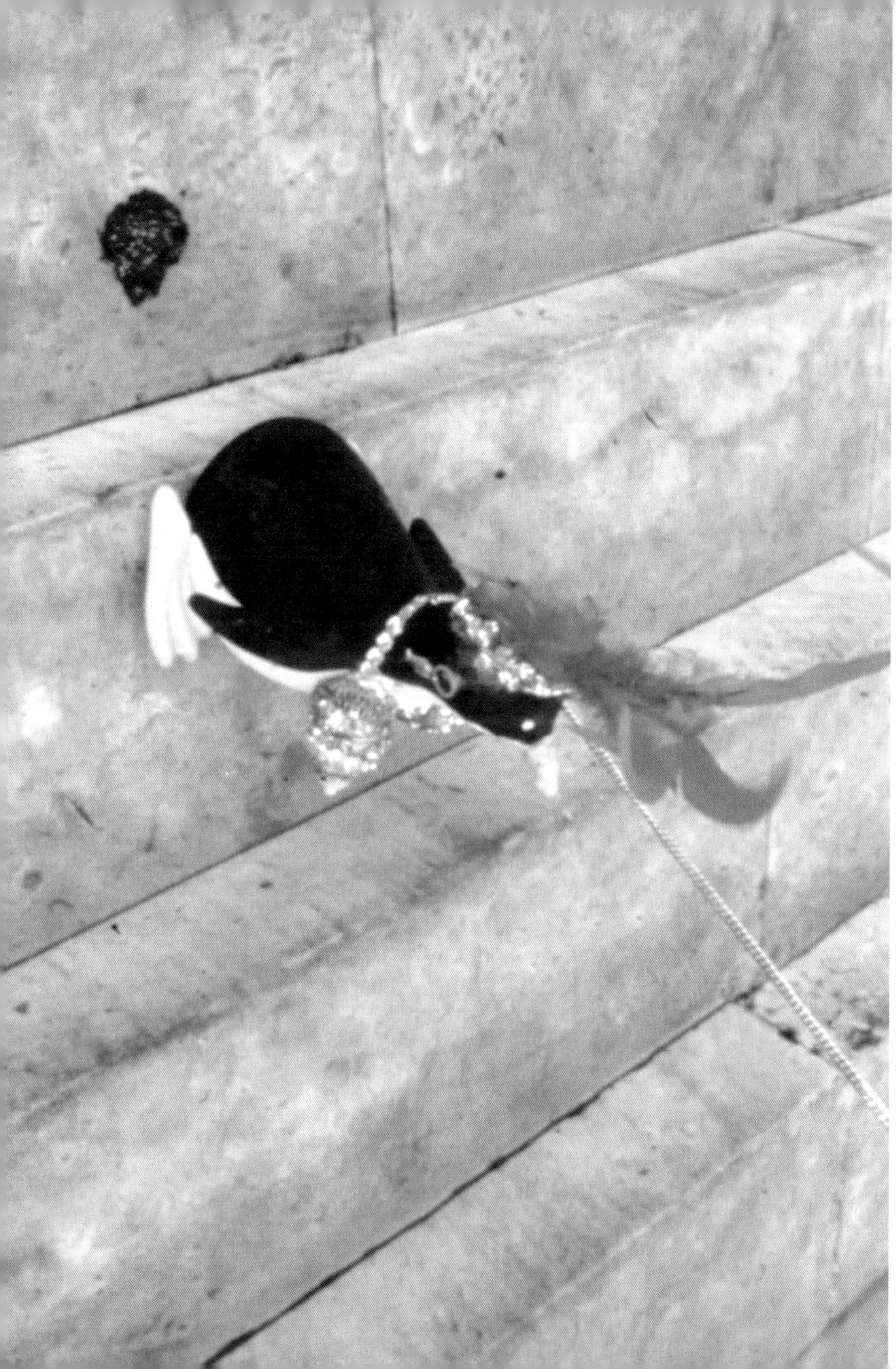

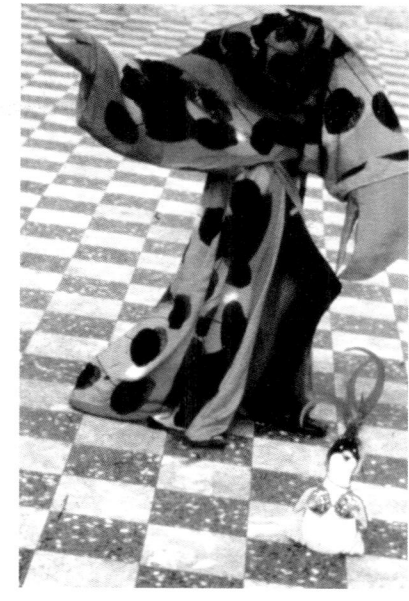

Smith appears in various roles including the Green Witch (bottom left), the Lobster (top right), and a masked pedestrian (top left) horrified to discover Yolanda shitting on the marble steps of Rome.

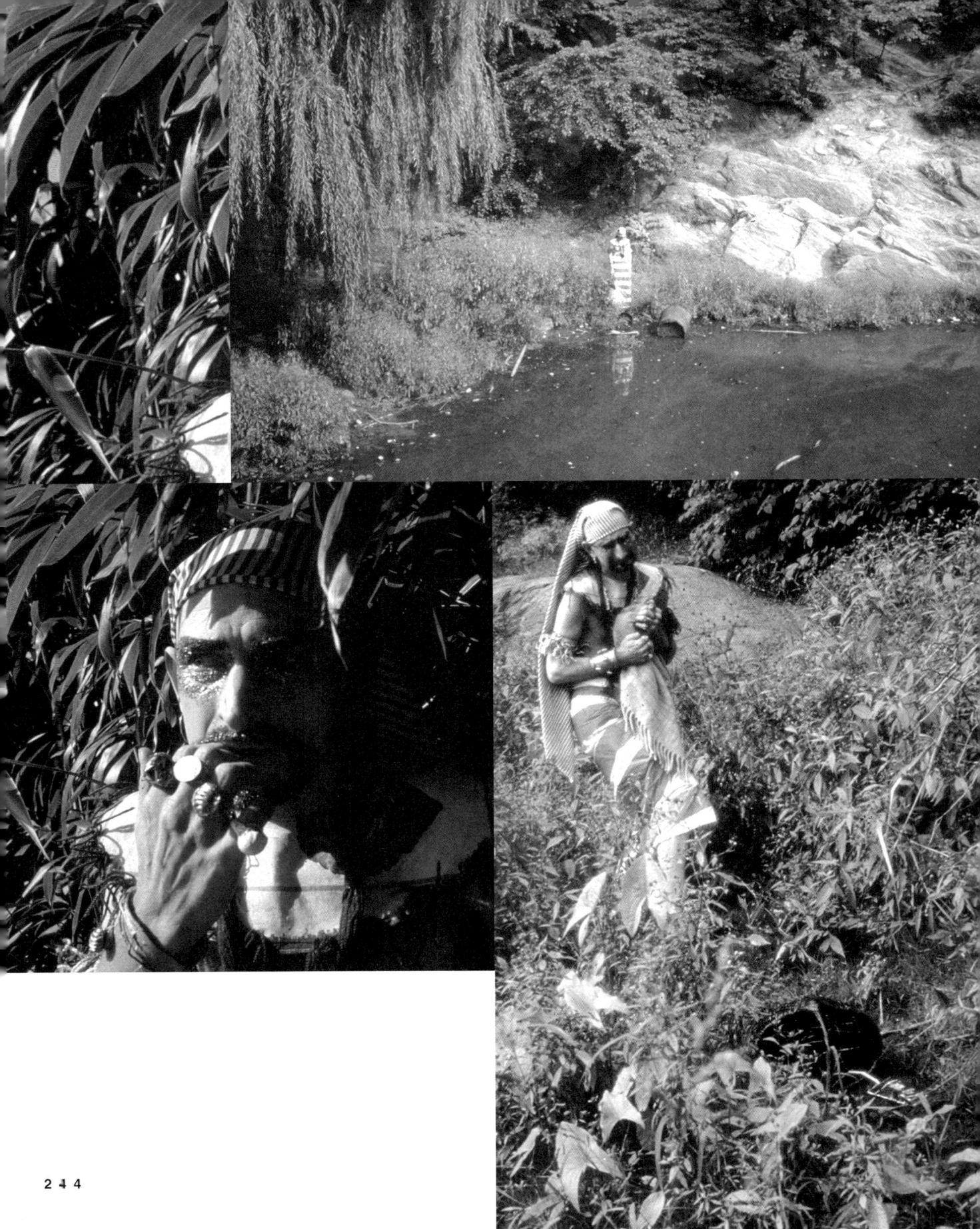

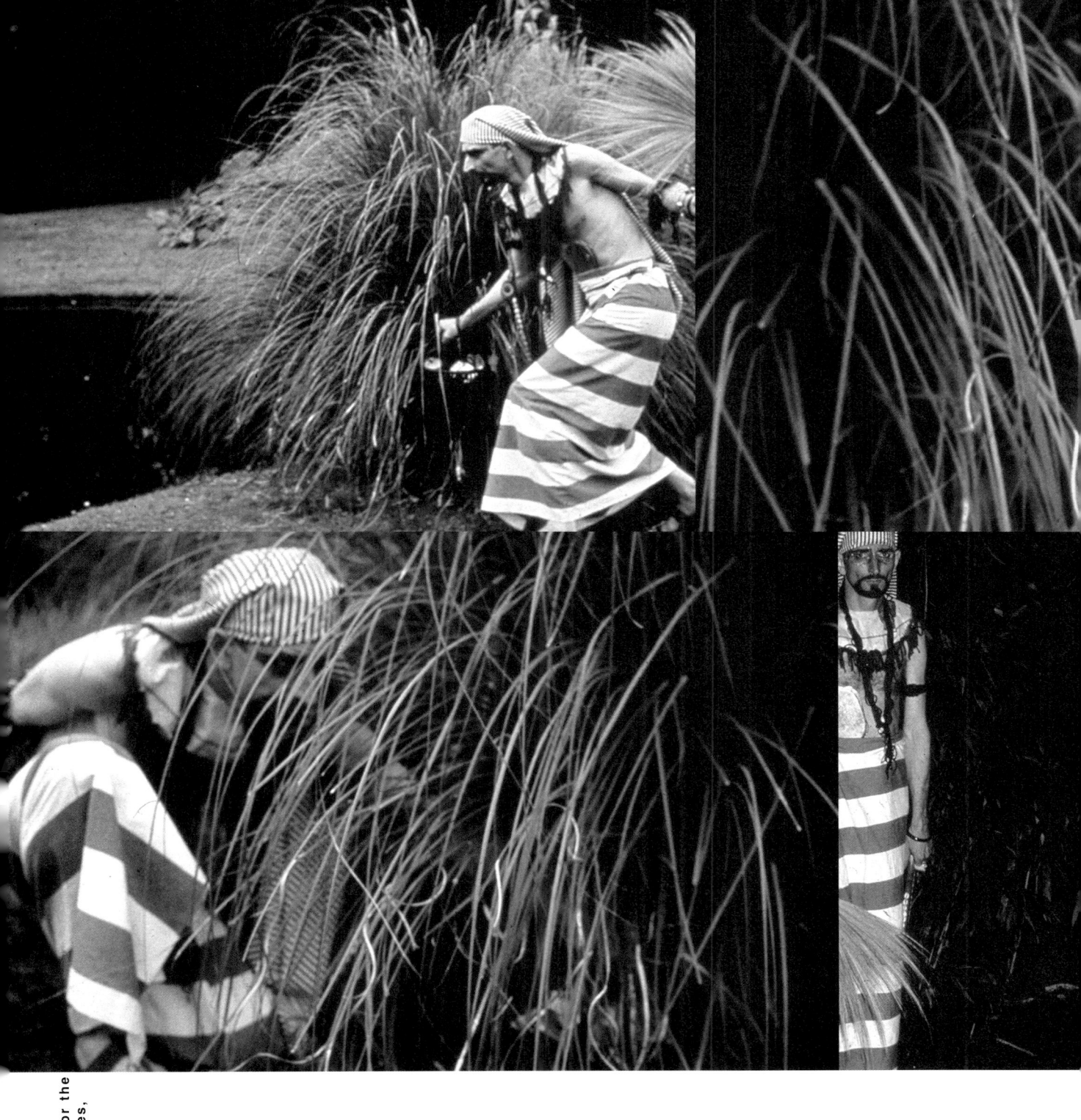

Smith and film artist
Babeth collaborate for the
slide sequence, Moses,
Cologne, 1974.

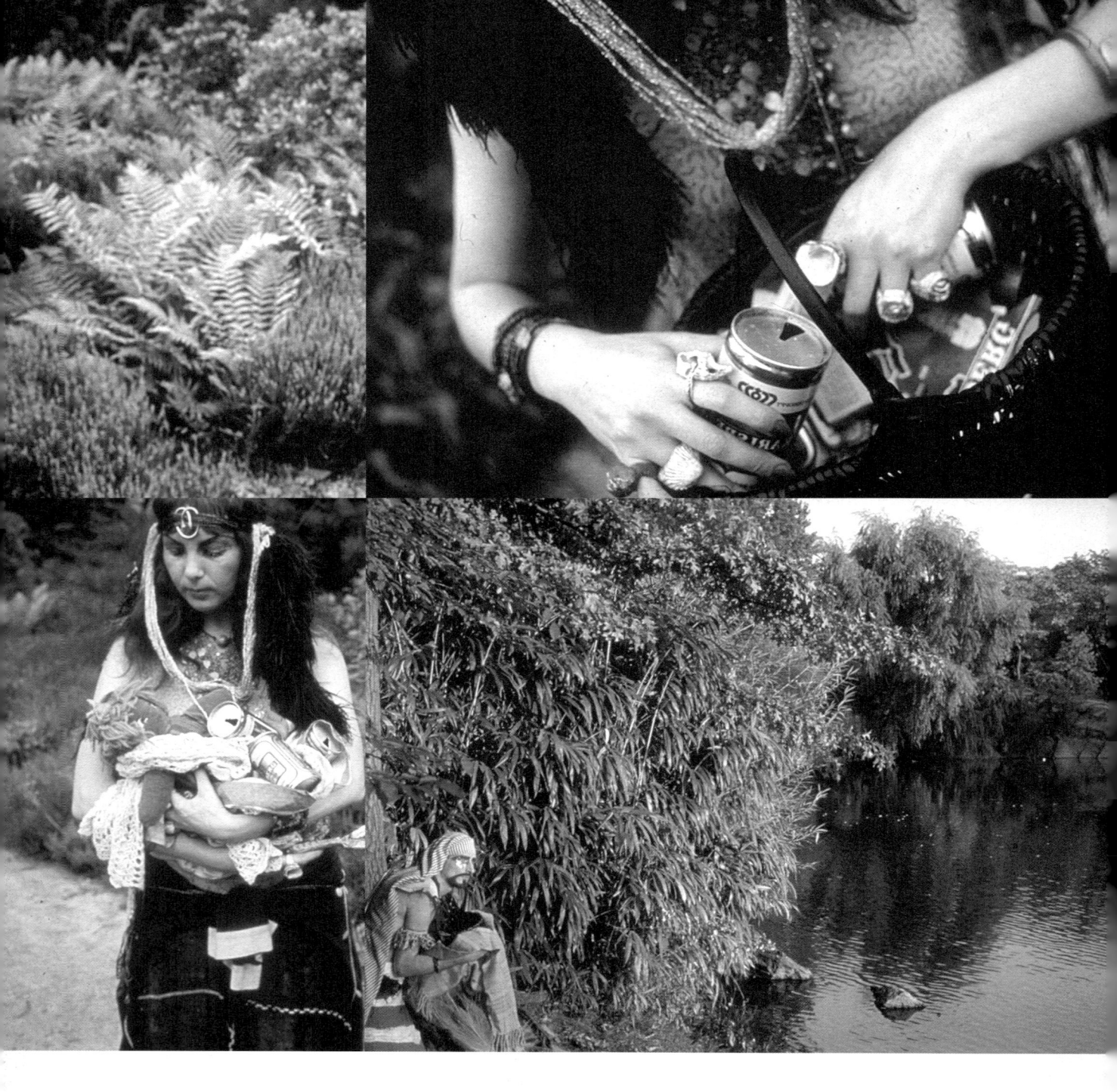

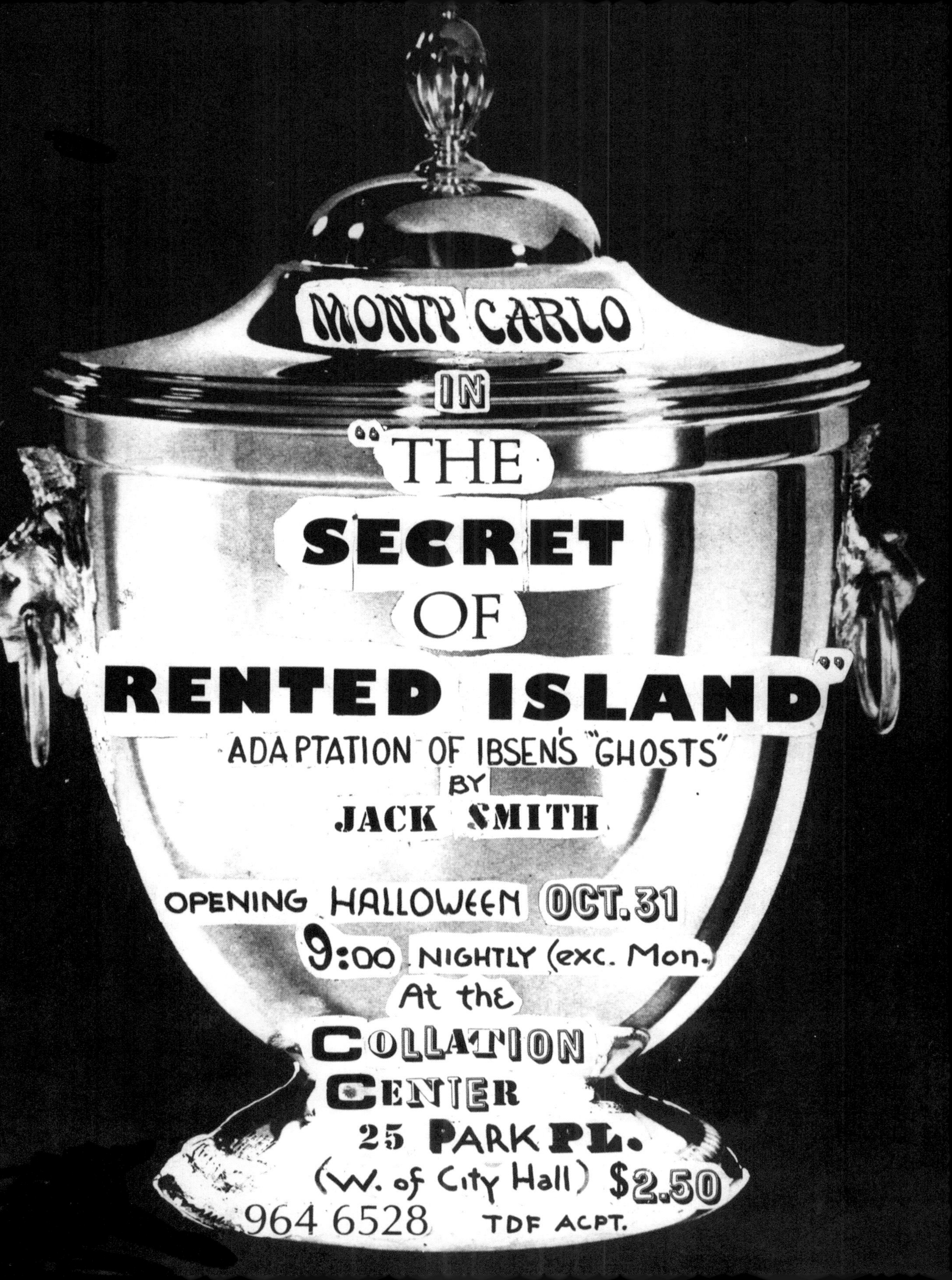

MONTE CARLO
IN
"THE
SECRET
OF
RENTED ISLAND"
ADAPTATION OF IBSEN'S "GHOSTS"
BY
JACK SMITH

OPENING HALLOWEEN OCT. 31
9:00 NIGHTLY (exc. Mon.
At the
COLLATION CENTER
25 PARK PL.
(W. of City Hall) $2.50
964 6528   TDF ACPT.

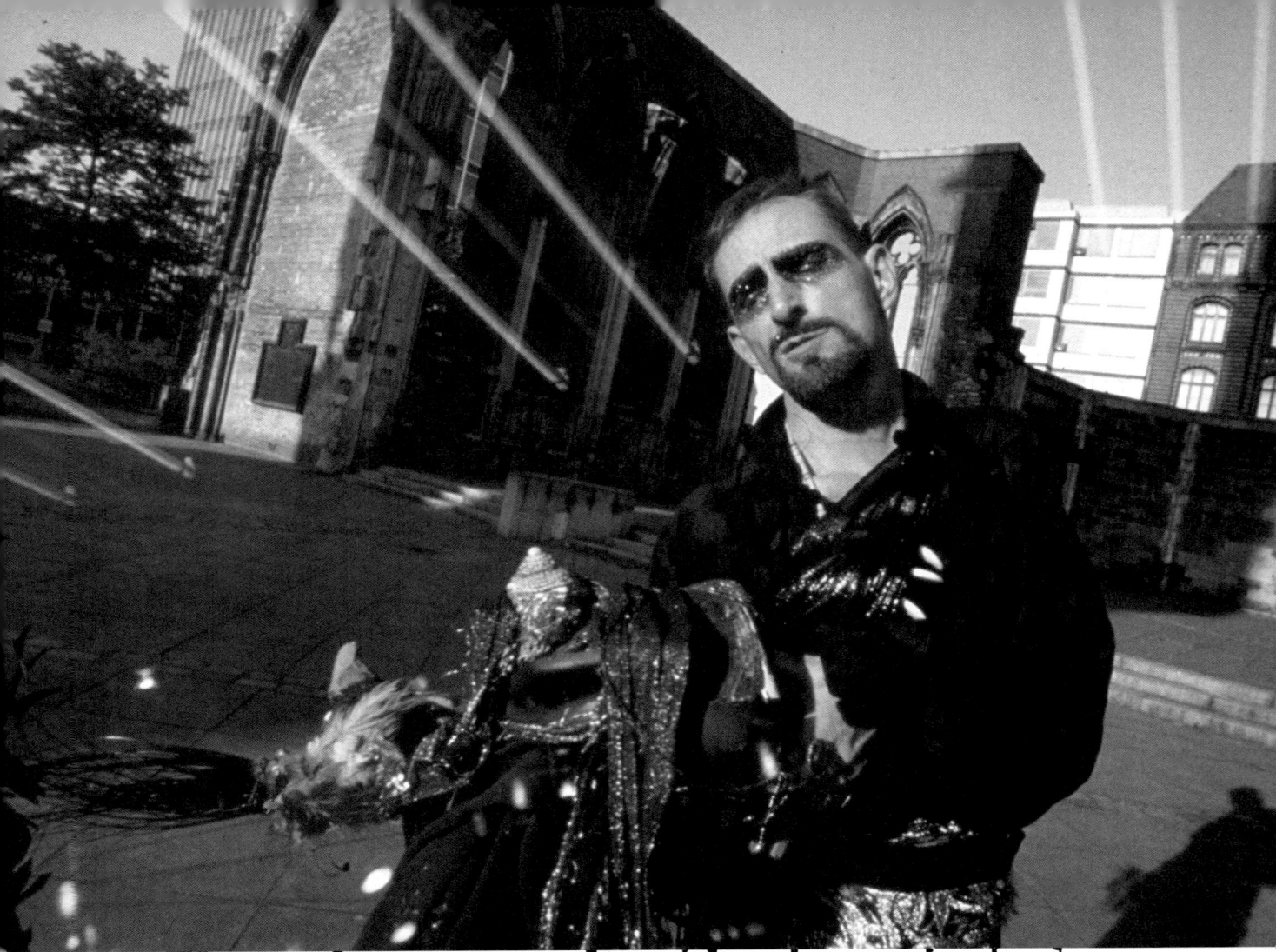

They have made their mistake.
They have let me live.

In this slide montage, Smith performs a version of I Danced with a Penguin, Hamburg, 1983.

248

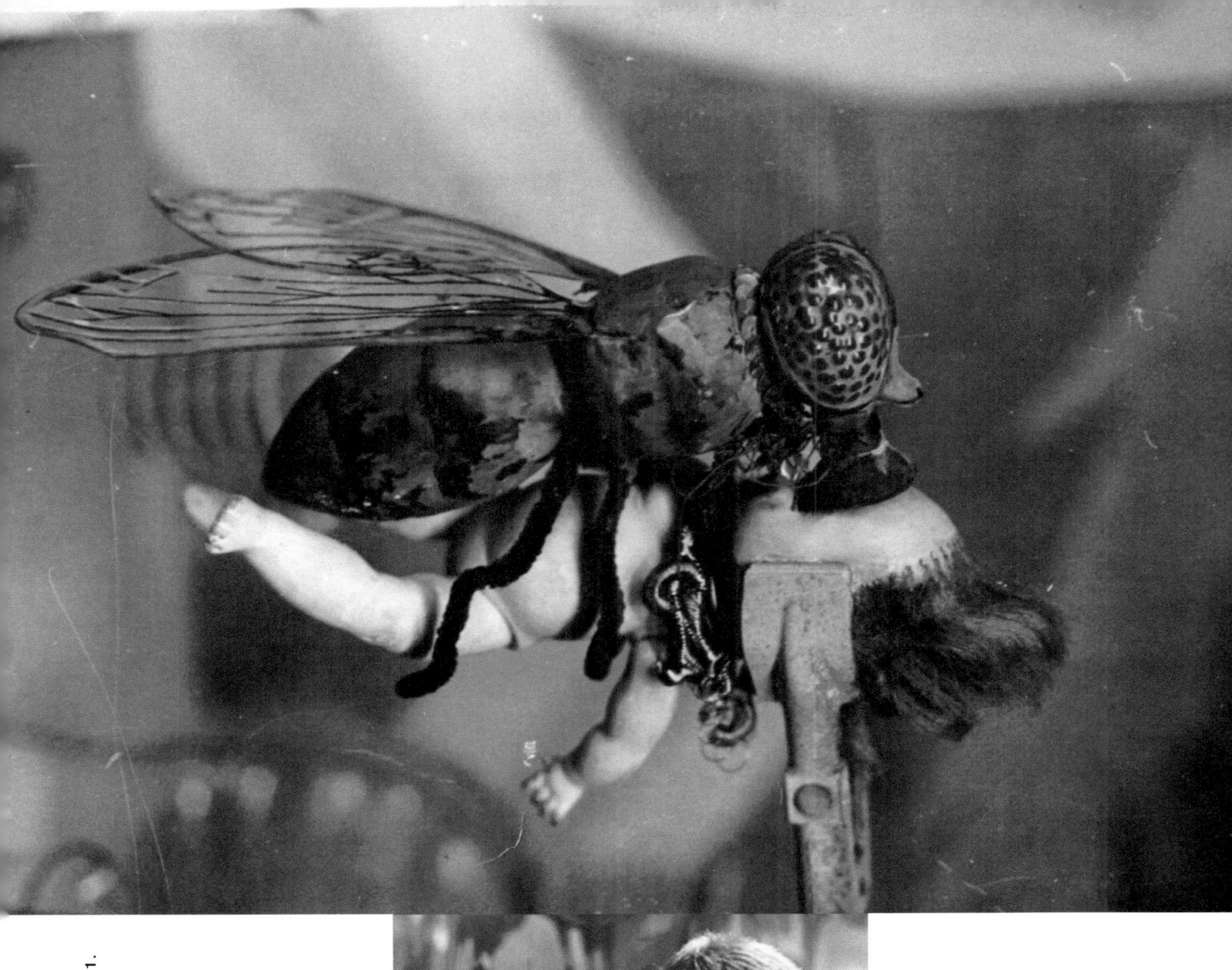

Smith admires a vampiristic assemblage, early
1960s. He used the detail in a later poster for
Penguin Rustling Out by the Old Archives, 1981.

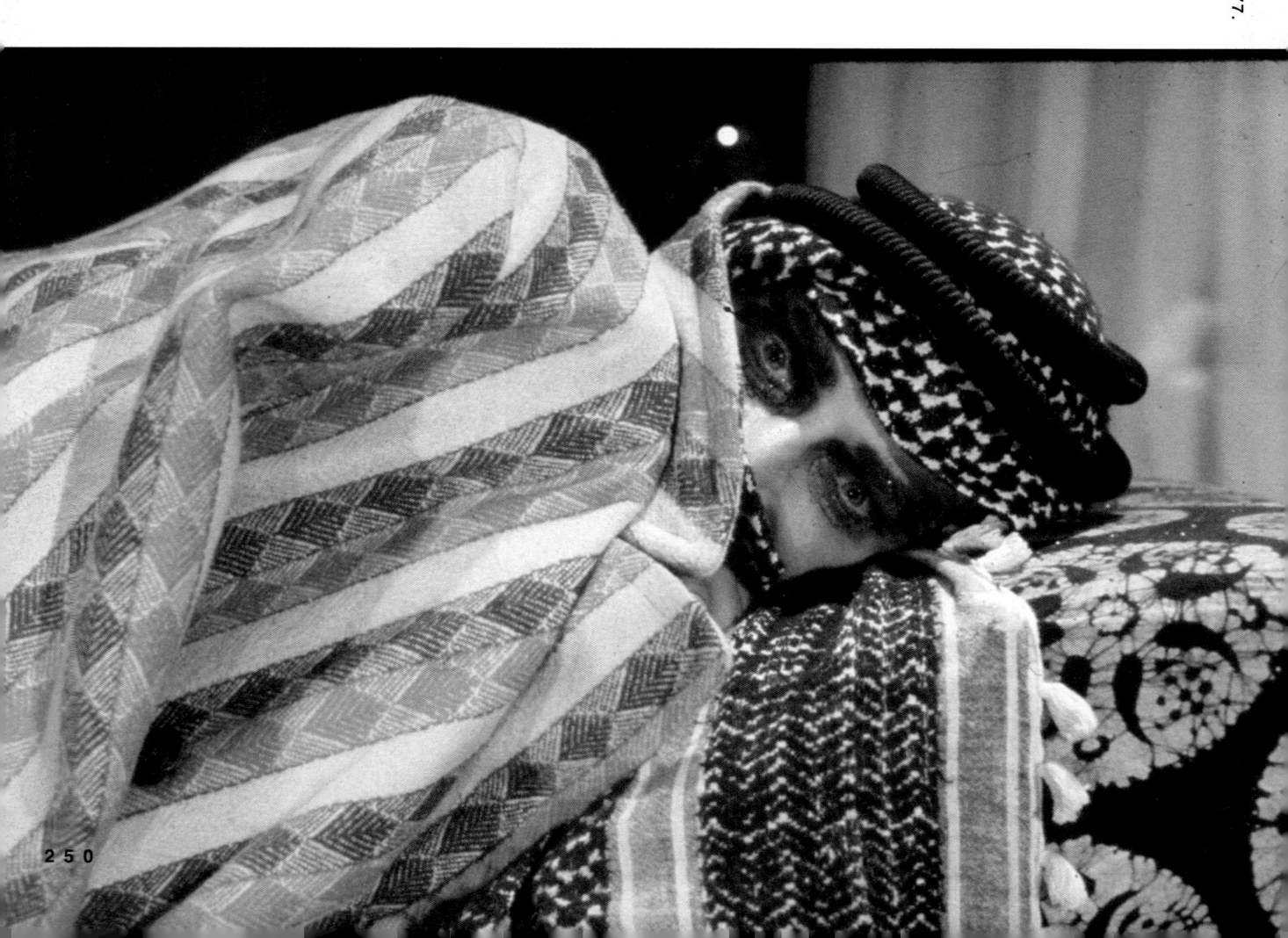

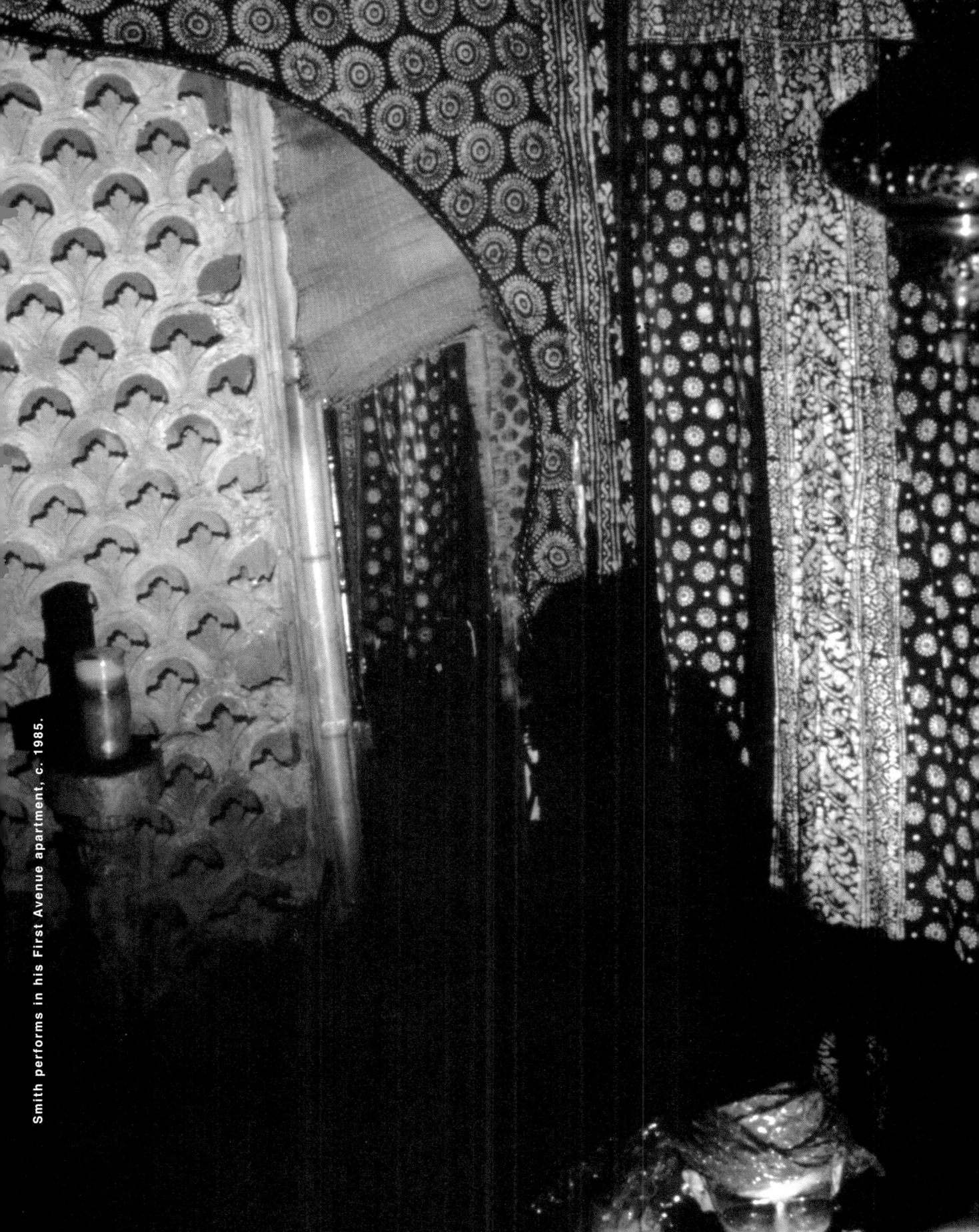

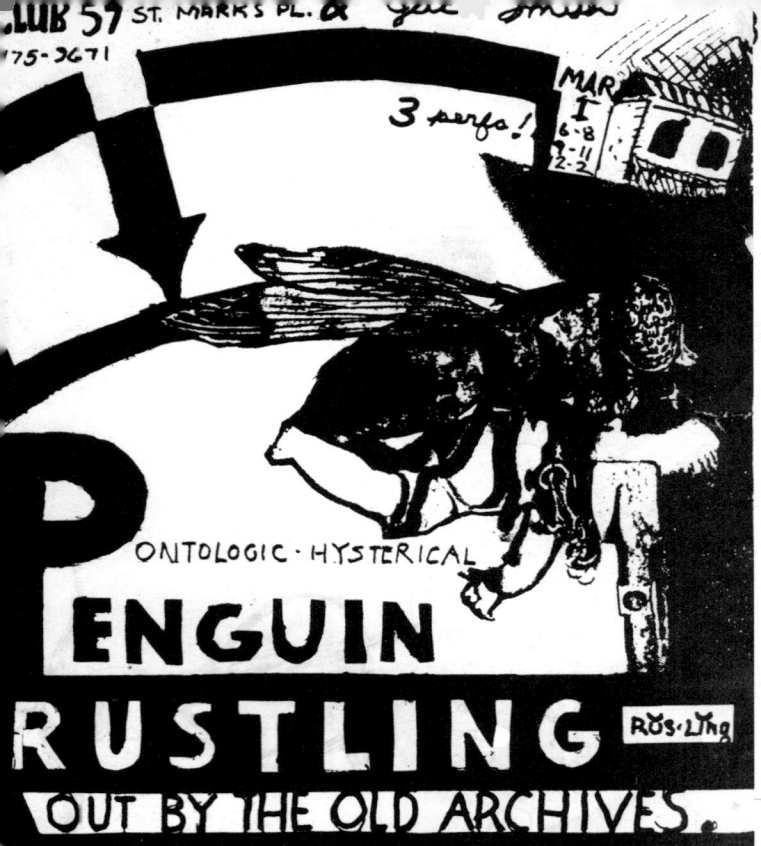

CLUB 57 ST. MARKS PL. & Jack Smith
75-2671

MAR 1
6-8
9-11
12-2

3 perfs!

ONTOLOGIC · HYSTERICAL

PENGUIN

RUSTLING   ROS·LINg

OUT BY THE OLD ARCHIVES.

BOILED LOBSTER-COLOR SLIDE SHOW   with

BELIEF IN BRAIN-PICKING is wh

IS

being taught

IN THE SCHOOLS

OF

CLAPTAIL

Lagoon.

A Jack Smith PROGRAM with JUNGLE BACK

What's underground about Marshmallows?

A tour through the underground night of Uncle Archives vaults of filmcrust. Guided by Jack Smith. Once a month performance & film

Smith used elements of his posters to stir interest in his performances and to attack his perceived enemies, including Jonas Mekas, Ellen Stewart of La Mama, the filmmaker Ken Jacobs, and theater director Richard Foreman.

252

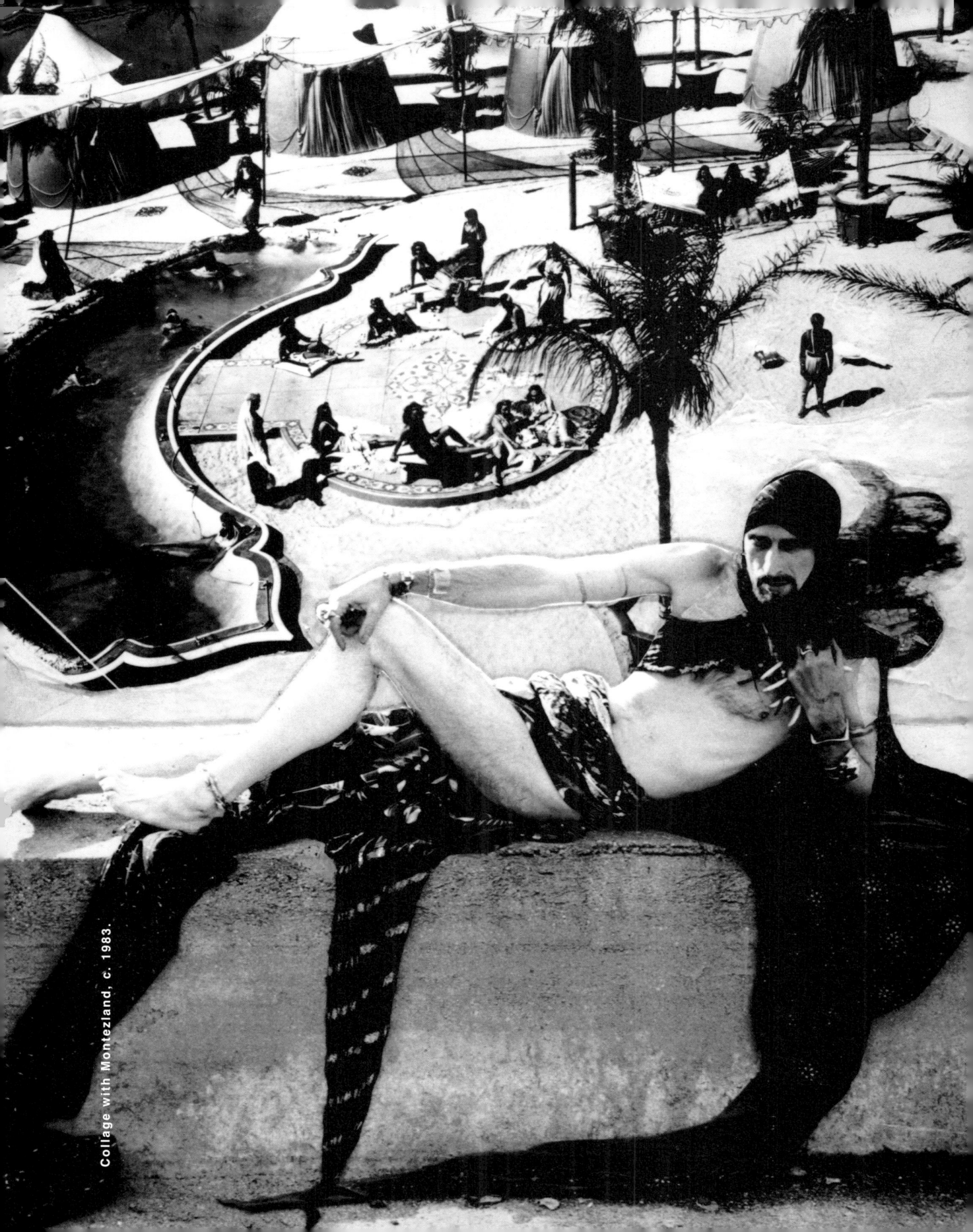

Collage with Montezland, c. 1983.

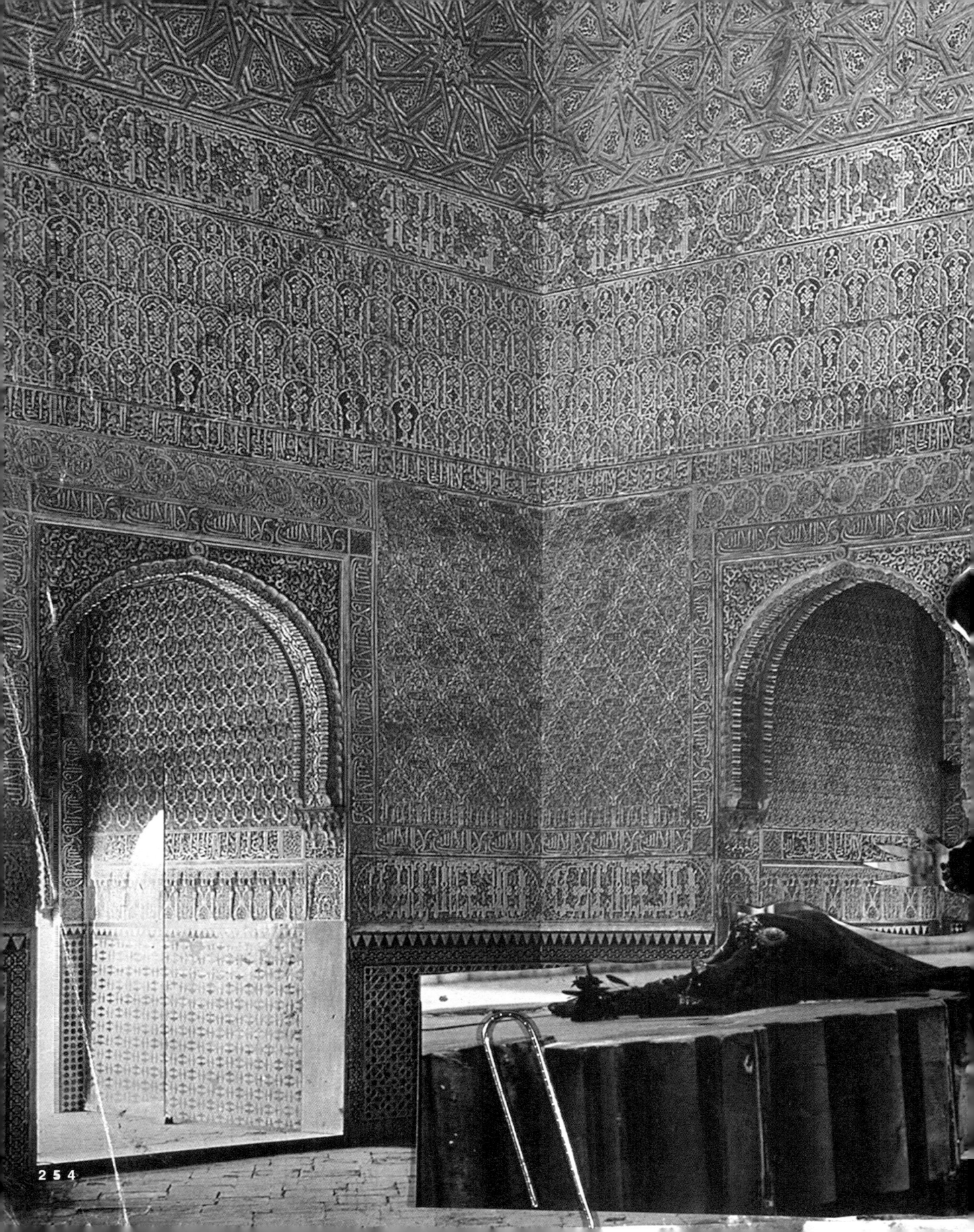

254

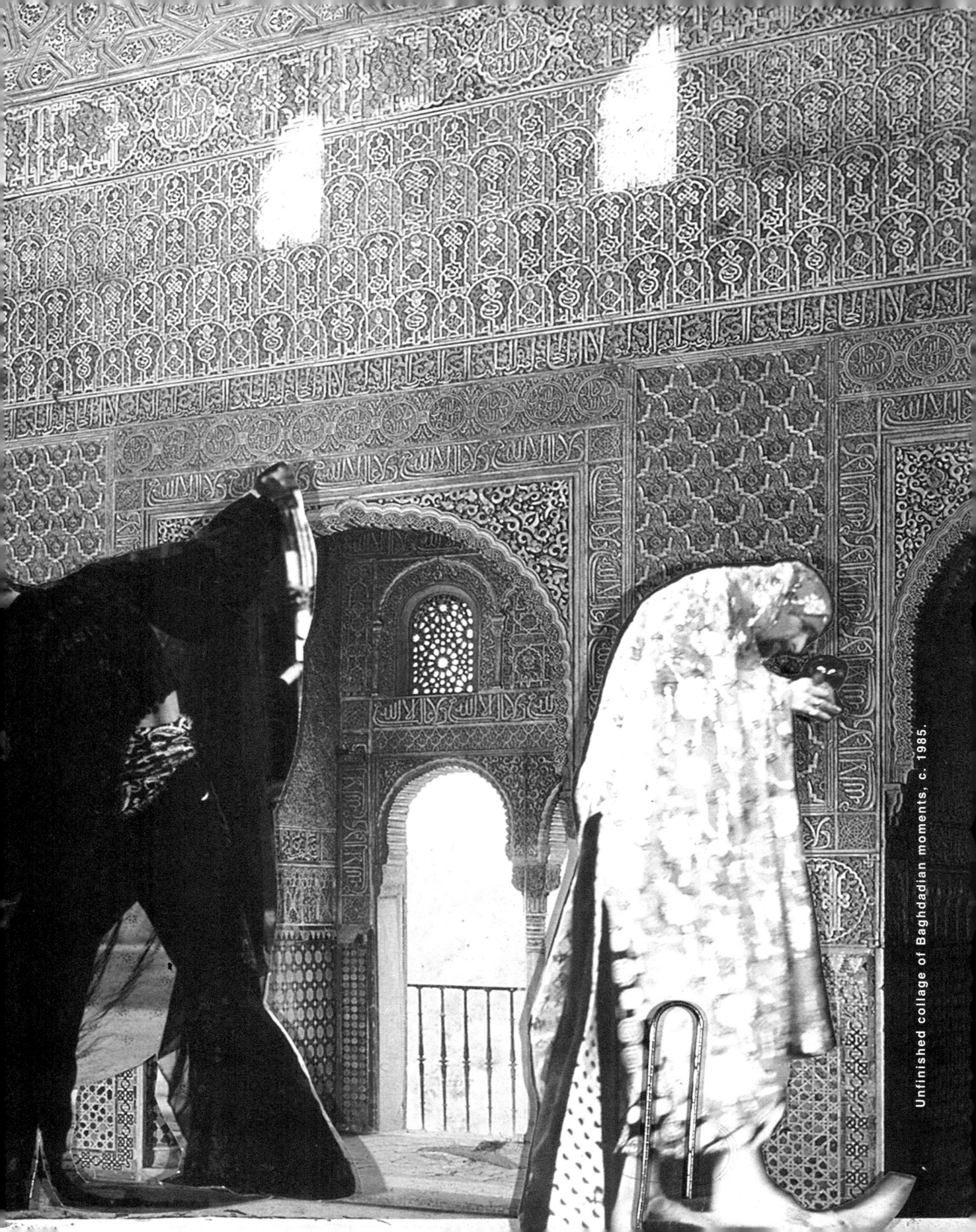

afterword

In the late 1980s, Jack Smith came to P. S. 1 Museum to discuss the possibility of an exhibition at The Clocktower Gallery, our Manhattan venue. This meeting, like many with Jack, can best be described as highly eventful, even operatic, but never quite materialized in a show. In fact, it followed several earlier and equally unsuccessful efforts to present this important, eccentric artist to a larger public. In 1979, I attempted to organize a performance series at a lower Manhattan strip parlor, the "Baby Doll Lounge." With some trepidation, I invited Jack to participate, and one winter's night we made a "field" inspection of the bar. Jack carefully inspected the flimsy stage and the non-existent lighting, but said little. We watched the girls for an hour or so in attentive silence, connected as appreciative members of the audience, and then went out into the night. The Baby Doll Lounge still stands at the corner of Church and White Streets, but our performance series never quite got off the ground. And, Jack Smith, after a career that spanned thirty years, is dead.

After Jack's death, Penny Arcade and J. Hoberman, founders of the Plaster Foundation, Inc. and caretakers of Jack Smith's personal archive, proposed an exhibition to me of undefined dimensions, to be drawn from the archives they have worked so hard to preserve. Having failed to exhibit Jack's work in his lifetime, I wanted to realize some kind of long-term installation room dedicated to displaying the evocative relics of his life as an artist. The late Anthony Vasconcellos, then managing director of the Institute, championed the proposal and pledged his time and the Institute's resources to defining and developing an exhibition.

In 1993, Tony asked Edward Leffingwell, who once served as the Institute's chief curator and program director, to direct a feisty team of curators, artist advisors, book publishers, and P. S. 1 staff in realizing a show and publication. He has devoted himself to the difficult task with diplomacy, good humor, acerbic wit, and a tireless devotion to getting Jack Smith the recognition he never received in his lifetime. The entire P. S. 1 staff, sharing Vasconcello's commitment and Leffingwell's enthusiasm, has contributed immeasurably to the project, particularly Lisa Bateman, who has acted as project manager. Dennis Szakacs, P. S. 1's former development director, was instrumental in the pursuit of additional financial backing, and encouraged the Institute's trustees to enthusiastically support the project. Martin Fritz, our current director of operations, shepherded the project to realization.

As the years have gone by, the ambitions of this project have expanded in ways suggested by Jack Smith's work. His legendary films, some of them thought to be lost, have been located and conserved by the careful and attentive hand of filmmaker Jerry Tartaglia. Through the diligence of the P. S. 1 staff, particularly Patrick Pardo and Mark Leyer, works on paper, photographs, costumes, and props have been identified and catalogued, and manuscripts and audio tapes transcribed. The presentation itself has been carefully readied for exhibition and tour by our able team of preparators, led by building director Hank Stahler. David Schwartz, curator of the American Museum of the Moving Image in Astoria, Queens, worked closely with J. Hoberman and Jerry Tartaglia to develop an accompanying film program intended to broaden the context of Jack's work in film. The designer Mary Brecht helped us to come to terms with costumes from the archives, conservator Martin Bansbach with many works on paper, and Joseph Santarromana with the digitalization of slide sequences.

Carole Kismaric, Marvin Heiferman, and Alanna Stang of LOOKOUT have packaged an

I WOULD SKEW anything to give you a moment of happiness.

exemplary record of this project in the form of this book. Working with designer Gary Koepke and his associates Joe Polevy, Greg Gorman, and Laurence King, they channeled Jack's spirit into its pages. Contributing authors Nayland Blake, J. Hoberman, Lawrence Rinder, and Ronald Tavel have created interpretive accounts that vivify this document. Each has given substantially to a new understanding of Jack's work in performance, film, photography, and creative writing. Ira Silverberg and Peter Ayrton of Serpent's Tail recognized early on the importance of publishing this work and committed themselves to doing so. As an editor of the publication and one of its writers, Edward Leffingwell has worked hand in hand with LOOKOUT, The Plaster Foundation, Inc., and P. S. 1 to shape this publication in a way that is faithful to the extravagant spirit of its subject.

At the time of this writing, the institutions participating in the exhibition's tour include: The Andy Warhol Museum, Pittsburgh; the University Art Museum, Berkeley; and Kunstwerke, Berlin. Mark Francis, curator of the Warhol Museum, was an early and enthusiastic supporter of the exhibition, and recognized its appropriateness to the collection and mission of his institute, as was our guest curator for Jack's early work in photography, Lawrence Rinder, of the Art Musuem at Berkeley. Klaus Biesenbach, director of Kunstwerke, joined us as our partner in organizing the European exhibition and its subsequent tour. We are particularly pleased to be working with such an adventurous European partner, and know that Jack Smith would feel at home with Kunstwerke.

We are thankful to all who have given generously of their time and expertise and to the legion of Jack Smith's associates and colleagues who have contributed to the gestation of this project. Among them are: Howard Guttenplan, the Millennium Film Workshop; Jonas Mekas, Anthology Film Archives; Charles Allcroft; Babeth; Barbara Becker; Kathrin Becker; Ira Cohen; Susanna De Maria Wilson; Sukdeo Doobay; Frederick and Isabel Eberstadt; Richard Foreman; Helen Gee; Ken and Flo Jacobs; Joan Jonas; Jerry Leiber; Steven Leiber; Taylor Mead; Malcolm Morley; Michael Oppedisano; Uzi Parnes; Richard Preston; Gaby Rodgers; Irving Rosenthal; Wieland Schuiz-Keil; Gwenn Thomas; John Vaccaro; Jeoffrey Wexler; Louis Walden; Robert Wilson; La Monte Young; and Marian Zazeela. We are particularly thankful to the photographers and writers who have helped us understand who Jack Smith is and what he means today.

Special thanks to the National Endowment for the Arts; the American Film Institute, National Center for Video and Film Preservation; the Judith Rothchild Foundation; the Plaster Foundation, Inc.; the New York State Council for the Arts; the Andy Warhol Foundation for the Visual Arts; and the Department of Cultural Affairs, the City of New York. Without their commitment this exhibition and publication would not have been possible.

If it is nearly ten years since Jack's last visit to P. S. 1, this project comes to fruition with the exhibition *Flaming Creature*, a tribute to the life work of one of America's most radical and influential artists. Like the reopening of a restored and expanded P. S. 1, an institution founded with ideas like Jack's in mind, let it be an accomplishment of truly Baghdadian distinction.

Alanna Heiss
President and Executive Director
P. S. 1, The Institute for Contemporary Art

an anecdoted chronology

1932 Jack Albert Smith is born on November 14 in Columbus, Ohio, the son of Alvin J. Smith of West Virginia and Chrystine Meyo of Hazelton, Pennsylvania.

c. 1939 Smith family moves to Texas. Alvin Smith dies in a boat accident. Chrystine Smith pursues a nursing career, and, with Jack and his sister, takes up residence in the trailer parks of Houston.

c. 1945 Smith's mother remarries and the family moves to Wisconsin.

1950 Graduating from high school in Kenosha, Smith induces his parents to buy him an 8mm motion picture camera; it is stolen shortly after he receives it.

Smith enrolls in a local community college

1951 Smith quits college and moves to Chicago where he works as an usher in the Orpheum Theatre and as a stock clerk in a department store.

1952 Smith moves to Los Angeles where he claims to have briefly studied movement with dancer Ruth St. Denis.

Smith begins a 16mm color harem film which he later titles *Buzzards Over Baghdad*.

1953 Smith moves to New York City, living in a hotel on 14th Street near Union Square.

1956 Attending film classes at CCNY, Smith meets aspiring filmmakers Ken Jacobs and Bob Fleischner.

1957 Smith appears in Ken Jacobs's *Saturday Afternoon Blood Sacrifice* and *Little Cobra Dance*, 16mm films shot in the streets of lower Manhattan.

Smith opens the Hyperbole Photography Studio in a storefront on Eighth Street.

1958-1959 Smith stars in Jacob's *Star Spangled to Death* and *Little Stabs at Happiness*.

1959 Smith shoots *Scotch Tape* on a single hundred-foot roll of Kodachrome film using a camera borrowed from Jacobs.

1960 Smith completes the film *Overstimulated*, shot in his Lower East Side apartment.

On August 9, Smith opens a solo exhibition of large color and black and white prints at the Limelight gallery, Seventh Avenue South.

The Museum of Modern Art, New York, acquires Smith's portrait of "Ouled Näil" and exhibits it in "Recent Acquisitions 1960-61."

1961 Smith joins Jacobs for the summer in Provincetown, Massachusetts, where he plays the Vampire Fairy in Jacobs's lyrical film shot in a cemetery, *The Death of P'town*.

1962 Smith films *Flaming Creatures* on sets on the roof of the Windsor Theater.

Piero Heliczer of the dead language press publishes 200 copies of *The Beautiful Book*, an artist's book of Smith's hand-tipped black and white small prints.

Film Culture 27 (Winter 1962-63) publishes Smith's essay "The Perfect Filmic Appositeness of Maria Montez," with a spread of photographs of Maria Montez.

1963 Smith begins work on his film *Normal Love*.

Flaming Creatures has its theatrical premiere on April 29 at midnight at the Bleecker Street Cinema.

On December 7, Jonas Mekas presents Smith with *Film Culture*'s Fifth Annual Independent Filmmaker Award.

During the third annual experimental film festival in Knokke-le-Zout, Belgium, *Flaming Creatures* is banned by the Belgian Ministry of Culture. In his hotel room, Mekas screens the film for Jean-Luc Godard, Agnes Varda, and Roman Polanski.

Film Culture 31 (Winter 1963-64) publishes Smith's essay "Belated Appreciation of V.S." and "The Memoirs of Maria Montez or Wait For Me At The Bottom Of The Pool."

1964 On February 3, *Flaming Creatures* and rushes of *Normal Love* are shown at the Gramercy Arts. The theater is closed two weeks later for screening unlicensed films.

On February 20, Smith projects Robert Adler's production slides of *Normal Love* at the New Bowery and broadcasts a tape of a radio speech by Antonin Artuad.

On March 3, *Flaming Creatures* and rushes for *Normal Love* are seized at the New Bowery Theatre by detectives from the New York City District Attorney's office.

The March 17 screenings of *Flaming Creatures* and Kenneth Anger's *Scorpio Rising* are shut down at the New Bowery Theatre.

On June 12, *Flaming Creatures* is declared obscene in New York Criminal Court.

Film Culture 33 (Summer 1964) publishes Smith's "Red Orchids." The issue contains photographs of himself as well as some of the principals of *Normal Love*.

Smith appears in various takes for the unreleased Warhol film *Batman/Dracula*.

Film Culture 35 (Winter 1964-65) publishes Smith's photographs in a spread called "The Moldy Hell of Men and Women."

1965 Smith presents "The Great Pasty Triumph, a solo exhibition of color photographs" on January 14 at Ferewhon Gallery, New York.

On April 1, Albuquerque, New Mexico, police confiscate *Flaming Creatures* during a screening sponsored by the Action Committee On Human Rights.

On August 11, Smith attends a benefit at the Broadway Central Hotel to contribute to the legal costs of two men charged with marijuana possession. A riot ensues, Smith assaults an officer, and is jailed.

Smith participates in "Young American Beatniks Morally Opposed to Prisons" at the Village Gate on August 22.

With an emphasis on the government's position on the possession of marijuana, and with specific reference to the war in Vietnam, Smith presents the performance *Rehearsal for the Destruction of Atlantis*, as part of the Expanded Cinema Festival organized by Mekas. Other performances are presented by Claes Oldenburg, Robert Rauschenberg, La Monte Young, Marian Zazeela, and Andy Warhol.

1966 Rock composer Jerry Leiber and his then wife, actress Gaby Rodgers, sponsor Smith's travel for a filmmaking trip to Carnival in Rio de Janeiro. On his return, he is convicted of charges relating to the Broadway Central event, and is placed on probation.

Smith publishes an edited performance script for *Rehearsal of the Destruction of Atlantis* in *Film Culture* 40 (Spring 1966).

The National Students Association files an amicus curiae brief in support of the *Flaming Creatures* case as appeals make their way to the U.S. Supreme Court.

Smith adapts stills from a film in progress (what would become *No President*) into an "underground movie flip book" and publishes them as "Buzzards Over Bagdad" in the December issue of *Aspen* magazine guest edited by Andy Warhol and David Dalton.

1967 On January 19, police seize a print of *Flaming Creatures* prior to its screening at the University of Michigan, Ann Arbor.

The U.S. Supreme Court refuses to review the appeal of the original conviction against *Flaming Creatures*. Associate Justice Abe Fortas publicly states that he would have reversed the original Criminal Court decision.

On November 9 and 14, Smith screens a new film program, "Horror and Fantasy at Midnight," which includes black and white footage of Smith's work in progress, *Kidnapping and Auctioning of Wendell Wilkie by the Love Bandit*, later titled *No President*.

Smith plays "Mr. X.," a bellhop, in The Ridiculous Theatre Company's presentation of Charles Ludlam's *Big Hotel* at Tambellini's Gate Theatre.

1968 Throughout the year, Smith presents a series of performances and slides at various downtown locations. These include *Clamericals of Clapitalism, Stepladder to Farblonjet*, and *Wait For Me at the Bottom of the Pool*.

In July, Strom Thurmond, ranking Republican on the Senate Judiciary Committee, arranges a screening of *Flaming Creatures* in the Senate office building, and furnishes stills to members of Congress and the press, claiming to have "shocked Washington's hardened press corps."

On September 4, details of the content of *Flaming Creatures* appear in the *Congressional Record*.

1969 On February 6, in South Bend, Indiana, members of the Citizens for Decent Literature and representatives of the prosecutor's office halt a screening of *Flaming Creatures* at a Notre Dame conference on pornography and censorship, falsely claiming that the film had been found obscene by the U.S. Supreme Court. The following day students are maced in a confrontation over the seizure of the film.

Smith screens *No President* at the Elgin and Bleecker Street Cinemas.

In December, Smith relocates to 36 Greene Street, where he inaugurates the Plaster Foundation Free Theater Series "every Saturday night for two years."

Smith appears as the Walrus in Robert Wilson's *The Life and Times of Sigmund Freud* at the Brooklyn Academy of Music, on December 18 and 20.

1970 Smith presents *10 Million B.C.* at 36 Greene Street. Performances run from January through April.

During April and May, Smith presents the performances *Technicolor Sunset Easter Pageant, Miracle of Farblonjet*, and *Withdrawal from Orchid Lagoon* at the Plaster Foundation.

Smith shows *No President* at the opening of the first New York Underground Film Festival on October 12 at Max's Kansas City, the New York hang out for artists, photographers, musicians, and the Warhol crowd.

The selection committee of Anthology Film Archives votes to include *Flaming Creatures* and *No President* in its collection.

During December, Smith presents *Claptailism of Palmola Christmas Spectacle* and *Gas Stations of the Cross Religious Spectacle* at the Plaster Foundation.

1971 On February 25, Smith, using the pseudonym Sharkbait Starflesh, appears as the Man with the Top Hat and Cape in Robert Wilson's *Deafman Glance* at the Brooklyn Academy of Music.

Evicted from his loft, Smith moves to a downstairs studio on Mercer Street.

Smith presents *Travelogue of Atlantis* (also known as "Boiled Lobster Sunset of Technicolor Sacred Landlord Paradise Slide Show Spectacle Starring Mario Montez") at the Brassiere Museum Theatre, Prince Street.

Smith opens *Sharkbait of Atlantis*, with his stars appearing in "Boiled Lobster Sunset Color Slides of Burning Beauty" at his Mercer Street studio.

1972 In the December 21 issue, *The Village Voice* publishes Smith's essay, "Taboo of Jingola: The Art of the Audience."

Smith begins work on the film project *Hamlet in the Rented World*.

1973 Smith completes the script for Modern Adaptation of R.B. Sheridan's "The Critic," variously titled *Theatrical Crooks, Lucky Landlordism of Rented Paradise*, and *Monkey Business of Atlantis*.

In the July 19 issue of *The Village Voice*, Smith publishes "Pink Flamingo Formulas in Focus," an article attacking film critics Jonas Mekas and Andrew Sarris and praising a John Waters film.

Smith presents *Sacred Landlordism of Lucky Paradise*, a slide show and performance, at the Onnasch Gallery, Spring Street.

1974 In Cologne, at the Kölner Kunstverein as part of Projekt '74, Smith collaborates with film artist Babeth in tableaux vivants for *Moses*, a movie in slides photographed by German filmmaker Wilhelm Hein.

In the summer, Smith travels to Rome and presents a slide exhibition at Fabio Sargentini's gallery. He continues making slide "movies" for later projection, featuring a toy penguin, Inez, also known as Yolanda la Pinguina.

Smith appears on the December cover of *Avalanche* magazine in a two-page, cartoon-style, photographic storyboard spread, "Fear Ritual of Shark Museum," with photographs by Gwenn Thomas.

1975 Smith concludes months of work on slide movies in and around Rome and returns to New York City.

Smith presents *Horror of the Rented World* at the Collective for Living Cinema on White Street. The slide show and performance mark the formal introduction of the penguin to Smith's repertory.

1976 On March 25, *Scotch Tape* is shown in Los Angeles at the International Film Exposition, as part of an evening billed as "Masters of American Independent Cinema."

Smith stages *How Can Uncle Fishhook Have a Free Bicentennial Zombie Underground?*, a slide show and performance at Artists Space, New York.

Smith opens the play *Secret of Rented Island*, an adaptation of Ibsen's *Ghosts* at the Collation Center near City Hall. The cast is partly live actors, partly toy animals.

1977 Smith re-stages *Rented Island as Orchid Rot of Rented Lagoon* and *A Dream of Rented Island*. He participates in the Cologne Art Fair, staging the performance "Irrational Landlordism of Baghdad," "a glimpse of a brassiere factory," in an art fair booth.

1978 Smith presents *I Was a Mekas Collaborator*, a comic performance that traces the development and decline of his relationship with Jonas Mekas.

Smith receives a National Endowment for the Arts grant for $10,000 for production costs of a new project, *Sinbad in the Rented World*. This film preoccupies Smith in the years to come.

1979 Smith presents film programs at lower Manhattan screening rooms.

1980 Smith presents film and slides in a program called "2 Nights in a Rented World," at the BFVF, Boston. The program leads to additional performances and screenings in the Boston area and encourages Smith to embark on a performance and lecture circuit.

On June 13-14, Smith performs as Sinbad Glick in *Exotic Landlordism of the World*, a featured performance of the Times Square Show, an experimental arts festival.

Smith appears as the hypnotist Dr. Shrinkelstein in Beth B. and Scott B.'s film *The Trap Door*, at the Bleecker Street Cinema.

Smith screens films at the Rocky Mountain Film Center, University of Colorado.

Smith appears as Sinbad Glick in "It's a Reagan World," a photospread in the *Soho Weekly News Winter Style Supplement*.

1981 Smith presents *Penguin Rustling Out by the Old Archives* at Club 57, St. Marks Place. His advertisements for the show lampoon Richard Foreman, Ken Jacobs, and Ellen Stewart.

On March 5, Smith receives a $3,500 grant from CAPS (Creative Artists Public Service Program).

Smith presents *Art Crust on Crab Lagoon* slide show at Artists Space.

Smith screens *Flaming Creatures* as part of The Restless Language film festival organized by curator and critic Germano Celant in Genoa.

Smith appears in *Penguin Panic in the Rented Desert* at Kathe Izzo's Eleventh Hour, a performance space in Boston.

Smith presents *What's Underground About Marshmallows*, a slide show and performance, at 814 Broadway.

1982 Smith opens *I Was a Male Yvonne de Carlo for the Lucky Landlord Underground*, at 1 Morton Street.

Smith requests and is granted an extension from the NEA for his *Sinbad* grant. He then proposes to the agency that his ongoing project be given a second grant; this request is denied.

Smith appears in *Impacted Croissants of Outer Space* at the Pyramid Club.

Smith's grant request to NYSCA (New York State Council for the Arts) is denied.

1983 Smith appears as the Bubble Goddess in Ela Troyano's *Bubble People (or Uulua)*, in a Pyramid Club

screening, on May 25.
During a festival in Hamburg, Smith performs *I Danced with a Penguin*.

1984 Smith performs with Ronald Tavel in *Clash of the Brassiere Goddesses* at the Pyramid Club, on April 28.

During the Personal Cinema Program at Millennium, Smith screens *Flaming Creatures* and *Normal Fantasy*, a version of *Normal Love*.

Smith presents a screening program, performance, and lecture at the Museum of Art, Carnegie Institute, Pittsburgh.

Smith presents *Brassieres of Uranus* in Forbidden Films Festival, Funnel Experimental Film Theatre, Toronto.

1985 Smith presents *Death of a Penguin* at Millennium.

Smith screens *Flaming Creatures,* Landlordism of Crab Lagoon (*Normal Love*), and *Scotch Tape* for the Visiting Filmmakers Series at the School of the Art Institute of Chicago.

1987 Smith stages "3 Oily Tuesdays with Jack Smith" at Limbo Café, New York City.

1988 Smith files for and receives Social Security benefits, disabled standing.

Smith participates in The First True Comedy Symposium, "The Artists Versus the Hippopotamus."

Smith cancels his appearance in William Niederkorn's production of *The Chaplin Acts*, due to his ill health.

1989 The New York Film Festival invites Smith to screen *Flaming Creatures.* The film is not screened at the festival until 1993.

In February, Smith receives treatment for AIDS related conditions at New York's Stuyvesant Polyclinic.

In early August, Smith is admitted to Cabrini Medical Center again and released in mid-August.

On August 19, Smith participates in The Double Symposium of Acting, The Second True Comedy Symposium.

In late August, Smith is admitted to Beth Israel Center.

On September 2, Smith participates in the second session of the Double Symposium on Acting.

On September 16, Smith dies from AIDS.

authors

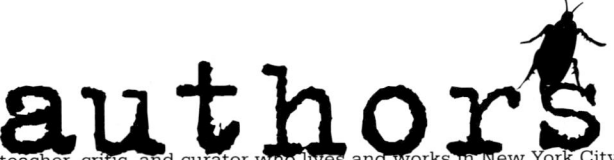

Nayland Blake is an artist, teacher, critic, and curator who lives and works in New York City. His work has been exhibited internationally since 1990 and is in the permanent collections of the Whitney Museum of American Art, The San Francisco Museum of Modern Art, and Boston's Museum of Fine Arts. In 1994, he was the co-curator of "In A Different Light," the first major museum exhibition to explore the impact of lesbian and gay artists on the art of the postwar era.

J. Hoberman is the senior film critic at *The Village Voice* and a contributing editor to *Sight and Sound*. His writings have been collected as *Vulgar Modernism* (Temple University Press), and he is the co-editor, with Ed Leffingwell, of *Wait for Me at the Bottom of the Pool: The Writings of Jack Smith* (High Risk/Serpent's Tail).

Edward Leffingwell is curatorial director of Flaming Creature. He is co-editor of *Wait For Me At The Bottom Of The Pool*. He has served as director of visual arts for the City of Los Angeles and as chief curator and program director for P. S. 1, is a corresponding editor for *Art in America*, and has organized retrospective exhibitions of the work of George Herms, John McCracken, and Michael Tracy.

Lawrence Rinder is curator for twentieth-century art at the Berkeley Art Museum. Among the exhibitions he has organized are *Knowledge of Higher Worlds: The Blackboard Drawings of Rudolf Steiner* (1997); *Louise Bourgeois: Drawings* (1996); and *In a Different Light* (1995). As curator of the MATRIX Program, he has organized exhibitions of work by Nayland Blake, Sophie Calle, Felix Gonzalez-Torres, Raymond Pettibon, Kiki Smith, Zoe Leonard, Charles Ray, Cindy Sherman, and Richard Tuttle, among others. His writing has been published in *Shift*, *Flash Art*, and *Artforum*, and in numerous catalogs and monographs.

Ronald Tavel founded and named The Theatre of the Ridiculous, the only extant, coherent theatrical movement of the American sixties. As Andy Warhol's screenwriter from 1964 to 1967 he wrote, and often directed and acted in, fourteen movies, eleven of which were recently restored by the Whitney Museum of American Art and currently are distributed through The Museum of Modern Art. His twenty-one screenplays and sketches and outlines for films are published this year, together with extensive commentaries and his Factory memoirs, by Sun & Moon Press, Los Angeles, in the *Complete Warhol Screenplays of Ronald Tavel*. Tavel wrote thirty-seven stage plays which Sun & Moon also plans to bring out, and a novel, *Street of Stairs* (Olympia Press). Ronald Tavel is represented by Helen Merrill, Ltd., New York City.

credits

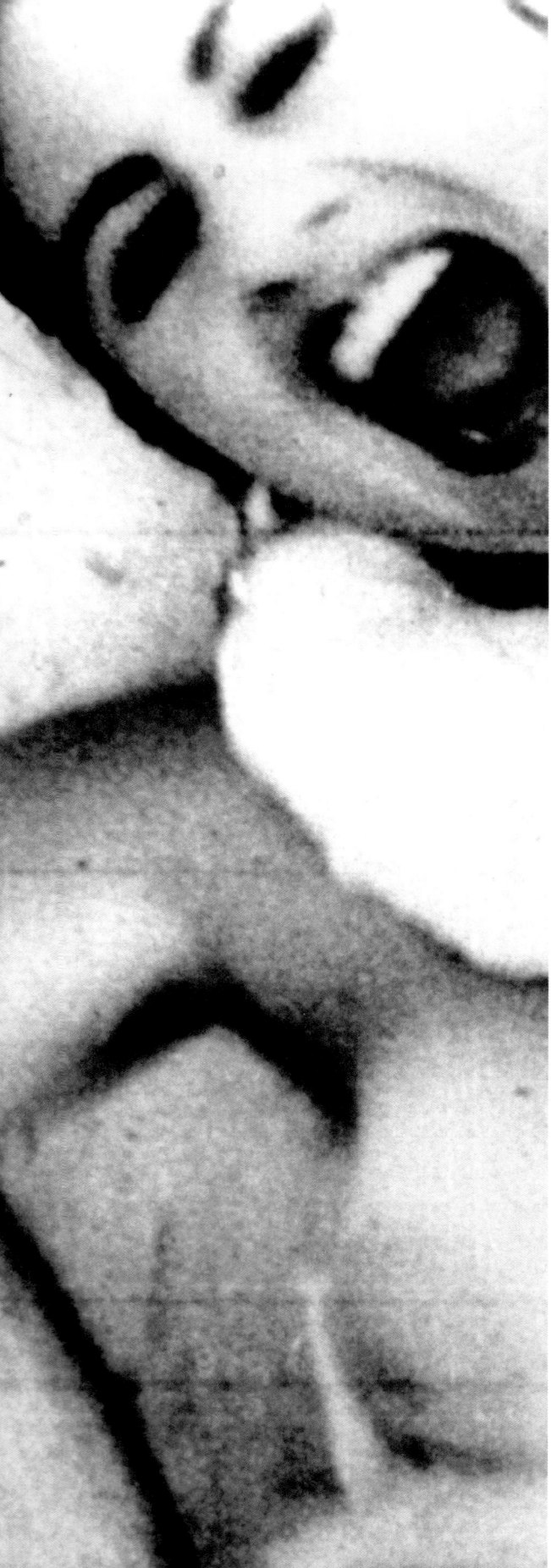

Asian Cultural Council
Australia Council for the Arts
Berlin Senate, Office for Cultural Affairs
Federal Office of Culture, Switzerland
Swiss Ministry of Home Affairs
Fundación Calara, Venezuela
The Irish American Cultural Institute
The Korean Culture and Arts Foundation
Ministry of Foreign Affairs, Norway
Royal Norwegian Consulate General
Stichting Fonds voor Beeldende Kunsten,
    The Netherlands

Contributors

Active Fire Extinguisher Co Inc
Alconda-Owsley Foundation
Emilio Ambasz
American Scandinavian Fund
Artforum International
Association Française d'Action Artistique
Sue and Joseph Berland
Ferris Booth Foundation
Ruth Bowman
Leo Castelli
Alfredo Ceibal
Adele Chatfield-Taylor
Citibank, N.A.
Eileen Cohen
Jane and John Comfort
Consolidated Edison Company of NY
Paula Cooper Gallery
Mr. and Mrs. Donald M. Cox
Gwen Darien
Marjorie Deane
Robert J. Denison
Beth Rudin DeWoody
Robert Djerejian
Marilynn Donini
Carol Eisenberg
Philip and Katherine Finkelpearl
Lawton W. Fitt
Susan and Arthur Fleischer
Richard Florsheim Art Fund
Arlyn and Edward Gardner
The Howard Gilman Foundation
Richard Gluckman
Goethe House New York
Carol and Arthur Goldberg
Peter A. Gordon
Agnes Gund
Mitchell Hauser
Rita E. Hauser
Akira Ikeda
J. P. Morgan & Co. Incorporated
E. William Judson
Ilya and Emilia Kabakov
Ada and Alex Katz
Harry and Nancy Koenigsberg
Edward and Phyllis Kwalwasser
Camille and Dennis LaBarre
Julie Lazar
Roy and Dorothy Lichtenstein
Vera List
Mrs. Richard D. Lombard
The Joe and Emily Lowe Foundation, Inc.
The John D. and Catherine T. MacArthur Foundation
Dr. Lester J. Mantell

Ronay and Richard Menschel
Sue and Eugene Mercy, Jr.
R.D. Merrill Foundation
The Joyce Mertz-Gilmore Foundation
Susan and Marvin Numeroff
Patricia and Morris Orden
Philip Morris Companies Inc.
Mary Ann Pierce
Marsha Plotnitsky (ICAR)
Jeff Preiss and Rebecca Quaytman
Hector and Erica Prud'homme
Renny Reynolds
George Rickey
Maria del Rio
W. M. Roth
Mr. and Mrs. Robert Ryman
Jane Safer
Barbara G. Sahlman
Mikael and Beth Salovaara
Joyce Pomeroy Schwartz
Vicki Sher
Fredrick Sherman
Roger Sherman
Ruth and Jerome A. Siegel
Lee Siegelson
J. L. H. Simonds
Nancy and Arnold Smoller
Constance and Anthony M. Solomon
Roger and Joan Sonnabend
  (Sonesta Charitable Foundation)
Jerry I. Speyer
Mr. and Mrs. Julian Taub
The Jane M. Timken Foundation
David Tofsky
Enzo Viscusi
The Andy Warhol Foundation for the Visual Arts, Inc.
William Wegman and Christine Burgin
The Norman and Rosita Winston Foundation, Inc.
Jerry Wolkoff
Virginia Wright
Anonymous

Staff

Alanna Heiss, President and Executive Director

Martin Fritz, Director of Operations
Hank Stahler, Building Director
Carole Kismaric, Publications Director

Kazue Kobata, Adjunct Curator

Kenneth Ansley, Finance/Systems Coordinator
Lisa Bateman, Special Projects Coordinator
Antoine Guerrero, Studio Program Coordinator
Kathy Kao, Fiscal Assistant
Marisa Morales, Office Coordinator
Kate Siamon, Assistant to the Director

James Acevedo, Preparator
Pablo Narvaez, Preparator
Flavia Rodriguez, Head Custodian

Bill Beirne, Education Coordinator
Antonia Perez, Art Educator

Liza Rios, Intern
Alfonso Spencer, Intern

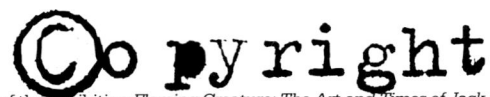

©opyright

Published by Serpent's Tail
4 Blackstock Mews
London, N4 2 BT ENGLAND
tel: 171-354 1949

Co-published by The Institute for Contemporary Art/P. S. 1
Museum
46-01 21st Street
Long Island City, New York 11101
tel: 718-784-2084

Packaged by Lookout
1024 Avenue of the Americas
New York, New York 10018
tel: 212-221-6463

Designed by Gary Koepke, Joe Polevy, and Greg Gorman

Printed and bound in Spain by Aries

Cataloging In Publication Data

Leffingwell, Edward (b.1941)
    underground culture, film making, theater, avant-garde,
    transvestites, drag queens, social history, performance
    art, biography, expanded cinema, art, 60s culture, New
    York downtown culture, photography, censorship

Library of Congress 96 - 070953
ISBN 1 85242 429 X

the Exhibition tour

The Institute for Contemporary Art/P. S. 1 Museum,
Long Island City, New York

The Andy Warhol Museum, Pittsburgh, Pennsylvania

Berkeley Art Museum, University of California, Berkeley

Kunstwerke Berlin, Institüt fur zeitgenössische Kunst, Berlin

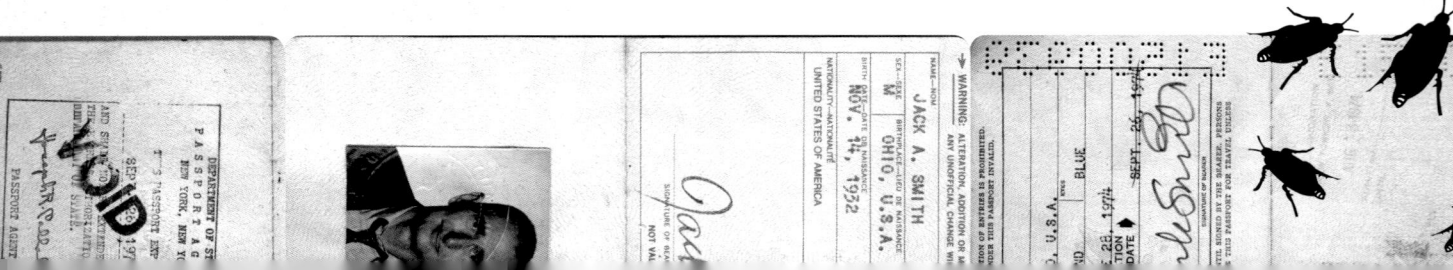